WITHDRAWN

McGraw-Hill Reading

Wonders

Mc
Graw
Hill

 Education

Bothell, WA • Chicago, IL • Columbus, OH • New York, NY

 TextEvaluator™

ETS and the ETS logo are registered trademarks of Educational Testing Service (ETS).
TextEvaluator is a trademark of Educational Testing Service.

Cover and Title Pages: Nathan Love

www.mheonline.com/readingwonders

C

Mc Graw Hill **Education**

Copyright © 2014 by The McGraw-Hill Companies, Inc.

All rights reserved. No part of this publication may be
reproduced or distributed in any form or by any means, or
stored in a database or retrieval system, without the prior
written consent of The McGraw-Hill Companies, Inc., including,
but not limited to, network storage or transmission, or
broadcast for distance learning.

Send all inquiries to:
McGraw-Hill Education
Two Penn Plaza
New York, New York 10121

Printed in the United States of America.

7 8 9 WEB 17 16 15 14

Common Core State Standards© Copyright 2010. National
Governors Association Center for Best Practices and Council of
Chief State School Officers. All rights reserved.

McGraw-Hill Reading Wonders

CCSS Reading/Language Arts Program

Program Authors

Dr. Diane August
Managing Director,
American Institutes for Research
Washington, D.C.

Dr. Donald Bear
Iowa State University
Ames, Iowa

Dr. Janice A. Dole
University of Utah
Salt Lake City, Utah

Dr. Jana Echevarria
California State University, Long Beach
Long Beach, California

Dr. Douglas Fisher
San Diego State University
San Diego, California

Dr. David J. Francis
University of Houston
Houston, Texas

Dr. Vicki Gibson
Educational Consultant
Gibson Hasbrouck and Associates
Wellesley, Massachusetts

Dr. Jan Hasbrouck
Educational Consultant
and Researcher
J.H. Consulting
Vancouver, Washington
Gibson Hasbrouck and Associates
Wellesley, Massachusetts

Margaret Kilgo
Educational Consultant
Kilgo Consulting, Inc.
Austin, Texas

Dr. Jay McTighe
Educational Consultant
Jay McTighe and Associates
Columbia, Maryland

Dr. Scott G. Paris
Vice President, Research
Educational Testing Service
Princeton, New Jersey

Dr. Timothy Shanahan
University of Illinois at Chicago
Chicago, Illinois

Dr. Josefina V. Tinajero
University of Texas at El Paso
El Paso, Texas

McGraw Hill Education

Bothell, WA • Chicago, IL • Columbus, OH • New York, NY

PROGRAM AUTHORS

Dr. Diane August

American Institutes for Research, Washington, D.C.

Managing Director focused on literacy and science for ELLs for the Education, Human Development and the Workforce Division

Dr. Donald R. Bear

Iowa State University

Professor, Iowa State University

Author of *Words Their Way, Words Their Way with English Learners, Vocabulary Their Way,* and *Words Their Way with Struggling Readers, 4–12*

Dr. Janice A. Dole

University of Utah

Professor, University of Utah

Director, Utah Center for Reading and Literacy

Content Facilitator, National Assessment of Educational Progress (NAEP)

CCSS Consultant to Literacy Coaches, Salt Lake City School District, Utah

Dr. Jana Echevarria

California State University, Long Beach

Professor Emerita of Education, California State University

Author of *Making Content Comprehensible for English Learners: The SIOP Model*

Dr. Douglas Fisher

San Diego State University

Co-Director, Center for the Advancement of Reading, California State University

Author of *Language Arts Workshop: Purposeful Reading and Writing Instruction* and *Reading for Information in Elementary School*

Dr. David J. Francis

University of Houston

Director of the Center for Research on Educational Achievement and Teaching of English Language Learners (CREATE)

Dr. Vicki Gibson

Educational Consultant Gibson Hasbrouck and Associates

Author of *Differentiated Instruction: Grouping for Success, Differentiated Instruction: Guidelines for Implementation,* and *Managing Behaviors to Support Differentiated Instruction*

Dr. Jan Hasbrouck

J.H. Consulting Gibson Hasbrouck and Associates

Developed Oral Reading Fluency Norms for Grades 1–8

Author of *The Reading Coach: A How-to Manual for Success* and *Educators as Physicians: Using RTI Assessments for Effective Decision-Making*

Margaret Kilgo

Educational Consultant Kilgo Consulting, Inc., Austin, TX

Developed Data-Driven Decisions process for evaluating student performance by standard

Member of Common Core State Standards Anchor Standards Committee for Reading and Writing

(Dole) Patrick Brennan; (Echevarria) Victoria Sanchez, CSULB; (Fisher) Courtesy of Douglas Fisher; (Gibson, Hasbrouck) Roger Pelissier; (Kilgo) Courtesy of Margaret Kilgo; (Paris) Courtesy of Scott G. Paris; (Shanahan; (Tinajero) Courtesy of Timothy Shanahan; (Tinajero) Courtesy of Josefina V. Tinajero; (Walker-Dalhouse) Dan Johnson, Marquette University; (others) McGraw-Hill Companies, Inc.

Dr. Scott G. Paris

Educational Testing Service,
Vice President, Research

Professor, Nanyang Technological
University, Singapore, 2008–2011
Professor of Education and Psychology,
University of Michigan, 1978–2008

Dr. Timothy Shanahan

University of Illinois at Chicago

Distinguished Professor, Urban Education
Director, UIC Center for Literacy
Chair, Department of Curriculum &
Instruction
Member, English Language Arts Work
Team and Writer of the Common Core
State Standards
President, International Reading
Association, 2006

Dr. Josefina V. Tinajero

University of Texas at El Paso

Dean of College of Education
President of TABE
Board of Directors for the American
Association of Colleges for Teacher
Education (AACTE)
Governing Board of the National Network
for Educational Renewal (NNER)

Consulting Authors

Kathy R. Bumgardner

National Literacy Consultant

Strategies Unlimited, Inc.
Gastonia, NC

Jay McTighe

Jay McTighe and Associates

Author of *The Understanding by Design
Guide to Creating High Quality Units* with
G. Wiggins; *Schooling by Design: Mission,
Action, Achievement* with G. Wiggins;
and *Differentiated Instruction and
Understanding By Design* with C. Tomlinson

Dr. Doris Walker-Dalhouse

Marquette University

Associate Professor, Department
of Educational Policy & Leadership
Author of articles on multicultural
literature, struggling readers, and
reading instruction in urban schools

Dinah Zike

Educational Consultant

Dinah-Might Activities, Inc.
San Antonio, TX

Program Reviewers

Kelly Aeppli-Campbell
Escambia County School District
Pensacola, FL

Marjorie J. Archer
Broward County Public Schools
Davie, FL

Whitney Augustine
Brevard Public Schools
Melbourne, FL

Antonio C. Campbell
Washington County School District
Saint George, UT

Helen Dunne
Gilbert Public School District
Gilbert, AZ

David P. Frydman
Clark County School District
Las Vegas, NV

Fran Gregory
Metropolitan Nashville Public Schools
Nashville, TN

Veronica Allen Hunt
Clark County School District
Las Vegas, NV

Michele Jacobs
Dee-Mack CUSD #701
Mackinaw, IL

LaVita Johnson Spears
Broward County Public Schools
Pembroke Pines, FL

Randall B. Kincaid
Sevier County Schools
Sevierville, TN

Matt Melamed
Community Consolidated School
   District 46
Grayslake, IL

Angela L. Reese,
Bay District Schools
Panama City, FL

Eddie Thompson
Fairfield City School District
Fairfield Township, OH

Patricia Vasseur Sosa
Miami-Dade County Public Schools
Miami, FL

Dr. Elizabeth Watson
Hazelwood School District
Hazelwood, MO

TEACHING WITH

INTRODUCE

Weekly Concept
Grade Appropriate
Topics, including Science
and Social Studies

• **Videos**
• **Photographs**
• **Interactive Graphic Organizers**

**Reading/Writing Workshop
Big Book and Little Book**

TEACH

Listening Comprehension
Complex Text

Close Reading
Shared Reading
Decodable Text

Minilessons
Phonics, High-Frequency
Words, Comprehension,
Writing Traits, Grammar

• **Visual Glossary**
• **Interactive Minilessons**
• **Interactive Graphic Organizers**

**Literature
Big Book**

Reading/Writing Workshop

APPLY

Close Reading
Anchor Texts
Extended Complex Texts
Application of
Strategies and Skills

• **eBooks**
• **Interactive Texts**
• **Listening Library**
• **English/Spanish Summaries**

Literature Anthology

DIFFERENTIATE

Leveled Readers
Small Group Instruction
with Differentiated Texts

- eBooks
- Interactive Texts
- Leveled Reader Search
- Listening Library
- Interactive Activities

Leveled Readers

INTEGRATE

Research and Inquiry
Short and Sustained Research
Projects

Text Connections
Reading Across Texts

Write About Reading
Analytical Writing

- Online Research
- Interactive Group
  Projects

Collection of Texts

ASSESS

Weekly Assessment

Unit Assessment

Benchmark Assessment

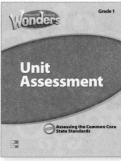

- Online Assessment
- Test Generator
- Reports

**Weekly
Assessment**

**Unit
Assessment**

**Benchmark
Assessment**

PROGRAM COMPONENTS

Big Book and Little Book of Reading/ Writing Workshop   **Literature Big Books**   **Literature Anthology**   **Interactive Read-Aloud Cards**   **Teacher Editions**   **Teaching Poster**

Leveled Readers   **Classroom Library Tradebooks**   **Your Turn Practice Book**   **Visual Vocabulary Cards**   **Leveled Workstation Activity Cards**

Photo Cards

CCSS Assessing the Common Core State Standards

could

Retelling Cards   **Sound-Spelling Cards**   **High-Frequency Word Cards**   **Response Board**   **Weekly Assessment**   **Unit Assessment**   **Benchmark Assessment**

Go Digital

For the Teacher

Plan
Customizable Lesson Plans

Assess
Online Assessments, Reports, and Scoring

Professional Development
Lesson and CCSS Videos

Teach
Classroom Presentation Tools, Instructional Lessons

Collaborate
Online Class Conversations, Interactive Group Projects

Additional Online Resources
Leveled Practice
Grammar Practice
Phonics/Spelling
ELL Activities
Genre Study
Reader's Theater
Tier 2 Intervention
Word-Building Cards

Manage and Assign
Student Grouping and Assignments

School to Home
Digital Open House Activities and Messages

For the Students

My To-Do List
Assignments
Assessments

Words to Know
Build Vocabulary

Read
eBooks
Interactive Texts

Play
Interactive Games

Write
Interactive Writing

School to Home
Activities for Home
Messages from the Teacher
Class Wall of Student Work

www.connected.mcgraw-hill.com

Meet the Meerkat. Text copyright © 2007 by Darrin Lunde. Illustrations copyright © 2007 by Patricia J. Wynne. Used with permission by Charlesbridge Publishing, Inc. All rights reserved.

UNIT 2 CONTENTS

Unit Planning

Unit Overview.. **x**

Unit Opener... **xii**

Weekly Lessons

Week 1 Jobs Around Town **T1**

Week 2 Buildings All Around **T78**

Week 3 A Community in Nature............................. **T156**

Week 4 Let's Help... **T234**

Week 5 Follow the Map.. **T312**

Week 6 Review and Assess.................................... **T390**

Model Lesson

Extended Lesson

Complex Text **T412**

Program Information

Scope and Sequence.. **BM1**

Index.. **BM10**

CCSS Correlations **CCSS1**

(t to r) Fuse/Getty Images; Sakis Papadopoulos/Robert Harding World Imagery/Getty Images;
Peter Scoones/Taxi/Getty Images; Jupiterimages/Foodpix/Getty Images; Jeff Greenberg/Alamy

UNIT OVERVIEW

Week 1	Week 2	Week 3
JOBS AROUND TOWN	**BUILDINGS ALL AROUND**	**A COMMUNITY IN NATURE**

READING

Week 1 — JOBS AROUND TOWN

ESSENTIAL QUESTION
What jobs need to be done in a community?

Build Background

CCSS **Oral Vocabulary**
L.1.5c *astonishing, community, equipment, fortunately, occupation*

CCSS **Word Work**
RF.1.2 Phonemic Awareness: Phoneme Blending, Phoneme Isolation, Phoneme Segmentation
RF.1.3 Phonics/Spelling: Short *e*
RF.1.3 Structural Analysis: Inflectional Endings -*ed*
RF.1.3g High-Frequency Words: *again, help, new, there, use*

CCSS **Comprehension**
Strategy: Make and Confirm Predictions
RL.1.3 Skill: Character, Setting, Events
Genre: Realistic Fiction

CCSS **Fluency**
RF.1.4b Intonation

Week 2 — BUILDINGS ALL AROUND

ESSENTIAL QUESTION
What buildings do you know? What are they made of?

Build Background

CCSS **Oral Vocabulary**
L.1.5c *collapsed, furious, materials, refused, shelter*

CCSS **Word Work**
RF.1.2 Phonological Awareness: Rhyme, Phoneme Identity, Phoneme Blending, Phoneme Segmentation
RF.1.3 Phonics/Spelling: Short *u*
RF.1.3 Structural Analysis: Contractions with -*'s*
RF.1.3g High-Frequency Words: *could, live, one, then, three*

CCSS **Comprehension**
Strategy: Make and Confirm Predictions
RL.1.3 Skill: Character, Setting, Events
Genre: Fantasy

CCSS **Fluency**
RF.1.4b Expression

Week 3 — A COMMUNITY IN NATURE

ESSENTIAL QUESTION
Where do animals live together?

Build Background

CCSS **Oral Vocabulary**
L.1.5c *depend, habitat, hibernate, tolerate, tranquil*

CCSS **Word Work**
RF.1.2 Phonemic Awareness: Phoneme Categorization, Phoneme Blending, Phoneme Substitution, Phoneme Segmentation
RF.1.3 Phonics/Spelling: End Blends
RF.1.3 Structural Analysis: Inflectional Endings -*ing*
RF.1.3g High-Frequency Words: *eat, no, of, under, who*

CCSS **Comprehension**
RL.1.1 Strategy: Reread
RI.1.2 Skill: Main Topic and Key Details
Genre: Informational Text/Nonfiction

CCSS **Fluency**
RF.1.4b Phrasing

LANGUAGE ARTS

Week 1

CCSS **Writing**
W.1.5 Trait: Organization

CCSS **Grammar**
RF.1.1 Nouns
L.1.2 Mechanics: Commas in a Series

Week 2

CCSS **Writing**
W.1.2 Trait: Organization

CCSS **Grammar**
RF.1.1 Singular and Plural Nouns
L.1.2 Mechanics: Apostrophes with Contractions

Week 3

CCSS **Writing**
W.1.2 Trait: Ideas

CCSS **Grammar**
RF.1.1 Possessive Nouns
L.1.2 Mechanics: Apostrophes with Possessive Nouns

(l to r) Fuse/Getty Images; Sakis Papadopoulos/Robert Harding World Imagery/Getty Images; Peter Scoones/Taxi/Getty Images; Jupiterimages/Foodpix/Getty Images; Jeff Greenberg/Alamy

Week 4	Week 5	Week 6
LET'S HELP	**FOLLOW THE MAP**	

Week 4 — LET'S HELP

ESSENTIAL QUESTION
How do people help out in the community?

Build Background

CCSS Oral Vocabulary
L.1.5c *admire, connections, enjoy, leadership, rely*

CCSS Word Work
RF.1.2 Phonemic Awareness: Phoneme Isolation, Phoneme Categorization, Phoneme Blending, Segmentation
RF.1.3 Phonics/Spelling: Consonant Digraphs *th, sh, -ng*
RF.1.3 Structural Analysis: Closed Syllables
RF.1.3g High-Frequency Words: *all, call, day, her, want*

CCSS Comprehension
RI.1.1 Strategy: Reread
RL.1.3 Skill: Character, Setting, Events
Genre: Fantasy

CCSS Fluency
RF.1.4b Intonation

CCSS Writing
W.1.3 Trait: Organization

CCSS Grammar
RF.1.1 Common and Proper Nouns
L.1.2 Mechanics: Capitalize Proper Nouns

Week 5 — FOLLOW THE MAP

ESSENTIAL QUESTION
How can you find your way around?

Build Background

CCSS Oral Vocabulary
L.1.5c *height, locate, model, route, separate*

CCSS Word Work
RF.1.2 Phonemic Awareness: Phoneme Segmentation, Phoneme Addition, Phoneme Blending
RF.1.3 Phonics/Spelling: Consonant Digraphs *ch, -tch, wh, ph*
RF.1.3 Structural Analysis: Inflectional Ending *-es*
RF.1.3g High-Frequency Words: *around, by, many, place, walk*

CCSS Comprehension
RI.1.1 Strategy: Reread
RI.1.2 Skill: Main Topic and Key Details
Genre: Informational Text/Nonfiction

CCSS Fluency
RF.1.4b Phrasing

CCSS Writing
W.1.5 Trait: Ideas

CCSS Grammar
RF.1.1 Irregular Plural Nouns
L.1.2 Mechanics: Capital Letters and Periods

Week 6

CCSS Reader's Theater
RF.1.4 Assign Roles
Fluency: Phrasing, Rate and Prosody

CCSS Reading Digitally
RI.1.5 Take Notes
W.1.6 Access Interactive Elements
Navigate Links

CCSS Research and Inquiry
W.1.7 Retell Information
Unit Projects
Presentation of Ideas

Unit 2 Assessment

Unit Assessment Book
pages 25–48

CCSS Writing
W.1.5 Celebrate: Share Your Writing
Portfolio Choice

Reading/Writing Workshop

Unit 2
Our Community

On My Street

Houses standing in a row,
One of them is mine, I know.

Many families on one street,
Each with friends it's
fun to meet.

Everywhere I look I see,
This neighborhood is
home to me.

—Constance Andrea Keremes

The Big Idea
What makes a community?

READING/WRITING WORKSHOP, pp. 6–7

The Big Idea *What makes a community?*

Talk About It

Have children read the Big Idea aloud. Ask them what they think a community is and if there can be different types of communities. Children may think a community is a group of people or a place where people live. They may suggest different communities such as a religious group, a neighborhood, or a group of friends.

Ask: *How can you be a good neighbor?* Have children discuss with partners or in groups, then share their ideas with the class. Let children know that they will discuss the Big Idea throughout the unit. Each week they will talk, read, and write about an Essential Question related to the Big Idea.

Read the Poem: "On My Street"

Read aloud "On My Street." Ask children questions to explore the theme.

→ What is the poem about?

→ Why does the speaker feel at home on this street?

→ What does it feel like to live on your street?

Personification Point out the phrase "houses standing." Have children stand up to show how houses stand. Ask: *Can houses really stand up like people do? Writers use imagery like this to help readers create a mental picture of what they are writing about.* Have children draw their own picture of houses standing.

RESEARCH AND INQUIRY

Weekly Projects Each week children will produce a project related to the Essential Question. They will then develop one of these projects more fully for the Unit Research Project. Through their research, children will focus their attention on:

→ writing in the voice of a community member.

→ brainstorming project topics.

→ collecting images and materials from multiple sources.

→ understanding maps.

Shared Research Board You may wish to develop a Shared Research Board. Children can post ideas and information about the unit theme. Children can post maps, materials, or facts they gather as they do their research. They can also post notes with questions they have as they conduct their research.

> ### WEEKLY PROJECTS
> Children work in pairs or small groups.
>
> **Week 1** Script About a Community Job, T44
>
> **Week 2** Building with Labels, T122
>
> **Week 3** Habitat Collage, T200
>
> **Week 4** Classroom Improvement List, T278
>
> **Week 5** Town Map, T356
>
> ### WEEK 6
> Children work in small groups to complete and present one of the following projects.
>
> → List of Questions → Plan
>
> → Diorama → Map
>
> → Collage

Go Digital

COLLABORATE
Post children's questions and monitor student online discussions. Create a Shared Research Board.

Go Digital! www.connected.mcgraw-hill.com

WRITING

Analytical Writing

Write About Reading As children read and reread for close reading of text, children will take notes and cite evidence to support their ideas and opinions.

Writing Every Day: Focus on Writing Traits Each week, children will focus on a writing trait. Children will draft and revise short writing entries in their writer's notebook, applying the trait to their writing.

> ### WEEKLY WRITING TRAITS
> **Week 1** Organization, T18
>
> **Week 2** Organization, T96
>
> **Week 3** Ideas, T174
>
> **Week 4** Organization, T252
>
> **Week 5** Ideas, T330

Go Digital

WRITING
Children can use the online writing tools.

Literature Big Book

Big Book and Little Book Reading/Writing Workshop

 👉 **Go Digital**

http://connected.mcgraw-hill.com

TEACH *AND* MODEL

Listening Comprehension

Comprehension Strategy *Make and Confirm Predictions* T10–T11

🔍 Close Reading

Shared Reading *Good Job, Ben!*, 14–23

Genre Realistic Fiction

Lexile 130

Words to Know T15

again, help, new, there, use

Minilessons ✔ Tested Skills  CCSS

✔ **Phonics**..Short *e*, T16–T17

✔ **Comprehension Skill**.....................Character, Setting, Events, T26–T27

✔ **Writing Traits**..................................Organization, T36–T37

✔ **Grammar**..Nouns, T37

JOBS AROUND TOWN
Essential Question
What jobs need to be done in a community?

WEEK 1

APPLY WITH CLOSE READING

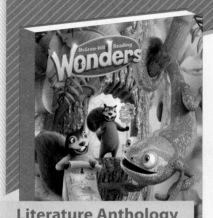

Literature Anthology

Complex Text

PAIRED READ

The Red Hat, 6–19
Genre Realistic Fiction
Lexile BR

"Firefighters at Work," 22–25
Genre Nonfiction
Lexile 290

Differentiated Text

Leveled Readers *Including Paired Reads*

APPROACHING
Lexile 70

ON LEVEL
Lexile 200

BEYOND
Lexile 330

ELL
Lexile 70

Extended Complex Text

The True Story of the 3 Little Pigs!
Genre
Fiction
Lexile 570

The Cow That Went Oink
Genre
Fiction
Lexile 270

Classroom Library lessons available online.

Classroom Library

TEACH AND MANAGE

How You Teach

INTRODUCE

Weekly Concept
Jobs Around Town

Reading/Writing Workshop
4–15

TEACH

Listening Comprehension
Millie Waits for the Mail

Close Reading
Good Job, Ben!

Minilessons
Character, Setting, Events; Realistic Fiction; Short *e*; High-Frequency Words

APPLY

Close Reading
The Red Hat
"Firefighters at Work"

👉 **Go Digital**

Interactive Whiteboard

Interactive Whiteboard

Mobile

How Students Practice

WEEKLY CONTRACT

PDF Online

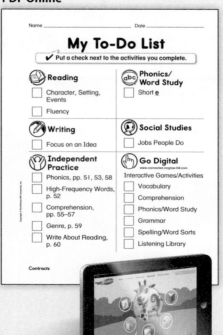

LEVELED PRACTICE AND ONLINE ACTIVITIES

Your Turn Practice Book
51–60

Leveled Readers

👉 **Go Digital**

Online To-Do List

Leveled Activities

Mobile

Go Digital! www.connected.mcgraw-hill.com

DIFFERENTIATE

SMALL GROUP INSTRUCTION

Leveled Readers

INTEGRATE

Research and Inquiry
Write a Script, T44–T45

Text Connections
Jobs Around Town, T46

Write About Reading
Analyze Character, Setting, Events, T47

ASSESS

**Weekly Assessment
51–60**

Mobile

**Online Research
and Writing**

**Online
Assessment**

LEVELED WORKSTATION CARDS

**More
Activities
on back**

6

People at Work

People do many kinds of jobs.

- Work with a partner.

- Draw two pictures of
people doing jobs.

SOCIAL ST

8

Organization: Focus on an Idea

I saw a nest.
It had birds in it.
They were babies!
The tree was tall.

- Tran had an idea for a story.
What was Tran's idea?

- Which sentence does not
focus on Tran's idea?

WRITING

6

Short e

peg   net

get

bed

- Think of words that rhyme with **leg**.
Write each word on a note card.

- Repeat with **set** and **bread**.

- Play a rhyming game with a
partner. Use this as an example:

  **What word rhymes with
  leg?** Choose the card.

- After the game, sort all the
cards by spelling patterns.

You need
› note cards
› pencils

PHONICS/WORD STUDY

3

Character, Setting, Events

A character is a person or animal in a story.
The setting is where a story takes place.
The events are what happen in a story.

- Reread a story you like.

- Make a Layered Book Foldable®.
Write **Who**, **Where**, and **What
Happens** on the layers.

- Fill in the book to tell
about the story.

Who
Where
What Happens

You need
› Layered Book
Foldable® Chart
› pencils or pens

READING

Go Digital! www.connected.mcgraw-hill.com • Interactive Games and Activities • Grade 1

DEVELOPING READERS AND WRITERS

Write to Sources and Research

Taking Notes, T35A

Character, Setting, Events, T35B

Make Connections: Essential Question, T35J

Research and Inquiry, T44

Analyze to Inform/Explain, T47

Comparing Texts, T53, T63, T67, T73

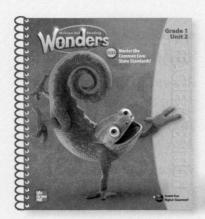

Teacher's Edition

Character, Setting, Events, pp. 55–57
Write About Reading, p. 60

Your Turn Practice Book

Interactive Whiteboard

Leveled Readers
Comparing Texts

Narrative Text
Story, T36–T37

Conferencing Routines
Peer Conferences, T42

Interactive Whiteboard

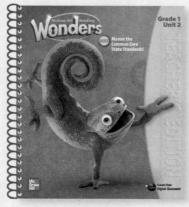

Teacher's Edition

Leveled Workstation Card
Story, Card 23

Writing Traits • **Shared and Interactive Writing**

Writing Trait: Organization
Story, T18

Conferencing Routines
Peer Conferences, T42

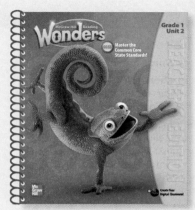

Teacher's Edition

Organization: Nouns, pp. 26–27

Reading/Writing Workshop

Leveled Workstation Card
Organization: Focus on an Idea, Card 8

Interactive Whiteboard

Grammar and Spelling

Grammar
Nouns, T19

Spelling
Words with Short *e*, T14

Interactive Whiteboard

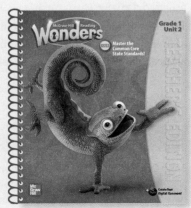

Teacher's Edition

Online Spelling and Grammar Games

Handwriting

SUGGESTED LESSON PLAN

✓ TESTED SKILLS

	DAY 1	DAY 2

READING

Whole Group

Teach, Model, and Apply

Reading/Writing Workshop

DAY 1

Build Background Jobs Around Town, T8–T9

Oral Vocabulary Words *occupation, community,* T8

Listening Comprehension
Big Book *Millie Waits for the Mail,* T10
Strategy: Make and Confirm Predictions, T11

Word Work T12–T15
Fluency: Sound-Spellings
Phonemic Awareness: Phoneme Blending
Phonics/Spelling: Introduce Short *e*
High-Frequency Words: *again, help, new, there, use*

Shared Reading *Good Job, Ben!* T16–T17

Practice Your Turn, p. 51

DAY 2

Oral Language Jobs Around Town, T20

Oral Vocabulary Words *equipment, fortunately, astonishing,* T20

Listening Comprehension Strategy: Make and Confirm Predictions, T21

Interactive Read-Aloud Cards "Jobs Around Town," T21

Word Work T22–T25
Fluency: Sound-Spellings
Phonemic Awareness: Phoneme Isolation
Phonics/Spelling: Review Short *e*
Structural Analysis: Inflectional Ending -*ed*
High-Frequency Words: *again, help, new, there, use*

Shared Reading *Good Job, Ben!* T26–T27

✓**Comprehension**
•Genre: Realistic Fiction, T26
•Skill: Character, Setting, Events, T27
Practice Your Turn, pp. 52–54

DIFFERENTIATED INSTRUCTION   Choose across the week to meet your children's needs.

Small Group

Approaching Level

Leveled Reader *Pick Up Day,* T52–T53
Phonemic Awareness Phoneme Blending, T54
Phonics Connect *e* and *ea* to /e/, T56
High-Frequency Words Review, T59

Leveled Reader *Pick Up Day,* T52–T53
Phonemic Awareness Phoneme Isolation, T54
Phonics Blend Words with Short *e*, T56
High-Frequency Words Reteach, T59
Comprehension Identify Characters, T60

On Level

Leveled Reader *Ben Brings the Mail,* T62–T63
Phonics Build Words with Short *e*, T64

Leveled Reader *Ben Brings the Mail,* T62–T63
High-Frequency Words Review Words, T64

Beyond Level

Leveled Reader *At Work with Mom,* T66–T67
Oral Vocabulary Multiple-Meaning Words, T68

Leveled Reader *At Work with Mom,* T66–T67
Oral Vocabulary Multiple-Meaning Words, T68

English Language Learners

Shared Read *Good Job, Ben!,* T70–T71
Phonemic Awareness Phoneme Blending, T54
Phonics Connect *e* and *ea* to /e/, T56
Vocabulary Preteach Oral Vocabulary, T74

Leveled Reader *Ben Brings the Mail,* T72–T73
Phonemic Awareness Phoneme Isolation, T54
Phonics Blend Words with Short *e*, T56
Vocabulary Preteach ELL Vocabulary, T74

LANGUAGE ARTS

Whole Group

Writing

Grammar

Shared Writing Writing Trait: Organization, T18
Story, T18

Grammar
•Nouns, T19

Mechanics: Commas in a Series, T19

Independent Writing Writing Trait: Organization, T28
Story, T28

Grammar
•Nouns, T29

Mechanics: Commas in a Series, T29

DAY 3	DAY 4	DAY 5 Review and Assess

READING

Oral Language Jobs Around Town, T30

Review Oral Vocabulary *occupation, community, equipment, fortunately, astonishing*, T30

Listening Comprehension
Big Book *Millie Waits for the Mail*, T31
•Strategy: Make and Confirm Predictions, T31
•Retelling, T31
•Fluency: Intonation, T31

Word Work T32–T35
Fluency: Sound-Spellings
Phonemic Awareness: Phoneme Blending
Phonics/Spelling: Blend Words with Short *e*
Structural Analysis: Inflectional Ending *-ed*
High-Frequency Words: *again, help, new, there, use*

Close Reading *The Red Hat*, T35A–T35J *Analytical Writing*

Practice Your Turn, pp. 55–57

Oral Language Jobs Around Town, T38

Comprehension Text Features: Labels, T39

Close Reading "Firefighters at Work," T39A–T39B

Word Work T40–T41
Fluency: Sound-Spellings
Phonemic Awareness: Phoneme Isolation
Phonics/Spelling: Build Words with Short *e*
Structural Analysis: Inflectional Ending *-ed*
High-Frequency Words: *again, help, new, there, use*

Integrate Ideas Research and Inquiry, T44–T45

Practice Your Turn, pp. 58–59

Integrate Ideas
•Text Connections, T46
• Write About Reading, T47 *Analytical Writing*

Word Work T48–T49
Fluency: Word Automaticity
Phonemic Awareness: Phoneme Blending/Segmentation
Phonics/Spelling: Blend and Build Words with Short *e*
Structural Analysis: Inflectional Ending *-ed*
High-Frequency Words: *again, help, new, there, use*

Practice Your Turn, p. 60

DIFFERENTIATED INSTRUCTION

Leveled Reader *Pick Up Day*, T52–T53
Phonemic Awareness Phoneme Blending, T55
Phonics Build Words with Short *e*, T57
Structural Analysis Review Inflectional Ending *-ed*, T58
Comprehension Review Character, Setting, Events, T61

Leveled Reader Paired Read: "The Recycling Center," T53 *Analytical Writing*
Phonemic Awareness Phoneme Isolation, T55
Phonics Blend Words with Short *e*, T57
Structural Analysis Reteach Inflectional Ending *-ed*, T58
Comprehension Read for Fluency, T60 ②

Leveled Reader Literature Circles, T53
Phonics Build Fluency with Phonics, T57
High-Frequency Words Cumulative Review, T59
Comprehension Self-Selected Reading, T61

Leveled Reader *Ben Brings the Mail*, T62–T63
Comprehension Review Character, Setting, Events, T65

Leveled Reader Paired Read: "At the Post Office," T63 *Analytical Writing*

Leveled Reader Literature Circles, T63
Comprehension Self-Selected Reading, T65

Leveled Reader *At Work with Mom*, T66–T67
Comprehension Review Character, Setting, Events, T69

Leveled Reader Paired Read: "Tools for the School Nurse," T67 *Analytical Writing*

Leveled Reader Literature Circles, T67
Comprehension Self-Selected Reading, T69

Leveled Reader *Ben Brings the Mail*, T72–T73
Phonemic Awareness Phoneme Blending, T55
Phonics Build Words with Short *e*, T57
Structural Analysis Reteach Inflectional Ending *-ed*, T58
High-Frequency Words Review Words, T75
Writing Writing Trait: Organization, T76

Leveled Reader Paired Read: "At the Post Office," T73 *Analytical Writing*
Phonemic Awareness Phoneme Isolation, T55
Structural Analysis Review Inflectional Ending *-ed*, T58
High-Frequency Words Reteach Words, T75
Grammar Nouns, T77

Leveled Reader Literature Circles, T73
Phonics Blend Words with Short *e*, T57
Spelling Words with Short *e*, T76

LANGUAGE ARTS

Independent Writing Writing Trait: Organization, T36
Story: Prewrite/Draft, T36–T37

Grammar
•Nouns, T37

Mechanics: Commas in a Series, T37

Independent Writing Writing Trait: Ideas, T42
Story: Revise/Proofread/Edit, T42–T43

Grammar
•Nouns, T43

Mechanics: Commas in a Series, T43

Independent Writing
Story: Publish and Present, T50

Grammar
•Nouns, T51

Mechanics: Commas in a Series, T51

DIFFERENTIATE TO ACCELERATE

  Scaffold to Access Complex Text

IF	the text complexity of a particular selection is too difficult for children
THEN	see the references noted in the chart below for scaffolded instruction to help children Access Complex Text.

Qualitative · Quantitative
Reader and Task
TEXT COMPLEXITY

	Big Book	**Reading/Writing Workshop**	**Literature Anthology**	**Leveled Readers**

Quantitative

Big Book
Millie Waits for the Mail
Lexile 610

Reading/Writing Workshop
Good Job, Ben!
Lexile 130

Literature Anthology
The Red Hat
Lexile BR

"Firefighters at Work"
Lexile 290

Leveled Readers
Approaching Level
Lexile 70

On Level
Lexile 200

Beyond Level
Lexile 330

ELL
Lexile 70

Qualitative

Big Book
What Makes the Text Complex?
- **Sentence Structure**, T31
- **Organization**, T31

 See Scaffolded Instruction in Teacher's Edition, T31

Reading/Writing Workshop
What Makes the Text Complex?
Foundational Skills
- Decoding with short *e*, T12–T13
- Reading words with inflectional ending -*ed*, T23
- Identifying high-frequency words, T15

See Scaffolded Instruction in Teacher's Edition, T12–T13, T15, and T23.

Literature Anthology
What Makes the Text Complex?
Foundational Skills
- Decoding with short *e*, T32–T33
- Reading words with inflectional ending -*ed*, T33
- Identifying high-frequency words, T35

Leveled Readers
What Makes the Text Complex?
Foundational Skills
- Decoding with short *e*
- Reading words with inflectional ending -*ed*
- Identifying high-frequency words
  again help new there use

See Level Up lessons online for Leveled Readers.

Reader and Task

Big Book
The Introduce the Concept lesson on pages T8–T9 will help determine the reader's knowledge and engagement in the weekly concept. See pages T10–T11, T31, and T44–T47 for questions and tasks for this text.

Reading/Writing Workshop
The Introduce the Concept lesson on pages T8–T9 will help determine the reader's knowledge and engagement in the weekly concept. See pages T16–T17, T26–T27, and T44–T47 for questions and tasks for this text.

Literature Anthology
The Introduce the Concept lesson on pages T8–T9 will help determine the reader's knowledge and engagement in the weekly concept. See pages T35A–T35J, T39A–T39B, and T44–T47 for questions and tasks for this text.

Leveled Readers
The Introduce the Concept lesson on pages T8–T9 will help determine the reader's knowledge and engagement in the weekly concept. See pages T52–T53, T62–T63, T66–T67, T72–T73, and T44–T47 for questions and tasks for this text.

Classroom Library Tradebooks: See pages T413–T415 for model lessons.

Monitor and *Differentiate*

IF you need to differentiate instruction

THEN use the Quick Checks to assess children's needs and select the appropriate small group instruction focus.

✓ Quick Check

Comprehension Strategy Make and Confirm Predictions, T11

Comprehension Skill Character, Setting, Events, T27

Phonics Words with Short *e*, T15, T25, T35, T41, T49

High-Frequency Words T15, T25, T35, T41, T49

If No →
| Approaching Level | **Reteach** T52–T61 |
| ELL | **Develop** T70–T77 |

If Yes →
| On Level | **Review** T62–T65 |
| Beyond Level | **Extend** T66–T69 |

Level Up with Leveled Readers

IF children can read their leveled text fluently and answer comprehension questions

THEN work with the next level up to accelerate children's reading with more complex text.

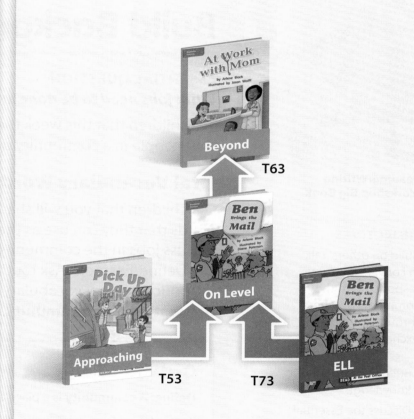

Beyond — T63

On Level

Approaching — T53

T73

ELL

ELL

ENGLISH LANGUAGE LEARNERS
SCAFFOLD

IF ELL students need additional support **THEN** scaffold instruction using the small group suggestions.

Shared Read	Leveled Reader	Phonemic Awareness	Phonics	Words to Know	Writing	Spelling	Grammar
Good Job, Ben!, T70–T71	*Ben Brings the Mail*, T72–T73 "At the Post Office," T73	Phoneme Blending, T54, T55 Phoneme Isolation, T54, T55	Words with Short *e*, T56–T57 Structural Analysis, T58	*again, help, new, there, use*, T75	Organization, T76	Words with Short *e*, T76	Nouns, T77

Note: Include ELL Students in all small groups based on their needs.

Materials

Reading/Writing Workshop
VOLUME 2

Reading/Writing Workshop Big Book
UNIT 2

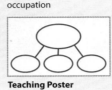

Literature Big Book
Millie Waits for the Mail

Visual Vocabulary Cards
community
occupation

Teaching Poster

| again |

High-Frequency Word Cards
again   there
help   use
new

| a | b | c |

Word-Building Cards

Think Aloud Clouds

Sound-Spelling Cards

→ Introduce the Concept

Reading/Writing Workshop Big Book

OBJECTIVES

CCSS Build on others' talk in conversations by responding to the comments of others through multiple exchanges. **SL.1.1b**

- Build background knowledge
- Discuss the Essential Question

ACADEMIC LANGUAGE

job, town, workers

MINILESSON 5 Mins

Build Background

ESSENTIAL QUESTION
What jobs need to be done in a community?

Tell children that this week they will be talking and reading about jobs that people in a community do.

Oral Vocabulary Words

Tell children that you will share some words that they can use as they discuss jobs in the community. Use the Define/Example/Ask routine to introduce the oral vocabulary words **occupation** and **community**.

Visual Vocabulary Cards

Oral Vocabulary Routine

Define: A **community** is a place and the people who live in it.

Example: Jan's community has two schools, one hospital, and three parks.

Ask: Are there any parks in your community?

Define: An **occupation** is a job someone does.

Example: Teacher, doctor, and truck driver are all good occupations.

Ask: What occupation would you like to have when you grow up?

Discuss the theme of *Jobs Around Town* and explain that there are many different kinds of jobs in your community. Have children name some jobs. *What jobs do people do in our community? How do these workers help the community?*

Go Digital

Jobs Around Town

Video

Photos

Visual Glossary

Graphic Organizer

READING/WRITING WORKSHOP, pp. 8–9

Talk About It: Jobs Around Town

Guide children to discuss how this job helps the community.

→ What is this man's occupation?

→ Why does this job need to be done?

Use Teaching Poster 40 and prompt children to complete the Word Web.

Children can look at pages 8–9 of their Reading/Writing Workshop and do the Talk About It activity with a partner.

Teaching Poster

Collaborative Conversations

Add New Ideas As children engage in partner, small-group, and whole-group discussions, encourage them to:

→ stay on topic.

→ connect their own ideas to the comments of others.

→ look for ways to connect their experiences to the conversation.

ENGLISH LANGUAGE LEARNERS SCAFFOLD

Beginning

Use Visuals Point to the man. *Is the man working in a grocery store? He is holding blueberries. Is he in the fruit and vegetable section of the grocery store? Point to another food.*

Intermediate

Describe Ask children to describe where the man is. Ask: *Where does this man work? What is his job?*

Advanced/Advanced High

Discuss Have children discuss what this man is doing. *What do you do at the grocery store? How could this man help you?*

→ # Listening Comprehension

Literature Big Book

OBJECTIVES

Demonstrate understanding of the organization and basic features of print. **RF.1.1**

- Reinforce concepts of print
- Develop concept understanding

ACADEMIC LANGUAGE

- *ellipses, dash, prediction*
- Cognates: *elipsis, predicción*

MINILESSON
10 Mins

Read the Literature Big Book

Connect to Concept: Jobs Around Town

Tell children that they will now read about a cow that always waits for the mail carrier. Ask: *Why do you think the cow waits for the mail carrier every day?*

Concepts of Print

Ellipses and Dashes Remind children that we read from the left to the right of the page, moving from the top line to the bottom line. As you read *Millie Waits for the Mail,* point out the dashes and ellipses. Explain that these symbols indicate that a long pause should be taken. When they are at the end of the last line on a page, these marks mean that the sentence continues on the next page. See prompts in the Big Book for modeling concepts of print.

Set a Purpose for Reading

→ Display the Big Book.

→ Read aloud the title and the names of the author and the illustrator.

→ Ask children to listen to the Big Book to find out why Millie waits for the mail carrier.

Go Digital

Millie Waits for the Mail

Make and Confirm Predictions

Strategy: Make and Confirm Predictions

❶ Explain Tell children that as they read the Big Book they can use the text and illustrations to make predictions about what will happen next. Then they can continue reading to find out whether their prediction was correct.

Think Aloud A prediction is an informed guess about what will happen in a story. When you make a prediction, you use the words and illustrations to help you guess what will happen. Today, as we read *Millie Waits for the Mail*, think about what may happen next. Then read on to find out if your prediction was correct.

❷ Model As you read, use the Think Aloud Cloud to model applying the strategy.

Think Aloud Remember that you can make predictions and then read on to see if you were correct. The text says there is something Millie loves more than anything else. I wonder what it is? I predict that what Millie loves more than anything else is getting a letter from the mail carrier, because the word *mail* is in the title. Let's read on to find out if my prediction is correct.

❸ Guided Practice As you continue to read, pause to prompt children to apply the strategy. Guide them to predict what might happen next and to use the evidence in the text and illustrations to confirm their predictions.

Respond to Reading

After reading, prompt children to share what they learned about Millie and the mail carrier. Discuss the predictions they made as they read and whether their predictions were correct.

ENGLISH LANGUAGE LEARNERS SCAFFOLD

Beginning

Predict Display pages 8 and 9 of *Millie Waits for the Mail. Let's make a prediction.* Point to the package. *Is the man dropping the package? Will the package break?*

Intermediate

Predict Display pages 8 and 9 of *Millie Waits for the Mail. What is happening here? Let's make a prediction. What do you think will happen to the package?*

Advanced/Advanced High

Predict Display pages 8 and 9 of *Millie Waits for the Mail. What do you think is inside the package? What do you think will happen to it? Why?*

Can children apply the strategy make and confirm predictions?

⬇

Small Group Instruction

If No →	Approaching	Reteach pp. T52–53
	ELL	Develop pp. T70–73
If Yes →	On Level	Review pp. T62–63
	Beyond Level	Extend pp. T66–67

→ # Word Work

Quick Review
Build Fluency: Sound-Spellings
Display the **Word-Building Cards:** *e, ea, sp, sn, sl, cr, fr, tr, o, pl, fl, cl, bl, i, a, s, r, l, t, m, n, c, p, b, f, g.* Have children say the sounds.

MINILESSON 5 Mins

Phonemic Awareness

OBJECTIVES

CCSS Orally produce single-syllable words by blending sounds (phonemes), including consonant blends. **RF.1.2b**

CCSS Decode regularly spelled one-syllable words. **RF.1.3b**

Phoneme Blending

① Model Show children how to blend phonemes to form words. *I am going to say three sounds. Then I will blend the three sounds together to make a word. The first sound is /l/. The middle sound is /e/. The last sound is /g/. Listen as I put the sounds together: /llleeeg/, leg. The word is leg.*

② Guided Practice/Practice Have children practice blending. Guide practice with the first word. *Listen carefully to these sounds. Put them together to make a word.*

/e/ /d/	/r/ /e/ /d/	/m/ /e/ /t/
/f/ /e/ /d/	/l/ /e/ /t/	/n/ /e/ /t/
/b/ /e/ /d/	/p/ /e/ /t/	/p/ /e/ /n/
/j/ /e/ /t/	/s/ /l/ /e/ /d/	/b/ /r/ /e/ /d/

MINILESSON 10 Mins

Phonics

SKILLS TRACE

SHORT e

Introduce Unit 2 Week 1 Day 1

Review Unit 2 Week 1 Days 2, 3, 4, 5

Assess Unit 2 Week 1

Introduce Short e

Sound-Spelling Card

① Model Display the *Egg* **Sound-Spelling Card.**
Teach /e/ spelled *e* and *ea* using *red* and *head.* Model writing the letter *e.* Use the handwriting models provided. *This is the Egg Sound-Spelling Card. The sound is /e/. The /e/ sound is spelled with the letter* e. *Sometimes it is spelled with the letters* ea. *Say it with me: /eee/. This sound is at the beginning of the word* egg. *Listen: /eeeg/, egg. I'll say /e/ as I write the letter.*

② Guided Practice/Practice Have children practice connecting the letter *e* to the sound /e/ by writing it. *Now do it with me. Say /e/ as I write the letter* e. *This time, write the letter* e *five times as you say the /e/ sound.* Continue with the letters *ea* for /e/.

Go Digital

Phonemic Awareness

Egg

Phonics

Handwriting

Blend Words with Short *e*

①Model Display **Word-Building Cards** *s, e, t.* Model how to blend the sounds. *This is the letter* s. *It stands for /s/. This is the letter* e. *It stands for /e/. This is the letter* t. *It stands for /t/. Listen as I blend these sounds together: /ssseeet/. Say it with me:* set.

Continue by modeling the words *beg, neck,* and *sweat.*

②Guided Practice/Practice Display the Day 1 Phonics Practice Activity. Read each word in the first row, blending the sounds; for example: */rrreeed/. The word is* red. Have children blend each word with you. Prompt children to read the connected text, sounding out the decodable words.

red	bed	bell	Ben	get	wet
jet	vet	men	ten	head	bread
set	sat	get	got	well	will
smell	sled	clap	flag	block	dress

Ten men met in a jet.

Did Jeff get a red sled?

Glen let Rex get the bread.

Also online

Day 1 Phonics Practice Activity

Corrective Feedback

Sound Error Model the sound that children missed, then have them repeat the sound. Say: *My turn.* Tap under the letter and say: *Sound? /e/ What's the sound?* Return to the beginning of the word. Say: *Let's start over.* Blend the word with children again.

Daily Handwriting

Throughout the week teach uppercase and lowercase letters *Ee* using the Handwriting models.

ENGLISH LANGUAGE LEARNERS

Phonemic Awareness: Minimal Contrasts Focus on articulation. Say /e/ and note your mouth position. Have children repeat. Use Sound-Spelling Cards. Repeat for /a/. Have children say both sounds, noticing the differences. Continue with *set/sat, bed/bad, met/mat.*

Phonics: Variations in Language In some languages, including Hmong and Khmer, there is no direct transfer for /e/. Emphasize /e/, and show correct mouth position. Practice with Approaching Level phonics lessons.

ON-LEVEL PRACTICE BOOK p. 51

The letters **e** or **ea** can make the short **e** sound.

leg   **bread**

A. Read the words in the box. Listen for the short **e** sound. Write the word that names each picture.

bed	vet	head	men

1. men   2. vet

3. head   4. bed

B. Write your own sentence using a word from the box.

5. Responses will vary.

APPROACHING p. 51	BEYOND p. 51	ELL p. 51

Word Work

Quick Review

High-Frequency Words: Read, Spell, and Write to review last week's high-frequency words: *jump, move, run, two.*

MINILESSON 5 Mins
Spelling

OBJECTIVES

CCSS Recognize and read grade-appropriate irregularly spelled words. **RF.1.3g**

CCSS Spell untaught words phonetically, drawing on phonemic awareness and spelling conventions. **L.1.2e**

Words with Short *e*

Dictation Use the Spelling Dictation routine to help children transfer their knowledge of sound-spellings to writing. Follow the Dictation routine.

Pretest After dictation, pronounce each spelling word. Read the sentence and pronounce the word again. Ask children to say each word softly, stretching the sounds, before writing it. After the pretest, display the spelling words and write each word as you say the letter names. Have children check their words.

leg	He scraped his **leg** when he fell.
beg	My dog likes to **beg** for food.
men	The **men** went to a party.
hen	A **hen** can lay eggs.
head	Cover your **head** with a hat.
bread	A sandwich needs two slices of **bread**.
grass	We played on the **grass** in the park.
spin	She watched the wheel **spin** around.
there	Please put the books over **there**.
again	We went skating **again** today.

For Approaching Level and Beyond Level children, refer to the Differentiated Spelling Lists for modified word lists.

Go Digital

Spelling Word Routine

they	together
how	eat

High-Frequency Word Routine

ENGLISH LANGUAGE LEARNERS

Pantomime Review the meanings of these words by using pictures, pantomime, or gestures when possible. Have children repeat or act out the word.

High-Frequency Words

again, help, new, there, use

1 Model Display the **High-Frequency Word Cards** *again, help, new, there,* and *use.* Use the Read/Spell/Write routine to teach each word.

→ **Read** Point to and say the word *again. This is the word* again. *Say it with me:* again. *Deb liked the book so much, she read it again.*

→ **Spell** *The word* again *is spelled a-g-a-i-n. Spell it with me.*

→ **Write** *Let's write the word in the air as we say each letter:* a-g-a-i-n.

→ Follow the same steps to introduce *help, new, there,* and *use.*

→ As children spell each word with you, point out the irregularities in sound-spellings, such as the /e/ sound spelled *ai* in the word *again.*

 → Have partners create sentences using each word.

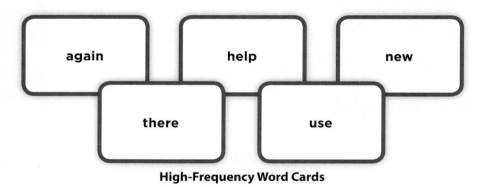

High-Frequency Word Cards

2 Guided Practice Have children read the sentences. Prompt them to identify the high-frequency words in connected text and to blend the decodable words.

1. Rex fell down **again**.
2. Can you **help** fix this mess?
3. Will you help the **new** kid?
4. **There** is my red pen!
5. Tell Ben to **use** a net.

Monitor and *Differentiate*

 Quick Check

Can children read and decode words with short *e*?

Can children recognize and read high-frequency words?

Small Group Instruction

If No → **Approaching** Reteach pp. T56–59

ELL Develop pp. T70–77

If Yes → **On Level** Review pp. T64–65

Beyond Level Extend pp. T68–69

→ # Shared Read

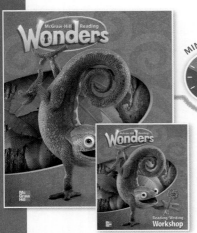

Reading/Writing Workshop Big Book and Reading/Writing Workshop

MINILESSON
10 Mins

Read *Good Job, Ben!*

Model Skills and Strategies

Tell children that you will now read a selection called *Good Job, Ben!* *As we read, look for the words* again, help, new, there, *and* use. *Look for words in which the letter* e *and the letters* ea *stand for the short* e *sound.*

Story Words Display the words *town, bus, books,* and *driver*. Spell the words and model reading them. Tell children that they will be reading them in the selection.

Guide children in reading *Good Job, Ben!* Point out the high-frequency words and words in which *e* and *ea* stand for the short *e* sound.

Genre: Realistic Fiction Tell children that *Good Job, Ben!* is realistic fiction. Explain to children that realistic fiction:

→ is an invented story that could happen in real life.

→ has made-up characters and events.

→ is not true, but could be based on real events.

Connect to Concept

ESSENTIAL QUESTION

Read together the Essential Question on page 14 of the Reading/Writing Workshop. Discuss the jobs the people in the story did. Guide children to connect what they have read to the Essential Question. *What jobs were done in this community? Why were they important?*

Go Digital

Good Job, Ben!

OBJECTIVES

CCSS Decode regularly spelled one-syllable words. **RF.1.3b**

CCSS Recognize and read grade-appropriate irregularly spelled words. **RF.1.3g**

Understand realistic fiction genre

ACADEMIC LANGUAGE

• *realistic fiction, prediction*

• Cognates: *ficción realista, predicción*

Good Job, Ben!

READING/WRITING WORKSHOP, pp. 14–23

Lexile 130

Partner Reading

Have partners use their Reading/Writing Workshop to review the skills and strategies.

→ Remind children that as they reread *Good Job, Ben!* they can use the text and illustrations to make predictions about what will happen next and then read on to see whether their predictions were correct.

→ Have children use pages 10–11 to review high-frequency words *again, help, new, there, use.*

→ Have children use pages 12–13 to review that the letters *e* and *ea* can stand for the short *e* sound. Guide them to blend the sounds to read the words.

→ Have children reread *Good Job, Ben!* with a partner. Guide them to apply the skills and strategies. Ask children to name features of the selection that tell them it is realistic fiction.

→ # Language Arts

Shared Writing

5 Mins
MINILESSON

Go Digital

OBJECTIVES

CCSS With guidance and support from adults, focus on a topic, respond to questions and suggestions from peers, and add details to strengthen writing as needed. **W.1.5**

CCSS Use common, proper, and possessive nouns. **L.1.1b**

ACADEMIC LANGUAGE

• *story, noun, comma*
• Cognate: *coma*

Writing Trait: Organization

❶ Model Tell children that they will now reread *Good Job, Ben!*, paying attention to how the story focuses on one idea. *Writers decide what they want to write about before they begin writing. They organize the sentences to go together and make sure that they are all about one idea.*

❷ Guided Practice/Practice Reread *Good Job, Ben!* Point out how the story is about one idea. Ask: *What is this story about?*

→ Prompt children to notice that starting on page 18, each page tells about a different job.

Story

Focus and Plan Tell children that this week they will be writing a story about jobs people do. Explain that a story is about a make-believe event. A story has characters, and it has a beginning, a middle, and an end.

 Brainstorm Use the Word Web on Teaching Poster 40 to help children brainstorm ideas for their stories. Ask children to name jobs they know about. Record children's ideas on the web.

Write Tell children that you will work together to write a story about a job. Model writing a story based on an idea on the web. Say: *Our story will be about one idea. It will have a beginning, a middle, and an end. Let's start the first sentence with* First. *Let's write a sentence that tells what happens first:* First, the baker mixed bread.

Work together to write a story about a baker with sentences that begin with *First, Next,* and *Last.*

Graphic Organizer

Writing

I see a fish.

Grammar

Grammar

MINILESSON 5 Mins

Nouns

① Model Tell children that a naming word is a noun. A noun names a person, place, or thing. Display the following sentences:

> A frog can hop.
>
> A crab swam.

Tell children *frog* and *crab* are nouns. Explain that every sentence has at least one noun.

To illustrate that a noun is a person, place, or thing, have each child name a noun they see in the classroom.

② Guided Practice/Practice Display the sentences below and read them aloud. Prompt children to chorally reread them with you. Have children work with a partner to identify the nouns.

> My mom claps. (mom)
>
> The glass fell. (glass)
>
> A man helps the little fox. (man, fox)

Talk About It Have partners orally generate sentences with nouns. Partners can take turns identifying the noun in each sentence.

Mechanics: Commas in a Series

① Model Tell children that when a writer uses three or more nouns in a list, there is a comma after all but the last noun. Display the following sentence:

> I play with dolls, blocks, and wigs.

Point out the list of three nouns and the comma after the first two nouns.

② Guided Practice Prompt children to complete the sentence frame.

> I like _____, _____, and _____.

ENGLISH LANGUAGE LEARNERS SCAFFOLD

Beginning

Demonstrate Comprehension Point to the two Model sentences. *Does* frog *name a thing? Show me how to hop. Is it a thing? No, so* hop *is not a noun. Does* crab *name a thing?* Restate responses in complete sentences.

Intermediate

Explain Ask children to circle the noun in the first Practice sentence. *How do you know this is a noun?* Continue with the second sentence. Allow children time to respond.

Advanced/Advanced High

Expand Write another sentence: *Dad grabs a box.* Have children identify the nouns. Have them tell why each is a noun. Restate children's responses.

Daily Wrap Up

→ Review the Essential Question and encourage children to discuss it using the oral vocabulary words. Ask: *What jobs did we talk about today? Are they done in our community?*

→ Prompt children to share the skills they learned. Ask: *How might you use those skills?*

Materials

Reading/Writing Workshop
VOLUME 2

Reading/Writing Workshop Big Book
UNIT 2

Visual Vocabulary Cards
astonishing
community
equipment
fortunately
occupation

High-Frequency Word Cards
again
help
new
there
use

Character	Setting	Events

Teaching Poster

Spelling Word Cards

Sound-Spelling Cards

a b c

Word-Building Cards

Interactive Read-Aloud Cards

(→) # Build the Concept

MINILESSON
5 Mins

Oral Language

Go Digital

school

Visual Glossary

"Jobs Around Town"

OBJECTIVES

CCSS
Ask and answer questions about key details in a text read aloud or information presented orally or through other media. **SL.1.2**

• Develop oral language

• Discuss the Essential Question

ACADEMIC LANGUAGE

• *supplies, predictions*

• Cognate: *predicciones*

ESSENTIAL QUESTION

Remind children that this week you've been talking and reading about jobs that need to be done in a community. Remind them of the man working in the grocery store, Millie and the mail carrier, and all the people Ben saw working in his community. Guide children to discuss the Essential Question using information from what they read and discussed on Day 1.

Oral Vocabulary Words

Review the oral vocabulary words *occupation* and *community*. Use the Define/Example/Ask routine to introduce the oral vocabulary words *astonishing*, *equipment*, and *fortunately*. Prompt children to use the words as they discuss jobs in the community.

Oral Vocabulary Routine

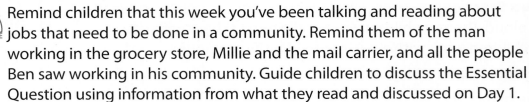

Define: Astonishing means "amazing" or "surprising."

Example: The number of stars in the sky was astonishing.

Ask: Which would be more astonishing: a baby playing baseball or a baby crying?

Define: Equipment is all the special things, or supplies, that you need to do something.

Example: When my family goes camping, we need sleeping bags and other special equipment.

Visual Vocabulary Cards

Ask: What equipment do you need to draw? To go fishing?

Define: Fortunately means "luckily."

Example: Fortunately, Tom's camera landed on soft carpet and did not break.

Ask: Finish this sentence: *It started to rain during the picnic. Fortunately, ____.*

Listening Comprehension

Read the Interactive Read Aloud

Strategy: Make and Confirm Predictions

Remind children that as they read, they can make predictions about what will happen next. Then they can use the words and illustrations to find out whether their prediction was correct. Model using the Think Aloud Cloud.

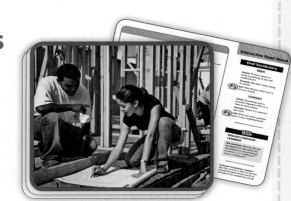

"Jobs Around Town"

Think Aloud When I read, I can guess what will happen next by thinking about the text and the illustrations. Then I will read on to see if my prediction was correct. That helps me better understand what I am reading. On the first card, I read about construction workers and how they help our community. I think that on the next cards I will learn about other workers who help our community. Let's keep reading to see if my prediction is correct.

Tell children that you will read "Jobs Around Town." Display the Interactive Read-Aloud Cards.

→ Pause as you read to model applying the strategy. Model using the text to confirm if your prediction was correct.

Make Connections

Discuss partners' responses to "Jobs Around Town." *Have you seen any of these workers in our community? What other workers have you seen in our community?*

ENGLISH LANGUAGE LEARNERS

Seek Clarification Some children may be confused by unfamiliar words. Encourage children to always seek clarification when they encounter a word or phrase that does not make sense to them. For example, *I don't understand this. Can you show me?*

 **Word Work**

Quick Review
Build Fluency: Sound-Spellings
Display the **Word-Building Cards:** *e, ea, sp, sn, sl, cr, fr, tr, o, pl, fl, cl, bl, i, a, s, r, l, t, m, n, c, p, b, f, g.* Have children say the sounds. Repeat, and vary the pace.

MINILESSON 5 Mins
Phonemic Awareness

OBJECTIVES

CCSS Isolate and pronounce initial, medial vowel, and final sounds (phonemes) in spoken single-syllable words. **RF.1.2c**

CCSS Decode regularly spelled one-syllable words. **RF.1.3b**

CCSS Read words with inflectional endings. **RF.1.3f**

Phoneme Isolation

❶ **Model** Show children how to isolate a phoneme in a word. *Listen carefully. I am going to say a word. Then I will say the middle sound in that word. What is the middle sound in /ssseeet/, set? That's right. The middle sound in set is /e/.*

❷ **Guided Practice/Practice** Have children practice isolating phonemes in a word. Do the first two together. *I am going to say more words. Tell me the middle sound in each word.*

men	red	hot	sit	leg
fell	map	head	get	beg

MINILESSON 5 Mins
Phonics

Review Short *e*

❶ **Model** Display the *Egg* **Sound-Spelling Card**. Review the sound /e/ spelled *e* and *ea* using the words *fell* and *bread*.

❷ **Guided Practice/Practice** Have children practice connecting the letter(s) and sound. Point to the Sound-Spelling Card. *What is this letter? What sound does it stand for? What are these letters? What sound do they stand for?*

Go Digital

Phonemic Awareness

Phonics

Structural Analysis

Handwriting

Blend Words with Short *e*

❶ Model Display **Word-Building Cards** *g, e, t.* Model how to generate and blend the sounds to say the word. *This is the letter* g. *It stands for /g/. This is the letter* e. *It stands for /e/. This is the letter* t. *It stands for /t/. Let's blend all three sounds: /geeet/. The word is* get.

Continue by modeling the words *leg, step, head,* and *deaf.*

❷ Guided Practice/Practice Repeat the routine with children with *let, ten, beg, neck, press, wet, stem, jet, fled, men, yes, smell, red.*

Build Words with Short *e*

❶ Model Display the Word-Building Cards *y, e, s.* Blend: /y/ /e/ /s/, /yeeesss/, *yes.*

→ Replace *s* with *t* and repeat with *yet.*

→ Change *y* to *b* and repeat with *bet.*

❷ Guided Practice/Practice Continue with *let, leg, beg, bag, big, bit, sit, set, met, wet, well.* Guide children to build and blend each word.

Structural Analysis

Inflectional Ending *-ed*

❶ Model Write and read aloud *yell* and *yelled.* Underline the *-ed.* Tell children that adding *-ed* to an action word makes it tell about something that has already happened.

Say *yell* and *yelled* again and have children listen for the /d/ sound at the end of *yelled.* Then write and say *dress, dressed, sweat,* and *sweated.* Point out that the letters *-ed* at the end of a word can stand for /d/ as in *yelled,* /t/ as in *dressed,* or /ed/ as in *sweated.* Say the word *sweated,* emphasizing the two syllables. Point out that adding *-ed* to the word *sweat* adds a word part, or syllable. Use each word in a sentence.

❷ Guided Practice/Practice Write the following words on the board: *mess, peck, smell, dread, spell.* Have children add *-ed* to each word, say each new word aloud, and then use each word in a sentence.

ENGLISH LANGUAGE LEARNERS

Build Vocabulary Review the meanings of example words that can be explained or demonstrated in a concrete way. For example, ask children to point to their *leg* and *neck.* Have them hold up *ten* fingers. Model the actions for *step* and *press,* saying, *"I can step on this rug."* and *"I can press my hands together."* and have children repeat. Provide sentence starters such as *"I will get ____"* for children to complete. Correct grammar and pronunciation as needed.

→ # Word Work

Quick Review

High-Frequency Words: Read, Spell and Write to review this week's high-frequency words: *again, help, new, there, use.*

MINILESSON 5 Mins

Spelling

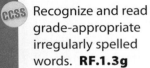

OBJECTIVES

CCSS Recognize and read grade-appropriate irregularly spelled words. **RF.1.3g**

CCSS Use conventional spelling for words with common spelling patterns and for frequently occurring irregular words. **L.1.2d**

Word Sort with *-eg, -en, -ead*

❶ **Model** Display the **Spelling Word Cards** from the Teacher's Resource Book, one at a time. Have children read each word, listening for short *e* and the ending sound.

Use cards for *peg, ten,* and *lead* to create a three-column chart. Say each word and pronounce the sounds: /p/ /e/ /g/; /t/ /e/ /n/; /l/ /e/ /d/. Say each word again, emphasizing the short *e* plus final consonant sounds (*-eg, -en, -ead*). Ask children to chorally spell each word.

❷ **Guided Practice/Practice** Have children place each Spelling Word Card in the column with the words containing the same final sounds and spellings (*-eg, -en, -ead*).

When completed, have children chorally read the words in each column. Then call out a word. Have a child find the word card and point to it as the class chorally spells the word.

Go Digital

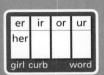

Spelling Word Sort

High-Frequency Word Routine

ANALYZE ERRORS/ARTICULATION SUPPORT

Use children's pretest errors to analyze spelling problems and provide corrective feedback. For example, the /e/ and /a/ sounds are formed in similar ways. Some children will substitute the letter *a* for the letter *e*.

Have children say /e/, paying attention to how it feels in the mouth. Repeat with /a/, noting how the face position changes slightly. Go back and forth between /e/ and /a/ to help children feel the difference.

Have children orally segment one of the spelling words. When children get to the /e/ sound, ask: *How does your mouth feel? What letter do we write for that sound?*

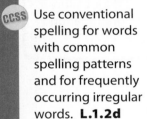

ENGLISH LANGUAGE LEARNERS

Provide Clues Practice spelling by helping children generate more words with medial short *e* patterns. Provide clues: *Think of a word that starts with t and rhymes with* men. Write the word and have children practice reading it. Correct their pronunciation, if needed.

High-Frequency Words

again, help, new, there, use

❶ Guided Practice Say each word and have children Read/Spell/Write it. Ask children to close their eyes, picture the word in their minds, and write it the way they see it. Display the high-frequency words for children to self-correct.

→ Point out unfamiliar sound-spellings, such as the /th/ sound spelled *th* in *there*.

❷ Practice Add the high-frequency words *again, help, new, there,* and *use* to the cumulative word bank.

→ Have children work with a partner to create sentences using the words.

→ Have children look at the words and compare their sounds and spellings to words from previous weeks.

→ Suggest that they write about jobs in their community.

Cumulative Review Review last week's words using the Read/Spell/Write routine.

→ Repeat the above routine, mixing the words and having children chorally say each one.

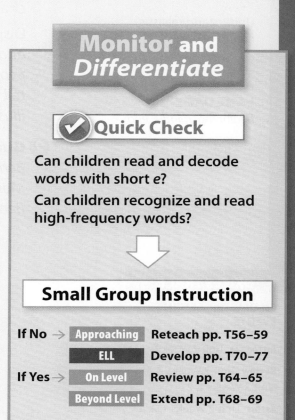

ON-LEVEL PRACTICE BOOK p. 52

A. Complete each sentence. Use one of the words in the box.

| again | help | new | there | use |

1. This hat is ___new___.
2. Ken will ___help___ me.
3. My cat is up ___there___.
4. We can ___use___ this.
5. Ned will try ___again___.

B. Write your own sentence using a word from the box.

6. Responses will vary.

| APPROACHING p. 52 | BEYOND p. 52 | ELL p. 52 |

Monitor and *Differentiate*

✔ Quick Check

Can children read and decode words with short *e*?

Can children recognize and read high-frequency words?

⬇

Small Group Instruction

If No → **Approaching** Reteach pp. T56–59
ELL Develop pp. T70–77
If Yes → **On Level** Review pp. T64–65
Beyond Level Extend pp. T68–69

Comprehension CLOSE READING

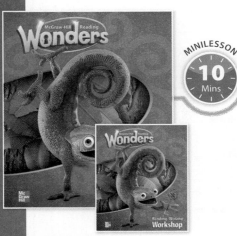

Reading/Writing Workshop Big Book and Reading/Writing Workshop

OBJECTIVES

CCSS Describe characters, settings, and major events in a story, using key details. **RL.1.3**

Understand realistic fiction genre

ACADEMIC LANGUAGE
beginning, middle, end

MINILESSON
10 Mins

Reread *Good Job, Ben!*

Genre: Realistic Fiction

❶ **Model** Tell children they will now reread the realistic fiction selection *Good Job, Ben!* Explain that as they read they will look for information in the text to help them understand the selection.

Review the characteristics of realistic fiction text:

→ has made-up characters and events

→ could happen in real life

→ has a beginning, a middle, and an end

Tell children that realistic fiction stories have a clear beginning, middle, and end. At the beginning of *Good Job, Ben!* we learn where the story takes place and who some of the characters are. In the middle of the story, we find out what the characters do. The events are presented in order. At the end, we find out the last thing the characters do.

Display pages 16 and 17: *This is the beginning of the story. I see a boy and a woman running to catch a bus. The words tell me that these people are Ben and his mom and that they are going to town. I can tell that this is realistic fiction because everything in the words and the illustrations could happen in real life.*

❷ **Guided Practice/Practice** Display pages 18 and 19 of *Good Job, Ben!* Say: *The middle of the story starts here. I can find out what Ben and Mom are doing by looking at the pictures and reading the text. What are Ben and Mom doing? What do they see? Could this happen in real life?*

Go Digital

Good Job, Ben!

Genre

Character, Setting, Events

SKILLS TRACE

CHARACTER, SETTING, EVENTS

Introduce Unit 2 Week 1

Review Unit 2 Weeks 2, 4; Unit 3 Weeks 1, 2

Assess Unit 2 Weeks 1, 2, 4

Skill: Character, Setting, Events

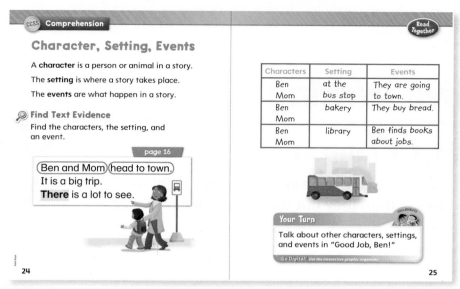

Reading/Writing Workshop, pp. 24–25

ON-LEVEL PRACTICE BOOK p. 57

A. Reread "A Fun Job."

Write <u>C</u> if the sentence and picture tell about a character.

Write <u>S</u> if the sentence and picture tell about a setting.

Write <u>E</u> if the sentence and picture tell about an event.

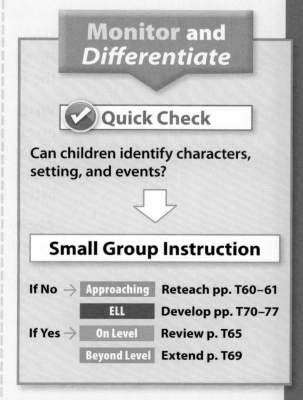

1. Ben likes his job.

　　　C

2. The shop has clocks.

　　　S

3. They fix the clock.

　　　E

APPROACHING p. 57	BEYOND p. 57	ELL p. 57

① Model Tell children that when they read realistic fiction, they can use the text to find the characters, settings, and events. Have children look at pages 24–25 in their Reading/Writing Workshop. Read together the definitions of character, setting, and events. *A character is a person or an animal in a story. The setting is where a story takes place. The events are what happens in a story.*

② Guided Practice/Practice Read together the Find Text Evidence section and model finding the characters, setting, and an event in *Good Job, Ben!* Point out the detail added to the graphic organizer.

On pages 16 and 17 we can find the characters, setting, and some events. The picture shows Mom and Ben. Mom and Ben are the characters. The text says that Mom and Ben head to town. This is an event. What is the setting?

Character	Setting	Events

Teaching Poster

Monitor and *Differentiate*

✓ **Quick Check**

Can children identify characters, setting, and events?

⬇

Small Group Instruction

If No → **Approaching** Reteach pp. T60–61

ELL Develop pp. T70–77

If Yes → **On Level** Review p. T65

Beyond Level Extend p. T69

→ # Language Arts

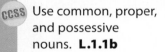

MINILESSON 5 Mins Interactive Writing

OBJECTIVES

CCSS With guidance and support from adults, focus on a topic, respond to questions and suggestions from peers, and add details to strengthen writing as needed. **W.1.5**

CCSS Use common, proper, and possessive nouns. **L.1.1b**

CCSS Use commas in dates and to separate single words in a series. **L.1.2c**

___

ACADEMIC LANGUAGE
• *events, order*
• Cognate: *orden*

Writing Trait: Organization

Review Tell children that writers decide what idea they want to write about in their stories. Then they put the information and events in order.

Story

Discuss Guide children to think of a job in the community they can write a story about. Refer to the Word Web children created on Day 1. List children's ideas. For example, *a crossing guard helping a child.*

Model/Apply Grammar Tell children that they will be working together to write a story about their idea. Remind them that every sentence has a noun and some sentences have more than one noun. Remind them that if they write three or more nouns in a list, they put a comma after all but the last one.

→ Write the sentence starter:

   First, _____.

Model choosing a noun and completing the sentence. For example, *First, the crossing guard asked Brad, Meg, and Ed to stand still.* Point out the nouns, and the commas used in the series.

Write Collaborate with children to write a beginning, a middle, and an ending sentence to form a story. Guide them to use the Word Web to get ideas. Work together to write sentences that show the order of events. As children create sentences, share the pen. Remind them to listen for the sounds in each word they write together.

Apply Writing Trait Review with children the story you wrote together on Day 1. Remind them how you used organization to write about one idea and put the events in order. Work together to write sentences that are about one idea and that begin *First, Then, Last.*

Go Digital

Graphic Organizer

Writing

I see a fish.

Grammar

Grammar

MINILESSON 5 Mins

Nouns

❶ Review Remind children that naming words are nouns. Nouns name persons, places, or things. Some nouns are *boy, house,* and *hat*. These three nouns name a person, a place, and a thing.

Write the following sentences:

> The frogs swim.
>
> The vet helps the cat.

Read the sentences aloud and have children chorally repeat. Guide children to circle the nouns in the sentences. (frogs, vet, cat)

❷ Guided Practice Write sample sentences. Read each sentence. Have children work in pairs to identify and circle each noun.

> The hen sits on the egg. (hen, egg)
>
> A dog slips. (dog)
>
> My sis sells socks. (sis, socks)
>
> The snack is hot. (snack)

❸ Practice Have children choose two nouns and write a sentence for each.

 Talk About It Have partners orally generate sentences with three or more nouns. Challenge them to use nouns that name a person, a place, and a thing in their sentences.

Mechanics: Commas in a Series

❶ Review Remind children that when a writer uses three or more nouns in a list, there is a comma after all but the last noun.

❷ Practice Display sentences with punctuation errors. Read each aloud. Have children work together to fix the sentences.

> I like figs yams and bread. (I like figs, yams, and bread.)
>
> Vic has pads pens, and clips. (Vic has pads, pens, and clips.)

ENGLISH LANGUAGE LEARNERS

Ask Guide children to circle the noun in the first Review example. *How do you know the word* frogs *is a noun? How many nouns are in this sentence?* Repeat with the second example sentence.

Find Noun Pictures Give pairs the Sound-Spelling Cards A–Z. Have them find pictures that are examples of a person (for example, *Queen*), a place (for example, *Volcano*), and a thing. Ask, *What is this? What makes it a noun?*

Daily Wrap Up

→ Discuss the Essential Question and encourage children to use the oral vocabulary words. *Name some jobs in our community that we learned about. How do these jobs help us?*

→ Prompt children to review and discuss the skills they used today by asking: *How will the skills you learned today help you read and write?*

Materials

Reading/Writing Workshop
VOLUME 2

Literature Anthology
VOLUME 2

Literature Big Book
Millie Waits for the Mail

Visual Vocabulary Cards

astonishing	again
community	help
equipment	new
fortunately	there
occupation	use

Teaching Poster

Response Board

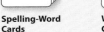
leg
Spelling-Word Cards

a b c
Word-Building Cards

→ Build the Concept

Oral Language
MINILESSON
5 Mins

Go Digital

Visual Glossary
school

Millie Waits for the Mail

Retell

OBJECTIVES

Retell stories, including key details, and demonstrate understanding of their central message or lesson. **RL.1.2**

Read grade-level text orally with accuracy, appropriate rate, and expression. **RF.1.4b**

Make and confirm predictions in a text

ACADEMIC LANGUAGE
• *exclamation mark, confirm*
• Cognate: *confirmar*

ESSENTIAL QUESTION
Remind children that this week you have been talking and reading about jobs in the community. Remind them of the mail carrier in *Millie Waits for the Mail*, the workers the child sees in *Good Job, Ben!* and the information they read about different jobs. Guide children to discuss the question using information from what they have read and talked about throughout the week.

Review Oral Vocabulary

Review the oral vocabulary words *community, occupation, equipment, fortunately, and astonishing* using the Define/Example/Ask routine. Encourage children to discuss jobs in the community when coming up with examples for each word.

Visual Vocabulary Cards

Listening Comprehension

MINILESSON
10 Mins

Reread Literature Big Book

Strategy: Make and Confirm Predictions

Remind children that as they read, they can make predictions. Then they can use the text evidence to confirm their predictions. *As we reread* Millie Waits for the Mail, *think about the predictions you made the first time we read it. Then think about the text and illustrations you used to see if you were correct.*

Read aloud *Millie Waits for the Mail*. Pause to model where you made and confirmed predictions when you first read it.

Literature Big Book

Model Retelling

Pause to retell portions of the selection. *I can use my own words to tell what happens in the story. So far, I have read that Millie waits for the mail carrier every day so she can jump out and scare him.*

→ After reading, model retelling the entire selection, using your own words to tell the important events in the correct order.

Model Fluency

Intonation Turn to page 20 of *Millie Waits for the Mail*. Point to the question marks and the exclamation marks. *When reading text with a question mark, your voice should rise, as when asking a question. When you read text with an exclamation mark, you should read it with strong emotion.*

→ Read aloud page 20 with slightly exaggerated intonation. Have children identify the question and exclamation marks and then reread the passage chorally. Repeat the reading to give children more practice with appropriate intonation.

ELL

ENGLISH LANGUAGE LEARNERS

Retell Guide children to retell by using a question prompt on each page. *What does Millie like to do?* Provide sentence starters for children to complete orally. *Millie likes to _____ the mail _____.*

Access Complex Text

If the complexity of the text makes it hard for children to read, use the Access Complex Text prompts.

Sentence Structure Some sentences contain ellipses and flow onto more than one page.

→ Remind children that in this text, the ellipses do not signal the end of a sentence. Use rising intonation on the words before the ellipses to indicate that the sentence is not complete. Then use falling intonation on the second part of the sentence.

Organization The jump in time at the end of the story may be confusing to some children.

→ Point out the differences in the illustrations on pages 4–5 and 24–25 (flowers blooming, more flies on flypaper, a chick in the red bucket). These differences show that a considerable amount of time has passed.

→  **Word Work**

Quick Review

Build Fluency: Sound-Spellings
Display the **Word-Building Cards:** *e, ea, sp, sn, sl, cr, fr, tr, o, pl, fl, cl, bl, i, a, s, r, l, t, m, n, c, p, b, f, g.* Have children say the sounds.

Phonemic Awareness

OBJECTIVES

 Decode regularly spelled one-syllable words. **RF.1.3b**

 Read words with inflectional endings. **RF.1.3f**

Phoneme Blending

❶ **Model** Place markers on the **Response Board** to show children how to orally blend phonemes. *I'm going to put one marker in each box as I say each sound. Then I will blend the sounds to form a word.* Place a marker for each sound you say: /m/ /e/ /t/. *This word has three sounds: /m/ /e/ /t/. Listen as I blend these sounds to form a word: /mmmeeet/,* met. *The word is* met.

❷ **Guided Practice/Practice** Have children practice blending. Do the first three words together. *Place a marker for each sound you hear. I will say one sound at a time. Then blend the sounds to say the word.*

/m/ /e/ /n/	/l/ /e/ /g/	/g/ /e/ t/
/r/ /e/ /d/	/b/ /e/ /d/	/p/ /e/ /n/
/s/ /m/ /e/ /l/	/d/ /r/ /e/ /s/	/s/ /t/ /e/ /p/

Phonics

Blend Words with Short *e*

❶ **Model** Display **Word-Building Cards** *s, t, e, p* to form the word *step.* Model how to generate and blend the sounds to say the word. *This is the letter* s. *It stands for /s/. This is the letter* t. *It stands for /t/. This is the letter* e. *It stands for /e/. This is the letter* p. *It stands for /p/. Listen as I blend these sounds together: /steeep/. Say it with me:* step.

Continue by modeling the words *pen, less,* and sweat.

❷ **Guided Practice/Practice** Review the words and sentences on the Day 3 Phonics Practice Activity with children. Read each word in the first row, blending the sounds; for example: /p/ /e/ /n/; /peeennn/. *The word is* pen.

Have children blend each word with you. Prompt children to read the connected text, sounding out the decodable words.

Go Digital

Phonemic Awareness

Phonics

Structural Analysis

Handwriting

pen	red	Rex	bell	gets	wet
Jen	ten	bed	deaf	vet	smell
yelled	dressed	headed	packed		
spelled	smelled	missed	sweated		
press	step	sled	bread	block	clock

Tell Meg to get ten eggs.

The red fox fled to its den.

Also online

Day 3 Phonics Practice Activity

MINILESSON
5 Mins

Structural Analysis

Inflectional Ending -*ed*

❶ **Model** Say the words *dress* and *dressed*. Ask children to listen closely to hear what is different. Point out the /t/ sound at the end of *dressed*.

→ Write the words *dress* and *dressed*. Underline the letters -*ed* at the end of *dressed*. Tell children that the letters -*ed* at the end of *dressed* mean that the action took place in the past.

❷ **Practice/Apply** Help children blend the words *yell, yelled, head, headed, pack, packed, grill, grilled, mix, mixed, mess, messed, lock,* and *locked*. Point out that the letters -*ed* at the end of a word can stand for /t/ as in *packed*, /d/ as in *yelled*, or /ed/ as in *headed*. Point out that adding -*ed* to some words, such as *head*, adds a word part, or syllable.

Corrective Feedback

Corrective Feedback Say: *My turn.* Model blending the word using the appropriate signaling procedures. Then lead children in blending the sounds. Say: *Do it with me.* You will respond with children to offer support. Then say: *Your turn. Blend.* Have children chorally blend. Return to the beginning of the word. Say: *Let's start over.*

 **Word Work**

MINILESSON
5 Mins

Spelling

OBJECTIVES

CCSS Recognize and read grade-appropriate irregularly spelled words. **RF.1.3g**

CCSS Use conventional spelling for words with common spelling patterns and for frequently occurring regular words. **L.1.2d**

-eg, -en, -ead Word Families

1 Model Make index cards for *-eg, -en, -ead* and form three columns in a pocket chart. Blend the sounds with children.

Hold up the *leg* **Spelling Word Card**. Say and spell it. Pronounce each sound clearly: /l/ /e/ /g/. Blend the sounds, stretching the vowel sound to emphasize it: /leeeg/. Repeat this step with *beg*. Place both words below the *-eg* card. Read and spell each spelling word together with children. Have children read each word. *What do you notice about these spelling words? They have the /e/ sound and they rhyme because they both end with /eg/ spelled e-g.*

2 Guided Practice/Practice Have children spell each word. Repeat the process with the *-en* and *-ead* words.

Display the words *grass, spin, there,* and *again* in a separate column. Read and spell the words together with children. Point out that these spelling words do not contain the /e/ sound spelled *e* or *ea.*

Conclude by asking children to orally generate additional words that rhyme with each word. Write the additional words on the board. Underline the common spelling patterns in the additional words. If necessary, point out the differences and explain why they are unusual.

Go Digital

Spelling Word Families

Visual Glossary

PHONICS/SPELLING PRACTICE BOOK p. 28

Read each word in the box. Say each word.

| leg | beg | men | hen |
| head | bread | there | again |

A. Use the clues to write a spelling word on the line.

1. starts like **miss** + ends like **ten** _____ men

2. starts like **look** + ends like **peg** _____ leg

3. starts like **hat** + ends like **ten** _____ hen

4. starts like **back** + ends like **peg** _____ beg

B. Write the spelling word on the line.

5. bread _____ bread   6. head _____ head

7. again _____ again   8. there _____ there

High-Frequency Words

again, help, new, there, use

❶ Guided Practice Say each word and have children Read/Spell/Write it. As children spell each word with you, point out unfamiliar sound-spellings, such as the *u_e* spelling for long *u* in *use*.

Use the **Visual Vocabulary Cards** to review this week's high-frequency words.

Visual Vocabulary Cards

❷ Practice Repeat the activity with last week's words.

Build Fluency: Word Automaticity

Have children read the following sentences aloud together at the same pace. Repeat several times.

Ben can go there again.

I will use a new pen.

Can you help Jeff?

Word Bank

Review the current and previous words in the word bank. Discuss with children which words should be removed, or added back, from previous high-frequency word lists. Remind children that the word bank should change as the class needs it to.

Monitor and Differentiate

Quick Check

Can children read and decode words with short *e*?

Can children recognize and read high-frequency words?

Small Group Instruction

If No →	Approaching	Reteach pp. T56–59
	ELL	Develop pp. T70–77
If Yes →	On Level	Review pp. T64–65
	Beyond Level	Extend pp. T68–69

Genre Realistic Fiction

Essential Question
What jobs need to be done in a community?
Read about a firefighter's exciting job.

Go Digital!

The Red Hat

17

by Eva Torres
illustrated by Vincent Nguyen

6

7

Literature Anthology

LITERATURE ANTHOLOGY, pp. 6–7

Develop Comprehension

CLOSE READING

Lexile BR

Read Literature Anthology

Review Genre: Realistic Fiction
Review with children the key characteristics of realistic fiction. It:

→ has made-up characters and events.

→ could happen in real life.

→ has a beginning, a middle, and an end.

Preview and Predict Display the illustration on pages 6 and 7. *Who might this selection be about? What might the character do? Let's find out.*

ESSENTIAL QUESTION
Read aloud the Essential Question: *What jobs need to be done in a community?* Tell children that as they read they should think about how firefighters help a community.

Story Words Read and spell the words *fire, truck,* and *thank.* Review word meaning. Tell children that they will read these words in the selection.

 Analytical Writing **Note Taking: Graphic Organizer** As children read the selection, guide them to fill in the graphic organizer on **Your Turn Practice Book** page 54 as you model recording details about the character, setting, and events of each section.

Jen has a **new** job.
She gets a red hat. **1**

8

She will **use** this hat a lot. **2**

9

LITERATURE ANTHOLOGY, pp. 8–9

1 Strategy: Make and Confirm Predictions

Teacher Think Aloud On these pages, I see a firefighter. She is getting a hat. The words tell me that this is Jen and that she has a new job. The words also tell me that she will use her red hat a lot. I can make a prediction that Jen will wear the hat when she works. As I read, I will use the words and illustrations to see if my prediction was correct.

2 Skill: Character, Setting, Events

Who is the main character? Where is she? What event has happened?

Character	Setting	Events
Jen	Outside a firehouse	She gets a hat.

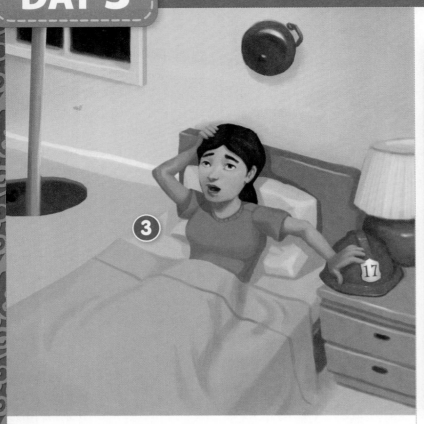

③

Jen is in bed.
There is a bell!
She grabs the red hat.

10

④

Jen can get down like this.
Go, Jen, go!

11

LITERATURE ANTHOLOGY, pp. 10–11

Develop Comprehension

CLOSE READING

③ Skill: Character, Setting, Events

Remember that the illustrations give information about a story, too. Sometimes the illustrations tell us things about the characters, setting, and events that we don't learn from the words. Look at the illustration on page 10. We read that Jen is in bed when the fire bell rings. Where is she sleeping when the fire bell rings? Yes, she is at the fire house. No wonder she heard the bell!

④ Strategy: Make and Confirm Predictions

Remember to check the predictions you made. I predicted that Jen would wear her hat when she works. On these pages I see and read about what Jen does. When the bell rings Jen grabs her hat. She is wearing it as she slides down the pole. This tells me that my prediction was correct. Now let's make a new prediction. The fire bell rang. What do you think will happen? Yes, I also think that Jen will go to put out a fire.

Jen hops on.
Go, Jen, go! **6**

12

It is a big fire!
Jen can **help**.

13

LITERATURE ANTHOLOGY, pp. 12–13

5 **Maintain Skill: Key Details**

There have been many details in the words and illustrations. Remember, we can think about the order of the details. The fire bell wakes Jen up. Then she slides down the pole. What detail do you see next? Look at the picture on page 12. What is Jen doing now? Yes, the next detail is that she hops on the fire truck.

6 **Author's Craft: Repetition**

Teacher Think Aloud Sometimes authors repeat words. This can add emphasis to an idea. On this page the author repeats the word *go* to emphasize that Jen is going fast.

7 **Skill: Character, Setting, Events**

Where is Jen now? What is happening there? What does Jen do? Let's add these details to the chart.

Character	Setting	Events
Jen	Outside a firehouse	She gets a hat.
Jen	At a fire	She helps put out a fire.

The fire is out.
Jen is wet.
Thank you, Jen!

14

Jen plays with Matt and Jill.
There is a bell **again**.

15

LITERATURE ANTHOLOGY, pp. 14–15

Develop Comprehension *CLOSE READING*

❽ Skill: Character, Setting, Events

Look at page 14. Where is Jen? Look at page 15.
Where is Jen now? What event happens?

Character	Setting	Events
Jen	Outside a firehouse	She gets a hat.
Jen	At a fire	She helps put out a fire.
Jen	Inside the firehouse	The fire bell rings.

❾ Strategy: Make and Confirm Predictions

Teacher Think Aloud Let's check whether our predictions were correct. We predicted that Jen puts out a fire. We read on page 14 that she does! Let's make a new prediction. What do you think will happen next? Tell why you think that.

Student Think Aloud The fire bell is ringing again. I think that Jen will help put out another fire.

Jen gets the red hat.
She gets in the truck.
Go, Jen, go!

16

Rex is up there.
He will not come to Jim.
Jen will help!

17

LITERATURE ANTHOLOGY, pp. 16–17

⑩ **Ask and Answer Questions**

Remember, as you read you can ask yourself questions about the story to better understand what happens. Then you can use the words and illustrations to find the answers. The answers to your questions will help you understand what you have read. Read page 16. I wonder where Jen is going? Now read page 17. Can you answer the question?

⑪ **Skill: Character, Setting, Events**

COLLABORATE Turn to a partner and discuss what you read and see on pages 16 and 17. Where is Jen? What is happening?

⑫ **Strategy: Make and Confirm Predictions**

Let's confirm the predictions we made. The fire bell rang again. We predicted Jen would put out another fire. Were we right? What *does* happen?

Jen gets Rex.

18

Jim is glad.
Rex is glad, too.
He has a new red bed.
Thank you, Jen!

19

LITERATURE ANTHOLOGY, pp. 18–19

Develop Comprehension

CLOSE READING

Skill: Characters, Setting, Events

COLLABORATE

Discuss with children new story events. *Talk with your partner about where Jen is and what event just happened. We can add those ideas to our chart.*

Character	Setting	Events
Jen	At a fire	She helps put out a fire.
Jen	Inside the fire house	The fire bell rings.
Jen	At a house	She saves a cat from a tree.

Return to Predictions and Purposes

Review children's predictions. Ask children if their predictions about the selection were correct. Guide them to use the evidence in the text to confirm whether their predictions turned out to be accurate. Prompt children to share what they learned about how firefighters help the community.

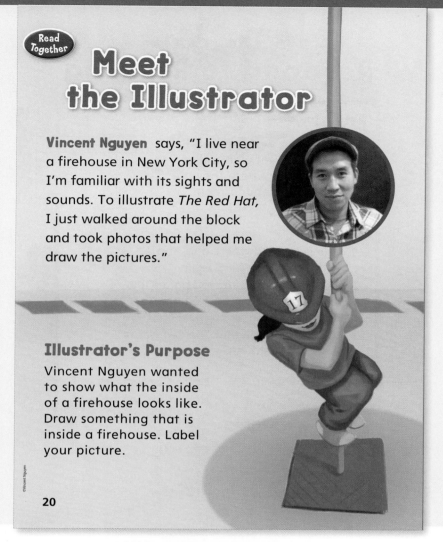

Meet the Illustrator

Vincent Nguyen says, "I live near a firehouse in New York City, so I'm familiar with its sights and sounds. To illustrate *The Red Hat,* I just walked around the block and took photos that helped me draw the pictures."

Illustrator's Purpose

Vincent Nguyen wanted to show what the inside of a firehouse looks like. Draw something that is inside a firehouse. Label your picture.

20

LITERATURE ANTHOLOGY, p. 20

Meet the Illustrator

Vincent Nguyen

Read aloud page 20 with children. Ask them why Nguyen took photos of a real firehouse. *Where did Nguyen take the photos? How did the photos help him draw the pictures?*

Illustrator's Purpose

Have children draw something that is inside a firehouse in their Response Journal. Have them label their drawing: *One thing inside a firehouse is a(n) _____.*

ILLUSTRATOR'S CRAFT

Focus on Points of View

Vincent Nguyen created the illustrations by looking at events from different angles. On page 16, for example, readers see the fire truck straight on as Jen drives the truck. On page 14 the illustration is drawn as if readers are kneeling alongside Jen. Point out the illustrations on pages 11 and 17. *On page 11 we look down as Jen slides down the pole. On page 17 we look up as she climbs. Seeing how far down she slides and how far up she climbs helps readers understand what Jen does.*

Respond to Reading

Retell

Use your own words to retell *The Red Hat*. Tell who the characters are, where they are, and what happens to them.

Character	Setting	Events

Text Evidence

1. Who is Jen and where does she work? **Character, Setting, Events**
2. What happens to the red hat at the beginning of the story? What happens to it at the end? **Character, Setting, Events**
3. How can you tell that *The Red Hat* is realistic fiction? **Genre**

Make Connections
? How does Jen help her community?
Essential Question

21

LITERATURE ANTHOLOGY, p. 21

Respond to Reading

Retelling

Guide children in retelling the selection. Remind them that as they read *The Red Hat*, they paid attention to who the characters are, what events happened, and where the events happened. Prompt children to use those details to retell the selection.

→ Have children use the details on their Character, Setting, Events chart to help them retell the selection.

Text Evidence

Guide children to use text evidence to answer the Text Evidence questions on Literature Anthology page 21. Model answering the questions as needed.

1. **Character, Setting, Events** To answer the first question, we need to look at details about Jen. Let's look back to pages 8 to 13. The details in the text tell us that Jen has a job helping to put out fires. She works in a firehouse and in a community.

2. Character, Setting, Events The question asks about the red hat at the beginning and at the end of the story. To answer this question, let's look for the red hat at the beginning and at the end of the story. At the beginning of the story, Jen gets the red hat. At the end of the story, the illustration shows us Rex the cat sleeps in Jen's red hat.

3. Genre This question asks how we know that the selection is realistic fiction. To answer this question, let's look back at the selection. On each page, we read about a character that is like a real person, events that are like what happens in real life, and places that are like real places. There is nothing in the story that could not happen in real life. This tells us that the selection is realistic fiction.

Make Connections

Essential Question Have children recall scenes from *The Red Hat* and think about how Jen helps the community. Prompt them to write a place where Jen goes on the fire truck. Have them share what Jen does there.

ELL

ENGLISH LANGUAGE LEARNERS

Retell Help children by looking at each page of the selection and asking a prompt such as: *Where is Jen when she gets the red hat?* Point to and identify the setting. *What is Jen doing?* Provide sentence frames to help children retell the selection such as: *Jen goes _____ when she _____.*

CONNECT TO CONTENT

COMPARE AND CONTRAST JOBS

Remind children that all week you have been comparing and contrasting different jobs people do in the community. Guide them to talk about the firefighters in *The Red Hat* and how they help the community. Remind children of the different jobs Ben saw people doing in *Good Job, Ben!* and the other workers they have read about this week. Prompt children to compare and contrast the different jobs. *How is a firefighter like a mail carrier? How are those jobs different? How does each job help the community?*

→ # Language Arts

Reading/Writing Workshop Big Book

OBJECTIVES

CCSS With guidance and support from adults, focus on a topic, respond to questions and suggestions from peers, and add details to strengthen writing as needed. **W.1.5**

CCSS Use common, proper, and possessive nouns. **L.1.1b**

CCSS Use commas in dates and to separate single words in a series. **L.1.2c**

ACADEMIC LANGUAGE
- *noun, commas, brainstorm*
- Cognate: *comas*

MINILESSON 5 Mins

Independent Writing

Writing Trait: Organization

1 Review Tell children they will write a draft. *Today you will write your story about someone who has a job in your community. Remember to write about one idea and include a beginning, a middle, and an end in your story.*

2 Guided Practice Have children open to page 26 in the Reading/Writing Workshop. Read the student model aloud. Point out how Jeff used the writing trait Organization to write about Ned's job. Guide children to identify what Ned's job is and what happens in the story.

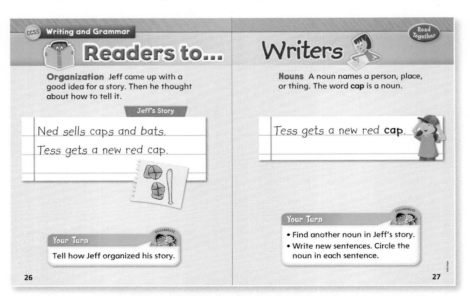

READING/WRITING WORKSHOP, pp. 26–27

Story

Model Have children look again at Jeff's story, noting his event and details. Before beginning their own writing process, have children complete the Your Turn to discuss Jeff's process.

Prewrite

Display the Word Web from Day 2. Tell children that to begin writing, they must choose one job. Preview the story ideas with children.

COLLABORATE **Brainstorm** Organize children into pairs based on the job they have chosen. Guide partners to use Teaching Poster 30 to organize their stories.

Go Digital

Present the Lesson

Graphic Organizer
Beginning
Middle
End

Writing

I see a fish.

Grammar

Draft

Have children write using their sequence charts. Remind them that a story is made up and has characters. Remind them to write about only one idea.

Apply Writing Trait Remind children that their stories should have one idea and a beginning, a middle, and an end.

Apply Grammar Tell children to think about the nouns they use. Remind them that every sentence has at least one noun. If they use three or more nouns in a list, they should put commas after all but the last noun.

As children work, conference with them to provide guidance.

Grammar
MINILESSON 5 Mins

Nouns

❶ **Review** Have children look at page 27 in the Reading/Writing Workshop. Remind them that a noun is a naming word. Have children identify the two nouns in the model sentence.

What are the nouns in this sentence: Tess gets a new red cap. *Which words name a person, place, or thing?* Tess *is a noun. It names a person.* Cap *is also a noun. It names a thing.*

❷ **Guided Practice/Practice** Guide children to identify a noun in Jeff's story. Remind children that every sentence has at least one noun, but some sentences may have more than one. Have children work with partners to write new sentences. Then have them circle the nouns in each sentence.

COLLABORATE **Talk About It** Have partners orally generate sentences about different jobs. Prompt them to name the nouns in each sentence.

Mechanics: Commas in a Series

❶ **Review** Remind children that when a writer uses three or more nouns in a list, there is a comma after all but the last noun.

❷ **Practice** Display the sentences. Read each aloud. Then have children fix each sentence.

I see frogs cats and dogs. (I see frogs, cats, and dogs.)

Fred sells cribs sleds and pots. (Fred sells cribs, sleds, and pots.)

ELL

ENGLISH LANGUAGE LEARNERS SCAFFOLD

Beginning

Demonstrate Comprehension Provide sentence frames for partners as they write their stories: _____ *has a job. The job is* _____. Model correct pronunciation as needed.

Intermediate

Explain Provide sentence starters for partners as they write their stories: *First,* _____. *Next,* _____. *Last,* _____. Repeat children's responses, correcting for grammar and pronunciation.

Advanced/Advanced High

Expand After children complete their stories, ask: *What idea did you write about? What nouns did you use? Why?* Elicit more details to support children's answers.

Daily Wrap Up

→ Review the Essential Question and encourage children to discuss it using the oral vocabulary words. Ask: *What jobs have you seen people do today?*

→ Prompt children to review and discuss skills they used today. Have them give examples of how they used each skill.

Materials

Literature Anthology
VOLUME 2

Visual Vocabulary Cards

astonishing   again
community   new
equipment   use
fortunately   help
occupation   there

Teaching Poster

Word-Building Cards

Dinah Zike's
FOLDABLES

Dinah Zike's Foldables®

leg

Spelling Word Cards

→ # Extend the Concept

MINILESSON
5 Mins

Oral Language

Go
Digital

OBJECTIVES
Use the illustrations and details in a text to describe its key ideas. **RI.1.7**

Review vocabulary

ACADEMIC LANGUAGE
• *label, illustration*
• Cognate: *illustración*

ESSENTIAL QUESTION

Remind children that this week they have been learning about jobs in the community. Guide children to discuss the question using information from what they have read and discussed.

Use the **Visual Vocabulary Cards** and the Define/Example/Ask routine to review the oral vocabulary words *occupation, community, equipment, fortunately,* and *astonishing.*

Guide children to use each word as they talk about what they have read and learned about what jobs are done in the community. Prompt children by asking questions.

→ What occupations have we read about?

→ What is a job people do in your community?

→ What special equipment do the construction workers use in *Good Job, Ben!*?

→ What would be an astonishing occupation to have?

→ Why is it fortunate to have firefighters in the community?

Review last week's oral vocabulary words *agree, difficult, exercise, exhausted,* and *physical.*

school

Visual Glossary

Teaching Poster

Firefighters
at Work

Firefighters at Work

Develop Comprehension

Text Feature: Labels

① **Explain** Tell children that they can use informational text selections to find facts and details about a topic. Explain that informational text often has illustrations with labels— words or phrases that name things in the illustrations.

Teaching Poster

② **Model** Display Teaching Poster 17. Point to the labels. *The labels help us understand what the pictures show.* Point to the builder's hat, jeans, and tool belt while you read the labels. *These labels tell us what the builder wears when she works. She wears a hard hat, jeans, and a tool belt.*

③ **Guided Practice/Practice** Read together the labels on the first illustration. Guide children to tell what the labels identify. *What parts of the picture do the labels name?* Repeat for the third illustration. Tell children to look for labels in the selection.

ELL

ENGLISH LANGUAGE LEARNERS SCAFFOLD

Beginning

Engage Use sentence frames to help children discuss the labels in the illustration. For example: *A _____ wears a _____.*

Intermediate

Describe Prompt children to think of more labels they can add to the illustration. *What else is the worker wearing?*

Advanced/Advanced High

Discuss Ask children to elaborate on the information in the labels. Ask: *Why does the worker wear these items? How do they help with the job?*

CCSS **Genre** Nonfiction

Compare Texts
Read about what real firefighters do.

Read Together

hat

Firefighters at Work

boots | pole

A bell rings at the firehouse. **Firefighters** slide down a pole. They put on special clothes fast!

22

The firefighters jump in a fire truck. The red truck speeds to the fire. It has a loud **siren** and a flashing red light. That tells cars to move away!

lights

ladder

① hose

23

Literature Anthology

LITERATURE ANTHOLOGY, pp. 22–23

Develop Comprehension

CLOSE READING

Lexile 290

Read Literature Anthology

Compare Texts

Remind children that in *The Red Hat*, they read about a firefighter named Jen. In "Firefighters at Work" they will read about the work that firefighters do. Have children make a prediction about what they will learn about firefighters in this selection. Then encourage them to think about the work Jen does as they read about these firefighters.

① Text Features: Labels

Teacher Think Aloud When I look at the photograph, I see many labels. They help me know what the things in the photograph are. The labels help me find the fire truck's hose and ladder in the photograph. I see also that the fire truck has flashing lights.

Content Words Point out the words *firehouse*, *firefighters*, *truck*, and *protect*. Prompt children to use context sentences to help them understand the words.

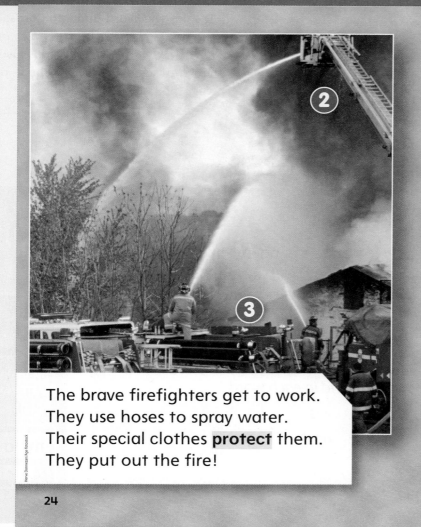

The brave firefighters get to work.
They use hoses to spray water.
Their special clothes **protect** them.
They put out the fire!

24

Now it is time for lunch.
They have lunch together.
Then they wait for the next bell. 4

Make Connections
How do firefighters
help the community?
Essential Question

25

LITERATURE ANTHOLOGY, pp. 24–25

② Strategy: Make and Confirm Predictions

Teacher Think Aloud I can look at the photographs to make a prediction. I predict I will learn what firefighters use to help them fight fires.

③ Text Features: Labels

Now the firefighters are putting out a fire. The labels on page 23 showed me the tools they use to put out a fire: hose and ladder. Do you see those tools in the photographs on page 24? How are they used? (The firefighters use the hoses to spray water and the ladder to get up high.)

④ Strategy: Make and Confirm Predictions

I predicted I would learn what firefighters use to fight fires. Use the text to confirm if I was correct. (Yes. The text tells about how firefighters use hoses and special clothes to help them put out fires.)

 Make Connections Have partners make connections between the firefighters they read about in *The Red Hat* and "Firefighters at Work."

 **Word Work**

Quick Review

Build Fluency: Sound-Spellings
Display the **Word-Building Cards:** *e, ea, sp, sn, sl, cr, fr, tr, o, pl, fl, cl, bl, i, a, s, r, l, t, m, n, c, p, b, f, g.* Have children say the sounds. Repeat, and vary the pace.

 MINILESSON 5 Mins

Phonemic Awareness

OBJECTIVES

CCSS Read words with inflectional endings. **RF.1.3f**

CCSS Recognize and read grade-appropriate irregularly spelled words. **RF.1.3g**

Decode and spell words with short *e*

Phoneme Isolation

1 **Model** Show children how to isolate a phoneme in a word. *Listen carefully. I am going to say a word. Then I will say the middle sound in that word. What is the middle sound in /ffffeeed/, fed? That's right. The middle sound in* fed *is /e/.*

2 **Guided Practice/Practice** Have children practice isolating phonemes in a word. Do the first two together. *I am going to say more words. Tell me the middle sound in each word.*

met	bed	bad	him	yes
bell	deaf	top	ten	neck

 MINILESSON 5 Mins

Phonics

Build Words with Short *e*

Review *The short* e *sound /e/ can be represented by the letters* e *or* ea. *We'll use* **Word-Building Cards** *to build words with short* e.

Place the letters *l, e, s, s. Let's blend the sounds together and read the word: /llleeesss/. Now let's change the* l *to* m. *Blend the sounds and read the word: /mmmeeesss/,* mess.

Continue with *set, bet, bat, bad, bed, fed, led, let, leg, lead, read, head, dead, deaf.*

Go Digital

Phonemic Awareness

Phonics

Structural Analysis

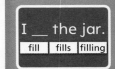

Spelling Word Sort

Visual Glossary

Structural Analysis

Inflectional Ending *-ed*

Review Write the words *spell* and *spelled* on the board and read them with children. Remind children that when *-ed* is added to action words, the ending sound of the new word can be /t/, /d/, or /ed/. Remind them that adding *-ed* to some words adds a word part, or syllable, as in *head* and *headed*.

Write the following words: *smell, trick, pack, sweat, dress.* Have children work in pairs to construct words that tell about actions in the past. Then have them write sentences with each word.

Spelling

Word Sort with *-eg, -en, -ead*

Review Provide pairs of children with copies of the **Spelling Word Cards**. While one partner reads the words one at a time, the other partner should orally segment the word and then write the word. After reading all the words, partners should switch roles.

Have children correct their own papers. Then have them sort the words by ending spelling pattern: *-eg, -en, -ead,* or no short *e* ending pattern.

High-Frequency Words

again, help, new, there, use

Review Display **Visual Vocabulary Cards** for high-frequency words *again, help, new, there, use.* Have children Read/Spell/Write each word.

→ Point to a word and call on a child to use it in a sentence.

→ Review last week's words using the same procedure.

Monitor and *Differentiate*

Quick Check

Can children read and decode words with short *e*?

Can children recognize and read high-frequency words?

Small Group Instruction

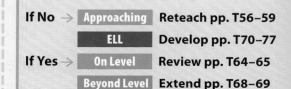

If No →	Approaching	Reteach pp. T56–59
	ELL	Develop pp. T70–77
If Yes →	On Level	Review pp. T64–65
	Beyond Level	Extend pp. T68–69

→ # Language Arts

MINILESSON 5 Mins
Independent Writing

Go Digital

Writing

📏 Make a capital letter.
Λ Add.
✐ Take out.

Proofreader's Marks

I see a fish.

Grammar

Story

Revise

Tell children that writers revise their writing to correct any mistakes and make their writing better. Explain that a writer might revise sentences in a story to make sure they all are about one idea and in an order that makes sense.

Apply Writing Trait: Ideas Explain that as writers revise, they might take out sentences that do not relate to the idea the writing is about. Display the following story:

> First, Deb got a job. Deb can spell well. Next, Deb helps Ben, Em, and Roz. Deb likes to jog. Last, Ben, Em, and Roz spell well, too.

Tell children that this story focuses on Deb's job of helping three children learn to spell. Point out that one sentence in the story is not about this idea. Guide children to see that the sentence about jogging does not belong in this story. Explain that to revise the story, they should take the sentence out.

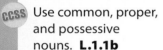 **Peer Review** Have children work in pairs to do a peer review, in which they will each read their partner's draft. They should take notes about what they like most, questions they have for the author, and ideas they think the author could include. Have partners discuss these topics. Provide time for them to make revisions to their stories.

Proofread/Edit

Apply Grammar Review proofreader's marks with children. Have them reread their drafts and fix mistakes. Remind them to make sure that:

→ every sentence has a noun.

→ all lists of three or more nouns have the necessary commas.

→ all words are spelled correctly.

→ all sentences are complete.

 Peer Edit Next, have partners exchange their drafts and take turns reading for the mistakes above. Encourage partners to discuss and fix errors together as they read.

OBJECTIVES

CCSS With guidance and support from adults, focus on a topic, respond to questions and suggestions from peers, and add details to strengthen writing as needed. **W.1.5**

CCSS Use common, proper, and possessive nouns. **L.1.1b**

ACADEMIC LANGUAGE
focuses, relate

Final Draft

After children have edited their own papers and finished their peer edits, have them write their final draft. Encourage them to create or find a photo or other visual that relates to their story. As children work, conference with them to provide guidance.

MINILESSON 5 Mins

Grammar

Nouns

1 Review Review with children that a noun is a naming word. It names a person, place, or thing. Have children name nouns they see around them.

2 Guided Practice Remind children that every sentence has at least one noun. Guide children to identify the noun, or nouns, as you say some sentences.

> My dad has a big red hat. (dad, hat)

> The man likes to dig rocks. (man, rocks)

Have children suggest replacement nouns for each sentence.

3 Practice Display the following words: *rock, dig, box, sis, yell, bed, up, mom, clock.* Have children identify the nouns.

Talk About It Have partners read aloud the stories they wrote. Partners can identify the nouns in each sentence.

Mechanics: Commas in a Series

1 Review Remind children that when there are three or more nouns in a list, there is a comma after all but the last noun.

2 Practice Display the sentences below. Read each aloud. Have children fix the sentences as a class.

> Nell plays tag blocks and dress up. (Nell plays tag, blocks, and dress up.)

> We use bats mitts, and caps. (We use bats, mitts, and caps.)

Daily Wrap Up

→ Have children discuss the Essential Question using the oral vocabulary words. Ask: *What job might you like to do in the future? Why?*

→ Prompt children to discuss the skills they practiced and learned today by asking, *What skills did you use today?*

Go Digital

www.connected.mcgraw-hill.com
RESOURCES
Research and Inquiry

→ **Wrap Up the Week**
Integrate Ideas

RESEARCH AND INQUIRY

Jobs Around Town

OBJECTIVES

CCSS Participate in shared research and writing projects (e.g., explore a number of "how-to" books on a given topic and use them to write a sequence of instructions). **W.1.7**

- Build background knowledge
- Research information using technology

ACADEMIC LANGUAGE
- *script, dialogue*
- Cognate: *diálogo*

Write a Script

COLLABORATE

Tell children that today they will do a research project with a partner to learn more about a job that helps the community. Review the steps in the research process.

STEP 1 ### Choose a Topic

Name examples of jobs in the community to prompt a brainstorming session. Guide partners to choose a job to write a script about.

STEP 2 ### Find Resources

Discuss how to use the selections to find information on partners' chosen jobs. Guide children to find additional information in reference materials and online. Tell them they can also speak to family members or other community members to learn about different jobs. Have them use the Research Process Checklist online.

Nurse – helps sick kids

Dinah Zike's
FOLDABLES

STEP 3 ### Keep Track of Ideas

Have children record their ideas in a Valley Fold Foldable®. Model recording details.

Collaborative Conversations

Add New Ideas Review with children that as they engage in partner, small-group, and whole-group discussions, they should:

→ stay on topic.

→ connect their own ideas to the comments of others.

→ look for ways to connect their experiences to the conversation.

Nurse: I am a nurse.
I help sick people get well.
I give them medicine.

STEP 4 Create the Project: Script

Explain the characteristics of a script.

→ **Words** A script gives the words that characters say in a play. In this project, one character talks about his or her job. The other character is someone related to the job.

→ **Play** A script is the written part of a play that can be performed on a stage.

Have pairs create scripts about their chosen jobs.

→ Guide partners to write sentences so that both partners can perform. For example, one child can be a nurse and the other, a patient.

→ Encourage partners to draw a picture of their worker.

→ Put the finished scripts together as a play for children to perform.

ENGLISH LANGUAGE LEARNERS

SCAFFOLD

Beginning	Intermediate	Advanced/High
Use Sentence Frames Use sentence frames to help children discuss their chosen job. For example: *A _____ helps the community by _____.*	**Discuss** Guide children to focus on the most important details about their job. Ask: *What does this community worker do? Where does he or she work?*	**Describe** Prompt children to explain why their chosen job is important to the community. Ask them to tell what might happen if nobody did the job.

Materials

Reading/Writing Workshop
VOLUME 2

Literature Anthology
VOLUME 2

Literature Big Book
Millie Waits for the Mail

Visual Vocabulary Cards

again
help
new
there
use

Teaching Poster

Interactive Read-Aloud Cards

Word-Building Cards

leg

Spelling Word Cards

→ # Integrate Ideas

TEXT CONNECTIONS

Connect to Essential Question

OBJECTIVES

 CCSS Identify basic similarities in and differences between two texts on the same topic (e.g., in illustrations, descriptions, or procedures). **RI.1.9**

• Develop answers to the Essential Question

• Make text connections to the world

ACADEMIC LANGUAGE

• *connections*

• Cognate: *conexiones*

Text to Text

Remind children that all week they have been reading selections about jobs that need to be done in a community. Now they can think about how the selections are similar. This is called making text connections. Model comparing texts using *Good Job, Ben!* and "Jobs Around Town."

Think Aloud *Good Job, Ben!* and "Jobs Around Town" are about jobs people do in the community. In both, I read about the important jobs people do that help the community. *Good Job, Ben!* is realistic fiction. The characters, settings, and events could happen in real life. "Jobs Around Town" is informational text. It tells about real people and places.

 Complete the Organizer Have children use the graphic organizer to help them discuss community jobs they read about.

→ Discuss and write about why the jobs need to be done in a community.

→ Discuss the different occupations that help a community.

Graphic Organizer

Text to Self

Have children discuss jobs people do in their own community and jobs they want to do. *Who do you know who has a job in your community? What is the job? What job would you want to do when you grow up? Why?*

Text to World

Have children discuss different types of jobs. Ask why each job is important. Then ask: *What would happen if no one did this job?*

WRITE ABOUT READING  *Analytical Writing*

OBJECTIVES

 Draw evidence from literary or informational texts to support analysis, reflection, and research. **W.4.9**

Analyze Character, Setting, Events

Explain to children that as a group you will write about one of the selections that they have read this week.

Using the evidence in the text, you will think about how the author used the character, setting, and events to tell the story.

Review the Character, Setting, Events chart you completed for *Good Job, Ben!* Guide children to analyze text evidence by asking "how" and "why" questions about the character, setting, and events.

→ *Why do you think the author wrote about the workers Ben met?*

→ *How did the author use the setting and events to tell about different jobs people do?*

→ *How did reading the selection help you understand community workers?*

Write an Analysis

Display the following sentence frames:

> In _____, the author wrote about the character _____.
>
> The author used the setting and events to tell about _____.
>
> The selection made us understand that _____.

Work with children to complete the sentence frames using the information about *Good Job, Ben!*

Select another realistic fiction selection you have read in this unit. Work with children to complete the sentence frames to write about how the author used characters, setting and events to tell about jobs.

RESEARCH AND INQUIRY *SOCIAL STUDIES*

OBJECTIVES

 Participate in shared research and writing projects. **W.1.7**

Wrap Up the Project

 Guide partners to share the job they chose. *What does a person in this job do? How does he or she help the community?* Then have children perform the class play. Have them use the Presentation Checklist online.

Word Work

Quick Review

Build Fluency: Sound-Spellings
Display the **Word-Building Cards:** *e, ea, sp, sn, sl, cr, fr, tr, o, pl, fl, cl, bl, i, a, s, r, l, t, m, n, c, p, b, f, g.* Have children say the sounds. Repeat, and vary the pace.

MINILESSON 5 Mins — Phonemic Awareness

OBJECTIVES

CCSS Orally produce single-syllable words by blending sounds (phonemes), including consonant blends. **RF.1.2b**

CCSS Decode regularly spelled one-syllable words. **RF.1.3b**

CCSS Read words with inflectional endings. **RF.1.3f**

Phoneme Blending

Review Guide children to blend phonemes to form words. *Listen as I say a group of sounds. Then blend those sounds to form a word.*

/m/ /e/ /n/   /l/ /e/ /s/   /b/ /e/ /d/   /n/ /e/ /k/

Phoneme Segmentation

Review Guide children to segment phonemes in words. *Now I am going to say a word. I want you to say each sound in the word.*

red   ten   yell   pen   sled

MINILESSON 5 Mins — Phonics

Blend and Build Words with Short *e*

Review Have children read and say the words *beg, fell, sled, men,* and *bread.* Then have children follow the word building routine with **Word-Building Cards** to build *leg, beg, peg, pen, men, den, ten, tell, bell, sell, well, swell, sweat.*

Word Automaticity Help children practice word automaticity. Display decodable words and point to each word as children chorally read it. Test how many words children can read in one minute. Model blending words children miss.

Go Digital

Phonemic Awareness

Phonics

Structural Analysis

Visual Glossary

Fluency: Word Automaticity

Structural Analysis

Inflectional Ending -ed

Review Have children explain when the -ed ending is used. Then have children practice writing words with -ed such as *yelled, spelled, headed, picked,* and *packed.*

Remind children that adding -ed to some words adds a word part, or syllable, such as in *head* and *headed.*

Spelling

Word Sort with -eg, -en, -ead

Review Have children use the **Spelling Word Cards** to sort the weekly words by vowel and ending sounds. Remind children that four of the words do not have the short *e* sound spelled *e* or *ea.*

Assess Assess children on their abilities to spell words in the -eg, -en, and -ead word families. Say each word and provide a sentence so that children can hear the words used in a correct context. Then allow them time to write down the words. To challenge children, you may wish to provide an additional word in each family in order to assess whether they understand the concept.

High-Frequency Words

again, help, new, there, use

Review Display **Visual Vocabulary Cards** *again, help, new, there, use.* Have children Read/Spell/Write each word. Have children write a sentence with each word.

Monitor and *Differentiate*

✓ Quick Check

Can children read and decode words with short *e*?

Can children recognize and read high-frequency words?

Small Group Instruction

If No →	Approaching	Reteach pp. T56–59
	ELL	Develop pp. T70–77
If Yes →	On Level	Review pp. T64–65
	Beyond Level	Extend pp. T68–69

→ # Language Arts

MINILESSON
5 Mins

Independent Writing

Go Digital

Writing

Checklists

I see a fish.

Grammar

OBJECTIVES

CCSS With guidance and support from adults, use a variety of digital tools to produce and publish writing, including in collaboration with peers. **W.1.6**

CCSS Use common, proper, and possessive nouns. **L.1.1b**

ACADEMIC LANGUAGE

• *presentation, story*

• Cognate: *presentación*

Story

Prepare

Review guidelines for making presentations with children.

→ Provide time for children to finish preparing their presentations. Remind them to practice using visuals if they have created any.

Present

Have children take turns giving presentations of their stories. Remind them to speak clearly. When listening to other stories, they should be polite and respectful, asking questions when appropriate and listening carefully when it is not appropriate to speak.

→ If possible, record the presentations so that children can self-evaluate.

Evaluate

Have children discuss their own presentations and evaluate their performance using the presentation rubric.

Use the teacher's rubric to evaluate children's writing. Have children add their writing to their Writer's Portfolio. Then have them discuss and write about how they have changed as writers throughout the year.

Publish

After children finish presenting their stories, discuss how the class will illustrate and then compile them into a book. Guide children to use digital tools to create the book. Title the book *Jobs in Our Community*. Allow children to design the cover of the book.

Grammar

Nouns

1 Review Have children describe what nouns are. Write the following sentence and have children identify the nouns:

A sled moves down the hill. (sled, hill)

2 Practice Ask: *How do I know which word or words in a sentence are nouns?*

Distribute one **Sound-Spelling Card** A–Z (do not use *jump*) to each child. Have each child name the pictured noun, tell whether it is a person, place, or thing, and then use the noun in a sentence.

Mechanics: Commas in a Series

1 Review Remind children that when there are three or more nouns in a list, there is a comma after each noun but the last one.

2 Practice Write the following sentences. Read each aloud. Have children fix the sentences.

Gran set hot dogs, ribs and ham on the grill. (Gran set hot dogs, ribs, and ham on the grill.)

Bev uses bricks blocks and clips to make a deck. (Bev uses bricks, blocks, and clips to make a deck.)

Mom grins at Mack Todd, and Bill. (Mom grins at Mack, Todd, and Bill.)

Wrap Up the Week

→ Review the Essential Question and encourage children to discuss using the oral vocabulary words.

→ Review that when children read they should identify and think about the characters, setting, and events. They can also make and confirm predictions as they read.

→ Review words with short *e* spelled *e* and *ea*. Remind children that the inflectional ending *-ed* at the end of an action word means the action happened in the past.

→ Use the Visual Vocabulary Cards to review the Words to Know.

→ Remind children that a story has characters and a beginning, a middle, and an end.

→ Approaching Level

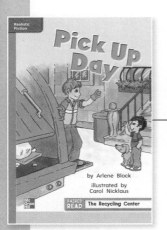

Lexile 70

 OBJECTIVES

Describe characters, setting, and major events in a story, using key details. **RL.1.3**

 With prompting and support, read prose and poetry of appropriate complexity for grade 1. **RL.1.10**

Make and confirm predictions

Leveled Reader: *Pick Up Day*

Before Reading

Preview and Predict

Have children turn to the title page. Read the title and the author's name and have children repeat. Preview the selection's illustrations. Prompt children to predict what the selection might be about.

Review Genre: Realistic Fiction

Have children recall that realistic fiction is an invented, or made-up, story, which could have happened in real life. It has invented, or make-believe, characters, settings, and events that could exist in real life.

ESSENTIAL QUESTION

Remind children of the Essential Question. Set a purpose for reading: *Let's read to find out what events happen on pick up day.*

Remind children that as they read a selection, they can ask questions about what they do not understand or what they want to know more about.

During Reading

Guided Comprehension

As children whisper read *Pick Up Day*, monitor and provide guidance, correcting blending and modeling the key strategies and skills.

Strategy: Make and Confirm Predictions

Remind children that they can use the words and illustrations to make predictions as they read. Model using the strategy: *On page 4 we learn the garbage truck is up the block. I predict the truck will stop at the boy's house.* Read page 5, point to the illustration, and confirm the prediction.

Skill: Character, Setting, Events

Remind children that a story has characters, a setting, and events. While reading, ask: *Who are the characters? Where does the story take place? What events happen?* Display a Character, Setting, Events chart for children to copy.

Go Digital

Pick Up Day

Graphic Organizer

Retell

Model recording children's answers in the character, setting, and events boxes. Have children copy the answers into their own charts.

Think Aloud On page 5 I see that Ted is on the truck. He is a character. The truck is on a city street. That is the setting. The garbage truck is stopping to pick up the garbage at the boy's house. That is one event.

Guide children to use the text and illustrations to complete the chart.

After Reading

Respond to Reading

Complete the Respond to Reading on page 12 after reading.

Retell

Have children take turns retelling the selection. Help children make a connection: *Have you ever seen a garbage truck? What do the workers on the truck do? In what ways are their jobs helpful to the community?*

Model Fluency

Read the sentences one at a time. Have children chorally repeat. Point out to children how your voice sounds at the end of a question and at the end of an exclamation.

Apply Have children practice repeated readings with partners. Provide feedback as needed.

PAIRED READ ...

Leveled Reader

"The Recycling Center"

Make Connections: Write About It · Analytical Writing

Before reading, ask children to note that the genre of this text is informational text. Discuss the Compare Texts direction. Ask children to tell how what they learned in *Pick Up Day* is related to what they read about in "The Recycling Center."

✎ *Analytical Writing*

COMPARE TEXTS

→ Have children use text evidence to compare realistic fiction to informational text.

Literature Circles

Lead children in conducting a literature circle using the Thinkmark questions to guide the discussion. You may wish to discuss what children have learned about community jobs from both selections in the Leveled Reader.

Level Up

Level-up lessons available online.

IF children can read *Pick Up Day* Approaching Level with fluency and correctly answer the Respond to Reading questions,

THEN tell children that they will read a selection on a similar topic.

• Use pages 2–4 of *Ben Brings the Mail* On Level to model using the Teaching Poster 28 to identify characters, setting, and events.

• Have children read the selection, checking their comprehension by using the graphic organizer.

→ Approaching Level

Phonemic Awareness

PHONEME BLENDING

TIER 2

OBJECTIVES

CCSS Orally produce single-syllable words by blending sounds (phonemes), including consonant blends. **RF.1.2b**

 I Do Explain to children that they will be blending sounds to form words. *Listen as I say two sounds: /e/ /g/. Say the sounds with me: /eee/ /g/. I'm going to blend the sounds together: /eee/ /g/, /eeeg/,* egg. *We blended the word* egg.

 We Do *Listen as I say three sounds: /j/ /e/ /t/. Repeat the sounds: /j/ /e/ /t/. Let's blend the sounds: /j/ /eee/ /t/, /jeeet/,* jet. *We made one word:* jet

Repeat this routine with the following words:

/b//e//t/   /f//e//l/   /l//e//t/   /m//e//t/   /p//e//n/   /r//e//d/
/w//e//t/   /s//e//l/   /g//e//t/   /h//e//n/

 You Do *It's your turn. I want you to blend the sounds I say together to form a word.*

/b//e//l/   /d//e//k/   /e//l//f/   /l//e//t/   /m//e//s/   /n//e//k/

Repeat the blending routine with additional short *e* words.

PHONEME ISOLATION

TIER 2

OBJECTIVES

CCSS Isolate and pronounce initial, medial vowel, and final sounds (phonemes) in spoken single-syllable words. **RF.1.2c**

 I Do Explain to children that they will listen for sounds at the beginning of words. *Listen as I say a word, and then identify the beginning sound in the word:* egg. *The beginning sound in* egg *is /e/.*

 We Do *Let's do some together. What sound do you hear at the beginning of this word:* bed? *I hear /b/ at the beginning of* bed.

Continue the routine with these words:

elf   leg   hem   pen   Ed   yes   elm   pen

 You Do *It's your turn. Tell me what sound you hear at the beginning of these words.*

mat   net   bin   yes   Sam   red   him   jet

Repeat the isolation routine with additional short *e* words.

PHONEME BLENDING

OBJECTIVES

CCSS Orally produce single-syllable words by blending sounds (phonemes), including consonant blends. **RF.1.2b**

 I Do Explain to children that they will be blending sounds to form words. *Listen as I say four sounds: /s/ /m/ /e/ /l/. Say the sounds with me: /s/ /m/ /e/ /l/. I'm going to blend the sounds together: /sss/ /mmm/ /eee/ /lll/, /sssmmmeeelll/,* smell. *We blended the word* smell.

 We Do *Listen as I say four sounds: /f/ /l/ /e/ /d/. Repeat the sounds: /f/ /l/ /e/ /d/. Let's blend the sounds: /fff/ /lll/ /eee/ /d/, /fffllleeed/,* fled. *We made one word:* fled.

Repeat this routine with the following words:

/b/ /r/ /e/ /d/   /d/ /e/ d/   /p/ /e/ /s/ /t/   /s/ /p/ /e/ /l/   /s/ /l/ /e/ /d/

 You Do *It's your turn. I want you to blend the sounds I say together to form a word.*

/r/ /e/ /d/   /d/ /e/ /f/   /h/ /e/ /d/   /s/ /p/ /e/ /l/   /d/ /r/ /e/ /s/

Repeat the blending routine with additional short *e* words.

PHONEME ISOLATION

OBJECTIVES

CCSS Isolate and pronounce initial, medial vowel, and final sounds (phonemes) in spoken single-syllable words. **RF.1.2c**

 I Do Explain to children that they will identify the middle sound in words. *I'll say a word and then say the middle sound. Listen: /mmmeeet/,* met. *I hear /e/ in the middle of* met.

 We Do *Let's do some together. What sound do you hear in the middle of* neck, */nnneeek/,* neck. *Yes! We all hear /e/ in the middle of* neck.

Repeat this routine with the following words:

cap   beg   not   lip   den   fat   pet   Pam

 You Do *It's your turn. What sound do you hear in the middle of each of these words?*

zip   tap   wet   tell   lap   fill   pin   bet

Repeat the isolation routine with additional single-syllable short *e* words.

 ENGLISH LANGUAGE LEARNERS

For the **ELLs** who need **phonemic awarenesss, phonics,** and **fluency** practice, use scaffolding methods as necessary to ensure children understand the meaning of the words. Refer to the Language Transfer Handbook for phonics elements that may not transfer in children's native languages.

→ Approaching Level

Phonics

CONNECT e AND ea TO /e/

OBJECTIVES

 Decode regularly spelled one-syllable words. **RF.1.3b**

 I Do Display the **Word-Building Card** e. *This is lowercase* e. *Watch and listen as I trace the letter* e *and say the sound it stands for.* Trace the letter e and say /e/ five times. Then say: *In some words the letters* e *and* a *together stand for the /e/ sound.* Display and trace ea together five times.

 We Do Repeat the routine with children. Have them take turns tracing lowercase e and ea and saying /e/ along with you: /e/. Repeat five times.

 You Do Have children write the letter e in the air with their fingers and say /e/ at least five times. Repeat with the letters ea.

Repeat having children air-write e and ea on paper while saying the sound /e/ throughout the week.

BLEND WORDS WITH SHORT e

OBJECTIVES

 Decode regularly spelled one-syllable words. **RF.1.3b**

Decode words with short e

 I Do Write the word *pet.* *Listen as I say the sound each letter stands for.* Point to each letter as you say the sound: /p/, /e/, /t/. *Now listen as I blend the sounds.* Point to each letter as you blend the sounds: /p/ /eee/ /t/, /peeet/, pet.

 We Do Guide children to blend the sounds and read the following words with you as you point to each letter: *men, hen, pen, peg, egg, let, met, well.*

 You Do Have children use Word-Building Cards to blend and read the following words on their own: *Ed, red, hem, led, bet, mess, less, fell, tell, fed.*

Repeat, blending additional short e words.

You may wish to review Phonics with **ELL** using this section.

BUILD WORDS WITH SHORT *e*

OBJECTIVES
Decode regularly spelled one-syllable words. **RF.1.3b**

Build and decode words with short *e*

I Do Display Word-Building Cards *t, e, n,* one at a time. Point to each letter as you say the letter and sound: *The letters* t, e, *and* n *stand for/t/, /eee/, and /nnn/. I can use these letters to build a word. Display the letters in a row. I can blend /t/ /eee/ /nnn/ together: /teeennn/,* ten.

We Do *Let's build a new word together.* Display the letters *h, e, a, d. Remember, the letters* ea *together can stand for the sound /e/. Let's blend and read the new word: /h/ /eee/ /d/, /heeed/,* head.

You Do Have children build and blend the words: *pet, let, met, bread, bet, bed, dead, red, fed, Ted.*

Repeat, building additional words with short *e.*

BLEND WORDS WITH SHORT *e*

OBJECTIVES
Decode regularly spelled one-syllable words. **RF.1.3b**

Decode words with short *e*

I Do Display Word-Building Cards *b, r, e, a, d. These are the letters* b *and* r. *They stand for the sounds /br/. These letters are* e, a. *Sometimes together they stand for /eee/. This is the letter* d. *It stands for /d/. Listen as I blend the sounds and read the word: /brrreeed/,* bread.

We Do *Let's blend some words together.* Blend the words *dread, sweat, fled, smell, deck, speck* with children.

You Do Display the words to the right. Have children blend and read the words.

bed	mess	step	press	fed	hem
neck	less	Glen	spell	head	bread
swell	dead	yes	leg	Ed	men
stem	egg	sped	Greg	wet	bell

My red dress is the best.

The men had bread and ham.

She had a red hat on her head.

BUILD FLUENCY WITH PHONICS

Sound-Spellings Fluency

Display the following Word-Building Cards: *e, ea, sp, sn, sl, cr, fr, tr, o, pl, fl, cl, bl, i, a, s, r, l, t, m, n, c, p, b, f, g.* Say the sounds. Have children echo the sounds. Repeat and vary the pace.

Fluency in Connected Text

Have children review *Good Job, Ben!* in their Reading/Writing Workshop. Identify short *e* words. Blend words as needed.

Have children reread the selection on their own or with a partner.

Approaching Level

Structural Analysis

REVIEW INFLECTIONAL ENDING -ed

OBJECTIVES

 Know and apply grade-level phonics and word analysis skills in decoding words. **RF.1.3**

 Read words with inflectional endings. **RF.1.3f**

Read words with the inflectional ending -ed

 I Do Write *yelled*. Read the word: /yyyeeellld/. Circle *yell* with your finger. *I know this is the word* yell. *The -ed ending is added to this word to tell me that it has already happened. This word is* yelled. *I can use* yell *and* yelled *in sentences. We'll yell for our team today. The girls yelled to their friends yesterday.*

We Do Write *fixed*. *Let's read this word:* /fffiiiikst/. *What word do you see that you know? Yes,* fix. *We know the* -ed *tells us that this is something that already happened. Remember,* -ed *can stand for the sound* /d/ *or* /t/. *In this word,* -ed *stands for* /t/. *Let's use* fix *and* fixed *in sentences.*

You Do Have partners read and determine the root word in each of the words below. Have them make up sentences for the root word and the word with the -*ed* ending:

smelled   messed   mixed   spilled   tossed   clicked

Repeat Have children create sentences with words ending in -*ed*.

RETEACH INFLECTIONAL ENDING -ed

OBJECTIVES

 Know and apply grade-level phonics and word analysis skills in decoding words. **RF.1.3**

 Read words with inflectional endings. **RF.1.3f**

Read words with the inflectional ending -ed

 I Do Write *press* and *pressed*. Read the word: /prrreeesss/. *This is the word* press. *Underline the letters* ed *in* pressed. *When I add* -ed, *it makes the word tell about something that already happened.* Add -*ed* to *press*. Read the word: /prrreeessst/. *If I pressed a button, it means I pressed it before.*

 We Do Write *swell* and *pass*. *Let's add* -ed. *Say* swelled: /sssweeellld/. *Say* passed: /paaasssd/. *Let's use the words* swelled *and* passed *in sentences.*

Repeat this routine with the following words:

head dread swell pick mix block land

 You Do *Now it's your turn. Add* -ed *to each word, read the word, and use it in a sentence.*

peck mess smell spell fill tick pass

Repeat reading and using additional words with -*ed* endings in sentences.

High-Frequency Words

REVIEW

OBJECTIVES

CCSS Recognize and read grade-appropriate irregularly spelled words. **RF.1.3g**

Review *again, help, new, there, use*

 I Do Use the **High-Frequency Word Cards** to **Read/Spell/Write** each high-frequency word. Use each word orally in a sentence.

 We Do Guide children to Read/Spell/Write each word on their **Response Boards**. Work together to generate oral sentences using the words.

 You Do Have each child do the Read/Spell/Write routine independently using the words *again, help, new, there, use.*

RETEACH

OBJECTIVES

CCSS Recognize and read grade-appropriate irregularly spelled words. **RF.1.3g**

CCSS Produce complete sentences when appropriate to task and situation. **SL.1.6**

Reteach *again, help, new, there, use*

 I Do Review the high-frequency words using the Read/Spell/Write routine. Write a sentence on the board for each high-frequency word.

 We Do Guide children to use the Read/Spell/Write routine. Work together to read and complete sentence starters: *(1) We will go again to ____. (2) I like to help ____. (3) This is a new ____. (4) There is my ____. (5) Can I use the ____?*

 You Do Say the word. Have children write the word and say a sentence. Display the word and have children self-correct.

Repeat for each high-frequency word.

CUMULATIVE REVIEW

OBJECTIVES

CCSS Recognize and read grade-appropriate irregularly spelled words. **RF.1.3g**

Review previously taught high-frequency words

 I Do Display the High-Frequency Word Cards from the previous weeks. Review each word using the Read/Spell/Write routine.

 We Do Have children write the words on their Response Boards. Complete sentences for each word: *Ben does not like ____. This class is very ____.*

 You Do Show each card and have children chorally read the words.

Fluency Display the High-Frequency Word Cards. Point to the words in random order. Have children chorally read. Repeat at a faster pace.

→ Approaching Level

Comprehension

READ FOR FLUENCY

OBJECTIVES

 Read with sufficient accuracy and fluency to support comprehension. **RF.1.4**

 Read grade-level text orally with accuracy, appropriate rate, and expression. **RF.1.4b**

I Do Read the first page of the Practice Book selection. Model using appropriate intonation and stressing important words.

We Do Read the next page of the Practice Book selection. Call attention to how you stress specific words and how your voice sounds when asking a question or reading the exclamation. Have children echo-read each sentence using appropriate intonation.

You Do Guide children to echo-read the whole passage, focusing on the questions and exclamations. Have partners then reread the passage chorally using correct intonation. Monitor children as they read.

IDENTIFY CHARACTERS

OBJECTIVES

 Ask and answer questions about key details in a text. **RL.1.1**

I Do Remind children that the key details are the important parts of a story. Explain that good readers use key details in the pictures and words to learn about the characters in a story.

We Do Read the Practice Book selection together. Ask about a character. Model identifying the details to answer the question.

Who is Ben? What does he do? How can you tell?

You Do Have children reread the passage chorally. Guide them to identify and share important details in the words and illustration that show other information about the characters and what they do.

REVIEW CHARACTER, SETTING, EVENTS

OBJECTIVES

 Describe characters, setting, and major events in a story, using key details. **RL.1.3**

 I Do

Remind children that the character is a person or animal in a story. The setting tells when and where the story takes place, and the events are the actions that take place in the story. *To understand a story, good readers recognize who, when, where, and what happens in the story.*

 We Do

Read the Practice Book selection together. Guide children to answer questions about the characters, setting, and events. *We read that this story is about Mom and Ben. It takes place at the clock store. How can we tell?*

 You Do

Have partners reread the sentences chorally. Guide children to record the information on a Character, Setting, Events chart.

SELF-SELECTED READING

OBJECTIVES

CCSS Describe characters, settings, and major events in a story, using key details. **RL.1.3**

CCSS With prompting and support, read prose and poetry of appropriate complexity for grade 1. **RL.1.10**

Apply the strategy and skill to read a text

Read Independently

Have children pick a realistic fiction selection for sustained silent reading. Remind them to:

→ recall or predict what the selection will be about before beginning to read.

→ identify the characters, setting, and events.

→ confirm if their predictions were correct.

Read Purposefully

Have children complete the Character, Setting, Events chart. After completing the chart, have partners:

→ share their charts.

→ tell how making predictions helped them understand the story.

On Level

Lexile 200

OBJECTIVES

 Describe characters, settings, and major events in a story, using key details. **RL.1.3**

 With prompting and support, read prose and poetry of appropriate complexity for grade 1. **RL.1.10**

Make and confirm predictions

Leveled Reader:
Ben Brings the Mail

Before Reading

Preview and Predict

Have children turn to the title page. Read the title and the author's name and have children repeat. Preview the selection's illustrations. Prompt children to predict what the selection might be about.

Review Genre: Realistic Fiction

Have children recall that realistic fiction is an invented or made-up story that could have happened in real life.

ESSENTIAL QUESTION

Remind children of the Essential Question: *What jobs need to be done in a community?* Set a purpose for reading: *Let's read to find out how bringing the mail helps the community.*

Remind children that as they read a selection, they can ask questions about what they do not understand or what they want to know more about.

During Reading

Guided Comprehension

As children whisper read *Ben Brings the Mail,* monitor and provide guidance, correcting blending and modeling the key strategies and skills.

Strategy: Make and Confirm Predictions

Remind children that they can use the words and illustrations to make predictions. They can read on to find out if their predictions are correct. Model the strategy: *On pages 2 and 3 the words and pictures tell me that the mail carrier is stopping. I predict he will bring mail to the people on the block.* Read page 4, point to the illustration, and confirm the prediction.

Skill: Character, Setting, Events

Remind children that stories have characters, settings, and events. While reading, ask: *Who are the characters? What is the setting? What happens?* Show a Character, Setting, Events chart for children to copy.

 Go Digital

 **Ben Brings the Mail**

Graphic Organizer

 **Retell**

T62 UNIT 2 WEEK 1

Model recording children's answers in the character, setting, and events boxes. Have children copy the answers into their own charts.

Think Aloud On page 4, I see a neighborhood street. That is the setting. I see Ben the mail carrier. He is a character. The words tell me that Ben gives a letter to Miss Deb. That is an event.

Guide children to use words and pictures to add characters, setting and events to their charts.

After Reading

Respond to Reading

Complete the Respond to Reading on page 12.

Retell

Have children take turns retelling the selection using the **Retelling Cards** as a guide. Help them make connections: *Do you see a mail carrier on your street or road? Does your mail carrier do what Ben does? How does your mail carrier help you?*

Model Fluency

Read the sentences one at a time as children chorally repeat. Show children how your voice sounds at the end of a question and exclamation.

Apply Have children practice reading with partners. Provide feedback.

PAIRED READ ...

"At the Post Office"

Make Connections: Write About It ✏️ *Analytical Writing*

Before reading, have children note that the genre of this text is informational text. Discuss the Compare Texts direction. Ask children how a mail carrier like Ben in *Ben Brings the Mail* and the post office workers in "At the Post Office" all help the community.

Leveled Reader

✏️ *Analytical Writing*

COMPARE TEXTS

→ Have children use text evidence to compare realistic fiction to informational text.

Literature Circles

Lead children in conducting a literature circle using the Thinkmark questions to guide the discussion. You may wish to discuss what children have learned about post office jobs from both selections in the Leveled Reader.

Level Up

Level-up lessons available online.

IF children can read *Ben Brings the Mail* On Level with fluency and correctly answer the Respond to Reading questions,

THEN tell children that they will read a story about another kind of community job.

• Use pages 2–4 of *At Work With Mom* Beyond Level to model using the Teaching Poster 28 to identify characters, setting, and events.

• Have children read the selection, checking their comprehension by using the graphic organizer.

On Level

Phonics

BUILD WORDS WITH SHORT *e*

OBJECTIVES

 Know and apply grade-level phonics and word analysis skills in decoding words. **RF.1.3**

 Decode regularly spelled one-syllable words. **RF.1.3b**

Build and decode words with short *e*.

 Display **Word-Building Cards** *p, e, n. The letters* p, e, n *stand for the sounds* /p/, /e/, *and* /n/. *I can use the letters to build a word. I will blend* /p/, /e/, *and* /n/: /peeennn/. *The word is* pen.

 Now let's build a word together. Let's use the cards for h, e, a, *and* d. Display the cards. *Let's blend:* /heeed/, head. *We made a word,* head.

Now let's build a new word. Let's change the letter h *to the letters* br. *Let's blend and read the new word:* /brrreeed/, bread. *The new word is* bread.

 Have children build and blend the words *hen, ten, den, deck, deaf, dead, read, dread.*

Repeat using additional words with short *e*.

High-Frequency Words

REVIEW WORDS

OBJECTIVES

 Recognize and read grade-appropriate irregularly spelled words. **RF.1.3g**

Review high-frequency words: *again, help, new, there, use*

 Use the **Read/Spell/Write** routine to review each word. Use each word orally in a sentence.

 Guide children to Read/Spell/Write each word using their **Response Boards**. Work together to create oral sentences using the words.

 Have children work with a partner to do the Read/Spell/Write routine on their own using the words *again, help, new, there,* and *use.* Have partners write sentences about this week's stories. Each sentence must contain at least one high-frequency word.

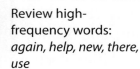

Comprehension

REVIEW CHARACTER, SETTING, EVENTS

OBJECTIVES
Describe characters, setting, and major events in a story, using key details. **RL.1.3**

 I Do
Remind children that a character is a person or an animal in a story. The setting tells when and where the story takes place, and the events are what actions take place. *The characters, setting, and events we read about in realistic fiction are like the people, places, and activities and experiences that might happen in real life.*

 We Do
Read aloud the first page of the Practice Book selection. Ask questions about the characters and setting. Discuss how children know the answers. *Who are the characters in the story? Where does the story take place?*

 You Do
Guide children to read the rest of the selection. Then have partners ask each other questions about the characters, setting, and events. Remind children to show where they find their answers.

SELF-SELECTED READING

OBJECTIVES
With prompting and support, read prose and poetry of appropriate complexity for grade 1. **RL.1.10**

Apply the strategy and skill to read a text

Read Independently

Have children pick a realistic fiction selection for sustained silent reading. Remind them to:

→ recall or predict what will happen next as they read the story.

→ identify the characters, setting, and important events in the story.

Read Purposefully

Have children complete the Character, Setting, Events chart. After completing the chart, have partners:

→ share and compare their charts.

→ tell about the predictions they made and which ones they could confirm.

→ identify characters, setting, and events that show that the selection is realistic fiction.

Beyond Level

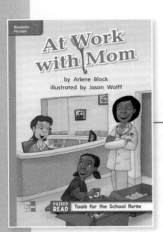

Lexile 330

OBJECTIVES

 Describe characters, setting, and major events in a story, using key details. **RL.1.3**

 With prompting and support, read prose of appropriate complexity for grade 1. **RL.1.10**

Make and confirm predictions

Leveled Reader: *At Work with Mom*

At Work with Mom

Graphic Organizer

Before Reading

Preview and Predict

Read the title and the author's name. Have children preview the title page and the illustrations. Ask: *What do you think this book will be about?*

Review Genre: Realistic Fiction

Have children recall that realistic fiction is an invented, or made-up story, which could have happened in real life. Prompt children to name key characteristics of realistic fiction. Tell them to look for these as they read the Leveled Reader.

ESSENTIAL QUESTION

Remind children of the Essential Question: *What jobs need to be done in a community?* Set a purpose for reading: *Let's read to find out what Jen's mom does and how she helps the community.*

During Reading

Guided Comprehension

Have children whisper read *At Work with Mom*. Have them place self-stick notes next to difficult words. Remind children that when they come to an unfamiliar word, they can look for familiar spellings. They will need to break longer words into smaller chunks and sound out each part.

Monitor children's reading. Stop periodically and ask open-ended questions to facilitate rich discussion, such as: *What does the author want us to know about Miss Rex's job?* Build on children's responses to develop deeper understanding of the text.

Strategy: Make and Confirm Predictions

Remind children that making and confirming predictions as they read will help them understand a selection. Say: *Use details in both the words and illustrations when you make and confirm predictions.*

Skill: Character, Setting, Events

Remind children that as they read a story, they should identify the characters, setting, and events. While reading, ask: *Who are the characters? Where does the story take place? What are the important events?* Display a Character, Setting, Events chart for children to copy.

Model how to record the information. Have children fill in their chart.

Think Aloud As I read pages 2 and 3 and look at the pictures, I learn that Dr. Deb is Jen's mom. They are two characters in the story. They are going to Dr. Deb's office. That is an event. Her office is the setting.

After Reading

Respond to Reading

Complete the Respond to Reading on page 12 after reading.

Retell

Have children take turns retelling the selection. Help children make a personal connection by writing about a visit to a doctor. *Write about a time you went to the doctor. Why did you go to the doctor? How did the doctor help you?*

PAIRED READ ...

"Tools for the School Nurse"

Make Connections: Write About It *Analytical Writing*

Before reading, ask children to preview the title page and prompt them to identify the genre. Discuss the Compare Texts direction. Have partners discuss how *At Work with Mom* is similar to "Tools for the School Nurse." Prompt children to share what they learned about medical tools.

Leveled Reader

Analytical Writing

COMPARE TEXTS

→ Have children use text evidence to compare realistic fiction to informational text.

Literature Circles

Lead children in conducting a literature circle using the Thinkmark questions to guide the discussion. You may wish to discuss what children have learned about how people in the health field help them from both selections in the Leveled Reader.

Gifted and Talented

SYNTHESIZE Challenge children to list different jobs in health care. Children should write about what jobs they think are most interesting. Encourage them to tell why they think the jobs are interesting and if they would consider any of them as their own careers.

EXTEND Have them use facts they learned from the week or do additional research to find out more about jobs in health care.

Beyond Level

Vocabulary

OBJECTIVES

 Use words and phrases acquired through conversation, reading and being read to, and responding to texts, including using frequently occurring conjunctions to signal simple relationships (e.g., *because*). **L.1.6**

Use multiple-meaning words in sentences

 I Do Review with children the meaning of the oral vocabulary word *occupation*.

Explain that some words have more than one meaning. *His occupation, or job, is a teacher.* Explain that *occupation* can have another meaning: a taking over of an area or place. *The occupation of the building will happen next week.*

 We Do Repeat the two meanings for *occupation*. Write and read each sentence aloud. Guide children to identify the definition used in each:

Many children are part of the occupation of the school.

The children voted for police officer as their favorite occupation.

 You Do Have partners take turns saying sentences for the different meanings of *occupation*. Have them tell which meaning is used in the other's sentence.

Repeat the routine by creating sentences for *community*.

 Gifted and Talented **Extend** Challenge children to share oral stories using one of the meanings of the word *occupation*. Have them tell their stories to a partner who has chosen to include the different meaning of *occupation* in his or her story. Have them discuss how their stories show the different meanings of the word.

Comprehension

REVIEW CHARACTER, SETTING, EVENTS

OBJECTIVES

 Describe characters, setting, and major events in a story, using key details. **RL.1.3**

 I Do Discuss how understanding the characters, setting, and events in a story helps readers to understand the story.

 We Do Read the Practice Book selection aloud. Model how to identify details to answer: *Who are the characters? What is the setting? Name one important event.*

 You Do Have children reread the Practice Book selection on their own. Have partners describe the characters and setting to each other by answering: *What do you know about Mom? What do you know about Ben? Why did the man come see them?*

SELF-SELECTED READING

OBJECTIVES

 Describe characters, setting, and major events in a story, using key details. **RL.1.3**

 With prompting and support, read prose and poetry of appropriate complexity for grade 1. **RL.1.10**

Apply the strategy and skill to read a text

Read Independently

Have children pick a realistic text selection for sustained silent reading. Tell them that they should predict what the story is about before reading. Have them complete a Character, Setting, Events chart as they read the story.

Read Purposefully

Have children record information in the Character, Setting, Events Chart. After reading, guide children to:

→ share the information they wrote on their charts with a partner.

→ tell their partner about the predictions they made and how they confirmed them.

 Independent Study Have children discuss why they did or did not like the stories they read. If they liked their story, challenge them to write sentences that tell others why they should read the book. If they did not like their story, challenge them to rewrite a section they would have liked to be different.

→ English Language Learners

Reading/Writing Workshop

 OBJECTIVES

 Describe characters, setting, and major events in a story, using key details. **RL.1.3**

With prompting and support, read prose and poetry of appropriate complexity for grade 1. **RL.1.10**

Make and confirm predictions

ACADEMIC LANGUAGE
• *prediction, confirm*
• Cognates: *predicción, confirmar*

Shared Read
Good Job, Ben!

Before Reading

Build Background

Read the Essential Question: *What jobs need to be done in a community?*

→ Explain the meaning of the Essential Question: *A community is a neighborhood. It is where people live near each other. People in the community need things done. Workers do jobs that help people who live in the community.*

→ **Model an answer:** *People in communities need workers to pick up their garbage. They need people to deliver their mail. They need schools and hospitals. They need to stay safe and healthy. Workers in the community do these and many other jobs.*

→ Ask children a question that ties the Essential Question to their own background knowledge: *Turn to a partner and talk about what jobs people do where you live. Who brings your mail? Who helps keep you safe? Who helps keep you healthy?* Call on several pairs.

During Reading

Interactive Question-Response

→ Ask questions that help children understand the meaning of the text after each paragraph.

→ Reinforce the meanings of key vocabulary by embedding the meanings in the questions.

→ Ask children questions that require them to use key vocabulary.

→ Reinforce comprehension strategies and skills of the week by modeling.

Go Digital

Good Job, Ben!

Character	Setting	Events

Graphic Organizer

Good Job, Ben!

Pages 14–15

Point to the title. *Listen as I read the title, or name, of this book.* Point to each word as you say the title. *Now let's say the title of the book together.* Have children chorally say: *The title of this book is* Good Job, Ben!

Explain and Model the Strategy Point to the illustration. *I see a boy is holding hands with a lady. They are leaving a classroom. I remember the title is* Good Job, Ben! *I predict, or guess, that this boy is Ben.*

Who do you predict, or guess, the woman is? What do you think they might do? (Ben's mother, They will go somewhere together.)

Pages 16–17

Read page 16. Point to each word as you read: "Ben and Mom head to town. It is a big trip. There is a lot to see." *What did you predict Ben and his mother would do? Do the words and picture on this page confirm, or show, your prediction was correct?* (sample answer: Yes, they will go somewhere together. They will go to town.)

Explain and Model Phonics Point to the sentence on page 16. *I will read each word in this sentence. Raise your hand when you hear a word that has the /e/ sound:* "Ben and Mom head to town." *Now let's say the words with the /e/ sound together: Ben, head.* Repeat with the sentence "Ben and Mom will get on the bus," on page 17.

Pages 18–19

Explain and Model High-Frequency Words
We see in the picture that a crossing guard can help Ben and Mom cross. Point to *help* on page 18. *This is the word* help. *Let's say it together.* Have children act out helping each other cross a street.

Explain and Model the Skill
After reading page 18, say: *I can use the words and picture to tell about an event. The crossing guard helped Ben and Mom cross the street.*

After reading page 19, say: *What event did you learn about in the words and picture on this page?* (Workers are fixing the road.)

Pages 20–21

Point to the baker. *Who is this and what does she do?* (a baker, bakes bread)

Repeat the same type of activity for the veterinarian on page 21.

Page 22–23

Explain and Model the Skill
Discuss the pictures on these pages. Read the words chorally with children. *The words and pictures show us Ben gets books about jobs. What is the setting?* (the library)

After Reading

Make Connections

→ Review the Essential Question.

→ English Language Learners

Lexile 70

OBJECTIVES

CCSS Describe characters, settings, and major events in a story, using key details. **RL.1.3**

CCSS Explain major differences between books that tell stories and books that give information, drawing on a wide reading of a range of text types. **RL.1.5**

CCSS With prompting and support, read prose and poetry of appropriate complexity for grade 1. **RL.1.10**

Make and confirm predictions

ACADEMIC LANGUAGE
• *predict, exclamations*
• Cognates: *predecir, exclamaciones*

Leveled Reader:
Ben Brings the Mail

Before Reading

Preview

Read the title. Ask: *What is the title?* Say it again. Repeat with the author's name. Preview the illustrations. Have children describe the pictures. Use simple language to tell about each page. Follow with questions, such as: *What is Ben doing here?*

ESSENTIAL QUESTION

Remind children of the Essential Question: *What jobs need to be done in a community?* Set a purpose for reading: *Let's read to find out how Ben's job helps the community.*

During Reading

Interactive Question-Response

Pages 2–3 Point to the illustrations on the pages. Read the labels to children and have them repeat: mail truck, mail. *Remember, when you guess what will happen, you are making a prediction. Talk with your partner about what you guess Ben will do.*

Pages 4–5 After reading these pages, point to the label and picture on page 5. *What is this?* (a letter) *What does Ben do?* (He delivers the letter to Miss Deb.) *Was your prediction about what Ben would do correct?*

Pages 6–7 After reading aloud page 6 ask: *The words say* "the ad will help Sam." *Look at the picture. Why is Sam sad?* (His bike is broken.) *What does the ad show?* (a place that fixes bikes) *How will it help Sam?* (Sam can take his bike there to be fixed.)

After reading page 7, say: *Tell your partner about the different things a mail carrier can deliver.* (letters, boxes, ads)

Pages 8–9 *What does Ben do if he can not give someone mail? Let's read the words that tell us:* Ben can use this box. *What is the box called?* (a mailbox) *Why doesn't Ben have mail for Rex?* (He is a dog.)

Pages 10–11 *Let's read the label together:* street. *Now let's reread these pages together. Tell your partner when you think Ben will be back. What do you think he will do when he comes back?*

Go Digital

Ben Brings the Mail

Graphic Organizer

Retell

After Reading

Respond to Reading

Revisit the Essential Question. Ask children to work with partners to answer the questions on page 12. Pair children with peers of varying language abilities.

Retell

Model retelling using the **Retelling Card** prompts. Say: *Look at the illustrations. Use details to help you retell the selection.* Help children make personal connections by asking: *Who delivers your mail? Where does he or she put your mail? What kind of mail does your family get?*

Intonation Fluency: Exclamations and Questions

Read the pages in the book, one at a time. Help children echo-read the pages expressively and with appropriate intonation. Remind them to read exclamations in a way that shows excitement.

Apply Have children practice reading with partners. Pair children with peers of varying language abilities.

PAIRED READ ...

"At the Post Office"

Make Connections:
Write About It *Analytical Writing*

Before reading, tell children to note that this text is informational text. Then discuss the Compare Texts direction.

After reading, ask children to make connections between the information they learned from "At the Post Office" and *Ben Brings the Mail*. Prompt children by providing a sentence frame: *Postal workers help the community by _____.*

Leveled Reader

Analytical Writing

COMPARE TEXTS

→ Have children use text evidence to compare realistic fiction to informational text.

Lead children in conducting a literature circle using the Thinkmark questions to guide the discussion. You may wish to discuss what children have learned about mail carriers from both selections in the leveled reader.

Level Up

Level-up lessons available online.

IF children can read *Ben Brings the Mail* **ELL Level** with fluency and correctly answer the Comprehension Check questions,

THEN tell children that they will read a more detailed version of the selection.

- Use pages 4–5 of *Ben Brings the Mail* **On Level** to model using Teaching Poster 28 to identify character, setting, and events.

- Have children read the selection, checking their comprehension by using the graphic organizer.

English Language Learners

Vocabulary

PRETEACH ORAL VOCABULARY

OBJECTIVES

 Produce complete sentences when appropriate to task and situation. **SL.1.6**

LANGUAGE OBJECTIVE

Preteach oral vocabulary words

 I Do Display images from the **Visual Vocabulary Cards** one at a time to preteach the oral vocabulary words *community* and *occupation*.

 We Do Display the image again. Model using sentences to describe the image.

You Do Display the word again. Have partners talk about how the pictures show the words *occupation* and *community*. Ask children to say each word three times.

Beginning	Intermediate	Advanced/High
Provide sentence frames: *An occupation is _____.* *In my community _____.*	Ask questions using the words: *What occupations do you know? Why do you like this community?*	Have partners write one sentence and one question for each word.

PRETEACH ELL VOCABULARY

OBJECTIVES

 Produce complete sentences when appropriate to task and situation. **SL.1.6**

LANGUAGE OBJECTIVE

Preteach ELL vocabulary words

 I Do Display images from the Visual Vocabulary Cards one at a time to preteach the ELL Vocabulary words *delivery* and *neighborhood*. Say each word and have children repeat it. Define the word in English.

 We Do Display the image again and guide children in explaining how it illustrates or demonstrates the word. Model using sentences to describe the image.

 You Do Display each word again and have children say the word and then spell it. Provide opportunities for children to use the words in speaking and writing. Provide sentence starters.

Beginning	Intermediate	Advanced/High
Help children draw a picture and write the word beneath it.	Have partners write one sentence for each word.	Challenge children to write two sentences for each word.

High-Frequency Words

OBJECTIVES

 Recognize and read grade-appropriate irregularly spelled words. **RF.1.3g**

LANGUAGE OBJECTIVE

Use high-frequency words: *again, help, new, there, use*

 I Do Display the **High-Frequency Word Cards** for *again, help, new, there,* and *use*. Read each word. Use the Read/Spell/Write routine to teach each word. Have children write the words on their **Response Boards**.

 We Do Write sentence frames on separate lines. Track the print as you guide children to read and complete the sentences: *(1) We will ____ again. (2) I can help you ____. (3) I have a new ____. (4) There is ____. (5) Can I use the ____?*

 You Do Display the High-Frequency Word Cards from previous weeks. Display one card at a time as children chorally read the word. Note words children need to review.

Beginning	Intermediate	Advanced/High
Point to and say each word for children to repeat.	Have children read each word as you display it.	Have children use each word in a sentence.

OBJECTIVES

 Recognize and read grade-appropriate irregularly spelled words. **RF.1.3g**

LANGUAGE OBJECTIVE

Reteach high-frequency words

 I Do Display each Visual Vocabulary Card and say the word aloud. Define the word in English, then in Spanish if appropriate, identifying any cognates.

 We Do Point to the image and explain how it illustrates the word. Have children repeat the word. Engage children in structured partner-talk about the image as prompted on the back of the card. Ask children to chorally say the word three times.

 You Do Display each visual card in random order, hiding the word. Have children identify and define the word in their own words.

Beginning	Intermediate	Advanced/High
Display an image and give children two word choices.	Provide definition starters for children, as necessary.	After children define the word, have them use it in a sentence.

English Language Learners
Writing/Spelling

WRITING TRAIT: ORGANIZATION

OBJECTIVES

With guidance and support from adults, focus on a topic, response to questions and suggestions from peers, and add details to strengthen writing as needed. **W.1.5**

LANGUAGE OBJECTIVE

Focus on an idea

 I Do

Explain that writers focus on the idea as they write. All their sentences tell about that idea. Say: *If I want to write about my job, every sentence I write will tell something about being a teacher.* Model writing sentences.

 We Do

Page through *Good Job, Ben!* Stop on one or two spreads and ask children what they learned about the job shown. Say: *Every sentence tells us about how someone does a certain job. What does this page tell about a job?*

 You Do

Have partners discuss a job they would like to write about. Have each partner write their idea and then write a sentence focusing on that idea.

Beginning	Intermediate	Advanced/High
Provide magazine pictures. Provide a sentence frame for children to complete to tell about a job someone is doing.	Show photos of everyday jobs. Provide sentence frames for children to complete to tell about the jobs.	Have children write three sentences about a job they know or like.

WORDS WITH SHORT *e*

OBJECTIVES

Use conventional spelling for words with common spelling patterns and for frequently occurring irregular words. **L.1.2d**

LANGUAGE OBJECTIVE

Spell words with short *e* spelled *e* and *ea*

 I Do

Read aloud the Spelling Words on page T14. Segment each word into sounds and attach a spelling to each sound. Point out the short *e* spelled *e* and *ea*. Read aloud, segment, and spell the remaining words and have children repeat.

 We Do

Read the sentence from the Dictation routine on page T14 aloud. Then, read the short *e* word slowly and ask children to repeat. Have them write the word. Repeat the process for the remaining sentences.

 You Do

Display the words. Have children work with a partner to check their spelling lists. Have children correct misspelled words on their list.

Beginning	Intermediate	Advanced/High
Help children copy the words with correct spelling and say the word.	After children have corrected their words, have pairs quiz each other.	Challenge children to think of other words that have the short *e* sound.

Grammar

NOUNS

OBJECTIVES

  Use common, proper, and possessive nouns. **L.1.1b**

  Use end punctuation for sentences. **L.1.2b**

LANGUAGE OBJECTIVE

Recognize that a noun names a person, place, animal, or thing

Language Transfers Handbook

TRANSFER SKILLS

Spanish, Cantonese, Korean, Hmong, Vietnamese, Haitian Creole, and Khmer speakers may omit adding *s* to plural nouns. At this point you can simply call their attention to the correct form for plural nouns when needed, explaining that when we use a noun that stands for more than one we usually add an *s*. Provide oral examples: *1 boy, 3 boys;* or written examples: *The cat sits. Three cats play.*

I Do Review that a noun is a naming word that names a person, place, or thing. Write the following sentence on the board: *The rock is black.* Read the sentence. Circle the word *rock. The word* rock *is a noun. It names a thing.*

We Do Write sentences and work with children to read them and circle the noun in each. Have them say *The word _____ is a noun.*

The frog can hop.

Ben likes to play.

My dog can beg.

The mops are wet.

You Do   Write the following sentence frames.

The _____ is hot. The _____ will sit.

Have partners copy and complete each frame with different nouns. Have them take turns reading the sentences aloud. Monitor children's pronunciation and answers.

Beginning	Intermediate	Advanced/High
Have children take turns naming objects in the classroom to complete the frame: *A _____ is a noun.*	Have one partner name a noun and the other create a sentence for it. Switch roles and repeat.	Have children write sentences about jobs, then share them with a partner. Have partners circle the nouns in each others' sentences.

PROGRESS MONITORING

Weekly Assessment

CCSS **TESTED SKILLS**

✔ **COMPREHENSION:**	✔ **PHONEMIC AWARENESS:**	✔ **PHONICS/STRUCTURAL ANALYSIS/HIGH-FREQUENCY WORDS:**
Character, Setting, Events **RL.1.3**	Phoneme Blending **RF.1.2b**	Short *e: e, ea* **RF.1.3b**
	Phoneme Isolation **RF.1.2c**	Inflectional Ending *-ed* **RF.1.3f**
	Phoneme Segmentation **RF.1.2d**	*again, help, new, there, use* **RF.1.3g**

Conduct group fluency assessments.

Assess fluency for one group of children per week using the **Letter Naming, Phoneme Segmentation,** and **Sight Word Fluency** assessments in *Reading Wonders Fluency Assessment.*

Go Digital! http://connected.mcgraw-hill.com

Using Assessment Results

TESTED SKILLS	If ...	Then ...
COMPREHENSION	Children answer 0–3 multiple-choice items correctly . . .	. . . assign Lessons 22–24 on Identify Character, Lessons 25–27 on Identify Setting, and Lessons 28–30 on Identify Plot Events from the ***Tier 2 Comprehension Intervention online PDFs.***
PHONEMIC AWARENESS	Children answer 0–1 multiple-choice items correctly . . .	. . . assign Lessons 62–66 on Phoneme Blending, Lessons 16–17 on Phoneme Isolation: Beginning Sounds, and Lessons 67–71 on Phoneme Segmenting from the ***Tier 2 Phonemic Awareness Intervention online PDFs.***
PHONICS/ STRUCTURAL ANALYSIS/HFW	Children answer 0–5 multiple-choice items correctly . . .	. . . assign Lesson 48 on Short *e* and Lesson 66 on Inflectional Ending -*ed* from the ***Tier 2 Phonics/Word Study Intervention online PDFs.***

Response to Intervention

Use children's assessment results to assist you in identifying children who will benefit from focused intervention.

Use the appropriate sections of the ***Placement and Diagnostic Assessment*** to designate children requiring:

2 **Intervention Online PDFs**

3 **WonderWorks Intervention Program**

WEEKLY OVERVIEW

Literature Big Book

**Big Book and Little Book
Reading/Writing Workshop**

 Go
Digital

http://connected.mcgraw-hill.com

TEACH AND MODEL

Listening Comprehension

Comprehension Strategy *Make and Confirm Predictions* T89

Close Reading

Shared Reading *Cubs in a Hut*, 34–43

Genre Fantasy

Lexile 390

Words to Know T93

could, live, one, then, three

Minilessons   ✔ Tested Skills CCSS

✔ **Phonics**................................... Short *u*, T94–T95

✔ **Comprehension Skill**.................. Character, Setting, Events, T105

✔ **Writing Traits**............................ Organization, T114

✔ **Grammar**................................... Singular and Plural Nouns, T115

Essential Question
What buildings do you know?
What are they made of?

WEEK 2

APPLY WITH CLOSE READING

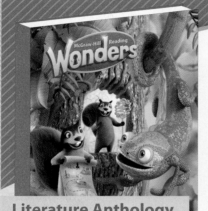

Literature Anthology

Complex Text

PAIRED READ

The Pigs, the Wolf, and the Mud, 26–41
Genre Fantasy
Lexile 320

"Homes Around the World," 44–47
Genre Nonfiction
Lexile 330

Differentiated Text

Leveled Readers *Including Paired Reads*

APPROACHING
Lexile 170

ON LEVEL
Lexile 150

BEYOND
Lexile 330

ELL
Lexile 10

Extended Complex Text

The True Story of the 3 Little Pigs!
Genre
Fiction
Lexile 570

The Cow That Went Oink
Genre
Fiction
Lexile 270

Classroom Library lessons available online.

Classroom Library

TEACH AND MANAGE

How You Teach

INTRODUCE

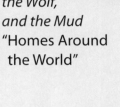

Weekly Concept
Buildings All Around

Reading/Writing Workshop
16–27

TEACH

Listening Comprehension
The 3 Little Dassies

Close Reading
Cubs in a Hut

Minilessons
Character, Setting, Events; Fantasy; Short *u*; High-Frequency Words

APPLY

Close Reading
The Pigs, the Wolf, and the Mud
"Homes Around the World"

 Go Digital **Interactive Whiteboard** **Interactive Whiteboard** **Mobile**

How Students Practice

WEEKLY CONTRACT

PDF Online

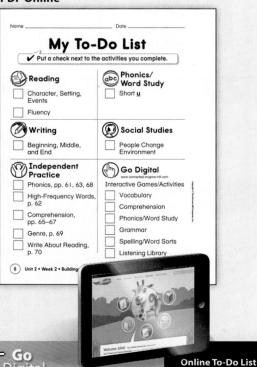

Name _____ Date _____

My To-Do List
✔ Put a check next to the activities you complete.

Reading
☐ Character, Setting, Events
☐ Fluency

Phonics/Word Study
☐ Short **u**

Writing
☐ Beginning, Middle, and End

Social Studies
☐ People Change Environment

Independent Practice
☐ Phonics, pp. 61, 63, 68
☐ High-Frequency Words, p. 62
☐ Comprehension, pp. 65–67
☐ Genre, p. 69
☐ Write About Reading, p. 70

Go Digital
www.connected.mcgraw-hill.com
Interactive Games/Activities
☐ Vocabulary
☐ Comprehension
☐ Phonics/Word Study
☐ Grammar
☐ Spelling/Word Sorts
☐ Listening Library

8 Unit 2 • Week 2 • Building

LEVELED PRACTICE and ONLINE ACTIVITIES

Your Turn Practice Book
61–70

Leveled Readers

 Go Digital **Online To-Do List**  **Leveled Activities**  **Mobile**

DIFFERENTIATE

SMALL GROUP INSTRUCTION

Leveled Readers

Mobile

INTEGRATE

Research and Inquiry
Draw and Label a Building, T122–T123

Text Connections
Buildings All Around, T124

Write About Reading
Analyze Character, Setting, Events, T125

Online Research and Writing

ASSESS

Wonders
Weekly Assessment

Weekly Assessment 61–70

Online Assessment

LEVELED WORKSTATION CARDS

7

Houses Around the World

People live in different kinds of houses.

- Pretend you lived somewhere that was very hot or very cold. What kind of house would you live in?

SOCIAL STUDIES

9

Organization: Beginning, Middle, End

Five fish went for a swim.
They saw a duck.
They saw a crab.

- Luis wrote a story.

- Luis's story has a beginning and a middle. It needs an end.

WRITING

7

Short u

-ug	-un	-ut

- Make a three-column chart. Write -ug, -un, and -ut at the top of the columns.

- Look at the words **bun, but, cut, dug, fun, hug, hut, jug, plug, run, spun,** and **tug.**

- Sort the words by spelling patterns. Write them in the correct column.

You need 20
› paper
› pencils or pens

PHONICS/WORD STUDY

Go Digital! www.connected.mcgraw-hill.com • Interactive Games and Activities • Grade 1   7

4

Character, Setting, Events

You can use illustrations to find out about the characters, setting, and events in a story.

- Talk about a Leveled Reader story with a partner.

- Look at the pictures on the Retelling Cards.

Retelling Cards

- Make a list of characters, settings, and events you see in the pictures.

You need 20
› Retelling Cards
› paper, pencils

READING

Go Digital! www.connected.mcgraw-hill.com • Interactive Games and Activities • Grade 1   4

DEVELOPING READERS AND WRITERS

Write to Sources and Research

Note Taking, T113A

Character, Setting, Events, T113B

Make Connections: Essential Question, T113J

Research and Inquiry, T122

Analyze to Inform/Explain, T125

Comparing Texts, T131, T141, T145, T151

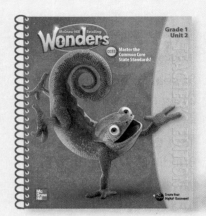

Teacher's Edition

Your Turn Practice Book

Character, Setting, Events, pp. 65–67
Write About Reading, p. 70

Leveled Readers
Comparing Texts

Interactive Whiteboard

Narrative Text
Story, T114–T115

Conferencing Routines
Peer Conferences, T120

Interactive Whiteboard

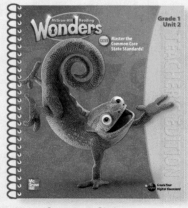

Teacher's Edition

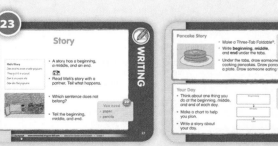

Leveled Workstation Card
Story, Card 23

Writing Traits • Shared and Interactive Writing

Writing Trait: Organization
Story, T96

Conferencing Routines
Peer Conferences, T120

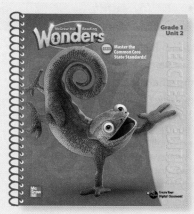

Teacher's Edition

Organization: Plurals, pp. 46–47

Reading/Writing Workshop

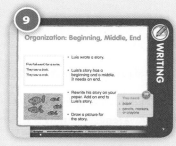

Leveled Workstation Card
Organization: Beginning, Middle, End, Card 9

Interactive Whiteboard

Grammar and Spelling

Grammar
Singular and Plural Nouns, T97

Spelling
Words with Short *u*, T92

Interactive Whiteboard

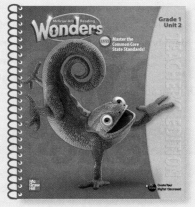

Teacher's Edition

Online Spelling and Grammar Games

Handwriting

SUGGESTED LESSON PLAN

	DAY 1	DAY 2
READING		
Teach, Model, and Apply *Whole Group*	**Build Background** Buildings All Around, T86–T87 **Oral Vocabulary Words** *shelter, materials,* T86 **Listening Comprehension** **Big Book** *The 3 Little Dassies,* T88 Strategy: Make and Confirm Predictions, T89 **Word Work** T90–T94 Fluency: Sound-Spellings Phonological Awareness: Rhyme Phonics/Spelling: Introduce Short *u* High-Frequency Words: *could, live, one, then, three* **Shared Reading** *Cubs in a Hut,* T94–T95 **Practice** Your Turn, p. 61	**Oral Language** Buildings All Around, T98 **Oral Vocabulary Words** *collapsed, furious, refused,* T98 **Listening Comprehension** Strategy: Make and Confirm Predictions, T99 **Interactive Read-Aloud Cards** "The Three Little Pigs," T99 **Word Work** T100–T103 Fluency: Sound-Spellings Phonemic Awareness: Phoneme Identity Phonics/Spelling: Review Short *u* Structural Analysis: Contractions with *'s* High-Frequency Words: *could, live, one, then, three* **Shared Reading** *Cubs in a Hut,* T104–T105 ✔**Comprehension** •Genre: Fantasy, T104 •Skill: Character, Setting, Events, T105 **Practice** Your Turn, pp. 62–64

DIFFERENTIATED INSTRUCTION Choose across the week to meet your student's needs.

Small Group	DAY 1	DAY 2
Approaching Level 	**Leveled Reader** *What a Nest!,* T130–T131 **Phonemic Awareness** Identify and Generate Rhyme, T132 **Phonics** Connect *u* to /u/, T134 **High-Frequency Words** Review, T137	**Leveled Reader** *What a Nest!,* T130–T131 **Phonemic Awareness** Phoneme Identity, T132 **Phonics** Blend Words with Short *u,* T134 **High-Frequency Words** Reteach, T137 **Comprehension** Key Details About Characters, T138
On Level 	**Leveled Reader** *Staying Afloat,* T140–T141 **Phonics** Build Words with Short *u,* T142	**Leveled Reader** *Staying Afloat,* T140–T141 **High-Frequency Words** Review Words, T142
Beyond Level	**Leveled Reader** *City Armadillo, Country Armadillo,* T144–T145 **Oral Vocabulary** Synonyms, T146	**Leveled Reader** *City Armadillo, Country Armadillo,* T144–T145 **Oral Vocabulary** Synonyms, T146
English Language Learners	**Shared Read** *Cubs in a Hut,* T148–T149 **Phonemic Awareness** Identify and Generate Rhyme, T132 **Phonics** Connect *u,* T134 **Vocabulary** Preteach Oral Vocabulary, T152	**Leveled Reader** *Staying Afloat,* T150–T151 **Phonemic Awareness** Phoneme Identity, T132 **Phonics** Blend Words with Short *u,* T134 **Vocabulary** Preteach ELL Vocabulary, T152

LANGUAGE ARTS

Writing Grammar *Whole Group*	DAY 1	DAY 2
	Shared Writing Writing Trait: Organization, T96 Story, T96 **Grammar** •Singular and Plural Nouns, T97 Mechanics: Apostrophe with Contractions, T97	**Independent Writing** Writing Trait: Organization, T106 Story, T107 **Grammar** •Singular and Plural Nouns, T107 Mechanics: Apostrophe with Contractions, T107

DAY 3	DAY 4	DAY 5 Review and Assess

READING

Oral Language Buildings All Around, T108

Review Oral Vocabulary *shelter, materials, collapsed, furious, refused,* T108

Listening Comprehension
Big Book *The 3 Little Dassies,* T109
•Strategy: Make and Confirm Predictions, T109
•Retelling, T109
•Fluency: Expression, T109

Word Work T110–T113
Fluency: Sound-Spellings
Phonemic Awareness: Phoneme Blending
Phonics/Spelling: Blend Words with Short *u*
Structural Analysis: Contractions with *'s*
High-Frequency Words: *could, live, one, then, three*

Close Reading *The Pigs, the Wolf, and the Mud,* T113A–T113J **Analytical Writing**

Practice Your Turn, pp. 65–67

Oral Language Buildings All Around, T116

Comprehension Text Features: Captions, T117

Close Reading "Homes Around the World," T117A–T117B

Word Work T118–T119
Fluency: Sound-Spellings
Phonemic Awareness: Phoneme Identity
Phonics/Spelling: Build Words with Short *u*
Structural Analysis: Contractions with *'s*
High-Frequency Words: *could, live, one, then, three*

Integrate Ideas Research and Inquiry, T122–T123

Practice Your Turn, pp. 68–69

Integrate Ideas
•Text Connections, T124
•Write About Reading, T125 **Analytical Writing**

Word Work T126–T127
Fluency: Word Automaticity
Phonemic Awareness: Phoneme Blending/Segmentation
Phonics/Spelling: Blend and Build Words with Short *u*
Structural Analysis: Contractions with *'s*
High-Frequency Words: *could, live, one, then, three*

Practice Your Turn, p. 70

DIFFERENTIATED INSTRUCTION

Leveled Reader *What a Nest!,* T130–T131
Phonemic Awareness Phoneme Blending, T133
Phonics Build Words with Short *u,* T135
Structural Analysis Review Contractions with *'s,* T136
Comprehension Review Character, Setting, Events, T139

Leveled Reader Paired Read: "Stone Castles," T131 **Analytical Writing**
Phonemic Awareness Phoneme Segmentation, T133
Phonics Blend Words with Short *u,* T135
Structural Analysis Reteach Contractions with *'s,* T136
Comprehension Read for Fluency, T138 **TIER 2**

Leveled Reader Literature Circles, T131
Phonics Build Fluency with Phonics, T135
High-Frequency Words Cumulative Review, T137
Comprehension Self-Selected Reading, T139

Leveled Reader *Staying Afloat,* T140–T141
Comprehension Review Character, Setting, Events, T143

Leveled Reader Paired Read: "A Day on a Houseboat," T141 **Analytical Writing**

Leveled Reader Literature Circles, T141
Comprehension Self-Selected Reading, T143

Leveled Reader *City Armadillo, Country Armadillo,* T144–T145
Comprehension Review Character, Setting, Events, T147

Leveled Reader Paired Read: "City or Country?", T145 **Analytical Writing**

Leveled Reader Literature Circles, T145
Comprehension Self-Selected Reading, T147

Leveled Reader *Staying Afloat,* T150–T151
Phonemic Awareness Phoneme Blending, T133
Phonics Build Words with Short *u,* T135
Structural Analysis Review Contractions with *'s,* T136
High-Frequency Words Review Words, T153
Writing Writing Trait: Organization, T154

Leveled Reader Paired Read: "A Day on a Houseboat," T151 **Analytical Writing**
Phonemic Awareness Phoneme Segmentation, T133
Structural Analysis Reteach Contractions with *'s,* T136
High-Frequency Words Reteach Words, T153
Grammar Singular and Plural Nouns, T155

Leveled Reader Literature Circles, T151
Phonics Blend Words with Short *u,* T135
Spelling Words with Short *u,* T154

LANGUAGE ARTS

Independent Writing Writing Trait: Organization, T114
Story: Prewrite/Draft, T114–T115

Grammar
•Singular and Plural Nouns, T115
Mechanics: Apostrophe with Contractions, T115

Independent Writing Writing Trait: Organization, T120
Story: Revise/Proofread/Edit, T120–T121

Grammar
•Singular and Plural Nouns, T121
Mechanics: Apostrophe with Contractions, T121

Independent Writing
Story: Publish and Present, T128

Grammar
•Singular and Plural Nouns, T129
Mechanics: Apostrophe with Contractions, T129

DIFFERENTIATE TO ACCELERATE

  Scaffold to Access Complex Text

IF ▶ the text complexity of a particular selection is too difficult for children

THEN ▶ see the references noted in the chart below for scaffolded instruction to help children Access Complex Text.

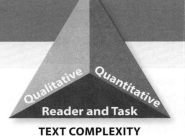

Qualitative / Quantitative
Reader and Task
TEXT COMPLEXITY

	Big Book	Reading/Writing Workshop	Literature Anthology	Leveled Readers
				 Approaching / On Level / Beyond / ELL
Quantitative	*The 3 Little Dassies* **Lexile** 780	*Cubs in a Hut* **Lexile** 390	*The Pigs, the Wolf, and the Mud* **Lexile** 320 "Homes Around the World" **Lexile** 330	**Approaching Level** **Lexile** 170 **On Level** **Lexile** 150 **Beyond Level** **Lexile** 330 **ELL** **Lexile** 10
Qualitative	What Makes the Text Complex? • **Vocabulary,** T109 **A C T** *See Scaffolded Instruction in Teacher's Edition,* T109.	What Makes the Text Complex? **Foundational Skills** • Decoding with short *u,* T90–T91 • Reading contractions with 's, T101 • Identifying high-frequency words, T93 *See Scaffolded Instruction in Teacher's Edition, T90–T91, T93, and T101.*	What Makes the Text Complex? **Foundational Skills** • Decoding with short *u,* T110–T111 • Reading contractions with 's, T111 • Identifying high-frequency words, T113	What Makes the Text Complex? **Foundational Skills** • Decoding with short *u* • Reading contractions with 's • Identifying high-frequency words *could live one then three* *See Level Up lessons online for Leveled Readers.*
Reader and Task	The Introduce the Concept lesson on pages T86–T87 will help determine the reader's knowledge and engagement in the weekly concept. See pages T88–T89, T109, and T122–T125 for questions and tasks for this text.	The Introduce the Concept lesson on pages T86–T87 will help determine the reader's knowledge and engagement in the weekly concept. See pages T94–T95, T104–T105, and T122–T125 for questions and tasks for this text.	The Introduce the Concept lesson on pages T86–T87 will help determine the reader's knowledge and engagement in the weekly concept. See pages T113A–T113J, T117A–T117B, and T122–T125 for questions and tasks for this text.	The Introduce the Concept lesson on pages T86–T87 will help determine the reader's knowledge and engagement in the weekly concept. See pages T130–T131, T140–T141, T144–T145, T150–T151, and T122–T125 for questions and tasks for this text.

Classroom Library Tradebooks: See pages T413–T415 for model lessons.

Monitor and *Differentiate*

IF → you need to differentiate instruction

THEN → use the Quick Checks to assess children's needs and select the appropriate small group instruction focus.

 **Quick Check**

Comprehension Strategy Make and Confirm Predictions, T89

Comprehension Skill Character, Setting, Events, T105

Phonics Words with Short *u*, T93, T103, T113, T119, T127

High-Frequency Words T93, T103, T113, T119, T127

If No → | **Approaching Level** | **Reteach** T130–T139
| **ELL** | **Develop** T148–T155
If Yes → | **On Level** | **Review** T140–T143
| **Beyond Level** | **Extend** T144–T147

Level Up with Leveled Readers

IF → children can read their leveled text fluently and answer comprehension questions

THEN → work with the next level up to accelerate children's reading with more complex text.

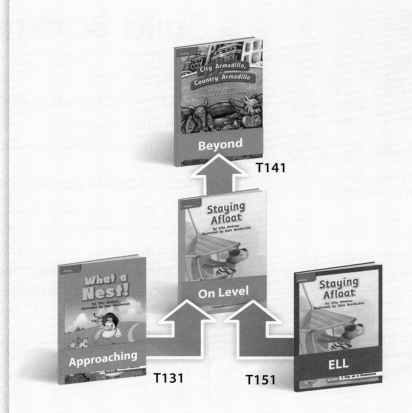

Beyond — T141

On Level

Approaching — T131

Staying Afloat — T151

ELL

ENGLISH LANGUAGE LEARNERS
ELL SCAFFOLD

IF ELL students need additional support **THEN** scaffold instruction using the small group suggestions.

Shared Read	Leveled Reader	Phonemic Awareness	Phonics	Words to Know	Writing	Spelling	Grammar
Cubs in a Hut, T148–T149	*Staying Afloat*, T150–T151 "A Day on a Houseboat," T151	Identify and Generate Rhyme, T132 Phoneme Identity, T132 Phoneme Blending, T133 Phoneme Segmentation , T133	Words with Short *u*, T134–T135 Structural Analysis, T136	*could, live, one, then, three*, T153	Organization, T154	Words with Short *u*, T154	Singular and Plural Nouns, T155

Note: Include ELL Students in all small groups based on their needs.

Materials

Reading/Writing Workshop
VOLUME 2

Reading/Writing Workshop Big Book
UNIT 2

Literature Big Book
The 3 Little Dassies

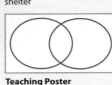

Visual Vocabulary Cards
materials
shelter

Teaching Poster

High-Frequency Word Cards

could   then
live   three
one

Word-Building Cards

Think Aloud Clouds

umbrella

Sound-Spelling Cards

Reading/Writing Workshop Big Book

OBJECTIVES

CCSS Follow agreed-upon rules for discussions (e.g., listening to others with care, speaking one at a time about the topics and texts under discussion). **SL.1.1a**

- Build background knowledge
- Discuss the Essential Question

ACADEMIC LANGUAGE
- *vocabulary, define, discuss*
- Cognates: *vocabulario, definir, discutir*

→ Introduce the Concept

MINILESSON
5 Mins

Build Background

ESSENTIAL QUESTION
What buildings do you know? What are they made of?

Tell children that this week they will be talking and reading about buildings and what they are made of.

Oral Vocabulary Words

Tell children that you will share some words that they can use as they discuss buildings. Use the Define/Example/Ask routine to introduce the oral vocabulary words **shelter** and **materials**.

Oral Vocabulary Routine   **Visual Vocabulary Cards**

Define: A **shelter** is a building that protects you or keeps you safe.

Example: When it started to rain, we ran into the shelter to stay warm and dry.

Ask: Is a house a kind of shelter? Why or why not?

Define: **Materials** are the things used to make something else.

Example: Wood, glue, nails, and paint are materials you will need to make a birdhouse.

Ask: What materials were used to make your desk and your chair?

Discuss the theme of "Buildings All Around." Have children describe some buildings they know. *What do the buildings look like? Where are they? What materials are they made of?*

Go Digital

Buildings All Around

Video

Photos

Visual Glossary

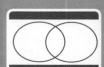

Graphic Organizer

READING/WRITING WORKSHOP, pp. 28–29

Talk About It: Buildings All Around

Guide children to discuss the buildings in this photo.

→ Look at the buildings at the front of the picture. What do you think they are made of? What do you think they are used for?

→ Look at the buildings in the background. How are they different from the others?

Use Teaching Poster 39 and prompt children to complete the Venn Diagram.

Children can look at page 29 of their Reading/Writing Workshop and do the Talk About It activity with a partner.

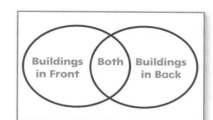

Teaching Poster

Collaborative Conversations

Take Turns Talking As children engage in partner, small-group, and whole-group discussions, encourage them to:

→ take turns talking and not speak over others.

→ raise their hand if they want to speak.

→ ask others to share their ideas and opinions.

ELL

ENGLISH LANGUAGE LEARNERS SCAFFOLD

Beginning

Use Visuals Point to the blue house. *This building is blue. Is it made of wood?* Point to the tall, black building. *Is this building tall or short? What color is it?* Use gestures as needed.

Intermediate

Describe Ask children to describe the buildings. *What do the buildings look like? What colors are they?*

Advanced/Advanced High

Discuss Have children elaborate on the buildings. *Which building do you like best? Why?* Repeat notable answers slowly and clearly to the class.

→ Listening Comprehension

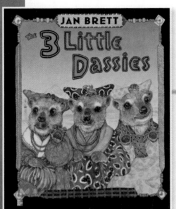

Literature Big Book

OBJECTIVES

CCSS Recognize the distinguishing features of a sentence (e.g., first word, capitalization, ending punctuation). **RF.1.1a**

• Reinforce concepts of print
• Develop concept understanding

ACADEMIC LANGUAGE
quotation, capital

Read the Literature Big Book

Connect to Concept: Buildings All Around

Tell children that they will now read about three little animals that each build a shelter. Ask: *What materials do you think the dassies will use?*

Concepts of Print

Quotations   Display *The 3 Little Dassies* and point out the quotation marks on page 3. Explain that quotation marks set off the words that characters say. The first quotation mark means that a character has started speaking. The second quotation mark means the character has finished speaking.

Point out that the first word after a quotation mark begins with a capital letter. Explain that this is because it is the first word of the character's sentence. See prompts in the Big Book for modeling concepts of print.

Set a Purpose for Reading

→   Display the Big Book.

→   Read aloud the title and the name of the author.

→   Ask children to listen to the Big Book to find out if the dassies are able to build good shelters.

Go Digital

The 3 Little Dassies

Make and Confirm Predictions

Strategy: Make and Confirm Predictions

❶ Explain Tell children that as you read the Big Book aloud, they can use the text and illustrations to make predictions about what will happen next. Then they can continue reading to find out whether their prediction was correct.

Think Aloud To make a prediction, think about the details in the text and the illustrations. Use the information to guess what will happen next. Today, as we read *The 3 Little Dassies*, think about what might happen next. Then we will read on to find out if your prediction was correct.

❷ Model As you read, use the Think Aloud Cloud to model applying the strategy.

Think Aloud Remember that you can make predictions and then read on to see if you were correct. The text says that Mimbi ran back into her grass house when she saw the eagle. I predict that Mimbi will try to warn her sisters about the eagle, because I know from the story that Mimbi loves her sisters. Let's read on to find out if my prediction is correct.

❸ Guided Practice As you continue to read the Big Book, pause to elicit predictions from children. Guide them in using clues in the text to make a prediction about what they think will happen. *What do you think might happen next? What in the story makes you think that?* Guide children to use the text and illustrations to confirm if their predictions were correct.

Respond to Reading

After reading, prompt children to share what they learned about building shelters. Discuss what predictions they made as they read and whether their predictions were correct. Prompt children to discuss the materials the dassies used to build their structures.

ENGLISH LANGUAGE LEARNERS SCAFFOLD

Beginning

Predict Display pages 20 and 21 of *The 3 Little Dassies*. Let's make a prediction. What will the eagle do?

Intermediate

Predict Display pages 20 and 21 of *The 3 Little Dassies*. Let's make a prediction. Will the eagle break Timbi's house? Do you think he will catch Timbi?

Advanced/Advanced High

Explain Display pages 20 and 21 of *The 3 Little Dassies*. Do you predict Timbi's house will break? Why or why not?

Monitor and *Differentiate*

 Quick Check

Can children apply the strategy make and confirm predictions?

Small Group Instruction

If No →	Approaching	Reteach pp. T130–131
	ELL	Develop pp. T148–151
If Yes →	On Level	Review pp. T140–141
	Beyond Level	Extend pp. T144–145

Word Work

Quick Review

Build Fluency: Sound-Spellings
Display the **Word-Building Cards:** *u, e, ea, sp, sn, sl, cr, fr, tr, o, pl, fl, cl, bl, i, a, s, r, l, t, n, m, c, p, b, f.* Have children say the sounds aloud.

MINILESSON 5 Mins

Phonological Awareness

OBJECTIVES

CCSS Decode regularly spelled one-syllable words. **RF.1.3b**

Identify and generate rhyming words

Identify and Generate Rhyme

1 Model Model for children how to identify and then generate rhyming words. *Listen carefully as I say two words:* bug, rug. Bug *and* rug *rhyme because they both end with the same sounds.* Bug *and* rug *end with /ug/. What is another word that rhymes with* bug *and* rug? *To figure that out, I think of words that end in /ug/.* Tug *rhymes with* bug *and* rug *because* tug *ends with /ug/.*

2 Guided Practice/Practice Have children practice identifying, then generating rhyming words. Do the first one with them. *I will say three words. Tell me which two words rhyme. Then say another word that rhymes with them.*

plum, gum, tag	bus, run, fun
nut, win, but	net, up, pup
hug, bug, hut	tub, block, rub

MINILESSON 10 Mins

Phonics

Sound-Spelling Card

Introduce Short *u*

1 Model Display the *Umbrella* **Sound-Spelling Card**. Teach /u/ spelled *u* using *up* and *sun*. Model writing the letter *u*. Use the handwriting models provided. *This is the* Umbrella *Sound-Spelling Card. The sound is /u/. The /u/ sound is spelled with the letter* u. *Say it with me: /uuu/. This is the sound at the beginning of the word* umbrella. *Listen: /uuu/,* umbrella. *I'll say /u/ as I write the letter* u *several times.*

2 Guided Practice/Practice Have children practice connecting the letter *u* to the sound /u/ by writing it. *Now do it with me. Say /u/ as I write the letter* u. *This time, write the letter* u *five times as you say the /u/ sound.*

SKILLS TRACE

SHORT *u*

Introduce Unit 2 Week 2 Day 1

Review Unit 2 Week 2 Days 2, 3, 4, 5

Assess Unit 2 Week 2

Go Digital

Phonological Awareness

Umbrella

Phonics

Handwriting

Blend Words with Short *u*

①Model Display the **Word-Building Cards** *f, u, n*. Model how to blend the sounds. *This is the letter* f. *It stands for /f/. This is the letter* u. *It stands for /u/. This is the letter* n. *It stands for /n/. Listen as I blend these sounds together: /fffuuunnn/. Say it with me:* fun.

Continue by modeling the words *hug, nut, fuzz,* and *plum*.

②Guided Practice/Practice Display the Day 1 Phonics Practice Activity. Read each word in the first row, blending the sounds; for example: */mmmuuud/. The word is* mud. Have children blend each word with you. Prompt children to read the connected text, sounding out the decodable words.

mud	bug	but	hut	fun	cub
up	us	duck	yuck	huff	stuff
rug	rag	luck	lock	truck	track
yelled	drum	skill	plum	head	puffed

Russ is as snug as a bug in his bed.

Gus plays drums and hums in the sun.

A hen clucks, but a duck quacks!

Also online

Day 1 Phonics Practice Activity

Corrective Feedback

Sound Error Model the sound that children missed, then have them repeat the sound. Say: *My turn.* Tap under the letter and say: *Sound? /u/ What's the sound?* Return to the beginning of the word. Say: *Let's start over.* Blend the word with children again.

Daily Handwriting

Throughout the week teach uppercase and lowercase letters *Uu* using the Handwriting models.

ELL

ENGLISH LANGUAGE LEARNERS

Phonological Awareness: Minimal Contrasts Focus on articulation. Say /u/ and note your mouth position. Have children repeat. Use Sound-Spelling Cards. Repeat for /o/. Have children say both sounds and notice the differences. Continue with: *hut/hit, nut/knot*.

Phonics: Variations in Language In Hmong, there is no direct transfer for /u/. In other languages, such as Spanish and Cantonese, there is an approximate transfer. Emphasize /u/, and show correct mouth position. Practice with Approaching Level phonics lessons.

ON-LEVEL PRACTICE BOOK p. 61

The letter **u** can make the short **u** sound you hear in **rug**.

A. Read the words. Listen for the short u sound. Write the word that names each picture.

cut	bug	hut	duck	pup

1. bug 2. pup

3. duck 4. cut

B. Write your own sentence using a word from the box.

5. Responses will vary.

APPROACHING p. 61	BEYOND p. 61	ELL p. 61

 **Word Work**

Quick Review

High-Frequency Words: Read, Spell, and Write to review last week's high-frequency words: *again, help, new, there, use.*

Spelling

5 Mins

Words with Short *u*

Dictation Use the Spelling Dictation routine to help children transfer their knowledge of sound-spellings to writing. Follow the Dictation routine.

Pretest After dictation, pronounce each spelling word. Read the sentence and pronounce the word again. Ask children to say each word softly, stretching the sounds, before writing it. After the pretest, display the spelling words and write each word as you say the letter names. Have children check their words.

run	I will **run** in the race tomorrow.
fun	Did you have **fun** at the party?
nut	A peanut is one kind of **nut**.
cut	I want to **cut** my hair.
bug	That is a really big **bug**!
rug	The cat naps on the **rug**.
men	Those **men** are my uncles.
head	Turn your **head** and look at me.
could	**Could** you help me, please?
one	I have **one** sister and one brother.

For Approaching Level and Beyond Level children, please refer to the Differentiated Spelling Lists for modified word lists.

OBJECTIVES

CCSS Recognize and read grade-appropriate irregularly spelled words. **RF.1.3g**

CCSS Use conventional spelling for words with common spelling patterns and for frequently occurring irregular words. **L.1.2d**

ENGLISH LANGUAGE LEARNERS

Pantomime Review the meanings of these words by using pictures, pantomime, or gestures when possible. Have children repeat or act out the word.

Go Digital

Spelling Word Routine

they	together
how	eat

High-Frequency Word Routine

High-Frequency Words

could, live, one, then, three

1 **Model** Display the **High-Frequency Word Cards** *could, live, one, then, three*. Use the Read/Spell/Write routine to teach each word.

→ **Read** Point to and say the word *could*. *This is the word* could. *Say it with me:* could. *Could you pass the nuts, please?*

→ **Spell** *The word could is spelled* c-o-u-l-d. *Spell it with me.*

→ **Write** *Let's write the word in the air as we say each letter:* c-o-u-l-d.

→ Follow the same steps to introduce *live, one, then,* and *three*.

→ As children spell each word with you, point out the irregularities in sound-spellings, such as the /ù/ sound spelled *oul* in the word *could*.

→ Have partners create sentences using each word.

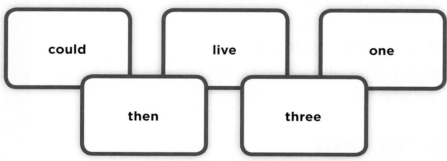

High-Frequency Word Cards

2 **Guided Practice** Have children read the sentences. Prompt them to identify the high-frequency words in connected text and to blend the decodable words.

1. I **could** pull a big sled.
2. Does a fox **live** in a den?
3. There is **one** frog on the log.
4. What did you do **then**?
5. **Three** black dogs run in the grass.

Monitor and *Differentiate*

✓ Quick Check

Can children read and decode words with short *u*?

Can children recognize and read high-frequency words?

Small Group Instruction

If No →	Approaching	Reteach pp. T134–137
	ELL	Develop pp. T148–155
If Yes →	On Level	Review pp. T142–143
	Beyond Level	Extend pp. T146–147

→ Shared Read

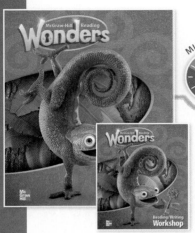

Reading/Writing Workshop Big Book and Reading/Writing Workshop

---

OBJECTIVES

 Decode regularly spelled one-syllable words. **RF.1.3b**

 Recognize and read grade-appropriate irregularly spelled words. **RF.1.3g**

Understand fantasy genre

ACADEMIC LANGUAGE

• *fantasy, predictions*

• Cognates: *fantasía, predicciones*

 MINILESSON 10 Mins

Read *Cubs in a Hut*

Model Skills and Strategies

Tell children that you will now read a selection called *Cubs in a Hut*. As we read, look for the words could, live, one, then, *and* three. Look for words with the /u/ sound.

Story Words Display the words *dry* and *night*. Spell the words and model reading them. Tell children that they will be reading the words in the selection.

Guide children in reading *Cubs in a Hut*. Point out the high-frequency words and words with the /u/ sound.

Genre: Fantasy Tell children that *Cubs in a Hut* is a fantasy. Explain to children that a fantasy story:

→ has made-up characters, settings, and events.

→ often has animal characters who talk and act like people.

→ has events that could not happen in real life.

Connect to Concept

ESSENTIAL QUESTION

 Read together the Essential Question on page 34 of the Reading/Writing Workshop. Discuss the materials that the three cubs use to make their hut. Guide children to connect what they have read to the Essential Question: *What are the buildings in the story made of?*

Go Digital

Cubs in a Hut

Cubs in a Hut

READING/WRITING WORKSHOP, pp. 34–43

Lexile 390

Partner Reading

Have partners use their Reading/Writing Workshop to review the skills and strategies.

→ Remind children that as they reread *Cubs in a Hut* they can use the words and illustrations to predict what will happen next in the story. Then they can read ahead to check their predictions.

→ Have children use pages 30–31 to review high-frequency words *could, live, one, then, three.*

→ Have children use pages 32–33 to review that the letter *u* can stand for the sound /u/. Guide them to blend the sounds to read the words.

→ Have children reread *Cubs in a Hut* with a partner. Guide them to apply the skills and strategies. Ask children to name features of the selection that tell them that it is a fantasy story.

→ # Language Arts

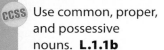 **MINILESSON** **5** Mins

Shared Writing

Go Digital

Graphic Organizer

Writing

I see a fish.

Grammar

Writing Trait: Organization

1 Model Tell children that they will now reread the fantasy *Cubs in a Hut*, paying attention to the way the author organizes information. *An author writes in a way that makes it easy to understand the order of the events that happen in a story.*

2 Guided Practice/Practice Reread *Cubs in a Hut*. Point out the story's organization. Ask: *What happens at the beginning of the story? What happens next?*

→ Prompt children to understand that the story has a clear beginning, middle, and end. First, the cubs decide to make the hut. Next, they plan and make the hut. Then the hut leaks. Last, they fix the leak.

Story

Focus and Plan Tell children that this week they will be writing a fantasy about building something. Remind children that a fantasy is a made-up story that could not happen in real life.

 Brainstorm Use Teaching Poster 30 to fill out a Sequence chart to help children organize events for a story about children who build a house out of fruit. Ask questions to prompt children to think about and identify the sequence of events. *What do the children do first? Where do they get the materials?* Record children's ideas on the chart.

Write Tell children that you will work together to write a fantasy about the children who made their house out of fruit. Model writing sentences based on the Teaching Poster. Say: *Let's start by telling what happens first. Let's write:* Nat and Kim made a house of fruit. First, they stuck the fruit together with honey.

Work together to write sentences that tell a clear beginning, middle, and end.

OBJECTIVES

CCSS Write narratives in which they recount two or more appropriately sequenced events, include some details regarding what happened, use temporal words to signal event order, and provide some sense of closure. **W.1.3**

CCSS Use common, proper, and possessive nouns. **L.1.1b**

- Identify and form singular and plural nouns
- Form contractions with *'s*

ACADEMIC LANGUAGE

- *organization, problem, solution, plural*
- Cognates: *organización, problema, solución, plural*

Grammar

Singular and Plural Nouns

1 Model Tell children that a singular noun names one person, one place, or one thing. Explain: *Some nouns name more than one person, place, or thing. These nouns are plural nouns. Usually you make a noun plural by adding* -s *to the end.*

Display the following sentences:

The <u>cat</u> is big.   The three <u>cats</u> nap.

Read the sentences with children. Underline the noun in each sentence. Point out that the word *cat* names one cat. It is a singular noun. Underline the *s* in *cats*. Point out that the word *cats* names more than one cat. It is a plural noun.

Tell children that if a noun ends in *-x, -s,* or *-ss*, you add *-es* to make the plural form. Display the following singular nouns in a column: *box, bus, boss*. Write the plural next to each.

2 Guided Practice/Practice Display the sentences below and read them aloud. Have pairs identify the noun that completes each sentence and identify it as singular or plural.

The six (<u>duck/ducks</u>) have many (<u>brick/bricks</u>). (ducks, plural; bricks, plural)

A (<u>frog/frogs</u>) got a lot of (<u>kiss/kisses</u>). (frog, singular; kisses, plural)

Talk About It Have partners work together to orally generate sentences using singular nouns. Challenge them to make the nouns plural using the same sentences.

Mechanics: Apostrophe with Contractions

1 Model Show children how to form contractions with *'s*. Write *it* and *is*. Beneath the words, write *it's*. Read the words aloud and have children listen for the differences. Explain that *it's* is a short way to say *it is*. Tell children that you can put two words together to make one word. An apostrophe takes the place of letters in the words. Use a similar procedure to teach contractions *she's, he's, where's*.

2 Guided Practice Write contractions with *'s* incorrectly. Ask children to correct your errors.

ELL
ENGLISH LANGUAGE LEARNERS SCAFFOLD

Beginning

Demonstrate Comprehension Explain singular and plural nouns. Read the first Model sentence. Point to the noun. *How many cats are there? Show me with your fingers.* Repeat with the second sentence. Allow children ample time to respond.

Intermediate

Explain Display the Model sentences. *What is the noun? How do you know if it is singular or plural?* Clarify responses by providing vocabulary.

Advanced/Advanced High

Expand Display the Guided Practice sentences. *How did you decide which noun is correct? How do you know if it is singular or plural?* Elicit more details to support children's answers.

Daily Wrap Up

→ Review the Essential Question and encourage children to discuss using the new oral vocabulary words. Ask: *What materials are different buildings made of?*

→ Prompt children to share what skills they've learned. How might they use those skills?

Materials

Reading/Writing Workshop
VOLUME 2

Reading/Writing Workshop Big Book
UNIT 2

Visual Vocabulary Cards
collapsed
furious
materials
refused
shelter

Teaching Poster

High-Frequency Word Cards
could   live   one   then   three

Word-Building Cards

Spelling Word Cards

umbrella
Sound-Spelling Cards

Interactive Read-Aloud Cards

→ Build the Concept

MINILESSON
5 Mins

Oral Language

Go Digital

school
Visual Glossary

"The Three Little Pigs"

OBJECTIVES

CCSS Ask and answer questions about key details in a text read aloud or information presented orally or through other media. **SL.1.2**

- Develop oral language
- Discuss the Essential Question

ACADEMIC LANGUAGE

- *predictions, illustrations*
- Cognates: *predicciones, ilustraciones*

ESSENTIAL QUESTION

Remind children that this week you have been talking and reading about buildings and what they are made of. Remind them of the houses and buildings in the city and how the cubs built a hut. Guide children to discuss the Essential Question using information from what they read on Day 1.

Oral Vocabulary Words

Review the oral vocabulary words *shelter* and *materials* from Day 1. Use the Define/Example/Ask routine to introduce the oral vocabulary words *collapsed, furious,* and *refused*. Prompt children to use the words as they discuss buildings and what they are made of.

Oral Vocabulary Routine

Define: If something **collapsed**, it fell down.

Example: The tent collapsed and fell on us!

Ask: What happens to a stack of blocks after it has collapsed?

Define: When someone gets very angry, he or she is **furious**.

Example: Billy was furious that he could not go out and play.

Ask: What might make you furious?

Define: If you **refused** to do something, you said firmly that you would not do it.

Example: My dog refused to go outside in the rain. He hates to get wet!

Ask: What have you refused to do?

Visual Vocabulary Cards

Listening Comprehension

MINILESSON
5 Mins

Read the Interactive Read Aloud

ELL

ENGLISH LANGUAGE LEARNERS

Request Assistance Remind children of expressions they can use to request assistance from the teacher or their partners, such as, *"Can you repeat that, please?"*

Strategy: Make and Confirm Predictions

Remind children that as they read, they can make predictions about what will happen next. Then they can use the words and illustrations to find out whether their prediction was correct. Model using the Think Aloud Cloud.

"The Three Little Pigs"

Think Aloud When I read, I can guess what will happen by thinking about the characters and what they might do next. That helps me better understand what I am reading. The little pig made a house of straw. I think that when the wolf comes, the little pig will run away. Let's read on to find out if my prediction is correct.

Tell children that you will read "The Three Little Pigs." Display the Interactive Read-Aloud Cards. Pause as you read to model applying the strategy.

→ Model using the text to confirm if your prediction was correct.

Make Connections

COLLABORATE

Discuss partners' responses to "The Three Little Pigs." *How are the pigs like the cubs who built a hut?*

→ # Word Work

Quick Review

Build Fluency: Sound-Spellings
Display the **Word-Building Cards**: *u, e, ea, sp, sn, sl, cr, fr, tr, o, pl, fl, cl, bl, i, a, s, r, l, t, n, m, c, p, b, f.* Have children say the sounds. Repeat, and vary the pace.

MINILESSON 5 Mins — Phonemic Awareness

OBJECTIVES

CCSS Isolate and pronounce initial, medial vowel, and final sounds (phonemes) in spoken single-syllable words. **RF.1.2c**

CCSS Decode regularly spelled one-syllable words. **RF.1.3b**

Read contractions with 's

Phoneme Identity

❶ **Model** Show children how to identify the same sound in a group of words. *Listen as I say three words:* mud, cub, fun. *I hear the same sound in the middle of* mud, cub, *and* fun. *Listen: /muuud/, /kuuub/, /fuuun/. The middle sound is /u/.*

❷ **Guided Practice/Practice** Have children practice identifying the same sound in a group of words. Do the first set together. *Listen as I say three words. Tell me the sound you hear in all three words. Let's do the first one together. Listen: /suuub/, /yuuum/, /fuuus/.*

sub, yum, fuss	bus, nut, huff	yes, fell, bed
bat, man, cap	hum, but, run	hot, log, sock

MINILESSON 5 Mins — Phonics

Review Short *u*

❶ **Model** Display the *Umbrella* **Sound-Spelling Card**. Review the sound /u/ spelled *u* using the words *us* and *bug*.

❷ **Guided Practice/Practice** Have children practice connecting the letter and sound. Point to the Sound-Spelling Card. *What is this letter? What sound does it stand for?*

Go Digital

Phonemic Awareness

Phonics

Structural Analysis

Handwriting

Blend Words with Short *u*

❶ Model Display **Word-Building Cards** *s, u, n* to form the word *sun*. Model how to generate and blend the sounds to say the word. *This is the letter* s. *It stands for /s/. This is the letter* u. *It stands for /u/. This is the letter* n. *It stands for /n/. Listen as I blend these sounds together: /sssuuunnn/. Say it with me:* sun.

Continue by modeling the words *buzz, luck, club,* and *truck.*

❷ Guided Practice/Practice Repeat the routine with children with *tub, rug, hug, cup, mug, snug, drum, pluck, stuck, cut, huff.*

Build Words with Short *u*

❶ Model Display the Word-Building Cards *c, u, t*. Blend: /k/ /u/ /t/, /kuuut/, *cut*.

Replace *c* with *h* and repeat with *hut*.

Change *t* to *m* and repeat with *hum*.

❷ Guided Practice/Practice Continue with *huff, puff, pup, cup, cub, club, cluck, pluck, plum, plug*. Guide children to build and blend each word.

ENGLISH LANGUAGE LEARNERS

Build Vocabulary Review the meanings of example words that can be explained or demonstrated in a concrete way. For example, ask children to point to or draw a picture of a *cup* or *mug*. Model the actions for *hug* and *hum* as you say, *I hug with my arms. I hum with my mouth.* Have children repeat. Provide sentence starters such as *I have fun when* ____ for children to complete. Correct grammar and pronunciation as needed.

MINILESSON 5 Mins

Structural Analysis

Contractions with *'s*

❶ Model Write and read aloud *he is* and *he's*. Explain to children that *he's* is a contraction. A contraction is when you put two words together to make one word. Point out that *he's* is a shorter way of writing and saying *he is*. Underline the *'s*. Explain that the apostrophe (') stands for the missing letter *i* in *is*. *You leave out one or more letters when you make a contraction.* Repeat for *she is/she's* and *it is/it's*.

Say *he's* and *she's* again and have children listen for the /z/ sound at the end. Then say *it's* and have children listen for the /s/ sound at the end. Use each word in a sentence.

❷ Guided Practice/Practice Write *he is, she is,* and *it is* on the board. Have children write the contraction for each word and then use the contraction in a sentence.

→ # Word Work

MINILESSON
5 Mins

Spelling

Word Sort with -un, -ut, -ug

❶ **Model** Display the **Spelling Word Cards** from the Teacher's Resource Book, one at a time. Have children read each word, listening for short *u* and the ending sound.

Use cards for *bun, hut,* and *dug* to create a three-column chart. Say each word and pronounce the sounds: /b/ /u/ /n/; /h/ /u/ /t/; /d/ /u/ /g/. Say each word again, emphasizing the short *u* plus final consonant sound. Ask children to chorally spell each word.

❷ **Guided Practice/Practice** Have children place each Spelling Word Card in the column with the words containing the same final sounds and spellings (*-un, -ut, -ug*).

When completed, have children chorally read the words in each column. Then call out a word. Have a child find the word card and point to it as the class chorally spells the word.

Go Digital

er	ir	or	ur
her			

girl curb   word

Spelling Word Sort

they	together
how	eat

High-Frequency Word Routine

OBJECTIVES

CCSS Recognize and read grade-appropriate irregularly spelled words. **RF.1.3g**

CCSS Use conventional spelling for words with common spelling patterns and for frequently occurring irregular words. **L.1.2d**

ANALYZE ERRORS/ARTICULATION SUPPORT

Use children's pretest errors to analyze spelling problems and provide corrective feedback. For example, the /u/ and /o/ sounds are formed in similar ways. Some children will substitute the letter *o* for the letter *u.*

Have children say /u/, paying attention to how it feels in the mouth. Repeat for /o/. Go back and forth to help children feel the difference.

Have children orally segment one of the spelling words. When you get to the /u/ sound, ask: *How does your mouth feel? What letter do we write for that sound?*

ENGLISH LANGUAGE LEARNERS

Provide Clues Practice spelling by helping children generate more words with medial short *u* patterns. Provide clues: *Think of a word that starts with* p *and rhymes with* cup. Write the word and have children practice reading it. Correct their pronunciation if needed.

MINILESSON
5 Mins

High-Frequency Words

could, live, one, then, three

① **Guided Practice** Say each word and have children Read/Spell/Write it. Ask children to close their eyes, picture the word in their minds, and write it the way they see it. Display the high-frequency words for children to self-correct.

→ Point out irregularities in sound-spellings, such as the /w/ sound spelled *o* in *one*.

② **Practice** Add the high-frequency words *could, live, one, then,* and *three* to the cumulative word bank.

COLLABORATE

→ Have children work with a partner to create sentences using the words.

→ Have children look at the words and compare their sounds and spellings to words from previous weeks.

→ Suggest that children write about buildings that people live in.

Cumulative Review Review last week's words using the Read/Spell/Write routine.

→ Repeat the above routine, mixing the words and having children chorally say each one.

ON-LEVEL PRACTICE BOOK p. 62

Complete each sentence. Use one of the words in the box.

| three | could | live | one | then |

1. I ____live____ in the city.

2. There is ____one____ duck.

3. Sam ____could____ not run.

4. She has ____three____ pups.

5. I run up the hill.
   ____Then____ I run down the hill.

| APPROACHING p. 62 | BEYOND p. 62 | ELL p. 62 |

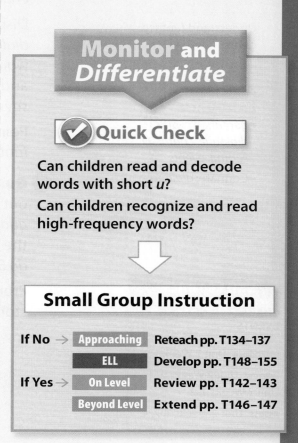

Monitor and *Differentiate*

✓ Quick Check

Can children read and decode words with short *u*?

Can children recognize and read high-frequency words?

Small Group Instruction

If No →	Approaching	Reteach pp. T134–137
	ELL	Develop pp. T148–155
If Yes →	On Level	Review pp. T142–143
	Beyond Level	Extend pp. T146–147

Comprehension

CLOSE READING

Reading/Writing Workshop Big Book and Reading/Writing Workshop

---

OBJECTIVES

CCSS Describe characters, settings, and major events in a story, using key details. **RL.1.3**

Understand fantasy genre

ACADEMIC LANGUAGE

• *quotation marks, dialogue, character, setting, events*
• Cognate: *diálogo*

MINILESSON
10 Mins

Reread *Cubs in a Hut*

Genre: Fantasy

❶ **Model** Tell children they will now reread the fantasy story *Cubs in a Hut*. Explain that as they read, they will look for information in the text and illustrations to help them understand the story.

Review the characteristics of a fantasy story. It:

→ has made-up characters, settings, and events.

→ could not happen in real life.

→ often has animal characters who talk and act like people.

→ can have dialogue.

Tell children that fantasy stories often have dialogue. Dialogue tells the reader what words the characters say aloud. In a story, the dialogue has quotation marks at the beginning and end of what the character says.

Display page 36 and read the first sentence: *This sentence includes dialogue. The quotation marks show you what Gus says. He says these words: "Let's make a hut."* Point out the quotation marks in the second and third sentences. *Russ says these words: "We could use mud." Bud says these words: "It will be fun!"*

Point out that the cubs are talking. *This tells me that the story is a fantasy.*

❷ **Guided Practice/Practice** Display page 38 of *Cubs in a Hut*. Point out the quotation marks in the second sentence. Say: *Look at the quotation marks. These show us that Russ says, "Let's move in!"* Point to the third sentence. Ask: *Where are the quotation marks? What words do Bud and Gus say?*

Prompt children to identify details that tell them that this is a fantasy story.

Go Digital

Cubs in a Hut

Genre

Character, Setting, Events

SKILLS TRACE

CHARACTER, SETTING, EVENTS

Introduce Unit 2 Week 1

Review Unit 2 Weeks 2, 4; Unit 3 Weeks 1, 2

Assess Unit 2 Weeks 1, 2, 4

Skill: Character, Setting, Events

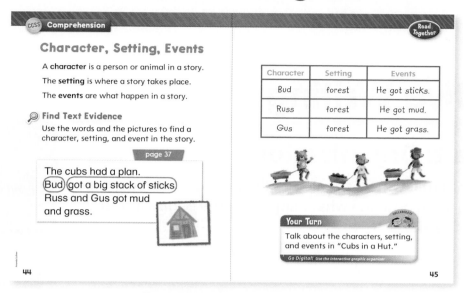

Reading/Writing Workshop, pp. 44–45

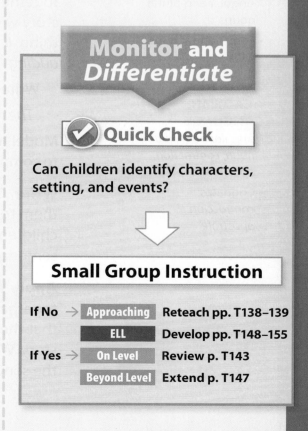

ON-LEVEL PRACTICE BOOK p. 67

Reread "Pals Play and Hum."
Follow the directions.

1. Write a sentence that tells where Bug is on page 1.

   _____

   Possible response: Bug is in a yard.

2. Write the word that tells what Duck can do.

   _____

   pluck

3. Write the word that tells what Frog can do.

   _____

   drum

4. Write a sentence that tells what the pals do.

   _____

   Possible response: The pals have fun.

APPROACHING p. 67	BEYOND p. 67	ELL p. 67

① **Model** Tell children that when they read realistic fiction they can use the text and illustrations to find the characters, settings, and events. Have children look at pages 44–45 in their Reading/Writing Workshop. Read together the definitions of Character, Setting, and Events. *A character is a person or animal in a story. The setting is where a story takes place. The events are what happens in a story.*

② **Guided Practice/Practice** Read together the Find Text Evidence section and model finding the characters, setting, and an event in the selection *Cubs in a Hut.* Point out the details added to the graphic organizer. *On page 37 we can find details about the characters, setting, and events. One of the characters is Bud. What does Bud do? He got sticks. This is an event. What other characters and events do we learn about? What is the setting?*

Character	Setting	Events

Teaching Poster

Monitor and *Differentiate*

✓ **Quick Check**

Can children identify characters, setting, and events?

⬇

Small Group Instruction

If No → **Approaching** Reteach pp. T138–139

ELL Develop pp. T148–155

If Yes → **On Level** Review p. T143

Beyond Level Extend p. T147

→ # Language Arts

Interactive Writing

Writing Trait: Organization

Review Tell children that writers should put their ideas in an order that makes sense. Writers can describe what happens at the beginning, in the middle, and at the end.

Story

Discuss Guide children to think of different characters and events they can write about for their fantasy about building something. For example, children might write about pigs that build a house out of mud and socks. Record all ideas, and then lead children to choose one. Prompt children to brainstorm events for the chosen story idea. Record their story events on a Sequence chart on Teaching Poster 30. Make sure they have a beginning, a middle, and an end.

Model/Apply Grammar Tell children that they will be working together to write a fantasy about building something. Remind them the story will include nouns, or names for a person, an animal, a place, or a thing. *If there is more than one of something, we make the noun a plural by adding -s or -es to the end of the noun.*

→ Write the sentence starter:

The pigs had a lot of _____ .

Model how to choose different plural nouns *(socks, boxes, bricks, glasses)* to complete this sentence. Remind children of the rules for using *-s* and *-es*.

Write Collaborate with children to write sentences for the story. Guide them to use the graphic organizer to sequence the events. Remind children to listen for the sounds in each word. As children create sentences, share the pen.

Apply Writing Trait Review with children the story you wrote together on Day 1. Remind them how they organized the sentences so that they told what happens at the beginning, middle, and end of the story. Work with children to use signal words *first, next,* and *last* to place the sentences into an order that makes sense.

OBJECTIVES

CCSS Write narratives in which they recount two or more appropriately sequenced events, include some details regarding what happened, use temporal words to signal event order, and provide some sense of closure. **W.1.3**

CCSS Use common, proper, and possessive nouns. **L.1.1b**

- Identify and form singular and plural nouns
- Form contractions with 's

ACADEMIC LANGUAGE

- *singular noun, plural noun, contraction, apostrophe*
- Cognates: *contracción, apóstrofe*

Go Digital

Graphic Organizer

Beginning
↓
Middle
↓
End

Writing

Grammar

I see a fish.

Grammar

Singular and Plural Nouns

1 Review Remind children that a singular noun names one person, place, or thing. Plural nouns name more than one person, place, or thing. Review that a noun is usually made plural by adding -s. When a noun ends with -x, -s, or -ss, you add -es.

→ Write the following sentences:

The foxes like socks. (foxes, plural; socks, plural)

The hen met many pigs. (hen, singular; pigs, plural)

Read the sentences aloud. Guide children to name each noun and tell if it is plural or singular. Have volunteers underline the endings in the plural nouns and explain the rule for adding -s or -es.

2 Guided Practice Write sample sentences. Read each sentence. Have children work in pairs to identify each noun and tell if it is singular or plural.

The kids make a school out of blocks.
(kids, plural; school, singular; blocks, plural)

The pigs had a cup and a glass.
(pigs, plural; cup, singular; glass, singular)

3 Practice Once children identify the nouns, have them write the other form of each noun. For example, if a noun is plural, have children write the singular form of the noun.

Talk About It Have partners work together to orally generate sentences with singular and plural nouns. Challenge them to create sentences that include at least one singular and one plural noun.

Mechanics: Apostrophes with Contractions

1 Review Remind children that a contraction is two words combined. *An apostrophe takes the place of certain letters. Many contractions are made with the word is. The apostrophe takes the place of the* i *in* is.

2 Practice Display these words. Have pairs combine the words correctly to form a contraction.

he is; where is; it is (he's, where's, it's)

ENGLISH LANGUAGE LEARNERS

Explain Read aloud the first Review sentence. Ask children to circle the words that name more than one of something. Have them complete the sentence frame: *A plural noun is a word that names _____.* Repeat correct answers slowly and clearly to the class.

Use Gestures Write and read aloud several nouns, both plural and singular. Have children hold up one finger if the noun is singular and names one person, place, or thing. If the noun is plural, have children hold up two or more fingers.

Daily Wrap Up

→ Discuss the Essential Question and encourage children to use the oral vocabulary words. Ask: *What kinds of materials would you like to use to build a house?*

→ Prompt children to review and discuss the skills they used today. *How will the skills you learned today help you read and write?*

Materials

Reading/Writing Workshop
VOLUME 2

Literature Anthology
VOLUME 2

Literature Big Book
The 3 Little Dassies

Visual Vocabulary Cards

collapsed	could
furious	live
materials	one
refused	then
shelter	three

a b c

Word-Building Cards

Teaching Poster

Response Board

Interactive Read-Aloud Cards

run

Spelling Word Cards

→ # Build the Concept

Go Digital

MINILESSON
5 Mins

Oral Language

OBJECTIVES

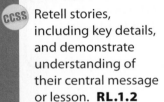

Retell stories, including key details, and demonstrate understanding of their central message or lesson. **RL.1.2**

Read grade-level text orally with accuracy, appropriate rate, and expression. **RF.1.4b**

Make and confirm predictions

ACADEMIC LANGUAGE

• *confirm, exclamation mark, emotion*

• Cognates: *confirmar, emoción*

ESSENTIAL QUESTION

Remind children that this week you have been talking and reading about buildings and what they are made of. Remind them of the shelters made by the animals in *The 3 Little Dassies*, *Cubs in a Hut*, and "The Three Little Pigs." Guide children to discuss the question using information from what they have read and talked about throughout the week.

Review Oral Vocabulary

Review the oral vocabulary words *shelter, materials, collapsed, furious,* and *refused* using the Define/Example/Ask routine. Encourage children to discuss buildings when coming up with examples for each word.

Visual Vocabulary Cards

Visual Glossary

The 3 Little Dassies

Retell

Listening Comprehension

MINILESSON 10 Mins

Reread the Big Book

Strategy: Make and Confirm Predictions

Remind children that as they read, they can use text evidence to make and confirm predictions. This can help them understand the characters and story events. *Think about the predictions you made when you first started reading this story. Were your predictions correct? Which pictures or words in the story did you use to make your predictions?*

Read aloud *The 3 Little Dassies*. Point out text evidence, such as pictures and events in the story, that could be used when making and confirming predictions.

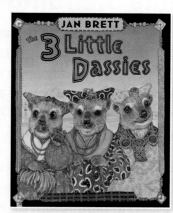

Literature Big Book

Model Retelling

Pause to retell portions of the selection. *I can use my own words to tell what happens in the story. I have read that the three little dassies set off to find a new place to live near the mountain. They hope their new home will be safe from eagles.*

→ After reading, model retelling the entire story, using your own words to tell the important events in the correct order.

Model Fluency

Expression Turn to page 31 of *The 3 Little Dassies*. Point to the quotation marks and the exclamation marks. *When reading text inside quotation marks, you should read it with lots of expression and speak the way you think the character would. If the text has an exclamation mark, you should read it with strong emotion.*

→ Read aloud page 31 with slightly exaggerated expression. Have children identify the quotation marks and exclamation marks and then reread the passage chorally. Repeat the reading to give children more practice reading with appropriate expression.

ELL

ENGLISH LANGUAGE LEARNERS

Retell Guide children to retell by using a question prompt on each page. *What does the first dassie use to make a house?* Provide sentence starters for children to complete orally. *The first dassie uses _____ to make a _____.*

Access Complex Text

If the complexity of the text makes it hard for children to read, use the Access Complex Text prompts.

Vocabulary Children may be unfamiliar with dassies.

→ Explain that a dassie is a small creature that lives in rocky regions in southern Africa. Dassies make their homes in nooks and crannies among large rocks. They enjoy sunning themselves on the rocks but will run for shelter when they sense danger. They are often hunted by jackals, lions, and eagles.

 **Word Work**

Quick Review

Build Fluency: Sound-Spellings
Display the **Word-Building Cards:** *u, e, ea, sp, sn, sl, cr, fr, tr, o, pl, fl, cl, bl, i, a, s, r, l, t, n, m, c, p, b, f.* Have children say the sounds.

Phonemic Awareness

Phoneme Blending

OBJECTIVES

CCSS Orally produce single-syllable words by blending sounds (phonemes), including consonant blends. **RF.1.2b**

CCSS Decode regularly spelled one-syllable words. **RF.1.3b**

Read contractions with *'s*

1 Model Place markers in the **Response Board** to represent sounds. Show children how to orally blend phonemes. *I am going to put one marker in each box as I say each sound. Then I will blend the sounds to form a word.* Place a marker for each sound as you say: */m/ /u/ /g/. This word has three sounds: /m/ /u/ /g/. Listen as I blend these sounds to form a word: /mmmuuug/,* mug. *The word is* mug.

2 Guided Practice/Practice Have children practice blending sounds to say a word. Do the first three together. *Let's do some together. I will say one sound at a time. Place a marker for each sound you hear. Then blend the sounds to say the word.*

| /u/ /p/ | /f/ /u/ n/ | /p/ /l/ /u/ /m/ |
| /k/ /u/ /p/ | /d/ /r/ /u/ /m/ | /s/ /t/ /u/ /k/ |

Phonics

Blend Words with Short *u*

1 Model Display **Word-Building Cards** *s, n, u, g.* Model how to blend the sounds. *This is the letter* s. *It stands for /s/. This is the letter* n. *It stands for /n/. This is the letter* u. *It stands for /u/. This is the letter* g. *It stands for /g/. Let's blend all four sounds: /snuuug/. The word is* snug.

Continue by modeling the words *duck, club, up,* and *plum.*

2 Guided Practice/Practice Review the words and sentences on the Day 3 Phonics Practice Activity with children. Read each word in the first row, blending the sounds; for example, */y/ /u/ /k/, /yuuuk/. The word is* yuck.

Have children blend each word with you. Prompt children to read the connected text, sounding out the decodable words.

Go Digital

Phonemic Awareness

Phonics

Structural Analysis

Handwriting

yuck	mud	huff	stuff	drum	snug
bug	plug	cub	fun	huts	stuck
puff	gruff	fluff	pluck	plus	dress
it's	she's	he's	what's	let's	buzz
cliff	track	truck	clock	cluck	puffed

Gus dug in the mud with us.

Bud huffs and puffs as he runs up a hill.

Also online

Day 3 Phonics Practice Activity

MINILESSON
5 Mins

Structural Analysis

Contractions with 's

❶ **Model** Write the word *she's*. Circle the *'s*. Tell children that the *'s* at the end shows that *she's* is a contraction. Remind them that a contraction is a word you make by putting two words together. When you do this, you replace one or more of the letters with an (') apostrophe. Write *she is* and model how to form the contraction by crossing out the *i* in *is* and replacing it with an apostrophe. Repeat for *let us* and the word *let's*.

❷ **Practice/Apply** Help children blend the contractions *he's* and *it's*. Point out that the letter *s* at the end can stand for /z/ as in *he's* or /s/ as in *it's*. Have children tell what two words each contraction stands for.

Corrective Feedback

Corrective Feedback Say: *My turn.* Model blending the word using the appropriate signaling procedures. Then lead children in blending the sounds. Say: *Do it with me.* You will respond with children to offer support. Then say: *Your turn. Blend.* Have children chorally blend. Return to the beginning of the word. Say: *Let's start over.*

→ Word Work

Quick Review
High-Frequency Words: Read, Spell, and Write to review this week's high-frequency words: *could, live, one, then, three.*

MINILESSON 5 Mins

Spelling

OBJECTIVES

CCSS Recognize and read grade-appropriate irregularly spelled words. **RF.1.3g**

CCSS Use conventional spelling for words with common spelling patterns and for frequently occurring irregular words. **L.1.2d**

-un, -ut, -ug Word Families

1 Model Make index cards for *-un, -ut, -ug* and form three columns in a pocket chart. Blend the sounds with children.

Hold up the *run* **Spelling Word Card**. Say and spell it. Pronounce each sound clearly: /r/ /u/ /n/. Blend the sounds, stretching the vowel sound to emphasize it: /ruuun/. Repeat this step with *fun*. Place both words below the *-un* card. Read and spell each spelling word together with children. Have children read each word. *What do you notice about these spelling words? They have the /u/ sound, and they rhyme because they both end with /un/ spelled* u-n.

2 Guided Practice/Practice Have children spell each word. Repeat the process with the *-ut* and *-ug* words.

Display the words *men, head, could,* and *one* in a separate column. Read and spell the words together with children. Point out that these spelling words do not contain the /u/ sound spelled *u*.

Conclude by asking children to orally generate additional words that rhyme with each word. Write the additional words on the board. Underline the common spelling patterns in the additional words. If necessary, point out the differences and explain why they are unusual.

PHONICS/SPELLING PRACTICE BOOK p. 33

A. Read the words in the box. Say each word. Then complete each word below to make a spelling word. Use each word once.

| run | fun | nut | cut |
| bug | rug | could | one |

1. c _o_ _u_ ld   5. b _u_ g

2. nu _t_   6. r _u_ n

3. r _u_ g   7. _o_ ne

4. f _u_ _n_   8. c _u_ _t_

B. Write your own sentence. Use one or two words from the box. Check that there are spaces between words.

Check spacing.

Possible response: There is a bug on the rug.

Go Digital

| er | ir | or | ur |
| her | | | |

girl curb   word

Spelling Word Families

school

Visual Glossary

MINILESSON
5 Mins

High-Frequency Words

could, live, one, then, three

❶ Guided Practice Say each word and have children Read/Spell/Write it. As children spell each word with you, point out the /th/ sounds (both voiced and unvoiced) spelled *th* in *then* and *three*.

Display **Visual Vocabulary Cards** to review this week's high-frequency words.

Visual Vocabulary Cards

❷ Practice Repeat the activity with last week's words.

Build Fluency: Word Automaticity

Have children read the following sentences aloud together at the same pace. Repeat several times.

> I had one dog.
>
> Then I got three cats.
>
> Could my dog live with three cats?

Word Bank

Review the current and previous words in the word bank. Discuss with children which words should be removed, or added back, from previous high-frequency word lists. Remind children that the word bank should change as the class needs it to.

Monitor and *Differentiate*

✓ **Quick Check**

Can children read and decode words with short *u*?

Can children recognize and read high-frequency words?

⬇

Small Group Instruction

If No →	**Approaching**	Reteach pp. T134–137
	ELL	Develop pp. T148–155
If Yes →	**On Level**	Review pp. T142–143
	Beyond Level	Extend pp. T146–147

Essential Question
What buildings do you know? What are they made of?
Read about three pigs who love mud and a wolf who doesn't.

Go Digital!

The Pigs, the Wolf, and the Mud
by Ellen Tarlow
illustrated by Pablo Bernasconi

26

27

LITERATURE ANTHOLOGY, pp. 26–27

Develop Comprehension
CLOSE READING
Lexile 320

Wonders
Literature Anthology

Literature Anthology

Read Literature Anthology

Review Genre: Fantasy
Review with children the key characteristics of a fantasy. It:

→ has made-up characters, settings, and events.

→ could not happen in real life.

→ often has dialogue.

Preview and Predict Display pages 26–27 and read aloud the title. Ask: *Which characters do you see in the picture? What are they doing? What do you think this story is about?*

ESSENTIAL QUESTION
Read aloud the Essential Question: *What buildings do you know? What are they made of?* Tell children that as they read they should think about the materials used in the story to make buildings.

Story Words Read and spell the words *wolf, rang, eat, and good-bye.* Review word meaning as needed. Tell children that they will read these words in the selection.

 Note Taking: Graphic Organizer As children read the selection, guide them to fill in the graphic organizer on **Your Turn Practice Book** page 64 as you model recording the character, setting, and event details of each section.

"It is a mess," said Pig **One**.
"But pigs like a mess," said Pig Two.
"Mud is fun!" yelled Pig Three. **1** **2**

Three pigs **lived** in a mud hut.

28

29

LITERATURE ANTHOLOGY, pp. 28–29

1 Skill: Character, Setting, Events

A character is a person or animal in a story. Let's look for information in the text about characters. Who are the story characters? Where are they? That is the setting. What are they doing? That is the event. Let's add these details to the chart.

Character	Setting	Events
Pig One, Pig Two, Pig Three	In the hut	Playing with mud

2 Strategy: Make and Confirm Predictions

Teacher Think Aloud Remember that you can make predictions and then read on to see if you were correct. On pages 28 and 29, the text and pictures tell us about the three pigs. They like a mess. Let's make a prediction about the pigs. I predict that the pigs will make a big mess. Let's read on to see if the prediction is correct.

"Get this!" yelled Pig One.
She tossed mud to Pig Two. **3**
"Mud is fun!" yelled Pig Three. **4**

30

The bell rang.
"Little pigs, pigs, pigs let me in."

31

LITERATURE ANTHOLOGY, pp. 30–31

Develop Comprehension CLOSE READING

3 Context Clues

If we don't know the meaning of the word *tossed*, we can look for context clues in the words around it. We can also use clues from the picture on the page. Look at the words around *tossed*, and look at the picture. What do you think the word *tossed* means? (The picture and the words "to Pig Two" tell that she is throwing mud. *Tossed* must mean "throw.")

4 Strategy: Make and Confirm Predictions

Teacher Think Aloud Let's check our prediction. We predicted that the pigs would make a mess. On page 30, I read that Pig One tosses mud. In the picture, I see two pigs throwing mud, and there is mud everywhere. My prediction was correct! The pigs made a mess. I will make another prediction to think about as I read. I predict that the pigs will clean up the mud.

"It is a big bad wolf!" said Pig One. **5**
"We can not let you in," yelled the
pigs. "You will eat us up."

32

"**Then** I will huff and puff,"
the wolf yelled back.
He huffed, huffed, huffed.
He puffed, puffed, puffed. **6**

33

LITERATURE ANTHOLOGY, pp. 32–33

5 Skill: Character, Setting, Events

Teacher Think Aloud On this page, I read about
a new character. It is the wolf. He is outside the
pigs' hut. I remember that the setting is where
events in a story happen. The wolf is outside. I will
add this character and setting to the chart.

Characters	Setting	Events
Pig One, Pig Two, Pig Three	Inside the mud hut	Playing with mud
The Wolf	Outside the mud hut	

6 Ask and Answer Questions

Remember, when you want to know something
in a story, you can ask yourself questions. You
can use the words and illustrations to find your
answers. The answers will help you understand
what you have read. Read page 32. We can ask
what the wolf will do if the pigs do not open the
door. Now let's read page 33. Can we answer the
question?

"Yuck!" said the wolf.
"I can not huff in mud.
I can not puff in mud." **7**

34

He rang the bell again.
"Pigs, pigs, pigs let me in!"
he yelled.
"We will not let you in!"
the pigs yelled back. **8**

35

LITERATURE ANTHOLOGY, pp. 34–35

Develop Comprehension *CLOSE READING*

7 Strategy: Make and Confirm Predictions

Teacher Think Aloud I will check my prediction. I predicted that the pigs would clean up the messy mud. They did not clean up the mud. My prediction was not correct. Actually, the mud is messier! Let's make new predictions. I predict that the wolf will not like the mud, so he will go away. What is your prediction?

Student Think Aloud I predict that the wolf will learn to like mud like the pigs do. They will all live happily ever after in the hut.

8 Skill: Character, Setting, Events

COLLABORATE Turn to a partner and discuss what the wolf does on these pages. (The wolf huffs, puffs, rings the bell, and yells.) **Add** this event to the chart.

Characters	Setting	Events
Pig One, Pig Two, Pig Three	Inside the mud hut	Play with mud
The Wolf	Outside the mud hut	Huffs and puffs, rings the bell, and yells

"Then I will kick, kick, kick,"
said the wolf.
He kicked, kicked, kicked.

36

The hut fell in! **9**
"Yuck!" said the wolf.
"I can not look at this mud." **10** **11**

37

LITERATURE ANTHOLOGY, pp. 36–37

9 Maintain Skill: Key Details

Remember that details happen in an order. Let's think about the key details so far in this story. Tell the details in the order that they appear in the story. (First, the pigs play with the mud in the hut. Next, the wolf comes to the hut. Then, he huffs and puffs, and kicks the hut. Last, the hut falls in!)

10 Author's Craft: Dialogue

Sometimes authors use dialogue to give information about what a character thinks. What does the dialogue on this page tell us about what the wolf thinks? (He does not like mud. He can not look at it.)

11 Skill: Character, Setting, Events

Let's add events to the chart. What does the wolf do? What happens to the mud hut?

Characters	Setting	Events
Pig One, Pig Two, Pig Three	Inside the mud hut	Play with mud
The Wolf	Outside the mud hut	Huffs and puffs, rings the bell, and yells
The Wolf	Inside the mud hut	Kicks the hut. It falls in

"You pigs are a big mess!"
"Yes!" yelled the pigs.
"Pigs like a big mess!" **12**

38

"But I do not!" yelled the
wolf. "I must get this mud
off. Good-bye, pigs." **13**

39

LITERATURE ANTHOLOGY, pp. 38–39

Develop Comprehension
CLOSE READING

12 Genre: Fantasy

Could the events in the story happen in real life? (no) What does that tell us about the story? (It is a fantasy.) Remember, fantasies often have dialogue. What is some dialogue on page 38? (The pigs say, "Pigs like a big mess!")

13 Retell

We can retell the events that happen in order using our own words. Let's tell what happens to the wolf in the story. (First, the wolf rings the bell. Then he huffs and puffs at the hut. Next, he kicks, and the hut falls in. Then the wolf falls into the mud. Last, the wolf runs away!)

"Let's make a hut," said Pig One.
"We **could** use bricks," said Pig Two.
"We could use sticks," said Pig Three.

40

"We will use mud," said Pig One.
"Mud is good!" said Pig Two.
"Mud is fun!" yelled Pig Three.
"Yuck!" said the wolf.

41

LITERATURE ANTHOLOGY, pp. 40–41

Skill: Character, Setting, Events

Prompt children to review the details they recorded about the characters, settings, and events. *Who are the characters in this story? What events happen? Where do things happen in the story?* Review and complete the Character, Setting, Events chart.

Return to Predictions and Purposes

Have partners review and discuss their predictions. *Turn to a partner and discuss the predictions that you made before you read the story. Tell your partner your predictions. Then think back to the story. Explain whether your predictions were correct and how you know. Use details from the story to explain.*

Character	Setting	Events
The Wolf	Inside the mud hut	Kicks the hut. It falls in
The Wolf	Inside the fallen-down mud hut	He does not like the mud. He leaves.
The Pigs	Outside where their hut used to be	They decide to build a hut out of mud.

Read Together

Meet the Illustrator

Pablo Bernasconi loves illustrating animals doing funny things. Pablo's studio is a mess, full of junk and papers. But Pablo loves being surrounded by his things, just as the pigs in the story love being surrounded by mud.

Illustrator's Purpose

Pablo Bernasconi likes to draw funny animals. Draw and write about an animal doing something you think is funny.

42

Respond to Reading

Retell

Use your own words to retell important events in *The Pigs, the Wolf, and the Mud.*

Text Evidence

1. What do the pigs like? **Character**

2. What does the wolf do when the pigs won't let him in the hut? **Character, Setting, Events**

3. How can you tell that *The Pigs, the Wolf, and the Mud* is a fantasy? **Genre**

Character	Setting	Events

Make Connections

? How is the pigs' hut like a building you know? How is it different? **Essential Question**

43

LITERATURE ANTHOLOGY, pp. 42–43

Meet the Illustrator

Pablo Bernasconi

Read aloud page 42. Point out that Pablo Bernasconi has a messy studio like the pigs' messy hut. Ask children what might be in Bernasconi's studio. *What materials would you keep in a studio? What do you think his studio looks like?*

Illustrator's Purpose

Have children draw and write about an animal doing something funny like making an unusual home in their Response Journal. *The _____ makes a home of _____.*

ILLUSTRATOR'S CRAFT

Focus on Characters' Actions

Explain that illustrators often show important details from a story.

→ Point out that in this story, many of the illustrations show important details about what the characters do. For example, on page 30, Pig One tosses mud to Pig Two. The illustration shows Pig One ready to toss a handful of mud.

→ Have children identify the characters' actions in other illustrations.

Respond to Reading

Retell

Guide children in retelling the selection. Remind them that as they read *The Pigs, the Wolf, and the Mud*, they paid attention to characters, setting, and events. Now they will use this information to retell the story.

→ Have children use the information they recorded on their Character, Setting, Events chart to help them retell the story.

Text Evidence

Guide children to use text evidence to answer the Text Evidence questions on Literature Anthology page 43. Model answering the questions as needed.

1. **Character** To answer the question, let's look in the story for information about the pigs. On pages 29 and 30, the pigs play with the mud. They say that mud is fun. This tells us they like mud. Let's look through the rest of the story for more evidence that the pigs like mud.

2. **Character, Setting, Events** The question asks what the wolf does after the pigs will not let him in on page 32. Let's look for what the wolf does after that. He huffs, puffs, and kicks. Then he knocks the hut in.

3. **Genre** This question asks how we can tell that *The Pigs, the Wolf, and the Mud* is a fantasy. To answer this question, we must remember that a fantasy is a made-up story. The characters, setting, or events could not exist or happen in real life. In this story, the characters are animals that talk, live in huts, and knock down a hut by huffing, puffing, and kicking. These things could not really exist or happen, so this story is a fantasy.

Make Connections

Essential Question Have children draw and label a building that they have seen or know about. Prompt them to discuss and list ways in which the building they chose and the pigs' hut are alike and different. Have them tell what each looks like, what each is made of, and how each is used.

ENGLISH LANGUAGE LEARNERS

Retell Help children by looking at each page of the story and asking a prompt such as: *Who is the story about? Which character does something on this page? What happens on this page? Where are the characters now?* Provide sentence starters to help children retell the selection, such as: *The pigs _____.*

Language Arts

Reading/Writing Workshop Big Book

OBJECTIVES

CCSS Write narratives in which they recount two or more appropriately sequenced events, include some details regarding what happened, use temporal words to signal event order, and provide some sense of closure. **W.1.3**

CCSS Use common, proper, and possessive nouns. **L.1.1b**

• Identify and form singular and plural nouns

• Form contractions with 's

ACADEMIC LANGUAGE

• *singular noun, plural noun, contraction, apostrophe*

• Cognates: *contracción, apóstrofe*

MINILESSON
5 Mins

Independent Writing

Writing Trait: Organization

① Review Tell children that today they will write a draft. *Think about the steps we have followed as we have written stories.*

② Guided Practice Have children open to page 46 in the Reading/Writing Workshop. Read the student model aloud. Point out how Judd used the writing trait, Organization. Guide children to identify and discuss what happened in the beginning, middle, and end of the story.

READING/WRITING WORKSHOP, pp. 46–47

Story

Model Have children look again at Judd's story, noting his characters and story organization. Have children complete the Your Turn.

Prewrite

Display the list of story ideas from Day 2. Guide children to choose a topic. Preview the topic choices.

 Brainstorm Place children in pairs based on the story idea they chose. Guide partners to use a Sequence chart to organize their story's beginning, middle, and end.

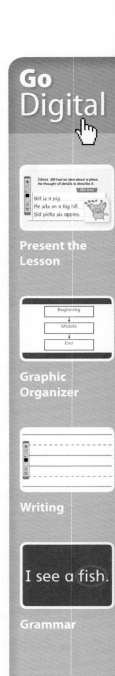

Go Digital

Present the Lesson

Graphic Organizer

Writing

Grammar

Draft

Have children write using their Sequence charts. Remind them that their story is a fantasy, so it tells about things that could not happen in real life.

Apply Writing Trait Remind children to tell the beginning, middle, and end. Provide sentence stems: *First, _____. Next, _____. Last, _____.*

Apply Grammar Have children think about the nouns they're using. Remind them to use -s and -es when there is more than one of something. Also remind children to use an apostrophe to form contractions with *'s.*

As children work, conference with them to provide guidance.

MINILESSON
5 Mins

Grammar

Singular and Plural Nouns

❶ **Review** Have children look at the Readers to Writers page in the Reading/Writing Workshop. Remind them that a plural noun means more than one. Most plural nouns end in -s. Nouns that end in -x, -s, or -ss use the -es ending. Have children identify the plural noun in the model sentence below.

Name the plural noun in this sentence: Six ducks lived in mud huts. *Which word names more than one?* Ducks *is a plural noun. Name another noun. Is it plural or singular?* Huts *is a plural noun, too.*

❷ **Guided Practice/Practice** Guide children to identify nouns in Judd's story and tell if they are singular or plural.

COLLABORATE

Talk About It Have partners create oral sentences about their story that use both singular and plural nouns.

Mechanics: Apostrophe with Contractions

❶ **Review** Remind children that an apostrophe takes the place of the letter or letters left out when two words combine to make a contraction.

❷ **Practice** Display incorrect contractions. Have children fix them.

it'is (it's)　h'es (he's)　whe'rs (where's)　sh'is (she's)

ENGLISH LANGUAGE LEARNERS SCAFFOLD

Beginning

Demonstrate Comprehension Provide additional sentence frames for partners as they write sentences: *The _____ use _____ to make _____.* Clarify children's responses as needed by providing vocabulary.

Intermediate

Explain Provide sequence sentence frames for partners as they write sentences: *In the beginning, the _____ _____. Then the _____ _____. Last, the _____ _____.* Clarify children's responses as needed by providing vocabulary.

Advanced/Advanced High

Expand After children complete their sentences, ask: *How did you organize your story? What happened first? Next? Last?* Allow children ample time to respond.

Daily Wrap Up

→ Review the Essential Question and encourage children to discuss using the oral vocabulary words. Ask: *What are different types of buildings?*

→ Prompt children to review and discuss the skills they used today. Guide them to give examples of how they used each skill.

Materials

Literature Anthology
VOLUME 2

Visual Vocabulary Cards

collapsed · could
furious · live
materials · one
refused · then
shelter · three

Teaching Poster

run

Spelling Word Cards

a b c

Word-Building Cards

Dinah Zike's
FOLDABLES

Dinah Zike's Foldables®

→ # Extend the Concept

MINILESSON 5 Mins

Oral Language

OBJECTIVES

CCSS

Know and use various text features (e.g., captions, bold print, subheadings, glossaries, indexes, electronic menus, icons) to locate key facts or information in a text. **RI.1.5**

Review vocabulary

ACADEMIC LANGUAGE

· caption, illustration
· Cognate: *ilustración*

ESSENTIAL QUESTION

Remind children that this week they have been learning about buildings and what they are made of. Guide children to discuss the question using information from what they have read and discussed.

Use the Visual Vocabulary Cards and the Define/Example/Ask routine to review the oral vocabulary words *shelter, materials, collapsed, furious,* and *refused.*

Guide children to use each word as they talk about what they have read and learned about buildings and what they are made of. Prompt children by asking questions.

→ What would be a good shelter if you lived in a very hot place?

→ What materials could you use to make a house?

→ What would you do if your shelter collapsed?

→ Would you be furious if your shelter collapsed? Why?

→ Would you refuse to live in a house made of mud? Why or why not?

Review last week's oral vocabulary words *astonishing, community, equipment, fortunately,* and *occupation.*

Go Digital

school

Visual Glossary

Teaching Poster

"Homes Around the World"

Develop Comprehension

Text Feature: Captions

1 **Explain** Remind children that they have been reading fiction about different types of buildings. Tell children they can use informational text selections to find facts and details about buildings. Explain that informational text often has photographs. These photographs often have captions—short descriptions giving information about the photograph.

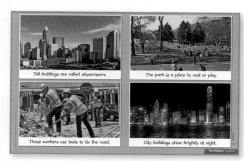

Teaching Poster

2 **Model** Display Teaching Poster 18. Read the first caption: *Tall buildings are called skyscrapers.* Say: *This caption gives information about the photograph. The caption tells us what the buildings in the photograph are called. This is information that we could not learn from the photograph itself.*

3 **Guided Practice/Practice** Read together the caption: *These workers use tools to fix the road.* Guide children to discuss the information in the caption. *What does the caption tell us? What information is in the caption but not in the photograph?* Tell children to look for captions as they read informational text selections.

ELL

ENGLISH LANGUAGE LEARNERS SCAFFOLD

Beginning

Use Sentence Frames Use sentence frames to help children discuss the photographs and captions. For example: *I see a _____. The buildings are _____.*

Intermediate

Describe Prompt children to describe what they see in the photographs and tell what they learn from the captions.

Advanced/Advanced High

Discuss Ask children to brainstorm their own captions for the photographs.

CCSS **Genre** Nonfiction

Read Together

Compare Texts
Read about the different
homes people make.

Homes Around the World

1 There are many kinds of **homes**.
People **build** their homes to fit
the place they live!

This home is built
into a rock.

This home is
made of wood.

This is a good home for a wet
place. There is a lot of water
here. The stilts help keep this
home dry.

44

45

LITERATURE ANTHOLOGY, pp. 44–45

Develop Comprehension

CLOSE READING

Lexile 330

Literature Anthology

Read Literature Anthology

Compare Texts

Remind children that in *The Pigs,
the Wolf, and the Mud*, they read about three pigs
who live in a mud hut. Tell children that in "Homes
Around the World," they will read about different
kinds of homes people build. Encourage children
to think about how these homes are like the pigs'
mud home, and how they are different.

1 Strategy: Make and Confirm Predictions

Teacher Think Aloud On these pages, I see
a title about homes and photographs of two
different types of homes—a home built into
a rock and a wooden home on stilts. I predict
that the next pages will tell about other kinds of
homes. I will read the selection to find out what it
is about. Then I will check whether my prediction
is correct.

Content Words Point out the words *homes*,
build, and *shelter*. Define the meaning of each
word for children.

This is a good home for a hot place. There is a lot of clay in this place. People use it to build homes. Clay keeps the home cool inside.

2 This home is made of clay.

3 An igloo is made of ice.

There is a lot of ice in this place. People can use it to build. This is an igloo. People don't live in igloos. But they are good **shelter** from the cold.

What is your home like?

Make Connections

 Which home do you think the pigs in *The Pigs, the Wolf, and the Mud* would like? Why? **Essential Question**

46

47

LITERATURE ANTHOLOGY, pp. 46–47

2 Text Features: Captions

Teacher Think Aloud When I look at this photograph, I wonder if this home is made of mud like the home of the three pigs in the story. I remember that a caption gives information about a photograph. I will read the caption to find out what this home is made of. The caption explains that the shelter is made of clay, not mud.

3 Text Feature: Captions

What important detail does the caption tell you about the igloo in the photograph? (Igloos are made of ice.)

Make Connections Have partners make connections between the homes they read about in "Homes Around the World" and *The Pigs, the Wolf, and the Mud.*

CONNECT TO CONTENT
ENVIRONMENTAL ADAPTATION

Guide children to discuss how the people using each type of shelter took advantage of or worked around the environment they were in. Say: *Why is the house on stilts? Why is the igloo made of ice?*

 **Word Work**

Quick Review

Build Fluency: Sound-Spellings
Display the **Word-Building Cards:** *u,
e, ea, sp, sn, sl, cr, fr, tr, o, pl, fl, cl,
bl, i, a, s, r, l, t, n, m, c, p, b, f.* Have
children say the sounds. Repeat, and
vary the pace.

 MINILESSON 5 Mins

Phonemic Awareness

Phoneme Identity

OBJECTIVES

 Isolate and pronounce initial, medial vowel, and final sounds (phonemes) in spoken single-syllable words. **RF.1.2c**

 Decode regularly spelled one-syllable words. **RF.1.3b**

- Spell words with short *u*
- Read contractions with *'s*

❶ **Model** Show children how to identify the same phoneme in a group of words. *Listen carefully as I say three words:* duck, jug, sub. *What sound do you hear that is the same in /duuuk/, /juuug/, and /suuub/? That's right. The middle sound is /u/.*

❷ **Guided Practice/Practice** Have children practice identifying the same phoneme in a group of words. Do the first two together. *I am going to say more words. Tell me the sound you hear that is the same in each group of words.*

fun, luck, mug	hop, lock, dot	run, huff, mud
ten, well, went	cup, cub, dug	fuzz, fun, hut

 MINILESSON 5 Mins

Phonics

Build Words with Short *u*

Review *The short* u *sound /uuu/ can be represented by the letter* u.
We'll use **Word-Building Cards** *to build words with short* u.

Place the letters *h, u, m. Let's blend the sounds together and read the word: /huuummm/. Now let's change the* h *to* y. *Blend the sounds and read the word: /yuuummm/.*

Continue with *yuck, tuck, tick, pick, pack, puck, muck, mud, mad, dad, dig, dug, lug, plug, slug.*

Go Digital

Phonemic Awareness

m	a
n	t	p

Phonics

I __ the jar.

| fill | fills | filling |

Structural Analysis

er	ir	or	ur
her			
girl curb			word

Spelling Word Sort

school

Visual Glossary

Structural Analysis

Contractions with 's

Review Write the word *it's* on the board and read it with children. Remind children that *it's* is a contraction. The apostrophe (') replaces the letters removed when the two words (*it* and *is*) are put together to make one word.

Write the following words: *it is, she is, he is, let us*. Have children work in pairs to construct contractions. Then have them write a sentence for each contraction.

Spelling

Word Sort with *-un, -ut, -ug*

Review Provide pairs of children with copies of the **Spelling Word Cards**. While one partner reads the words one at a time, the other partner should orally segment the word and then write the word. After reading all the words, partners should switch roles.

Have children correct their own papers. Then have them sort the words by ending spelling pattern: *-un, -ut, -ug,* or no short *u* ending.

High-Frequency Words

could, live, one, then, three

Review Display **Visual Vocabulary Cards** for high-frequency words *could, live, one, then, three*. Have children Read/Spell/Write each word.

→ Point to a word and call on a child to use it in a sentence.

→ Review last week's words using the same procedure.

Monitor and *Differentiate*

✓ **Quick Check**

Can children read and decode words with short *u*?

Can children recognize and read high-frequency words?

⬇

Small Group Instruction

If No →	Approaching	Reteach pp. T134–137
	ELL	Develop pp. T148–155
If Yes →	On Level	Review pp. T142–143
	Beyond Level	Extend pp. T146–147

→ # Language Arts

MINILESSON
5 Mins

Independent Writing

Go Digital

Writing

━━ Make a capital letter.
Λ Add.
✐ Take out.

Proofreader's Marks

I see a fish.

Grammar

OBJECTIVES

CCSS With guidance and support from adults, focus on a topic, respond to questions and suggestions from peers, and add details to strengthen writing as needed. **W.1.5**

CCSS Use common, proper, and possessive nouns. **L.1.1b**

- Identify and form singular and plural nouns
- Form contractions with 's

ACADEMIC LANGUAGE
- *improve, order*
- Cognate: *orden*

Story

Revise

Explain to children that revising helps make their ideas clearer and their writing more interesting.

Apply Writing Trait: Organization Explain that as writers revise, they move sentences to improve the story's organization. They may add words to tell the beginning, middle, and end. Display the following story:

> The ducks got bread.
>
> The ducks made a house with the bread.
>
> The ducks made a house of grass.
>
> The red birds ate the bread.

Guide children to switch the order of the last two sentences. Then model adding words to signal event order *(first, next, last)*.

 Peer Review Have children work in pairs to do a peer review. They should take notes about what they like most, questions they have for the author, and ideas they think the author could include. Provide time for them to discuss and make revisions.

Proofread/Edit

Apply Grammar Review proofreader's marks with children. Have them reread their drafts and fix mistakes. Remind them to make sure that:

→ all plural nouns are formed correctly.

→ apostrophes in contractions are in the correct place.

→ all words are spelled correctly.

→ all sentences are complete.

 Peer Edit Next, have partners exchange their drafts and take turns reading for the above mistakes. Encourage partners to discuss and fix errors together as they read.

Final Draft

After children have edited their own papers and finished their peer edits, have them write their final draft. Encourage them to create or find a photo or other visual that relates to their writing. As children work, conference with them to provide guidance.

MINILESSON
5 Mins

Grammar

Singular and Plural Nouns

❶ **Review** Remind children that you add *-s* to most singular nouns to name more than one person, place, or thing, but sometimes you must add *-es* to form the plural. Recall that we add *-es* to nouns that end with *-x, -s,* or *-ss*. Ask: *What are some plural nouns?*

❷ **Guided Practice** Display the following singular nouns: *bus, clock, egg, mess.* Guide children to form the plural for each noun.

❸ **Practice** Display the following singular nouns: *class, box, mutt, drum.* Have partners form the plural for each noun.

Talk About It Have partners work together to orally generate sentences with the Practice activity words. Challenge them to create sentences for both the singular and plural forms of each word.

Mechanics: Apostrophe with Contractions

❶ **Review** Remind children that a contraction is a word you make when you put two words together but leave out one or more letters. An apostrophe takes the place of the letter or letters left out. Many contractions are made with the word *is*. The apostrophe takes the place of the *i* in *is*.

❷ **Practice** Provide partners with word cards for *it's, she's, he's, where's.* Have one child read one contraction at a time. The partner writes the word, checks it, and makes necessary corrections. Partners then switch roles.

Daily Wrap Up

→ Review the Essential Question and encourage children to discuss using the oral vocabulary words. Ask: *What materials would you like to use to build a school?*

→ Prompt children to discuss the skills they practiced and learned today. Guide them to share examples of each skill.

👈 **Go** Digital

www.connected.mcgraw-hill.com
RESOURCES
Research and Inquiry

→ **Wrap Up the Week**
Integrate Ideas

RESEARCH AND INQUIRY

Buildings All Around

OBJECTIVES

CCSS Participate in shared research and writing projects (e.g., explore a number of "how-to" books on a given topic and use them to write a sequence of instruction). **W.1.7**

- Build background knowledge
- Research information using technology

ACADEMIC LANGUAGE
- *materials*
- Cognate: *materiales*

Draw and Label a Building

 Review the steps in the research process. Tell children that today they will do a research project with a partner to learn more about a building in their town or community and what it is made of.

STEP 1 **Choose a Topic**

Name some familiar buildings or types of buildings to prompt a brainstorming session. Guide partners to choose a building to research.

STEP 2 **Find Resources**

Discuss how to use the selections, reference materials, and online sources to find information on their chosen building. Have children use the Research Process Checklist online.

STEP 3 **Keep Track of Ideas**

Have children record their ideas in an Accordion Book Foldable®. Model recording details.

Dinah Zike's
FOLDABLES

Collaborative Conversations

Take Turns Talking Review with children that as they engage in partner, small-group, and whole-group discussions, they should:

→ take turns talking and not speak over others.

→ raise their hand if they want to speak.

→ ask others to share their ideas and opinions.

**STEP 4 Create the Project:
Drawing with Labels**

Remind children of the characteristics of labels.

→ **Information** Labels give information about parts
of an illustration. In this project, the labels give
information about the materials used to make the
building.

→ **Arrows** A label can have an arrow to show what
part of the illustration the label tells about.

Have children create a drawing of their chosen
building.

→ Guide them to label their drawing with the names of the materials
used to construct the building.

ENGLISH LANGUAGE LEARNERS

ELL SCAFFOLD

Beginning	Intermediate	Advanced/High
Use Sentence Frames Use sentence frames to help children discuss their buildings. For example: *This building is made of _____ and _____.*	**Discuss** Guide children to focus on the materials the building is made of. Ask: *What are the walls made of? What are the windows made of?*	**Describe** Prompt children to elaborate on the building's materials. Ask: *What else can be made using these materials? Where else have you seen them?*

Materials

Reading/Writing Workshop
VOLUME 2

Literature Anthology
VOLUME 2

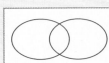

Literature Big Book
The 3 Little Dassies

Visual Vocabulary Cards

could
live
one
then
three

Teaching Poster

Word-Building Cards

Interactive Read-Aloud Cards

Spelling Word Cards

→ Integrate Ideas

TEXT CONNECTIONS

Connect to Essential Question

OBJECTIVES

 Compare and contrast the adventures and experiences of characters in stories. **RL.1.9**

• Develop answers to the Essential Question

• Make text connections to the world

ACADEMIC LANGUAGE

• dwellings, habitat, needs, protection

• Cognates: *hábitat, protección*

Text to Text

Remind children that all week they have been reading selections about buildings and what they are made of. Tell them that now they can think about how the selections are similar to one another. This is called making connections across texts. Model comparing texts using *Cubs in a Hut* and "The Three Little Pigs."

Think Aloud *Cubs in a Hut* and "The Three Little Pigs" are both about animal characters and the homes they build. Even though the homes are different, the cubs and pigs both use sticks to build their homes.

 Complete the Organizer Have children use the Word Web to help them discuss buildings they read about and what they are made of.

→ Discuss and write about two different buildings we read about. Describe what they are used for and what they are made of.

→ Discuss all the different materials that buildings can be made of.

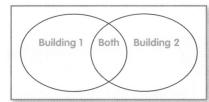

Teaching Poster

Text to Self

Have children discuss homes, schools, or other buildings in their community. Ask: *What are they made of? Which do you like best? Why?*

Text to World

Have children discuss different types of homes around the world. Ask: *Why are homes different in different places? How would a home in a hot place be different from a home in a cold place? Would both those homes be good shelters? Why?*

WRITE ABOUT READING  *Analytical Writing*

OBJECTIVES

 Draw evidence from literary or informational texts to support analysis, reflection, and research. **W.4.9**

Analyze Character, Setting, Events

Explain to children that as a group you will write about one of the selections that they have read this week.

Using the evidence in the text, you will think about how the author used the character, setting, and events to tell the story.

Review the Character, Setting, Events chart you completed for *Cubs in a Hut*. Guide children to analyze text evidence by asking "how" and "why" questions about the characters, setting, and events.

→ *Why might the author have wanted to write about three characters?*

→ *How did the author use the setting (the hut) to tell events in the story?*

→ *How did reading the selection help you understand why there are many different kinds of homes?*

Write an Analysis

Display the following sentence frames:

In _____, the author wrote about _____.

The author told about _____ characters who lived in a _____.

In the story, the characters _____.

The selection helped us understand that _____.

Work with children to complete the sentence frames using the information about *Cubs in a Hut*.

Select another story you have read in this unit. Work with children to complete similar sentence frames to write about how the author used characters, setting, and events to tell about homes or buildings.

RESEARCH AND INQUIRY

OBJECTIVES

 Participate in shared research and writing projects. **W.1.7**

Wrap Up the Project

 Guide partners to share the information about their building. *What building did you choose? What does it look like? What is it made of? What is the building used for?* Have them use the Presentation Checklist online.

→ # Word Work

Quick Review

Build Fluency: Sound-Spellings
Display the **Word-Building Cards**: *u, e, ea, sp, sn, sl, cr, fr, tr, o, pl, fl, cl, bl, i, a, s, r, l, t, n, m, c, p, b, f.* Have children say the sounds. Repeat, and vary the pace.

MINILESSON 5 Mins

Phonemic Awareness

OBJECTIVES

CCSS Segment spoken single-syllable words into their complete sequence of individual sounds (phonemes). **RF.1.2d**

CCSS Decode regularly spelled one-syllable words. **RF.1.3b**

- Read contractions with 's
- Spell words with short *u*

Phoneme Blending

Review Guide children to blend phonemes to form words. *Listen as I say a group of sounds. Then blend those sounds to form a word.*

/s/ /u/ /n/   /b/ /u/ /g/   /d/ /r/ /u/ /m/   /f/ /l/ /u/ /f/

Phoneme Segmentation

Review Guide children to segment phonemes in words. *Now I am going to say a word. I want you to say each sound in the word.*

fun   luck   cluck   plus   truck   spun

MINILESSON 5 Mins

Phonics

Blend and Build Words with Short *u*

Review Have children read and say the words *fun, rub, snug,* and *drum.* Then have children follow the word-building routine with **Word-Building Cards** to build *gum, hum, hug, pug, plug, plus, pluck, puck, puff, huff, hut, but, bun, fun, sun, sub.*

Word Automaticity Help children practice word automaticity. Display decodable words and point to each word as children chorally read it. Test how many words children can read in one minute. Model blending words children miss.

Go Digital

Phonemic Awareness

Phonics

Structural Analysis

Visual Glossary

Fluency: Word Automaticity

Structural Analysis

Contractions with 's

Review Have children explain what a contraction is and how to form one. Then have children practice writing and reading the contractions for *he is, she is, it is,* and *let us.*

Spelling

Word Sort with *-un, -ut, -ug*

Review Have children use the **Spelling Word Cards** to sort the weekly words by vowel and ending sounds. Remind children that four of the words do not have the short *u* sound spelled *u.*

Assess children on their abilities to spell words in the *-un, -ut,* and *-ug* word families. Say each word and provide a sentence so that children can hear the words used in a correct context. Then allow them time to write down the words. In order to challenge children, you may wish to provide an additional word in each family in order to assess whether they understand the concept.

High-Frequency Words

could, live, one, then, three

Review Display **Visual Vocabulary Cards** *could, live, one, then, three.* Have children Read/Spell/Write each word. Have children write a sentence with each word.

Monitor and *Differentiate*

 Quick Check

Can children read and decode words with short *u*?

Can children recognize and read high-frequency words?

↓

Small Group Instruction

If No →	**Approaching**	Reteach pp. T134–137
	ELL	Develop pp. T148–155
If Yes →	**On Level**	Review pp. T142–143
	Beyond Level	Extend pp. T146–147

Language Arts

 MINILESSON
5 Mins

Independent Writing

Go
Digital

Writing

Checklists

I see a fish.

Grammar

OBJECTIVES

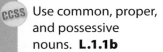

CCSS With guidance from adults, use a variety of digital tools to produce and publish writing, including in collaboration with peers. **W.1.6**

CCSS Use common, proper, and possessive nouns. **L.1.1b**

Present a story

ACADEMIC LANGUAGE

• *presentation, fantasy*

• Cognates: *presentación, fantasía*

Story

Prepare

Review guidelines for making presentations with children.

→ Provide time for children to finish preparing their presentations. Remind them to practice using a drawing of the characters or building and any other visual they are using.

Present

Have children take turns giving presentations of their fantasy stories. Remind them to speak clearly. When listening to other stories, they should be polite and respectful, asking questions when appropriate and listening carefully when it is not appropriate to speak.

→ If possible, record the presentation so that children can self-evaluate.

Evaluate

Have children discuss their own presentations and evaluate their performance using the presentation rubric.

Use the teacher's rubric to evaluate children's writing. Have children add their writing to their Writer's Portfolio. Then have them discuss and write about how they have become better writers.

Publish

After children finish presenting their stories, discuss how the class will publish a class book of all the stories. Have children suggest how to organize the book with stories and illustrations. Guide them to use digital tools to create the book.

Grammar

Singular and Plural Nouns

1 Review Have children explain the difference between a singular noun and a plural noun. Ask them to tell how plural nouns are formed. Write the following sentence and have children identify the plural nouns:

> The hen put the eggs in boxes.

2 Practice Ask: *How do I know if each noun is singular or plural?*

Display the following nouns: *map, box, bug, bus, hut.* Read each noun aloud. Have children choose two nouns and write two sentences using the plural form of each noun.

Mechanics: Apostrophe with Contractions

1 Review Remind children that a contraction is two words put together. An apostrophe takes the place of the letter or letters left out. Many contractions are made with the word *is*. The apostrophe takes the place of the *i* in *is*.

2 Practice Write the following sentences. Read each aloud. Have children fix the contraction in each sentence.

> Wher'is the truck? (Where's)
>
> It'is here. (It's)
>
> Sh'es sad. (She's)

Wrap Up the Week

→ Review the Essential Question and encourage children to discuss using the oral vocabulary words.

→ Review that making and confirming predictions and identifying the characters, setting, and events helps readers better understand stories.

→ Review blending words with short *u*. Remind children that an apostrophe stands for letters left out when you combine two words into a contraction.

→ Use the Visual Vocabulary Cards to review the Words to Know.

→ Remind children that a fantasy is a made-up story that has characters, a setting, or events that could not exist.

→ Approaching Level

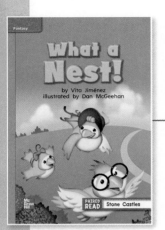

Lexile 170

 OBJECTIVES

Describe characters, settings, and major events in a story, using key details. **RL.1.3**

 With prompting and support, read prose and poetry of appropriate complexity for grade 1. **RL.1.10**

Make and confirm predictions

Leveled Reader:
What a Nest!

Before Reading

Preview and Predict

Have children turn to the title page. Read the title and the author's and the illustrator's names and have children repeat. Preview the selection's illustrations. Prompt children to predict what the selection might be about.

Review Genre: Fantasy

Have children recall that a fantasy is a story that has invented characters, settings, or other elements that could not exist in real life.

ESSENTIAL QUESTION

Remind children of the Essential Question. Set a purpose for reading: *Let's read to find out what a nest is made of.*

Remind children that as they read a selection, they can ask questions about what they do not understand or want to know more about.

During Reading

Guided Comprehension

As children whisper read *What a Nest!,* monitor and provide guidance, correcting blending and modeling the key strategies and skills.

Strategy: Make and Confirm Predictions

Remind children to make predictions about story events and read on to confirm them. Model the strategy: *On pages 2 and 3 we learn the birds need a place to live. They fly over a castle. I predict that will be their home. I'll read on to find out.* Read page 4. Point to the illustration to confirm the prediction.

Skill: Character, Setting, Events

Remind children that characters are the people or animals in a story; the setting is where the story takes place; the events are what happens. Children will find details about them in the text and illustrations. While reading, ask: *Who are the characters? What is the setting? What events happen?* Display a Character, Setting, Events chart for children to copy.

Go Digital

What a Nest!

Graphic Organizer

Retell

Model recording children's answers in the character, setting, and events boxes. Have children copy the answers into their own charts.

Think Aloud On page 4, I see and read that Bert is going to get twigs to build the nest. Bert is a character. He is getting twigs. That is an event. The picture shows the top of a castle. That is the setting.

Guide children to use the text and illustrations to complete the chart.

After Reading

Respond to Reading

Complete the Respond to Reading on page 12 after reading.

Retell

Have children take turns retelling the selection using the **Retelling Cards** as a guide. Help them make a connection: *Where have you seen a bird's nest? What was it made of?*

Model Fluency

Read the sentences one at a time. Have children chorally repeat. Point out to children how your voice sounds at the end of an exclamation.

Apply Have children practice repeated readings with partners.

PAIRED READ ...

"Stone Castles"

Make Connections: Write About It 🖊 *Analytical Writing*

Before reading, ask children to note that the genre of this text is informational text. Then discuss the Compare Texts direction. Ask children to tell how what they read in "Stone Castles" can help them understand *What a Nest!* Guide children to realize that one book helped them understand the setting of the other.

Leveled Reader

Analytical Writing

COMPARE TEXTS
→ Have children use text evidence to compare fantasy to informational text.

Literature Circles

Lead children in conducting a literature circle using the Thinkmark questions to guide the discussion. You may wish to discuss what children have learned about materials used for shelters in both selections in the Leveled Reader.

Level Up

Level-up lessons available online.

IF children can read *What a Nest!* Approaching Level with fluency and correctly answer the Respond to Reading questions,

THEN tell children that they will read a story about another kind of building.

• Use pages 2–4 of *Staying Afloat* On Level to model using Teaching Poster 28 to identify characters, setting, and events.

• Have children read the selection, checking their comprehension by using the graphic organizer.

Approaching Level

Phonemic Awareness

TIER 2

IDENTIFY AND GENERATE RHYME

 OBJECTIVES

Isolate and pronounce initial, medial vowel, and final sounds (phonemes) in spoken single-syllable words. **RF.1.2c**

Identify and generate rhyming words

 I Do
Explain to children that they will be identifying words that rhyme. *Listen as I say two words:* fun, run. Fun *and* run *rhyme because they both end in /un/. Listen: /f/ /un/; /r/ /un/. Now listen to this word:* sun. Sun *ends in /un/. Listen: /s/ /un/.* Sun *rhymes with* fun *and* run.

 We Do
Listen to these words: bug, dug. *Listen for the ending sounds: /b/ /ug/, /d/ /ug/.* Bug *and* dug *end the same. That means they rhyme. What other words rhyme with* bug *and* dug? Rug *ends in /ug/.* Rug *rhymes with* bug *and* dug.

Have children stand if the words rhyme. Ask what other words rhyme.

big, wig (fig)   drum, hum (gum)   mug, red

 You Do
It's your turn. Tell which two words in each group rhyme. Then say other words that rhyme with them.

tub, fin, cub   back, tug, mug   shut, but, red

Repeat the rhyming routine with additional short *u* rhyming words.

TIER 2

PHONEME IDENTITY

OBJECTIVES

Isolate and pronounce initial, medial vowel, and final sounds (phonemes) in spoken single-syllable words. **RF.1.2c**

 I Do
Explain to children that they will be identifying the same sound in a group of words. *Listen as I say three words:* cup, hum, rub. *I hear the /u/ sound in the middle of* cup, hum, *and* rub. *Listen: /kuuup/, /huuum/, /ruuub/. The middle sound is /u/.*

 We Do
Listen as I say three words: duck, but, mud. *Repeat the words:* duck, but, mud. *What sound do you hear in the middle of /duuuk/, /buuut/, /muuud/?*

Repeat this routine with the following words:

run, cub, bus   sad, bag, hat   hill, mitt, dig

 You Do
It's your turn. What sound do you hear in the middle of each group of words?

lock, top, jog   nut, bud, rug   bed, net, well

Repeat the isolation routine with additional short *u* words.

PHONEME BLENDING

OBJECTIVES

Orally produce single-syllable words by blending sounds (phonemes), including consonant blends. **RF.1.2b**

 I Do

Explain to children that they will be blending sounds to form words. *Listen as I say two sounds: /uuu/ /p/. Say the sounds with me: /uuu/ /p/. I'm going to blend the sounds together: /uuu/ /p/, /uuup/, up. I blended the word* up.

 We Do

Listen as I say two sounds: /uuu/ /sss/. Repeat the sounds: /uuu/ /sss/. Let's blend the sounds: /uuu/ /sss/, /uuusss/, us. *We made one word:* us.

Repeat this routine with the following words:

/f//u//n/ /b//u//s/ /k//u//p/ /d//u//k/ /m//u//g/ /s//u//n/
/d//r//u//m/ /k//l//u//b/

 You Do

It's your turn. Blend the sounds I say together to form a word.

/t//u//b/ /b//u//g/ /k//u//t/ /m//u//d/ /p//u//p/

Repeat the blending routine with additional short *u* words.

PHONEME SEGMENTATION

OBJECTIVES

Segment spoken single-syllable words into their complete sequence of individual sounds (phonemes). **RF.1.2d**

 I Do

Explain to children that they will be segmenting words into sounds. Listen as I say a word: *up*. *I hear two sounds: /uuu/ and /p/. There are two sounds in the word* up: */uuu/ and /p/.*

 We Do

Let's do some together. I am going to say a word: /duuug/. How many sounds do you hear? The sounds in dug *are /d/ /uuu/ and /g/. There are three sounds.*

Repeat this routine with the following words:

us sun bug fuzz gum drum

 You Do

I'll say a word. Tell me how many sounds you hear. Then tell me the sounds.

run fuss rub bun cuff plum stuff truck plus

 ENGLISH LANGUAGE LEARNERS

For the **ELLs** who need **phonemic awareness**, **phonics**, and **fluency** practice, use scaffolding methods as necessary to ensure children understand the meaning of the words. Refer to the Language Transfer Handbook for phonics elements that may not transfer in children's native languages.

Approaching Level

Phonics

CONNECT *u* TO /u/

 TIER 2

OBJECTIVES

 Decode regularly spelled one-syllable words. **RF.1.3b**

I Do Display the **Word-Building Card** *u. This is lowercase* u. *I am going to trace the letter* u *while I say /uuu/, the sound that the letter* u *stands for.* Trace the letter *u* while saying /uuu/ five times.

We Do *Now do it with me.* Have children take turns saying /uuu/ while using their fingers to trace the lowercase *u* in the air. Then have them say /uuu/ as they use their fingers to trace the letter *u* five more times.

You Do Have children connect the letter *u* to the sound /u/ by saying /uuu/ as they trace a lowercase *u* on paper five to ten times. Then ask them to write the letter *u* while saying /uuu/ five to ten times.

Repeat, connecting the letter *u* to the sound /u/ through tracing and writing the letters *Uu* throughout the week.

BLEND WORDS WITH SHORT *u*

 TIER 2

OBJECTIVES

 Decode regularly spelled one-syllable words. **RF.1.3b**

Decode words with short *u*

I Do Display Word-Building Cards *s, u, n. This is the letter* s. *It stands for /s/. Say it with me: /s/. This is the letter* u. *It stands for /u/. Let's say it together: /u/. This is the letter* n. *It stands for /n/. I'll blend the sounds together: /sssuuunnn/,* sun.

We Do Guide children to blend the sounds and read: *us, up, nut, cup, duck, club.*

You Do Have children use Word-Building Cards to blend and read: *mug, fun, tub, hut, mud, luck, fluff, drum, plus, slug, stun.*

Repeat, blending additional short *u* words.

You may wish to review Phonics with **ELL** using this section.

BUILD WORDS WITH SHORT *u*

OBJECTIVES

 Decode regularly spelled one-syllable words. **RF.1.3b**

Build and decode words with short *u*

 I Do Display Word-Building Cards *u, s. These are the letters* u *and* s. *They stand for /uuu/ and /sss/. I will blend /uuu/ and /sss/ together: /uuusss/,* us.

 We Do *Now let's do one together.* Make the word *us* using Word-Building Cards. Place the letter *b* in front of *us. Let's blend: /b/ /uuusss/, /buuusss/,* bus.

I am going to change the letter s *in* bus *to the letter* t. *Change* s *to* t. *Let's blend and read the new word: /b/ /uuu/ /t/, /buuut/,* but.

 You Do Have children build the words: *nut, hut, hum, hug, bug, tug, tuck, stuck.*

Repeat, building additional words with short *u*.

BLEND WORDS WITH SHORT *u*

OBJECTIVES

 Decode regularly spelled one-syllable words. **RF.1.3b**

Decode words with short *u*

 I Do Display Word-Building Cards *m, u, g. This is the letter* m. *It stands for /m/. This is the letter* u. *It stands for /u/. This is the letter* g. *It stands for /g/. Listen as I blend all three sounds: /mmmuuug/,* mug. *The word is* mug.

 We Do Let's do some together. Blend and read the words *up, tub, jug, buzz,* and *plum* with children.

You Do Display the words to the right. Have children blend and read the words.

mud	cup	fun	rub	sun	duck
cut	run	bud	pup	cub	plug
dug	net	bun	sit	black	snug
drop	bed	fluff	brick	fuzz	truck

The truck is stuck in the mud.

Six ducks run in the sun.

Do Russ and Gus have a cub or a pup?

BUILD FLUENCY WITH PHONICS

Sound-Spellings Fluency

Display the following Word-Building Cards: *u, e, ea, sp, sn, sl, cr, fr, tr, o, pl, fl, cl, bl, i, a, s, r, l, t, n, m, c, p, b, f.* Have children chorally say the sounds. Repeat and vary the pace.

Fluency in Connected Text

Have children review *Cubs in a Hut* in their Reading/Writing Workshop. Identify short *u* words. Blend words as needed.

Have children reread the selection on their own or with a partner.

→ Approaching Level

Structural Analysis

REVIEW CONTRACTIONS WITH 's

OBJECTIVES

 Know and apply grade-level phonics and word analysis skills in decoding words. **RF.1.3**

Read contractions with *'s*

 I Do Write *he's*. Read the word: /hēz/. *I look at the word* he's *and I see a word I know:* he. *The* 's *tells me this word is a contraction.* He's *is a short way of saying* he is. *I'm going to use* he is *and* he's. *He is happy. He's happy. They mean the same thing.*

 We Do Write *she's*. *Let's read this word:* /shēz/. *If we look at* she's, *is there a word we know? Yes,* she. *We know that* 's *tells us the word is a contraction. What two words does* she's *stand for? Let's use* she is *and* she's *in sentences.*

 You Do Display the contractions *he's, she's,* and *it's*. Ask partners to identify the two words each contraction stands for. Have them use the contractions in sentences.

Repeat Have partners use the contractions *he's, she's,* and *it's* in sentences. One partner can say a sentence with *he is, she is,* or *it is*. The other partner can say the sentence with a contraction.

RETEACH CONTRACTIONS WITH 's

OBJECTIVES

 Know and apply grade-level phonics and word analysis skills in decoding words. **RF.1.3**

Read contractions with *'s*

 I Do Write *it is* and *it's*. Read the words. Circle the *'s* in *it's*. *When I see* 's *at the end of the word* it, *I know the word is a contraction. The contraction* it's *is a short way of saying* it is. *Listen: It is raining today. It's raining today.*

 We Do Write *he*. *Let's add* 's. *Say* he's. *What two words does* he's *stand for? Yes,* he is. *Write* he is. *Let's use* he is *and* he's *in sentences. Say a sentence for* he is. Have children substitute *he's* for *he is* in the sentence.

Repeat this routine with *she's*.

 You Do Have partners take turns using the contractions *it's, he's,* and *she's* in sentences. Guide children as needed.

High-Frequency Words

REVIEW

OBJECTIVES

 Recognize and read grade-appropriate irregularly spelled words. **RF.1.3g**

Review *could, live, one, then, three*

 Use the **High-Frequency Word Cards** to **Read/Spell/Write** each high-frequency word. Use each word orally in a sentence.

 Guide children to Read/Spell/Write each word on their **Response Boards**. Help them generate oral sentences for the words.

 Have partners work together to Read/Spell/Write the words *could, live, one, then,* and *three*. Ask them to say sentences for the words.

RETEACH

OBJECTIVES

 Recognize and read grade-appropriate irregularly spelled words. **RF.1.3g**

 Review the high-frequency words using the Read/Spell/Write routine. Write and read a sentence for each word.

 Guide children in using the Read/Spell/Write routine. Ask them to complete sentence starters: *(1) I could go ____. (2) I live ____. (3) One day, ____. (4) I wake up. Then I ____. (5) I see three ____.*

 Ask children to work with partners to say and spell the words. Have one partner say a word and the other spell it. Have children self-correct.

CUMULATIVE REVIEW

OBJECTIVES

 Recognize and read grade-appropriate irregularly spelled words. **RF.1.3g**

Review previously taught high-frequency words

 Display the High-Frequency Word Cards from the previous weeks. Use the Read/Spell/Write routine to review each word.

 Guide children as they Read/Spell/Write the words on their Response Boards. Have students complete sentence frames for the words. *I have a new ____. It will be fun to make ____.*

 Show each card and have children chorally read. Mix and repeat.

Fluency Display the High-Frequency Word Cards. Point to words in random order. Have children chorally read. Repeat at a faster pace.

Approaching Level

Comprehension

READ FOR FLUENCY

TIER 2

OBJECTIVES

 Read grade-level text orally with accuracy, appropriate rate, and expression. **RF.1.4b**

I Do Read the first page of the Practice Book story aloud. Model using appropriate expression when reading dialogue and exclamations.

We Do Read the next page and have children repeat each sentence after you. Point out how you use appropriate expression.

You Do Have children read the rest of the story aloud. Remind them to use appropriate expression when they read dialogue and exclamations.

IDENTIFY CHARACTERS

TIER 2

OBJECTIVES

 Describe characters, settings, and major events in a story, using key details. **RL.1.3**

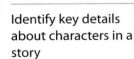 Use illustrations in a story to describe its characters, setting, or events. **RL.1.7**

Identify key details about characters in a story

I Do Remind children about stories they have been reading. *When I read a story, I look for the key details about the characters. I use the pictures and words to find the characters in a story.*

We Do Read the first two pages of the Practice Book story aloud. Pause to point out key details that tell about the characters. Identify details and explain to children why they are important. *We learn that Bee and Duck are characters in this story. The pictures show Bee humming into a microphone and Duck playing guitar. The words tell us what the characters can do.*

You Do Guide children as they read the rest of the Practice Book story. Prompt them to identify key details that tell about other characters and to tell why they are important.

REVIEW CHARACTER, SETTING, EVENTS

OBJECTIVES

CCSS Describe characters, settings, and major events in a story, using key details. **RL.1.3**

Apply skill to identify the characters, setting, and events in a story

I Do Remind children that a fantasy story has characters, a setting, and events that could not happen in real life. *Characters are who the story is about. The setting tells where and when the story takes place. The events tell what happens. Key details tell about the characters, setting, and events.*

We Do Read the first two pages of the Practice Book story together. Pause to point out key details that tell about the characters, setting, and events. *What characters did we read about?* Add the characters to a Character, Setting, Events chart.

You Do Ask: *What did we read about the setting and events?* Add these items to the chart. Continue by guiding children as they read to tell about characters, setting, and events in the rest of the story.

SELF-SELECTED READING

OBJECTIVES

CCSS Describe characters, settings, and major events in a story, using key details. **RL.1.3**

CCSS With prompting and support, read prose and poetry of appropriate complexity for grade 1. **RL.1.10**

Apply the strategy and skill to read a text

Read Independently

Have children pick a fantasy for sustained silent reading. Remind them that:

→ they can find information in both the text and illustrations about the characters, setting, and events.

→ as they read, they should make and confirm predictions about the story.

Read Purposefully

Have children record details about the characters, setting, and events on a Character, Setting, and Events chart. After reading, guide children to participate in a group discussion about the story they read. Guide children to:

→ share the information they recorded on their chart.

→ tell which characters were their favorites and why.

→ share predictions they made and tell if their predictions were correct.

→ On Level

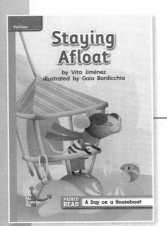

Lexile 150

OBJECTIVES

 Describe characters, setting, and major events in a story, using key details. **RL.1.3**

 With prompting and support, read prose and poetry of appropriate complexity for grade 1. **RL.1.10**

Make and confirm predictions

Leveled Reader:
Staying Afloat

Before Reading

Preview and Predict

Have children turn to the title page. Read the title and the author's name and have children repeat. Preview the selection's illustrations. Prompt children to predict what the selection might be about.

Review Genre: Fantasy

Have children recall that a fantasy is a story that has invented characters, setting, or other elements that could not exist in real life.

ESSENTIAL QUESTION

Remind children of the Essential Question: *What buildings do you know? What are they made of?* Set a purpose for reading: *Let's read to find out if Sam can help Bob with a houseboat.*

Remind children that as they read a selection, they can ask questions about what they do not understand or want to know more about.

During Reading

Guided Comprehension

As children whisper read *Staying Afloat*, monitor and provide guidance, correcting blending and modeling the key strategies and skills.

Strategy: Make and Confirm Predictions

Remind children to make predictions as they read and to check their predictions as they read on. Model the strategy: *On page 5 I read that Bob wants Sam to help him make a boat. I predict that Sam will help.* Read page 6 to confirm the prediction.

Skill: Character, Setting, Events

Remind children that characters are the people or animals in a story; the setting is where and when a story takes place; the events are what happens. These details will help children understand the story. While reading, ask: *Who are the characters? What is the setting? What events happen?* Show the Character, Setting, Events chart for children to copy.

Go
Digital

Staying Afloat

Graphic Organizer

Retell

Model recording children's answers in the character, setting, and events boxes. Have children copy the answers into their own charts.

Think Aloud On page 5, I see the mice on the riverbank. That is the setting. I read that Sam sees Bob. They are the characters. The words tell me that Bob asks Sam to help him build a boat. That is an event.

Guide children to use words and pictures to add characters, setting, and events to their charts.

After Reading

Respond to Reading

Complete the Respond to Reading on page 12.

Retell

Have children take turns retelling the selection using the **Retelling Cards** as a guide. Help them make a connection: *Have you ever been in a boat? Did you like it? Why or why not? Do you know what the boat was made of? Do you think a boat made of paper is safe? Why or why not?*

Model Fluency

Read the sentences one at a time. Have children chorally repeat. Point out to children how your voice sounds at the end of an exclamation and how it changes when reading dialogue.

Apply Have children practice reading with partners. Provide feedback.

PAIRED READ ...

"A Day on a Houseboat"

Make Connections: Write About It ✏️ *Analytical Writing*

Before reading, ask children to note that the text's genre is informational text. Then discuss the Compare Texts direction. After reading, ask: *How does "A Day on a Houseboat" help you better understand* Staying Afloat?

Leveled Reader

✏️ *Analytical Writing*

COMPARE TEXTS

→ Have children use text evidence to compare fantasy to informational text.

Literature Circles

Lead children in conducting a literature circle using the Thinkmark questions to guide the discussion. You may wish to discuss what children have learned about houseboats from both selections in the leveled reader.

Level Up

Level-up lessons available online.

IF children can read *Staying Afloat*, On Level with fluency and correctly answer the Respond to Reading questions,

THEN tell children that they will read a story about another type of building.

- Use pages 2–4 of *City Armadillo, Country Armadillo* Beyond Level to model using Teaching Poster 35 to identify characters, setting, and events.

- Have children read the selection, checking their comprehension by using the graphic organizer.

On Level

Phonics

BUILD WORDS WITH SHORT *u*

OBJECTIVES

 Decode regularly spelled one-syllable words. **RF.1.3b**

Build and decode words with short *u*

 I Do Display **Word-Building Cards** f, u, n. *These are the letters* f, u, *and* n. *They stand for /f/, /u/, and /n/. I will blend /f/, /u/, and /n/ together: /fffuuunnn/,* fun. *The word is* fun.

 We Do *We blended the word* fun *together: /fffuuunnn/,* fun. *Now let's change the letter* f *to* r. Make the change, then say: *Let's blend and read the new word together: /r/ /u/ /n/, /rrruuunnn/,* run. *The new word is* run.

 You Do Have children build and blend these words: *rut, but, bun, bud, mud, mug, pug, pup, puck, tuck, truck.*

Repeat with additional short *u* words.

High-Frequency Words

REVIEW WORDS

OBJECTIVES

 Recognize and read grade-appropriate irregularly spelled words. **RF.1.3g**

Review high-frequency words *could, live, one, then, three*

 I Do Use the **Read/Spell/Write** routine to review each word. Use each word orally in a sentence.

 We Do Guide children to Read/Spell/Write each word using their **Response Boards**. Then have partners say sentences for the words. Have one partner say a sentence but leave out the word. Ask the other partner to tell which word completes the sentence.

 You Do Have partners use the Read/Spell/Write routine with the words *could, live, one, then,* and *three.* Ask them to write sentences about this week's stories. Explain that each sentence should use at least one high-frequency word.

Comprehension

REVIEW CHARACTER, SETTING, EVENTS

OBJECTIVES

 Describe characters, settings, and major events in a story, using key details. **RL.1.3**

 Use illustrations and details in a story to describe its characters, setting, or events. **RL.1.7**

 Remind children that characters are who the story is about; setting is when and where the story takes place; and events are what happens. *When we read fantasy, we look for details about the characters, setting, and events. The details can be found in the words and pictures.*

 Read the first two pages of the Practice Book story aloud. Pause to point out information about characters, setting, and events. *We read about some characters. What characters did we read about? What can they do? What is the setting? How do you know?*

 Guide children to read the rest of the Practice Book story. Remind them to look for key details about characters, setting, and events. Then invite children to discuss and describe the characters, setting, and events.

SELF-SELECTED READING

OBJECTIVES

 With prompting and support, read prose and poetry of appropriate complexity for grade 1. **RL.1.10**

Apply the strategy and skill to read a text

Read Independently

Have children pick a fantasy for sustained silent reading. Remind them to:

→ look for important details that describe the characters, setting, and events.

→ make and confirm predictions about the story.

Read Purposefully

Have children record details on a Character, Setting, and Events chart. After reading, guide partners to:

→ share the information they recorded on their chart.

→ tell which characters were their favorites and why.

→ share predictions they made and tell if their predictions were correct.

Beyond Level

Lexile 330

 OBJECTIVES

Describe characters, settings, and major events in a story, using key details. **RL.1.3**

Make and confirm predictions

Leveled Reader:
City Armadillo, Country Armadillo

Before Reading

Preview and Predict

Read the title and the author's name. Have children preview the title page and the illustrations. Ask: *What do you think this book will be about?*

Review Genre: Fantasy

Have children recall that a fantasy is a story that has invented characters, setting, or other elements that could not exist in real life.

ESSENTIAL QUESTION

Remind children of the Essential Question: *What buildings do you know? What are they made of?* Set a purpose for reading: *Let's read to find out how city life and country life are the same and how they are different for two armadillos.*

During Reading

Guided Comprehension

Have children whisper read *City Armadillo, Country Armadillo*. Have them place self-stick notes next to difficult words. Remind children that when they come to an unfamiliar word, they can look for familiar spellings. They will need to break longer words into smaller chunks and sound out each part.

Monitor children's reading. Stop periodically and ask open-ended questions to facilitate rich discussion, such as *What does the author want us to know about city life and country life?* Build on children's responses to develop deeper understanding of the text.

Strategy: Make and Confirm Predictions

Remind children to make and confirm predictions as they read. Say: *Making and confirming predictions helps you understand what you read. Use details from the words and illustrations to make a prediction. Then read on to confirm your prediction.*

Go Digital

City Armadillo, Country Armadillo

Graphic Organizer

Skill: Character, Setting, Events

Remind children that stories have characters, a setting, and events. While reading, ask: *Who are the characters? Where and when does the story take place? What events happen?* Then ask: *How does identifying these help you understand the story?* Display a Character, Setting, Events chart for children to copy.

Model how to record the character, setting, and events. Have children fill in their charts.

Think Aloud As I read pages 4 and 5 and look at the pictures, I learn that Steve will visit Tommy. Steve and Tommy are characters in the story. Steve goes to the city to visit Tommy. That is an event. The city is a setting in this story.

After Reading

Respond to Reading

Complete the Respond to Reading on page 12 after reading.

Retell

Have children take turns retelling the selection. Help children make a personal connection by writing about a place in the city or country. *Write about a place in the city or the country that you have been to. What buildings did you see? What did you do?*

PAIRED READ ...

"City or Country?"

Make Connections: Write About It
Analytical Writing

Leveled Reader

Before reading, ask children to preview the title page and prompt them to identify the genre as informational text. Discuss the Compare Texts direction. Have partners discuss what they learned from *City Armadillo, Country Armadillo* and "City or Country?"

Analytical Writing

COMPARE TEXTS

→ Have children use text evidence to compare fantasy to informational text.

Literature Circles

Lead children in conducting a literature circle using the Thinkmark questions to guide the discussion. You may wish to discuss what children have learned about city and country life from both selections in the Leveled Reader.

Gifted and Talented

SYNTHESIZE Challenge children to think of the kinds of buildings they have visited and write about the buildings they like most. Encourage them to tell why they like those buildings and where they can be found.

EXTEND Have them use facts they learned from the week or do additional research to find out more about buildings in different places.

Beyond Level

Vocabulary

ORAL VOCABULARY: SYNONYMS

OBJECTIVES

 Use sentence-level context as a clue to the meaning of a word or phrase. **L.1.4a**

 Use words and phrases acquired through conversations, reading and being read to, and responding to texts, including using frequently occurring conjunctions to signal simple relationships (e.g., *because*). **L.1.6**

 I Do Review the meaning of the oral vocabulary word *shelter*. Remind children that a synonym is a word that means almost the same thing as another word. *A synonym for* shelter *is* refuge. *A refuge is a place that keeps you safe. The hut in the woods was our refuge from the storm.*

 We Do Have children take turns using the word *refuge* in sentences. Ask what could be a refuge and what it might be a refuge from. Explain that other synonyms for *shelter* are *sanctuary* and *haven*. Ask children what they picture when they hear each of these words.

Have partners discuss the meaning of the oral vocabulary word *furious*. Explain that other synonyms for *furious* are *enraged* and *irate*.

 You Do Have partners use the word *shelter* and at least one of its synonyms in sentences. Have partners ask and answer questions using the words *enraged* and *irate*.

 Gifted and Talented **Extend** Have children act out a short skit using the oral vocabulary words *shelter* and *furious* correctly. Challenge them to include at least two synonyms they learned in their skit.

Comprehension

REVIEW CHARACTER, SETTING, EVENTS

OBJECTIVES

 Describe characters, settings, and major events in a story, using key details. **RL.1.3**

 Use illustrations and details in a story to describe its characters, setting, or events. **RL.1.7**

 I Do Discuss with children what characters, setting, and events are. Prompt them to tell how key details help them describe a story's characters, setting, and events.

We Do Guide children in reading the first two pages of the Practice Book story aloud. Pause to prompt children to identify characters, setting, and events. Have them share key details that help children describe them. *Who are some characters in the story? What is the setting? How do you know?*

You Do Have children read the rest of the Practice Book story independently. Remind them to identify key details about characters, setting, and events. Then invite children to use the details to describe the characters, setting, and events.

SELF-SELECTED READING

OBJECTIVES

 With prompting and support, read prose and poetry of appropriate complexity for grade 1. **RL.1.10**

Apply the strategy and skill to read a text

Read Independently

Have children pick a fantasy for sustained silent reading. Tell them that they should use a Character, Setting, and Events chart to record details about the characters, setting, and events in their story. Remind them to make and confirm predictions as they read the story.

Read Purposefully

Have children record details on a Character, Setting, and Events chart. After reading, guide children to:

→ tell what they liked about the story and share the information they recorded on their chart with a partner.

→ discuss with their partner the predictions they made and how they confirmed them.

→ record information about the story in a reading response journal.

Gifted and Talented **Independent Study** Have children compare their self-selected fantasy selection to the fantasy selections they read this week. What did they like or not like about their selection? Challenge them to write a review of their selection using key details to support their responses.

English Language Learners

Reading/Writing Workshop

OBJECTIVES

Describe characters, settings, and major events in a story, using key details. **RL.1.3**

Make and confirm predictions

ACADEMIC LANGUAGE

- *prediction, confirm*
- Cognates: *predicción, confirmar*

Shared Read
Cubs in a Hut

Cubs in a Hut

Graphic Organizer

Before Reading

Build Background

Read the Essential Question: *What buildings do you know? What are they made of?*

→ Explain the meaning of the Essential Question: *A building is a kind of shelter. People live in some buildings. They work in other buildings. Buildings are made of different kinds of materials.*

→ **Model an answer:** *Some buildings are made of wood. Some are made of stone. Different parts of buildings are also made of different kinds of materials. Windows are made of glass. Some chimneys are made of brick.*

→ Ask children a question that ties the Essential Question to their own background knowledge: *Turn to a partner and talk about what our school building is made of. Does our school building have bricks in the walls? Is it made of stone? It is made of wood?* Call on several pairs.

During Reading

Interactive Question-Response

→ Ask questions that help children understand the meaning of the text after each paragraph.

→ Reinforce the meanings of key vocabulary by explaining meanings that are embedded in the questions.

→ Ask children questions that require them to use key vocabulary.

→ Reinforce the comprehension strategies and skills of the week by modeling.

Cubs in a Hut

Pages 34–35

Point to the title. *Listen as I read the title, or name, of this book.* Point to each word as you say the title. *Now let's say the title of the book together.* Have children chorally say: *The title of this book is* Cubs in a Hut.

Pages 36–37

Explain and Model the Skill Point to the picture and say: *The picture shows three cubs.* After reading both pages, ask: *Who are the characters in this story?* (Bud, Gus, and Russ are the characters.)

Explain and Model the Strategy Before reading, point to the illustration. *The cubs are getting some mud, grass, and sticks. They have a plan. I predict, or guess, that they will work together to build the hut.*

What do you predict, or guess, will happen? Do you think they will work together? (They will work together to get the job done; they will play or live in the hut.)

Pages 38–39

Explain and Model the Strategy Read page 38. Point to each word as you read. "The cubs did a very good job." *What did you predict? Do the words and picture on this page confirm, or show, that your prediction was correct?* (Yes, the picture shows the cubs holding tools. They are excited to have finished their project. They worked together like I predicted. The words say they did a good job and that they want to move into the hut.)

Explain and Model Phonics Point to the first sentence on page 39. *I will read each word in this sentence. Raise your hand when you hear a word that has the /u/ sound.* "The cubs set up rugs and beds." *Now let's say the words with the /u/ sound together:* cubs, up, rugs.

Pages 40–41

Explain and Model High-Frequency Words
Have children chorally read as you point to each word: "Then one night three cubs got up." Point to *one. This is the word* one. *Let's say it together.* Have children hold up one finger. Repeat with the word *three.*

Explain and Model the Skill Point to the picture and say: *The picture shows the cubs are in their hut.* After reading both pages, ask: *What is the setting in this part of the story? What is the event?* (The setting is inside the hut. The event is that the roof is leaking. Water is dripping on the cubs.)

What do you think will happen? What will the cubs do? (I predict that the cubs will fix the hut and stop the leak.)

Pages 42–43

Explain and Model the Strategy Talk about the illustrations. Point to each word as you read: "We must fix it, " said Bud. *What did you predict would happen? Do the words and picture on this page confirm, or show, that your prediction was correct?* (Yes, the cubs fixed the hut.)

After Reading

Make Connections

→ Review the Essential Question.

English Language Learners

Lexile 10

 OBJECTIVES

Describe characters, settings, and major events in a story, using key details. **RL.1.3**

Make and confirm predictions

ACADEMIC LANGUAGE

• predict, confirm
• Cognates: *predicción, confirmar*

Leveled Reader: *Staying Afloat*

Before Reading

Preview

Read the title. Ask: *What is the title? Say it again.* Repeat with the author's name. Preview the illustrations. Have children describe the pictures. Use simple language to tell about each page. Follow with questions, such as: *Who is this character? Where does this part of the story take place?*

ESSENTIAL QUESTION

Remind children of the Essential Question. Say: *Let's read to find out what makes Sam's house so special.* Encourage children to ask for help when they do not understand a word or phrase.

During Reading

Interactive Question-Response

Pages 2–3 *What is the character's name?* (Sam) *Yes, this is Sam. He is telling this story. Let's read the labels on these pages. Say them with me:* Sam, boat. *Tell your partner a sentence using both words in the sentence. Then tell me about where Sam lives.*

Pages 4–5 After reading pages 4 and 5 aloud, reread them chorally with children. *Look at the illustrations with your partner. Talk about what the pictures show. Tell which characters you see. Tell about the setting in this part of the story.*

Pages 6–7 *Remember, when you read you can stop and predict, or guess, what will happen. What do you think will happen next? Why do you think so? Use the words and pictures to help you make your prediction.* (I predict that the boat will not float. It is made of cardboard. The picture shows the waves going into the boat. The words say the "waves jump in.")

Pages 8–9 *Look at the pictures on pages 8 and 9. Talk with your partner about what the pictures show. Talk about whether or not your prediction was correct. Tell how you know.*

Pages 10–11 *Let's read pages 10 and 11.* Have children read with you. *Look at the pictures. How is this new boat different from the old boat?*

Go Digital

Staying Afloat

Graphic Organizer

Retell

After Reading

Respond to Reading

Revisit the Essential Question. Ask partners to work together to fill in the graphic organizers and answer the questions on page 12. Pair children with peers of varying language abilities.

Retell

Model retelling using the **Retelling Card** prompts. Say: *Look at the illustrations. Use details to help retell the selection.* Help children make personal connections: *How is your house like Sam's? How is it different?*

Expression Fluency: Dialogue, Exclamations

Read the sentences in the book, one at a time. Help children echo-read the pages expressively and with appropriate intonation. Remind them to read exclamations in a way that shows excitement and to read dialogue the way the characters might really sound.

Apply Have children practice reading with partners. Pair children with peers of varying language abilities. Provide feedback as needed.

PAIRED READ ...

"A Day on a Houseboat"

Make Connections:
Write About It *Analytical Writing*

Before reading, tell children to note that this text is informational text. Then discuss the Compare Texts direction.

Leveled Reader

After reading, ask children to make connections between the information they learned from "A Day on a Houseboat" and *Staying Afloat*. Prompt children by providing a sentence frame: *A houseboat needs ____.*

Analytical Writing

COMPARE TEXTS

→ Have children use text evidence to compare fantasy to informational text.

Literature Circles

Lead children in conducting a literature circle using the Thinkmark questions to guide the discussion. You may wish to discuss what children have learned about houseboats from both selections in the Leveled Reader.

Level Up

Level-up lessons available online.

IF children can read *Staying Afloat* **ELL Level** with fluency and correctly answer the Respond to Reading questions,

THEN tell children that they will read a more detailed version of the story.

• Use pages 2–4 of *Staying Afloat* **On Level** to model using Teaching Poster 35 to identify character, setting, and events.

• Have children read the selection, checking their comprehension by using the graphic organizer.

English Language Learners
Vocabulary

PRETEACH ORAL VOCABULARY

OBJECTIVES

Produce complete sentences when appropriate to task and situation. **SL.1.6**

LANGUAGE OBJECTIVE

Preteach oral vocabulary words

 I Do Display images from the **Visual Vocabulary Cards** one at a time to preteach the oral vocabulary words *shelter* and *materials*.

We Do Display each image again and guide children with questions to show how it illustrates or demonstrates the word. Model using sentences to describe the image.

 You Do Display the word again and have children talk to a partner about how this picture demonstrates the word.

Beginning	Intermediate	Advanced/High
Provide sentences for children to complete: *The dog took shelter in _____. He used materials to _____.*	Have partners use each word in a sentence.	Have children write sentences using the words *shelter* and *materials*.

PRETEACH ELL VOCABULARY

OBJECTIVES

Produce complete sentences when appropriate to task and situation. **SL.1.6**

LANGUAGE OBJECTIVE

Preteach ELL vocabulary words

 I Do Display images from the Visual Vocabulary Cards one at a time to review the ELL Vocabulary words *construction* and *sink* and follow the routine. Say each word and have children repeat it. Define the word in English.

 We Do Display each image again and explain how it illustrates or demonstrates the word. Model using sentences to describe the image.

 You Do Display each word again and have children say the word and then spell it. Provide opportunities for children to use the words in speaking and writing. Provide sentence starters.

Beginning	Intermediate	Advanced/High
Help children repeat the sentences aloud and fill in the correct word.	Have children read the sentences they wrote.	Have children create their own sentences using the words.

High-Frequency Words

REVIEW WORDS

CCSS

OBJECTIVES

Recognize and read grade-appropriate irregularly spelled words. **RF.1.3g**

LANGUAGE OBJECTIVE

Review high-frequency words *could, live, one, then, three*

 I Do Display the **High-Frequency Word Cards** for *could, live, one, then,* and *three*. Use the Read/Spell/Write routine to teach each word. Have children write the words on their **Response Boards**.

 We Do Write sentence frames on separate lines. Track the print as children read and complete the sentences: *(1) Could you help me _____? (2) I live _____. (3) I have one new _____. (4) We can run. Then we can _____. (5) I see one _____, two _____, and three _____.*

 You Do Display the High-Frequency Word Cards from the previous five weeks. Display one card at a time as children chorally read the word. Mix and repeat. Note words that children need to review.

Beginning	Intermediate	Advanced/High
Point to and say each word for children to repeat.	Have children read each word as you display it.	Have children say each word and then use it in a sentence.

RETEACH WORDS

CCSS

OBJECTIVES

Recognize and read grade-appropriate irregularly spelled words. **RF.1.3g**

LANGUAGE OBJECTIVE

Reteach high-frequency words

 I Do Display each Visual Vocabulary Card and say the word aloud. Define the word in English and, if appropriate, in Spanish. Identify any cognates.

 We Do Point to each image again, one at a time, and explain how it illustrates or demonstrates the word. Ask children to repeat the word. Engage children in structured partner-talk about the image as prompted on the back of the card. Ask children to chorally say the word three times.

 You Do Display each visual in random order, hiding the word. Have children identify the word and define it in their own words.

Beginning	Intermediate	Advanced/High
Display an image and give children two word choices.	Provide sentence starters for children, as necessary.	Have children use each word in a sentence.

English Language Learners
Writing/Spelling

WRITING TRAIT: ORGANIZATION

OBJECTIVES

Write narratives in which they recount two or more appropriately sequenced events, include some details regarding what happened, use temporal words to signal event order, and provide some sense of closure. **W.1.3**

LANGUAGE OBJECTIVE

Use organization to write a story with a beginning, middle, and end

 Explain that writers organize a story into a beginning, a middle, and an end. Discuss a familiar story, such as *The Three Little Pigs*, with children. Help them tell what happens at the beginning, the middle, and the end.

 Read aloud pages 36–37 of *Cubs in a Hut*. Ask what happens at the beginning of the story. (The cubs decide to make a hut.) Repeat the exercise for the middle and the end of the story.

 Have children write three sentences to tell a short story with a beginning, a middle, and an end.

Beginning	Intermediate	Advanced/High
Help children write their sentences. Provide sentence frames for them to copy and complete.	Ask children to list the events that take place in the beginning, middle, and end of their story. Repeat their responses. Provide sentence frames, if necessary.	Remind children to include a beginning, middle, and end. Ask: *How does the story begin? Who are the characters? Where does the story take place? How does the story end?*

WORDS WITH SHORT *u*

OBJECTIVES

Use conventional spelling for words with common spelling patterns and for frequently occurring irregular words. **L.1.2d**

LANGUAGE OBJECTIVE

Spell words with short *u*

 Read aloud the Spelling Words on page T92. Segment the first word into sounds and attach a spelling to each sound. Point out the short /u/. Continue with remaining words.

 Read aloud the first sentence from the Dictation routine on page T92. Then read the short *u* word slowly and ask children to repeat. Have them write the word. Repeat the process for the remaining sentences.

 Display the words. Have children work with a partner to check their spelling lists. Have children correct misspelled words on their lists.

Beginning	Intermediate	Advanced/High
Help children say the words and copy them with the correct spelling.	After children have corrected their words, have pairs quiz each other.	Challenge children to think of other words that have the short *u* sound.

Grammar

SINGULAR AND PLURAL NOUNS

OBJECTIVES

CCSS Use common, proper, and possessive nouns. **L.1.1b**

LANGUAGE OBJECTIVE

Recognize the -s, -es plural forms for nouns

Language Transfers Handbook

The Cantonese, Haitian Creole, Hmong, Korean, Vietnamese, and Khmer languages do not use a plural marker. Children who speak these languages may forget the plural marker when forming plural nouns. Provide extra support by having them repeat singular and plural noun pairs.

 I Do

Review that nouns name people, places, or things. *A singular noun names one person, place, or thing. A plural noun names more than one. I add -s to most nouns to make them mean "more than one." I add -es to nouns that end in* x, s, *or* ss.

Write *duck* and *ducks*. Circle the -s. *I add* -s *to* duck *to make it mean "more than one duck."* Write these sentences: *I see one duck. I see two ducks.* Hold up one finger as you read the first sentence and two fingers as you read the second. Repeat with *fox* and *foxes*.

 We Do

Write the sentences provided below on the board. Have children read each sentence, circle each noun, and tell if it is singular or plural. Have them say: *I know the noun is _____ because it does/does not end in* -s *or* -es.

There are two cups in this bag.

The truck has boxes in it.

I see buses at my school.

Can a cat play the drums?

 You Do

Write the following sentence frames on the board:

We go on a trip. I get one new _____. I pack three _____.

Pair children and have them complete each sentence frame. Circulate, listen in, and take note of each child's language use and proficiency.

Beginning	Intermediate	Advanced/High
Have children hold up one finger and say *I have one finger*. Have them hold up ten fingers and say *I have ten fingers*. Continue with ears, hands, eyes, nose, knees.	Ask children to point out one object in the classroom. Then have them point out multiple objects. Have them use sentences to tell how many objects they find.	Have children write sentences using the singular and plural versions of three words.

PROGRESS MONITORING

Weekly Assessment

✔ **COMPREHENSION:**
Character, Setting,
Events **RL.1.3**

Use Illustrations
RL.1.7

✔ **PHONEMIC AWARENESS:**
Identify and Generate
Rhyme **RF.1.2c**

Phoneme Identity **RF.1.2c**

Phoneme Blending **RF.1.2b**

Phoneme Segmentation **RF.1.2d**

✔ **PHONICS/STRUCTURAL ANALYSIS/HIGH-FREQUENCY WORDS:**
Short *u* **RF.1.3b**

Contractions with *'s* **L.1.1**

could, live, one, then, three **RF.1.3g**

Conduct group fluency assessments.

Assess fluency for one group of children per week using the
Letter Naming, Phoneme Segmentation, and **Sight Word Fluency** assessments in *Reading Wonders Fluency Assessment.*

Go Digital! http://connected.mcgraw-hill.com

Using Assessment Results

TESTED SKILLS	If ...	Then ...
COMPREHENSION	Children answer 0–3 multiple-choice items correctly . . .	. . . assign Lessons 22–24 on Identify Character, Lessons 25–27 on Identify Setting, Lessons 28–30 on Identify Plot Events, and Lesson 94 on Using Illustrations from the ***Tier 2 Comprehension Intervention online PDFs.***
PHONEMIC AWARENESS	Children answer 0–1 multiple-choice items correctly . . .	. . . assign Lessons 6–8 on Identify Rhyme, Lessons 49–50 on Phoneme Identity: Medial Sounds (short vowels), Lessons 62–66 on Phoneme Blending, and Lessons 67–71 on Phoneme Segmenting from the ***Tier 2 Phonemic Awareness Intervention online PDFs.***
PHONICS/ STRUCTURAL ANALYSIS/HFW	Children answer 0–5 multiple-choice items correctly . . .	. . . assign Lesson 49 on Short *u* from the ***Tier 2 Phonics/Word Study Intervention online PDFs.***

Response to Intervention

Use children's assessment results to assist you in identifying children who will benefit from focused intervention.

Use the appropriate sections of the ***Placement and Diagnostic Assessment*** to designate children requiring:

TIER 2 **Intervention Online PDFs**

TIER 3 **WonderWorks Intervention Program**

Literature Big Book

**Big Book and Little Book
Reading/Writing Workshop**

 **Go** Digital

http://connected.mcgraw-hill.com

TEACH AND MODEL

Listening Comprehension

Comprehension Strategy *Reread* T166–T167

Close Reading

Shared Reading *The Best Spot,* 54–63

Genre Nonfiction

Lexile 160

Words to Know T171

eat, no, of, under, who

Minilessons   ✔ **Tested Skills** CCSS

✔ **Phonics** .... End Blends, T172–T173

✔ **Comprehension Skill** .... Main Topic and Key Details, T183

✔ **Writing Traits** .... Ideas, T192

✔ **Grammar** .... Possessive Nouns, T193

APPLY WITH CLOSE READING

Literature Anthology

Complex Text

PAIRED READ

At a Pond, 48–59
Genre Nonfiction
Lexile 190

"Way Down Deep," 62–63
Genre Poetry
Lexile NP

NP = Non-Prose

Differentiated Text

Leveled Readers *Including Paired Reads*

APPROACHING
Lexile 170

ON LEVEL
Lexile 210

BEYOND
Lexile 370

ELL
Lexile 170

Extended Complex Text

Cactus Hotel
Genre
Nonfiction
Lexile 700

Meet the Meerkat
Genre
Nonfiction

Lexile 340

Classroom
Library
lessons available
online.

Classroom Library

"Cover" from the book *Cactus Hotel* by Brenda Z. Guiberson. Illustrated by Megan Lloyd. Copyright text © 1991 by Brenda Z. Guiberson. Illustrations © 1991 by Megan Lloyd. Reprinted by permission of Henry Holt and Company, LLC.; *Meet the Meerkat*. Text copyright © 2007 by Darrin Lunde. Illustrations copyright © 2007 by Patricia J. Wynne. Used with permission by Charlesbridge Publishing, Inc. All rights reserved.

TEACH AND MANAGE

How You Teach

INTRODUCE

Weekly Concept
A Community in Nature

Reading/Writing Workshop
28–39

TEACH

Listening Comprehension
Babies in the Bayou

Close Reading
The Best Spot

Minilessons
Main Topic and Key Details, Nonfiction, End Blends, High-Frequency Words

APPLY

Close Reading
At a Pond
"Way Down Deep"

 Go Digital

 Interactive Whiteboard

 Interactive Whiteboard

 Mobile

---

How Students Practice

WEEKLY CONTRACT

PDF Online

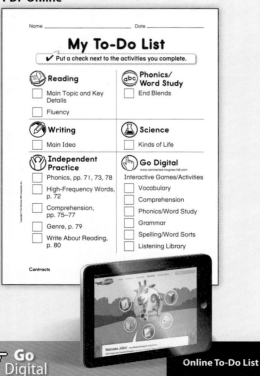

Name _____ Date _____

My To-Do List
✔ Put a check next to the activities you complete.

📖 **Reading**
☐ Main Topic and Key Details
☐ Fluency

✏️ **Writing**
☐ Main Idea

✋ **Independent Practice**
☐ Phonics, pp. 71, 73, 78
☐ High-Frequency Words, p. 72
☐ Comprehension, pp. 75–77
☐ Genre, p. 79
☐ Write About Reading, p. 80

🔤 **Phonics/ Word Study**
☐ End Blends

🧪 **Science**
☐ Kinds of Life

👆 **Go Digital**
www.connected.mcgraw-hill.com
Interactive Games/Activities
☐ Vocabulary
☐ Comprehension
☐ Phonics/Word Study
☐ Grammar
☐ Spelling/Word Sorts
☐ Listening Library

Contracts

LEVELED PRACTICE AND ONLINE ACTIVITIES

Your Turn Practice Book
71–80

Leveled Readers

 Go Digital

 Online To-Do List

 Leveled Activities

Mobile

DIFFERENTIATE

SMALL GROUP INSTRUCTION

Leveled Readers

Mobile

INTEGRATE

Research and Inquiry
Make a Collage, T200–T201

Text Connections
A Community in Nature, T202

Write About Reading
Analyze Main Topic and Key Details, T203

Online Research and Writing

ASSESS

Weekly Assessment 71–80

Online Assessment

LEVELED WORKSTATION CARDS

More Activities on back

8

Animal Homes

Animals live on land, in the air, and in the water.

- Draw a picture of an animal that lives in the water. Write the animal's name.

- Draw a picture of an animal that lives

SCIENCE

8

Organization: Focus on an Idea

I saw a nest.
It had birds in it.
They were babies!
The tree was tall.

- Tran had an idea for a story. What was Tran's idea?

- Which sentence does not focus on Tran's idea?

WRITING

8

End Blends

| p | o | n | d |

- Use the Word-Building Cards. Build the word **pond**.

- Build and write more words that end in **-nd**.

pond

- Now make words that end with **-nk** or **-st**.

- Draw a picture of one of the words. Label it.

You need 20
› Word-Building Cards
› paper
› pencils, crayons, or markers

PHONICS/WORD STUDY

5

Main Topic and Key Details

The main topic is what the selection is about. Key details give information about the main topic.

- Read a nonfiction story.

- Use a Shutter Foldable®.

The | Story

- Decide what the selection is about. Write it on the inside.

- Write a key detail on each tab.

You need 20
› Shutter Foldable®
› pencils, crayons, or markers

READING

DEVELOPING READERS AND WRITERS

Write to Sources and Research

Note Taking, T191A

Main Topic and Key Details, T191B

Author's Purpose, T191G

Make Connections: Essential Question, T191H

Research and Inquiry, T200

Analyze to Inform/Explain, T203

Comparing Texts, T209, T219, T223, T229

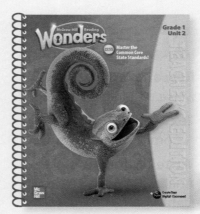

Teacher's Edition

Your Turn Practice Book

Main Topic and Key Details, pp. 75–77
Write About Reading, p. 80

Leveled Readers
Comparing Texts

Interactive Whiteboard

Narrative Text
Sentences That Explain, T192–T193

Conferencing Routines
Peer Conferences, T198

Interactive Whiteboard

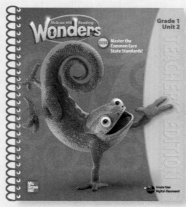

Teacher's Edition

Leveled Workstation Card
Sentences That Explain, Card 24

Writing Traits • Shared and Interactive Writing

Writing Trait: Ideas
Sentences That Explain, T174

Conferencing Routines
Peer Conferences, T198

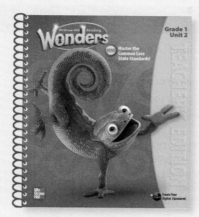

Teacher's Edition

Ideas: Possessive Nouns, pp. 66–67

Reading/Writing Workshop

Leveled Workstation Card
Organization: Focus on an Idea, Card 8

Interactive Whiteboard

Grammar and Spelling

Grammar
Possessive Nouns, T175

Spelling
Words with End Blends, T170

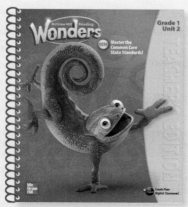

Teacher's Edition

Interactive Whiteboard

Online Spelling and Grammar Games

Handwriting

SUGGESTED LESSON PLAN

		DAY 1	DAY 2

READING

Whole Group

Teach, Model, and Apply

Reading/Writing Workshop

DAY 1

Build Background A Community in Nature, T164–T165

Oral Vocabulary Words *depend, habitat,* T164

Big Book *Babies in the Bayou,* T166

Listening Comprehension Strategy: Reread, T167

Word Work T168–T171
Fluency: Sound-Spellings
Phonemic Awareness: Phoneme Categorization
Phonics/Spelling: Introduce End Blends
High-Frequency Words: *eat, no, of, under, who*

Shared Reading *The Best Spot,* T172–T173

Practice Your Turn, p. 71

DAY 2

Oral Language A Community in Nature, T176

Oral Vocabulary Words *hibernate, tolerate, tranquil,* T176

Listening Comprehension Strategy: Reread, T177

Interactive Read-Aloud Cards "Animals in the Desert," T177

Word Work T178–T181
Fluency: Sound-Spellings
Phonemic Awareness: Phoneme Blending
Phonics/Spelling: Review End Blends
Structural Analysis: Inflectional Ending *-ing*
High-Frequency Words: *eat, no, of, under, who*

Shared Reading *The Best Spot,* T182–T183

✓**Comprehension**
•Genre: Informational Text/Nonfiction, T182
•Skill: Main Topic and Key Details, T183

Practice Your Turn, pp. 72–74

DIFFERENTIATED INSTRUCTION   Choose across the week to meet your children's needs.

Small Group

Approaching Level

DAY 1
Leveled Reader *Meerkat Family,* T208–T209
Phonemic Awareness Phoneme Categorization, T210 ②
Phonics Connect to Consonant Blends, T212 ②
High-Frequency Words Review, T215

DAY 2
Leveled Reader *Meerkat Family,* T208–T209
Phonemic Awareness Phoneme Blending, T210 ②
Phonics Blend Words with End Blends, T212 ②
High-Frequency Words Reteach, T215
Comprehension Identify Key Details, T216 ②

On Level

DAY 1
Leveled Reader *Meerkat Family,* T218–T219
Phonics Build Words with End Blends, T220

DAY 2
Leveled Reader *Meerkat Family,* T218–T219
High Frequency Words Review Words, T220

Beyond Level

DAY 1
Leveled Reader *Meerkat Family,* T222–T223
Oral Vocabulary Context Clues, T224

DAY 2
Leveled Reader *Meerkat Family,* T222–T223
Oral Vocabulary Context Clues, T224

English Language Learners

DAY 1
Shared Read *The Best Spot,* T226–T227
Phonemic Awareness Phoneme Categorization, T210
Phonics Connect to Consonant Blends, T212
Vocabulary
Preteach Oral Vocabulary, T230

DAY 2
Leveled Reader *Meerkat Family,* T228–T229
Phonemic Awareness Phoneme Blending, T210
Phonics Blend Words with End Blends, T212
Vocabulary Preteach ELL Vocabulary, T230

LANGUAGE ARTS

Whole Group

Writing

Grammar

DAY 1
Shared Writing Writing Trait: Ideas, T174
Sentences That Explain, T174

Grammar
•Possessive Nouns, T175

Mechanics: Apostrophe with Possessive Nouns, T175

DAY 2
Interactive Writing Writing Trait: Ideas, T184
Sentences That Explain, T184

Grammar
•Possessive Nouns, T185

Mechanics: Apostrophe with Possessive Nouns, T185

DAY 3	DAY 4	DAY 5 Review and Assess

READING

Oral Language A Community in Nature, T186
Review Oral Vocabulary *depend, habitat, hibernate, tolerate, tranquil,* T186
Listening Comprehension
Big Book *Babies in the Bayou,* T187
•Strategy: Reread, T187
•Retelling, T187
•Fluency: Phrasing, T187
Word Work T188–T191
Fluency: Sound-Spellings
Phonemic Awareness: Phoneme Substitution
Phonics/Spelling: Blend Words with End Blends
Structural Analysis: Inflectional Ending -ing
High-Frequency Words: *eat, no, of, under, who*
Close Reading *At a Pond,* T191A–T191H ● *Analytical Writing*
Practice Your Turn, pp. 75–77

Oral Language A Community in Nature, T194
Comprehension Literary Element: Repetition, T194
Close Reading "Way Down Deep," T195
Word Work T196–T197
Fluency: Sound-Spellings
Phonemic Awareness: Phoneme Categorization
Phonics/Spelling: Build Words with End Blends
Structural Analysis: Inflectional Ending -ing
High-Frequency Words: *eat, no, of, under, who*
Integrate Ideas Research and Inquiry, T200–T201
Practice Your Turn, pp. 78–79

Integrate Ideas
•Text Connections, T202
•Write About Reading, T203 ● *Analytical Writing*
Word Work T204–T205
Fluency: Word Automaticity
Phonemic Awareness: Phoneme Blending/Segmentation
Phonics/Spelling: Blend and Build Words with End Blends
Structural Analysis: Inflectional Ending -ing
High-Frequency Words: *eat, no, of, under, who*
Practice Your Turn, p. 80

DIFFERENTIATED INSTRUCTION

Leveled Reader *Meerkat Family,* T208–T209
Phonemic Awareness Phoneme Substitution, T211
Phonics Build Words with End Blends, T213
Structural Analysis Review Inflectional Ending -ing, T214
Comprehension Review Main Topic and Key Details, T217

Leveled Reader Paired Read: "I Live in a House," T209 ● *Analytical Writing*
Phonemic Awareness Phoneme Segmentation, T211
Phonics Blend Words with End Blends, T213
Structural Analysis Reteach Inflectional Ending -ing, T214
Comprehension Read for Fluency, T216 ②

Leveled Reader Literature Circles, T209
Phonics Build Fluency with Phonics, T213
High-Frequency Words Cumulative Review, T215
Comprehension Self-Selected Reading, T217

Leveled Reader *Meerkat Family,* T218–T219
Comprehension Review Main Topic and Key Details, T221

Leveled Reader Paired Read: "I Live in a House," T219 ● *Analytical Writing*

Leveled Reader Literature Circles, T219
Comprehension Self-Selected Reading, T221

Leveled Reader *Meerkat Family,* T222–T223
Comprehension Review Main Topic and Key Details, T225

Leveled Reader Paired Read: "I Live in a House," T223 ● *Analytical Writing*

Leveled Reader Literature Circles, T223
Comprehension Self-Selected Reading, T225

Leveled Reader *Meerkat Family,* T228–T229
Phonemic Awareness Phoneme Substitution, T211
Phonics Build Words with End Blends, T213
Structural Analysis Review Inflectional Ending -ing, T214
High-Frequency Words Review Words, T231
Writing Writing Trait: Ideas, T232

Leveled Reader Paired Read: "I Live in a House," T229 ● *Analytical Writing*
Phonemic Awareness Phoneme Segmentation, T211
Structural Analysis Reteach Inflectional Ending -ing, T214
High-Frequency Words Reteach Words, T231
Grammar Possessive Nouns, T233

Leveled Reader Literature Circles, T229
Phonics Blend Words with End Blends, T213
Spelling Words with End Blends, T232

LANGUAGE ARTS

Independent Writing Writing Trait: Ideas, T192
Sentences That Explain: Prewrite/Draft, T192–T193
Grammar
•Possessive Nouns, T193
Mechanics: Apostrophe with Possessive Nouns, T193

Independent Writing Writing Trait: Ideas, T198
Sentences That Explain: Revise/Proofread/Edit, T198–T199
Grammar
•Possessive Nouns, T199
Mechanics: Apostrophe with Possessive Nouns, T199

Independent Writing
Sentences That Explain: Publish and Present, T206
Grammar
•Possessive Nouns, T207
Mechanics: Apostrophe with Possessive Nouns, T207

DIFFERENTIATE TO ACCELERATE

 Scaffold to Access Complex Text

> **IF** the text complexity of a particular selection is too difficult for children
>
> **THEN** see the references noted in the chart below for scaffolded instruction to help children Access Complex Text.

Qualitative · Quantitative
Reader and Task
TEXT COMPLEXITY

Big Book	**Reading/Writing Workshop**	**Literature Anthology**	**Leveled Readers**

Quantitative

Big Book	Reading/Writing Workshop	Literature Anthology	Leveled Readers	
Babies in the Bayou **Lexile** 710	*The Best Spot* **Lexile** 160	*At a Pond* **Lexile** 190	**Approaching Level** **Lexile** 170	**On Level** **Lexile** 210
		"Way Down Deep" **Lexile** NP	**Beyond Level** **Lexile** 370	**ELL** **Lexile** 170

Qualitative

Big Book	Reading/Writing Workshop	Literature Anthology	Leveled Readers
What Makes the Text Complex? • **Purpose,** T187 • **Organization,** T187 **A C T** *See Scaffolded Instruction in Teacher's Edition, T187.*	**What Makes the Text Complex?** **Foundational Skills** • Decoding with end blends, T168–T169 • Reading words with inflectional ending *-ing*, T179 • Identifying high-frequency words, T171 *See Scaffolded Instruction in Teacher's Edition, T168–T169, T171, and T179.*	**What Makes the Text Complex?** **Foundational Skills** • Decoding with end blends, T188–T189 • Reading words with inflectional ending *-ing*, T189 • Identifying high-frequency words, T191	**What Makes the Text Complex?** **Foundational Skills** • Decoding with end blends • Reading words with inflectional ending *-ing*, • Identifying high-frequency words *eat no of under who* *See Level Up lessons online for Leveled Readers.*

Reader and Task

Big Book	Reading/Writing Workshop	Literature Anthology	Leveled Readers
The Introduce the Concept lesson on pages T164–T165 will help determine the reader's knowledge and engagement in the weekly concept. See pages T166–T167, T187, and T200–T203 for questions and tasks for this text.	The Introduce the Concept lesson on pages T164–T165 will help determine the reader's knowledge and engagement in the weekly concept. See pages T172–T173, T182–T183, and T200–T203 for questions and tasks for this text.	The Introduce the Concept lesson on pages T164–T165 will help determine the reader's knowledge and engagement in the weekly concept. See pages T191A–T191H, T195, and T200–T203 for questions and tasks for this text.	The Introduce the Concept lesson on pages T164–T165 will help determine the reader's knowledge and engagement in the weekly concept. See pages T208–T209, T218–T219, T222–T223, T228–T229, and T200–T203 for questions and tasks for this text.

Classroom Library Tradebooks: See pages T413–T415 for model lessons.

Monitor and *Differentiate*

IF → you need to differentiate instruction

THEN → use the Quick Checks to assess children's needs and select the appropriate small group instruction focus.

✓ Quick Check

Comprehension Strategy Reread, T167

Comprehension Skill Main Topic and Key Details, T183

Phonics End Blends, T171, T181, T191, T197, T205

High-Frequency Words T171, T181, T191, T197, T205

If No →
Approaching Level	**Reteach** T208–T217
ELL	**Develop** T226–T233

If Yes →
On Level	**Review** T218–T221
Beyond Level	**Extend** T222–T225

Level Up with Leveled Readers

IF → children can read their leveled text fluently and answer comprehension questions

THEN → work with the next level up to accelerate children's reading with more complex text.

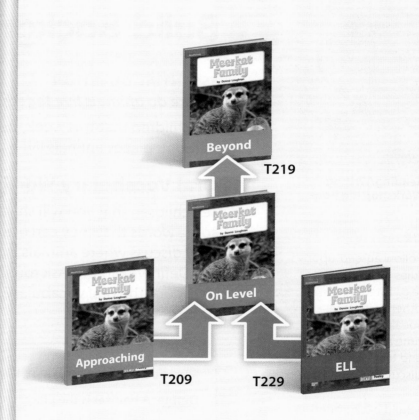

Beyond — T219

On Level

Approaching — T209   T229   ELL

ENGLISH LANGUAGE LEARNERS SCAFFOLD

IF ELL students need additional support **THEN** scaffold instruction using the small group suggestions.

Shared Read	Leveled Reader	Phonemic Awareness	Phonics	Words to Know	Writing	Spelling	Grammar
The Best Spot, T226–T227	*Meerkat Family,* T228–T229 "I Live in a House," T229	Phoneme Categorization, T210 Phoneme Blending, T210 Phoneme Substitution, T211 Phoneme Segmentation, T211	Words with End Blends, T212–T213 Structural Analysis, T214	*eat, no, of, under, who,* T215	Ideas, T232	Words with End Blends, T232	Possessive Nouns, T233

Note: Include ELL Students in all small groups based on their needs.

Materials

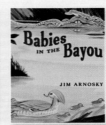

Reading/Writing Workshop
VOLUME 2

Reading/Writing Workshop Big Book
UNIT 2

Literature Big Book
Babies in the Bayou

Visual Vocabulary Cards
depend   habitat

Teaching Poster

eat

High-Frequency Word Cards
eat   under
no   who
of

a b c
Word-Building Cards

Think Aloud Clouds

Nn
n
kn_ gn
nest
Sound-Spelling Cards

Reading/Writing Workshop Big Book

OBJECTIVES

CCSS Follow agreed-upon rules for discussions (e.g., listening to others with care, speaking one at a time about the topics and texts under discussion). **SL.1.1a**

• Build background knowledge
• Discuss the Essential Question

ACADEMIC LANGUAGE
• *rely, community, nature*
• Cognates: *comunidad, naturaleza*

(→) # Introduce the Concept

MINILESSON · 5 Mins

Build Background

ESSENTIAL QUESTION
Where do animals live together?

Tell children that this week they will be talking and reading about the different places animals live.

Oral Vocabulary Words

Tell children that you will share some words that they can use as they discuss where animals live. Use the Define/Example/Ask routine to introduce the oral vocabulary words **habitat** and **depend**.

Oral Vocabulary Routine

Visual Vocabulary Cards

Define: A **habitat** is the place where an animal lives in nature.

Example: A black bear's habitat is the forest.

Ask: What is the habitat of dolphins and whales?

Define: When you **depend** on something, you rely on it for the things you need.

Example: Babies depend on their parents for food and shelter.

Ask: Whom do you depend on for the things you need?

Discuss the theme of "A Community in Nature." Have children tell about animals they know about. *What kind of habitat do they live in? Why do you think they live there?*

Go Digital

A Community in Nature

Video

school
Visual Glossary

Graphic Organizer

READING/WRITING WORKSHOP, pp. 48–49

Talk About It: A Community in Nature

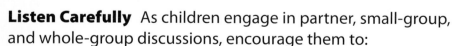

Guide children to discuss the penguins and their habitat.

→ Describe this habitat. What do you see?

→ Is this a good habitat for the penguins? Why?

Use Teaching Poster 40 and prompt children to complete the Word Web by filling in what the habitat is like.

Children can look at page 49 of their Reading/Writing Workshop and do the Talk About It activity with a partner.

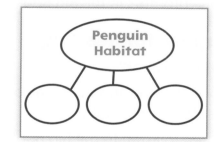

Teaching Poster

Collaborative Conversations

Listen Carefully As children engage in partner, small-group, and whole-group discussions, encourage them to:

→ Always look at the speaker.

→ Respect others by not interrupting them.

→ Repeat others' ideas to check understanding.

ENGLISH LANGUAGE LEARNERS SCAFFOLD

Beginning

Use Visuals Point to the penguins. *These are penguins. Do penguins swim in the water? What are the penguins standing on?*

Intermediate

Describe Ask children to describe the penguins and their habitat. *What do the penguins look like? Is their habitat warm or cold?*

Advanced/Advanced High

Discuss Have children elaborate on the penguins in the photo. *What is their habitat like?*

→ Listening Comprehension

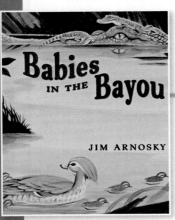

Literature Big Book

MINILESSON
10 Mins

Read the Literature Big Book

Connect to Concept: A Community in Nature

Tell children that they will now read about baby animals that live in a special habitat called a bayou—a warm, swampy area. Ask: *Can you guess what kinds of animals live in a bayou?*

Concepts of Print

Distinguish Sentences Remind children that sentences begin with a capital letter and end with a punctuation mark. As you read *Babies in the Bayou*, point out the capital letter at the beginning of each sentence as well as the end punctuation. Explain that some pages contain only part of a sentence, and that you must turn the page to read the end of the sentence. See prompts in the Big Book for modeling concepts of print.

Set a Purpose for Reading

→ Display the Big Book.

→ Read aloud the title and the name of the author. Explain that the author is also the illustrator.

→ Ask children to listen to the Big Book to find out what kinds of animals live in a bayou.

OBJECTIVES

CCSS Recognize the distinguishing features of a sentence (e.g., first word, capitalization, ending punctuation). **RF.1.1a**

- Reinforce concepts of print
- Develop concept understanding

ACADEMIC LANGUAGE

- *reread, information, facts, details*
- Cognates: *información, detalles*

Go Digital

Babies in the Bayou

When I read _____, I had to reread...

Reread

Strategy: Reread

❶ Explain Tell children that if they do not understand something they read in the Big Book, they can go back and reread the text. Explain that when you reread, you go back and read something again. Rereading can help them understand the text better and remember important information.

Think Aloud *Rereading parts of a book when you don't understand can help you to better understand what you read. It can also help you remember important information. Today, as we read Babies in the Bayou, remember that you can go back and reread parts of the text to make sure that you understand all the facts and details of the selection.*

❷ Model As you read, use the Think Aloud Cloud to model applying the strategy.

Think Aloud *Remember that you can reread parts of the text to make sure you understood correctly. There is a lot of information on these pages. I am not sure that I understood what it was about. When I reread the pages, I understand that the baby alligators are sleeping on a log while their mother guards them.*

❸ Guided Practice As you continue to read the Big Book, pause to elicit questions from children. Guide them to reread the text to answer their questions. *Remember, you can reread parts of the text to help you understand and answer questions.*

Respond to Reading

After reading, prompt children to share what they learned about the baby animals in the bayou. Discuss what parts they needed to reread and how rereading helped them to understand all the facts and details. Prompt children to talk about what they might hear and feel if they were in the bayou.

ENGLISH LANGUAGE LEARNERS SCAFFOLD

Beginning

Engage Display pages 12 and 13 of *Babies in the Bayou*. *I didn't understand this part. Let's reread it.* Reread the pages. *Do the babies have black rings on their tails? Do they have black fur on their faces?*

Intermediate

Describe Display pages 6 and 7 of *Babies in the Bayou*. *I do not understand who is sleeping on a log, the alligator or her babies. Let's reread the page.* Reread the pages. *Who is sleeping on the log?*

Advanced/Advanced High

Explain Display pages 26 through 29 of *Babies in the Bayou*. *I do not understand what the danger is. Let's reread this part.* Reread the pages. *Can you explain what the danger is?*

Monitor and *Differentiate*

 Quick Check

Can children apply the strategy reread?

Small Group Instruction

If No →	**Approaching**	Reteach pp. T208–209
	ELL	Develop pp. T226–229
If Yes →	**On Level**	Review pp. T218–219
	Beyond Level	Extend pp. T222–223

→  # Word Work

Quick Review

Build Fluency: Sound-Spellings
Display the **Word-Building Cards:** *nd, nk, nt, st, sk, mp, u, e, ea, sp, sn, sl, cr, fr, tr, o, pl, fl, cl, bl, i, a, s, r, l, t.*
Have children say the sounds.

 5 Mins MINILESSON

Phonemic Awareness

OBJECTIVES

CCSS Isolate and pronounce initial, medial vowel, and final sounds (phonemes) in spoken single-syllable words. **RF.1.2c**

CCSS Decode regularly spelled one-syllable words. **RF.1.3b**

Phoneme Categorization

❶ **Model** Listen to the ending sounds in these words: *last, send, rest.* Two of the words end with /st/. One does not. That's right, the words *last* and *rest* end with /st/. The word *send* does not end with /st/. It does not belong.

❷ **Guided Practice/Practice** Say the words. Have children identify the word that does not end with the chosen blend. Guide practice with the first example.

Listen for /nd/: band, back, land.

Listen for /nk/: sink, hunk, hand.

Listen for /mp/: lamp, last, jump.

Listen for /nt/: help, ant, sent.

Listen for /sk/: ask, list, desk.

10 Mins MINILESSON

Phonics

Introduce End Blends

Sound-Spelling Card

❶ **Model** Display **Sound-Spelling Card** *nest.*
Teach /st/ spelled *st.* Model writing the letters *st.* Use the handwriting models provided. *This is the Nest Sound-Spelling Card. The last two sounds are /st/. They are spelled with the letters st. Say it with me: /st/. These are the sounds at the end of the word* nest. *Listen: /n/ /e/ /st/.* Repeat for these ending consonant blends: *nk, nd, nt, sk, mp.*

❷ **Guided Practice/Practice** Have children practice connecting the letters *s* and *t* to the sounds /st/ by writing them. *Now do it with me. Say /st/ as I write the letters s and t. This time, write the letters s and t five times as you say the /st/ sounds.* Repeat for *nk, nd, nt, sk,* and *mp.*

Go Digital

Phonemic Awareness

nest

Phonics

Handwriting

SKILLS TRACE

END BLENDS

Introduce Unit 2 Week 3 Day 1

Review Unit 2 Week 3 Days 2, 3, 4, 5

Assess Unit 2 Week 3

Blend Words with End Blends

❶ Model Display **Word-Building Cards** *v, e, s, t*. Model how to blend the sounds. This is the letter *v*. It stands for /v/. This is the letter *e*. It stands for /e/. These are the letters *s* and *t*. When I blend them together they stand for /st/. Listen as I blend these sounds together: /v/ /e/ /st/, /vvveeest/. Say it with me: *vest*.

Continue by modeling the words *hand, pink, vent, clamp,* and *desk*.

❷ Guided Practice/Practice Display the Day 1 Phonics Practice Activity. Read each word in the first row, blending the sounds; for example: /aaand/. The word is and. Have children blend each word with you. Prompt children to read the connected text, sounding out the decodable words.

and	nest	sand	plant	last	trunk
end	ant	must	hunt	went	crisp
ask	mask	bump	jump	romp	stomp
blink	desk	spent	clump	stand	trust

An ant is not fast.

Is the test on the desk?

The skunk is in the tent!

Also online

Day 1 Phonics Practice Activity

Corrective Feedback

Sound Error Model the sound that children missed, then have them repeat the sounds. Say: *My turn*. Tap under the letter and say: *Sounds? /st/ What are the sounds?* Return to the beginning of the word. Say: *Let's start over*. Blend the word with children again.

Daily Handwriting

Throughout the week teach uppercase and lowercase letters *Tt* using the Handwriting models.

ENGLISH LANGUAGE LEARNERS

Phonemic Awareness: Minimal Contrasts Focus on articulation. Make the /st/ sounds, clearly pronouncing each sound. Have children repeat. Then say *pat* and *past*. Have children repeat, noticing the differences. Continue by having children say minimal-contrast word pairs, such as *pet/pest, deck/desk; lit/list*.

Phonics: Variations in Language Many languages have few or limited consonant blends. In addition, one or more of the letters in a blend might not transfer or have only an approximate transfer. For example, in Vietnamese and Hmong, there is an approximate transfer for /t/. Emphasize the individual sounds in a consonant blend and show correct mouth position. Practice with Approaching Level phonics lessons.

ON-LEVEL PRACTICE BOOK p. 71

Sometimes words end with a **blend** of sounds. You can hear each consonant sound in an **end blend**.

nest   sink

A. Read the words in the box. Listen for the end blend. Write the word that names each picture. Underline the end blend.

list	hand	tent	bank	desk	lamp

1. tent
2. lamp
3. hand
4. desk
5. list
6. bank

B. Write your own sentence using a word from the box.

7. Responses will vary.

APPROACHING p. 71	BEYOND p. 71	ELL p. 71

 **Word Work**

Quick Review

High-Frequency Words: Read, Spell, and Write to review last week's high-frequency words: *could, live, one, then, three.*

MINILESSON 5 Mins

Spelling

OBJECTIVES

CCSS Recognize and read grade-appropriate irregularly spelled words. **RF.1.3g**

CCSS Spell untaught words phonetically, drawing on phonemic awareness and spelling conventions. **L.1.2e**

Words with End Blends

Dictation Use the Spelling Dictation routine to help children transfer their knowledge of sound-spellings to writing. Follow the Dictation routine.

Pretest After dictation, pronounce each spelling word. Read the sentence and pronounce the word again. Ask children to say each word softly, stretching the sounds, before writing it. After the pretest, display the spelling words and write each word as you say the letter names. Have children check their words.

lend	Can you **lend** me your pencil?
send	I will **send** the letter tomorrow.
fast	**Fast** is the opposite of slow.
past	He stayed up **past** his bedtime.
sink	We put the dirty dishes in the **sink**.
wink	I'll **wink** my eye if I know the answer.
run	If I **run** to school I won't be late.
bug	A fly is one kind of **bug**.
of	My house is made **of** brick.
who	**Who** is sitting next to you?

For Approaching Level and Beyond Level children, refer to the Differentiated Spelling Lists for modified word lists.

Go Digital

Spelling Word Routine

they	together
how	eat

High-Frequency Word Routine

ENGLISH LANGUAGE LEARNERS

Pantomime Review the meanings of these words by using pictures, pantomime, or gestures when possible. Have children repeat or act out the word.

MINILESSON 5 Mins

High-Frequency Words

eat, no, of, under, who

1 Model Display the **High-Frequency Word Cards** *eat, no, of, under,* and *who*. Use the Read/Spell/Write routine to teach each word.

→ **Read** Point to and say the word *eat. This is the word* eat. *Say it with me:* eat. *We will eat sandwiches for lunch.*

→ **Spell** *The word eat is spelled* e-a-t. *Spell it with me.*

→ **Write** *Let's write the word in the air as we say each letter:* e-a-t.

→ Follow the same steps to introduce *no, of, under,* and *who.*

→ As children spell each word with you, point out the irregularities in sound-spellings, such as the /u/ sound spelled *o* in the word *of.*

→ Have partners create sentences using each word.

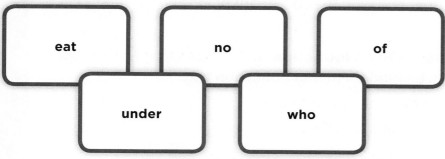

High-Frequency Word Cards

2 Guided Practice Have children read the sentences. Prompt them to identify the high-frequency words in connected text and to blend the decodable words.

1. What do you like to **eat**?

2. **No**, you can not go.

3. The trunk has lots **of** stuff in it.

4. The dog hid **under** the bed.

5. **Who** is it?

Monitor and *Differentiate*

 **Quick Check**

Can children read and decode words with ending consonant blends?

Can children recognize and read high-frequency words?

↓

Small Group Instruction

If No →	Approaching	Reteach pp. T212–215
	ELL	Develop pp. T226–233
If Yes →	On Level	Review pp. T220–221
	Beyond Level	Extend pp. T224–225

→ Shared Read

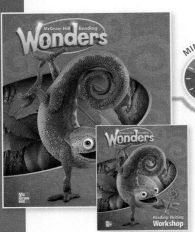

**Reading/Writing
Workshop Big Book
and Reading/Writing
Workshop**

OBJECTIVES

 Decode regularly
spelled one-syllable
words. **RF.1.3b**

 Recognize and read
grade-appropriate
irregularly spelled
words. **RF.1.3g**

Understand
nonfiction genre

**ACADEMIC
LANGUAGE**

• *nonfiction,
information, reread*

• Cognates: *no ficción,
información*

 MINILESSON 10 Mins

Read *The Best Spot*

Model Skills and Strategies

Tell children that you will now read a selection called *The Best Spot. As
we read, look for the words* eat, no, of, under, *and* who. *Look for words that
end with the consonant blends* nd, nk, nt, st, sk, *and* mp.

Story Words Display the words *forest, animals, deer, rabbit,* and *wasp*.
Spell the words and model reading them. Review word meanings
as needed. Tell children that they will be reading these words in the
selection.

Guide children in reading *The Best Spot*. Point out the high-frequency
words and words that end with the consonant blends *nd, nk, nt, st, sk,*
and *mp*.

Genre: Informational Text/Nonfiction Tell children that *The Best Spot*
is a nonfiction text. Remind them that nonfiction text:

→ tells about real people, places, or things.

→ tells information about a specific topic.

→ gives information and facts.

Connect to Concept

ESSENTIAL QUESTION

Read together the Essential Question on page 54 of the Reading/Writing
Workshop. Discuss how the habitats in the selection are alike and
different. Prompt children to share observations they made about the
animals in the selection. Guide children to connect what they have read
to the Essential Question. *Where do these animals live?*

**Go
Digital**

The Best Spot

The Best Spot

READING/WRITING WORKSHOP, pp. 54–63

Lexile 160

Partner Reading

Have partners use their Reading/Writing Workshop to review the skills and strategies.

→ Remind children that as they reread *The Best Spot* they can go back and reread parts of the text they did not understand the first time or want to remember better.

→ Have children use pages 50–51 to review high-frequency words *eat, no, of, under, who.*

→ Have children use pages 52–53 to review the consonant blends *nd, nk, nt, st, sk,* and *mp.* Guide them to blend the sounds to read the words.

→ Have children reread *The Best Spot* with a partner. Guide them to apply the skills and strategies. Ask children to name features of the selection that tell them that it is nonfiction.

→ # Language Arts

Go Digital

Graphic Organizer

Writing

I see a fish.

Grammar

MINILESSON 5 Mins

Shared Writing

OBJECTIVES

 Write informative/explanatory texts in which they name a topic, supply some facts about the topic, and provide some sense of closure. **W.1.2**

 Use common, proper, and possessive nouns. **L.1.1b**

ACADEMIC LANGUAGE
• *main idea, nonfiction, possessive*
• Cognate: *posesivo*

Writing Trait: Ideas

1 Model Tell children that they will now reread *The Best Spot*, paying attention to the main topic of the selection. Say: *An author writes about one idea, or topic. All the details the writer includes explain information about the topic.*

2 Guided Practice/Practice Reread *The Best Spot*. Point out the main topic. Ask: *What is the main topic, or what is the selection about?*

→ Prompt children to understand that the author first states the main topic. Then the author writes sentences that explain information about the animals that live in the forest.

Sentences That Explain

Focus and Plan Tell children that this week they will be writing sentences that explain facts about a place animals live together. Explain that the sentences will be nonfiction, which means they will give true information.

 Brainstorm Use the Word Web on Teaching Poster 40 to help children organize information about animals that live together in the forest. Say: *The main topic is animals that live together in the forest. Let's write that in the big circle of our web. What are some details we read about?* Record children's ideas on the web.

Write Tell children that you will work together to write nonfiction sentences that explain facts about animals that live together in the forest. Model writing sentences based on the Word Web. Say: *Let's start by telling the main topic. Let's write:* Animals live together in the forest. *Next let's write sentences that explain facts about the animals. Let's write:* Rabbits live in the forest.

Work together to write sentences that explain.

Grammar

MINILESSON 5 Mins

Possessive Nouns

1 Model Tell children that writers use an apostrophe and the letter *s* at the end of many nouns to say that someone or something owns something. Display the following sentences:

> Meg's dog is wet!
>
> The dog's bed is red.

Explain that *Meg's* and *dog's* are possessive nouns. In the first sentence the dog belongs to Meg. In the second sentence the bed belongs to the dog.

2 Guided Practice/Practice Display the sentences below and read them aloud. Prompt children to chorally reread them with you. Have children work with a partner to circle the possessive noun in each sentence. Then have them underline what item is owned.

> The hen's eggs are in the nest. (hen's; eggs)
>
> The duck's bill is wet. (duck's; bill)

Talk About It Have partners work together to orally generate sentences with possessive nouns while talking about features of the animals they have read about.

Mechanics: Apostrophe with Possessive Nouns

1 Model Explain to children that writers use an apostrophe followed by the letter *s* to form a possessive noun.

2 Guided Practice Prompt children to correct the possessive noun in each sentence.

> This is Dons' pet. (Don's)
>
> The cubs mom is in the den. (cub's)

ELL

ENGLISH LANGUAGE LEARNERS SCAFFOLD

Beginning

Demonstrate Comprehension Explain that writers add apostrophe *s* to show ownership. Read the first Model Sentence. *Show me the possessive noun. Yes, Meg's. The dog belongs to Meg.* Repeat with the second sentence. Allow time to respond.

Intermediate

Explain Ask children to circle the possessive nouns in the Practice examples. *How do you know it is possessive? What belongs to _____?* Correct responses as needed.

Advanced/Advanced High

Expand Display the Practice sentences. Have children find the plural noun in the Practice sentences. *How can you tell the difference between a possessive noun and a plural noun?*

Daily Wrap Up

→ Review the Essential Question and encourage children to discuss using the new oral vocabulary words. Ask: *What did you learn about how animals live together in a forest habitat?*

→ Prompt children to share what skills they learned. *How might they use those skills?*

Materials

Reading/Writing Workshop
VOLUME 2

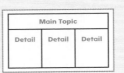

Reading/Writing Workshop Big Book
UNIT 2

Visual Vocabulary Cards

depend
habitat
hibernate
tolerate
tranquil

Main Topic		
Detail	Detail	Detail

Teaching Poster

eat

High-Frequency Word Cards
eat no of under who

a b c

Word-Building Cards

lend

Spelling Word Cards

Interactive Read-Aloud Cards

→ # Build the Concept

MINILESSON
5 Mins

Oral Language

OBJECTIVES

Ask and answer questions about key details in a text read aloud or information presented orally or through other media. **SL.1.2**

• Develop oral language

• Discuss the Essential Question

ACADEMIC LANGUAGE

• *communities, reread, detail*

• Cognates: *comunidades, detalle*

ESSENTIAL QUESTION

Remind children that this week you have been talking and reading about communities in nature. Remind them of the penguins and their rocky habitat and all the animals in the forest. Guide children to discuss the Essential Question using information from what they read and talked about on Day 1.

Oral Vocabulary Words

Review the oral vocabulary words *habitat* and *depend* from Day 1. Use the Define/Example/Ask routine to introduce the oral vocabulary words *hibernate, tranquil,* and *tolerate.* Prompt children to use the words as they discuss where animals live.

Oral Vocabulary Routine

Define: To **hibernate** is to spend the winter sleeping in a shelter.

Example: The bear wants to hibernate in a warm cave through the long winter.

Ask: Where might be a good place for an animal to hibernate?

Define: **Tranquil** means "calm and peaceful."

Example: The family spent a tranquil day by the lake.

Ask: What is your favorite tranquil place?

Define: **Tolerate** means "put up with something unpleasant."

Example: The hardy oak tree can tolerate the harsh winter.

Ask: Can you tolerate loud music? Can you tolerate itchy clothes? Why or why not?

Visual Vocabulary Cards

Go Digital

school

Visual Glossary

"Animals in the Desert"

Listening Comprehension

MINILESSON
5 Mins

Read the Interactive Read Aloud

ENGLISH LANGUAGE LEARNERS

Directionality Ask children to point to where you start reading. (top left) Ask where you finish reading on the card. (bottom right)

Strategy: Reread

Remind children that as they read, they can go back and reread parts of a selection that they did not understand. They can also reread to help them remember important information. Model using the Think Aloud Cloud.

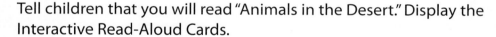

"Animals in the Desert"

Think Aloud As I read, I will check that I understood the important details. If I am not sure, I will reread a sentence or two. This will help me to be sure that I understand and can remember all of the important details.

Tell children that you will read "Animals in the Desert." Display the Interactive Read-Aloud Cards.

→ Pause to model rereading to check your comprehension. Prompt children to check if they understand what you have read. If they are not sure, reread the section and guide them to listen carefully for the important details.

Make Connections

COLLABORATE

Guide partners to discuss what they learned about animals living together in the desert habitat. Prompt children to share how rereading helped them to better understand the selection. Ask: *What observations did you make about the animals as you listened to the words and looked at the pictures? How are the animals in the desert like the animals in* The Best Spot?

(t) Richard Cummins/Corbis; (r) Royalty-Free/Corbis; (l) altrendo nature/Altrendo/Getty Images; (c) GOODSHOOT/Alamy

Word Work

Quick Review

Build Fluency: Sound-Spellings
Display the **Word-Building Cards:** *nd, nk, nt, st, sk, mp, u, e, ea, sp, sn, sl, cr, fr, tr, o, pl, fl, cl, bl, i, a, s, r, l, t*. Have children say the sounds. Repeat, and vary the pace.

MINILESSON 5 Mins

Phonemic Awareness

Go Digital

Phoneme Blending

OBJECTIVES

CCSS Orally produce single-syllable words by blending sounds (phonemes), including consonant blends. **RF.1.2b**

CCSS Decode regularly spelled one-syllable words. **RF.1.3b**

CCSS Read words with inflectional endings. **RF.1.3f**

1 Model Show children how to blend phonemes. *Listen as I say the sounds in a word*: /b/ /e/ /s/ /t/. *Now I will blend the sounds together and say the word*: /beeest/, *best*. *Let's say the word together*: best.

2 Guided Practice/Practice Have children practice blending sounds to form words. *I am going to say some words sound by sound*. Blend the sounds together to say the word.

/s/ /a/ /n/ /d/   /j/ /u/ /n/ /k/   /m/ /i/ /n/ /t/
/a/ /s/ /k/   /p/ /a/ /s/ /t/   /l/ /a/ /m/ /p/

Phonemic Awareness

MINILESSON 5 Mins

Phonics

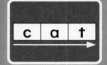

Phonics

Review End Blends

1 Model Display **Word-Building Cards** *s* and *k*. Review the sounds /sk/ spelled *sk* using the words *mask* and *disk*. Repeat for other ending consonant blends: *nd, nk, nt, st,* and *mp*.

2 Guided Practice/Practice Have children practice connecting the letters and sounds. Point to the Word-Building Cards. *What are these letters? What sounds do they stand for?*

Structural Analysis

Handwriting

Blend Words with End Blends

1 Model Display **Word-Building Cards** *l, a, m, p* to form the word *lamp*. Model how to generate and blend the sounds to say the word. *This is the letter* l. *It stands for /l/. This is the letter* a. *It stands for /a/. This is the letter* m *and this is the letter* p. *Together they stand for the sounds /mp/. Listen as I blend these sounds together*: /llllaaamp/. *Say it with me*: lamp.

Continue by modeling the words *pond, last, blank, mint,* and *desk*.

2 Guided Practice/Practice Repeat the routine with children with *fast, bend, junk, hint, task, ramp, blast, clump, grunt, stand*.

Build Words with End Blends

1 Model Display the Word-Building Cards *p, e, s, t*. Blend: /p/ /e/ /s/ /t/, /peeest/, *pest*.

→ Replace *e* with *a* and repeat with *past*.

→ Change *p* to *l* and repeat with *last*.

2 Guided Practice/Practice Continue with *land, lend, lent, sent, send, sand, sad, had, hand, band, brand, land, last, fast, fat, fit, fist, mist, mink, pink*. Guide children to build and blend each word.

MINILESSON
5 Mins

Structural Analysis

Inflectional Ending *-ing*

1 Model Write and read aloud *bend* and *bending*. Underline the *-ing*. Tell children that adding *-ing* to an action word makes it tell about something that is happening now. *Can I bend?* Bend as you say, *I am bending*.

Remind children that every word has beats, or syllables. Explain that each syllable in a word has one vowel sound. Say the word *bend* and have children tell how many syllables they hear. Then say *bending*, and have children clap the syllables. Point out that adding *-ing* to *bend* adds a syllable.

2 Guided Practice/Practice Write the following words on the board: *jump, yell, hunt, rest, ask, bump, spell*. Have children add *-ing* to each word and then use each word in a sentence.

ELL

ENGLISH LANGUAGE LEARNERS

Build Vocabulary Review the meanings of example words that can be explained or demonstrated in a concrete way. For example, ask several children to *stand* in line and point to the *last* one in line. Model the action for *bend*, saying, *"I can bend and touch the floor."* and have children repeat. Provide sentence frames such as *"A _____ is fast."* for children to complete. Correct grammar and pronunciation as needed.

→ # Word Work

⏱ 5 Mins — MINILESSON
Spelling

OBJECTIVES

CCSS Recognize and read grade-appropriate irregularly spelled words. **RF.1.3g**

CCSS Use conventional spelling for words with common spelling patterns and for frequently occurring irregular words. **L.1.2d**

Word Sort with *-end, -ast, -ink*

1 Model Display the **Spelling Word Cards** from the Teacher's Resource Book, one at a time. Have children read each word, listening for the ending consonant blend sounds.

Use cards for *bend, last,* and *pink* to create a three-column chart. Say each word and pronounce the sounds: /b/ /e/ /n/ /d/; /l/ /a/ /s/ /t/; /p/ /i/ /n/ /k/. Say each word again, emphasizing the vowel and ending consonant blend sounds. Ask children to chorally spell each word.

2 Guided Practice/Practice Have children place each Spelling Word Card in the column with the words containing the same ending consonant blend sounds and spellings.

When completed, have children chorally read the words in each column. Then call out a word. Have a child find the word card and point to it as the class chorally spells the word.

ANALYZE ERRORS/ARTICULATION SUPPORT

Use children's pretest errors to analyze spelling problems and provide corrective feedback. For example, some children will leave off one of the letters in a final blend.

Distribute **Response Boards** to children. Clearly pronounce one of the spelling words, emphasizing the final blend. Have children repeat.

Guide children to segment the word, placing one counter onto each box for each sound in the word. Then help children replace each counter with a letter. Continue with the rest of the spelling words.

Go Digital

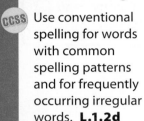

er	ir	or	ur
her			
girl curb			word

Spelling Word Sort

they	together
how	eat

High-Frequency Word Routine

ELL
ENGLISH LANGUAGE LEARNERS

Provide Clues Practice spelling by helping children generate more words with *-end, -ast,* and *-ink* patterns. Provide clues: *Think of a word that starts with* p *and rhymes with* sink. Write the word and have children practice reading it. Correct their pronunciation if needed.

High-Frequency Words

eat, no, of, under, who

1 Guided Practice Say each word and have children Read/Spell/Write it. Ask children to close their eyes, picture the word in their minds, and write it the way they see it. Display the high-frequency words for children to self-correct.

→ Point out irregularities in sound-spellings, such as the /h/ sound spelled *wh* in *who*.

2 Practice Add the high-frequency words *eat, no, of, under,* and *who* to the cumulative word bank.

→ Have children work with a partner to create sentences using the words.

→ Have children look at the words and compare their sounds and spellings to words from previous weeks.

→ Suggest that they write about animals and where they live.

Cumulative Review Review last week's words using the Read/Spell/Write routine.

→ Repeat the above routine, mixing the words and having children chorally say each one.

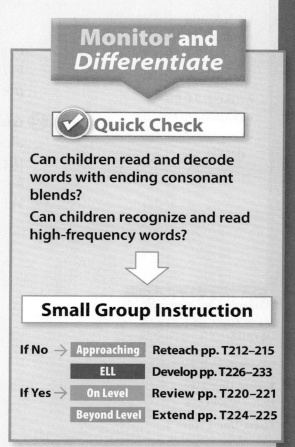

Comprehension CLOSE READING

**Reading/Writing
Workshop Big Book
and Reading/Writing
Workshop**

OBJECTIVES

CCSS Identify the main
topic and retell
key details of a
text. **RI.1.2**

Understand
nonfiction genre

**ACADEMIC
LANGUAGE**

• *diagram, detail, topic*

• Cognates: *diagrama,
detalle*

MINILESSON 10 Mins Reread *The Best Spot*

Genre: Informational Text/Nonfiction

❶ **Model** Tell children they will now reread the informational selection
The Best Spot. Explain that as they read they will look for information
in the text to help them understand the selection.

Review the characteristics of informational nonfiction text. It:

→ tells information and facts about real people, places, or things.

→ presents information about a specific topic.

→ can present information in different text features, such as
diagrams.

Tell children that informational nonfiction selections provide facts
and details. Explain that they sometimes have diagrams. *Diagrams
are pictures that show the parts of something. They have labels that
name the parts and help us to locate information.*

Display page 61 of *The Best Spot.* Say: *I can see a diagram of an ant
colony. Each label names a part of the colony or tells what is happening
in the colony. I can use this diagram to locate the names of the parts of
the colony.*

❷ **Guided Practice/Practice** Point out the label *Food* and read it
aloud. Say: *This label tells me important information about this part of
the ant colony. It tells me that this room of the colony is where the ants
keep food. This is an important detail.* Point out the label *Eggs* and ask:
What do we learn from this part of the diagram?

**Go
Digital**

The Best Spot

Genre

**Main Topic and
Key Details**

SKILLS TRACE

**MAIN TOPIC AND KEY
DETAILS**

Introduce Unit 2 Week 3

Review Unit 2 Week 5;
Unit 3 Weeks 4, 5

Assess Unit 2 Week 3

Skill: Main Topic and Key Details

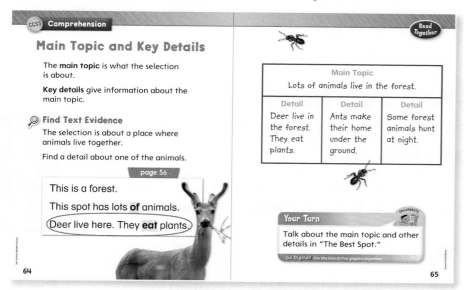

Reading/Writing Workshop, pp. 64–65

ON-LEVEL PRACTICE BOOK p. 77

A. Reread "Big Rock Pond." Write the main topic to tell what it is about. Write the key details to tell more about the topic. Use the sentences from the box.

> Bugs buzz.
> Frogs jump.
> Things live at the pond.
> Bats spin.

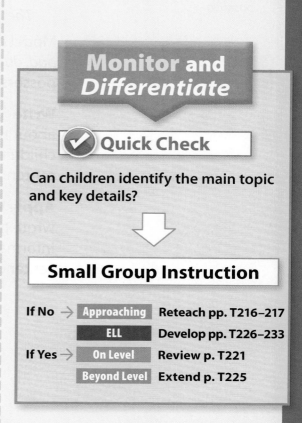

Topic:

_____
Things live at the pond.
_____

Key Detail: Bugs buzz.
_____

Key Detail: Frogs jump.
_____

Key Detail: Bats spin.
_____

APPROACHING p. 77	BEYOND p. 77	ELL p. 77

1 Model Tell children that when they read informational nonfiction they can use the text to find the main topic and key details. Have children look at pages 64–65 in their Reading/Writing Workshop. Read together the definition of Main Topic and Key Details. *The main topic is what the selection is about. Key details give information about the main topic.*

2 Guided Practice/Practice Read together the Find Text Evidence section and model finding the main topic and a key detail in the selection *The Best Spot*. Point out the main topic and key detail added to the graphic organizer. *The main topic of this selection is the many animals who live together in the forest. On page 56 we can find a detail in the text about deer. The text says this is a forest. It says that deer live there and that they eat plants. This is a key detail. It gives information about the main topic of the selection. What key detail can you find about ants?*

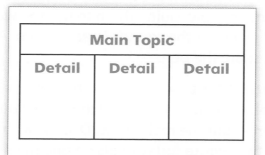

Teaching Poster

Monitor and *Differentiate*

✓ **Quick Check**

Can children identify the main topic and key details?

↓

Small Group Instruction

If No → **Approaching** Reteach pp. T216–217
ELL Develop pp. T226–233
If Yes → **On Level** Review p. T221
Beyond Level Extend p. T225

→ Language Arts

MINILESSON
5 Mins

Interactive Writing

OBJECTIVES

CCSS Write informative/explanatory texts in which they name a topic, supply some facts about the topic, and provide some sense of closure. **W.1.2**

CCSS Use common, proper, and possessive nouns. **L.1.1b**

ACADEMIC LANGUAGE

• *main idea, explain, possessive*

• Cognates: *explicar, posesivo*

Writing Trait: Ideas

Review Tell children that writers tell about one main topic. They include sentences that explain information about the main topic.

Sentences That Explain

Discuss Guide children to think of different places animals live together, such as a pond, that they can use as a main topic to write sentences. Record their ideas on a blank Word Web using Teaching Poster 40.

Model/Apply Grammar Tell children that they will be working together to write sentences that explain the chosen topic. Remind them that they can include possessive nouns to show that an animal has something.

→ Write the sentence starter:

   The _____ _____ is in the pond.

Model how to choose different phrases with possessive nouns (*frog's pad, duck's nest*) to complete this sentence. Model adding *'s* to form a possessive noun.

Write Collaborate with children to write sentences that explain facts about the main topic. Guide them to use the web to get details. Remind children to listen for the sounds in each word. As children create sentences, share the pen.

Apply Writing Trait Review with children the sentences that you wrote together on Day 1. Remind them how the sentences explain information about the main topic. Discuss with children how the sentences they wrote today focus on one main topic.

Go Digital

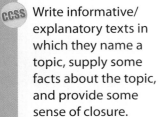

Graphic Organizer

Writing

I see a fish.

Grammar

Grammar

5 Mins

Possessive Nouns

1 Review Remind children that writers use a possessive noun to say that someone or something owns something. To form a possessive noun, the writer adds an apostrophe and the letter *s*.

→ Write the following sentences:

Nell's pig Pat lives in a pen. (Nell's; pig)

The pig's pen has lots of mud. (pig's; pen)

Read the sentences aloud and have children chorally repeat. Guide children to circle the possessive noun in each sentence and identify what the person or animal owns.

2 Guided Practice Write sample sentences. Read each sentence. Have children work in pairs to identify each possessive noun and what is owned.

The kid's tent is up. (kid's; tent)

Ken's dog spots a frog. (Ken's; dog)

3 Practice Have partners write a sentence about each other using a possessive. *My friend's hair is brown. This is Dan's lunch.*

Talk About It Have partners work together to orally generate more sentences with possessive nouns that tell about each other.

Mechanics: Apostrophe with Possessive Nouns

1 Review Remind children that to form a possessive, they should add apostrophe *s* to a noun to show someone or something owns something.

2 Practice Display sentences with incorrect possessive nouns. Read the sentences aloud. Have children work together to fix them.

The schools bricks are red. (school's)

The foxs' kit likes to play. (fox's)

The crabs legs can move fast! (crab's)

ENGLISH LANGUAGE LEARNERS

Explain Read aloud the first Review sentence. Have children circle the possessive noun. Then have them underline the noun that tells what is owned. Have them complete the sentence frame: _____ *belongs to* _____. Clarify children's responses as needed by providing vocabulary.

Use Non-Verbal Cues Write an apostrophe and an *s* on two index cards. Display the first sentence from the Mechanics Practice activity, omitting the final *s* in *schools*: *The school bricks are red.* Have children use the index cards to correct the possessive noun in the sentence. Repeat with the other two sentences.

Daily Wrap Up

→ Discuss the Essential Question and encourage children to use the oral vocabulary words. Ask: *What are some places where animals live together?*

→ Prompt children to review and discuss the skills they used today by asking: *How will the skills you learned today help you?*

Materials

Reading/Writing Workshop
VOLUME 2

Literature Anthology
VOLUME 2

Literature Big Book
Babies in the Bayou

Visual Vocabulary Cards

depend	of
eat	tranquil
habitat	tolerate
hibernate	under
no	who

Teaching Poster

Main Topic

Detail	Detail	Detail

a b c

Word-Building Cards

lend

Spelling Word Cards

(→) # Build the Concept

Go Digital

MINILESSON 5 Mins

Oral Language

ESSENTIAL QUESTION

Remind children that this week you have been talking and reading about animal communities. Remind them of the babies in the bayou, the creatures in the woodland area, and the different habitats they read about. Guide children to discuss the question using information from what they have read and talked about throughout the week.

Review Oral Vocabulary

Review the oral vocabulary words *depend, habitat, hibernate, tranquil,* and *tolerate* using the Define/Example/Ask routine. Encourage children to discuss animal communities when coming up with examples for each word.

Visual Vocabulary Cards

OBJECTIVES

 Identify the main topic and retell key details of a text. **RI.1.2**

 Read grade-level text orally with accuracy, appropriate rate, and expression. **RF.1.4b**

Reread text

ACADEMIC LANGUAGE
• *rhythm, repeated*
• Cognate: *ritmo*

Visual Glossary

Babies in the Bayou

Retell

Listening Comprehension

CLOSE READING

MINILESSON 10 Mins

Reread Literature Big Book

Strategy: Reread

Remind children that as they read, they can go back and reread parts they did not understand. This can help them better understand and remember the facts and details in the text. *As we read* Babies in the Bayou, *we can stop and reread sentences that are not clear to us or we want to remember better.*

Read aloud *Babies in the Bayou.* Pause to model rereading. Encourage children to say which details they had trouble understanding and find evidence in the text and illustrations to aid them as you model rereading.

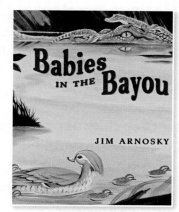

Literature Big Book

Model Retelling

Pause to retell portions of the selection. *I can use my own words to explain the facts and details I have read. So far, I have read the bayou is a place with shallow water and mossy trees. There are birds that walk in the water.*

→ After reading, model retelling the entire selection, using your own words to tell the important facts and details in the correct order.

Model Fluency

Phrasing Turn to page 8 of *Babies in the Bayou.* Read the first line and explain that these words are repeated throughout the text. *When you read repeated words, you can read them with rhythm.*

→ Read aloud pages 12 through 17 with slightly exaggerated rhythm on the phrase *there are babies in the bayou.* Have children identify the repeated words. Repeat the reading to give children more practice with appropriate phrasing.

ELL

ENGLISH LANGUAGE LEARNERS

Retell Guide children to retell by using a question prompt on each page. *What do the baby alligators look like?* Provide sentence starters for children to complete orally. *The baby alligators have black and yellow ____ and sharp white ____.*

A C T

Access Complex Text

If the complexity of the text makes it hard for children to read, use the Access Complex Text prompts.

Purpose Children may not grasp the true informational purpose of the text because it uses imagery and poetic language to present scientific facts.

→ Help children identify the facts presented in the text.

Organization The text lacks a strong organizational pattern.

→ Help children to see how the text moves from one animal to the next; for example, the author mentions raccoons eating turtle eggs and then gives facts and details about turtles.

→ # Word Work

Quick Review
Build Fluency: Sound-Spellings
Display the **Word-Building Cards:** *nd, nk, nt, st, sk, mp, u, e, ea, sp, sn, sl, cr, fr, tr, o, pl, fl, cl, bl, i, a, s, r, l, t.*
Have children say the sounds.

MINILESSON 5 Mins

Phonemic Awareness

OBJECTIVES

CCSS Isolate and pronounce initial, medial vowel, and final sounds (phonemes) in spoken single-syllable words. **RF.1.2c**

CCSS Decode regularly spelled one-syllable words. **RF.1.3b**

CCSS Read words with inflectional endings. **RF.1.3f**

Phoneme Substitution

❶ **Model** Show children how to orally substitute sounds. *I am going to say a word: /b/ /a/ /n/ /d/,* band. *Now I will change a sound to make a new word. Change the /a/ to /e/. The vowel sound of the new word is /e/. The new word is /b/ /e/ /n/ /d/,* bend.

❷ **Guided Practice/Practice** Have children practice substituting sounds with these examples. Say the first word in each pair and the sound substitution. Do the first row with children. *Listen to each word I say. Then we will change a sound to make a new word.*

tank/sank	hint/tint	lost/cost
hunt/hunk	limp/lamp	send/sent
band/sand	past/pest	blend/blonde

MINILESSON 5 Mins

Phonics

Blend Words with End Blends

❶ **Model** Display **Word-Building Cards** *s, t, u, m, p.* Model how to blend the sounds. These are the letters *s* and *t.* They stand for the sounds /st/. This is the letter *u.* It stands for /u/. These are the letters *m* and *p.* They stand for the sounds /mp/. *Let's blend these sounds:* /stuuump/. *The word is* stump.

Continue by modeling the words *end, sunk,* and *drink.*

❷ **Guided Practice/Practice** Review the words and sentences on the Day 3 Phonics Practice Activity with children. Read each word in the first row, blending the sounds, for example: /r/ /e/ /s/ /t/; /rrreeest/. *The word is* rest.

→ Have children blend each word with you. Prompt children to read the connected text, sounding out the decodable words.

Go Digital

Phonemic Awareness

Phonics

Structural Analysis

Handwriting

rest pond jump ant and land

rent dusk brand disk bank past

hunting bending printing jumping

drinking planting asking standing

sweated buzzed stuffed it's

Ask Gus to dust the lamp.

Fix the tent and we can go camping.

Also online

Day 3 Phonics Practice Activity

MINILESSON
5 Mins

Structural Analysis

Inflectional Ending *-ing*

❶ **Model** Say the words *jump* and *jumping*. Ask children to listen closely to hear what is different. Point out the *-ing* ending in *jumping*.

→ Write the words *jump* and *jumping*. Underline the letters *-ing* in *jumping*. Tell children that the letters *-ing* at the end of *jumping* mean that the action is taking place now. *I am jumping.*

❷ **Practice/Apply** Help children blend the words *blink, blinking, mend, mending, bust, busting, plant, planting, camp,* and *camping*. Remind children that each syllable in a word has a vowel sound. *Adding the letters* -ing *at the end of a word adds a syllable.*

Corrective Feedback

Corrective Feedback Say: *My turn.* Model blending the word using the appropriate signaling procedures. Then lead children in blending the sounds. Say: *Do it with me.* You will respond with children to offer support. Then say: *Your turn. Blend.* Have children chorally blend. Return to the beginning of the word. Say: *Let's start over.*

 **Word Work**

Quick Review

High-Frequency Words: Read, Spell, and Write to review this week's high-frequency words: *eat, no, of, under, who.*

MINILESSON **5** Mins

Spelling

OBJECTIVES

CCSS Recognize and read grade-appropriate irregularly spelled words. **RF.1.3g**

CCSS Use conventional spelling for words with common spelling patterns and for frequently occurring irregular words. **L.1.2d**

-end, -ast, -ink Word Families

❶ **Model** Display index cards for *-end, -ast, -ink* and form three columns in a pocket chart. Blend the sounds with children.

Hold up the *lend* **Spelling Word Card**. Say and spell it. Pronounce each sound clearly: /l/ /e/ /n/ /d/. Blend the sounds, emphasizing the ending consonant blend: /leeend/. Repeat this step with *send*. Place both words below the *-end* card. Read and spell each spelling word together with children. Have children read each word. *What do you notice about these spelling words? They rhyme because they both end with the /end/ sounds spelled* e-n-d.

❷ **Guided Practice/Practice** Have children spell each word. Repeat the process with the *-ast* and *-ink* words.

Display the words *run, bug, of,* and *who* in a separate column. Read and spell the words together with children. Point out that these spelling words do not end with *-end, -ast,* or *-ink*.

Conclude by asking children to orally generate additional words that rhyme with each word. Write the additional words on the board. Underline the common spelling patterns in the additional words. If necessary, point out the differences and explain why they are unusual.

PHONICS/SPELLING PRACTICE BOOK p. 38

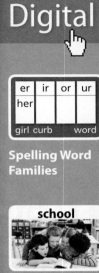

Go
Digital

er	ir	or	ur
her			
girl	curb		word

Spelling Word Families

school

Visual Glossary

lend	send	fast	past
sink	wink	of	who

A. Write the spelling words that have the spelling pattern.

nk 1. ___sink___ 2. ___wink___

nd 3. ___lend___ 4. ___send___

st 5. ___fast___ 6. ___past___

In 1–6, order of words may vary.

B. Write the two spelling words that rhyme with each of these words.

7. bend ___send___ ___lend___

8. pink ___sink___ ___wink___

In 7–8, order of words may vary.

High-Frequency Words

eat, no, of, under, who

❶ Guided Practice Say each word and have children Read/
Spell/Write it. As children spell each word with you, point out
irregularities in sound-spellings, such as /v/ spelled *f* in *of*.

→ Display the **Visual Vocabulary Cards** to review this week's
high-frequency words.

Visual Vocabulary Cards

❷ Practice Repeat the activity with last week's words.

Build Fluency: Word Automaticity

Have children read the following sentences together at the same
pace. Repeat several times.

> A frog can eat a lot of bugs.
>
> Who is under the mask?
>
> No, I do not like it.

Word Bank

Review the current and previous words in the word bank. Discuss
with children which words should be removed, or added back, from
previous high-frequency word lists. Remind children that the word
bank should change as the class needs it to.

Monitor and *Differentiate*

✅ **Quick Check**

Can children read and decode
words with ending consonant
blends?

Can children recognize and read
high-frequency words?

Small Group Instruction

If No → **Approaching** Reteach pp. T212–215

ELL Develop pp. T226–233

If Yes → **On Level** Review pp. T220–221

Beyond Level Extend pp. T224–225

CCSS **Genre** Nonfiction

Essential Question
Where do animals live together?
Read about animals that live at a pond.

Go Digital!

At a Pond
by Nancy Finton

48

49

LITERATURE ANTHOLOGY, pp. 48–49

Literature Anthology

Develop Comprehension   CLOSE READING

Lexile 190

Read Literature Anthology

Review Genre: Informational Text/Nonfiction Review with children the key characteristics of nonfiction:

→ Provides facts and details about real people, places, events, or things.

→ Presents information about a specific topic.

Preview and Predict Read the title on page 49 and look at the picture. *What might this selection be about? What might we learn as we read? Let's find out.*

ESSENTIAL QUESTION
Read aloud the Essential Question: *Where do animals live together?* Tell children that as they read they should think about the types of animals that live together at a pond.

Story Words Read and spell the words *water, turtle,* and *dragonfly.* Review the meaning of each word. Tell children that they will read these words in the selection.

 Analytical Writing **Note Taking: Graphic Organizer** As children read the selection, guide them to fill in the graphic organizer on **Your Turn Practice Book** page 74 as you model recording the main topic and the key details of each section.

Who lives at a pond? ❶

50

Who is **under** the water? ❷
Who is on the land?
Who can fly to the pond?
Let's see!

51

LITERATURE ANTHOLOGY, pp. 50–51

❶ **Strategy: Reread**

Teacher Think Aloud I know it's important to understand what a selection is about right from the beginning. I'm going to reread the first two pages to make sure I know what this selection is about. Now that I have checked my understanding, I know that this selection is about animals that live in a pond. Not only that, it's about animals under the water in the pond, animals on the land around the pond, and animals that are flying in the air above the pond.

❷ **Skill: Main Topic and Key Details**

Teacher Think Aloud Remember, the main topic is what the selection is all about: animals that live at a pond. Let's add this information to our chart.

Main Topic: Animals at a pond		
Detail	Detail	Detail

3 Frogs live at a pond.
They swim and hop and jump.
Frogs rest on plants on the pond.

52

This frog is hunting for bugs.
It sees a bug.
Will it get a snack?
It has to be quick! Yum, yum!

53

LITERATURE ANTHOLOGY, pp. 52–53

Develop Comprehension CLOSE READING

❸ Ask and Answer Questions

Teacher Think Aloud We can check our understanding as we read by asking questions. We can ask: *What do frogs do at the pond?* We can use the text and photographs to find the answer. On page 52, we read that frogs swim, hop, jump, and rest on plants. We can ask: *What do frogs eat?* On page 53 we read they eat bugs.

❹ Maintain Skill: Key Details

Remember, photographs in informational text can show key details that help you to better understand the text. With a partner, look at the photographs on pages 52 and 53. What key details do you learn from these photographs?

SCIENCE CONNECT TO CONTENT
HABITATS AND ORGANISMS

Point out that this selection is about one environment and the animals that live there. Explain that the pond is a habitat for many animals. Prompt children to name some of the animals that live at the pond. Guide children to recall other environments they have read about (the bayou, the forest, and the desert) and the animals that live in each.

STEM

5 Ducks come to the pond.
They **eat** lots **of** bugs and plants.
This duck dips its bill to get bugs.
Dip, dip, dip!

54

Ducks make nests on land. **6**
They use twigs and grass.
Who is in the eggs?
Quack, quack, quack! **7**

55

LITERATURE ANTHOLOGY, pp. 54–55

5 ## Strategy: Reread

Teacher Think Aloud I will stop to make sure I understand what I have just read. I realize I don't understand whether ducks live in the water or on the land. I will reread these pages to find the information I may have missed. Now I understand that they do some things in the water and some things on land. I can also tell from the photo that they do some things in the air. They fly!

6 ## Author's Craft: Sentence Structure

Instead of stating a fact, the author chose to ask a question: *Who is in the eggs?* Does she give us the answer? (No, but she gives us a clue.)

7 ## Skill: Main Topic and Key Details

Let's review the text on pages 52 to 55. What key details did we learn about frogs and ducks? Let's add this information to the Main Topic and Details chart.

Main Topic: Animals at a pond		
Detail Frogs swim, hop, jump, rest on plants, eat bugs	**Detail** Ducks eat bugs and plants, make nests on land	**Detail**

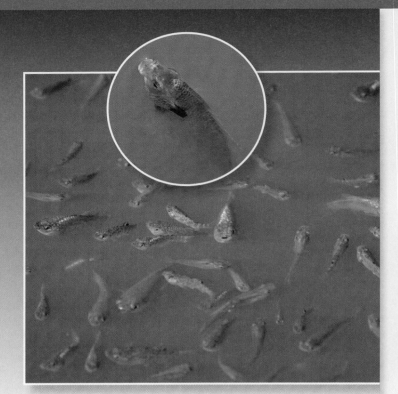

8 Turtles can be on land and in water.
They swim and swim.
Then they stop and rest in the sun.

56

Can fish be on land? **No!** **9**
Fish live in water.
They swim, swim, swim.
A big fish comes up to eat. Gulp!

57

LITERATURE ANTHOLOGY, pp. 56–57

Develop Comprehension

CLOSE READING

8 Strategy: Reread

Teacher Think Aloud After reading pages 56 and 57, we should stop and make sure we understand what we have read. What should we do if we realize there was something we didn't quite understand?

Student Think Aloud I'm confused about turtles. I think it said they can be on land and in water. I'll read again and make sure I understood that right. Yes! The first sentence on page 56 says "Turtles can be on land and in water." This means turtles are different from fish that can only swim in water.

9 Skill: Main Topic and Key Details

Turn to a partner and discuss what you have read on pages 56 and 57. Let's add these important details to the Main Topic and Details chart.

Main Topic: Animals at a pond		
Detail Ducks eat bugs and plants, make nests on land	**Detail** Turtles on land or in water rest in sun	**Detail** Fish only swim in water

Bugs like water.
Lots of bugs live at a pond.
A dragonfly is a big bug.
You can see it at a pond.

58

Look at the animals at a pond.
Who are they?

egret

raccoon

newt

goldfish

toad

beaver

59

LITERATURE ANTHOLOGY, pp. 58–59

Skill: Main Topic and Key Details

Review the Main Topic and Details chart with children. *Let's take a last look at our chart. What was the main topic of the selection? What were the key details? Are all of the details about the main topic? Is our chart complete, or is there anything else we should add?*

Return to Predictions and Purposes

Review children's predictions. Ask if their predictions were correct. Guide them to use evidence in the text to confirm whether their predictions were accurate. Discuss what children learned about animals at the pond by reading the selection.

Main Topic: Animals at a pond		
Detail Turtles on land or in water rest in sun	**Detail** Fish only swim in water	**Detail** Bugs, lots of different kinds

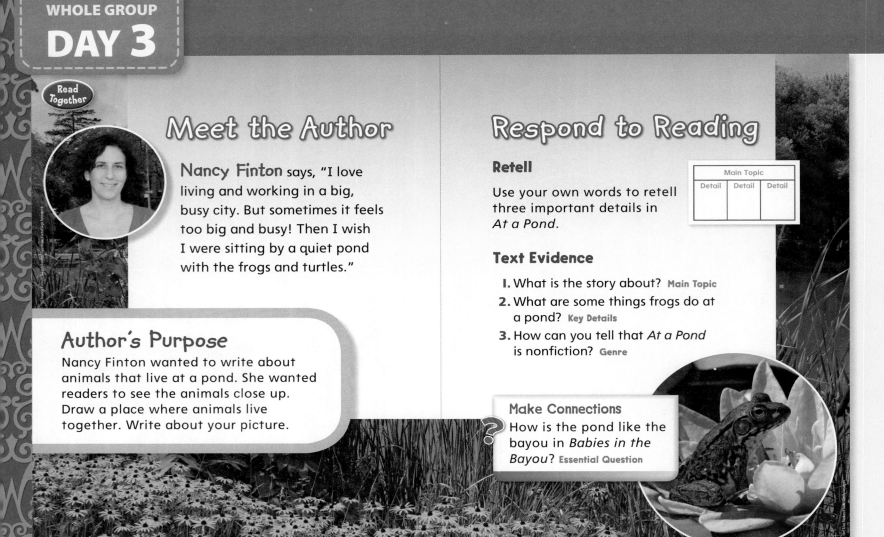

Read Together

Meet the Author

Nancy Finton says, "I love living and working in a big, busy city. But sometimes it feels too big and busy! Then I wish I were sitting by a quiet pond with the frogs and turtles."

Author's Purpose

Nancy Finton wanted to write about animals that live at a pond. She wanted readers to see the animals close up. Draw a place where animals live together. Write about your picture.

Respond to Reading

Retell

Use your own words to retell three important details in *At a Pond*.

Main Topic		
Detail	Detail	Detail

Text Evidence

1. What is the story about? **Main Topic**
2. What are some things frogs do at a pond? **Key Details**
3. How can you tell that *At a Pond* is nonfiction? **Genre**

Make Connections

How is the pond like the bayou in *Babies in the Bayou*? **Essential Question**

60   61

LITERATURE ANTHOLOGY, pp. 60–61

Meet the Author

Nancy Finton

Read aloud page 60 with children. Ask them why they think Nancy Finton chose to write about the animals that live together at a pond. *What do you think Nancy Finton likes about the city? What do you think she likes about the pond?*

Author's Purpose

Have children draw a picture of an animal habitat in their Response Journals. Provide a sentence starter children can use to tell about their picture. *Animals live in/at/on _____.* Challenge children to add a sentence with repetition.

AUTHOR'S CRAFT

Focus on Repetition

The author of *At a Pond* makes the text more interesting and fun by repeating certain words. Let's reread to find where the author repeats certain words. What words does she repeat on page 53? (Yum, yum!) On page 54? (Dip, dip, dip.) Page 55? (Quack, quack, quack!) Page 57? (Swim, swim, swim.) What do all of these words have in common? They are related to the animals' actions and sounds. They help tell key details about what the animal is doing.

Respond to Reading

Retelling

Guide children in retelling the selection. Remind them that as they read *At a Pond* they paid attention to the main topic and key details and reread when they weren't sure they understood the text. Now they will use that information to retell the selection.

→ Have children use the information they recorded on their Main Topic and Key Details chart to help them retell the selection.

Text Evidence

Guide children to use text evidence to answer the Text Evidence questions on Literature Anthology page 61. Model answering the questions as needed.

1. **Main Topic** To determine the main topic of this selection, we need to look back at pages 48–51. The text clearly tells us that we are going to see who lives at a pond, so we know the selection is about animals that live at and around a pond. We can confirm that this is the main topic by looking at the key details in the pages that follow to make sure they support that topic.

2. **Key Details** To answer this question, we need to look at the key details in the text. Let's look back at pages 52–53. The details in the text tell us that frogs swim, hop, jump, rest on plants, and hunt for bugs.

3. **Genre** This question asks how we know that the selection is nonfiction. To answer this question, let's look back at the selection. On each page we read facts about animals that live at a pond. There are photographs of the animals, and they are real animals in the world around us. The author presents information about a specific topic. All of these are clues that *At a Pond* is a nonfiction text.

Make Connections

Essential Question Have children work with a partner to brainstorm ways that the pond habitat in *At a Pond* is like the bayou habitat in *Babies in the Bayou*. Then have partners list their ideas and share them with the class.

ENGLISH LANGUAGE LEARNERS

Retell Help children by looking at each page of the selection and prompting them with a question, such as *What animals are on this page? What do they do?* Point to and identify the animals and use body language and gestures to demonstrate what they do. Provide sentence starters to help children retell the selection, such as *Frogs live at the pond. They _____.*

→ # Language Arts

Reading/Writing Workshop Big Book

OBJECTIVES

CCSS Write informative/ explanatory texts in which they name a topic, supply some facts about the topic, and provide some sense of closure. **W.1.2**

CCSS Use common, proper, and possessive nouns. **L.1.1b**

ACADEMIC LANGUAGE
prewrite, draft

MINILESSON
5 Mins

Independent Writing

Writing Trait: Ideas

❶ **Practice** Tell children that they will write a draft. Say: *Think about how we have written sentences that explain a main topic.*

❷ **Guided Practice** Have children open to the Readers to Writers page in the Reading/Writing Workshop. Read the student model aloud. Point out how Brent focused on the writing trait by having one idea, or topic. Guide children to identify and discuss his idea.

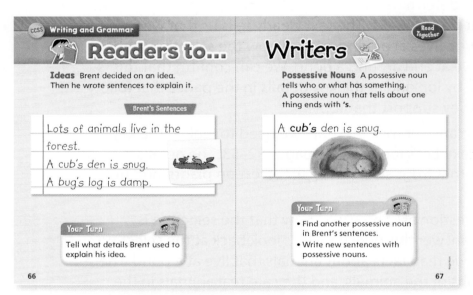

READING/WRITING WORKSHOP, pp. 66–67

Sentences That Explain

Model Have children look again at Brent's sentences, noting his topic and information he explains. Have them complete the Your Turn.

Prewrite

Display the list of topic ideas from Day 2. Guide children to choose a topic. Preview the topic choices.

Brainstorm Place children in pairs based on the topic they have chosen. Guide partners to use a Word Web to organize their ideas.

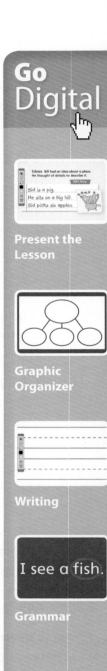

Go Digital

Present the Lesson

Graphic Organizer

Writing

I see a fish.

Grammar

Draft

Have children write using details from their Word Webs to write sentences that explain. Prompt them to include a topic sentence.

Apply Writing Trait Remind children to only write about one topic or idea.

Apply Grammar Have children think about the nouns they are using. When appropriate, remind them to add *'s* to form a possessive noun.

As children work, conference with them to provide guidance.

MINILESSON

5 Mins

Grammar

Possessive Nouns

❶ Review Have children look at the Readers to Writers page in the Reading/Writing Workshop. Remind them that a possessive noun tells who or what has something. Have children identify the possessive noun in the model sentence.

Find the possessive noun in the sentence *A cub's den is snug. Which word tells who or what has something?* Cub's *is the possessive noun. What belongs to the cub? The den belongs to the cub.*

❷ Guided Practice/Practice Guide children to identify another possessive noun in Brent's sentences. Have children write another sentence with a possessive noun that Brent could add to his paper.

COLLABORATE

Talk About It Have partners work together to orally generate sentences more with possessive nouns to add to Brent's writing.

Mechanics: Apostrophe with Possessive Nouns

❶ Review Remind children that to form a possessive, add apostrophe *s* to a noun to show someone or something owns something.

❷ Practice Display the incorrect sentences. Have children fix them.

> this hogs' pal is a pig. (This hog's pal is a pig.)
>
> Where is frogs pond (Where is frog's pond?)

ELL

ENGLISH LANGUAGE LEARNERS SCAFFOLD

Beginning

Expand Provide sentence frames for partners as they write sentences: _____ *live in a* _____. Clarify children's responses as needed by providing vocabulary.

Intermediate

Narrate Encourage children to talk about their topics. *What animals live together in a pond?* Repeat children's responses, correcting grammar or pronunciation as needed. Provide sentence frames, then have children complete and read them.

Advanced/Advanced High

Elaborate Prompt children to offer details in their sentences. *What does a duck do in a pond? Let's include that in your sentences that describe animals that live together in a pond.* Help children transfer these details to their writing.

Daily Wrap Up

→ Review the Essential Question and encourage children to discuss it using the oral vocabulary words. Ask: *What habitats have you learned about? How do animals live together in each habitat?*

→ Prompt children to review and discuss the skills they used today. Guide them to give examples of how they used each skill.

Materials

Visual Vocabulary Cards

depend   of
eat   tranquil
habitat   tolerate
hibernate   under
no   who

Spelling Word Cards

lend

Word-Building Cards

a b c

Dinah Zike's FOLDABLES

Dinah Zike's Foldables®

Literature Anthology
VOLUME 2

Teaching Poster

→ Extend the Concept

MINILESSON

5 Mins

Oral Language

CCSS

OBJECTIVES

Identify words and phrases in stories or poems that suggest feelings or appeal to the senses. **RL.1.4**

Review vocabulary

ACADEMIC LANGUAGE

• *repetition*
• Cognate: *repetición*

ESSENTIAL QUESTION

Remind children that this week they have been learning about communities in nature. Guide children to discuss the question using information from what they have read and talked about.

Use the Define/Example/Ask routine to review the oral vocabulary words *depend, habitat, hibernate, tranquil,* and *tolerate.* Then review last week's words *collapsed, furious, materials, refused,* and *shelter.*

Literary Element: Repetition

① Explain Remind children that they have been reading informational text about where animals live. Explain that they can also read poetry about animal habitats. Tell children that poetry selections provide information in a way that entertains the senses. Explain that poems often have repetition, or repeated words or phrases. Repetition can make a poem fun to read and hear.

Teaching Poster

② Model Display Teaching Poster 23. Read the first three lines of the poem. Point out that the first and the third lines are the same. *The author repeated the line* Foxes have a lot of fun. *This repetition gives the poem a good rhythm and makes it more interesting.*

③ Guided Practice/Practice Read together the rest of the poem. *What line did the author repeat? Why do you think the author repeated that line?* Tell children to listen for repetition as they read poetry.

Go Digital

Visual Glossary

Teaching Poster

"Way Down Deep"

CCSS **Genre** Poetry

Compare Texts
Read about animals that live in the water.

Read Together

Way Down Deep
by Mary Ann Hoberman

Underneath the water
Way down deep
In sand and stones and seaweed
Starfish creep
Snails inch slowly
Oysters sleep
❶ Underneath the water
Way down deep. ❷

Make Connections
How is under the sea like the pond? How is it different? **Essential Question**

62

63

LITERATURE ANTHOLOGY, pp. 62–63

Develop Comprehension CLOSE READING

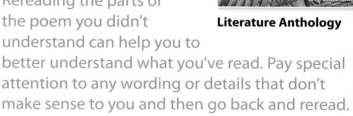
Literature Anthology

Read Literature Anthology

Compare Texts

Tell children that as they read they should think about how the animals and habitat in "Way Down Deep" are similar to those in *At a Pond*.

❶ Literary Element: Repetition

The poet repeats certain phrases in this poem. What phrases does she repeat? (Underneath the water/ Way down deep) Why do you think the author repeats "Underneath the water / Way down deep"? (This gives the poem a pattern and a rhythm that makes it sound a bit like a song.)

❷ Strategy: Reread

Teacher Think Aloud
Rereading the parts of the poem you didn't understand can help you to better understand what you've read. Pay special attention to any wording or details that don't make sense to you and then go back and reread.

Make Connections Have partners make connections between the animals and their habitat in "Way Down Deep" and those in *At a Pond. How are they similar? How are they different?*

→ # Word Work

Quick Review

Build Fluency: Sound-Spellings
Display the **Word-Building Cards:**
nd, nk, nt, st, sk, mp, u, e, ea, sp,
sn, sl, cr, fr, tr, o, pl, fl, cl, bl, i, a, s,
r, l, t. Have children say the sounds.
Repeat, and vary the pace.

Phonemic Awareness

OBJECTIVES

CCSS Isolate and pronounce initial, medial vowel, and final sounds (phonemes) in spoken single-syllable words. **RF.1.2c**

CCSS Read words with inflectional endings. **RF.1.3f**

Phoneme Categorization

1 Model Show children how to categorize phonemes using a group of words. Listen as I say three words: *ramp, clank, blimp.* I hear the same end sounds /mp/ in *ramp* and *blimp. Clank* does not end with /mp/. *Clank* does not belong.

2 Guided Practice/Practice Have children practice identifying the word that does not belong. Guide practice with the first set.

lump, limp, land	slant, mist, hunt
pink, blank, jump	desk, list, dust

Phonics

Build Words with End Blends

Review *The sounds /nk/ can be represented by the letters* nk. *We'll use the* **Word-Building Cards** *to build words with* nk *and other ending blends.*

Place the letters *s, i, n, k. Let's blend the sounds together and read the word: /sssiiink/. Now let's change the s to r. Blend the sounds and read the word: /rrriiink/, rink.*

Continue with *risk, disk, desk, dent, went, wet, let, lent, lint, lit, lip, limp, blimp.*

**Go
Digital**

**Phonemic
Awareness**

Phonics

**Structural
Analysis**

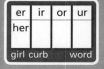

**Spelling Word
Sort**

Visual Glossary

Structural Analysis

Inflectional Ending -*ing*

Review Write the words *drink* and *drinking* on the board and read them with children. *Adding* -ing *to an action word means the action is happening now. I am drinking.* Remind children that adding -*ing* to a word adds a syllable.

Write the following words: *spend, list, print, trust, spell, stomp.* Have children work in pairs to construct words that tell about actions happening now by adding -*ing*. Then have them read the new words aloud and write sentences with each word.

Spelling

Word Sort with -*end, -ast, -ink*

Review Provide pairs of children with copies of the **Spelling Word Cards**. While one partner reads the words one at a time, the other partner should orally segment the word and then write the word. After reading all the words, partners should switch roles.

Have children correct their own papers. Then have them sort the words by ending spelling pattern: -*end, -ast, -ink,* or no consonant-blend ending.

High-Frequency Words

eat, no, of, under, who

Review Display **Visual Vocabulary Cards** for high-frequency words *eat, no, of, under, who.* Have children Read/Spell/Write each word.

→ Point to a word and call on a child to use it in a sentence.

→ Review last week's words using the same procedure.

Monitor and *Differentiate*

✓ Quick Check

Can children read and decode words with ending consonant blends?

Can children recognize and read high-frequency words?

⬇

Small Group Instruction

If No →	Approaching	Reteach pp. T212–215
	ELL	Develop pp. T226–233
If Yes →	On Level	Review pp. T220–221
	Beyond Level	Extend pp. T224–225

Language Arts

Independent Writing

Sentences That Explain

Go Digital

Revise

Explain to children that revising helps make their ideas clearer and more interesting.

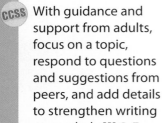

OBJECTIVES

CCSS With guidance and support from adults, focus on a topic, respond to questions and suggestions from peers, and add details to strengthen writing as needed. **W.1.5**

CCSS Use common, proper, and possessive nouns. **L.1.1b**

ACADEMIC LANGUAGE
clearer, topic

Apply Writing Trait: Ideas Explain that as writers revise, they make sure all of their sentences are about one main topic. Display the following sentences that explain information about animals that live together in a pond:

1. Animals live together in a pond.
2. Fish swim in schools.
3. I have a pet fish.
4. Mom duck swims with the kids.

Read the sentences aloud. Guide children to identify the sentence that does not tell about the idea. Model deleting it.

 Peer Review Have children work in pairs to do a peer review. They should take notes about what they like most, questions they have for the author, and ideas they think the author could include. Provide time for them to discuss making revisions.

Proofread/Edit

Apply Grammar Review proofreader's marks with children. Have them reread their drafts and fix mistakes. Remind them to make sure that:

→ all possessive nouns are formed correctly.

→ all words are spelled correctly.

→ all sentences are complete.

 Peer Edit Next, have partners exchange their drafts and take turns reading for the mistakes above. Encourage partners to discuss and fix errors together as they read.

Writing

Make a capital letter.
∧ Add.
✄ Take out.

Proofreader's Marks

I see a fish.

Grammar

Final Draft

After children have edited their own papers and finished their peer edits, have them write their final draft. As children work, conference with them to provide guidance. Encourage them to create or find a photo or other visual that relates to their writing.

MINILESSON
5 Mins

Grammar

Possessive Nouns

1 Review Remind children that a possessive noun shows that someone or something owns something. Hold up a book and say: *This book belongs to me. How can you use a possessive noun to say this book belongs to me?* (my teacher's book)

2 Guided Practice Guide children to identify the possessive noun and identify what belongs to whom as you say the following sentences:

The lion's teeth are sharp. (lion's; teeth)

The shark's home is the ocean. (shark's; home)

COLLABORATE

Talk About It Have partners work together to orally generate sentences with possessive nouns about animals and their homes.

Mechanics: Apostrophe with Possessive Nouns

1 Review Remind children that a possessive noun ends with 's.

2 Practice Display the sentences below. Read each aloud. Have children fix the sentences as a class.

Here is a hens nest (Here is a hen's nest.)

this mans' kid's are here. (This man's kids are here.)

Daily Wrap Up

→ Review the Essential Question and encourage children to discuss using the oral vocabulary words. Ask: *What animals live in a habitat near your home?*

→ Prompt children to discuss the skills they practiced today. Have them share examples of each skill.

☞ **Go** Digital

www.connected.mcgraw-hill.com
RESOURCES
Research and Inquiry

→ # Wrap Up the Week
Integrate Ideas

RESEARCH AND INQUIRY

A Community in Nature

OBJECTIVES

CCSS Participate in a shared research and writing project (e.g., explore a number of "how-to" books on a given topic and use them to write a sequence of instructions). **W.1.7**

- Build background knowledge
- Research information using technology

ACADEMIC LANGUAGE
- *habitat, collage*
- Cognates: *hábitat, collage*

Make a Collage

Review the steps in the research process. Tell children that today they will do a research project with a partner to create a collage about a habitat and the animals that live in it.

STEP 1 **Choose a Topic**

Name common animal habitats to prompt a brainstorming session. Guide partners to choose an animal habitat to research.

STEP 2 **Find Resources**

Discuss how to use the selections to find information on their chosen habitat. Remind children that they can find more details in reference materials and online. Have them use the Research Process Checklist online.

STEP 3 **Keep Track of Ideas**

Have children record their ideas in an Accordion Foldable®. Model recording details.

Desert lizards snakes cactus eagles coyotes

Dinah Zike's
FOLDABLES

Collaborative Conversations

Listen Carefully Review with children that as they engage in partner, small-group, and whole-group discussions, they should:

→ always look at the speaker.

→ respect others by not interrupting them.

→ repeat others' ideas to check understanding.

Desert

STEM

STEP 4 **Create the Project: Collage**

Explain the characteristics of a collage.

→ **Text** A collage can have a title. In this project, the title of the collage will be the name of an animal habitat. Other text can be labels or short captions.

→ **Mixed Materials** Collages can be made from many materials, such as magazines, newspapers, packaging, scraps of fabric, and other craft materials. They can have small items, such as tiny plastic toys.

→ **Images** A collage can have images. For this project, collages will have images of animals and plants that live in the habitat.

Have partners create a collage about their chosen habitat and the animals that live in it.

→ Have children write the name of the habitat as the title.

→ Encourage children to write labels and captions.

ELL ENGLISH LANGUAGE LEARNERS
SCAFFOLD

Beginning	Intermediate	Advanced/High
Use Sentence Frames Use sentence frames to help children discuss their habitat. For example: *You can find _____ in this habitat.*	**Discuss** Guide children to focus on the most important details about their habitat. Ask: *Is this habitat wet or dry? Is it hot or cold? What kinds of animals live there?*	**Describe** Prompt children to brainstorm words that describe the habitat. Encourage them to find images that illustrate each word. For example, if the habitat is rocky, they can cut out photos of rocks.

Materials

Reading/Writing Workshop
VOLUME 2

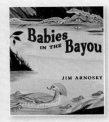

Literature Anthology
VOLUME 2

Literature Big Book
Babies in the Bayou

Visual Vocabulary Cards
eat
no
of
under
who

Teaching Poster

Spelling Word Cards

Word-Building Cards

→ Integrate Ideas

TEXT CONNECTIONS

Connect to Essential Question

OBJECTIVES

 Identify basic similarities in and differences between two texts on the same topic (e.g., in illustrations, descriptions, or procedures). **RI.1.9**

- Develop answers to the Essential Question
- Make text connections to the world

ACADEMIC LANGUAGE

- *organize, evidence*
- Cognates: *organizar, evidencia*

Text to Text

Remind children that all week they have been reading selections about animals that live in different environments. Tell them now they can make connections across texts by thinking about how the texts are similar. Model comparing text using *Babies in the Bayou* and *The Best Spot*.

Think Aloud *The Best Spot* and *Babies in the Bayou* are both about places where animals live together. *The Best Spot* tells about animals in a forest, and *Babies in the Bayou* tells about animals in the bayou. The animals in both places get the shelter and food they need from their special habitat.

 Complete the Organizer Have children use the Word Web to help them organize the information from this week's selections.

→ Discuss and write about the habitats. What features are important in each?

→ How do the animals depend on their habitat for the things they need?

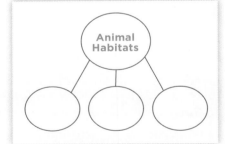

Teaching Poster

Text to Self

Have children discuss the different places they have seen animals living together. *Where have you seen animals living together? How are these places different from the places you read about this week? How are they the same?*

Text to World

Have children talk about habitats they would like to visit. *What faraway place would you like to visit to see animals living together? What might you see there?* If necessary, suggest options such as beach, jungle, or the North Pole.

WRITE ABOUT READING  Analytical Writing

OBJECTIVES

 Draw evidence from literary or informational texts to support analysis, reflection, and research. **W.4.9**

Analyze Main Topic and Key Details

Explain to children that as a group you will write about one of the selections they have read this week.

Using the evidence in the text, we will think about how the author used the main topic and key details to write about the topic.

Review the Main Topic and Details chart you completed for *The Best Spot*. Guide children to analyze the text evidence by asking "how" and "why" questions about the main topic and details.

→ *Why might the author have wanted to write about the creatures that live in the woods?*

→ *How did the author use details to help explain the main topic?*

→ *How did reading the piece help you better understand the main topic?*

Write an Analysis

Display the following sentence frames:

> *In _____, the author wrote about _____.*
>
> *The author used the details _____ and _____ to support the main topic.*
>
> *The selection made us understand _____.*

Work with children to complete the sentence frames using the information about *The Best Spot*.

Select another informational text selection you have read this week. Work with children to complete similar sentence frames to write about how the author used the main topic and key details.

RESEARCH AND INQUIRY SCIENCE

OBJECTIVES

 Participate in a shared research and writing projects. **W.1.7**

Wrap Up the Project

 COLLABORATE Guide partners to share their collages. *What habitat did you choose? Why did you choose this habitat?* Prompt partners to point out details in the images they used. Have them share the information they learned about their animal habitat. Have them use the Presentation Checklist online.

STEM

 → **Word Work**

Quick Review

Build Fluency: Sound-Spellings:
Display the **Word-Building Cards**
*nd, nk, nt, st, sk, mp, u, e, ea, sp,
sn, sl, cr, fr, tr, o, pl, fl, cl, bl, i, a, s,
r, l, t.* Have children say the sounds.
Repeat, and vary the pace.

 MINILESSON 5 Mins

Phonemic Awareness

OBJECTIVES

CCSS Segment spoken single-syllable words into their complete sequence of individual sounds (phonemes). **RF.1.2d**

CCSS Decode regularly spelled one-syllable words. **RF.1.3b**

CCSS Read words with inflectional endings. **RF.1.3f**

Phoneme Blending

Review Guide children to blend phonemes to form words. *Listen as I say a group of sounds. Then blend those sounds to form a word.*

/h/ /a/ /n/ /d/   /l/ /a/ /n/ /d/   /l/ /a/ /s/ /t/   /l/ /i/ /n/ /k/

Phoneme Segmentation

Review Guide children to segment phonemes in words. *Now I am going to say a word. I want you to say each sound in the word.*

ant   pant   fast   pest   tusk   frost   spend

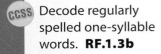 MINILESSON 5 Mins

Phonics

Blend and Build Words with End Blends

Review Have children read and say the words *hand, trunk, tent, fast, dusk,* and *lamp.* Have children use **Word-Building Cards** to build *link, clink, clank, bank, band, bend, bent, best, bet, net, nest, rest, west.*

Word Automaticity Help children practice word automaticity. Display decodable words and point to each word as children chorally read it. Test how many words children can read in one minute. Model blending words children miss.

Go Digital

Phonemic Awareness

Phonics

Structural Analysis

Visual Glossary

Fluency: Word Automaticity

Structural Analysis

Inflectional Ending -ing

Review Have children explain when the -ing ending is used. Then have children practice writing words with -ing such as *landing, ending, jumping, buzzing,* and *smelling.* Remind children that adding -ing to a word adds a syllable, such as in *dunk* and *dunking.*

Spelling

Word Sort with -end, -ast, -ink

Review Have children use the **Spelling Word Cards** to sort the weekly words by vowel and ending consonant blend sounds. Remind children that four of the words do not end in -end, -ast, or -ink.

Assess Assess children on their abilities to spell words in the -end, -ast, and -ink word families. Say each word and provide a sentence so that children can hear the words used in a correct context. Then allow them time to write down the words. In order to challenge children, you may wish to provide an additional word in each family in order to assess whether they understand the concept.

High-Frequency Words

eat, no, of, under, who

Review Display **Visual Vocabulary Cards** *eat, no, of, under, who.* Have children Read/Spell/Write each word. Have children write a sentence with each word.

Monitor and *Differentiate*

 Quick Check

Can children read and decode words with ending consonant blends?

Can children recognize and read high-frequency words?

Small Group Instruction

If No →	**Approaching**	Reteach pp. T212–215
	ELL	Develop pp. T226–233
If Yes →	**On Level**	Review pp. T220–221
	Beyond Level	Extend pp. T224–225

→ # Language Arts

MINILESSON
5 Mins

Independent Writing

Sentences That Explain

Prepare

Review guidelines for making presentations with children.

→ Provide time for children to finish preparing their presentations. Remind them to practice using a photo or drawing of their chosen habitat and any other visual they are using.

Present

Have children take turns giving presentations of their sentences that explain. Remind them to speak clearly. When listening to others, they should be polite and respectful, asking questions when appropriate and listening carefully when it is not appropriate to speak.

→ If possible, record the presentation so that children can self-evaluate.

Evaluate

Have children discuss their own presentations and evaluate their performance using the presentation rubric.

Use the teacher's rubric to evaluate children's writing. Have children add their writing to their Writer's Portfolio. Then have them discuss and write about how they have become better writers.

Publish

After children finish presenting their sentences that explain, discuss how the class will display their sentences that explain on a bulletin board. Suggest to children that they illustrate their writing more. Vote on how to organize the bulletin board, such as grouping students' writing by places where animals live. Guide children to use digital tools to create the bulletin board.

OBJECTIVES

CCSS With guidance from adults, use a variety of digital tools to produce and publish writing, including in collaboration with peers. **W.1.6**

CCSS Use common, proper, and possessive nouns. **L.1.1b**

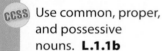

ACADEMIC LANGUAGE
- *vote, organize*
- Cognates: *votar, organizar*

Go Digital

Writing

Checklists

I see a fish.

Grammar

Grammar

Possessive Nouns

1 Review Have children describe what possessive nouns are and how they are used. Write the following sentence and have children identify the possessive noun:

> There's the skunk's den! (skunk's)

2 Practice Ask: *How do I know if a word is a possessive noun?*

Write sentences that are missing a possessive noun. Read each sentence.

> _____ dog is lost.
>
> This is _____ snack.

→ Have children work in pairs to complete each sentence with a possessive noun. Have pairs write the possessive noun on the board to complete and share the sentences.

Mechanics: Apostrophe with Possessive Nouns

1 Review Remind children that writers add an apostrophe followed by the letter *s* to form a possessive noun.

2 Practice Write the following sentences. Read each aloud. Have children fix the sentences.

> Here's a cubs den's. (Here's a cub's den.)
>
> grams' dog is running. (Gram's dog is running.)
>
> This hens egg's Are big. (This hen's eggs are big.)

Wrap Up the Week

→ Review the Essential Question and encourage children to discuss using the oral vocabulary words.

→ Review that when children read a text, they should look for key details about the main topic. They can also reread to better understand the information.

→ Review blending words with end blends. Remind children that a possessive noun, formed by adding 's, tells who or what owns something.

→ Use the Visual Vocabulary Cards to review the Words to Know.

→ Remind children that nonfiction text explains facts about a topic.

Approaching Level

Lexile 170

OBJECTIVES

 Identify the main topic and retell key details of a text. **RI.1.2**

Leveled Reader:
Meerkat Family

Go Digital

Meerkat Family

Graphic Organizer

Retell

Before Reading

Preview and Predict

Have children turn to the title page. Read the title and the author's name and have children repeat. Preview the selection's photographs. Prompt children to predict what the selection might be about.

Review Genre: Informational Text/Nonfiction

Help children to recall that a nonfiction selection tells information and facts about real people, places, or things. The selection presents facts about a specific topic.

ESSENTIAL QUESTION

Remind children of the Essential Question: *Where do animals live together?* Set a purpose for reading: *Let's read to find out where meerkats live together.*

Remind children that as they read a selection, they can ask questions about what they do not understand or what they want to know more about.

During Reading

Guided Comprehension

As children whisper read *Meerkat Family*, monitor and provide guidance, correcting blending and modeling the key strategies and skills.

Strategy: Reread

Remind children as they read that they can reread if they don't understand something. Model using the strategy on pages 2–3: *I'm going to reread these two pages to make sure I know what I'm reading about. Now I know that this selection is about meerkats.* Tell children they can also reread to remember important information.

Skill: Main Topic and Key Details

Remind children the main topic is what the selection is mainly about. Details tell about the topic. *Let's look for key details as we read.* Display a Main Topic and Key Details chart for children to copy.

Model recording children's answers in the details boxes. Have children record the answers in their own charts.

Think Aloud The key details give important information about the meerkats. On page 5, I read that meerkats eat bugs and plants. They also look out for birds. Let's add these details to the Key Details chart.

Guide children to add additional key details to the chart. Then help them determine the main topic.

After Reading

Respond to Reading

Have children complete the Respond to Reading on page 12.

Retell

Have children take turns retelling key facts from the selection, using the **Retelling Cards** as a guide. Help children make a personal connection by asking: *Have you seen other animals living together? Where were they?*

Model Fluency

Read the sentences one at a time. Have children chorally repeat. Point out how you phrase repeated words in the selection.

Apply Have partners practice reading. Provide feedback as needed.

PAIRED READ ...

"I Live in a House!"

Make Connections: Write About It *Analytical Writing*

Before reading, ask children to note that the genre of this text is poetry. Discuss the Compare Texts direction. After reading, ask children to make connections between the information they learned from "I Live in a House!" and *Meerkat Family*.

Leveled Reader

FOCUS ON SCIENCE

Children can extend their knowledge of where animals live by completing the science activity on page 16.
STEM

Literature Circles

Lead children in conducting a literature circle using the Thinkmark questions to guide the discussion. You may wish to discuss what children have learned about animals and where they live from both selections in the Leveled Reader.

Level Up

Level-up lessons available online.

IF children can read *Meerkat Family* **Approaching Level** with fluency and correctly answer the Respond to Reading questions,

THEN tell children that they will read a more detailed version of the selection.

- Use pages 10–11 of *Meerkat Family* **On Level** to model using Teaching Poster 29 to identify the key details and main topic.

- Have children read the selection, checking their comprehension by using the graphic organizer.

Approaching Level

Phonemic Awareness

PHONEME CATEGORIZATION

TIER 2

OBJECTIVES

 Isolate and pronounce initial, medial vowel, and final sounds (phonemes) in spoken single-syllable words. **RF.1.2c**

Categorize words by phoneme

I Do Explain to children that they will listen for a word that does not belong. *Listen as I say three words:* band, end, fist. *I heard the sounds /nd/ at the end of* band *and* end. *I heard /st/ at the end of* fist. Fist *does not belong.*

We Do *Listen as I say three words:* mask, sip, desk. *Which two words end with the same sounds? Yes,* mask *and* desk *end with /sk/.* Sip *does not end with the /sk/ sounds.* Sip *does not belong.*

Repeat the routine with these words:

stuff, camp, jump   prep, list, fast   bent, sent, junk

You Do *It's your turn. Which words go together? Which word does not belong?*

sank, yank, damp   pond, cask, wind   junk, clink, hand

Repeat the categorization routine with additional end-blend words.

PHONEME BLENDING

TIER 2

OBJECTIVES

 Orally produce single-syllable words by blending sounds (phonemes), including consonant blends. **RF.1.2b**

I Do Explain to children that they will blend sounds to form words. *Listen as I say three sounds: /e/ /n/ /d/. Now say the sounds with me: /e/ /n/ /d/. Listen as I blend the sounds together: /eeennnd/,* end. *I blended the word* end. *Say the word with me:* end.

We Do *Listen as I say three sounds: /a/ /n/ /t/. Repeat the sounds with me: /a/ /n/ /t/. Let's blend the sounds together: /aaannnt/,* ant. *We said one word:* ant.

Repeat the routine with these words:

/a/ /s/ /k/   /f/ /a/ /s/ /t/   /t/ /ā/ /n/ /k/   /b/ /u/ /m/ /p/

You Do *It's your turn. Blend the sounds that I say to form a word.*

/p/ /ō/ /s/ /t/   /f/ /ī/ /n/ /d/   /t/ /a/ /s/ /k/   /l/ /i/ /m/ /p/

Repeat the blending routine with additional words with end blends.

PHONEME SUBSTITUTION

CCSS

OBJECTIVES

Isolate and pronounce initial, medial vowel, and final sounds (phonemes) in spoken single-syllable words. **RF.1.2.c**

Substitute sounds in words to form new words

 I Do Explain that children will substitute phonemes. *Listen as I say this word:* band. *Now I'll change one sound from /a/ to /e/: /beeennnd/. The new word is* bend.

 We Do *Listen as I say a word:* send. *Say the word with me:* send. *Let's change one sound. Let's change /d/ to /t/. Let's say the new word together:* sent.

Repeat the routine with these pairs of words:

hand, land   end, and   sand, band

 You Do *Now you try it. Change one sound to form a new word.*

mint, mist   rest, rust   lift, list   ant, and

Repeat the substitution routine with additional words with end blends.

PHONEME SEGMENTATION

CCSS

OBJECTIVES

Segment spoken single-syllable words into their complete sequence of individual sounds (phonemes). **RF.1.2d**

 I Do Explain to children that they will segment words into sounds. *Listen to this word:* fist. *I hear four sounds: /f/, /i/, /s/, and /t/. There are four sounds in the word* fist.

 We Do *Let's try it together. I'll say a word:* lamp. *How many sounds do you hear? Yes, there are four sounds in* lamp. *The four sounds are /l/, /a/, /m/, and /p/.*

Repeat the routine with these words:

fun   fund   net   nest

 You Do *I'll say a word. Hold up a finger for each sound that you hear. Then say the sounds.*

tank   mint   crisp   blimp   tusk   guest

ELL ENGLISH LANGUAGE LEARNERS

For the **ELLs** who need **phonemic awareness, phonics**, and **fluency** practice, use scaffolding methods as necessary to ensure children understand the meaning of the words. Refer to the Language Transfer Handbook for phonics elements that may not transfer in children's native languages.

→ Approaching Level

Phonics

CONNECT TO CONSONANT BLENDS

 TIER 2

 OBJECTIVES

Decode regularly spelled one-syllable words. **RF.1.3b**

I Do Display the **Word-Building Cards** n and d. *These are lowercase* n *and* d. *I'm going to write the letters as I blend those sounds. Trace the letters five times while saying /nnnd/.* Repeat for the blends *nk, nt, st, sk, mp.*

We Do *Let's do it together.* Have children trace the letters that stand for each blend with their finger while saying the sounds the letters stand for.

You Do Have children connect the letters of each blend to the sounds by tracing the letters with their finger while saying the sounds. Then have them write the blends while saying the sounds.

Repeat and connect the letters that stand for the blends to their sounds throughout the week.

BLEND WORDS WITH END BLENDS

TIER 2

 OBJECTIVES

Decode regularly spelled one-syllable words. **RF.1.3b**

I Do Display Word-Building Cards e, n, and d. *This is the letter* e. *It stands for /e/. Say it with me: /eee/. These letters are* n *and* d. *Let's blend both sounds: /nnnd/. Now let's blend all of the sounds together to make a word: /eeennnd/,* end. *The word is* end.

We Do Guide children to blend the sounds and read: *sunk, dent, best, ask, camp.*

You Do Have children blend the sounds and decode: *band, dunk, bent, test, bump, band, fist.*

Repeat, blending words with end blends.

You may wish to review Phonics with **ELL** using this section.

BUILD WORDS WITH END BLENDS

OBJECTIVES

 Decode regularly spelled one-syllable words. **RF.1.3b**

Build and decode words with ending consonant blends

 I Do Display **Word-Building Cards** *d, e. I will blend these sounds together: /deee/.* Add cards *s, k. Let's blend all the sounds: /deeessk/,* desk. *The word is* desk.

 We Do *Now let's try it together.* Display the cards *p, o, n, d. Point to the letters n and d. Let's blend all the sounds to say the word: /pooonnnd/,* pond. *The word is* pond.

 You Do Have children build and decode these words: *and, sand, send, sent, tent, tint, mint, mist, must, just, jump, bump.*

Repeat, building additional words with end blends.

BLEND WORDS WITH END BLENDS

OBJECTIVES

 Decode regularly spelled one-syllable words. **RF.1.3b**

Blend and decode words with ending consonant blends

 I Do Display Word-Building Cards *d, u, s, t. Point to each letter. The letters stand for these sounds: /d/ /u/ /s/ /t/. I will blend the four sounds: /duuussst/,* dust. *The word is* dust.

 We Do *Let's do some together.* Blend and read the words *lamp, mask, tent, bank,* and *end* with children.

 You Do Display the words to the right. Have children blend and read the words.

hand	send	wind	tank	sink	hint
lint	went	fast	lost	rest	ask
mask	camp	bump	clunk	print	dump
trunk	spend	Brent	cost	dust	test

The trunk is lost.

Send the mask to Brent.

I went to camp.

BUILD FLUENCY WITH PHONICS

Sound-Spellings Fluency

Display the following Word-Building Cards *nd, nk, nt, st, sk, mp, u, e, ea, sp, sn, sl, cr, fr, tr, o, pl, fl, cl, bl, i, a, s, r, l, t.* Have children chorally say the sounds. Repeat and vary the pace.

Fluency in Connected Text

Have children review *The Best Spot* in their Reading/Writing Workshop. Identify words with ending consonant blends. Blend words as needed.

Have children reread the selection on their own or with a partner.

→ Approaching Level

Structural Analysis

REVIEW INFLECTIONAL ENDING -ing

 CCSS

OBJECTIVES
Read words with inflectional endings. **RF.1.3f**

Review words with the inflectional ending -ing

 I Do Write *jumping*. Say the word and have children repeat it with you. *I look at the word* jumping *and I see a smaller word that I know:* jump. *The* -ing *ending can tell me that an action is happening right now: I am jumping over the puddle.* Jump as you repeat the sentence.

 We Do Write *looking*. Say the word and have children repeat it. *Do you see a smaller word that you know? Yes,* look! *The* -ing *ending means that an action is happening right now. Let's use* looking *in a sentence.*

 You Do Give partners several words with -ing endings. Have children find the root word and say a sentence that includes the word.

Repeat Have partners take turns asking each other questions using words with the -ing ending.

RETEACH INFLECTIONAL ENDING -ing

 CCSS

OBJECTIVES
Read words with inflectional endings. **RF.1.3f**

Read words with the inflectional ending -ing

 I Do Write *pull* and *pulling*. Read the word: *pulling*. Circle the letters -ing. *When I add the letters* -ing *to a verb, it can mean that the action is happening right now. If I am pulling something, I am pulling it right now.*

 We Do Write *camp* and *hunt* and read the words with children. Say: *Let's add* -ing. Add the ending to each root word and then read the words with children. *Let's think of sentences that use these words.*

Repeat this routine with the following examples:

bend   dust   add   spell   sink   ask   pump

 You Do Have children add -ing to verbs. Help them repeat the words. *Now it's your turn. Add* -ing *to each word. Say the word and use each word in a sentence.*

look   list   lend   bump   land   rent   stomp

Repeat Have children add the suffix -ing to more verbs.

High-Frequency Words

REVIEW

OBJECTIVES

Recognize and read grade-appropriate irregularly spelled words. **RF.1.3g**

Review *eat, no, of, under, who*

 Use the **High-Frequency Word Cards** to **Read/Spell/Write** each high-frequency word. Use each word orally in a sentence.

 Guide children to Read/Spell/Write each word on their **Response Boards**. Help them create oral sentences that include the words.

 Have partners do the Read/Spell/Write routine on their own using the words *eat, no, of, under,* and *who.*

RETEACH

OBJECTIVES

Recognize and read grade-appropriate irregularly spelled words. **RF.1.3g**

 Review the high-frequency words using the Read/Spell/Write routine. Write a sentence for each high-frequency word.

 Guide children to use the Read/Spell/Write routine. Use sentence starters: *(1) My dog will eat ____. (2) No, I will not ____. (3) I have a lot of ____. (4) The pup is under the ____. (5) Who will fix ____?*

 Ask children to close their eyes, picture the word, and then write it as they see it. Have children self-correct.

CUMULATIVE REVIEW

OBJECTIVES

Recognize and read grade-appropriate irregularly spelled words. **RF.1.3g**

Review previously taught high-frequency words

 Display the High-Frequency Word Cards from the previous weeks. Review each word using the Read/Spell/Write routine.

 Have children write each word on their Response Boards. Complete sentences for each word, such as: *I have a new ____. I live ____.*

 Show each card and have children chorally read. Mix and repeat.

Fluency Display the High-Frequency Word Cards. Point to the words in random order. Have children chorally read each word. Repeat at a faster pace.

Approaching Level

Comprehension

READFOR FLUENCY

 TIER 2

OBJECTIVES
 Read with sufficient accuracy and fluency to support comprehension. **RF.1.4**

I Do Read the first sentence in the Practice Book selection. Model pausing at commas and using appropriate phrasing for repeated words.

We Do Read the next sentence and have children repeat each sentence after you. Discuss how you slightly pause between each repeated verb.

You Do Have children read the rest of the selection aloud. Remind them to look for patterns and repeated words as they read.

IDENTIFY KEY DETAILS

TIER 2

OBJECTIVES
Ask and answer questions about the key details in a text. **RI.1.1**

I Do Remind children that they have been reading an informational story. Explain that they can look for important details in the illustrations and the text.

We Do Ask children to look closely at the illustrations in the Practice Book selection. Guide them to point out key details in the pictures. *We see a boy and his mother sitting on a rock by a pond. We see a bug, two frogs, and three bats at the pond. These are important key details.*

You Do Help children read the Practice Book selection. After each sentence, ask them to identify key details. Ask them to explain why the detail is important.

REVIEW MAIN TOPIC AND KEY DETAILS

OBJECTIVES

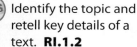

Identify the topic and retell key details of a text. **RI.1.2**

I Do Remind children that informational selections have a main topic. *The main topic is what the story is mostly about. The key details help to explain more about the main topic.*

We Do Read the title and the first two pages of the Practice Book selection together. Discuss key details in the illustrations. Guide children to identify the main topic. *What is this selection mainly about? Yes, Big Rock Pond!*

You Do Help children read the rest of the selection. Then reread each sentence and discuss the important detail in each sentence. Record it on a Main Topic and Details chart. Use the information in the chart to help children identify the main topic of the selection.

SELF-SELECTED READING

OBJECTIVES

Identify the topic and retell key details of a text. **RI.1.2**

With prompting and support, read informational texts appropriately complex for grade 1. **RI.1.10**

Apply the strategy and skill to read a text

Read Independently

Have children choose a nonfiction selection for sustained silent reading. Remind them that:

→ the main topic is what the selection is mainly about. Key details give information about the main topic.

→ they can find key details in the words and illustrations.

→ they should reread if they don't understand something they have read.

Read Purposefully

Guide children to record the topic and key details on a Main Topic and Details chart. After reading, guide them in a group discussion about the selection they read. Guide children to:

→ share the information they recorded on their chart.

→ connect what they learned to their real-life experiences.

→ On Level

Lexile 210

 OBJECTIVES

Identify the main topic and retell key details of a text. **RI.1.1**

Leveled Reader:
Meerkat Family

Go Digital

Meerkat Family

Graphic Organizer

Before Reading

Preview and Predict

Have children turn to the title page. Read the title and the author's name and have children repeat. Preview the selection's photographs. Prompt children to predict what the selection might be about.

Review Genre: Informational Text/Nonfiction

Have children recall that a nonfiction selection provides information about real people, places, or things. The selection presents facts about a specific topic.

ESSENTIAL QUESTION

Remind children of the Essential Question: *Where do animals live together?* Set a purpose for reading: *Let's read how meerkats live together.*

Remind children that as they read a selection, they can ask questions about what they do not understand or what they want to know more about.

Retell

During Reading

Guided Comprehension

As children whisper read *Meerkat Family*, monitor and provide guidance, correcting blending, and modeling the key strategies and skills.

Strategy: Reread

Remind children as they read that they should reread if they don't understand something they have read. Model using the strategy on pages 7–8: *I read the rooms in a burrow stay cool. How can they do that? I will reread. On page 7 I read that the burrows are underground. That would help them stay cool.* Tell children they can also reread to remember important information.

Skill: Main Topic and Key Details

Remind children that the main topic is what the selection is mostly about. Facts and details tell about the topic. *Let's look for important details as we read.* Display a Main Topic and Key Detail chart for children to copy.

Model recording answers in the details boxes. Have children record the answers into their charts.

Think Aloud As I read, I will look for the important, or key, details. I can find them in the text or in the photos. These details help me understand and remember the information about meerkats. They also connect to the main topic.

After children finish reading the selection, provide time for them to complete the chart.

After Reading

Respond to Reading

Complete the Respond to Reading on page 12 after reading.

Retell

Have children take turns retelling key details from the selection, using the **Retelling Cards** as a guide. Help children make a connection by asking: *What other animals do you know that live together? Where do they live?*

Model Fluency

Read the sentences one at a time. Have children chorally repeat. Point out how you pause when you see a comma or punctuation mark. Demonstrate how to read with phrasing.

Apply Have partners practice reading. Provide feedback as needed.

PAIRED READ ...

"I Live in a House!"

Make Connections: Write About It

Before reading, ask children to note the genre of this text is poetry. Then discuss the Compare Texts direction. After reading, ask children to make a connection between *Meerkat Family* and "I Live in a House."

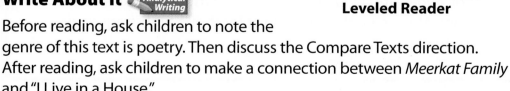

Leveled Reader

FOCUS ON SCIENCE

Children can extend their knowledge of where animals live by completing the science activity on page 16.

STEM

Literature Circles

Lead children in conducting a literature circle using the Thinkmark questions to guide the discussion. You may wish to discuss what children have learned about where animals live from both selections in the Leveled Reader.

Level Up

Level-up lessons available online.

IF children can read *Meerkat Family* **On Level** with fluency and correctly answer the Respond to Reading questions,

THEN tell children that they will read a more detailed version of the selection.

- Use pages 8–9 of *Meerkat Family* **Beyond Level** to model using Teaching Poster 29 to identify the key details.

- Have children read the selection, checking their comprehension by using the graphic organizer.

On Level

Phonics

BUILD WORDS WITH END BLENDS

 OBJECTIVES

Decode regularly spelled one-syllable words. **RF.1.3b**

Build and decode words with ending consonant blends

 I Do

Display **Word-Building Cards** b, u, m, p. *These are the letters* b, u, m, p. *They stand for* /b/ /u/ /m/ /p/. *I'll blend the sounds together:* /buuummmp/, *bump. The word is* bump.

 We Do

Let's do one together. Make the word *bank* using Word-Building Cards. *Let's blend the word:* /b/ /a/ /n/ /k/, /baaannnk/, bank. *The word is* bank.

 You Do

Have children build and blend these words: *hand, land, lend, mend, mind, mint, mist, must, dust, dump, damp, clamp, clank.*

Repeat with other words with ending consonant blends.

High-Frequency Words

REVIEW WORDS

 OBJECTIVES

Recognize and read grade-appropriate irregularly spelled words. **RF.1.3g**

Review high-frequency words *eat, no, of, under, who*

 I Do

Use the **Read/Spell/Write** routine to review each new word. Use each word in a sentence.

 We Do

Guide children to Read/Spell/Write each word using their **Response Boards**. Work with the group to generate oral sentences using the words.

 You Do

Have partners work together to do the Read/Spell/Write routine using the words *eat, no, of, under,* and *who*. Ask children to write sentences about this week's stories. Make sure they include at least one high-frequency word in each sentence.

Comprehension

REVIEW MAIN TOPIC AND KEY DETAILS

OBJECTIVES
Identify the topic and retell key details of a text. **RI.1.2**

 I Do

Remind children that as they read informational selections, they can look for key details to help them understand what they read. These key details will help them identify the main topic. *When we read, we look for important details in the words and pictures or photographs. These details help us understand the main topic, what the selection is mostly about.*

 We Do

Read the first two sentences of the Practice Book selection aloud. Stop and point out the key detail in each sentence. Ask children to explain why these details are important. *We read about what a bug can do at Big Rock Pond. Why is that an important detail?*

 You Do

Guide children to read the remainder of the Practice Book selection. Remind them to find the key details as they read. Then have partners discuss how these details connect to the main topic.

SELF-SELECTED READING

OBJECTIVES
Identify the topic and retell key details of a text. **RI.1.2**

With prompting and support, read informational texts appropriately complex for grade 1. **RI.1.10**

Apply the strategy and skill to read a text

Read Independently

Have children choose a nonfiction selection for sustained silent reading. Remind them to:

→ look for key details to help them understand what they are reading.

→ use details to understand the main topic of the selection.

→ reread when they don't understand something they have read or want to remember something important.

Read Purposefully

Have children record the important details on a Main Topic and Details chart. Then help partners to:

→ share the information they recorded on the chart and tell each other about the stories they read.

→ discuss how the key details connect to the main idea.

→ Beyond Level

Lexile 370

Leveled Reader:
Meerkat Family

**Go
Digital**

Meerkat Family

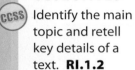

**Graphic
Organizer**

Before Reading

Preview and Predict

Read the title and author name. Have children preview the title page and the photographs. Ask: *What do you think this book will be about?*

Review Genre: Informational Text/Nonfiction

Have children recall that a nonfiction selection tells information about real people, places, or things. The selection presents facts about a specific topic.

ESSENTIAL QUESTION

Remind children of the Essential Question: *Where do animals live together?* Have children set a purpose for reading by saying: *What do you want to find out about meerkats and how they live together?*

During Reading

Guided Comprehension

Have children whisper read *Meerkat Family*. Have them place self-stick notes next to difficult words. Remind children that when they come to an unfamiliar word, they can look for familiar spellings. They will need to break longer words into smaller chunks and sound out each part.

Monitor children's reading. Stop periodically and ask open-ended questions to facilitate rich discussion, such as: *Why do you think a burrow is a safe and comfortable place for a meerkat family to live?*

Strategy: Reread

Remind children that they can reread to help them understand and remember information in a selection. *If you don't understand something that you read, pause and reread. Look for more information in the details and the photos.*

OBJECTIVES

 Identify the main topic and retell key details of a text. **RI.1.2**

Skill: Main Topic and Key Details

Remind children that as they read a selection, they can use words and photos to find important, or key details. After children finish the selection, say: *Key details are pieces of important information that tell about the main topic. What are some of the key details in this selection?* Display a Main Topic and Key Details chart for children to copy.

Model recording children's answers in the details boxes. Have children record the details in their chart.

Think Aloud As I read the selection, I am going to look for important pieces of information. I'll think about what all these details tell about. That's the main topic.

After Reading

Respond to Reading

Have children complete the Respond to Reading on page 12 after reading.

Retell

Have children take turns retelling important information from the selection. Have children make a personal connection by writing about other animal homes. Say: *Write about how a meerkat family is similar to a human family. What are some differences?*

PAIRED READ ...

"I Live in a House!"

Make Connections: Write About It

Before reading "I Live in a House!" have children preview the title page and identify the genre. Then discuss the Compare Texts direction. After reading, have partners discuss information they learned. Ask children to make connections by comparing and contrasting the selections.

Leveled Reader

FOCUS ON SCIENCE

Children can extend their knowledge of where animals live by completing the science activity on page 16.

Literature Circles

Lead children in conducting a literature circle using the Thinkmark questions to guide the discussion. You may wish to discuss what children have learned about where animals live from both selections in the Leveled Reader.

Gifted and Talented

SYNTHESIZE Challenge children to think about a different animal that interests them and where the animal lives. Have them draw a picture to show the animal's habitat. Help them to label the picture with key details.

EXTEND Have children do additional research to find out more about the animal that they chose. Help them add details to their picture. Then provide time for children to share their information.

Beyond Level
Vocabulary

OBJECTIVES

 Use sentence-level context as a clue to the meaning of a word or phrase. **L.1.4a**

 I Do

Explain to children that other words in a sentence can help to explain the meaning of a particular word. *Sometimes the words that come before or after an unknown word can help explain its meaning.* Review the meaning of the oral vocabulary word *habitat*.

Write the sentence: *The pond is a good* habitat *for the frog. The word* pond *helps us understand that a habitat is a place where an animal lives.*

 We Do

Then focus on the oral vocabulary word *depend*. Say the sentence: *We depend on the bus to get to school.* Talk about how the words in the sentence help them figure out the meaning of the word *depend*.

 You Do

Have partners take turns using the words *habitat* and *depend* in sentences. Discuss how context clues help with the meanings of the words. Have partners share their sentences with the group.

 Gifted and Talented

Extend Have children pick an animal and draw a picture that shows how the animal depends on its habitat to live. Challenge them to present their pictures to the whole class. While presenting, they should use the words *habitat* and *depend* in context-rich sentences that help define the words.

Comprehension

REVIEW MAIN TOPIC AND KEY DETAILS

OBJECTIVES

 Identify the topic and retell key details of a text. **RI.1.2**

 I Do Talk about how children can find key details in words, photographs, and pictures. Discuss how they can use key details to understand what they read.

 We Do Have children read the first two sentences of the Practice Book selection. As you read, stop to identify key details and discuss why they are important. *What key detail did we read? Why is it important? How does it connect to the main topic?*

 You Do Have children read the rest of the Practice Book selection independently. Encourage them to pause and look for important details as they read. Talk about how the details connect to the main topic.

SELF-SELECTED READING

OBJECTIVES

 Identify the topic and retell key details of a text. **RI.1.2**

 With prompting and support, read informational texts appropriately complex for grade 1. **RI.1.10**

Apply strategy and skill to read a text

Read Independently

Have children choose a nonfiction selection for sustained silent reading. Tell them that they should use a Main Topic and Details chart. Remind them to reread when they do not understand something they have read or if they want to remember something important.

Read Purposefully

Have children record the key details and topic on a Main Topic and Details chart. After reading, guide children to:

→ share the information they recorded on the chart with a partner.

→ record information about the selection in a reading response journal.

 Independent Study Have children write letters to the authors of the selections they read. Tell them to include information they learned from the selection and ask what else they would like to know about the topic.

English Language Learners

Reading/Writing Workshop

OBJECTIVES

Ask and answer questions about key details in a text. **RI.1.2**

Shared Read:
The Best Spot

Go Digital

The Best Spot

| Main Topic | | |
| Detail | Detail | Detail |

Graphic Organizer

Before Reading

Build Background

Read the Essential Question: *Where do animals live together?*

→ Explain the meaning of the Essential Question: *Some animals live in groups. Others live alone. Many different animals can live in one area.*

→ **Model an answer:** *Some animals live on land. Some animals live in the ocean. Others live near a pond or a stream.*

→ Ask children a question that ties the Essential Question to their own background knowledge: *Turn to a partner and think of an animal that you know about. Does that animal live alone or in a group? Where might it live?* Call on several pairs.

During Reading

Interactive Question-Response

→ Ask questions that help children understand the meaning of the text after each paragraph.

→ Reinforce the meanings of key vocabulary by providing meanings embedded in the questions.

→ Ask children questions that require them to use key vocabulary.

→ Reinforce comprehension strategies and skills of the week by modeling.

The Best Spot

Pages 54–55

Point to the title. *Listen as I read the title of the selection.* Point to each word as you read it. *What is the title?* (The Best Spot) *The word* spot *can mean different things. Let's figure out what it means here.*

Point to the animals in the illustration. *What animals do you see?* (birds, deer, rabbit) *I also see trees and plants. I think the word* spot *in this title means a particular place, the forest. Let's read to find out why this spot is the best for the animals.*

Pages 56–57

Explain and Model the Skill *Let's look for key details as we read the selection. This will help us figure out the main topic. I see a deer in this picture. Point to it. What is the deer doing?* (eating) Read pages 56 and 57. *What does the deer eat?* (plants) *What other animal lives in this spot?* (rabbit)

What do these two animals have in common? (They both live in the forest.)

Pages 58–59

Look at the picture on page 58. Who lives in the nest? (birds) *Let's read these two pages together.*

Explain and Model the Strategy Reread to help children understand why the mom gets bugs. *I read the text, but I don't really understand why the mom gets bugs. I can reread and look at the picture. I see that the baby birds want to eat the bugs. Now I understand this detail better.*

How are a bird nest and a wasp nest alike? How are they different? (The nests are different shapes and made from different things. The bird nest is open at the top. They are both in a tree. Animals live in both nests.)

Pages 60–61

What insect do you see in the photos and diagram? (ants) *Let's read these pages together. Where do these ants live?* (the forest, underground)

What do the ants do under the ground? Use the diagram to find out. (dig, collect/store food, raise young)

Explain and Model High-Frequency Words Demonstrate how the word *under* means "below."

Point to the word under *on page 61. Under means "below." Put your finger under your chin.*

Page 62

Let's look for details in the picture to understand what is happening. Who is taking care of the baby foxes, the kits? (the mom fox) *Let's read the first two sentences:* Fox kits hop on a stump. Mom fox lets the kits run and jump.

What do you think dad fox is hunting for? (small animals)

Explain and Model Phonics *Reread the first sentence with me. Which word ends with the /mp/ sound?* (stump) *Listen as I read the second sentence. Which word ends with the /mp/ sound?* (jump)

Page 63

Let's read this page together. What is the skunk doing? (hunting)

Why do you think the forest is the best spot for the animals? (They can find places to live and food to eat.)

After Reading

Make Connections

→ Review the Essential Question.

→ English Language Learners

Lexile 170

OBJECTIVES

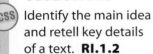
Identify the main idea and retell key details of a text. **RI.1.2**

Leveled Reader:
Meerkat Family

Go Digital

Before Reading

Preview

Read the title. Ask: *What is the title? Say it with me.* Repeat with the author's name. Preview the selection's photographs. Help children describe the images. Use simple language to tell about each page. Ask questions, such as: *Do meerkats have spots? Point to a spot. What color are their noses? What other animals have black noses?*

ESSENTIAL QUESTION

Remind children of the Essential Question: *Where do animals live together?* Say: *Let's read to find out how meerkats live together.* Encourage children to ask for help when they encounter a confusing word or phrase.

During Reading

Interactive Question-Response

Pages 2–3 Point to the photos on pages 2 and 3. *What does a meerkat look like? What does it have on its face? Now let's read together the sentence that tells about their eyes:* "Meerkats have bright eyes."

Pages 4–5 *What are the meerkats doing on page 5?* (eating) *Let's read the label together:* bug. *Now let's read the sentences on this page to see what else meerkats eat.* (plants and small animals)

Pages 6–7 *Let's read the first sentence on page 7:* "Meerkats live in burrows." *Point to the label on the photo. This is the word* burrow. *Where are burrows? Let's look for the sentence on this page that tells us.* ("Burrows are under the ground.")

Pages 8–9 *Look at the picture on pages 8 and 9. It shows what a burrow looks like. Tell your partner what you see. Point to parts of the picture to help.*

Pages 10–11 *What do you see in the photos on pages 10 and 11?* Point to the adult and baby meerkats. *Let's read these two pages together to learn about baby meerkats.* After reading, ask: *Who takes care of the baby meerkats?* (the adult meerkats)

Meerkat Family

Graphic Organizer

Retell

After Reading

Respond to Reading

Revisit the Essential Question. Ask children to work with partners to fill in the graphic organizer and answer the questions on page 12. Pair children with peers of varying language abilities.

Retell

Model retelling using the **Retelling Card** prompts. Then guide children to retell key details in the selection to a partner.

Fluency: Appropriate Phrasing

Read the sentences in the book, one at a time. Help children echo read the pages expressively and with appropriate phrasing. Remind them to pause when they see a comma or end punctuation mark.

Apply Have children practice reading with a partner. Pair children with peers of varying language abilities. Provide feedback as needed.

PAIRED READ ...

Leveled Reader

"I Live in a House!"

Make Connections:
Write About It *Analytical Writing*

Before reading, ask children to note that the genre of this text is poetry. Then discuss the Compare Texts direction. After reading, ask children to make connections between the information they learned from "I Live in a House!" and *Meerkat Family*. Prompt children by providing sentence frames: Children and meerkat babies live with _____.

FOCUS ON SCIENCE

Children can extend their knowledge of where animals live by completing the science activity on page 16.

STEM

Literature Circles

Lead children in conducting a literature circle using the Thinkmark questions to guide the discussion. You may wish to discuss what children have learned about animal communities from both selections in the Leveled Reader.

Level Up

Level-up lessons available online.

IF children can read *Meerkat Family*, **ELL Level** with fluency and correctly answer the Respond to Reading questions,

THEN tell children that they will read a more detailed version of the selection.

• Use pages 8–9 of *Meerkat Family* **On Level** to model using Teaching Poster 29 to identify the main topic and key details.

• Have children read the selection, checking their comprehension by using the graphic organizer.

English Language Learners
Vocabulary

PRETEACH ORAL VOCABULARY

 OBJECTIVES
Produce complete sentences when appropriate to task and situation. **SL.1.6**

LANGUAGE OBJECTIVE

Preteach oral vocabulary words

 I Do Display the image from the **Visual Vocabulary Cards** one at a time to preteach the oral vocabulary words *habitat* and *depend*.

 We Do Display the images again and talk about how they illustrate or demonstrate the words. Model using sentences to describe the image.

 You Do Display the words again and have partners discuss how the pictures demonstrate the word *habitat* and *depend*.

Beginning	Intermediate	Advanced/High
Provide sentence frames: *A habitat _____. Animals depend on _____.*	Have children ask a question about the picture using the words.	Have children write sentences using each word..

RETEACH ELL VOCABULARY

 OBJECTIVES
Produce complete sentences when appropriate to task and situation. **SL.1.6**

LANGUAGE OBJECTIVE

Reteach ELL vocabulary words

 I Do Display images from the Visual Vocabulary Cards one at a time to preteach the ELL Vocabulary words *environment* and *survival* and follow the routine. Say the word and have children repeat it.

We Do Display the image again and explain how it illustrates the word. Model using sentences to describe the image.

 You Do Display the word again. Have children say and spell the word. Provide opportunities for children to use the words in speaking and writing. Provide sentence starters.

Beginning	Intermediate	Advanced/High
Help children write the completed sentences and read them aloud.	Have children read the completed sentences they wrote.	Have children create their own sentences using the words.

High-Frequency Words

REVIEW WORDS

CCSS

OBJECTIVES

Recognize and read grade-appropriate irregularly spelled words. **RF.1.3g**

LANGUAGE OBJECTIVE

Review high-frequency words *eat, not, of, under, who*

I Do

Display the **High-Frequency Word Cards** for *eat, no, of, under,* and *who.* Read each word. Use the **Read/Spell/Write** routine to teach each word. Help children write each word on their **Reponse Boards**.

We Do

Write sentence frames. Track the print as children read and complete the sentences: **(1)** *I will eat _____.* **(2)** *No, we did not _____.* **(3)** *Some of us can _____.* **(4)** *The pup is under the _____.* **(5)** *Who can fix _____?*

You Do

Display the High-Frequency Word Cards from the previous weeks. Display one card at a time as children chorally read the word. Mix and repeat. Note words children need to review.

Beginning	Intermediate	Advanced/High
Point to and say each word for children to repeat.	Have children read each word as you display it.	Have children say the word and then use it in a sentence.

RETEACH WORDS

OBJECTIVES

Recognize and read grade-appropriate irregularly spelled words. **RF.1.3g**

LANGUAGE OBJECTIVE

Reteach high-frequency words

I Do

Display each **Visual Vocabulary Card** and say the word aloud. Define the word in English and, if appropriate, in Spanish. Identify any cognates.

We Do

Point to the image again and explain how it illustrates or demonstrates the word. Ask children to repeat the word. Engage children in structured partner-talk about the image as prompted on the back of the card. Ask children to chorally say the word three times.

You Do

Display each visual in random order, hiding the word. Have children identify the word and explain it in their own words.

Beginning	Intermediate	Advanced/High
Display an image and give children two word choices.	Provide definition starters for children, as necessary.	Have partners take turns saying a sentence but leaving out the word. Ask the other to tell what word completes the sentence.

English Language Learners
Writing/Spelling

WRITING TRAIT: IDEAS

OBJECTIVES
Identify the main topic and retell key details of a text. **RI.1.2**

LANGUAGE OBJECTIVE

Write a sentences that focus on a main topic

 I Do
Explain that writers need to focus on one idea, or topic, when they write information texts, or nonfiction. All the sentences in the selection should tell something about that idea.

 We Do
Read pages 56 and 57 of *The Best Spot*. Talk about what the text on these pages is mostly about. *The writer tells us what the main topic is. What animals did we read about? Where do they live?*

 You Do
We're going to write sentences about another place where animals live: a pond. *The pond is your main topic. Write three sentences that focus on animals and plants at a pond.* Have children work with a partner.

Beginning	Intermediate	Advanced/High
Provide a sentence starters: *Near the pond _____. Fish swim _____.*	Have partners list plants and animals near a pond and then write sentences.	Challenge partners to write two more sentences about the main topic.

WORDS WITH END BLENDS

OBJECTIVES
Use conventional spelling for words with common spelling patterns and for frequently occurring irregular words. **L.1.2d**

LANGUAGE OBJECTIVE

Spell words with ending consonant blends

 I Do
Read aloud the Spelling Words on page T170. Write *lend* on the board and circle the letters *nd*. Point out that when these letters appear together, we say both sounds. Segment and read the word. Continue with the rest of the words and have children repeat.

 We Do
Read the first sentence from Dictation Routine on page T170 aloud. Slowly read the word with the ending blend. Ask children to repeat and write the word. Repeat the process for the remaining sentences.

 You Do
Display the words. Have partners check their spelling lists. Help children correct any misspelled words.

Beginning	Intermediate	Advanced/High
Help children write the word and repeat it after you.	Have partners use Word-Building Cards to form, say, and spell each word.	Challenge children to dictate or write a sentence with each word.

Grammar

POSSESSIVE NOUNS

OBJECTIVES

Use common, proper, and possessive nouns. **L.1.1b**

LANGUAGE OBJECTIVE

Recognize the possessive form of nouns

Language Transfers Handbook

TRANSFER SKILLS

Spanish, Hmong, Vietnamese, and Haitian Creole speakers may use prepositions to describe possessives, saying *the leg of the dog* rather than *the dog's leg*. Although the construction is grammatically correct it is not used typically. Provide practice in changing to possessives, such as: *the head of the cat* (*the cat's head*); *the pen of Kim* (*Kim's pen*); *the fin of the fish* (*the fish's fin*).

 I Do

Review that a possessive noun is a noun that shows ownership. Hand a pen to a child. Point to the pen and say: *This is [Lisa's] pen.* Write: *This is Lisa's pen.* Read the sentence. Circle the word *Lisa's*. Say: *The word* Lisa *is a noun. It ends with an apostrophe -s. This shows that the pen belongs to Lisa.*

 We Do

Write sentences and work with children to read them and circle the possessive noun in each. Have them say: *The _____ belongs to _____.*

The box's top is bent .

The clock's hands do not move.

Tim's hat is red.

The frog's back is green.

 You Do

Write the following sentence frames.

The (cat) milk spilled.

(Ted) dog can run fast.

Have partners make the noun in parentheses a possessive noun, then read the sentence aloud. Monitor children's answers and pronunciation as they read the sentences aloud.

Beginning	Intermediate	Advanced/High
One partner holds up an object and the other says the name as a possessive noun and object: *Ann's pencil.* Switch roles and repeat.	One partner names an object as a possessive noun: *book's.* The other says a sentence that includes the possessive: *The book's cover is red.* Switch roles and repeat.	Have children write and read sentences about helping in the community, using possessive nouns. Have partners circle the possessive nouns in each others' sentences.

PROGRESS MONITORING

Weekly Assessment

CCSS TESTED SKILLS

✓ COMPREHENSION:	✓ PHONEMIC AWARENESS:	✓ PHONICS/STRUCTURAL ANALYSIS/HIGH-FREQUENCY WORDS:
Main Topic and Key Details **RI.1.2**	Phoneme Categorization **RF.1.2c**	Ending Consonant Blends: *nd, nk, nt, st, sk, mp* **RF.1.3**
	Phoneme Blending **RF.1.2b**	Inflectional Ending *-ing* **RF.1.3f**
	Phoneme Substitution **RF.1.2c**	*eat, no, of, under, who* **RF.1.3g**
	Phoneme Segmentation **RF.1.2d**	

FLUENCY ←

Conduct group fluency assessments.

Assess fluency for one group of children per week using the **Letter Naming, Phoneme Segmentation,** and **Sight Word Fluency** assessments in *Reading Wonders Fluency Assessment.*

Go Digital! http://connected.mcgraw-hill.com

Using Assessment Results

✓ TESTED SKILLS	If ...	Then ...
COMPREHENSION	Children answer 0–3 multiple-choice items correctly ...	... assign Lessons 85–87 on Main Idea and Details from the ***Tier 2 Comprehension Intervention online PDFs.***
PHONEMIC AWARENESS	Children answer 0–1 multiple-choice items correctly ...	... assign Lessons 31–32 on Phoneme Categorization: Ending Sounds, Lessons 62–66 on Phoneme Blending, Lessons 84–89 on Phoneme Substitution, and Lessons 67–71 on Phoneme Segmenting from the ***Tier 2 Phonemic Awareness Intervention online PDFs.***
PHONICS/ STRUCTURAL ANALYSIS/HFW	Children answer 0–5 multiple-choice items correctly ...	... assign Lesson 51 on Short Vowels: Final Blends and Lesson 67 on Inflectional Ending *-ing* from the ***Tier 2 Phonics/Word Study Intervention online PDFs.***

Response to Intervention

Use children's assessment results to assist you in identifying children who will benefit from focused intervention.

Use the appropriate sections of the ***Placement and Diagnostic Assessment*** to designate children requiring:

TIER 2 **Intervention Online PDFs**

TIER 3 **WonderWorks Intervention Program**

TEACH AND MODEL

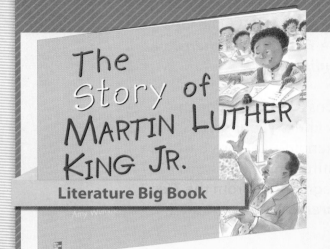

The Story of MARTIN LUTHER KING JR.
Literature Big Book

Big Book and Little Book
Reading/Writing Workshop

Listening Comprehension

Comprehension Strategy *Reread* T244–T245

Close Reading

Shared Reading *Thump Thump Helps Out,* 74–83
Genre Fantasy
Lexile 510

Words to Know T249

all, call, day, her, want

Minilessons   ✓ **Tested Skills** CCSS

✓ **Phonics** .... Consonant Digraphs *th, sh, -ng,* T250–T251
✓ **Comprehension Skill** .... Character, Setting, Events, T261
✓ **Writing Traits** .... Organization, T270
✓ **Grammar** .... Common and Proper Nouns, T271

☞ **Go Digital**

http://connected.mcgraw-hill.com

LET'S HELP
Essential Question
How do people help out in the community?

WEEK 4 →

APPLY WITH CLOSE READING

Literature Anthology

Complex Text

PAIRED READ →

Nell's Books, 64–79
Genre Fantasy
Lexile 200

"Kids Can Help!," 82–85
Genre Nonfiction
Lexile 350

Differentiated Text

Leveled Readers *Including Paired Reads*

APPROACHING
Lexile 40

ON LEVEL
Lexile 200

BEYOND
Lexile 390

ELL
Lexile 190

Extended Complex Text

The True Story of the 3 Little Pigs!
Genre
Fiction
Lexile 570

The Cow That Went Oink
Genre
Fiction
Lexile 270

Classroom Library lessons available online.

Classroom Library

TEACH AND MANAGE

How You Teach

INTRODUCE

Weekly Concept
Let's Help

Reading/Writing Workshop
40–51

TEACH

Listening Comprehension
The Story of Martin Luther King Jr.

Close Reading
Thump Thump Helps Out

Minilessons
Character, Setting, Events; Fantasy; Consonant Digraphs *th*, *sh*, *-ng*; High-Frequency Words

APPLY

Close Reading
Nell's Books
"Kids Can Help!"

 Go Digital

Interactive Whiteboard

Interactive Whiteboard

Mobile

How Students Practice

WEEKLY CONTRACT

PDF Online

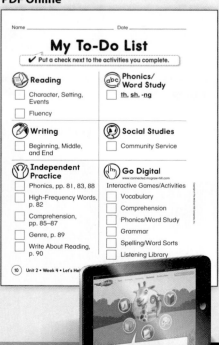

LEVELED PRACTICE AND ONLINE ACTIVITIES

Your Turn Practice Book
81–90

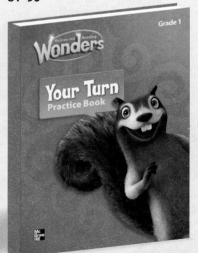

Leveled Readers

 **Go Digital**

Online To-Do List

Leveled Activities

Mobile

DIFFERENTIATE

SMALL GROUP INSTRUCTION

Leveled Readers

Mobile

INTEGRATE

Research and Inquiry
Make a List, T278–T279

Text Connections
Let's Help, T280

Write About Reading
Analyze Character, Setting,
Events, T281

**Online Research
and Writing**

ASSESS

Wonders
**Weekly
Assessment**

**Weekly Assessment
81–90**

**Online
Assessment**

LEVELED WORKSTATION CARDS

More
Activities
on back

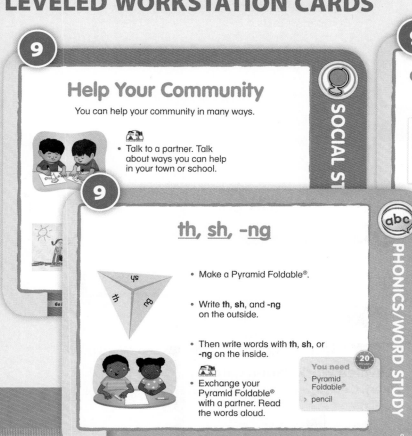

9

Help Your Community

You can help your community in many ways.

- Talk to a partner. Talk about ways you can help in your town or school.

SOCIAL STUDIES

9

th, sh, -ng

- Make a Pyramid Foldable®.

- Write **th**, **sh**, and **-ng** on the outside.

- Then write words with **th**, **sh**, or **-ng** on the inside.

- Exchange your Pyramid Foldable® with a partner. Read the words aloud.

You need
> Pyramid Foldable®
> pencil

20 Minutes

PHONICS/WORD STUDY

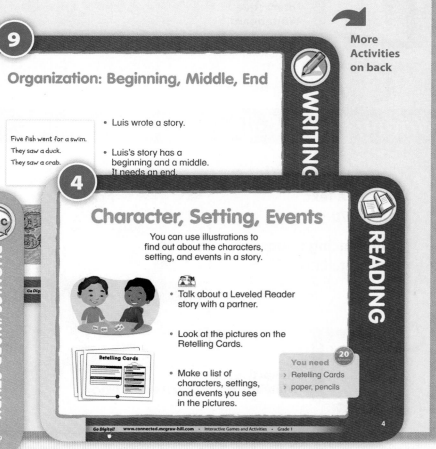

9

Organization: Beginning, Middle, End

- Luis wrote a story.

Five fish went for a swim.
They saw a duck.
They saw a crab.

- Luis's story has a beginning and a middle. It needs an end.

WRITING

4

Character, Setting, Events

You can use illustrations to find out about the characters, setting, and events in a story.

- Talk about a Leveled Reader story with a partner.

- Look at the pictures on the Retelling Cards.

Retelling Cards

- Make a list of characters, settings, and events you see in the pictures.

You need
> Retelling Cards
> paper, pencils

20 Minutes

READING

Write About Reading • Analytical Writing

Write to Sources and Research

Note Taking, T269A

Character, Setting, Events, T269B

Author's Purpose, T269I

Make Connections: Essential Question, T269J

Research and Inquiry, T278

Analyze to Inform/Explain, T281

Comparing Texts, T287, T297, T301, T307

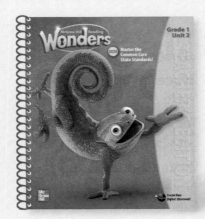

Teacher's Edition

Your Turn Practice Book

Character, Setting, Events, pp. 85–87
Write About Reading, p. 90

Interactive Whiteboard

Leveled Readers
Comparing Texts

Writing Process • Independent Writing

Narrative Text
Story, T270–T271

Conferencing Routines
Peer Conferences, T276

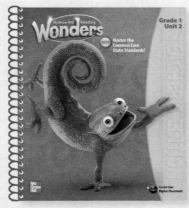

Teacher's Edition

Interactive Whiteboard

 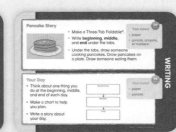

Leveled Workstation Card
Story, Card 23

Writing Traits • Shared and Interactive Writing

Writing Trait: Organization
Story, T252

Conferencing Routines
Peer Conferences, T276

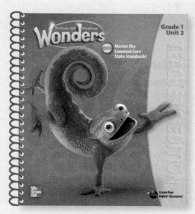

Teacher's Edition

Organization: Proper
Nouns, pp. 86–87

Reading/Writing Workshop

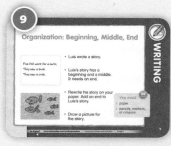
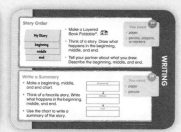

Leveled Workstation Card
Organization: Beginning, Middle, End, Card 9

Go Digital

Interactive Whiteboard

Grammar and Spelling

Grammar
Common and Proper Nouns, T253

Spelling
Words with *th*, *sh*, *-ng*, T248

Go Digital

Interactive Whiteboard

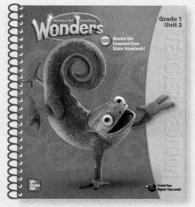

Teacher's Edition

Go Digital

Online Spelling and Grammar Games

Handwriting

SUGGESTED LESSON PLAN

✓ TESTED SKILLS CCSS

	DAY 1	**DAY 2**

READING

Whole Group

Teach, Model, and Apply

Reading/Writing Workshop

DAY 1

Build Background Let's Help, T242–T243
Oral Vocabulary Words *leadership, admire,* T242
Listening Comprehension
Big Book *The Story of Martin Luther King Jr.,* T244 Strategy: Reread, T245
Word Work T246–T251
Fluency: Sound-Spellings
Phonemic Awareness: Phoneme Isolation
Phonics/Spelling: Introduce *th, sh, -ng*
High-Frequency Words: *all, call, day, her, want*
Shared Reading *Thump Thump Helps Out,* T250–T251
Practice Your Turn, p. 81

DAY 2

Oral Language Let's Help, T254
Oral Vocabulary Words *connections, enjoy, rely,* T254
Listening Comprehension Strategy: Reread, T255
Interactive Read-Aloud Cards "Luis's Library," T255
Word Work T256–T259
Fluency: Sound-Spellings
Phonemic Awareness: Phoneme Categorization
Phonics/Spelling: Review Consonant Digraphs
Structural Analysis: Closed Syllables
High-Frequency Words: *all, call, day, her, want*
Shared Reading *Thump Thump Helps Out,* T260–T261
✓**Comprehension**
•Genre: Fantasy, T260
•Skill: Character, Setting, Events, T261
Practice Your Turn, pp. 82–84

DIFFERENTIATED INSTRUCTION   Choose across the week to meet your children's needs.

Small Group

Approaching Level

DAY 1

Leveled Reader *The Sick Tree,* T286–T287
Phonemic Awareness Phoneme Isolation, T288 ②
Phonics Connect to Consonant Digraphs, T290 ②
High-Frequency Words Review, T293

DAY 2

Leveled Reader *The Sick Tree,* T286–T287
Phonemic Awareness Phoneme Categorization, T289 ②
Phonics Blend Words with Consonant Digraphs, T291 ②
High-Frequency Words Reteach, T293
Comprehension Key Details, T294 ②

On Level

DAY 1

Leveled Reader *Squirrels Help,* T296–T297
Phonics Build Words with *th, sh, -ng,* T298

DAY 2

Leveled Reader *Squirrels Help,* T296–T297
High Frequency Words Review Words, T298

Beyond Level

DAY 1

Leveled Reader *Wow, Kitty!,* T300–T301
Oral Vocabulary Antonyms, T302

DAY 2

Leveled Reader *Wow, Kitty!,* T300–T301
Oral Vocabulary Antonyms, T302

English Language Learners

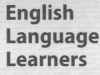

DAY 1

Shared Read *Thump Thump Helps Out,* T304–T305
Phonemic Awareness Phoneme Isolation, T288
Phonics Connect to Consonant Digraphs, T290
Vocabulary Preteach Oral Vocabulary, T308

DAY 2

Leveled Reader *Squirrels Help,* T306–T307
Phonemic Awareness Phoneme Categorization, T288
Phonics Blend Words with *th, sh, -ng,* T291
Vocabulary Preteach ELL Vocabulary, T308

LANGUAGE ARTS

Whole Group

Writing
Grammar

DAY 1

Shared Writing Writing Trait: Organization, T252
Story, T252
Grammar
•Common and Proper Nouns, T253
Mechanics: Capitalize Proper Nouns, T253

DAY 2

Interactive Writing Writing Trait: Organization, T252
Story, T252
Grammar
•Common and Proper Nouns, T253
Mechanics: Capitalize Proper Nouns, T253

DAY 3	DAY 4	DAY 5 Review and Assess

READING

Oral Language Let's Help, T264	**Oral Language** Let's Help, T272	**Integrate Ideas**
Review Oral Vocabulary *admire, connections, enjoy, leadership, rely*, T264	**Comprehension** Text Feature: List, T273	• Text Connections, T280
Listening Comprehension	**Close Reading** "Kids Can Help!", T273A–T273B	• Write About Reading, T281 *Analytical Writing*
Big Book *The Story of Martin Luther King Jr.*, T265	**Word Work** T274–T275	**Word Work** T282–T283
• Strategy: Reread, T265	Fluency: Sound-Spellings	Fluency: Word Automaticity
• Retelling, T265	Phonemic Awareness: Phoneme Categorization	Phonemic Awareness: Phoneme Blending/ Segmentation
• Fluency: Intonation, T265	Phonics/Spelling: Build Words with *th, sh, -ng*	Phonics/Spelling: Blend and Build Words with *th, sh, -ng*
Word Work T266–T268	Structural Analysis Closed Syllables	Structural Analysis: Closed Syllables
Fluency: Sound-Spellings	High-Frequency Words: *all, call, day, her, want*	High-Frequency Words: *all, call, day, her, want*
Phonemic Awareness: Phoneme Blending	**Integrate Ideas** Research and Inquiry, T278–T279	**Practice** Your Turn, p. 90
Phonics/Spelling: Blend Words with *th, sh, -ng*	**Practice** Your Turn, pp. 88–89	
Structural Analysis: Closed Syllables		
High-Frequency Words: *all, call, day, her, want*		
Close Reading *Nell's Books*, T269A–T269J *Analytical Writing*		
Practice Your Turn, pp. 85–87		

DIFFERENTIATED INSTRUCTION

Leveled Reader *The Sick Tree*, T286–T287	**Leveled Reader** Paired Read: "Beach Clean-Up," T287 *Analytical Writing*	**Leveled Reader** Literature Circles, T287
Phonemic Awareness Phoneme Blending, T289	**Phonemic Awareness** Phoneme Categorization, T289	**Phonics** Build Fluency with Phonics, T291
Phonics Build Words with Consonant Digraphs, T291	**Phonics** Blend Words with *th, sh, -ng*, T291	**High-Frequency Words** Cumulative Review, T293
Structural Analysis Review Closed Syllables, T292	**Structural Analysis** Reteach Closed Syllables, T292	**Comprehension** Self-Selected Reading, T295
Comprehension Review Character, Setting, Events, T295	**Comprehension** Read for Fluency, T294 ②	

Leveled Reader *Squirrels Help*, T296–T297	**Leveled Reader** Paired Read: "Food Drive," T297 *Analytical Writing*	**Leveled Reader** Literature Circles, T297
Comprehension Review Character, Setting, Events, T299		**Comprehension** Self-Selected Reading, T299

Leveled Reader *Wow, Kitty!*, T300–T301	**Leveled Reader** Paired Read: "Sharing Skills," T301 *Analytical Writing*	**Leveled Reader** Literature Circles, T301
Comprehension Review Character, Setting, Events, T303		**Comprehension** Self-Selected Reading, T303

Leveled Reader *Squirrels Help*, T306–T307	**Leveled Reader** Paired Read: "Food Drive," T307 *Analytical Writing*	**Leveled Reader** Literature Circles, T307
Phonemic Awareness Phoneme Blending, T289	**Phonemic Awareness** Phoneme Categorization, T289	**Phonics** Blend Words with *th, sh, -ng*, T291
Phonics Build Words with *th, sh, -ng*, T291	**Structural Analysis** Reteach Closed Syllables, T292	**Spelling** Words with Consonant Digraphs *th, sh, -ng*, T310
Structural Analysis Review Closed Syllables, T292	**High-Frequency Words** Reteach Words, T309	
High-Frequency Words Review Words, T309	**Grammar** Common and Proper Nouns, T311	
Writing Writing Trait: Organization, T310		

LANGUAGE ARTS

Independent Writing Writing Trait: Organization, T270 Story: Prewrite/Draft, T270–T271	**Independent Writing** Writing Trait: Organization, T276 Story: Revise/Proofread/Edit, T276–T277	**Independent Writing** Story: Publish and Present, T284
Grammar • Common and Proper Nouns, T271	**Grammar** • Common and Proper Nouns, T277	**Grammar** • Common and Proper Nouns, T285
Mechanics: Capitalize Proper Nouns, T271	Mechanics: Capitalize Proper Nouns, T277	Mechanics: Capitalize Proper Nouns, T285

DIFFERENTIATE TO ACCELERATE

 A C T Scaffold to **A**ccess **C**omplex **T**ext

IF the text complexity of a particular selection is too difficult for children

THEN see the references noted in the chart below for scaffolded instruction to help children Access Complex Text.

Qualitative   Quantitative
Reader and Task
TEXT COMPLEXITY

	Big Book	Reading/Writing Workshop	Literature Anthology	Leveled Readers

Quantitative	*The Story of Martin Luther King Jr.* **Lexile** 510	*Thump Thump Helps Out* **Lexile** 510	*Nell's Books* **Lexile** 200 "Kids Can Help" **Lexile** 350	**Approaching Level** **Lexile** 40 **Beyond Level** **Lexile** 390 — **On Level** **Lexile** 200 **ELL** **Lexile** 190
Qualitative	What Makes the Text Complex? · **Genre,** T265 · **Lack of Prior Knowledge,** T265 **A C T** *See Scaffolded Instruction in Teacher's Edition, T265.*	What Makes the Text Complex? **Foundational Skills** · Decoding with *th, sh, -ng,* T246–T247 · Reading words with closed syllables, T257 · Identifying high-frequency words, T249 *See Scaffolded Instruction in Teacher's Edition, T246–T247, T249, and T257.*	What Makes the Text Complex? **Foundational Skills** · Decoding with *th, sh, -ng,* T266–T267 · Reading words with closed syllables, T267 · Identifying high-frequency words, T269	What Makes the Text Complex? **Foundational Skills** · Decoding with *th, sh, -ng* · Reading words with closed syllables · Identifying high-frequency words *all call day her want* *See Level Up lessons online for Leveled Readers.*
Reader and Task	The Introduce the Concept lesson on pages T242–T243 will help determine the reader's knowledge and engagement in the weekly concept. See pages T244–T245, T265, and T278–T281 for questions and tasks for this text.	The Introduce the Concept lesson on pages T242–T243 will help determine the reader's knowledge and engagement in the weekly concept. See pages T250–T251, T260–T261, and T278–T281 for questions and tasks for this text.	The Introduce the Concept lesson on pages T242–T243 will help determine the reader's knowledge and engagement in the weekly concept. See pages T269A–T269J, T273A–T273B, and T278–T281 for questions and tasks for this text.	The Introduce the Concept lesson on pages T242–T243 will help determine the reader's knowledge and engagement in the weekly concept. See pages T286–T287, T296–T297, T300–T301, T306–T307, and T278–T281 for questions and tasks for this text.

Classroom Library Tradebooks: See pages T413–T415 for model lessons.

Go Digital! www.connected.mcgraw-hill.com

Monitor and *Differentiate*

IF you need to differentiate instruction

THEN use the Quick Checks to assess children's needs and select the appropriate small group instruction focus.

 Quick Check

Comprehension Strategy Reread, T245

Comprehension Skill Character, Setting, Events, T261

Phonics Consonant Digraphs *th*, *sh*, *-ng*, T249, T259, T269, T275, T283

High-Frequency Words T249, T259, T269, T275, T283

If No → | Approaching Level | Reteach T286–T295
| ELL | Develop T304–T311

If Yes → | On Level | Review T296–T299
| Beyond Level | Extend T300–T303

Level Up with Leveled Readers

IF children can read their leveled text fluently and answer comprehension questions

THEN work with the next level up to accelerate children's reading with more complex text.

Beyond — T297

Squirrels Help — On Level

The Sick Tree — Approaching — T287

Squirrels Help — ELL — T307

ENGLISH LANGUAGE LEARNERS SCAFFOLD

IF ELL students need additional support **THEN** scaffold instruction using the small group suggestions.

Shared Read	Leveled Reader	Phonemic Awareness	Phonics	Words to Know	Writing	Spelling	Grammar
Thump Thump Helps Out, T304–T305	*Squirrels Help*, T306–T307 "Food Drive," T307	Phoneme Isolation, T288 Phoneme Categorization, T288 Phoneme Blending, T289 Phoneme Categorization, T289	Words with Consonant Digraphs *th*, *sh*, *-ng*, T290–T291 Structural Analysis, T292	*all, call, day, her, want*, T293	Organization, T310	Words with Consonant Digraphs *th*, *sh*, *-ng*, T310	Common and Proper Nouns, T311

Note: Include ELL Students in all small groups based on their needs.

Materials

Reading/Writing Workshop
VOLUME 2

Reading/Writing Workshop Big Book
UNIT 2

Literature Big Book
The Story of Martin Luther King Jr.

Visual Vocabulary Cards
admire
leadership

High-Frequency Word Cards
all   her
call   want
day

Word-Building Cards

Teaching Poster

Think Aloud Clouds

Sound-Spelling Cards

→ # Introduce the Concept

Reading/Writing Workshop Big Book

OBJECTIVES

CCSS Ask questions to clear up any confusion about the topics and texts under discussion. **SL.1.1c**

- Build background knowledge
- Discuss the Essential Question

ACADEMIC LANGUAGE

- *communities, principal*
- Cognates: *comunidades, principal*

(MINILESSON 5 Mins) ## Build Background

ESSENTIAL QUESTION
How do people help out in the community?

Tell children that this week they will be talking and reading about ways that people can help their communities.

Oral Vocabulary Words

Tell children that you will share some words that they can use as they discuss how people help in the community. Use the Define/Example/Ask routine to introduce the oral vocabulary words **leadership** and **admire**.

Visual Vocabulary Cards

Oral Vocabulary Routine

<u>Define:</u> **Leadership** is the ability to guide a group of people, or the action of leading others.

<u>Example:</u> Thanks to Coach Jackson's leadership, the team won the game.

<u>Ask:</u> How can good leadership from the principal help our school?

<u>Define:</u> When you **admire** someone, you approve of and like that person.

<u>Example:</u> Amy admires her neighbors because they helped clean up the park.

<u>Ask:</u> Whom do you admire?

Discuss the theme of "Let's Help" and explain that there are many ways people can help out and make their communities better. Have children tell about ways they have helped their communities. *What did you do? How did you help?*

Go Digital

Let's Help

Video

Visual Glossary

Graphic Organizer

READING/WRITING WORKSHOP, pp. 68–69

ELL

ENGLISH LANGUAGE LEARNERS SCAFFOLD

Beginning

Use Visuals Point to the photo of the children. *The children are in a garden. Are they planting flowers? Are they working together?*

Intermediate

Describe Ask children to describe the scene. *What tools are the children using? What are the children planting?* Correct grammar and punctuation as needed.

Advanced/Advanced High

Discuss Have children elaborate on the garden. *What is in the garden? What are the children doing there?* Repeat children's responses slowly and clearly.

Talk About It: Let's Help

Guide children to discuss what the children are doing.

→ Where are the children?

→ What are they doing? How do you think they might feel?

Use Teaching Poster 40 and prompt children to complete the Word Web by telling different ways the children in the garden could be helping the community.

Have children look at page 68 of their Reading/Writing Workshop and do the Talk About It activity with a partner.

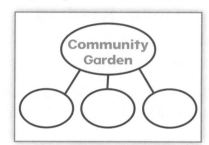

Teaching Poster

Collaborative Conversations

Ask and Answer Questions As children engage in partner, small-group, and whole-group discussions, encourage them to:

→ ask questions about ideas they do not understand.

→ give others a chance to think after asking a question.

→ write down questions they want to ask the teacher or the whole class.

→ # Listening Comprehension

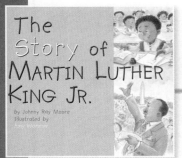

Literature Big Book

OBJECTIVES

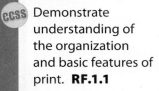 Demonstrate understanding of the organization and basic features of print. **RF.1.1**

Develop concept understanding

ACADEMIC LANGUAGE
reread, highlight

Read the Literature Big Book

MINILESSON 10 Mins

Connect to Concept: Let's Help

Tell children that they will now read about a boy who wanted his community to be fair for everyone. Ask: *What do you already know about Martin Luther King Jr.?*

Concepts of Print

Special Text Treatments As you read *The Story of Martin Luther King Jr.*, point out the words in color print. Explain that the author used different colors to highlight important words. Have children identify the words in color print. Point out to children that some pages contain only part of a sentence, and that you must turn the page to read the end of the sentence. See prompts in the Big Book for modeling concepts of print.

Set a Purpose for Reading

→ Display the Big Book.

→ Read aloud the title, and the names of the author and the illustrator.

→ Ask children to listen to the Big Book to find out what problems Martin Luther King Jr. saw in his community.

Go Digital

The Story of Martin Luther King Jr.

Reread

Strategy: Reread

1 Explain Tell children that if they do not understand something they read in the Big Book, or if they think something is important, they can go back and reread the text. Explain that when you reread, you go back and read something again. Rereading can help them clear up any confusion they had while reading and can help them remember important information.

Think Aloud Rereading a section of text can help clear up any questions you had. Today, as we read *The Story of Martin Luther King Jr.*, remember that you can go back and reread parts of the text to make sure that you understand all the facts and details of the selection.

2 Model As you read, use the Think Aloud Cloud to model applying the strategy.

Think Aloud Remember that you can reread parts of the text to make sure you understood correctly. There is a lot of information on these pages. I am not sure that I understood the information about Martin at school. When I reread the page, I understand that Martin liked school and always did extra work.

3 Guided Practice As you continue to read the Big Book, pause to elicit questions from children. Guide them to reread the text to answer their questions. *Remember, you can reread parts of the text to help you understand and answer questions.* Also have children point out important information they want to reread to better remember.

Respond to Reading

After reading, prompt children to share what they learned about Martin Luther King Jr. and how he helped his community. Discuss which parts they reread and ask questions to check their understanding of those parts.

ELL

ENGLISH LANGUAGE LEARNERS SCAFFOLD

Beginning

Engage Display pages 10 and 11. *Are the children at school? Are they playing? I don't understand what is wrong with Martin's school.* Reread the text. *Is Martin's school old? Does it need to be fixed? Show me something that needs to be fixed.* Allow children ample time to respond.

Intermediate

Describe Display pages 10 and 11. Ask children to describe the illustration. *Is the equipment old or new? How do you know?* Model correct pronunciation as needed. *What can we do if we do not understand what is wrong with Martin's school?*

Advanced/Advanced High

Describe Have children reread pages 10 and 11 and explain what is wrong with Martin's school. Elicit details to support their answers.

Monitor and *Differentiate*

✓ Quick Check

Can children apply the reread strategy?

Small Group Instruction

If No → **Approaching**   Reteach pp. T286–287

ELL   Develop pp. T304–311

If Yes → **On Level**   Review pp. T298–299

Beyond Level   Extend pp. T302–303

→ # Word Work

Quick Review
Build Fluency: Sound-Spellings
Display the **Word-Building Cards:**
th, sh, ng, nd, nk, nt, st, sk, mp, u, e, ea, sp, sn, sl, cr, fr, tr, o, pl, fl, cl, bl, i, a, s. Have children say the sounds.

Phonemic Awareness
5 Mins

OBJECTIVES

 Isolate and pronounce initial, medial vowel, and final sounds (phonemes) in spoken single-syllable words. **RF.1.2c**

Decode regularly spelled one-syllable words. **RF.1.3b**

Phoneme Isolation

1 Model Show children how to isolate sounds in words. *Listen as I say a word:* thin. *The beginning sound in* thin *is /th/. Say the sound with me: /th/.* Repeat with *wash* for final sounds.

2 Guided Practice/Practice Have children practice isolating initial and final sounds. *Listen to these words. Say the beginning sound you hear.*

thump   shoe   them   thick   ship   shell

Now say the end sound you hear in these words.

fish   path   rang   teeth   cash   wing

Phonics
10 Mins

Sound-Spelling Card

Introduce *th, sh, -ng*

1 Model Display the *Thumb* **Sound-Spelling Card**. Teach both sounds of /th/ using *thank* and *them*. Model writing the letters *th*. Use the Handwriting models provided. *This is the* Thumb *Sound-Spelling Card. The beginning sound is /th/. Stretch the target sound. The /th/ sound is spelled* th. *Say it with me: /th/. This is the sound at the beginning of* thumb. *Listen:* thumb. *I'll say /th/ as I write the letters several times.* Repeat for *sh* and *ng*. Use *Shell* and *Sing* Sound-Spelling Cards.

2 Guided Practice/Practice Have children practice connecting the letters *t* and *h* to /th/ by writing them. *Say /th/ as I write* t *and* h. *Now, write the letters* t *and* h *five times as you say /th/.* Repeat for *sh, -ng*.

SKILLS TRACE

SHORT *e*

Introduce Unit 2 Week 1 Day 1

Review Unit 2 Week 1 Days 2, 3, 4, 5

Assess Unit 2 Week 1

Go Digital

Phonemic Awareness

Thumb

Phonics

Handwriting

Blend Words with *th, sh, -ng*

1 Model Display **Word-Building Cards** *t, h, i, n*. Model how to blend the sounds. *These are the letters* th. *Together, they stand for /th/. This is the letter* i. *It stands for /i/. This is the letter* n. *Listen as I blend these sounds together: /thiiin/. Say it with me.*

Continue by modeling the words *ship, sing, math,* and *wish.*

2 Guided Practice/Practice Display the Day 1 Phonics Practice Activity. Read each word in the first row, blending the sounds; for example, /shooop/. The word is *shop.* Have children blend each word with you. Prompt children to read the connected text, sounding out the decodable words.

shop	wish	then	that	hush	crash
sing	sang	bang	long	this	thump
hip	ship	hot	shot	mat	math
desks	think	bring	lump	grand	clang

Thank you for handing that shell to me.

Beth thinks she spots a fish in the pond!

He rushed to the ship to bring his bag.

Also online

Day 1 Phonics Practice Activity

Corrective Feedback

Sound Error Model the sound that children missed, then have them repeat the sound. Say: *My turn.* Tap under the letter and say: *Sound? /th/ What's the sound?* Return to the beginning of the word. Say: *Let's start over.* Blend the word with children again.

Daily Handwriting

Throughout the week teach uppercase and lowercase letters *Ff* using the Handwriting models.

ENGLISH LANGUAGE LEARNERS

Phonemic Awareness: Minimal Contrasts Focus on articulation. Say /sh/ and note your mouth position. Have children repeat. Use Sound-Spelling Cards. Repeat for /th/. Have children say both sounds, noticing the differences. Continue with: *shot/thought, mash/math, shin/thin.*

Phonics: Variations in Language In some languages, including Spanish, Cantonese, and Khmer, there is no direct transfer for the /sh/ sound. Emphasize /sh/, and show correct mouth position. Practice with Approaching Level phonics lessons.

ON-LEVEL PRACTICE BOOK p. 81

The letters **sh** make the ending sound in **fish**.
The letters **th** make the beginning sound in **thin**.
The letters **ng** make the ending sound in **ring**.

Read each sentence. Circle the word that has sh, th, or ng. Write the word.

1. Here is a (fresh) plum.   fresh

2. Min and Dan like to (sing).   sing

3. A bug can (sting)!   sting

4. Say (thank) you for a gift.   thank

5. Sam and Dad pick up (shells).   shells

6. I like to play (with) my pals.   with

APPROACHING	BEYOND	ELL
p. 81	p. 81	p. 81

→ # Word Work

Quick Review

High-Frequency Words: Read, Spell, and Write to review last week's high-frequency words: *eat, no, of, under, who.*

MINILESSON 5 Mins

Spelling

OBJECTIVES

CCSS Recognize and read grade-appropriate irregularly spelled words. **RF.1.3g**

CCSS Spell untaught words phonetically, drawing on phonemic awareness and spelling conventions. **L.1.2e**

Words with *th, sh, -ng*

Dictation Use the Spelling Dictation routine to help children transfer their growing knowledge of sound-spellings to writing. Follow the Dictation routine.

Pretest After dictation, pronounce each spelling word. Read the sentence and pronounce the word again. Ask children to say each word softly, stretching the sounds, before writing it. After the pretest, display the spelling words and write each word as you say the letter names. Have children check their words.

fish	**Fish** swim in the pond.
shop	Dad and I **shop** for new shoes.
ship	A **ship** is a very big boat.
with	Put your backpack **with** the others.
thing	What is that **thing** on your desk?
sang	The girls **sang** together at the party.
fast	I ran as **fast** as I could in the race.
wink	Dad likes to **wink** when he makes a joke.
want	I **want** to go to sleep.
call	We got a **call** from Grandma.

For Approaching Level and Beyond Level children, refer to the Differentiated Spelling Lists for modified word lists.

Go Digital

Spelling Word Routine

they	together
how	eat

High-Frequency Word Routine

ENGLISH LANGUAGE LEARNERS

Pantomime Review the meanings of these words by using pictures, pantomime, or gestures when possible. Have children repeat or act out the word.

MINILESSON 5 Mins

High-Frequency Words

all, call, day, her, want

① Model Display the **High-Frequency Word** Cards *all, call, day, her,* and *want*. Use the Read/Spell/Write routine to teach each word.

→ **Read** Point to and say the word *all. This is the word* all. *Say it with me:* all. *I see all the students.*

→ **Spell** *The word all is spelled* a-l-l. *Spell it with me.*

→ **Write** *Let's write the word in the air as we say each letter:* a-l-l.

→ Follow the same steps to introduce *call, day, her,* and *want.*

→ As children spell each word with you, point out the irregularities in sound-spellings, such as the /o/ sound spelled *a* in *want.*

→ Have partners create sentences using each word.

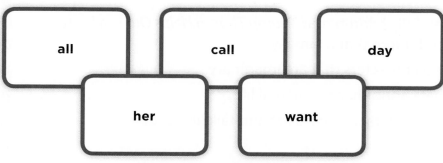

| all | call | day |

| her | want |

High-Frequency Word Cards

② Guided Practice Have children read the sentences. Prompt them to identify the high-frequency words in connected text and to blend the decodable words.

1. I see **all** the kids in the class.
2. I think I will **call** Seth.
3. I spent the **day** at the shop.
4. Beth lost **her** big bag.
5. Do you **want** to sing a song with me?

Monitor and *Differentiate*

✓ Quick Check

Can children read and decode words with consonant digraphs *th, sh, -ng?*

Can children recognize and read high-frequency words?

⬇

Small Group Instruction

If No →	Approaching	Reteach pp. T290–293
	ELL	Develop pp. T304–311
If Yes →	On Level	Review pp. T298–299
	Beyond Level	Extend pp. T302–303

→ # Shared Read

Reading/Writing Workshop Big Book and Reading/Writing Workshop

---

OBJECTIVES

 Decode regularly spelled one-syllable words. **RF.1.3b**

 Recognize and read grade-appropriate irregularly spelled words. **RF.1.3g**

Understand fantasy genre

ACADEMIC LANGUAGE
- *fantasy, imaginary*
- Cognates: *fantasía, imaginario/a*

MINILESSON
10 Mins

Read *Thump Thump Helps Out*

Model Skills and Strategies

Tell children that you will now read a selection called *Thump Thump Helps Out*. Say: *As we read, look for the words* all, call, day, her, *and* want. *Look for words with the letter pairs* th, sh, *and* -ng.

Story Words Display the words *heard, home, loud,* and *needs*. Spell the words and model reading them. Tell children that they will be reading the words in the selection.

Guide children in reading *Thump Thump Helps Out*. Point out the high-frequency words and words with the letter pairs *th, sh,* and *-ng*.

Genre: Fantasy Tell children that *Thump Thump Helps Out* is a fantasy story. Explain to children that a fantasy:

→ has events and characters that are imaginary.

→ has events that cannot happen in real life.

→ often has animal characters who act and talk like people.

Connect to Concept

ESSENTIAL QUESTION

 Read together the Essential Question on page 74 of the Reading/Writing Workshop. Discuss what Thump Thump does to help his community. Guide children to connect what they have read to the Essential Question: *How do people help out in the community?*

Go Digital

Thump Thump Helps Out

Thump Thump Helps Out

READING/WRITING WORKSHOP, pp. 74–83
Lexile 510

Partner Reading

Have partners use their Reading/Writing Workshop to review the skills and strategies.

→ Remind children that as they reread *Thump Thump Helps Out*, they can take note of sections they found confusing. Then they can go back and read them again.

→ Have children use pages 70–71 to review high-frequency words *all, call, day, her, want.*

→ Have children use pages 72–73 to review the digraphs *th, sh,* and *-ng.* Guide them to blend the sounds to read the words.

→ Have children reread *Thump Thump Helps Out* with a partner. Guide them to apply the skills and strategies. Ask children to name features of the selection that tell them that it is fantasy text.

Language Arts

 MINILESSON 5 Mins

Shared Writing

OBJECTIVES

CCSS Write narratives in which they recount two or more appropriately sequenced events, include some details regarding what happened, use temporal words to signal event order, and provide some sense of closure. **W.1.3**

CCSS Use common, proper, and possessive nouns. **L.1.1b**

Capitalize proper nouns

ACADEMIC LANGUAGE
story, common noun, proper noun

Writing Trait: Organization

1 Model Tell children that they will now reread *Thump Thump Helps Out*, paying attention to how the author organized the events in the story. Explain: *A story needs a beginning, a middle, and an end.*

2 Guided Practice/Practice Reread *Thump Thump Helps Out*. Point out how the story has three parts: a beginning, a middle, and an end. Ask: *What happens at the beginning? What happens in the middle? What happens at the end?*

Story

Focus and Plan Tell children that this week they will be writing a story about people in a community helping each other. Explain that their story will be about a make-believe event. Tell them their story must have characters, and a beginning, middle, and end.

Brainstorm Use the Word Web on Teaching Poster 40 to help children brainstorm ideas for their stories. Ask children to name ways people in a community can work together. As needed, prompt them with ideas such as recycling, planting in a community garden, putting on a bake sale, or sorting canned goods at a food pantry. Record children's ideas on the Word Web.

Write Tell children that you will work together to write a story about helping in a community event. Model writing a story based on an idea on the Word Web. Say: *My story will have a beginning, a middle, and an end. I will start the first sentence with the word* first. *Let's write a sentence that tells what happens first in our story:* First, Cass went with her mom and dad to the community garden.

Work together to write a story about a child helping to plant a community garden with sentences that start with *First, Next,* and *Last.*

Go Digital

Graphic Organizer

Writing

I see a fish.

Grammar

Grammar

MINILESSON 5 Mins

Common and Proper Nouns

1 Model Remind children that a common noun names a person, place, or thing and begins with a lowercase letter. Explain that the names of particular people, pets, places, and things are called proper nouns. Explain that a proper noun begins with a capital letter. Display the following sentences:

> Seth has a drum.
>
> Miss Gum is at West School.
>
> My dog Bing runs fast.

Point out that *Seth, Miss Gum, West School,* and *Bing* are proper nouns, and *drum* and *dog* are common nouns.

Have children identify which proper nouns name people, which name places, and which name pets.

2 Guided Practice/Practice Display the sentences below and read them aloud. Prompt children to chorally reread them with you. Have children work with a partner to identify the proper nouns.

> We swim in Glass Pond. (Glass Pond)
>
> Grant, Beth, and Russ snack on nuts. (Grant, Beth, Russ)

Ask children to identify any common nouns. (nuts)

Talk About It Have partners work together to orally generate sentences with common and proper nouns. Challenge them to create sentences that have at least one common and one proper noun.

Mechanics: Capitalize Proper Nouns

1 Model Remind children that a proper noun always begins with a capital letter. Display the following sentence:

> My cat Dot likes to play.

Point out the proper noun (Dot) and the common noun (cat).

2 Guided Practice Prompt children to correct each sentence.

> gran calls her pet cat king kong. (Gran, King Kong)
>
> trish spent all day at lost pond. (Trish, Lost Pond)

ENGLISH LANGUAGE LEARNERS SCAFFOLD

Beginning

Demonstrate Comprehension Point to the Model sentences. *Does* Seth *name a particular person? Is* West School *a proper noun? Name another proper noun.* Allow children ample time to respond.

Intermediate

Explain Ask children to circle the proper noun in the first example sentence. *How do you know this is a proper noun?* Continue with the second sentence. Clarify children's responses by providing prompts as needed.

Advanced/Advanced High

Expand Write another set of words: *shell, tent, Sam.* Have children identify the common nouns and the proper noun. Have them tell how they know. Model correct pronunciation as needed.

Daily Wrap Up

→ Review the Essential Question and encourage children to discuss it using the new oral vocabulary words. Ask: *What are some ways to help the community?*

→ Prompt children to share what skills they learned. Ask: *What skills help you become a better writer? What skills help you become a better reader?*

Materials

Reading/Writing Workshop
VOLUME 2

Reading/Writing Workshop Big Book
UNIT 2

Visual Vocabulary Cards
admire
connections
enjoy
leadership
rely

all

High-Frequency Word Cards
all
call
day
her
want

Character	Setting	Point of View

Teaching Poster

a b c

Word-Building Cards

fish

Spelling Word Cards

Interactive Read-Aloud Cards

sh

shell

Sound-Spelling Cards

→ # Build the Concept

MINILESSON 5 Mins

Oral Language

OBJECTIVES

Ask and answer questions about key details in a text read aloud or information presented orally or through other media. **SL.1.2**

- Develop oral language
- Discuss the Essential Question

ACADEMIC LANGUAGE

- *reread, details, community*
- Cognates: *detalles, comunidad*

ESSENTIAL QUESTION

Remind children that this week you have been talking and reading about how people can help out in the community. Remind them of the children working in the community garden and how Thump Thump helped the community. Guide children to discuss the Essential Question using information from what they read on Day 1.

Oral Vocabulary Words

Review the oral vocabulary words *admire* and *leadership* from Day 1. Use the Define/Example/Ask routine to introduce the oral vocabulary words *connections*, *enjoy*, and *rely*. Prompt children to use the words as they discuss ways to help out in a community.

Oral Vocabulary Routine

Define: **Connections** are links between two or more things.

Example: The connections between people in a community can be strong.

Ask: What are some connections between you and your neighbors?

Define: If you **enjoy** something, you like it.

Example: Cats enjoy being petted.

Ask: What is something you enjoy doing with friends?

Define: When you know you can trust someone to help, you **rely** on that person.

Example: Children rely on their parents for many things they need.

Ask: Whom do you rely on to get to and from school every day?

Visual Vocabulary Cards

Go Digital

school

Visual Glossary

"Luis's Library"

Listening Comprehension

MINILESSON
5 Mins

Read the Interactive Read Aloud

Strategy: Reread

Remind children that as they read, they can go back and reread parts they did not understand or important information they want to remember. Model the strategy using the Think Aloud Cloud.

Think Aloud As I read, I will check that I understood the events and what the people are doing. If I am not sure, I will reread a sentence or two. That can help me to be sure that I understand what the selection is about.

"Luis's Library"

Tell children that you will read "Luis's Library," a nonfiction informational text about a traveling librarian. Display the Interactive Read-Aloud Cards.

→ Pause to model rereading to check your comprehension. Prompt children to check if they understand what you have read. If they are not sure, reread the section and guide them to listen carefully for the details about the people and events.

Make Connections

COLLABORATE

Discuss partners' responses to "Luis's Library." Prompt children to discuss how Luis helped out his community. Then ask: *How do you think we get books in our school library? What is a way that you might help our school community get books?*

ELL

ENGLISH LANGUAGE LEARNERS

Non-verbal Cues Remind children that they can use non-verbal cues to share information when they are not able to do so verbally. Encourage children to use pantomime or draw.

 → **Word Work**

Quick Review

Build Fluency: Sound-Spellings
Display the **Word-Building Cards:**
th, sh, ng, nd, nk, nt, st, sk, mp, u, e, ea, sp, sn, sl, cr, fr, tr, o, pl, fl, cl, bl, i, a, s. Have children say the sounds. Repeat, and vary the pace.

MINILESSON 5 Mins — Phonemic Awareness

OBJECTIVES

ccss Know the spelling-sound correspondences for common consonant digraphs. **RF.1.3a**

ccss Decode two-syllable words following basic patterns by breaking the words into syllables. **RF.1.3e**

Blend and build words with consonant digraphs

Phoneme Categorization

1 Model Show children how to categorize phonemes. *Listen to these words:* wish, bank, ship. *The words* wish *and* ship *have the sound /i/. The word* bank *does not. It doesn't belong.*

2 Guided Practice/Practice Have children identify the word that does not belong with the others. *I will say three words. Tell me which word does not belong and why:* sing, math, smash. Sing *does not belong because* math *and* smash *have the sound /a/;* sing *does not.* Repeat with the following examples.

moth, path, shop

crash, rush, blush

head, mesh, long

MINILESSON 5 Mins — Phonics

Review Consonant Digraphs *th, sh, -ng*

1 Model Display the *Shell* **Sound-Spelling Card**. Review the sound /sh/ spelled *sh* using the words *ship* and *trash.* Repeat with the *Thumb* and *Sing* Sound-Spelling Cards and the words *that, path,* and *ring.*

2 Guided Practice/Practice Have children practice connecting the letters and sound. Point to the Sound-Spelling Card. *What are these letters? What sound do they stand for?*

Go Digital

Phonemic Awareness

Phonics

I __ the jar.

| fill | fills | filling |

Structural Analysis

A A
a a

Handwriting

Blend Words with *th, sh, -ng*

❶ Model Display **Word-Building Cards** *r, i, n, g* to form the word *ring*. Model how to generate and blend the sounds to say the word. *This is the letter* r. *It stands for /r/. This is the letter* i. *It stands for /i/. These are the letters* n *and* g. *Together they stand for /ng/. Listen as I blend these sounds together: /riiing/, ring.*

Continue by modeling the words *flash, thick, shock,* and *cloth*.

❷ Guided Practice/Practice Repeat the routine with children with *that, thump, moth, shed, trash, shell, wing, bring, stung.*

Build Words with *th, sh, -ng*

❶ Model Display the Word-Building Cards *t, h, i, n, g*. Blend: /th/ /i/ /ng/, /thiiinnng/, *thing*.

Replace *th* with *w* and repeat with *wing*.

Change *w* to *s* and repeat with *sing*.

❷ Guided Practice/Practice Continue with *sling, sting, sing, ring, bring, wing, thing, think, thin, than*. Guide children to build and blend each word.

ENGLISH LANGUAGE LEARNERS

Build Vocabulary Review the meanings of example words that can be explained or demonstrated in a concrete way. For example, ask children to point to the trash can for *trash*. Model *wing* by flapping your arms, saying, *I can flap my wings,* and have children repeat. Provide sentence starters such as "I will bring _____" for children to complete. Correct grammar and pronunciation as needed.

Structural Analysis

MINILESSON
5 Mins

Closed Syllables

❶ Model Write and read aloud *cabin*. Say the word slowly, clapping for each syllable. Have children repeat. Point out that *cabin* has two syllables, or word parts. Draw a line between the two syllables: *cab/in*. Explain that when a syllable ends in a consonant and has one vowel letter, the vowel sound is usually short. Point to *cab*. *Cab* ends with *b* and has one vowel letter, so the vowel sound in *cab* is /a/, the short *a* sound. This is called a closed syllable. Knowing this will help children read multisyllabic words. Repeat with the syllable *in*.

❷ Guided Practice/Practice Write the following words on the board: *napkin, dentist, mitten, rabbit, picnic, helping, wishing*. Help children divide each word into syllables (e.g., divide between the two consonants in the middle of a word or divide before the *-ing* ending), then read the words. Help them identifying the short vowel sounds and then make a list of all the closed syllables.

→ # Word Work

Quick Review

High-Frequency Words: Read, Spell and Write to review this week's high-frequency words: *all, call, day, her, want.*

MINILESSON **5** Mins

Spelling

OBJECTIVES

CCSS Use conventional spelling for words with common spelling patterns and for frequently occurring irregular words. **L.1.2d**

Word Sort with *th, sh, -ng*

1 **Model** Display the **Spelling Word Cards** from the Teacher's Resource Book, one at a time. Have children read each word, listening for the consonant digraph.

Use cards for digraphs *th, sh,* and *-ng* to create a three-column chart. Say each digraph and pronounce the sounds: *The letters* th *are pronounced /th/;* sh *is /sh/; and* -ng *is /ng/.* Have children repeat the spelling and pronunciation of each digraph.

2 **Guided Practice/Practice** Have children place each Spelling Word Card in the column with the word containing the same consonant digraph *(th, sh, -ng).*

When completed, have children chorally read the words in each column. Then call out a word. Have a child find the word card and point to it as the class chorally spells the word.

ANALYZE ERRORS/ARTICULATION SUPPORT

Use children's pretest errors to analyze spelling problems and provide corrective feedback. For example, some children will write only one letter for the digraph, such as *t* for *th,* or they will replace the digraph with another letter, such as *f* for *th.*

Create word sorts to analyze consonant and consonant-digraph spelling patterns. Make index cards for *th/t, sh/s, -ng/g* and display them. Also make cards for *sop, sip, wit, tin, sag.*

Have children sort the spelling words and the five words above and then chorally read the words.

Go Digital

Spelling Word Sort

| they | together |
| how | eat |

High-Frequency Word Routine

ENGLISH LANGUAGE LEARNERS

Provide Clues Practice spelling by helping children generate more words with consonant digraphs *th, sh, -ng. Think of a word that starts with* d *and rhymes with* fish. Write the word and have children practice reading it. Correct their pronunciation, if needed.

MINILESSON 5 Mins

High-Frequency Words

all, call, day, her, want

1 Guided Practice Say each word and have children Read/Spell/Write it. Ask children to close their eyes, picture the word in their minds, and write it the way they see it. Display the high-frequency words for children to self-correct.

→ Point out the *-all* spelling pattern in both *all* and *call*.

2 Practice Add the high-frequency words *all, call, day, her,* and *want* to the cumulative word bank.

COLLABORATE

→ Have children work with a partner to create sentences using the words.

→ Have children look at the words and compare their sounds and spellings to words from previous weeks.

→ Suggest that they write about helping in the community.

Cumulative Review Review last week's words using the Read/Spell/Write routine.

→ Repeat the above routine, mixing the words and having children chorally say each one.

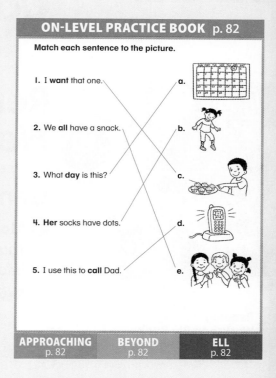

ON-LEVEL PRACTICE BOOK p. 82

Match each sentence to the picture.

1. I **want** that one.
2. We **all** have a snack.
3. What **day** is this?
4. **Her** socks have dots.
5. I use this to **call** Dad.

| APPROACHING p. 82 | BEYOND p. 82 | ELL p. 82 |

Monitor and *Differentiate*

✓ **Quick Check**

Can children read and decode words with consonant digraphs *th, sh, -ng*?

Can children recognize and read high-frequency words?

Small Group Instruction

If No → **Approaching** Reteach pp. T290–293

ELL Develop pp. T304–311

If Yes → **On Level** Review pp. T298–299

Beyond Level Extend pp. T302–303

Comprehension

CLOSE READING

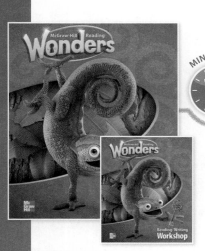

Reading/Writing Workshop Big Book and Reading/Writing Workshop

---

OBJECTIVES

CCSS Describe characters, settings, and major events in a story, using key details. **RL.1.3**

Understand fantasy genre

ACADEMIC LANGUAGE

• illustrations, character, setting, events

• Cognate: *ilustraciones*

SKILLS TRACE

CHARACTER, SETTING, EVENTS

Introduce Unit 2 Week 1

Review Unit 2 Weeks 2, 4; Unit 3 Weeks 1, 2 Days 2, 3, 4

Assess Unit 2 Weeks 1, 2, 4

Reread *Thump Thump Helps Out*

MINILESSON 10 Mins

Genre: Fantasy

1 Model Tell children they will now reread the fantasy story *Thump Thump Helps Out*. Explain that as they read they will look for information in the text to help them understand the selection.

Review the characteristics of fantasy:

→ has events and characters that are imaginary.

→ has events that cannot happen in real life.

→ often has animal characters who act and talk like people.

→ often has illustrations.

Tell children that fantasy stories usually have illustrations. They are usually drawings, like those in *Thump Thump Helps Out*. The illustrations may show the characters, setting, or events of the story. Readers can learn many key details by looking at the illustrations.

Display pages 76 and 77: *This illustration shows many details. I see a lot of rabbits, so I know that this story is all about rabbits. I see one rabbit singing and tapping his foot. I can tell this story is a fantasy, because rabbits do not sing or wear clothes in real life.*

2 Guided Practice/Practice Display pages 78 and 79 of *Thump Thump Helps Out*. Say: *There is a lot going on in this illustration. What do you see? Could this happen in real life? What is something in the illustration that could not happen in real life?*

Go Digital

Thump Thump Helps Out

Genre

Character, Setting, Events

Skill: Character, Setting, Events

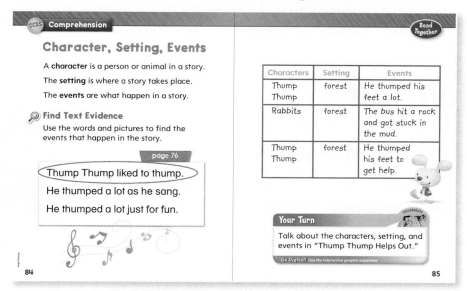

Reading/Writing Workshop, pp. 84–85

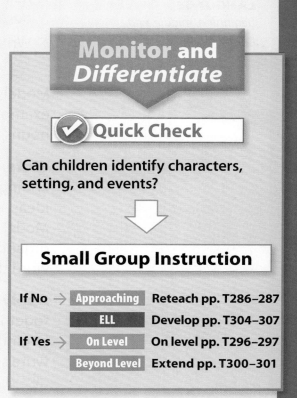

| APPROACHING p. 87 | BEYOND p. 87 | ELL p. 87 |

1 Model Tell children that when they read fantasy stories they can use the text and the illustrations to find the characters, settings, and events. Have children look at pages 84–85 in their Reading/Writing Workshop. Read together the definitions of character, setting, and events. *A character is a person or animal in a story. The setting is where a story takes place. The events are what happens in a story.*

2 Guided Practice/Practice Read together the Find Text Evidence section and model finding the characters, setting, and an event in *Thump Thump Helps Out*. Point out the detail added to the graphic organizer. *On pages 76 and 77, we can find the characters, setting, and events. One of the characters is Thump Thump. The text tells us what he does. It says he liked to thump while he sang. It says he thumped a lot just for fun. This is an event. What other characters and events do we learn about in the rest of the story? What is the setting?*

Character	Setting	Events

Teaching Poster

Monitor and *Differentiate*

✓ Quick Check

Can children identify characters, setting, and events?

⬇

Small Group Instruction

If No → **Approaching** Reteach pp. T286–287

ELL Develop pp. T304–307

If Yes → **On Level** On level pp. T296–297

Beyond Level Extend pp. T300–301

COMPREHENSION **T261**

Language Arts

MINILESSON
5 Mins

Interactive Writing

Writing Trait: Organization

Review Tell children that writers put the events in their stories in order. Writers write stories with a beginning, a middle, and an end.

Story

Discuss Guide children to choose one idea from the Day 1 Word Web, such as sorting food at a food bank. Guide children to think of ideas for a story about that topic. Record their ideas on another Word Web using Teaching Poster 40.

Model/Apply Grammar Tell children that they will be working together to write a story about their idea. Remind them that a story has a beginning, a middle, and an end. Remind them that a proper noun is the name of a particular person, pet, place, or thing. A proper noun begins with a capital letter.

→ Ask: *What is the name of your main character? This is the name of a particular person. It is a proper noun.*

→ Write the sentence frame:

＿＿＿＿＿ *will help* ＿＿＿＿＿.

Model using the character's name and completing the sentence. For example, *Ling will help pick up trash*. Point out proper and common nouns. Model capitalizing the proper noun.

Write Collaborate with children to write a beginning, middle, and ending sentence to form a story. Guide them to use the web to get ideas. Work together to write sentences that show the order of events. Model using the sequence of events organizer on Teaching Poster 30 to organize the sentences. Remind children to listen for the sounds in each word they write together. As children create sentences, share the pen.

Apply Writing Trait Review with children the story you wrote together on Day 1. Remind them how they used organization to show a beginning, middle, and end to the story. Work together with children to write sentences that begin with *First, Next, Last*.

OBJECTIVES

CCSS Write narratives in which they recount two or more appropriately sequenced events, include some details regarding what happened, use temporal words to signal event order, and provide some sense of closure. **W.1.3**

CCSS Use common, proper, and possessive nouns. **L.1.1b**

ACADEMIC LANGUAGE
beginning, middle, end, proper noun

Go Digital

Beginning
↓
Middle
↓
End

Graphic Organizer

Writing

I see a fish.

Grammar

Grammar

Common and Proper Nouns

1 Review Remind children that the names of particular people, pets, places, and things are called proper nouns. Remind them that a proper noun begins with a capital letter.

→ Write the following sentences:

We went to Grand Cliff with Max the dog.

Kip and Jon use a map.

Read the sentences aloud and have children chorally repeat. Guide children to circle the proper nouns and underline the common nouns in the sentences.

2 Guided Practice Write sample sentences. Read each sentence. Have children work in pairs to identify and circle each proper noun.

Bev gets Scott a snack.

Gramps lives at the top of Trent Hill.

Clint puts the dish in the sink.

My pet pig Ping likes to eat yams.

3 Practice Have children identify the circled words as people, places, things, or pets.

Talk About It Have partners work together to orally generate sentences about helping out. Challenge them to create sentences with more than one common noun or proper noun.

Mechanics: Capitalize Proper Nouns

1 Review Remind children that a proper noun always begins with a capital letter.

2 Practice Display sentences with capitalization errors. Read each aloud. Have children work together to fix the sentences.

Will hank go to peck School with us? (Will Hank go to Peck School with us?)

dan and jen had a Picnic by the pond. (Dad and Jen had a picnic by the pond.)

ENGLISH LANGUAGE LEARNERS

Explain Ask children to circle the proper nouns in the first example. *How do you know* Grand Cliff *and* Max *are proper nouns? How many proper nouns are in the second sentence?*

Proper Noun Walk Take children on a walk to locate proper nouns. Guide them to identify each one and write it in a list. For example, the names of teachers, the principal, the school, and other examples you encounter.

Daily Wrap Up

→ Discuss the Essential Question and encourage children to use the oral vocabulary words. *How have you helped your community?*

→ Prompt children to review and discuss the skills they used today. *How will the skills you learned today help you become a better reader and writer?*

Materials

Reading/Writing Workshop
VOLUME 2

Literature Anthology
VOLUME 2

Literature Big Book
The Story of Martin Luther King Jr.

Visual Vocabulary Cards

admire   leadership
connections   rely
enjoy

Teaching Poster

Word-Building Cards

 fish

Spelling Word Cards

Interactive Read-Aloud Cards

→ Build the Concept

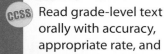
MINILESSON
5 Mins

Oral Language

Go Digital

OBJECTIVES

Read grade-level text orally with accuracy, appropriate rate, and expression. **RF.1.4b**

Reread text

ACADEMIC LANGUAGE
• *emphasize, stress*
• Cognate: *enfatizar*

ESSENTIAL QUESTION

Remind children that this week you are talking and reading about how people can help their communities. Remind them of the children planting flowers, the problems Martin faced in *The Story of Martin Luther King Jr.*, and the way both animals and kids worked together on projects for their communities. Guide children to discuss the question using information from what they have read and talked about throughout the week.

Review Oral Vocabulary

Review the oral vocabulary words *admire, leadership, enjoy, rely,* and *connections* using the Define/Example/Ask routine. Encourage children to discuss ways to help their community when coming up with examples for each word.

school
Visual Glossary

The Story of Martin Luther King Jr.

Retell

Visual Vocabulary Cards

Listening Comprehension

CLOSE READING

MINILESSON
10 Mins

Reread Literature Big Book

Strategy: Reread

Remind children that as they read, they can go back and reread parts they did not understand or want to remember better. This can help them to better understand the facts and details in the text. As we reread *The Story of Martin Luther King Jr.,* we can stop and reread sentences that are not clear to us.

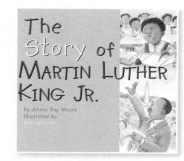

Literature Big Book

Read aloud *The Story of Martin Luther King Jr.* Pause to model rereading. Encourage children to say which details they had trouble understanding and help them reread to find information in the text and illustrations.

Model Retelling

Pause to retell portions of the selection. *I can put facts and details from the text into my own words. So far, I have read that Martin was the son of a preacher and a teacher. He was born in 1929 in Atlanta, Georgia.*

→ After reading, retell the selection, using your own words to tell the important facts and details in the correct order.

Model Fluency

Intonation Turn to page 8 of *The Story of Martin Luther King Jr.* Point out the word *more* in brown text. Explain that the author set the word in colored text in order to emphasize it. When you read emphasized words, you can stress them by reading them a little bit louder than the other words.

→ Read aloud page 11 with slightly exaggerated stress on the words set in colored print. Have children identify the emphasized words. Repeat the reading to give children more practice with appropriate intonation.

ELL

ENGLISH LANGUAGE LEARNERS

Retell Guide children to retell by using a question prompt on each page. *What job did Martin's father have?* Provide sentence starters for children to complete orally. *Martin's father was a ____.*

A C T

Access Complex Text

If the complexity of the text makes it hard for children to read, use the Access Complex Text prompts.

Genre Children may mistakenly think of the text as fiction because it is presented like a story.

→ Remind children that Martin Luther King Jr. was a real person and that the problems presented in the text really existed.

Lack of Prior Knowledge Children may be unfamiliar with segregation.

→ Explain that in some places in the past, there were laws that kept black people from mixing with white people and that Martin Luther King Jr. worked to end these laws.

 → **Word Work**

Quick Review

Build Fluency: Sound-Spellings
Display the **Word-Building Cards:**
th, sh, ng, nd, nk, nt, st, sk, mp, u, e, ea, sp, sn, sl, cr, fr, tr, o, pl, fl, cl, bl, i, a, s. Have children say the sounds.

 MINILESSON **5** Mins

Phonemic Awareness

OBJECTIVES

CCSS Know the spelling-sound correspondences for common consonant digraphs. **RF.1.3a**

CCSS Decode two-syllable words following basic patterns by breaking the words into syllables. **RF.1.3e**

Phoneme Blending

❶ **Model** Show children how to orally blend phonemes. *Listen as I say the sounds in a word: /sh/ /e/ /l/. Now I will blend the sounds together and say the word: /sheeelll/,* shell. *Let's say the word together:* shell. Repeat with /th/ /i/ /k/, *thick;* /h/ /a/ /ng/, *hang;* /s/ /ou/ /th/, *south;* /b/ /r/ /u/ /sh/, *brush.*

❷ **Guided Practice/Practice** Have children practice blending phonemes. *Let's do some together. I am going to say some words, sound by sound. Listen as I say a word. Blend the sounds together to say the word.* Do the first three with children.

/th/ /a/ /n/	/b/ /r/ /o/ /th/	/b/ /a/ /ng/
/sh/ /a/ /k/	/m/ /a/ /sh/	/s/ /t/ /i/ /ng/
/sh/ /i/ /p/	/th/ /i/ /n/	/k/ /i/ /ng/

 Go Digital

Phonemic Awareness

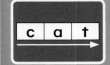

Phonics

 MINILESSON **5** Mins

Phonics

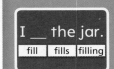

Structural Analysis

Blend Words with *th, sh, -ng*

❶ **Model** Display **Word-Building Cards** *s, t, i, n, g.* Model how to blend the sounds. *This is the letter* s. *It stands for /s/. This is the letter* t. *It stands for /t/. This is the letter* i. *It stands for /i/. These are the letters* ng. *Together they stand for /ng/. Let's blend the sounds: /stiiing/. The word is* sting.

Continue by modeling the words *shop, moth, this,* and *fresh.*

❷ **Guided Practice/Practice** Review the words and sentences on the Day 3 Phonics Practice Activity with children. Read each word in the first row, blending the sounds; for example: /sh/, /i/, /p/; /shiiip/.

→ Have children blend each word with you. Prompt them to read the connected text, sounding out the decodable words.

Handwriting

ship	shop	shell	wish	fish	dish
this	that	thing	think	long	song
singing	rushing	bringing	clanging	banging	
rabbit	basket	picnic	selfish	absent	sting
stand	hump	thump	desks	vents	

We thank Seth for singing with us.

The king wished for a ship filled with fish!

Also online

Day 3 Phonics Practice Activity

Structural Analysis

Closed Syllables

❶ Model Write and read aloud *rabbit*. Say the word slowly, clapping for each syllable. Have children repeat. Draw a line between the two syllables: *rab/bit*. Remind children that when a syllable ends in a consonant and has one vowel letter, the vowel sound is usually short. Point to *rab*. Rab *ends with* b *and has one vowel letter, so the vowel sound in* rab *is /a/, the short* a *sound. This is a closed syllable.* Repeat with the syllable *bit*. Continue modeling with *button*. Explain to children that they may need to approximate sounds in multisyllabic words.

❷ Practice/Apply Help children divide the words *singing, thinking, basket, pocket,* and *finish* into syllables. Have children identify the vowel sound in each syllable and how they know the vowel sounds are short. Help them identify these as closed syllables. Then, have children blend the words.

Corrective Feedback

Corrective Feedback Say: *My turn.* Model blending the word using the appropriate signaling procedures. Then lead children in blending the sounds. Say: *Do it with me.* You will respond with children to offer support. Then say: *Your turn. Blend.* Have children chorally blend. Return to the beginning of the word. Say: *Let's start over.*

 **Word Work**

Quick Review

High-Frequency Words: Read, Spell and Write to review this week's high-frequency words: *all, call, day, her, want.*

 MINILESSON **5** Mins

Spelling

OBJECTIVES

 Recognize and read grade-appropriate irregularly spelled words. **RF.1.3g**

 Use conventional spelling for words with common spelling patterns and for frequently occurring irregular words. **L.1.2d**

- Spell words with consonant digraphs
- Recognize and read high-frequency words

Consonant Digraphs *th, sh, -ng*

1 **Model** Make index cards for *th, sh, -ng* and form three columns in a pocket chart. Blend the sounds with children.

Hold up the *fish* **Spelling Word Card**. Say and spell it. Pronounce each sound clearly: /f/ /i/ /sh/. Blend the sounds, stretching the digraph sound to emphasize it. Repeat this step with *shop* and *ship.* Place the words below the *sh* card. Read and spell each spelling word together with children. Have children read each word. Ask: *What do you notice about these spelling words? Yes, they have the /sh/ sound spelled* s-h.

2 **Guided Practice/Practice** Have children spell each word. Repeat the process with the *th* and *-ng* words.

Display the words *fast, wink, want,* and *call* in a separate column. Read and spell the words together with children. Point out that these spelling words do not contain consonant digraphs *th, sh,* or *-ng.*

Conclude by asking children to orally generate additional words that have the /th/, /sh/, and /ng/ sounds. Write the additional words on the board. Underline the common spelling patterns in the additional words. If necessary, point out the differences and explain why they are unusual.

Go Digital

Spelling Word Sort

Visual Glossary

PHONICS/SPELLING PRACTICE BOOK p. 43

Read the words in the box. Say each word.

| fish | shop | ship | with |
| thing | sang | want | call |

Complete each spelling word with the letter **a**.

1. c __a__ ll   2. s __a__ ng

3. w __a__ nt

Complete each spelling word with the letter i.

4. sh __i__ p   5. th __i__ ng

6. f __i__ sh   7. w __i__ th

Complete the spelling word with the letter o.

8. sh __o__ p

MINILESSON 5 Mins

High-Frequency Words

all, call, day, her, want

1 Guided Practice Say each word and have children Read/Spell/Write it. As children spell each word with you, point out sound-spellings children have learned, such as the ending consonant blend /nt/ in *want*.

Display **Visual Vocabulary Cards** to review this week's high-frequency words.

Visual Vocabulary Cards

2 Practice Repeat the activity with last week's words.

Build Fluency: Word Automaticity

Have children read the following sentences aloud together at the same pace. Repeat several times.

I want to call Beth.

I will ask her to bring a sled.

We will play all day!

Word Bank

Review the current and previous words in the word bank. Discuss with children which words should be removed, or added back, from previous high-frequency word lists. Remind children that the word bank should change as the class needs it to.

Monitor and *Differentiate*

✓ **Quick Check**

Can children read and decode words with consonant digraphs *th, sh, -ng*?

Can children recognize and read high-frequency words?

Small Group Instruction

If No →	Approaching	Reteach pp. T290–293
	ELL	Develop pp. T304–311
If Yes →	On Level	Review pp. T298–299
	Beyond Level	Extend pp. T302–303

©The McGraw-Hill Companies, Inc./Emilie Chollat

CCSS Genre Fantasy

Essential Question
How do people help out in the community?
Read about an elephant who loves books.

Go Digital!

Nell's Books

by Miriam Cohen
Illustrated by Emilie Chollat

64   65

LITERATURE ANTHOLOGY, pp. 64–65

Literature Anthology

Develop Comprehension CLOSE READING

Lexile 200

Read Literature Anthology

Review Genre: Fantasy
Review with children the key characteristics of fantasy:

→ Has made-up characters, settings, and events that could not happen in real life.

→ Often has illustrations

Preview and Predict Direct children's attention to pages 64–65. Read the title and have children look at the illustrations. *What might this story be about? Which character do you think is Nell? Why? Let's find out.*

ESSENTIAL QUESTION
Read aloud the Essential Question: *How do people help out in the community?* Tell children that as they read they should think about how Nell and the other story characters help in their community.

Story Words Read and spell the words *books, read, rained,* and *heard.* Review the meaning of each word. Tell children that they will read these words in the selection.

Analytical Writing

Note Taking: Graphic Organizer As children read the selection, guide them to fill in the graphic organizer on **Your Turn Practice Book** page 84 as you model recording the character, setting, and events key details of each section.

Nell liked to read.
She liked it a lot.
Nell could sit and read **all day** long.

66

"Will you play with us, Nell?"
called Cat and Dog.
"Shh!" said Nell. "I am reading." **①**

② 67

LITERATURE ANTHOLOGY, pp. 66–67

① Strategy: Reread

Teacher Think Aloud On page 67, the text says Dog and Cat ask Nell to play, but she says she is reading. I'm not sure I understand why Nell doesn't want to play. I will reread page 66 to see if it helps me understand. I reread that Nell likes to read a lot; she could sit and read all day. Now I understand that Nell would rather read than play with Dog and Cat.

② Skill: Character, Setting, Events

Teacher Think Aloud As we read, we can use the text and illustrations to learn about the characters, setting, and events in a story. Who are the characters? Where are they? What has happened? Let's add these details to our chart.

Characters	Setting	Events
Nell, Dog, Cat	outdoors	Nell reads. Dog and Cat ask Nell to play.

"Will you shop with me, Nell?"
asked Pig. ❸
"Shh!" said Nell. "This is good!" ❹

68

"That Nell is not fun at all,"
said Dog.
"She just reads," said Cat.
"She will not do a thing!"

69

©the McGraw-Hill Companies, Inc./Emilie Chollet

LITERATURE ANTHOLOGY, pp. 68–69

Develop Comprehension

CLOSE READING

❸ Skill: Character, Setting, Events

What new character do we meet? What is the setting? What event happens? Let's add that information to our chart.

❹ Maintain Skill: Key Details

Remember that illustrations can include key details to help you understand a story. Let's look at the illustration on page 68. What key detail tells us what Nell is talking about when she says "Shh! This is good!"? (In the illustration, she is reading a book. This key detail tells us that she is talking about the book.)

Characters	Setting	Events
Nell, Dog, Cat	outdoors	Nell reads. Dog and Cat ask her to play.
Nell, Pig	indoors	Pig asks Nell to go shopping.

Then one day it rained.
Dog and Cat set up a tent.
Pig got dressed up for fun.
"This is good," said Dog.
"Yes!" said Pig and Cat.

70

It rained the next day, too.
"We **want** to go out," said Dog.
"We are sick of tents and dressing up,"
said Pig and Cat. 5 6

71

LITERATURE ANTHOLOGY, pp. 70–71

❺ Strategy: Reread

Teacher Think Aloud I read Pig and Cat say they are sick of tents and dressing up. I'm confused by what they mean. I will go back and reread to see if there are details I missed. Now I see that when it rained the previous day, Dog, Cat, and Pig set up a tent and dressed up to have fun indoors. I understand that by the second rainy day they got bored playing in the tent and dressing up.

❻ Skill: Characters, Setting, Events

Discuss with a partner what you have read about the characters on these pages. Where are they? What can you tell about them from what they say and do? What can you tell from the illustrations?

Characters	Setting	Events
Nell, Dog, Cat	outdoors	Nell reads. Dog and Cat ask Nell to play.
Nell, Pig	indoors	Pig asks Nell to go shopping.
Dog, Cat, Pig	indoors	Dog, Cat, and Pig set up a tent and dress up.

Nell went to **her** shelf. **7**
"Here, Dog," she said.
"I think you will like this."
"Yuck!" said Dog.

72

"This will be fun for Pig," said Nell.
"Cat, you will like this a lot." **8** **9**
"Ick!" said Cat and Pig.
"Shh!" said Nell. "Let's read."

73

LITERATURE ANTHOLOGY, pp. 72–73

Develop Comprehension

CLOSE READING

7 Skill: Character, Setting, Events

Teacher Think Aloud I read Nell took books from her shelf and gave her friends books she thought they'd like. This tells me Nell is a good friend. She cares about her friends because she knows they are sick of being indoors. She loves reading so much and she thinks they will, too.

What do you learn about the other characters?

Student Think Aloud I read that Dog said, "Yuck!" and Cat and Pig said, "Ick!" when Nell gave them books. This tells me that they don't like to read.

Let's add these details to our chart.

8 Author's Craft: Dialogue

The author is using dialogue to help tell the story. Dialogue tells the reader what a character is saying. There has been dialogue on almost every page of the story. Who is talking on this page? (Nell, Cat, and Pig) Yes, Nell, Cat, and Pig are all speaking the dialogue. What does the dialogue tell us about these characters? (that Nell wants her friends to read)

9 Genre: Fantasy

What are some details that tell us that this story is a fantasy? (It has illustrations and animal characters that act like people.)

Dog read in his tent.
Pig read in a tub.
Cat read in a pot. 10

74

They read all day long.
"This is fun!" said Cat
and Dog and Pig. 11

75

LITERATURE ANTHOLOGY, pp. 74–75

10 **Strategy: Reread**

Teacher Think Aloud In the beginning and middle of the story, Nell was the only one reading. Now everyone is reading. I'm going to reread a few pages, to be sure I understand why. Now I understand. The characters were stuck indoors because of rain. When Dog, Cat, and Pig became bored, Nell gave them each a book to read. That's why they're all reading now.

11 **Skill: Characters, Setting, Events**

Turn to a partner and discuss what you have read about the characters on these pages. What are they doing now? What can you tell about them?

Characters	Setting	Events
Nell, Dog, Cat, Pig	indoors	Nell gives books to her friends. They do not want to read.
Dog, Cat, Pig	indoors	Dog, Cat, and Pig have fun reading.

The next day, Nell heard clanging.
She heard banging.
"Nell, come quick!" called Dog.

76

"We did this is for you," said Dog.
"You can hand out books to all,"
said Cat.
"Nell is good at that," said Pig.
"That is just my wish!" said Nell.

77

LITERATURE ANTHOLOGY, pp. 76–77

Develop Comprehension *CLOSE READING*

⑫ Maintain Skill: Key Details

Remember that illustrations in a story can include important information that helps us understand the characters, setting, or events. Sometimes the illustrations can include details that are not in the words. The text on page 77 tells us that Dog, Pig, and Cat did something for Nell. Look at the illustration. What did they do? (They made a bookmobile, a kind of traveling library.) What can you tell from the illustration about how Dog, Pig and Cat feel about the bookmobile? (They look happy.)

⑬ Context Clues

Teacher Think Aloud If I don't know the meaning of a word or words in a story, I can look at the illustrations and at the other words in the sentence for clues to figure out the meaning. Cat says Nell can *hand out* books. The illustration shows a truck full of books. Other words in the sentence are *to all*. I think *hand out* means to give out or distribute. I think Cat wants Nell to drive the truck around the community giving out books to others.

Nell got in.
"Let's hand out books," she said.

78

"Shh!"said Dog and Cat and Pig.
"Let us read!"

79

LITERATURE ANTHOLOGY, pp. 78–79

Skill: Character, Setting, Events

Guide children to complete the chart by adding details about the characters, setting, and events in the end of the story. *Where are the characters now? What are they doing?* Review the completed chart with children and discuss the characters, settings, and events.

Return to Predictions and Purposes

Review children's predictions. Ask children if their story predictions were correct. Guide them to use evidence in the text to confirm whether their predictions were accurate. Discuss what children learned about ways to help out in a community.

Characters	Setting	Events
Nell, Dog, Cat, Pig	indoors	Nell gives books to her friends. They do not want to read.
Dog, Cat, Pig	indoors	Dog, Cat, and Pig have fun reading.
Nell, Dog, Cat, Pig	outdoors	Dog, Cat, and Pig make a bookmobile so Nell can hand out books.

Meet the Author

Miriam Cohen says, "I have always loved elephants because they are smart animals that do nice things for other elephants. I imagined an elephant that was so smart she could read. I had fun writing about how she shared her love of books with her friends."

Author's Purpose

Miriam Cohen wanted to tell about an animal that helps its community. Draw an animal helping its community. Write about it.

80

Respond to Reading

Retell

Use your own words to retell important events in *Nell's Books*.

Character	Setting	Events

Text Evidence

1. What do Dog, Pig, and Cat learn from Nell? **Character, Setting, Events**
2. What did Cat, Dog, and Pig do to help the community? **Character, Setting, Events**
3. How can you tell that *Nell's Books* is a fantasy? **Genre**

Make Connections

How does giving books out help a community? **Essential Question**

81

LITERATURE ANTHOLOGY, pp. 80–81

Meet the Author

Miriam Cohen

Read aloud page 80 with children. Ask them why they think Miriam Cohen made Nell an elephant instead of a different animal. *How do you think Miriam Cohen got the idea for writing the story? What made her enjoy writing the story?*

Author's Purpose

Help children brainstorm a list of ways people help in their community. Tell them to draw a picture of an animal character, showing it helping. Have chidren write a sentence of dialogue that tells how the character helps. *"I like to _____."*

AUTHOR'S CRAFT

Focus on Dialogue

In her story, Miriam Cohen uses dialogue to help the reader understand the characters. Dialogue helps make the characters in the story more real.

→ What did Pig and Cat say that told you they were bored playing indoors? ("We are sick of tents and dressing up.")

→ Why do you think Dog said, "Yuck!" when he got a book? (He didn't like to read.)

→ What did Dog, Cat, and Pig say at the end that told you they like reading? ("Shh! Let us read!")

Respond to Reading

Retelling

Guide children in retelling the story. Remind them that as they read *Nell's Books* they paid attention to the characters, setting, and events, and reread parts of the story. Now they will use that information to retell the story.

→ Have children use the information they recorded on their Character, Setting, Events charts to help them retell the story.

Text Evidence

Guide children to use text evidence to answer the Text Evidence questions on Literature Anthology page 81. Model answering the questions as needed.

1. **Character, Setting, Events** To answer the question, we need to look back at details in the text that tell us what the characters say and do. The text on page 66 tells us that Nell liked to read a lot. The text on pages 72–73 tells us that when Nell gave Dog, Pig, and Cat books to read, they said, "Yuck," and "Ick." Then on pages 74–75, the text tells us they read all day and said it was fun. The characters learned to love reading because of Nell.

2. **Character, Setting, Events** The question asks about events in the end of the story. To figure this out we need to think about details in the text and pictures that tell what happened. After Dog, Cat, and Pig saw how much fun it was to read the books that Nell shared with them, the text and illustrations show us that they made a bookmobile for Nell so she could share her books with others. The bookmobile would help the whole community.

3. **Genre** This question asks how we know that the selection is a fantasy. To answer this, we must remember that a fantasy is a made-up story about characters and events that could not really happen. The characters in this story are animals that talk and do things like people, such as read and set up a bookmobile. Real animals do not talk, read, or drive cars. These are clues that *Nell's Books* is a fantasy.

Make Connections

Essential Question Have children draw a picture and label it to show how they get books in their community. Guide children to share their work with a partner and talk about how giving out books helps a community.

ELL

ENGLISH LANGUAGE LEARNERS

Retell Help children by looking at each page of the story and asking a prompt, such as, *What characters are on this page? Where are they?* Point to and identify the characters and where they are. *What are the characters doing?* Provide sentence starters to help children retell the story, such as: *Nell is ____. Dog, Cat, and Pig are ____.*

SOCIAL STUDIES

CONNECT TO CONTENT

HELPING THE COMMUNITY

Remind children thay have been reading and talking about ways that we can participate in the community. Guide children to think about how Nell and her friends participated in their community. Ask: *How does Nell help her friends? What do Nell and her friends do to help the larger community?* Prompt children to discuss how giving out books can help the people in the community.

→ # Language Arts

Reading/Writing Workshop Big Book

OBJECTIVES

CCSS Write narratives in which they recount two or more appropriately sequenced events, include some details regarding what happened, use temporal words to signal event order, and provide some sense of closure. **W.1.3**

CCSS Use common, proper, and possessive nouns. **L.1.1b**

ACADEMIC LANGUAGE

• *organization, proper nouns*

• Cognate: *organización*

MINILESSON
5 Mins

Independent Writing

Writing Trait: Organization

① **Review** Tell children that today they will write a draft. *Today you will write your own story about people helping in their community. Remember that a story has a beginning, a middle, and an end.*

② **Guided Practice** Have children open to the Readers to Writers page in the Reading/Writing Workshop. Read the student model aloud. Point out how Trish used organization. Guide children to identify the beginning, middle, and end of Trish's story.

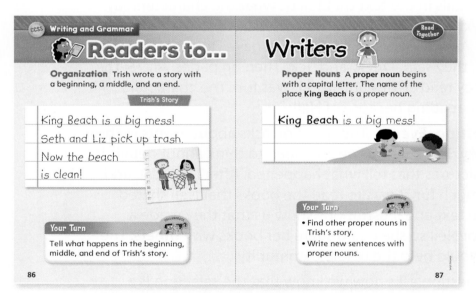

READING/WRITING WORKSHOP, pp. 86–87

Story

Model Have children look again at Trish's story, noting her topic and organization. Have them complete the Your Turn to discuss her process.

Prewrite

Display the Word Web of ideas from Day 2. Preview the story ideas with children. Tell children that to begin writing, they must first choose an idea.

Brainstorm Place children in pairs based on the ideas they chose. Have them use a Sequence organizer to organize their drafts.

Go Digital

Present the Lesson

Graphic Organizer

Writing

I see a fish.

Grammar

Draft

Have children write their drafts using sequence charts. Remind them that their story should be make-believe and have characters.

Apply Writing Trait As children write their drafts, remind them that their stories should have a beginning, middle, and end. Encourage them to begin sentences with *First, Next, Last*.

Apply Grammar Tell children to think about the nouns they use. Remind them if they use proper nouns, they must capitalize them.

As children work, conference with them to provide guidance.

Grammar

Common and Proper Nouns

❶ **Review** Have children look at the Readers to Writers page in the Reading/Writing Workshop. Remind them a proper noun names particular people, places, or things. Look at the model sentence.

Ask: *What is the proper noun in this sentence:* King Beach is a big mess! *Which words name a particular place?* King Beach *is a proper noun. It names a particular place.*

❷ **Guided Practice/Practice** Guide children to identify the proper nouns in Trish's story.

Have children work with partners to write new sentences about people. Then have them circle the proper nouns in each sentence.

Talk About It Have partners work together to orally generate sentences to add to Trish's story. Challenge them to create sentences with different proper nouns.

Mechanics: Capitalize Proper Nouns

❶ **Review** Remind children that a proper noun begins with a capital letter.

❷ **Practice** Display the following groups of words. Read them aloud. Then have children circle the proper nouns.

cloth, Seth, Greg (Seth, Greg)

pen, Frog Pond, eggs (Frog Pond)

Dad, Beth, day (Dad, Beth)

ELL

ENGLISH LANGUAGE LEARNERS SCAFFOLD

Beginning

Demonstrate Comprehension Help children start writing by providing sentence frames: *My character's name is _____. My character helps _____.* Allow children ample time to respond.

Intermediate

Explain Provide sentence frames for partners as they write their stories: *First, _____ helped _____. Next, _____. Last, _____.* Have children complete them orally before they write them.

Advanced/Advanced High

Expand Before children write their stories, ask: *What idea will you write about? What proper nouns could you use?*

Daily Wrap Up

→ Review the Essential Question and encourage children to discuss using the oral vocabulary words. Ask: *How can you help our school today?*

→ Prompt children to review and discuss the skills they used today.

Materials

Visual Vocabulary Cards

admire	all
leadership	call
enjoy	day
rely	her
connections	want

 Spelling Word Cards

 **Word-Building Cards**

Literature Anthology
VOLUME 2

Teaching Poster

Dinah Zike's Foldables®

→ # Extend the Concept

MINILESSON
5 Mins

Oral Language

OBJECTIVES

Know and use various text features (e.g., headings, tables of contents, glossaries, electronic menus, icons) to locate key facts or information in a text. **RI.1.5**

Review vocabulary

ACADEMIC LANGUAGE
• *list, information*
• Cognates: *lista, información*

ESSENTIAL QUESTION

Remind children that this week they have been learning about ways people can help out in their community. Guide children to discuss the question using information from what they have read and discussed.

Use the **Visual Vocabulary Cards** and the Define/Example/Ask routine to review the oral vocabulary words *admire, leadership, enjoy, rely,* and *connections*.

Guide children to use each word as they talk about what they have read and learned about how people help out in the community. Prompt children by asking questions.

→ Who is a hero you admire?

→ How does a team coach show leadership?

→ What do you enjoy doing with people in your community?

→ Who do you rely on to help you get to school?

→ How can you make connections between the stories you have read this week?

Review oral vocabulary words from last week: *habitat, depend, hibernate, tranquil, tolerate.*

Go Digital

Visual Glossary

Teaching Poster

"Kids Can Help"

Develop Comprehension

Text Feature: List

1 Explain Tell children that they can use informational text selections to find facts and details about how people help in the community. Explain that informational text sometimes includes a list, a written set of connected items. A list can use numbers to set off each new item in the list.

Teaching Poster

2 Model Display Teaching Poster 14. Read the title of the list. Point out the numbers. *This is a list of things to do. The person who wrote the list has to do four things.* Read the first item on the list. *The first thing the person must do is feed the dog.*

3 Guided Practice/Practice Read together items 2–4. Guide children to discuss the things the person needs to do. *What is the second thing the person needs to do? What else does he or she need to do? Why do you think the person wrote this list?* Help children think of other things lists can be used for. Tell children to look for a list as they read informational text.

ENGLISH LANGUAGE LEARNERS SCAFFOLD

Beginning

Use Sentence Frames Use sentence frames to help children discuss the list. For example: *The child must do ____ things today. First, she must ____. Next, she must ____.*

Intermediate

Describe Ask children to describe what they can learn from the list. *What kind of pet does the child have? Does she like to spend time outside?*

Advanced/Advanced High

Discuss Ask children to create their own list of things they must do at school today. Guide them to list the items in the order they will be done.

CCSS **Genre** Nonfiction

Compare Texts
Read about how kids can help out.

Read Together

Kids Can Help!

How can kids help the **neighborhood**?

Kids can help grow a **garden**! It is fun to plant seeds and help them grow.

A community garden is a great place to help. The plants are pretty to look at. And everyone can enjoy fresh fruits and vegetables.

82

83

LITERATURE ANTHOLOGY, pp. 82–83

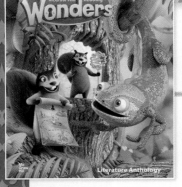

Literature Anthology

Develop Comprehension

CLOSE READING

Lexile 350

Read Literature Anthology

Compare Texts

Review with children that in *Nell's Books*, Nell helps her community. Tell them that now they will read a nonfiction selection about how children can help a neighborhood. Have them think about how these kids are like Nell and her friends.

Content Words Point out the words *neighborhood, garden,* and *recycle*. Prompt children to use context sentences to help them understand the words.

❶ Strategy: Reread

Teacher Think Aloud I want to make sure I understand and can remember what people do in a community garden. I will reread the text and look at the photograph. Now I understand that kids and grown-ups plant seeds and help to grow fruits and vegetables for everyone to share.

Kids can help clean the playground. They can pick up trash. They can **recycle** cans and bottles.

Recycling makes the neighborhood clean. Recycling helps our Earth, too.

84

Do you want to help your neighborhood? Think about what you can do.

② ③

How We Can Help

1. Plant a garden.
2. Clean the playground.
3. Recycle cans and bottles.

Make Connections

How does a garden help a community? **Essential Question**

85

LITERATURE ANTHOLOGY, pp. 84–85

② Text Features: List

Teacher Think Aloud I read about some ways kids can help in their neighborhood. Now I see a list in the photo on page 85. I know that a list can help organize ideas so I can understand and remember them better. Let's read this list together.

③ Text Features: List

What information is organized on this list? (ways you can help in your neighborhood) How does the list help you? (It helps me remember what the kids in the selection do. It helps me plan things I can do.) What could you add to this list?

 Make Connections Have partners make connections between how Nell helped her community and how the kids in this selection are helping.

→

Quick Review

Build Fluency: Sound-Spellings
Display the **Word-Building Cards:**
th, sh, ng, nd, nk, nt, st, sk, mp, u, e, ea, sp, sn, sl, cr, fr, tr, o, pl, fl, cl, bl, i, a, s. Have children say the sounds. Repeat, and vary the pace.

 MINILESSON 5 Mins

Phonemic Awareness

OBJECTIVES

CCSS Isolate and pronounce initial, medial vowel, and final sounds (phonemes) in spoken single-syllable words. **RF.1.2c**

CCSS Know the spelling-sound correspondences for common consonant digraphs. **RF.1.3a**

CCSS Decode two-syllable words following basic patterns by breaking the words into syllables. **RF.1.3e**

Phoneme Categorization

❶ **Model** Show children how to categorize phonemes. *Listen as I say three words: truck, hang, thump. Truck and thump both have the /u/ sound in the middle, but hang does not. Hang does not belong.*

❷ **Guided Practice/Practice** Have children practice categorizing phonemes. Guide practice with the first set. *Listen to these words. Two words have the same middle sound. Which word does not belong?*

head, hug, hunk	swum, jump, think	lost, shop, brush
blush, cash, stump	ship, trick, rush	stung, cost, rush

MINILESSON 5 Mins

Phonics

Build Words with *th, sh, -ng*

Review The sound /th/ is represented by the letters *th*. The sound /sh/ is represented by the letters *sh*. The sound /ng/ is represented by the letters *ng*. We'll use **Word-Building Cards** to build words with *sh, th,* and *-ng*.

Place the letters *m, a, t, h*. Say: *Let's blend the sounds together and read the word: /mmmaaath/.* Now change the *th* to *sh*. Blend the sounds and read the word: /mmmaaash/, *mash*.

Continue with *rash, rang, ring, thing, thick, sick, sack, shack, shock, shop, hop, hot, lot, log, long.*

Go Digital

Phonemic Awareness

Phonics

Structural Analysis

Spelling Word Sort

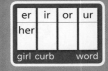

Visual Glossary

Structural Analysis

Closed Syllables

Review Write the words *selfish* and *ringing* on the board and divide them into syllables. Read the words with the children. Remind children that when a syllable has only one vowel letter and ends with a consonant, the vowel sound is usually short. This is called a closed syllable. Have children come to the board and circle the closed syllables. Ask others to explain why they are closed. Remind children that they may have to approximate sounds in order to read the multisyllabic words correctly.

Write the following words: *dentist, wishing, mitten, rabbit, thinking*. Have children work in pairs to divide the words and pronounce them. Then have them write sentences with those words.

Spelling

Word Sort with *th, sh, -ng*

Review Provide pairs of children with copies of the **Spelling Word Cards**. While one partner reads the words one at a time, the other partner should orally segment the word and then write the word. After reading all the words, partners should switch roles.

Have children correct their own papers. Then have them sort the words by consonant digraph spelling pattern: words with *th, sh, -ng,* or no consonant digraphs.

High-Frequency Words

all, call, day, her, want

Review Display **Visual Vocabulary Cards** for high-frequency words *all, call, day, her, want*. Have children Read/Spell/Write each word.

→ Point to a word and call on a child to use it in a sentence.

→ Review last week's words using the same procedure.

Monitor and *Differentiate*

 Quick Check

Can children read and decode words with consonant digraphs *th, sh, -ng*?

Can children recognize and read high-frequency words?

Small Group Instruction

If No →	Approaching	Reteach pp. T290–293
	ELL	Develop pp. T304–311
If Yes →	On Level	Review pp. T298–299
	Beyond Level	Extend pp. T302–303

→ # Language Arts

MINILESSON
5 Mins

Independent Writing

OBJECTIVES

CCSS With guidance and support from adults, focus on a topic, respond to questions and suggestions from peers, and add details to strengthen writing as needed. **W.1.5**

CCSS Use common, proper, and possessive nouns. **L.1.1b**

ACADEMIC LANGUAGE

• *organize, review, common nouns, proper nouns*

• Cognate: *organizar*

Story

Revise

Tell children that writers revise their writing to make their writing more clear to a reader. Explain that a writer might change the order of sentences in a story to make sure they are in the correct order.

Apply Writing Trait: Organization Explain that as writers revise, they move ideas around so they are organized to show a beginning, a middle, and an end. Display the following story:

> The box is ready to go. Jet helps set cans in a box. Jet and Dad will help again in three days. Dad sets yams and bread in the box.

Tell children that this story is not organized correctly. Help children organize the sentences by adding *First, Next, Last* to the sentences. Show children how to rewrite the sentences in order.

Peer Review Have children work in pairs to do a peer review, which means they will each read their partner's draft. They should take notes about what they like most, questions they have for the author, and ideas they think the author could include. Have partners discuss these topics. Provide time for them to make revisions to their stories.

Proofread/Edit

Apply Grammar Review proofreader's marks with children. Have them reread their drafts and fix mistakes. Remind them to make sure that:

→ every sentence has a noun.

→ proper nouns begin with capital letters.

→ all words are spelled correctly.

→ all sentences are complete.

Peer Edit Next, have partners exchange their drafts and take turns reading for the above mistakes. Encourage partners to discuss and fix errors together as they read.

Go Digital

Writing

━ Make a capital letter.
Λ Add.
✔ Take out.

Proofreader's Marks

I see a fish.

Grammar

Final Draft

After children have edited their own papers and finished their peer edits, have them write their final draft. Encourage them to create or find a photo or other visual that relates to their writing. As children work, conference with them to provide guidance.

Grammar

Common and Proper Nouns

1 Review Review with children that a proper noun names particular people, pets, places, and things. Proper nouns begin with a capital letter. Write *person, pet,* and *place* on cards. Have each child pick a card and name a proper noun that fits the category.

2 Guided Practice Guide children to underline the common nouns in these sentences and circle the proper nouns.

> Dad and Clem went to Kent on a bus.
>
> My dog Shep swam in Fish Pond.
>
> Miss Smith sings a song in Red Hall.

3 Practice Have partners make a two-column chart with the headings "Proper Nouns" and "Common Nouns." Have each pair choose a book from the class library and find at least five common nouns and five proper nouns. Have partners share their charts with the class.

 Talk About It Have partners work together to orally generate more sentences with the common and proper nouns they listed on their charts.

Mechanics: Capitalize Proper Nouns

1 Review Remind children that a proper noun begins with a capital letter.

2 Practice Display the sentences below. Read each aloud. Have children fix the sentences as a class.

> brent and fran live in red rock. (Brent and Fran live in Red Rock.)
>
> My Cat fluff can jump on the Bed. (My cat Fluff can jump on the bed.)

Daily Wrap Up

→ Review the Essential Question and encourage children to discuss using the oral vocabulary words.

→ Prompt children to discuss the skills they practiced and learned today.

Go Digital
www.connected.mcgraw-hill.com
RESOURCES
Research and Inquiry

→ **Wrap Up the Week**
Integrate Ideas

RESEARCH AND INQUIRY

Let's Help

OBJECTIVES

 Participate in shared research and writing projects (e.g., explore a number of "how-to" books on a given topic and use them to write a sequence of instructions). **W.1.7**

- Build background knowledge
- Research using information technology

ACADEMIC LANGUAGE
list, brainstorm, improve

Make a List

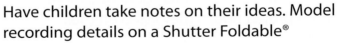 Review the steps in the research process. Tell children that today they will do a research project with a group to make a list of ways they can make the classroom a better place.

STEP 1 ### Choose a Topic

Guide groups to think of things that need improvement in the classroom, such as adding books to the class library.

STEP 2 ### Find Resources

Discuss how to use the selections, reference materials, and online sources to research and brainstorm ways to improve the classroom community. Have children use the Research Process Checklist online.

STEP 3 ### Keep Track of Ideas

Have children take notes on their ideas. Model recording details on a Shutter Foldable®

Our Classroom   How Can We Make It Better?

Dinah Zike's
FOLDABLES

Collaborative Conversations

Ask and Answer Questions Review with children that as they engage in partner, small-group, and whole-group discussions, they should:

→ ask questions about ideas they do not understand.

→ give others a chance to think after asking a question.

→ write down questions they want to ask the teacher or the whole class.

STEP 4 **Create the Project: List of Ways to Improve the Classroom**

Explain the characteristics of a list.

→ **Items** A list shows a set of connected items.

→ **Text** A list uses words to describe or explain ideas.

→ **Numbers** A list can use numbers to set off each new item in the list.

Have children create a list of things that would improve their classroom community.

→ Guide them to write their ideas as phrases or in sentence form.

→ Prompt children to share their lists with other groups. Have them ask and answer questions about the items on other groups' lists.

How to Make Our Classroom Better

1. Have a craft table.

2. Bring in new books.

3. Have soft chairs for reading.

4. Get new toys.

ENGLISH LANGUAGE LEARNERS

ELL SCAFFOLD

Beginning	Intermediate	Advanced/High
Use Sentence Frames Use sentence frames to help children discuss the classroom and ways to improve it. For example: *Our classroom needs _____. We want _____ in our classroom.*	**Discuss** Guide children to focus on how their suggestions would help the children in the classroom. Ask: *How will the children use that? Why will they enjoy having that in the classroom?*	**Describe** Prompt children to elaborate on their ideas. Ask them to explain how their suggested changes would improve the classroom.

Materials

Reading/Writing Workshop
VOLUME 2

Literature Anthology
VOLUME 2

Literature Big Book
The Story of Martin Luther King Jr.

Visual Vocabulary Cards
all
call
day
her
want

Teaching Poster

Word-Building Cards

fish

Spelling Word Cards

→ Integrate Ideas

TEXT CONNECTIONS

Connect to Essential Question

OBJECTIVES

Identify basic similarities in and differences between two texts on the same topic (e.g., in illustrations, descriptions, or procedures). **RI.1.9**

- Develop answers to the Essential Question
- Make text connections to the world

ACADEMIC LANGUAGE
community

Text to Text

Remind children they have been reading selections about how people can help their communities. Tell them now they can make connections across texts by thinking about how the selections were similar. Model comparing texts using *The Story of Martin Luther King Jr.* and "Luis's Library."

Think Aloud *The Story of Martin Luther King Jr.* and "Luis's Library" are both about people who help people in their countries. Martin Luther King Jr. helped his fellow citizens gain equal rights. Luis Soriano helps children in his country have books in areas that do not have libraries.

Complete the Organizer Have children use the graphic organizer to help them organize the information from this week's selections.

→ Discuss and write about how the people they read about helped their communities.

→ Discuss other ways people can help their communities.

Ways to Help Your Community

Teaching Poster

Text to Self

Have children discuss ways they help. *What do you do at school to help your teacher or your friends? How could you help your community outside of school?*

Text to World

Have children discuss what they have learned. *Why do people help in their communities? How do you feel about helping out? What do you think are the most important ways people can help?*

WRITE ABOUT READING *Analytical Writing*

OBJECTIVES

CCSS Draw evidence from literary or informational texts to support analysis, reflection, and research. **W.4.9**

Analyze Character, Setting, Events

Explain to children that as a group they will write about one of the selections that they have read this week.

Tell children that using the evidence in the text, they will think about how the author described characters, setting, and events in a story.

Review the Character, Setting, Events chart for *Thump Thump Helps Out*. Guide children to analyze the text evidence by asking "who," "where," and "how" questions about the characters, setting, and events.

→ *Who are the characters the author writes about?*

→ *Where does the story take place? What are some events? What clues does the author give to help you identify the setting and events?*

→ *How do details in the text help you understand the characters, setting, and events?*

Write an Analysis

Display the following sentence frames:

> In _____, the author wrote about _____.
>
> The author used details like _____, _____, and _____ to help you understand characters, setting, and events in the story.
>
> The story helped us understand _____.

Guide children to complete the sentence frames.

Select another fantasy story you have read this week. Work with children to complete the sentence frames to write about how the author described characters, setting, and events.

RESEARCH AND INQUIRY SOCIAL STUDIES

OBJECTIVES

CCSS Participate in shared research and writing projects. **W.1.7**

Wrap Up the Project

 Guide partners to share information from their lists about making their classroom a better place. Have children use the Presentation Checklist online. *What ideas did you have about improving our classroom?*

→ # Word Work

Quick Review

Build Fluency: Sound-Spellings
Display the **Word-Building Cards:**
th, sh, ng, nd, nk, nt, st, sk, mp, u, e, ea, sp, sn, sl, cr, fr, tr, o, pl, fl, cl, bl, i, a, s. Have children say the sounds. Repeat, and vary the pace.

MINILESSON 5 Mins

Phonemic Awareness

OBJECTIVES

CCSS Segment spoken single-syllable words into their complete sequence of individual sounds (phonemes). **RF.1.2d**

CCSS Decode two-syllable words following basic patterns by breaking the words into syllables. **RF.1.3e**

Phoneme Blending

Review Guide children to blend phonemes to form words. *Listen as I say a group of sounds.* Then blend the sounds to form a word.

/k/ /a/ /sh/	/th/ /i/ /k/	/s/ /i/ /ng/
/s/ /t/ /u/ /ng/	/b/ /r/ /i/ /ng/	/s/ /m/ /a/ /sh/

Phoneme Segmentation

Review Guide children to segment phonemes in words. *I am going to say a word. Tell me the sounds you hear in the word.*

thin   fish   ship   flash   cling   math   sing

MINILESSON 5 Mins

Phonics

Blend and Build Words with *th, sh, -ng*

Review Have children read and say the words *thank, with, shell, wish,* and *stung.* Then have children follow the word-building routine with **Word-Building Cards** to build *hip, ship, shop, shot, hot, pot, pin, win, wing, ding, dish, dash, clash, bash, bath, bang, sang, song.*

Word Automaticity Help children practice word automaticity. Display decodable words and point to each word as children chorally read it. Test how many words children can read in one minute. Model blending words children miss.

Go Digital

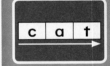

Phonemic Awareness

Phonics

Structural Analysis

Visual Glossary

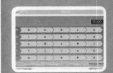

Fluency: Word Automaticity

Structural Analysis

Closed Syllables

Review Write the word *pocket*. Have children read it and divide it into syllables. Have them identify the vowel sounds and explain why the syllables are closed syllables. Then have children practice writing and reading more words with closed syllables, such as *basket, finish, helping, fishing,* and *jumping*.

Spelling

Word Sort with *th, sh, -ng*

Review Have children use the **Spelling Word Cards** to sort the weekly words by consonant digraphs. Remind children that four of the words do not have the *th, sh,* or *-ng* spellings.

Assess Assess children on their abilities to spell words with consonant digraphs *th, sh,* and *-ng*. Say each word and provide a sentence so that children can hear the words used in a correct context. Then allow them time to write down the words. In order to challenge children, you may wish to provide an additional word with each spelling in order to assess whether they understand the concept.

High-Frequency Words

all, call, day, her, want

Review Display **Visual Vocabulary Cards** *all, call, day, her, want*. Have children Read/Spell/Write each word. Have children write a sentence with each word.

Monitor and *Differentiate*

✓ Quick Check

Can children read and decode words with consonant digraphs *th, sh, -ng*?

Can children recognize and read high-frequency words?

⬇

Small Group Instruction

If No →  **Approaching** Reteach pp. T290–298

  ELL Develop pp. T304–311

If Yes → **On Level** Review pp. T298–299

  Beyond Level Extend pp. T302–303

Language Arts

 MINILESSON 5 Mins

Independent Writing

OBJECTIVES

CCSS With guidance and support from adults, use a variety of digital tools to produce and publish writing, including in collaboration with peers. **W.1.6**

CCSS Use common, proper, and possessive nouns. **L.1.1b**

ACADEMIC LANGUAGE

• *presentation, common and proper nouns*

• Cognate: *presentación*

Story

Prepare

Review guidelines for making presentations with children.

→ Provide time for children to finish preparing their presentations. Remind them to practice using visuals if they have created any.

Present

Have children take turns giving presentations of their community-helping stories. Remind them to speak clearly. When listening to other stories, they should be polite and respectful, asking questions when appropriate and listening carefully when it is not appropriate to speak.

→ If possible, record the presentations so children can self-evaluate.

Evaluate

Have children discuss their own presentations and evaluate their performance using the presentation rubric.

Use the teacher's rubric to evaluate children's writing. Have children add their writing to their Writer's Portfolio. Then have them discuss and write about how they have changed as writers throughout the year.

Publish

After children finish presenting their stories, guide them to use digital tools in their writing. Discuss how the class can post the stories on a class blog. Post the stories and encourage parents to read them.

Go Digital

Writing

Checklists

I see a fish.

Grammar

Grammar

Common and Proper Nouns

❶ Review Have children describe proper nouns. Write the following sentence and have children identify the proper nouns:

Ken and Len like to eat Fizz Puffs.

❷ Practice Ask: *How do I know which words in a sentence are proper nouns?*

Write a dialogue. Have pairs of children each take a part and read the dialogue aloud, filling in proper nouns.

First Person: *My name is _____. Who are you?*

Second Person: *My name is _____.*

First Person: *I live on [name of street]. I go to [name of school].*

Second Person: *My pet is _____. I like [name of cereal].*

Children can act out the dialogue for the class and have the class identify the proper nouns.

Mechanics: Capitalize Proper Nouns

❶ Review Remind children that proper nouns begin with a capital letter.

❷ Practice Write the following sentences. Read each aloud. Have children fix the sentences.

mom and lin went camping at grand hill. (Mom and Lin went camping at Grand Hill.)

Miss wong likes to Fish on a dock at swan pond. (Miss Wong likes to fish on a dock at Swan Pond.)

My pet fish lil eats and swims. (My pet fish Lil eats and swims.)

Wrap Up the Week

→ Review the Essential Question and encourage children to discuss using the oral vocabulary words.

→ Review that children can reread parts of a story to better understand it and should identify the characters, setting, and events of a story.

→ Review words with *th, sh,* and *-ng.* Remind children that when a syllable has only one vowel and ends with a consonant, the vowel sound is short.

→ Use the Visual Vocabulary Cards to review the Words to Know.

→ Remind children that a story is organized so it has a beginning, middle, and end.

→ Approaching Level

by Sarah Hughes
illustrated by
Viviana Garofoli

PAIRED READ Beach Clean-Up

Lexile 40

OBJECTIVES

Describe characters, settings, and major events in a story, using key details. **RL.1.3**

Leveled Reader:
The Sick Tree

Go
Digital

The Sick Tree

Before Reading

Preview and Predict

Have children turn to the title page. Read the title and the author's name and have children repeat. Preview the selection's illustrations. Prompt children to predict what the selection might be about.

Review Genre: Fantasy

Have children recall that a fantasy is a story that has invented characters, setting, or other elements that could not exist in real life.

ESSENTIAL QUESTION

Remind children of the Essential Question: *How do people help out in the community?* Set a purpose for reading: *Let's read to find out how the birds help the sick tree.*

Remind children that as they read a selection, they can ask questions about what they do not understand or what they want to know more about.

Character	Setting	Events

Graphic Organizer

Retell

During Reading

Guided Comprehension

As children that whisper read *The Sick Tree,* monitor and provide guidance, correcting blending and modeling the key strategies and skills.

Strategy: Reread

Remind children that if they don't understand something, they can go back and reread. Model the strategy. *I don't understand this sentence on page 3: "We will make it better." I reread page 2 and understand the birds think the tree is sick because the leaves are falling. So they want to make the tree better.*

Skill: Character, Setting, Events

Remind children that the characters are the people or animals in a story; the setting is where the story takes place; the events are what happens. *Who are the characters? Where does the story take place? What are the important events?* Display a Character, Setting, Events chart for children to copy.

Model recording children's answers in the character, setting, and events boxes. Have children copy the answers into their own charts.

Think Aloud I can tell from the picture on page 4 that the story takes place in the woods. That is the setting. I read one of the birds is Trish. That bird is a character. Trish tapes a leaf to the tree. That is an event.

Guide children to use the text and illustrations to complete the chart.

After Reading

Respond to Reading

Complete the Respond to Reading on page 12 after reading.

Retell

Have children take turns retelling the selection, using the **Retelling Cards** to guide them. Help children make a connection by asking: *Have you ever tried to help save a plant or help an animal? Why did the plant or animal need help? What did you do to help?*

Model Fluency

Read the sentences one at a time. Have children read chorally. Point out to children how your voice sounds when you stress important words.

Apply Have children practice repeated readings with partners. Provide feedback as needed.

PAIRED READ ...

"Beach Clean-Up"

Make Connections:
Write About It 🖊 *Analytical Writing*

Before reading, ask children to note that the genre of this text is informational text. Then discuss the Make Connections direction. After reading, ask children to say one word that tells about what both "Beach Clean-Up" and *The Sick Tree* are about.

Leveled Reader

🖊 *Analytical Writing*

COMPARE TEXTS

→ Have children use text evidence to compare fantasy to informational text.

Literature Circles

Lead children in conducting a literature circle using the Thinkmark questions to guide the discussion. You may wish to discuss what children have learned about helping others in both selections in the Leveled Reader.

Level Up

Level-up lessons available online.

IF children can read *The Sick Tree*, Approaching Level with fluency and correctly answer the Respond to Reading questions,

THEN tell children that they will read another story about helping out.

• Use pages 2–5 of *Squirrels Help* On Level to model using Teaching Poster 28 to identify characters, setting, and events.

• Have children read the selection, checking their comprehension by using the graphic organizer.

→ Approaching Level

Phonemic Awareness

PHONEME ISOLATION

OBJECTIVES

 Isolate and pronounce initial, medial vowel, and final sounds (phonemes) in spoken single-syllable words. **RF.1.2c**

 I Do   Explain to children that they will listen for specific sounds in words. *I'll say a word and then say the beginning sound. Listen:* thin. *The beginning sound is /th/. Now I'll say a new word and then say the ending sound. Listen:* sing. *I hear /ng/ at the end of* sing.

 We Do   *Let's do one together. Listen for the beginning sound in this word:* ship. *What sound do you hear at the beginning of* ship? *That's right, /sh/.*

Repeat the routine with these words: beginning sound—*that, spill, shell, them, shut, thumb;* ending sound—*path, ring, dish, moth, clasp, long, fish.*

 You Do   *It's your turn.* Have children isolate the beginning sound in these words: *there, shop, speck, then, that.* Have them isolate the ending sound in these words: *with, wish, strong, cloth, cling, rash.*

PHONEME CATEGORIZATION

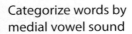
OBJECTIVES

 Isolate and pronounce initial, medial vowel, and final sounds (phonemes) in spoken single-syllable words. **RF.1.2c**

Categorize words by medial vowel sound

 I Do   Explain to children that they will be categorizing sounds today. *Listen as I say three words:* shut, thud, skill. *When I say* shut *and* thud *I can hear the /u/ sound in the middle of each word.* Skill *has the /i/ sound in the middle.* Skill *does not belong.*

 We Do   *Listen as I say three words:* sing, hush, this. *Two of the words have the same sound in the middle, /i/ :* sing *and* this. *The word* hush *does not have /i/. It does not belong.*

Repeat this routine for medial vowel with the following groups of words:

crash, brush, that   wing, thump, rush   flap, flush, sung

 You Do   *It's your turn. Which words go together and which word does not belong?*

shock, flop, hug   them, hung, blush   lung, wish, rig

PHONEME BLENDING

OBJECTIVES

 Orally produce single-syllable words by blending sounds (phonemes), including consonant blends. **RF.1.2b**

 I Do Tell children they will be blending sounds to form words. *Listen as I say three sounds: /sh/ /e/ /l/. Say them with me: /sh/ /e/ /l/. I'm going to blend the sounds together: /sh/ /eee/ /lll/, /sheeelll/,* shell. *We blended the word* shell.

 We Do *Listen as I say three sounds: /th/ /e/ /m/. Repeat the sounds: /th/ /e/ /m/. Let's blend the sounds: /th/ /eee/ /mmm/, /theeemmm/,* them. *We made* them.

Repeat this routine with the following words:

/sh/ /u/ /t/   /th/ /i/ /ng/   /s/ /a/ /ng/   /m/ /a/ /sh/   /sh/ /o/ /p/

 You Do *It's your turn. I want you to blend the sounds I say together to form a word.*

/m/ /a/ /th/   /th/ /a/ /t/   /sh/ /a/ /k/   /k/ /a/ /sh/   /r/ /a/ /ng/

PHONEME CATEGORIZATION

OBJECTIVES

 Isolate and pronounce initial, medial vowel, and final sounds (phonemes) in spoken single-syllable words. **RF.1.2c**

Categorize words by medial phoneme

 I Do Explain to children that they will be categorizing sounds. *Listen as I say three words:* ship, that, this. Ship *and* this *both have the /i/ sound in the middle.* That *does not have /i/.* That *has the /a/ sound.* That *does not belong.*

 We Do *Listen as I say three words:* shop, block, them. *Two have the same vowel sound, /o/:* shop, block. Them *does not have the /o/ sound. It does not belong.*

Repeat this routine with the following words:

that, trash, song   crush, thin, fill   shed, then, hung

 You Do *It's your turn. Listen for the middle sound. Which words go together and which word does not?*

thick, shack, path   crib, then, wish   fresh, Beth, dash

ENGLISH LANGUAGE LEARNERS

For the **ELLs** who need **phonemic awareness, phonics**, and **fluency** practice, use scaffolding methods as necessary to ensure children understand the meaning of the words. Refer to the Language Transfer Handbook for phonics elements that may not transfer in children's native languages.

→ Approaching Level

Phonics

CONNECT *th, sh, -ng* TO /th/, /sh/, /ng/

TIER 2

 CCSS

OBJECTIVES

Know the spelling-sound correspondences for common consonant digraphs. **RF.1.3a**

 I Do Display **Word-Building Cards** for *s* and *h*. *These are the letters* sh. *Watch and listen as I trace the letters and say the sound they stand for.* Trace the letters *sh* and say /sh/ five times. Repeat for Word-Building Cards *n* and *g* and the /ng/ sound and then *t* and *h* and the /th/ sound heard at the beginning of *then* and *this.*

 We Do *Now do it with me.* Have children trace the *sh, ng,* and *th* on the Word-Building Cards with their fingers while saying the sounds. Have each child say all three sounds several times.

 You Do Have children connect the letters *th, sh, -ng* to the sounds /th/, /sh/, /ng/ by tracing each letter pair with their finger while saying /th/, /sh/, and /ng/. Once children have traced on paper five to ten times, they should write the letters while saying the appropriate sounds five to ten times.

Repeat, connecting these consonant digraphs with the sounds they stand for throughout the week.

BLEND WORDS WITH *th, sh, -ng*

TIER 2

 CCSS

OBJECTIVES

Know the spelling-sound correspondences for common consonant digraphs. **RF.1.3a**

Decode words with *th, sh,* and *-ng*

 I Do Display Word-Building Cards *t, h, i, n. Listen as I say the sounds the letters stand for.* Point to each card as you say the sound: /th/ /i/ /n/. *Now listen as I blend the sounds:* /th/ /iii/ /nnn/; /thiiinnn/; thin.

 We Do Guide children to blend the sounds and read: *fish, sing, path, sting, shut, thick.*

 You Do Have children blend and decode the following words on their own: *this, them, that, shop, shack, shut, sang, wing, sung, gash, cloth.*

Repeat, blending additional *th, sh,* and *-ng* words.

You may wish to review Phonics with **ELL** using this section.

BUILD WORDS WITH *th, sh, -ng*

OBJECTIVES

Know the spelling-sound correspondences for common consonant digraphs. **RF.1.3a**

Build and decode words with *th, sh, -ng*

 I Do Display **Word-Building Cards** *b, a, th,* one at a time. Point to each card as you say the letter and sound: *The letters* b, a, *and* th *stand for the sounds* /b/, /a/, *and* /th/. *I can use these letters to build a word.* Display letters in a row. *I can blend* /b/ /aaa/ /th/ *together:* /baaath/, bath.

 We Do *Let's build a new word together. Let's change the* th *in* bath *to* ng. *Let's blend and read the new word:* /b/ /aaa/ /ng/, /baang/, bang.

You Do Have children use the Word-Building Cards to continue building the words *sang, sing, wing, thing, this, thin, shin, ship,* and *shop.*

BLEND WORDS WITH *th, sh, -ng*

OBJECTIVES

Know the spelling-sound correspondences for common consonant digraphs. **RF.1.3a**

Decode regularly spelled one-syllable words. **RF.1.3b**

Blend and decode words with *th, sh, -ng*

 I Do Display Word-Building Cards *th, i, ng.* Hold up each card as you name the letters and say each sound: *The letters* th *stand for* /th/. *The letter* i *stands for* /i/. *The letters* ng *stand for* /ng/. Point to each card as you blend. *Listen as I blend the sounds and read the word:* /thiiing/, thing.

 We Do *Let's blend some words together.* Blend and read the words with children: *this, thick, thing, breath, clash, sting, bring, shack, smash.*

 You Do Display the words to the right. Have children blend and read the words.

sling	song	trash	thin	them	cash
than	crush	with	long	hang	thank
brush	fresh	thump	fling	lung	cloth
shut	flash	that	wing	rang	wish

She can bring that thing to me.

This shell can go in the trash.

We sing with them on the path to school.

BUILD FLUENCY WITH PHONICS

Sound-Spellings Fluency

Display the following Word-Building Cards: *th, sh, ng, nd, nk, nt, st, sk, mp, u, e, ea, sp, sn, sl, cr, fr, tr, o, pl, fl, cl, bl, i, a, s.* Have children chorally say the sounds. Repeat and vary the pace.

Fluency in Connected Text

Have children review *Thump Thump Helps Out* in their Reading/Writing Workshop. Identify words with *th, sh, -ng.* Blend words as needed.

Have children reread on their own or with a partner.

→ Approaching Level

Structural Analysis

REVIEW CLOSED SYLLABLES

OBJECTIVES

 Know and apply grade-level phonics and word analysis skills in decoding words. **RF.1.3**

Read words with closed syllables

 I Do Write *ship*. Say: *When a word with one vowel* [point to the *i*] *letter ends with a consonant* [point to the *p*], *the vowel sound is usually short. Listen: /shiiip/.*

 We Do Write *hang*. *Let's decide if this word is a closed syllable word. How many vowel letters does it have? Yes, it has one vowel:* a. *Does it end in a consonant? Right! It does end with two consonants, but together they stand for one consonant sound, /ng/. What sound does the vowel stand for? Yes, it is a short a: /a/. So it is a closed syllable. Let's read the word together: /haaang/; hang.*

 You Do Write the words below on the board. Have one partner choose a word and tell the other if it is a closed syllable word and why. Then have the other partner read the word. Switch roles and repeat.

shop   this   shack   thin   thing   song   hang   that

Repeat Have children read additional closed syllable words.

RETEACH CLOSED SYLLABLES

OBJECTIVES

 Know and apply grade-level phonics and word analysis skills in decoding words. **RF.1.3**

Read words with closed syllables

 I Do Write *thin*. Circle the *i*. Put a check next to the *n*. *This word has one vowel and ends in a consonant, so the vowel sound is short* i. *This makes thin a closed syllable.* Say the sentence, stressing the word *thin*: *My dog is <u>thin</u>.*

 We Do Write *gong*. Circle the *o*. Put a check next to the *ng*. Remind children that *ng* stands for one sound. Discuss with children why this is a closed syllable word. Read the word together and have the group create a sentence for it.

 You Do *Now it's your turn. Circle the vowel. Check that the word ends in one consonant sound. Read the word and use it in a sentence.*

ring   shock   shed   thick   truck   ship   moth

Repeat identifying, reading, and using closed syllable words in sentences.

High-Frequency Words

REVIEW

OBJECTIVES

Recognize and read grade-appropriate irregularly spelled words. **RF.1.3g**

Review high-frequency words *all, call, day, her, want*

 I Do Use the **High-Frequency Word Cards** to **Read/Spell/Write** each high-frequency word. Use each word orally in a sentence.

 We Do Guide children to Read/Spell/Write each word on their **Response Boards**. Work together to generate oral sentences using the words.

 You Do Have each child do the Read/Spell/Write routine on his or her own using the words *all, call, day, her, want*.

RETEACH

OBJECTIVES

Recognize and read grade-appropriate irregularly spelled words. **RF.1.3g**

 I Do Review the high-frequency words using the Read/Spell/Write routine. Give an oral sentence for each high-frequency word.

 We Do Guide children to use the Read/Spell/Write routine. Read and complete sentence starters together: *(1) All of the dogs _____. (2) I will call my _____. (3) What day will we _____? (4) Will you tell her to _____? (5) I do not want _____.*

 You Do Say the word. Have children write the word and say a sentence. Display the word and have children self-correct.

Repeat for each high-frequency word.

CUMULATIVE REVIEW

OBJECTIVES

Recognize and read grade-appropriate irregularly spelled words. **RF.1.3g**

Review previously taught high-frequency words

 I Do Display the High-Frequency Word Cards from the previous weeks. Review each word using the Read/Spell/Write routine.

 We Do Have children write the words on their Response Boards. Complete sentences for each word: *We will eat _____. I have no _____. The cost of this rug is _____. The box is under the _____. Who is _____?*

 You Do Show each card and have children chorally read each word. Mix and repeat.

Fluency Display each word. Have children chorally read the words, then read them again at a faster pace.

→ # Approaching Level

Comprehension

READ FOR FLUENCY

OBJECTIVES

 Read grade-level text orally with accuracy, appropriate rate, and expression. **RF.1.4b**

 I Do Read the first two lines of the Practice Book selection. Model using appropriate intonation and stressing important words in each sentence.

 We Do Read the rest of the Practice Book selection. Call attention to how you stress specific words and how your voice changes tone. Have children underline the words you stress and then echo read each sentence using appropriate intonation.

 You Do Have children work with a partner and take turns rereading the passage. Remind them to use proper intonation, stressing the important words they underlined. Monitor children as they read to check for correct intonation, stress, and pronunciation.

IDENTIFY KEY DETAILS

OBJECTIVES

CCSS Ask and answer questions about key details in a text. **RL.1.1**

 I Do Remind children that the key details are the important pieces of information in a story. Stress that key details can help them learn about and understand characters.

 We Do Read the Practice Book passage together. Model identifying the details to answer questions about a character. *What do the dogs want to do? What does Shep make? How do you know?*

 You Do Have children reread the passage chorally. Guide them to identify and share important details in the words and illustrations that help them understand the story and its characters.

REVIEW CHARACTER, SETTING, EVENTS

OBJECTIVES

 Describe characters, settings, and major events in a story, using key details. **RL.1.3**

 I Do Remind children that the characters in a fantasy story are often animals. The setting tells when and where the story takes place, and the events are the actions that take place in the story. Identifying these parts of the story helps readers understand what the story is about.

 We Do Read the first two pages of the Practice Book selection together. Point out the characters, setting, and events in the words and illustration. *We read that this story is about Rex and Shep and their friends. Those are the characters. What type of creatures are they? What events took place?*

 You Do Have children read the rest of the story. Have them work in pairs as you guide them to complete a Character, Setting, Events chart.

SELF-SELECTED READING

OBJECTIVES

 Describe characters, settings, and major events in a story, using key details. **RL.1.3**

 With prompting and support, read prose and poetry of appropriate complexity for grade 1. **RL.1.10**

Apply the strategy and skill to read a text.

Read Independently

Have children pick a fantasy selection for sustained silent reading. Remind them to:

→ reread any parts that they do not understand.

→ identify the characters, setting, and events.

→ note the parts of the story that could not happen in real life.

Read Purposefully

Have children complete the Character, Setting, Events chart. After completing the chart, have partners:

→ share their charts and tell each other about the story they read.

→ tell if they reread any parts of the story and if so, why.

On Level

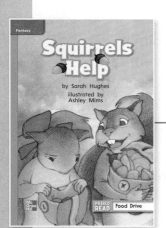

Lexile 200

 OBJECTIVES

Describe characters, settings, and major events in a story, using key details. **RL.1.3**

Leveled Reader:
Squirrels Help

Go Digital

Squirrels Help

Before Reading

Preview and Predict

Have children turn to the title page. Read the title and the author's name and have children repeat. Preview the selection's illustrations. Prompt children to predict what the selection might be about.

Review Genre: Fantasy

Have children recall that a fantasy is a story that has invented characters, setting, or other elements that could not exist in real life.

ESSENTIAL QUESTION

Remind children of the Essential Question: *How can people help out in the community?* Set a purpose for reading: *Let's read to find out how squirrels help.*

Remind children that as they read a selection, they can ask questions about what they do not understand or what they want to know more about.

Character	Setting	Events

Graphic Organizer

Retell

During Reading

Guided Comprehension

As children whisper read *Squirrels Help*, monitor and provide guidance, correcting blending and modeling the key strategies and skills.

Strategy: Reread

Remind children to reread if they don't understand something they've just read. Model using the strategy on page 5. *I am confused. Is Tom talking to Sue or Dad? I will reread this page.* Reread page 5 aloud. *Now I understand. Tom is asking Dad if they can help Sue.*

Skill: Character, Setting, Events

Remind children that stories include characters, a setting, and events. After reading, ask: *Who are the story characters? What is the setting? What are the important events?* Display a Character, Setting, Events chart for children to copy.

Model recording answers for children. Have children copy the answers into their own charts.

Think Aloud On page 6, I see the squirrels are in the woods. That is the setting. I read about Sue and Tom. They are characters. I also read that Tom shows Sue where to find nuts. That is an event.

Guide children to use the words and pictures to add characters, setting, and events to their charts.

After Reading

Respond to Reading

Have children complete the Respond to Reading on page 12.

Retell

Have children take turns retelling the selection, using the **Retelling Cards** to guide them. Help children make a connection by asking: *Have you ever helped a friend? Has a friend ever helped you? Tell me what happened. Tell me how you felt.*

Model Fluency

Read the sentences one at a time. Have children chorally repeat. Point out to children how your voice sounds when you stress important words in the story.

Apply Have partners practice reading. Provide feedback as needed.

PAIRED READ ...

"Food Drive"

Make Connections:
Write About It

Ask children to note this is informational text. Then discuss the Compare Texts direction. After reading, ask children to tell one thing they learned in both *Squirrels Help* and "Food Drive." Guide children to realize both books showed the importance of helping others have enough food.

Leveled Reader

Analytical Writing

COMPARE TEXTS

→ Have children use text evidence to compare fantasy to informational text.

Literature Circles

Lead children in conducting a literature circle using the Thinkmark questions to guide the discussion. You may wish to discuss what children have learned about helping others from both selections in the Leveled Reader.

Level Up

Level-up lessons available online.

IF children can read *Squirrels Help* On Level with fluency and correctly answer the Respond to Reading questions,

THEN tell children that they will read a longer story about helping out.

• Use pages 2–5 of *Wow, Kitty!* Beyond Level to model using Teaching Poster 28 to identify characters, setting, and events.

• Have children read the selection, checking their comprehension by using the graphic organizer.

On Level

Phonics

BUILD WORDS WITH *th, sh, -ng*

OBJECTIVES

Know the spelling-sound correspondences for common consonant digraphs. **RF.1.3a**

Build and decode words with consonant digraphs *th, sh,* and *-ng*

 I Do Display and point to **Word-Building Cards** *sh, o, p. These are the letters* sh, o, *and* p. *They stand for /sh/, /o/, and /p/. I will blend /sh/, /o/, and /p/ together: /shooop/,* shop. *The word is* shop.

 We Do *Now let's build a word together. Let's make the word using the Word-Building Cards* th, a, *and* t. *Display the cards. Let's blend: /th/ /aaa/ /t/, /thaaat/,* that. *We made the word* that.

 You Do *Now let's change the* t *at the end to* n. *Let's blend and read the new word: /th/ /aaa/ /nnn/, /thaaannn/,* than. *The new word is* than.

Have children build and blend the following words: *this, thin, shin, ship, shop, shock, shack, shall, shell*. Continue with *ring, rang, rank, sank, sang, sing, song*.

Repeat with additional words with *th, sh,* and *-ng*.

High-Frequency Words

REVIEW WORDS

OBJECTIVES

Recognize and read grade-appropriate irregularly spelled words. **RF.1.3g**

Review high-frequency words: *all, call, day, her, want*

 I Do Use the **Read/Spell/Write** routine to review each word. Use each word orally in a sentence.

 We Do Guide children to Read/Spell/Write each word using their **Response Boards**. Work together to create oral sentences using the words.

 You Do Have partners work together using the Read/Spell/Write routine with the words *all, call, day, her,* and *want*. Have partners then write sentences about the stories they have read this week. Each sentence must contain at least one high-frequency word.

Comprehension

REVIEW CHARACTER, SETTING, EVENTS

OBJECTIVES

 Describe characters, settings, and major events in a story, using key details. **RL.1.3**

 I Do Remind children that a character is a person or animal in a story. The setting tells when and where the story takes place, and the events are what happens in the story. *When we read a fantasy story, the characters, setting, and events are things that could not exist or happen in real life.*

We Do Read aloud the first three sentences of the Practice Book selection and look at the picture. Ask questions about the characters. Have children point out key details in the words and pictures. *Who are the characters? What are they doing? How do you know?*

 You Do Guide children to read the rest of the Practice Book selection. Then have partners ask each other questions about the characters, setting, and events. Remind children to show where they find their answers using both the words and the illustrations.

SELF-SELECTED READING

OBJECTIVES

 Describe characters, settings, and major events in a story, using key details. **RL.1.3**

With prompting and support, read prose and poetry of appropriate complexity for grade 1. **RL.1.10**

Apply the strategy and skill to read a text

Read Independently

Have children pick a fantasy selection for sustained silent reading. Remind them to:

→ reread any parts of the story that they do not understand.

→ identify characters, settings, or events that could not happen in real life.

Read Purposefully

Have children complete information in the Character, Setting, Events chart. After completing the chart, have partners:

→ share and compare their charts.

→ tell what parts of their story they reread and if they liked those parts.

→ identify characters, setting, and events that let them know the story is a fantasy.

→ Beyond Level

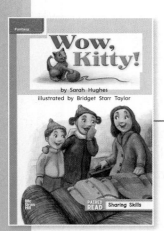

Lexile 390

 OBJECTIVES

Describe characters, settings, and major events in a story, using key details. **RL.1.3**

Leveled Reader: *Wow, Kitty!*

Go Digital

Wow, Kitty!

Graphic Organizer

Before Reading

Preview and Predict

Read the title and author name. Have children preview the title page and the illustrations. Ask: *What do you think this book will be about?*

Review Genre: Fantasy

Have children recall that a fantasy is a story that has invented characters, setting, or other elements that could not exist in real life.

ESSENTIAL QUESTION

Remind children of the Essential Question: *How can people help out in the community?* Set a purpose for reading: *Let's read to find out what is so special about Kitty.*

During Reading

Guided Comprehension

Have children whisper read *Wow, Kitty!*. Have them place self-stick notes next to difficult words. Remind children that when they come to an unfamiliar word, they can look for familiar spellings. They will need to break longer words into smaller chunks and sound out each part.

Monitor children's reading. Stop periodically and ask open-ended questions to facilitate rich discussion, such as, *What do you think is actually happening overnight?* Build on children's responses to develop deeper understanding of the text.

Strategy: Reread

Remind children to reread text if they don't understand something they've read. Say: *Sometimes when we read we don't understand what the author has said. When that happens, reread the sentence or paragraph. Sometimes you might need to read an earlier page. Rereading can also help you remember important information.*

Skill: Character, Setting, Events

Have children review what the characters, setting, and events in a story are. Remind them that they can find key details about these in the text and illustrations. *Who are the characters? What is the setting? What are the important events?* Display a Character, Setting, Events chart for children to copy.

Think Aloud As I read pages 2 and 3 and look at the illustrations, I learn that Mom, Dad, Deb, and Nick are in their home. This tells me the characters and setting. I see a cat, too. That's another character.

Model how to record the character, setting, and events. Have children fill in their chart.

After Reading

Respond to Reading

Have children complete the Respond to Reading on page 12.

Retell

Have children take turns retelling the selection. Help children make a personal connection by writing about something someone made for them or they made for someone else. *What was made? Who made it? For whom? How did it help? How did you feel?*

PAIRED READ ...

Leveled Reader

"Sharing Skills"

Make Connections: Write About It 🖍️ *Analytical Writing*

Before reading, ask children to preview the title page and prompt them to identify the genre as informational text. Discuss the Compare Texts direction. After reading, have partners compare what they read about in "Sharing Skills" and *Wow, Kitty!*

Analytical Writing

COMPARE TEXTS

→ Have children use text evidence to compare fantasy to informational text.

Literature Circles

Lead children in conducting a literature circle using the Thinkmark questions to guide the discussion. You may wish to discuss what children have learned about doing things for others from both selections in the Leveled Reader.

Gifted and Talented

SYNTHESIZE Challenge children to think of what their special talents are and how they can use them to help others. Encourage them to tell who they could help and how.

EXTEND Have them use facts they learned from the week or do additional research to find out more about how people can help in their community.

Beyond Level

Vocabulary

ORAL VOCABULARY: ANTONYMS

OBJECTIVES

 Identify real-life connections between words and their use. **L.1.5c**

Determine the meaning of antonyms and use them in sentences

 I Do Review the meaning of the oral vocabulary word *enjoy*. Remind children that antonyms are word pairs that have opposite meanings.

If someone enjoys *something, it means he or she likes it. People who do not* enjoy *something* detest *it.* Enjoy *and* detest *are antonyms.*

Continue with: *When you* admire *someone, you like the things that person does. When you* disapprove *of someone, you do not like the things he or she does.* Admire *and* disapprove *are antonyms.*

 We Do Guide children to share ideas about what people might enjoy and what they might detest. Then have them take turns completing this sentence frame: *I admire _____, but I disapprove of _____.*

 You Do Have partners create new sentences using the word pairs *enjoy/detest* and *admire/disapprove*. Remind them that their sentences should show how each pair of words are antonyms.

 Gifted and Talented **Extend** Have partners discuss times they have enjoyed an activity and detested an activity. Challenge them to think of qualities they admire or disapprove of in others. Have them share their ideas with another pair.

Comprehension

REVIEW CHARACTER, SETTING, EVENTS

OBJECTIVES

Describe characters, settings, and major events in a story, using key details. **RL.1.3**

 I Do
Remind children that to understand a story, readers need to identify and understand the characters, setting, and events. Discuss what each story element is.

 We Do
Guide children in reading the first three sentences of the Practice Book selection aloud. *Who are the characters?* Discuss what the illustrations show about the characters. *What did we learn about Shep so far?*

 You Do
Have children read the rest of the Practice Book selection on their own. Remind them to think about what the characters are like, where the story takes place, and what the important events are. Then have them discuss the story with a partner and record their information on a Character, Setting, Events chart.

SELF-SELECTED READING

OBJECTIVES

Describe characters, settings, and major events in a story, using key details. **RL.1.3**

With prompting and support, read prose and poetry of appropriate complexity for grade 1. **RL.1.10**

Apply the strategy and skill to read a text

Read Independently

Have children pick a fantasy selection for sustained silent reading. Have them complete a Character, Setting, Events chart as they read the story. Remind them to reread any parts of the selection that they do not understand.

Read Purposefully

Have children record information in the Character, Setting, Events chart. After reading, guide children to:

→ share their charts with a partner and discuss whether or not they had to reread parts of the selection and why.

→ discuss how the characters, setting, and events show that the story is a fantasy.

 Independent Study Tell children to draw their favorite scene from the story they read and write a caption explaining what is happening. Challenge them to share their pictures with the class.

English Language Learners

Reading/Writing Workshop

OBJECTIVES

Describe characters, settings, and major events in a story, using key details. **RL.1.3**

Shared Read:
Thump Thump Helps Out

Go Digital

Thump Thump Helps Out

Graphic Organizer

Before Reading

Build Background

Read the Essential Question: *How do people help out in the community?*

→ Explain the meaning of the Essential Question: *Your community is your neighborhood. It is where you live, play, go to school, and shop. People help you and others in your community in many different ways.*

→ **Model an answer:** *We can help by keeping our neighborhood clean and by asking our neighbors if they need help. Some people give food to food banks. They help senior citizens with errands or plant gardens to make the neighborhood look nice.*

→ Ask children a question that ties the Essential Question to their own background knowledge: *Turn to a partner and talk about how you or someone you know helps out in your community.* Call on several pairs.

During Reading

Interactive Question-Response

→ Ask questions that help children understand the meaning of the text after each paragraph.

→ Reinforce the meanings of key vocabulary by providing meanings embedded in the questions.

→ Ask children questions that require them to use key vocabulary.

→ Reinforce comprehension strategies and skills of the week by modeling.

Thump Thump Helps Out

Pages 74–75

Point to the title. *Listen as I read the title.* Point to each word as you say the title. *Now let's say the title together.* Have children chorally say: *The title is Thump Thump Helps Out.*

Pages 76–77

Explain and Model the Strategy After reading aloud pages 76 and 77 say, *I do not understand what the rabbits do not like. I will reread these pages and look at the pictures to help me understand.* Reread the page and point to Thump Thump in the picture. *Now I see. The other rabbits do not like it when Thump Thump thumps his foot.*

Pages 78–79

Explain and Model Phonics Point to the third sentence on page 78. *I will read each word. Raise your hand when you hear a word that has the sound /sh/: "Bang! Crash! Clunk!" Now let's say the word with the /sh/ sound:* crash.

Explain and Model High-Frequency Words Have children choral read as you point to each word: "But not one big rabbit heard her call." Point to *call*. *This is the word* call. *Let's say it together.* Have children act out how they would call for help like Miss Sheldon did.

What events have taken place in the story? (Thump Thump's bus hit a rock; the kids are stuck.)

Pages 80–81

Explain and Model the Skill Point to the picture. Say: *The picture shows Thump Thump standing outside the school bus. I think he may try to help. Let's read to see what happens next in the story.*

What does Thump Thump do? Did it help? (Thump Thump thumps. The big rabbits hear his thumping and come to help fix the bus.)

Explain and Model Phonics Have children echo read each sentence on page 80. After each sentence have them repeat the words that begin with the /th/ sound: *Thump, Thump; think; thumped, thumped, thumped.* Point to each word as children say it.

Pages 82–83

Explain and Model the Strategy Read pages 82 and 83. *I'm not sure why the big rabbits need Thump Thump's help. I will reread these two pages to make sure I understand why they are asking him for help. Now that I have reread the pages, I see that the big rabbits want Thump Thump to thump if there's ever a rabbit who needs help.*

Explain and Model High-Frequency Words Have children choral read the second sentence on page 82. Point to *want*. *This is the word* want. *Let's say it together. When you want something, you hope you can get it.*

How does the story end? (The big rabbits ask Thump Thump to thump if a rabbit needs help. He still helps by thumping to this day.)

After Reading

Make Connections

→ Review the Essential Question.

English Language Learners

Lexile 190

OBJECTIVES

Describe characters, settings, and major events in a story, using key details. **RL.1.3**

Leveled Reader:
Squirrels Help

Before Reading

Preview

Read the title. Ask: *What is the title?* Say it again. Repeat with the author's name. Preview the illustrations. Have children describe the pictures. Use simple language to tell about each page. Follow with questions, such as, *What does this picture show about the story?*

ESSENTIAL QUESTION

Remind children of the Essential Question: *How do people help out in the community?* Say: *Let's read to find out how other squirrels can help Sue.* Encourage children to ask for help when they do not understand a word or phrase.

During Reading

Interactive Question-Response

Pages 2–3 *Look at the pictures and the labels. Say each label after me:* squirrel, Sue. *The first sentence tells what the squirrels are doing. Let's read it together:* "The squirrels look for nuts." *Let's look at the pictures again. What do you see?* (squirrels gathering nuts) *Does Sue look happy?* (no)

Pages 4–5 *Look at page 4. Who has a lot of nuts?* (Tom) *Why is Sue sad?* (She only found three nuts) *Tom asks Dad if they can help Sue. Let's read together what Dad says:* We can help. *How might they help Sue?*

Pages 6–7 *Let's read the label on page 6 together:* stream. *Point to the stream in the picture. Tom says that is a good spot. What is it a good spot, or place, for?* (collecting nuts) *How do you think Sue feels now?* (happy)

Pages 8–9 *It's winter now. Look at the picture. How do you know it's winter?* (snow on the ground; trees are bare) *Sue is pinning a note for Tom on the tree. What does the note say?* (Thanks!) *Why is Sue glad Tom helped her?* (She had nuts during the winter.)

Pages 10–11 *Look at page 11. Sue and the other squirrel seem excited in this picture. Why?* (Now they know where to find nuts.) *Do you remember what happened to Sue at the beginning of the story? How is the end different?*

Go Digital

Squirrels Help

Graphic Organizer

Retell

Literature Circles

Lead children in conducting a literature circle using the Thinkmark questions to guide the discussion. You may wish to discuss what children have learned about helping others in both selections in the Leveled Reader.

After Reading

Respond to Reading

Revisit the Essential Question. Ask children to work with partners to fill in the graphic organizer and answer the questions on page 12. Pair children with peers of varying language abilities.

Retell

Model retelling using the **Retelling Card** prompts. Say: *Look at the illustrations. Use details to help you retell the selection.* Help children make personal connections by asking: *Have you ever seen a squirrel? Where? What did it look like? What was it doing?*

Intonation Fluency: Stress Important Words

Read the pages in the book, one at a time. Help children echo read the pages expressively and with appropriate intonation. Remind them to stress important words when they read aloud.

Apply Have children practice reading with partners. Pair children with peers of varying language abilities. Provide feedback as needed.

Level Up

Level-up lessons available online.

IF children can read *Squirrels Help* **ELL Level** with fluency and correctly answer the Respond to Reading questions,

THEN tell children that they will read a more detailed version of the story.

- Use pages 2–4 of *Squirrels Help* **On Level** to model using Teaching Poster 28 to identify character, setting, and events.

- Have children read the selection, checking their comprehension by using the graphic organizer.

PAIRED READ ...

Leveled Reader

"Food Drive"

Make Connections: Write About It ✎ *Analytical Writing*

Before reading, ask children to note that this text is informational text. Then discuss the Compare Texts direction.

After reading, ask children to make connections between what they learned from "Food Drive" and *Squirrels Help*. Prompt children by providing sentence starters: *Animals and people need food to _____. Animals and people can help _____.*

✎ *Analytical Writing*

COMPARE TEXTS

→ Have children use text evidence to compare fantasy to informational text.

English Language Learners
Vocabulary

PRETEACH ORAL VOCABULARY

OBJECTIVES
Produce complete sentences when appropriate to task and situation. **SL.1.6**

LANGUAGE OBJECTIVE
Preteach oral vocabulary words

 I Do Display images from the **Visual Vocabulary Cards** one at a time to preteach the oral vocabulary words *leadership* and *admire*.

 We Do Display the images again and explain how they illustrate or demonstrate the words. Model using sentences to describe the image.

 **You Do** Have partners talk to each other about how the picture demonstrates the word *leadership*.

Beginning	Intermediate	Advanced/High
Ask children to show how someone with leadership or they admire might act.	Provide sentence starters for children to use to tell about the images.	Have children use the words in sentences about the pictures.

PRETEACH ELL VOCABULARY

OBJECTIVES
Produce complete sentences when appropriate to task and situation. **SL.1.6**

LANGUAGE OBJECTIVE
Preteach ELL vocabulary words

 I Do Display images from the Visual Vocabulary Cards one at a time to preteach the ELL Vocabulary words *helpful* and *prepare* and follow the routine. Say the words and have children repeat. Define the word in English.

 We Do Display an image again and explain how it illustrates or demonstrates the word. Model using sentences to describe the image.

 You Do Display the word again and have children say the word and then spell it. Provide opportunities for children to use the words in speaking and writing. Provide sentence starters.

Beginning	Intermediate	Advanced/High
Say the word and a simple sentence with the word for children to repeat.	Have children complete the sentence starters and read their sentences aloud.	Have children write their own sentences using the word and then read them.

High-Frequency Words

REVIEW WORDS

OBJECTIVES

Recognize and read grade-appropriate irregularly spelled words. **RF.1.3g**

Use sentence-level context as a clue to the meaning of a word or phrase. **L.1.4.a**

LANGUAGE OBJECTIVE

Review high-frequency words *all, call, day, her, want*

 Display the **High-Frequency Word Cards** for *all, call, day, her,* and *want.* Read each word. Use the **Read/Spell/Write** routine to teach each word. Have children write the words on their **Response Boards**.

 Write sentence frames on separate lines. Track the print as you guide children to read and complete the sentences: (1) *We will all _____.* (2) *I will call _____.* (3) *What day is _____?* (4) *Her dress is _____.* (5) *I want _____.*

 Display the High-Frequency Word Cards from the previous weeks. Display one card at a time as children chorally read the word. Mix and repeat. Note words children need to review.

Beginning	Intermediate	Advanced/High
Point to and say each word for children to repeat.	Have children read each word as you display it.	Have children say each word and then use it in a sentence.

RETEACH WORDS

OBJECTIVES

Recognize and read grade-appropriate irregularly spelled words. **RF.1.3g**

LANGUAGE OBJECTIVE

Use high-frequency words

 Display each Visual Vocabulary Card and say the word aloud. Define the word in English, then in Spanish if appropriate, identifying any cognates.

 Point to the image again and explain how it illustrates or demonstrates the word. Ask children to repeat the word. Engage children in structured partner-talk about the image as prompted on the back of the card. Ask children to chorally say the word three times.

 Display each visual in random order, hiding the word. Have children identify and define the word in their own words.

Beginning	Intermediate	Advanced/High
Display an image and give children two word choices. They choose the correct word.	Provide sentence starters for children using the words.	After children define each word, have them use it in a sentence.

English Language Learners
Writing/Spelling

WRITING TRAIT: ORGANIZATION

OBJECTIVES

 With guidance and support from adults, focus on a topic, respond to questions and suggestions from peers, and add details to strengthen writing as needed. **W.1.5**

LANGUAGE OBJECTIVE

Write in sequence

 I Do Explain that writers include a beginning, middle, and end when they write a story. Write and read the following sentences: *Dan and Nell Duck jump in the pond. They play all day. Then they eat and nap.* Help children identify the beginning, middle, and end of the story.

 We Do Help children recall the story "Thump Thump Helps Out." Guide them in telling what happened in the beginning, middle, and end. Explain that the writer wrote the events in the order in which they happened.

 You Do Have children write three sentences about a person who did something to help others. Remind them to write the sentences in the order in which things happened to show the beginning, middle, and end.

Beginning	Intermediate	Advanced/High
Have children draw three pictures in order showing what happened. Have them number the pictures: 1, 2, 3.	Help children tell a story using sentence frames. *First he/she ____ . Then ____ . Last ____ .*	Have children to write a three-sentence story that has a beginning, middle, and end.

WORDS WITH CONSONANT DIGRAPHS *th, sh, -ng*

OBJECTIVES

 Use conventional spelling for words with common spelling pattern and for frequently occurring irregular words. **L.1.2d**

LANGUAGE OBJECTIVE

Spell words with *th, sh,* and *-ng*

 I Do Read aloud the Spelling Words on page T248. Segment the first word into sounds and attach a spelling to each sound. Point out the *sh* sound and spelling. Read aloud, segment, and spell the remaining words and have children repeat.

 We Do Read the first sentence from Dictation Routine on page T248 aloud. Then, read the *sh* word slowly and have children repeat. Have them write it. Repeat the process for the remaining sentences and words with *th, sh,* and *-ng.*

 You Do Display the words. Have children work with a partner to check their spelling lists. Have children correct misspelled words on their list.

Beginning	Intermediate	Advanced/High
Help children copy the words with correct spelling and say the word.	After children have corrected their words, have pairs quiz each other.	Challenge children to think of other words that have *th, sh,* and *-ng.*

Grammar

COMMON AND PROPER NOUNS

OBJECTIVES

 CCSS Use common, proper, and possessive nouns. **L.1.1b**

LANGUAGE OBJECTIVE

Recognize the difference between common and proper nouns

Language Transfers Handbook

TRANSFER SKILLS

Cantonese, Haitian Creole, Hmong, Korean, Vietnamese, and Khmer speakers may omit -s in third-person singular present-tense verbs when creating sentences (*The cat see the mat.*). Point it out and emphasize the -s when giving examples.

 I Do Explain that a common noun names any person, animal, place, or thing. Write the sentence: *The school is big.* Read the sentence and circle the word *school*. Say: School *is a common noun.* Then replace *The school* with *Mill Glen School*. Read the sentence again and identify *Mill Glen School* as a proper noun. *Proper nouns name particular people, places, or things. Proper nouns begin with uppercase letters.*

We Do Point to objects in the classroom, including individual children and classroom pets. With children say each name and write it on the board; for example, *book, chair, Maria, paper, floor, Rob.* Help children identify each as a common noun or a proper noun. Then have them identify the proper nouns in the sentences below by saying: *The proper noun is _____ .*

I like my classes at Big Rock School.

My dog Jack likes to sit.

 You Do Write the following nouns on the board:

cat   Nick   pot   Gran   bell   bank   desk

Ask partners to identify the common nouns and the proper nouns. Observe and help if children are having difficulty. Ask questions such as: *Is a* pot *a particular thing? Can it be any* pot *at all? Is* pot *a common noun or a proper noun?*

Beginning	Intermediate	Advanced/High
Point to classroom objects and people. Ask questions: *Is this a plant? Is* plant *a proper name? Is this a girl? What is the girl's proper name?*	Ask children to choose a photograph in the Big Book and say examples of common nouns they see. Encourage them to use complete sentences.	Ask children to choose a photograph in the Big Book and describe it using common and proper nouns. Help them make a list of the nouns that they use.

PROGRESS MONITORING

Weekly Assessment

✓**COMPREHENSION:**
Character, Setting, Events **RL.1.3**
Use Illustrations **RL.1.7**

✓**PHONEMIC AWARENESS:**
Phoneme Isolation **RF.1.2c**
Phoneme Categorization **RF.1.2c**
Phoneme Blending **RF.1.2b**
Phoneme Segmentation **RF.1.2d**

✓**PHONICS/STRUCTURAL ANALYSIS/HIGH-FREQUENCY WORDS:**
Consonant Digraphs *th, sh, -ng* **RF.1.3a**
Closed Syllables **RF.1.3d, e**
all, call, day, her, want **RF.1.3g**

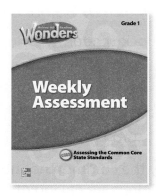

FLUENCY ←

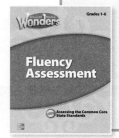

Conduct group fluency assessments.

Assess fluency for one group of children per week using the **Letter Naming, Phoneme Segmentation,** and **Sight Word Fluency** assessments in *Reading Wonders Fluency Assessment.*

Go Digital! http://connected.mcgraw-hill.com

Using Assessment Results

✓ TESTED SKILLS	If ...	Then ...
COMPREHENSION	Children answer 0–3 multiple-choice items correctly . . .	. . . assign Lessons 22–24 on Identify Character, Lessons 25–27 on Identify Setting, Lessons 28–30 on Identify Plot Events, and Lesson 94 on Using Illustrations from the *Tier 2 Comprehension Intervention online PDFs*.
PHONEMIC AWARENESS	Children answer 0–1 multiple-choice items correctly . . .	. . . assign Lessons 16–17 on Phoneme Isolation: Beginning Sounds, Lessons 27–29 on Phoneme Isolation: Ending Sounds, Lessons 53–54 on Phoneme Categorization: Medial Sounds, Lessons 62–66 on Phoneme Blending, and Lessons 67–71 on Phoneme Segmenting from the *Tier 2 Phonemic Awareness Intervention online PDFs*.
PHONICS/ STRUCTURAL ANALYSIS/HFW	Children answer 0–5 multiple-choice items correctly . . .	. . . assign Lesson 52 on Short Vowels: Digraphs (*th, sh, -ng*) and Lesson 106 on Closed Syllables from the *Tier 2 Phonics/Word Study Intervention online PDFs*.

Response to Intervention

Use children's assessment results to assist you in identifying children who will benefit from focused intervention.

Use the appropriate sections of the ***Placement and Diagnostic Assessment*** to designate children requiring:

TIER 2 **Intervention Online PDFs**

TIER 3 **WonderWorks Intervention Program**

Literature Big Book

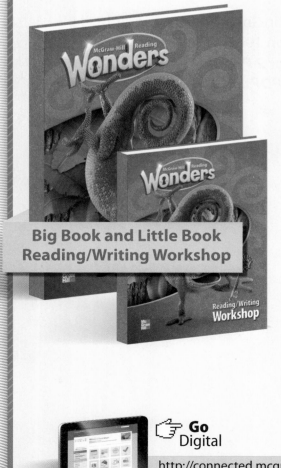

**Big Book and Little Book
Reading/Writing Workshop**

☞ **Go**
Digital

http://connected.mcgraw-hill.com

TEACH AND MODEL

Listening Comprehension

Comprehension Strategy *Reread* T322–T323

🔍 Close Reading

Shared Reading *Which Way on the Map?*, 94–103

Genre Nonfiction

Lexile 160

Words to Know T327

around, by, many, place, walk

Minilessons   ✔ **Tested Skills**

✔ **Phonics**..Consonant Digraphs, T328–T329

✔ **Comprehension Skill**.........................Main Topic and Key Details, T338–T339

✔ **Writing Traits**....................................Ideas, T348

✔ **Grammar**...Irregular Plural Nouns, T349

FOLLOW THE MAP
Essential Question
How can you find your way around?

WEEK 5

APPLY WITH CLOSE READING

Complex Text

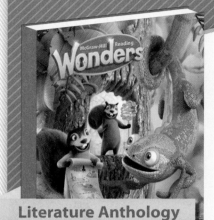

Literature Anthology

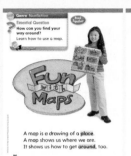

PAIRED READ

Fun with Maps, 86–93
Genre Nonfiction
Lexile NP

"North, East, South, or West?", 94–95
Genre Nonfiction
Lexile 360

NP = Non-Prose

Differentiated Text

Leveled Readers   *Including Paired Reads*

APPROACHING
Lexile 130

ON LEVEL
Lexile 230

BEYOND
Lexile 420

ELL
Lexile 60

Extended Complex Text

Cactus Hotel
Genre
Nonfiction
Lexile 700

Meet the Meerkat
Genre
Nonfiction
Lexile 340

Classroom Library lessons available online.

Classroom Library

"Cover" from the book *Cactus Hotel* by Brenda Z. Guiberson. Illustrated by Megan Lloyd. Copyright text © 1991 by Brenda Z. Guiberson. Illustrations © 1991 by Megan Lloyd. Reprinted by permission of Henry Holt and Company, LLC.; *Meet the Meerkat*. Text copyright © 2007 by Darrin Lunde. Illustrations copyright © 2007 by Patricia J. Wynne. Used with permission by Charlesbridge Publishing, Inc. All rights reserved.

TEACH AND MANAGE

How You Teach

INTRODUCE

Weekly Concept
Follow the Map

Reading/Writing Workshop
52–63

TEACH

Listening Comprehension
Me on the Map

Close Reading
Which Way on the Map?

Minilessons
Main Topic and Key Details,
Nonfiction, Consonant Digraphs,
High-Frequency Words

APPLY

Close Reading
Fun with Maps
"North, East,
 South, or West?"

 Go Digital   Interactive Whiteboard   Interactive Whiteboard   Mobile

How Students Practice

WEEKLY CONTRACT

PDF Online

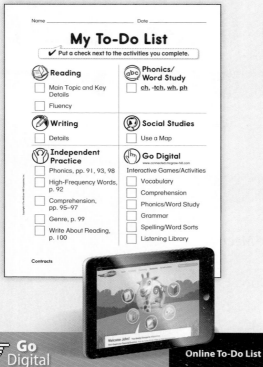

Name _____   Date _____

My To-Do List
✔ Put a check next to the activities you complete.

Reading
☐ Main Topic and Key Details
☐ Fluency

Phonics/ Word Study
☐ ch, -tch, wh, ph

Writing
☐ Details

Social Studies
☐ Use a Map

Independent Practice
☐ Phonics, pp. 91, 93, 98
☐ High-Frequency Words, p. 92
☐ Comprehension, pp. 95–97
☐ Genre, p. 99
☐ Write About Reading, p. 100

Go Digital
www.connected.mcgraw-hill.com
Interactive Games/Activities
☐ Vocabulary
☐ Comprehension
☐ Phonics/Word Study
☐ Grammar
☐ Spelling/Word Sorts
☐ Listening Library

Contracts

LEVELED PRACTICE AND ONLINE ACTIVITIES

Your Turn Practice Book
91–100

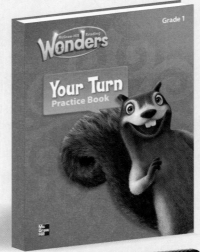

Leveled Readers

 Go Digital   Online To-Do List

 Leveled Activities

 Mobile

DIFFERENTIATE

SMALL GROUP INSTRUCTION

Leveled Readers

Mobile

INTEGRATE

Research and Inquiry
Make a Map, T356–T357

Text Connections
Follow the Map, T358

Write About Reading
Analyze Main Topic and Key Details, T359

Online Research and Writing

ASSESS

Weekly Assessment
91–100

Online Assessment

LEVELED WORKSTATION CARDS

More Activities on back

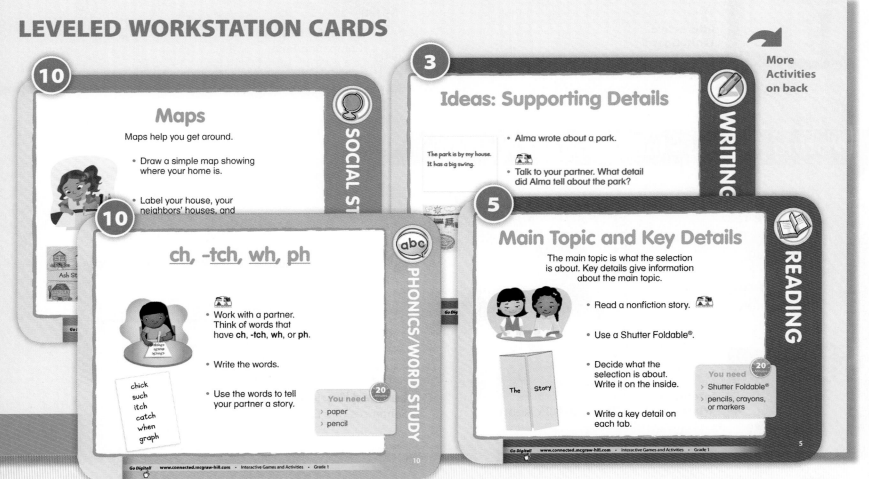

10

Maps

Maps help you get around.

- Draw a simple map showing where your home is.

- Label your house, your neighbors' houses, and

SOCIAL STUDIES

Ash St

Go

10

ch, -tch, wh, ph

- Work with a partner. Think of words that have **ch**, **-tch**, **wh**, or **ph**.

- Write the words.

- Use the words to tell your partner a story.

chick
such
itch
catch
when
graph

You need
> paper
> pencil
20 minutes

PHONICS/WORD STUDY

Go Digital! www.connected.mcgraw-hill.com · Interactive Games and Activities · Grade 1

10

3

Ideas: Supporting Details

The park is by my house. It has a big swing.

- Alma wrote about a park.

- Talk to your partner. What detail did Alma tell about the park?

WRITING

5

Main Topic and Key Details

The main topic is what the selection is about. Key details give information about the main topic.

- Read a nonfiction story.

- Use a Shutter Foldable®.

- Decide what the selection is about. Write it on the inside.

The Story

- Write a key detail on each tab.

You need
> Shutter Foldable®
> pencils, crayons, or markers
20 minutes

READING

Go Digital! www.connected.mcgraw-hill.com · Interactive Games and Activities · Grade 1

5

DEVELOPING READERS AND WRITERS

Write to Sources and Research

Note Taking, T347A

Main Topic and Key Details, T347B

Research and Inquiry, T356

Analyze to Inform/Explain, T359

Comparing Texts, T365, T375, T379, T385

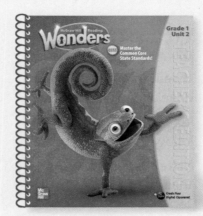

Teacher's Edition

Your Turn Practice Book

Main Topic and Key Details, pp. 95–97
Write About Reading, p. 100

Leveled Readers
Comparing Texts

Interactive Whiteboard

Narrative Text
Sentences That Explain, T348–T349

Conferencing Routines
Peer Conferences, T354

Interactive Whiteboard

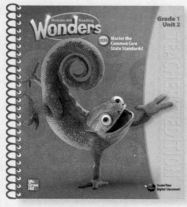

Teacher's Edition

 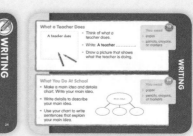

Leveled Workstation Card
Sentences That Explain, Card 24

Writing Traits • **Shared and Interactive Writing**

Writing Trait: Ideas
Sentences That Explain, T330

Conferencing Routines
Peer Conferences, T354

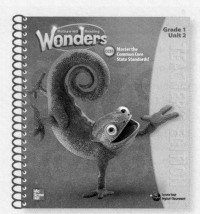

Teacher's Edition

Ideas: Irregular Plural Nouns, pp. 106–107

Reading/Writing Workshop

Leveled Workstation Card
Ideas: Supporting Details, Card 3

Interactive Whiteboard

Grammar and Spelling

Grammar
Irregular Plural Nouns, T331

Spelling
Words with *ch, -tch, wh, ph,* T326

Interactive Whiteboard

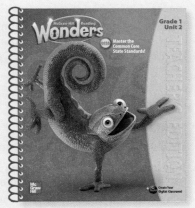

Teacher's Edition

Online Spelling and Grammar Games

Handwriting

SUGGESTED LESSON PLAN

✓ TESTED SKILLS 〔CCSS〕   DAY 1   DAY 2

READING

Whole Group

Teach, Model, and Apply

Reading/Writing Workshop

DAY 1

Build Background Follow the Map, T320–T321

Oral Vocabulary Words *locate, route,* T320

Listening Comprehension

Big Book *Me on the Map,* T322
Strategy: Reread, T323

Word Work T324–T327
Fluency: Sound-Spellings
Phonemic Awareness: Phoneme Segmentation
Phonics/Spelling: Introduce Consonant Digraphs *ch, -tch, wh, ph*
High-Frequency Words: *around, by, many, place, walk*

Shared Reading *Which Way on the Map?,* T328–T329

Practice Your Turn, p. 91

DAY 2

Oral Language Follow the Map, T332

Oral Vocabulary Words *height, model, separate,* T332

Listening Comprehension Strategy: Reread, T333

Interactive Read-Aloud Cards "Map It!", T333

Word Work T334–T337
Fluency: Sound-Spellings
Phonemic Awareness: Phoneme Addition
Phonics/Spelling: Review Consonant Digraphs *ch, -tch, wh, ph*
Structural Analysis: Inflectional Ending *-es*
High-Frequency Words: *around, by, many, place, walk*

Shared Reading *Which Way on the Map?,* T338–T339

✓**Comprehension**
•Genre: Informational Text/Nonfiction, T338
•Skill: Main Topic and Key Details, T339

Practice Your Turn, pp. 92–94

DIFFERENTIATED INSTRUCTION   Choose across the week to meet your children's needs.

Small Group

Approaching Level

DAY 1

Leveled Reader *How Maps Help,* T364–T365

Phonemic Awareness Phoneme Segmentation, T366 ②

Phonics Connect *ch, -tch* to /ch/, *wh* to /hw/, *ph* to /f/, T368 ②

High-Frequency Words Review, T371

DAY 2

Leveled Reader *How Maps Help,* T364–T365

Phonemic Awareness Phoneme Blending, T366 ②

Phonics Blend Words with *ch, -tch, wh, ph,* T368 ②

High-Frequency Words Reteach, T371

Comprehension Identify Key Details, T372 ②

On Level

DAY 1

Leveled Reader *How Maps Help,* T374–T375

Phonics Build Words with Consonant Digraphs *ch, -tch, wh, ph,* T376

DAY 2

Leveled Reader *How Maps Help,* T374–T375

High Frequency Words Review Words, T376

Beyond Level

DAY 1

Leveled Reader *How Maps Help,* T378–T379

Oral Vocabulary Synonyms, T380

DAY 2

Leveled Reader *How Maps Help,* T378–T379

Oral Vocabulary Synonyms, T380

English Language Learners

DAY 1

Shared Read *Which Way on the Map?,* T382–T383

Phonemic Awareness Phoneme Segmentation, T366

Phonics Connect *ch, -tch* to /ch/, *wh* to /hw/, *ph* to /f/, T368

Vocabulary
Preteach Oral Vocabulary, T386

DAY 2

Leveled Reader *How Maps Help,* T384–T385

Phonemic Awareness Phoneme Blending, T366

Phonics Blend Words with *ch, -tch, wh, ph,* T368

Vocabulary Preteach ELL Vocabulary, T386

LANGUAGE ARTS

Whole Group

Writing

Grammar

DAY 1

Shared Writing Writing Trait: Ideas, T330
Sentences That Explain, T330

Grammar
•Irregular Plural Nouns, T331

Mechanics: Capital Letters and Periods, T331

DAY 2

Independent Writing Writing Trait: Ideas, T340
Sentences That Explain, T340

Grammar
•Irregular Plural Nouns, T341

Mechanics: Capital Letters and Periods, T341

DAY 3	DAY 4	DAY 5 Review and Assess

READING

Oral Language Follow the Map, T342

Review Oral Vocabulary *height, locate, model, route, separate*, T342

Listening Comprehension
Big Book *Me on the Map*, T343
•Strategy: Reread, T343
•Retelling, T343
•Fluency: Phrasing, T343

Word Work T344–T347
Fluency: Sound-Spellings
Phonemic Awareness: Phoneme Blending
Phonics/Spelling: Blend Words with Consonant Digraphs *ch, -tch, wh, ph*
Structural Analysis: Inflectional Ending *-es*
High-Frequency Words: *around, by, many, place, walk*

Close Reading *Fun with Maps*,
T347A–T347F *Analytical Writing*

Practice Your Turn, pp. 95–97

Oral Language Follow the Map, T350

Comprehension Text Feature: Map, T350

Close Reading "North, East, South, or West?", T351

Word Work T352–T353
Fluency: Sound-Spellings
Phonemic Awareness: Phoneme Addition
Phonics/Spelling: Build Words with *ch, -tch, wh, ph*
Structural Analysis: Inflectional Ending *-es*
High-Frequency Words: *around, by, many, place, walk*

Integrate Ideas Research and Inquiry, T356–T357

Practice Your Turn, pp. 98–99

Integrate Ideas
•Text Connections, T358
•Write About Reading, T359 *Analytical Writing*

Word Work T360–T361
Fluency: Word Automaticity
Phonemic Awareness: Phoneme Blending/Segmentation
Phonics/Spelling: Blend and Build with *ch, -tch, wh, ph*
Structural Analysis: Inflectional Ending *-es*
High-Frequency Words: *around, by, many, place, walk*

Practice Your Turn, p. 100

DIFFERENTIATED INSTRUCTION

Leveled Reader *How Maps Help*, T364–T365
Phonemic Awareness Phoneme Segmentation, T367
Phonics Build Words with *ch, -tch, wh, ph*, T369
Structural Analysis Review Inflectional Ending *-es*, T370
Comprehension Review Main Topic and Key Details, T373

Leveled Reader Paired Read: "On the Map," T365 *Analytical Writing*
Phonemic Awareness Phoneme Addition, T367
Phonics Blend Words with *ch, -tch, wh, ph*, T369
Structural Analysis Reteach Inflectional Ending *-es*, T370
Comprehension Read for Fluency, T372 ②

Leveled Reader Literature Circles, T365
Phonics Build Fluency with Phonics, T369
High-Frequency Words Cumulative Review, T371
Comprehension Self-Selected Reading, T373

Leveled Reader *How Maps Help*, T374–T375
Comprehension Review Main Topic and Key Details, T377

Leveled Reader Paired Read: "On the Map," T375 *Analytical Writing*

Leveled Reader Literature Circles, T375
Comprehension Self-Selected Reading, T377

Leveled Reader *How Maps Help*, T378–T379
Comprehension Review Main Topic and Key Details, T381

Leveled Reader Paired Read: "On the Map," T379 *Analytical Writing*

Leveled Reader Literature Circles, T379
Comprehension Self-Selected Reading, T381

Leveled Reader *How Maps Help*, T384–T385
Phonemic Awareness Phoneme Segmentation, T367
Phonics Build Words with *ch, -tch, wh, ph*, T369
Structural Analysis Review Inflectional Ending *-es*, T370
High-Frequency Words Review Words, T387
Writing Writing Trait: Ideas, T388

Leveled Reader Paired Read: "On the Map," T385 *Analytical Writing*
Phonemic Awareness Phoneme Addition, T367
Structural Analysis Reteach Inflectional Ending *-es*, T370
High-Frequency Words Reteach Words, T387
Grammar Irregular Plural Nouns, T389

Leveled Reader Literature Circles, T385
Phonics Blend Words with *ch, -tch, wh, ph*, T369
Spelling Words with Consonant Digraphs *ch, -tch, wh, ph*, T388

LANGUAGE ARTS

Independent Writing Writing Trait: Ideas, T348
Sentences That Explain: Prewrite/Draft, T348–T349

Grammar
•Irregular Plural Nouns, T349

Mechanics: Capital Letters and Periods, T349

Independent Writing Writing Trait: Ideas, T354
Sentences That Explain:
Revise/Proofread/Edit, T354–T355

Grammar
•Irregular Plural Nouns, T355

Mechanics: Capital Letters and Periods, T355

Independent Writing
Sentences That Explain: Publish and Present, T362

Grammar
•Irregular Plural Nouns, T363

Mechanics: Capital Letters and Periods, T363

DIFFERENTIATE TO ACCELERATE

A C T Scaffold to Access Complex Text

IF the text complexity of a particular selection is too difficult for children

THEN see the references noted in the chart below for scaffolded instruction to help children Access Complex Text.

Qualitative / Quantitative

Reader and Task

TEXT COMPLEXITY

	Big Book 	**Reading/Writing Workshop** 	**Literature Anthology** 	**Leveled Readers** 
Quantitative	*Me on the Map* **Lexile** 300	*Which Way on the Map?* **Lexile** 160	*Fun with Maps* **Lexile** NP "North, East, South, or West?" **Lexile** 360	**Approaching Level** **Lexile** 130 **On Level** **Lexile** 230 **Beyond Level** **Lexile** 420 **ELL** **Lexile** 60
Qualitative	**What Makes the Text Complex?** • **Purpose,** T343 • **Organization,** T343 A C T *See Scaffolded Instruction in Teacher's Edition, T343.*	**What Makes the Text Complex?** **Foundational Skills** • Decoding with consonant digraphs *ch, -tch, wh,* and *ph,* T324–T325 • Reading words with inflectional ending *-es,* T335 • Identifying high-frequency words, T327 *See Scaffolded Instruction in Teacher's Edition, T324–T325, T327, and T335.*	**What Makes the Text Complex?** **Foundational Skills** • Decoding with consonant digraphs *ch, -tch, wh,* and *ph,* T344–T345 • Reading words with inflectional ending *-es,* T345 • Identifying high-frequency words, T347	**What Makes the Text Complex?** **Foundational Skills** • Decoding with consonant digraphs *ch, -tch, wh,* and *ph* • Reading words with inflectional ending *-es* • Identifying high-frequency words *around by many place walk* *See Level Up lessons online for Leveled Readers.*
Reader and Task	The Introduce the Concept lesson on pages T320–T321 will help determine the reader's knowledge and engagement in the weekly concept. See pages T322–T323, T343, and T356–T359 for questions and tasks for this text.	The Introduce the Concept lesson on pages T320–T321 will help determine the reader's knowledge and engagement in the weekly concept. See pages T328–T329, T338–T339, and T356–T359 for questions and tasks for this text.	The Introduce the Concept lesson on pages T320–T321 will help determine the reader's knowledge and engagement in the weekly concept. See pages T347A–T347F, T351, and T356–T359 for questions and tasks for this text.	The Introduce the Concept lesson on pages T320–T321 will help determine the reader's knowledge and engagement in the weekly concept. See pages T364–T365, T374–T375, T378–T379, T384–T385, and T356–T359 for questions and tasks for this text.

Classroom Library Tradebooks: See pages T413–T415 for model lessons.

Monitor and *Differentiate*

IF ► you need to differentiate instruction

THEN ► use the Quick Checks to assess children's needs and select the appropriate small group instruction focus.

✔ Quick Check

Comprehension Strategy Reread, T323

Comprehension Skill Main Topic and Key Details, T339

Phonics Consonant Digraphs *ch, -tch, wh, ph*, T327, T337, T347, T353, T361

High-Frequency Words T327, T337, T347, T353, T361

If No →
| Approaching Level | Reteach T364–T373 |
| ELL | Develop T382–T389 |

If Yes →
| On Level | Review T374–T377 |
| Beyond Level | Extend T378–T381 |

Level Up with Leveled Readers

IF ► children can read their leveled text fluently and answer comprehension questions

THEN ► work with the next level up to accelerate children's reading with more complex text.

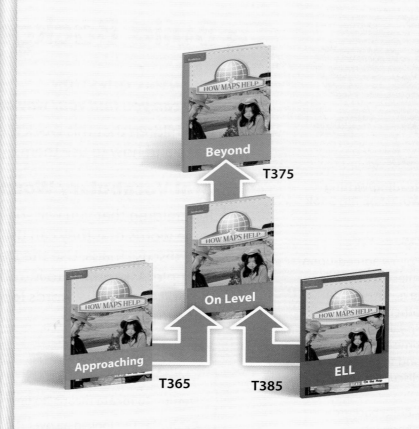

Beyond
T375

On Level

Approaching
T365

T385

ELL

IF ► ELL students need additional support **THEN** ► scaffold instruction using the small group suggestions.

Shared Read	Leveled Reader	Phonemic Awareness	Phonics	Words to Know	Writing	Spelling	Grammar
Which Way on the Map?, T382–T383	*How Maps Help*, T384–T385 "On the Map," T385	Phoneme Segmentation, T366 Phoneme Blending, T366 Phoneme Segmentation, T367 Phoneme Addition, T367	Words with Consonant Digraphs *ch, -tch, wh, ph*, T368–T369 Structural Analysis, T370	*around, by, many, place, walk*, T371	Ideas, T388	Words with Consonant Digraphs *ch, -tch, wh, ph*, T388	Irregular Plural Nouns, T389

Note: Include ELL Students in all small groups based on their needs.

Materials

Reading/Writing Workshop
VOLUME 2

Reading/Writing Workshop Big Book
UNIT 2

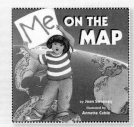
Literature Big Book
Me On the Map

Visual Vocabulary Cards
locate   route

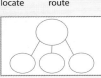
Think Aloud Clouds

Teaching Poster

around
High-Frequency Word Cards
around   place
by   walk
many

a b c
Word-Building Cards

ch
tch
cheese
Sound-Spelling Cards

→ # Introduce the Concept

Reading/Writing Workshop Big Book

OBJECTIVES

CCSS Follow agreed-upon rules for discussions (e.g., listening to others with care, speaking one at a time about the topics and texts under discussion). **SL.1.1a**

- Build background knowledge
- Discuss the Essential Question

ACADEMIC LANGUAGE

- *follow, map*
- Cognate: *mapa*

MINILESSON 5 Mins

Build Background

ESSENTIAL QUESTION

How can you find your way around?

Tell children that this week they will be talking and reading about maps and how to use them.

Oral Vocabulary Words

Tell children that you will share some words that they can use as they discuss maps. Use the Define/Example/Ask routine to introduce the oral vocabulary words **locate** and **route**.

Visual Vocabulary Cards

Oral Vocabulary Routine

Define: To **locate** means "to find."

Example: Tim looked all over the house to locate his missing shoe.

Ask: How can you locate information in a book?

Define: A **route** is the road or way to take to get somewhere.

Example: We take the same route to school every day.

Ask: What do you see on your route to school?

Discuss the theme of "Follow the Map." Have children discuss how maps help us. *What can you use a map to locate? How could you use a map to plan a new route?*

Go Digital

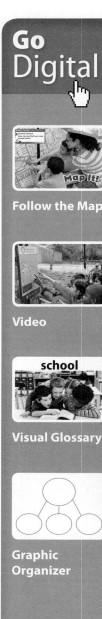
Follow the Map

Video

school
Visual Glossary

Graphic Organizer

David R Frazier Photolibrary Inc/Alamy

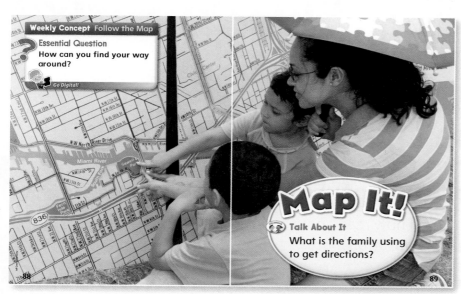

READING/WRITING WORKSHOP, pp. 88–89

Talk About It: Follow the Map

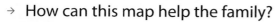

Guide children to discuss how the family is using the map.

→ What does this map show?

→ How can this map help the family?

→ What do you think the family is trying to locate on the map?

Use Teaching Poster 40 and prompt children to complete the Word Web by sharing words to describe what they see in the photograph.

Children can look at page 89 of their Reading/Writing Workshop and do the Talk About It activity with a partner.

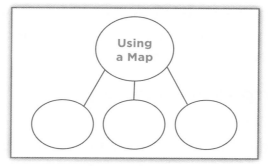

Teaching Poster

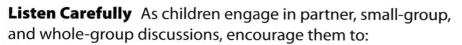

Collaborative Conversations

Listen Carefully As children engage in partner, small-group, and whole-group discussions, encourage them to:

→ always look at the speaker.

→ respect others by not interrupting them.

→ repeat others' ideas to check understanding.

ELL

ENGLISH LANGUAGE LEARNERS SCAFFOLD

Beginning

Use Visuals Point to the map. *This is a map. Does it show streets? Does it show a river? What else does it show?*

Intermediate

Describe Ask children to describe the map and the family. *What is the family doing? What are they looking at on the map?*

Advanced/Advanced High

Discuss Have children elaborate on the scene. *Why might the family be looking at the map? What information can they get from the map?* Elicit more details to support children's answers.

→ # Listening Comprehension

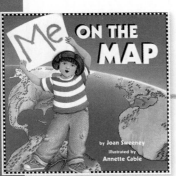

Literature Big Book

OBJECTIVES

CCSS Recognize the distinguishing features of a sentence (e.g., first word, capitalization, ending punctuation).
RF.1.1a

Develop concept understanding

ACADEMIC LANGUAGE

• map, left, right, top, bottom, label
• Cognate: *mapa*

MINILESSON
10 Mins

Read the Literature Big Book

Connect to Concept: Follow the Map

Tell children that they will now read about a girl and her maps. Ask: *What kinds of places can be on maps?*

Concepts of Print

Reading Sentences Across Pages Tell children that text can appear on different places on a page. Display pages 4 and 5 of *Me on the Map* and point out the sentences as you read the text. Explain that even when the sentences are placed all over a page, we read them one page at a time, from left to right and from top to bottom. Point out that the first word of each sentence always begins with a capital letter. Have children identify the first word of each sentence and the direction of text in *Me on the Map*.

Point out the labels on the map on page 6. Explain that the labels name what each part of the map represents. See prompts in the Big Book for modeling concepts of print.

Set a Purpose for Reading

→ Display the Big Book.

→ Read aloud the title and the names of the author and the illustrator.

→ Ask children to listen to the Big Book to find out what kind of maps the girl has.

Go Digital

Me on the Map

Reread

Strategy: Reread

❶ Explain Tell children that if they do not understand something they read in the Big Book, they can go back and reread the text. Explain that when you reread, you go back and read something again. Rereading can help them clear up any confusion they had while reading.

Think Aloud Rereading a section of text can help you answer any questions you had about it. Today, as we read *Me on the Map*, remember that you can go back and reread parts of the text to make sure that you understand all the details.

❷ Model As you read, use the Think Aloud Cloud to model applying the strategy.

Think Aloud Remember that you can reread parts of the text to make sure you understood everything. There are a lot of details on these pages. I'm not sure if the house in the small picture is the same as the house on the map. I will reread page 6: "This is my house. This is a map of my house." Now I understand that the house in the picture and the house on the map are the same house.

❸ Guided Practice As you continue to read the Big Book, pause to elicit questions from children. Guide them in rereading parts they did not understand. *Did you understand how the girl finds her state on the map? What can we do if we do not understand?* Pause to check children's understanding and reread sections as needed.

Respond to Reading

After reading, prompt children to share what they learned about maps. Discuss what parts you reread and how rereading helped them to understand the events and details.

ELL

ENGLISH LANGUAGE LEARNERS SCAFFOLD

Beginning

Engage Display page 7. *Are these houses? Are the same houses on the map? I'm not sure what the map shows.* Reread the text. *Does the map show the houses on the girl's street?* Allow children time to respond. *Show me the girl's house on the map.*

Intermediate

Describe Display pages 8 and 9. Ask children to describe the illustrations. *What do you see on page 8? How are the map and the illustration on page 8 alike?* Repeat correct answers clearly. *What can we do if we do not understand these pages?*

Advanced/Advanced High

Describe Display pages 10 and 11. *What does the map show? How are the illustration on page 10 and the map related?* Have children reread to check their understanding of the details. Correct their responses as needed.

Monitor and *Differentiate*

 Quick Check

Can children apply the strategy reread?

⬇

Small Group Instruction

If No →	**Approaching**	Reteach pp. T364–T365
	ELL	Develop pp. T382–T385
If Yes →	**On Level**	Review pp. T374–T375
	Beyond Level	Extend pp. T378–T379

→  # Word Work

Quick Review

Build Fluency: Sound-Spellings
Display the **Word-Building Cards:** *ch, tch, wh, ph, th, sh, ng, nd, nk, nt, st, sk, mp, u, e, ea, sp, sn, sl, cr, fr, tr, o, pl, fl, cl.* Have children say the sounds.

Phonemic Awareness
5 Mins

Phoneme Segmentation

OBJECTIVES

CCSS Segment spoken single-syllable words into their complete sequence of individual sounds (phonemes). **RF.1.2d**

CCSS Know the spelling-sound correspondences for common consonant digraphs (two letters that represent one sound). **RF.1.3a**

1 Model Use the **Response Board** to show children how to segment a word into phonemes. *Listen as I say a word:* chin. *I want to know how many sounds are in the word* chin. *I will place a marker in a box for each sound I hear. Listen: /ch/ /i/ /n/. The first sound is /ch/. The middle sound is /i/. The last sound is /n/. I will place three markers because I hear three sounds in the word. Say the three sounds in* chin *with me: /ch/ /i/ /n/.*

2 Guided Practice/Practice Have children practice segmenting words. Guide practice with the first two words. *I am going to say some words. Say each sound in the word and place a marker in a box for the sound you hear. Then tell me how many sounds are in each word.*

itch (2)	whale (3)	whiz (3)	chip (3)
phone (3)	why (2)	much (3)	chops (4)

Phonics
10 Mins

Sound-Spelling Card

Introduce Consonant Digraphs *ch, -tch, wh, ph*

1 Model Display the *Cheese* **Sound-Spelling Card.** Teach the sound /ch/ spelled *ch* and *-tch* using *cheese* and *match.* Model writing the letters *ch* and *tch.* Use the handwriting models provided. *This is the* Cheese *Sound-Spelling Card. The sound is /ch/. The /ch/ sound is spelled with the letters* ch. *Say it with me: /ch/. This is the sound at the beginning of the word* cheese: */ch/ /ē/ /z/. Sometimes at the end of a word the /ch/ sound is spelled -tch, as in* match. *I'll say /ch/ as I write the letters* ch *and* tch *several times.* Repeat with the *Whale* and *Fire* Sound-Spelling Cards for /hw/*wh* and /f/*ph.*

2 Guided Practice/Practice Have children practice connecting the letters *ch* and *tch* to the sound /ch/ by writing them. *Say /ch/ as I write the letters* ch *and* tch. *This time, write the letters* ch *and* tch *five times each as you say the /ch/ sound.* Repeat for /hw/*wh* and /f/*ph.*

Go Digital

Phonemic Awareness

Cheese
Phonics

Handwriting

Blend Words with *ch, -tch, wh, ph*

① Model Display **Word-Building Cards** *w, h, i, z*. Model how to blend the sounds. *These are the letters* w *and* h. *Together they stand for* /hw/. *This is the letter* i. *It stands for* /i/. *This is the letter* z. *It stands for* /z/. *Listen as I blend these sounds together:* /hwiiizzz/. *Say it with me.*

Continue by modeling the words *chop, much, pitch,* and *graph*.

② Guided Practice/Practice Display the Day 1 Phonics Practice Activity. Read each word in the first row, blending the sounds; for example: /sssuuuch/. *The word is* such. Have children blend each word with you. Prompt children to read the connected text, sounding out the decodable words.

such	chat	check	lunch	which	catch
rich	chin	graph	inch	Mitch	Steph
whip	whiz	bunch	bench	chest	chess
wing	shop	thin	bring	grand	stuff

Chet will pitch.

Steph will catch.

Which lunch will Mitch pick?

Also online

Day 1 Phonics Practice Activity

Corrective Feedback

Sound Error Model the sound that children missed, then have them repeat the sound. Say: *My turn.* Tap under the letter and say: *Sound? /ch/ What's the sound?* Return to the beginning of the word. Say: *Let's start over.* Blend the word with children again.

 Daily Handwriting

Throughout the week, teach uppercase and lowercase letters *Cc* using the Handwriting models.

ENGLISH LANGUAGE LEARNERS

Phonemic Awareness: Minimal Contrasts Focus on articulation. Say /hw/ and note your mouth position. Use Sound-Spelling Cards. Repeat for /ch/. Have children say both sounds, noticing the differences. Continue with: *cheat/ wheat, whip/chip.*

Phonics: Variations in Language In some languages, including Spanish, Cantonese, Vietnamese, and Hmong, there is no direct sound transfer for /hw/. Emphasize /hw/ and show correct mouth position. Practice with Approaching Level phonics lessons.

ON-LEVEL PRACTICE BOOK p. 91

The letters **ch** and **tch** stand for the sound you hear at the beginning of **chip** and the end of **ditch**. The letters **wh** stand for the sound at the beginning of **when**. The letters **ph** stand for the sound at the end of **graph**.

Read the words in the box. Match each word with a sound-spelling below. Write the word.

whisk	chin	Phil	graph
pitch	lunch	when	catch

1. wh	whisk		when
2. ch	lunch		chin
3. ph	graph		Phil
4. tch	catch		pitch

APPROACHING p. 91	BEYOND p. 91	ELL p. 91

Word Work

Quick Review

High-Frequency Words: Read, Spell, and Write to review last week's high-frequency words: *all, call, day, her, want.*

MINILESSON **5** Mins

Spelling

OBJECTIVES

CCSS Recognize and read grade-appropriate irregularly spelled words. **RF.1.3g**

CCSS Use conventional spelling for words with common spelling patterns and for frequently occurring irregular words. **L.1.2d**

Words with *ch, -tch, wh, ph*

Dictation Use the Spelling Dictation routine to help children transfer their growing knowledge of sound-spellings to writing. Follow the Dictation routine.

Pretest After dictation, pronounce each spelling word. Read the sentence and pronounce the word again. Ask children to say each word softly, stretching the sounds, before writing it. After the pretest, display the spelling words and write each word as you say the letter names. Have children check their words.

whip	The recipe says to **whip** the eggs.
whale	That **whale** is really big!
catch	I can **catch** the ball with two hands.
match	Her red shoes **match** her red dress.
chin	The baby has food on his **chin**.
graph	The **graph** shows more girls than boys.
shop	Dad and I **shop** for a new coat.
with	Our dog comes everywhere **with** us.
many	There were **many** people at the show.
around	He got dizzy from spinning **around**.

For Approaching Level and Beyond Level children, refer to the Differentiated Spelling Lists for modified words lists.

Go Digital

Spelling Word Routine

they	together
how	eat

High-Frequency Word Routine

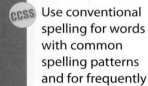

ENGLISH LANGUAGE LEARNERS

Pantomime Review the meaning of these words by using pictures, pantomime, or gestures when possible. Have children repeat or act out the word.

High-Frequency Words

around, by, many, place, walk

❶ Model Display the **High-Frequency Word Cards** *around, by, many, place,* and *walk*. Use the Read/Spell/Write routine to teach each word.

→ **Read** Point to and say the word *around. This is the word* around. *Say it with me:* around. *The dog ran around in circles.*

→ **Spell** *The word* around *is spelled* a-r-o-u-n-d. *Spell it with me.*

→ **Write** *Let's write the word* around *in the air as we say each letter:* a-r-o-u-n-d.

→ Follow the same steps to introduce *by, many, place,* and *walk.*

→ As children spell each word with you, point out irregularities in sound-spellings, such as the /e/ sound spelled *a* in *many.*

→ Have partners create sentences using each word.

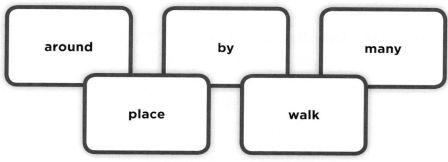

around

by

many

place

walk

High-Frequency Word Cards

❷ Guided Practice Have children read the sentences. Prompt them to identify the high-frequency words in connected text and to blend the decodable words.

1. The top spins **around**.

2. I sat **by** Chad at lunch.

3. **Many** kids like to run.

4. This is a good **place** to sit.

5. **Walk** with me.

Monitor and
Differentiate

 Quick Check

Can children read and decode words with consonant digraphs *ch, –tch, wh, ph*?

Can children recognize and read high-frequency words?

⬇

Small Group Instruction

If No →	Approaching	Reteach pp. T368–T369
	ELL	Develop pp. T382–T389
If Yes →	On Level	Review pp. T376–T377
	Beyond Level	Extend pp. T380–T381

→ Shared Read

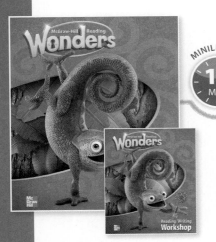

Read *Which Way on the Map?*

Model Skills and Strategies

Tell children that you will now read a nonfiction selection called *Which Way on the Map? As we read, look for the words* around, by, many, place, and walk. *Look for words where two or more letters stand for one sound, such as ch, -tch, wh,* and *ph.*

Story Words Display the words *lake, letter, each, people, shows,* and *town.* Spell each word and model reading it. Tell children that they will be reading the words in the selection.

Guide children in reading *Which Way on the Map?* Point out the high-frequency words and words in which digraphs *ch, -tch, wh,* and *ph* stand for one sound.

Genre: Informational Text/Nonfiction Tell children that *Which Way on the Map?* is a nonfiction selection. Remind children that informational nonfiction:

→ tells about real people, places, things, or events.

→ presents facts and information about a topic.

→ often uses photographs and illustrations to give information.

Connect to Concept

ESSENTIAL QUESTION

Read together the Essential Question on page 94 of the Reading/Writing Workshop. Discuss some places in your community that could be shown on a map. Guide children to connect what they have read to the Essential Question: *How can you find your way around?*

Reading/Writing Workshop Big Book and Reading/Writing Workshop

OBJECTIVES

 Decode regularly spelled one-syllable words. **RF.1.3b**

 Recognize and read grade-appropriate irregularly spelled words. **RF.1.3g**

Understand nonfiction genre

ACADEMIC LANGUAGE
• *nonfiction, map*
• Cognates: *no ficción, mapa*

Which Way on the Map?

Which Way on the Map?

READING/WRITING WORKSHOP, pp. 94–103
Lexile 160

Partner Reading

Have partners use their Reading/Writing Workshop to review the skills and strategies.

→ Remind children that as they reread *Which Way on the Map?* they can reread certain sections to make sure they understand what they are reading. Remind children that they can also reread to answer questions that they might have as they read.

Have children use pages 90–91 to review high-frequency words *walk, around, place, many,* and *by.*

→ Have children use pages 92–93 to review that the letters *ch, -tch, wh,* and *ph* can stand for one sound. Guide them to blend the sounds to read the words.

→ Have children reread *Which Way on the Map?* with a partner. Guide them to apply the skills and strategies. Ask children to name features of the selection that tell them that it is a nonfiction selection.

→ # Language Arts

MINILESSON
5
Mins

Shared Writing

Go Digital

Graphic Organizer

Writing

I see a fish.

Grammar

OBJECTIVES

CCSS With guidance and support from adults, focus on a topic, respond to questions and suggestions from peers, and add details to strengthen writing as needed. **W.1.5**

- Use irregular plural nouns
- Capitalize the first word in a sentence
- Use periods at the end of statements

ACADEMIC LANGUAGE

- *idea, details, noun*
- Cognates: *idea, detalles*

Writing Trait: Ideas

1 Model Tell children that they will now reread *Which Way on the Map?*, paying attention to what idea the author wrote about and what details tell about the idea. *Authors think of an idea before they begin writing. They include details in their writing to make the ideas easier to understand.*

2 Guided Practice/Practice Reread *Which Way on the Map?* Point out the details that support the writer's idea. Ask: *What details tell about the school? What details tell about the park?*

→ Prompt children to understand that the author gives details that tell about each place on the map. The author doesn't name the place, just gives details as clues. The details tell about the author's idea of describing places on a map.

Sentences That Explain

Focus and Plan Tell children that this week they will be writing sentences that tell about a place on a map. Explain that the sentences will be nonfiction. They will explain facts about the place.

 Brainstorm Use the Word Web on Teaching Poster 40 to help children organize information about a place on a map. Say: *The idea we will write about is a restaurant that serves lunch. What are some details we can write about it?* Record children's ideas on the web.

Write Tell children that you will work together to write sentences that explain facts about the restaurant on the map. Model writing sentences based on the Word Web. Say: *Let's start by telling the idea. Let's write:* This restaurant is in Chatham. *Next let's write sentences that explain facts about the place. Let's write:* Many people eat there.

Work together to write sentences that explain.

Grammar

MINILESSON
5 Mins

Irregular Plural Nouns

❶ Model Remind children that a noun names a person, place, or thing. Remind them that you add *-s* or *-es* to most nouns to name more than one, but other nouns change spelling completely. Display the following list:

One	More Than One
man	men
woman	women
child	children

Read each pair of words and have children repeat. Also say the following pairs and have children repeat: *person/people, mouse/mice, tooth/teeth.*

❷ Guided Practice/Practice Display the sentences below as you read each sentence aloud. Have children identify the plural noun in the sentence.

Two children play catch. (children)

Men and women are eating lunch. (men, women)

A few people run on the track. (people)

Talk About It Assign partners one singular and one irregular plural noun such as *woman/women*. Have them make up and tell each other sentences using each plural noun.

Mechanics: Capital Letters and Periods

❶ Model Remind children that a statement always begins with a capital letter and ends with a period.

❷ Guided Practice Have children correct each sentence.

the children jump in (The children jump in.)

six men Go fishing (Six men go fishing.)

ENGLISH LANGUAGE LEARNERS SCAFFOLD

Beginning

Demonstrate Comprehension Point to each Practice sentence. *Does* [children] *tell about one or more than one?* Repeat with each sentence. Restate responses in complete sentences.

Intermediate

Explain Display the Practice sentences. *Which words tell about more than one person?* Repeat correct answers slowly and clearly.

Advanced/Advanced High

Expand Display the Guided Practice sentences. *What does* children *mean?* Repeat with each plural noun. Model correct pronunciation as needed.

Daily Wrap Up

→ Review the Essential Question and encourage children to discuss it using the oral vocabulary words. Ask: *What can you use to find your way around?*

→ Prompt children to share the skills they learned. Ask: *How might you use those skills?*

Materials

Reading/Writing Workshop
VOLUME 2

Reading/Writing Workshop Big Book
UNIT 2

Visual Vocabulary Cards

height   route
locate   separate
model

whip

Spelling Word Cards

a b c

Word-Building Cards

Main Topic		
Detail	Detail	Detail

Teaching Poster

Interactive Read-Aloud Cards

ch
tch
cheese

Sound-Spelling Cards

→ # Build the Concept

MINILESSON
5 Mins

Oral Language

OBJECTIVES

CCSS Ask and answer questions about key details in a text read aloud or information presented orally or through other media. **SL.1.2**

• Develop oral language

• Discuss the Essential Question

ACADEMIC LANGUAGE

• *reread, text, map, feature*

• Cognates: *texto, mapa*

ESSENTIAL QUESTION

Remind children that this week you've been talking and reading about maps and how to use them. Remind them of how the family located places on the map of the city and the maps of the children's town. Guide children to discuss the Essential Question using information from what they read on Day 1.

Oral Vocabulary Words

Review the oral vocabulary words *locate* and *route* from Day 1. Use the Define/Example/Ask routine to introduce the oral vocabulary words *height*, *model*, and *separate*. Prompt children to use the words as they discuss maps.

Oral Vocabulary Routine

<u>Define:</u> The **height** of something is how tall it is.

<u>Example:</u> Lana's height is three feet, five inches.

<u>Ask:</u> How can you measure your height?

<u>Define:</u> A **model** is a small copy of something large.

<u>Example:</u> Grandpa built a model of an airplane.

<u>Ask:</u> Have you ever seen a model? What was it of?

<u>Define:</u> When you **separate** two things, you keep them apart from each other.

<u>Example:</u> Workers at the animal shelter separate the cats and dogs so they will not fight.

<u>Ask:</u> Why might it be a good idea to separate cats and birds?

Visual Vocabulary Cards

Go Digital

school

Visual Glossary

"Map It!"

Listening Comprehension

MINILESSON
5 Mins

Read the Interactive Read Aloud

Strategy: Reread

Remind children that as they read, they can go back and reread parts they did not understand. Model using the Think Aloud Cloud.

When I read, I can reread parts of the text to make sure I understood correctly. That helps me better understand what I am reading. I am not sure that I understood how to use the scale feature on a map. When I reread, I can look at the illustrations again and think about the details that confused me. Now I understand how to use this feature.

"Map It!"

Tell children that you will be reading a nonfiction text about the features on a map. Display the Interactive Read-Aloud Cards as you read "Map It!"

→ Pause to model using the strategy. Prompt children to identify parts of the selection that they did not understand. Guide them to go back and reread those parts.

Make Connections

COLLABORATE

Guide children to discuss what they learned about maps in the selection. *What do different features on a map tell us? How can we use them to find our way around?*

ELL

ENGLISH LANGUAGE LEARNERS

Seek Clarification Some children may be confused by unfamiliar words. Encourage children to always seek clarification when they encounter a word or phrase that does not make sense to them. For example, *I don't understand this. Can you show me?*

Word Work

Quick Review

Build Fluency: Sound-Spellings
Display the **Word-Building Cards:**
ch, tch, wh, ph, th, sh, ng, nd, nk, nt, st, sk, mp, u, e, ea, sp, sn, sl, cr, fr, tr, o, pl, fl, cl. Have children say the sounds. Repeat and vary the pace.

OBJECTIVES

CCSS Know the spelling-sound correspondences for common consonant digraphs (two letters that represent one sound). **RF.1.3a**

CCSS Decode regularly spelled one-syllable words. **RF.1.3b**

CCSS Read words with inflectional endings. **RF.1.3f**

MINILESSON 5 Mins

Phonemic Awareness

Phoneme Addition

❶ **Model** Show children how to add a phoneme to a word to create a new word. *Listen carefully. I am going to say a word:* at. *Now I am going to repeat the word and add the sound /ch/ to the beginning to make a new word: /ch/ /at/,* chat. *The new word is* chat.

❷ **Guided Practice/Practice** Have children practice adding phonemes. Guide practice with the first two. *I am going to say more sounds and words. Add the sound to the beginning of the word to get a new word. Tell me the word.*

ill, /ch/ (chill)   eat, /hw/ (wheat)   in, /ch/ (chin)

ant, /ch/ (chant)   am, /hw/ (wham)   at, /ch/ (chat)

MINILESSON 5 Mins

Phonics

Review Consonant Digraphs *ch, -tch, wh, ph*

❶ **Model** Display the *Cheese* **Sound-Spelling Card**. Review the sound /ch/ spelled *ch* and *-tch* using the words *chat, lunch,* and *patch.* Repeat with the *Whale* and *Fire* Sound-Spelling Cards and the words *when* and *Phil.*

❷ **Guided Practice/Practice** Have children practice connecting the letters and sound. Point to the Sound-Spelling Card. *What are these letters? What sound do they stand for?*

Go Digital

Phonemic Awareness

Phonics

I __ the jar.
| fill | fills | filling |

Structural Analysis

Handwriting

Blend Words with *ch, -tch, wh, ph*

1 Model Display **Word-Building Cards** *c, h, i, l, l* to form the word *chill*. Model how to generate and blend the sounds to say the word. *These are the letters* c *and* h. *Together they stand for /ch/. This is the letter* i. *It stands for /i/. These are the letter* ll. *Together they stand for /ll/. Let's blend these sounds together: /chiiilll/. Say it with me:* chill.

Continue by modeling the words *chess, fetch, whiz,* and *Steph*.

2 Guided Practice/Practice Repeat the routine with children with *whack, which, when, graph, chick, chest, lunch, pitch, catch, sketch*.

Build Words with *ch, -tch, wh, ph*

1 Model Display the Word-Building Cards *l, u, n, c, h*. Blend: /l/ /u/ /n/ /ch/, /llluuunnnch/, *lunch*.

→ Replace *l* with *m* and repeat with *munch*.

→ Replace *m* with *b* and repeat with *bunch*.

2 Guided Practice/Practice Continue with *punch, pinch, inch, itch, ditch, hitch, pitch, patch, pat, hat, chat, chap, chop, chip, whip, whim, whiz, which*. Guide children to build and blend each word.

MINILESSON
5 Mins

Structural Analysis

Inflectional Ending *-es*

1 Model Write and read aloud *patch* and *patches*. Underline the letters *-es*. Explain that we add *-es* to some naming words to make them mean "more than one." *The letters* -es *at the end of* patches *mean there is more than one patch. We add* -es *when the word ends in* ch, tch, sh, x, z, *or* ss.

Say *patch* and *patches* again and have children listen for the /z/ sound at the end of *patches*. Remind children that the letter *s* can sometimes stand for the /z/ sound; the *-es* in *patches* stands for /əz/. Say the word *patches* again, emphasizing the two syllables. Point out that adding *-es* to the word *patch* adds a word part, or syllable. Use each word in a sentence.

2 Guided Practice/Practice Write the following words: *lunch, ranch, match, ditch, box, wish, kiss, buzz*. Have children add *-es* to each word and then use each word in a sentence.

ELL

ENGLISH LANGUAGE LEARNERS

Build Vocabulary Review the meanings of example words that can be explained or demonstrated in a concrete way. For example, ask children to point to their *chest* and to their *chin*. Model the action for *catch* by tossing a ball (or small object) in the air and catching it, saying, "*I can catch the ball,*" and have children repeat. Provide sentence starters, such as *For lunch I like* _____ for children to complete. Correct grammar and pronunciation as needed.

→ # Word Work

Quick Review

High-Frequency Words: Read, Spell, and Write to review this week's high-frequency words: *around, by, many, place, walk.*

MINILESSON 5 Mins Spelling

OBJECTIVES

CCSS Recognize and read grade-appropriate irregularly spelled words. **RF.1.3g**

CCSS Use conventional spelling for words with common spelling patterns and for frequently occurring irregular words. **L.1.2d**

Word Sort with *ch, -tch, wh, ph*

❶ **Model** Display the **Spelling Word Cards** from the Teacher's Resource Book. Have children read each word, listening for the consonant digraph.

Use cards for *chat, pitch, wham,* and *Phil* to create a four-column chart. Say each word and pronounce the sounds, emphasizing the digraph in each. *The letters* ch *and* -tch *are pronounced /ch/,* wh *is /hw/, and* ph *is /f/.* Have children chorally spell each word.

❷ **Guided Practice/Practice** Have children place each Spelling Word Card in the column for the word containing the same consonant digraph sound and spelling. When completed, have children read the words in each column. Then call out a word. Have a child find the word card and point to it as the class spells the word.

ANALYZE ERRORS/ARTICULATION SUPPORT

Use children's pretest errors to analyze spelling problems and provide corrective feedback. For example, some children will substitute the letter *j* for *ch.* Additionally, they might confuse the name of the letter h (*aitch*) with the sound /ch/, or write only one letter for the digraph, such as *c* for *ch.*

Work with children to recognize the difference in the sounds and spellings in minimal contrast pairs, such as *junk/chunk, hill/chill, jug/chug, cop/chop.*

Say each word. Have children repeat. Isolate the /ch/ sound in the second word of the pair and focus on how the mouth forms that sound. Then have children write the word.

Go Digital

Spelling Word Sort

High-Frequency Word Routine

ENGLISH LANGUAGE LEARNERS

Provide Clues Practice spelling by helping children generate more words with consonant digraphs *ch, -tch, wh,* and *ph.* Provide clues: *Think of a word that begins with* ch *and rhymes with* stop. Write the word and have children practice reading it. Correct their pronunciation, if needed.

MINILESSON 5 Mins

High-Frequency Words

around, by, many, place, walk

1 Guided Practice Say each word and have children Read/Spell/Write it. Ask children to close their eyes, picture the word in their minds, and write it the way they see it. Display the high-frequency words for children to self-correct.

→ Point out sound-spelling patterns that have not yet been taught, such as the /ī/ sound spelled *y* in *by* and the /ē/ sound spelled *y* in *many*.

2 Practice Add the high-frequency words *around*, *by*, *many*, *place*, and *walk* to the cumulative word bank.

→ Have children work with a partner to create sentences using the words.

→ Have children look at the words and compare their sounds and spellings to words from previous weeks.

→ Suggest that they write about ways to find their way around a place, like their school or town.

Cumulative Review Review last week's words using the Read/Spell/Write routine.

→ Repeat the above routine, mixing the words and having children chorally say each one.

ON-LEVEL PRACTICE BOOK p. 92

A. Complete each sentence. Use one of the words in the box.

| walk | many | by | place | around |

1. Ned sits _____ **by** _____ the tree.

2. She has _____ **many** _____ socks.

3. This is a good _____ **place** _____ to eat.

4. Ed will _____ **walk** _____ fast.

5. We go _____ **around** _____ the rock.

B. Write your own sentence using a word from the box.

6. Responses will vary.

| APPROACHING p. 92 | BEYOND p. 92 | ELL p. 92 |

Monitor and Differentiate

✓ **Quick Check**

Can children read and decode words with consonant digraphs *ch*, –*tch*, *wh*, *ph*?

Can children recognize and read high-frequency words?

Small Group Instruction

If No →	Approaching	Reteach pp. T368–T369
	ELL	Develop pp. T382–T389
If Yes →	On Level	Review pp. T376–T377
	Beyond Level	Extend pp. T380–T381

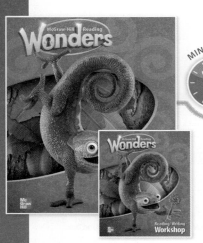

Reading/Writing Workshop Big Book and Reading/Writing Workshop

OBJECTIVES

 Identify the main topic and retell key details of a text. **RI.1.2**

Understand nonfiction genre

ACADEMIC LANGUAGE

- *nonfiction, main topic, key details*
- Cognate: *no ficción*

Comprehension · CLOSE READING

MINILESSON 10 Mins

Reread *Which Way on the Map?*

Genre: Informational Text/Nonfiction

1 Model Tell children they will now reread the nonfiction selection *Which Way on the Map?* Explain that as they read, they will look for information in the text to help them understand the selection. Review the characteristics of informational nonfiction. It:

→ tells about real people, places, things, or events.

→ presents facts and information about a topic.

→ can use text features like maps to give information.

Tell children that a nonfiction selection is about real things. *We can learn about real things in a nonfiction selection. The text, pictures, and photos will give facts and interesting details.*

Display pages 96–97. *This nonfiction selection gives information about a map. It helps us learn how to use a map to locate places in town.*

2 Guided Practice/Practice Display and read aloud pages 98 and 99 of *Which Way on the Map?* Say: *The photo shows what the school looks like. The map shows its location. The text, the map, and the photo give information about how to use a map. Can you find this building on the map?*

Go Digital

Which Way on the Map?

Genre

Main Topic and Key Details

Skill: Main Topic and Key Details

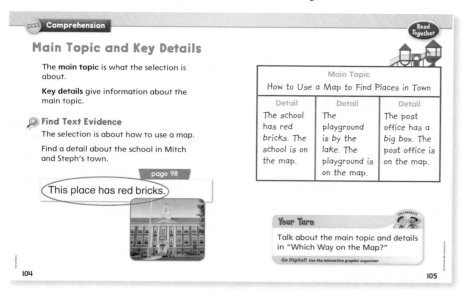

Reading/Writing Workshop, pp. 104–105

ON-LEVEL PRACTICE BOOK p. 97

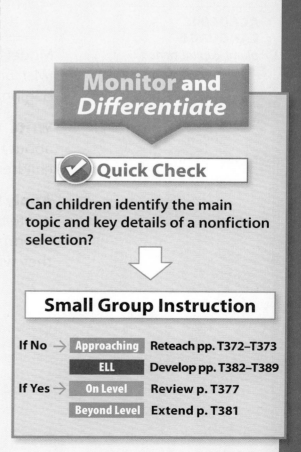

Read the story and follow the directions.

1. Write the word that tells you what chicks do.

   hatch

2. Write the word that tells what kids play.

   catch

3. Write what buses do.

   They whiz by.

4. Write the main topic of "Look Around."

   Possible Response: There are lots of things to see.

APPROACHING p. 97	BEYOND p. 97	ELL p. 97

❶ Model Tell children that when they read nonfiction, they can think about what the selection is about. Have children look at pages 104–105 in their Reading/Writing Workshop. Read together the definition of main topic and key details. *The main topic is what the selection is about. Key details give information about the main topic.*

❷ Guided Practice/Practice Read together the Find Text Evidence section and model using clues to find the main topic and key details of *Which Way on the Map?* Point out the information added to the graphic organizer. *The main topic of the selection is how to use a map to find places. The photo and text on page 98 show a large building with red bricks. This is a school. We can find the school on the map. Those are key details. The details are added to the Main Topic and Details chart. What other details can we find about the main topic?*

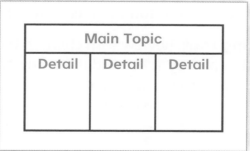

Teaching Poster

Monitor and Differentiate

✓ **Quick Check**

Can children identify the main topic and key details of a nonfiction selection?

⬇

Small Group Instruction

If No → Approaching Reteach pp. T372–T373
            ELL   Develop pp. T382–T389
If Yes → On Level   Review p. T377
            Beyond Level Extend p. T381

COMPREHENSION **T339**

Language Arts

MINILESSON

5 Mins

Interactive Writing

OBJECTIVES

CCSS Write informative/ explanatory texts in which they name a topic, supply some facts about the topic, and provide some sense of closure. **W.1.2**

• Use irregular plural nouns

• Capitalize first word in a sentence

• Use periods at end of statements

ACADEMIC LANGUAGE
plural, capital, period

Writing Trait: Ideas

Review Tell children that they should think of an idea before they begin writing. Then they should include details that tell about the idea and that help readers understand the idea.

Sentences That Explain

Discuss Guide children to think of a place on a map from their reading or one they have used in the classroom, such as a post office. Record their ideas on a Word Web.

Model/Apply Grammar Tell children that they will be working together to write sentences that explain the chosen topic. Remind them that some nouns that name more than one do not end in *-s* or *-es*.

→ Write the sentence starter:

_____ *in the post office.*

Model how to choose different phrases with irregular plural nouns (*Men buy stamps; People stand in line*) to complete the sentence. Model beginning the sentence with a capital letter and ending with a period.

Write Collaborate with children to write sentences that explain facts about the idea. Guide them to use the Word Web to get details. Remind children to listen for the sounds in each word.

Apply Writing Trait Review with children the sentences that you wrote together on Day 1. Remind them how the sentences explain information about the idea. Discuss with children how the sentences they wrote today focus on one idea.

Go Digital

Graphic Organizer

Writing

I see a fish.

Grammar

Grammar

5 Mins

Irregular Plural Nouns

❶ Review Remind children that the spelling of some nouns changes when the noun is plural.

Write the following sentences:

A man walked by. Then two men walked by. (men)

A woman claps her hands. Three women stand up. (women)

My tooth came out! What can I do with my teeth? (teeth)

A mouse sits in the grass. Do mice live here? (mice)

Read the sentences aloud and have children chorally repeat. Have children tell you which nouns name more than one.

❷ Guided Practice Write the sentence frames below. Read each sentence and the choices to complete it. Have children tell you the correct noun to complete the sentence.

The two _____ (child, children) run to school. (children)

The three kids eat lunch with one _____ (woman, women). (woman)

Many _____ (man, men) help dig the ditch. (men)

❸ Practice Have partners write or say a sentence about people at school using irregular plural nouns such as: *Children play outside. The women watch the children.*

Talk About It Have partners work together to orally generate sentences with irregular plural nouns.

Mechanics: Capital Letters and Periods

❶ Review Remind children that all statements begin with a capital letter and end with a period.

❷ Practice Prompt children to correct each sentence.

i have socks on my feet (I have socks on my feet.)

two men play chess (Two men play chess.)

ENGLISH LANGUAGE LEARNERS

Explain Display the first pair of Model sentences. Ask children to underline the noun that names one. Then have them circle the noun that names more than one. Have them complete the sentence frame: *A plural noun is a word that _____.* Clarify children's responses as needed by providing vocabulary.

Match Write each of the following words on an index card: *child, children, man, men, woman, women.* Mix up the cards. Have children match the singular and plural forms of each word.

Daily Wrap Up

→ Discuss the Essential Question and encourage children to use the oral vocabulary words. *How do maps help?*

→ Prompt children to discuss what they learned: *How will today's skills help you read and write?*

Materials

Reading/Writing Workshop
VOLUME 2

Literature Anthology
VOLUME 2

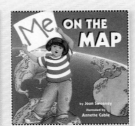
Literature Big Book
Me on the Map

Visual Vocabulary Cards

height   around
locate   by
model   many
route   place
separate walk

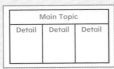
Teaching Poster

Spelling Word Cards

Word-Building Cards

→ Build the Concept

Go Digital

Visual Glossary

MINILESSON 5 Mins

Oral Language

 OBJECTIVES

 Participate in collaborative conversations with diverse partners about grade 1 topics and texts with peers and adults in small and larger groups. **SL.1.1**

 Retell stories, including key details, and demonstrate understanding of their central message or lesson. **RL.1.2**

ACADEMIC LANGUAGE
• *reread, patterns, repeated*
• Cognate: *patrones*

ESSENTIAL QUESTION

Remind children that this week you have been talking and reading about how we use maps. Remind them of the family looking at the city map, the maps the girl had, and the different types of maps they read about. Guide children to discuss the Essential Question using information from what they have read and talked about throughout the week.

Review Oral Vocabulary

Review the oral vocabulary words *height, locate, model, route,* and *separate* using the Define/Example/Ask routine. Encourage children to discuss how we use maps when coming up with examples for each word.

Me on the Map

Retell

Visual Vocabulary Cards

Listening Comprehension

MINILESSON
10 Mins

Reread Literature Big Book

Strategy: Reread

Remind children that as they read, they can reread sections that are unclear to them. This can help them better understand the events and details in the text. *As we reread* Me on the Map, *we can stop and reread parts that are not clear to us.*

Read aloud *Me on the Map*. Pause to model rereading. Prompt children to identify key details using evidence in the text and illustrations.

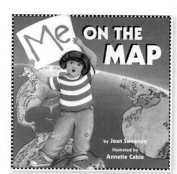

Literature Big Book

Model Retelling

Pause to retell portions of the selection. *I can put details and events into my own words. I have read that the girl has a map of her room and a map of her house. I can tell from the illustrations that she drew the maps herself.*

→ After reading, retell the selection, using your own words to tell the important events and details in the correct order.

Model Fluency

Phrasing Turn to pages 4 and 5 of *Me on the Map*. Read the text and explain that the phrase *This is* repeats throughout the first part of the text. Read aloud page 19 and have children identify the repeated phrase. *When you read repeated words, you can read them with rhythm.*

→ Read aloud pages 22 and 23 with slightly exaggerated rhythm on the phrases *And in my* and *I find*. Have children identify the repeated words. Repeat the reading to give children more practice with appropriate phrasing.

ELL

ENGLISH LANGUAGE LEARNERS

Retell Guide children to retell by using a question prompt on each page. *What does the girl find on this map?* Provide sentence starters for children to complete orally. *The girl finds _____.*

ACT

Access Complex Text

If the complexity of the text makes it hard for children to read, use the Access Complex Text prompts.

Purpose The text explains how to use maps and the relationship of small geographic areas to larger areas.

→ Explain that maps can show a small area, such as a room, or a larger area that contains the smaller one, such as a city.

Organization Children must understand how the featured land areas expand and then contract over the course of the story.

→ Help children grasp the concept by using hand and arm gestures to represent how the size of the area featured on each map increases on each page during the first part of the story and decreases during the second part.

→ Word Work

Quick Review

Build Fluency: Sound-Spellings
Display the **Word-Building Cards:** *ch, tch, wh, ph, th, sh, ng, nd, nk, nt, st, sk, mp, u, e, ea, sp, sn, sl, cr, fr, tr, o, pl, fl, cl.* Have children say the sounds.

Phonemic Awareness

OBJECTIVES

CCSS Know the spelling-sound correspondences for common consonant digraphs (two letters that represent one sound). **RF.1.3a**

CCSS Read words with inflectional endings. **RF.1.3f**

Phoneme Blending

❶ **Model** Show children how to orally blend phonemes. *Listen as I say the sounds in a word: /hw/ /i/ /ch/. Now I will blend the sounds together and say the word: /hwiiich/,* which. *Let's say the word together:* which. Repeat with */ch/ /a/ /t/,* chat; */b/ /e/ /n/ /ch/,* bench; */p/ /i/ /ch/,* pitch; */f/ /ō/ /n/,* phone.

❷ **Guided Practice/Practice** Have children practice blending phonemes. *Let's do some together. I am going to say some words sound by sound. Listen as I say a word. Blend the sounds together to say the word.* Do the first three with children.

/b/ /a/ /ch/	/ch/ /o/ /p/	/hw/ /e/ /n/
/ch/ /i/ /p/	/d/ /i/ /ch/	/hw/ /i/ /s/ /k/
/m/ /a/ /ch/	/f/ /e/ /ch/	/g/ /r/ /a/ /f/

Phonics

Blend Words with *ch, -tch, wh, ph*

❶ **Model** Display **Word-Building Cards** *p, i, t, c, h.* Model how to blend the sounds. *This is the letter* p. *It stands for /p/. This is the letter* i. *It stands for /i/. These are the letters* tch. *Together they stand for /ch/. Let's blend the sounds: /piiich/. The word is* pitch.

Continue by modeling the words *check, crunch, whiff,* and *graph.*

❷ **Guided Practice/Practice** Review the following words and sentences on the Day 3 Phonics Practice Activity with children. Read each word in the first row, blending the sounds; for example, */chaaat/. The word is* chat.

Have children blend each word with you. Prompt children to read the connected text, sounding out the decodable words.

Go Digital

Phonemic Awareness

Phonics

Structural Analysis

Handwriting

chat	lunch	check	pitch	catch
such	which	when	graph	rich
chat	cat	catch	whiz	whip

benches	bunches	lunches	inches
patches	wishes	dishes	sketches

When will the chick hatch?

A chunk of lunch fell on Steph's chin.

Also online

Day 3 Phonics Practice Activity

MINILESSON
5 Mins

Structural Analysis

Inflectional Ending -es

① Model Write the words *inch, inches, stitch, stitches* and read them with children. Underline the letters *-es*. Remind children that when *-es* is added to a naming word, it changes the meaning of the word to mean there is more than one. It also adds a syllable. Read the words and have children read them. Have them clap out the syllables.

② Practice/Apply Help children blend the words *bench, benches, sketch, sketches*. Point out that the letters *-es* at the end of a word can stand for /əz/.

Corrective Feedback

Corrective Feedback Say *My turn*. Model blending using the appropriate signaling procedures. Then lead children in blending the sounds. Say: *Do it with me*. You will respond with children to offer support. Then say: *Your turn. Blend*. Have children chorally blend. Return to the beginning of the word. Say: *Let's start over*.

→ Word Work

Quick Review

High-Frequency Words: Read, Spell, and Write to review this week's high-frequency words: *around, by, many, place, walk*.

MINILESSON
5 Mins

Spelling

OBJECTIVES

CCSS Recognize and read grade-appropriate irregularly spelled words. **RF.1.3g**

CCSS Use conventional spelling for words with common spelling patterns and for frequently occurring irregular words. **L.1.2d**

Word Sort with *ch, -tch, wh, ph*

① Model Make index cards for *ch, -tch, wh,* and *ph* and form four columns in a pocket chart. Blend the sounds with children.

Hold up the *whip* **Spelling Word Card**. Say and spell it. Pronounce each sound clearly: /hw/ /i/ /p/. Blend the sounds, emphasizing the digraph. Repeat this step with *whale*. Place the words below the *wh* card. Read and spell each spelling word together with children. Have children read each word. *What do you notice about these spelling words? Yes, they have the /hw/ sound spelled* w-h.

② Guided Practice/Practice Have children spell each word. Repeat the process with the *-tch, ch,* and *ph* words.

Display the words *shop, with, many,* and *around* in a separate column. Read and spell the words together with children. Point out that these spelling words do not contain consonant digraphs *ch, -tch, wh,* or *ph*.

Conclude by asking children to orally generate additional words that rhyme with each word or contain the same consonant digraph. Write the additional words on the board. Underline the common spelling patterns in the additional words. If necessary, point out the differences and explain why they are unusual.

Go Digital

Spelling Word Sort

Visual Glossary

PHONICS/SPELLING PRACTICE BOOK p. 48

Read the spelling words in the box.

| whip | whale | catch | match |
| chin | graph | many | around |

Find the spelling words in the puzzle.
Draw a circle around each word.

x	b	l	e	w	h	i	p	s
o	g	r	a	p	h	a	p	k
w	h	a	l	e	v	u	o	s
b	m	t	a	r	o	u	n	d
k	i	x	m	n	e	q	r	w
e	m	a	t	c	h	m	j	r
i	p	h	n	d	j	l	l	a
c	e	o	c	h	i	n	x	e
e	y	v	m	a	n	y	k	u
s	o	r	c	a	t	c	h	t

MINILESSON 5 Mins

High-Frequency Words

around, by, many, place, walk

❶ Guided Practice Say each word and have children Read/Spell/Write it. As children spell each word with you, point out the *l* in *walk*, which some children might omit.

→ Display **Visual Vocabulary Cards** to review this week's high-frequency words.

Visual Vocabulary Cards

❷ Practice Repeat the activity with last week's words.

Build Fluency: Word Automaticity

Have children read the following sentences aloud together at the same pace. Repeat several times.

I can walk around the block.

Many branches fell.

Place the cup by the dish.

Word Bank

Review the current and previous words in the word bank. Discuss with children which words should be removed, or added back, from previous high-frequency word lists. Remind children that the word bank should change as the class needs it to.

Monitor and *Differentiate*

 Quick Check

Can children read and decode words with consonant digraphs *ch, –tch, wh, ph*?

Can children recognize and read high-frequency words?

Small Group Instruction

If No →	Approaching	Reteach pp. T368–T369
	ELL	Develop pp. T382–T389
If Yes →	On Level	Review pp. T376–T377
	Beyond Level	Extend pp. T380–T381

CCSS **Genre** Nonfiction

Essential Question
How can you find your way around?
Learn how to use a map.

Go Digital!

Read Together

A map is a drawing of a **place**.
A map shows us where we are.
It shows us how to get **around**, too.

86

Phil's Room

A map can be of a small place.
This is a map of Phil's room.
How **many** windows do you see?
What is next to Phil's bed?
What is **by** the door?

87

LITERATURE ANTHOLOGY, pp. 86–87

Develop Comprehension
CLOSE READING

Literature Anthology

Read Literature Anthology

Review Genre: Informational Text/Nonfiction Review with children the key characteristics of nonfiction. It:

→ provides facts and details about real people, places, events, or things.

→ presents information about a specific topic.

→ can include text features such as maps.

Preview and Predict Display pages 86 and 87. Read the title and discuss the illustrations. Ask: *What might this selection be about? What do you think we will learn as we read? Let's find out.*

ESSENTIAL QUESTION

Read aloud the Essential Question: *How can you find your way around?* Tell children that as they read they should think about how they can use different kinds of maps to find their way.

Story Words Read, spell, and define the words *room, town, park,* and *islands*. Explain that they will read these words in the selection.

Analytical Writing **Note Taking: Graphic Organizer** As children read the selection, guide them to fill in the graphic organizer on **Your Turn Practice Book** page 94 as you model recording the main topic and the key details of each section.

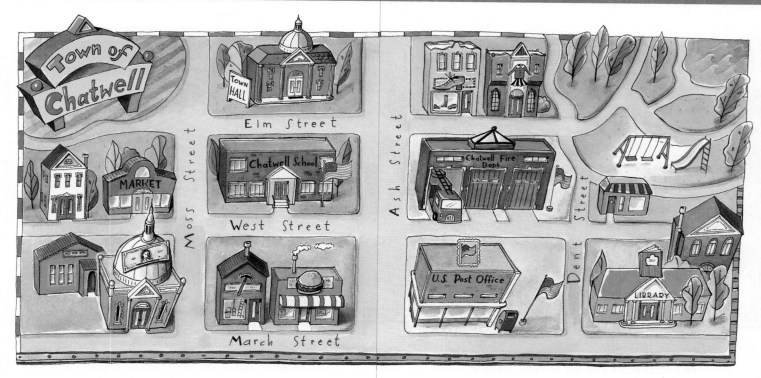

A map can be of a big place. This is a map of a town. What places do you see on the map?

Which street is the market on? What is by the firehouse? How would you **walk** from the school to the library?

88

89

LITERATURE ANTHOLOGY, pp. 88–89

❶ Strategy: Reread

Teacher Think Aloud I remember that if something doesn't make sense the first time I read it, I can reread to see if there was something I missed. I'm a little confused after reading pages 88 and 89. I thought I read that maps were of small places. But now it says maps can be of big places. I'll read again from the beginning. Now I understand. Maps can be of small places *and* maps can be of big places.

❷ Skill: Main Topic and Key Details

What is the main topic? (maps) What is a key detail about maps on page 86? What is a key detail on pages 87 and 88? Let's add those to our chart.

Main Topic Maps		
Detail Maps show us where we are and how to get around.	**Detail** There are maps for all kinds of places.	**Detail**

A map can be of a fun place.
This is a map of a park.
The symbols on maps stand for real ③
things. On this map, 🪑 stands for
a place to eat lunch.

90

A key tells what the symbols mean. ④
Match the symbol in the key with
the one on the map.
What symbol stands for the pond?
What does 🛝 stand for?

91

LITERATURE ANTHOLOGY, pp. 90–91

Develop Comprehension

CLOSE READING

③ Strategy: Reread

Teacher Think Aloud I am not sure if I understand
what I read about symbols and map keys. I will
reread these pages to check my understanding.
A symbol stands for something. The map key lists
the symbols and tells what each one stands for.
So, we can use the map key to read the symbols.

④ Skill: Main Topic and Key Details

Teacher Think Aloud When I read pages 90 and
91, I find out that a map can be of a fun place.
That goes along with a detail we know: There are
maps for all kinds of places. But there's another
key detail here. What do you think it is?

Student Think Aloud On pages 90 and 91, I
read that maps have symbols that stand for real
things. The key tells me what each symbol means.
I will add that to my Main Topic and Details chart.

Main Topic		
Maps		
Detail	**Detail**	**Detail**
Maps show us where we are and how to get around.	There are maps for all kinds of places.	Maps have symbols and a key that tells what the symbols stand for.

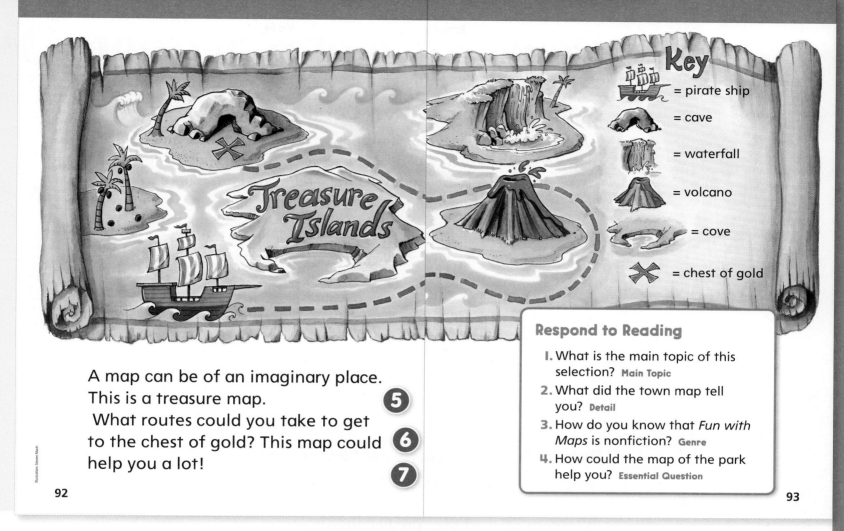

A map can be of an imaginary place. This is a treasure map. **(5)**
What routes could you take to get to the chest of gold? This map could **(6)** help you a lot! **(7)**

92

Respond to Reading

1. What is the main topic of this selection? **Main Topic**
2. What did the town map tell you? **Detail**
3. How do you know that *Fun with Maps* is nonfiction? **Genre**
4. How could the map of the park help you? **Essential Question**

93

LITERATURE ANTHOLOGY, pp. 92–93

(5) Skill: Main Topic and Key Details

On page 92 we read that a map can be of an imaginary place. That's another key detail. Do you think we should add it to our chart? Why or why not? (We don't need to add it to our chart because we already have the detail "There are maps for all kinds of places." An imaginary place is just one more kind of place.)

(6) Word Categories

We can sort words into categories. What category might you put *treasure, chest,* and *gold* into? (Possible answer: fantasy words)

(7) Maintain Skill: Key Details

The text on page 92 asks how we could find the chest of gold. Do you see the chest of gold marked on the map? (No, it is not there.) Let's look in the map key. Does that help you find the chest of gold? (Yes. The key tells us that the big X is a symbol for a chest of gold.) Now can you find the chest of gold on the map? How? (Yes, we see the big X on the map. That tells us where the chest of gold is.)

Develop Comprehension

CLOSE READING

Skill: Main Topic and Key Details

Guide children to review the information on the Main Topic and Details chart. *Let's take a last look at our Main Topic and Details chart. What was the main topic of the selection? What were the key details? Is our chart complete or is there anything else we should add?*

<table>
<tr><td colspan="3" align="center">**Main Topic**
Maps</td></tr>
<tr><td align="center">**Detail**
Maps show us where we are and how to get around.</td><td align="center">**Detail**
There are maps for all kinds of places.</td><td align="center">**Detail**
Maps have symbols and a key that tells what the symbols stand for.</td></tr>
</table>

Return to Predictions and Purposes

Review children's predictions. Ask children if their predictions about the selection were correct. Guide them to use the evidence in the text to confirm whether their predictions turned out to be accurate. Discuss what children learned from the selection. Did they learn anything new about maps?

Respond to Reading

Retelling

Guide children in retelling the selection. Remind them that as they read *Fun with Maps,* they paid attention to the main topic and key details and reread when there was something they didn't understand. Now they will use what they learned to retell the selection.

→ Have children use the information they recorded on their Main Topic and Details chart to help them retell the selection.

Text Evidence

Guide children to use text evidence to answer the Respond to Reading questions on Literature Anthology page 93. Model answering the questions as needed.

1. **Main Topic** This question asks what the main topic of the selection is. To answer it, we should look back at the selection. On page 86 we read the title *Fun with Maps,* which suggests that the topic of the selection is maps. The first paragraph is also all about maps. If we look at our Main Topic and Details chart, all the details we wrote were about maps, too. So we can tell the main topic of the selection is maps.

2. **Detail** Question 2 asks what the town map tells us. To answer the question, we should look at the town map on pages 88 and 89, as well as the text about the map. The town map tells us where certain places are in the town, such as the market and the firehouse. It also tells us the names of the streets in the town.

3. **Genre** To answer the question about how we know the selection is nonfiction, let's look back at the selection. On each page we see real maps of real places, like a bedroom, a town, and a park. Even though there is a map of an imaginary place, the information about the map is factual. These are clues that *Fun with Maps* is nonfiction.

4. **Essential Question** Question 4 asks how the map of the park could help us. Let's look back at pages 90 and 91 to answer the question. The map of Bell Park has symbols that stand for real places in the park. By looking at the key, I can figure out what the symbols stand for. I find out where to go in the park to eat, to play, or to listen to music. If I were to visit Bell Park, the map would help me figure out how to get around.

ENGLISH LANGUAGE LEARNERS

Retell Help children by looking at each page of the selection and asking a question, such as, *What is this a map of? What do you see on this map?* Provide sentence starters to help children retell the selection, such as, *This is a map of _____. It has symbols for _____.*

CONNECT TO CONTENT
SOCIAL STUDIES
USING A MAP

Remind children that this week they've been reading about maps and how they can use maps to locate and identify a variety of man-made and physical features. Ask students to discuss what they learned about maps from the selection. Talk about the different ways that they can use maps. Provide a collection of maps of a variety of places, such as towns, parks, shopping malls, and schools. Distribute the maps to pairs. Have each pair study their map, and then share with the class what the map shows and any interesting features they see on it.

→ # Language Arts

Reading/Writing Workshop Big Book

OBJECTIVES

CCSS Write informative/ explanatory texts in which they name a topic, supply some facts about the topic, and provide some sense of closure. **W.1.2**

- Use irregular plural nouns
- Capitalize first word in a sentence
- Use periods at end of statements

ACADEMIC LANGUAGE
prewrite, draft

MINILESSON
5 Mins

Independent Writing

Writing Trait: Ideas

❶ Review Tell children that they will write a draft. *Think about the steps we have followed as we wrote sentences that explain an idea.*

❷ Guided Practice Have children open to the Readers to Writers page in the Reading/Writing Workshop. Read the student model aloud. Point out how Chad used the writing trait Ideas. Guide children to identify and discuss the shop Chad wrote about.

Reading/Writing Workshop, pp. 106–107

Sentences That Explain

Model Have children look again at Chad's sentences, noting his idea and how he explains it. Have children complete the Your Turn.

Prewrite

Display the list of topic ideas from Day 2. Guide children to choose a topic. Preview the topic choices.

COLLABORATE
Brainstorm Place children in pairs based on the topic they have chosen. Guide partners to use a Word Web to organize their ideas.

Go Digital

Present the Lesson

Graphic Organizer

Writing

I see a fish.

Grammar

Draft

Have children use details from their Word Webs to write sentences that explain their chosen idea. Prompt them to include a sentence that tells the idea they are writing about.

Apply Writing Trait Remind children to only write about one idea.

Apply Grammar Remind children that the spelling of some nouns changes when the noun names more than one.

As children work, conference with them to provide guidance.

Grammar

MINILESSON 5 Mins

Irregular Plural Nouns

❶ Review Have children look at the Readers to Writers pages in the Reading/Writing Workshop. Remind them that a plural noun names more than one. Have children identify the plural nouns in the model sentence.

Ask: *What are the plural nouns in this sentence?* It sells ball caps for children. *Which words tell about more than one?* Caps *and* children *are plural nouns. Which noun did not have* -s *added to name more than one?* (children)

❷ Guided Practice/Practice Have children identify other irregular plural nouns in Chad's sentences. Have them dictate sentences with an irregular plural noun that Chad could add to his paper. Write children's suggestions.

Talk About It Have partners work together to orally generate sentences with irregular plural nouns.

COLLABORATE

Mechanics: Capital Letters and Periods

❶ Review Remind children that all statements begin with a capital letter and end with a period.

❷ Practice Display the incorrect sentences. Have children fix them.

the mice munch on a Plum (The mice munch on a plum.)

the Women thank the man for his help (The women thank the man for his help.)

ENGLISH LANGUAGE LEARNERS SCAFFOLD

Beginning

Expand Provide sentence frames for partners as they write sentences: *This _____ is by a _____. It _____.* Clarify children's responses as needed by providing vocabulary.

Intermediate

Narrate Encourage children to talk about their Word Webs. *What details explain about your place?* Repeat children's responses, correcting grammar or pronunciation as needed. Provide sentence frames; then have children complete and read them.

Advanced/Advanced High

Elaborate Prompt children to offer details in their sentences: *What do people do in a [location]? Let's include that in your sentences that tell about this place on the map.* Help children transfer these details to their writing.

Daily Wrap Up

→ Review the Essential Question and encourage children to discuss using the oral vocabulary words. Ask: *What kinds of places can be found on a map?*

→ Prompt children to review and discuss the skills they used today. Guide them to give examples of how they used each skill.

Materials

Wonders
Literature Anthology
VOLUME 2

Visual Vocabulary Cards

height   around
locate   by
model   many
route   place
separate   walk

Teaching Poster

a b c

Word-Building Cards

Dinah Zike's
FOLDABLES

Dinah Zike's Foldables®

whip

Spelling Word Cards

→ # Extend the Concept

MINILESSON
5
Mins

Oral Language

OBJECTIVES

CCSS Know and use various text features (e.g., headings, tables of contents, glossaries, electronic menus, icons) to locate key facts or information in a text. **RI.1.5**

Review vocabulary

ACADEMIC LANGUAGE
• *map, grounds, field*
• Cognate: *mapa*

ESSENTIAL QUESTION

Remind children that this week they have been learning about maps. Guide children to discuss the Essential Question using information from what they have read and discussed.

Use the Define/Example/Ask routine to review the oral vocabulary words *height, locate, model, route,* and *separate.* Then review last week's oral vocabulary words *leadership, admire, enjoy, rely,* and *connections.*

Text Feature: Map

1 Explain Tell children that they can use informational text selections to find facts and details. Explain that informational text sometimes includes a map—a picture that shows where places are found. A map sometimes has a title that tells about the map and a key that shows what the symbols on the map stand for.

Teaching Poster

2 Model Display Teaching Poster 19. *This is a map of the area around a school. You could use this map to find your way around the grounds of this school.* Point out the map key. *The key shows each symbol used on the map. It lists what each symbol stands for. We use the key to find things on the map.*

3 Guided Practice/Practice Guide children to identify the map's features. *Where is the soccer field? The key shows us the map symbol for soccer field. How can you get from the school building to the field?* Tell children to look for maps when reading informational text.

Go Digital

school

Visual Glossary

Teaching Poster

"North, East, South, or West?"

CCSS **Genre** Nonfiction

Compare Texts
Read about the directions on a map.

Read Together

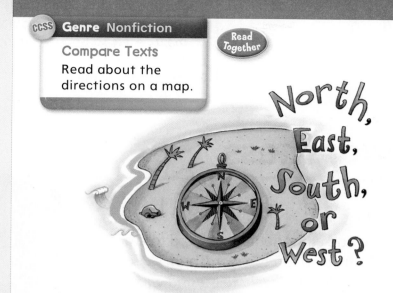

North, East, South, or West?

1 Many maps show directions. North, East, South, and West are directions. Directions tell us which way to go.

Look at the map of the zoo. Find each direction. Is the lion north or south of the snack bar? Are the chimps closer to the east or west?

Chester Zoo

2

Key
N = North
E = East
S = South
W = West

Make Connections
? What is north of the baseball field on the map of Bell Park?
Essential Question

94

95

LITERATURE ANTHOLOGY, pp. 94–95   **Lexile** 360

Develop Comprehension   CLOSE READING

Read Literature Anthology

Compare Texts

Tell children that as they read they should think about how the map features are like the ones in *Which Way on the Map?*

1 Strategy: Reread

Teacher Think Aloud If something I read doesn't make sense, I can go back and reread to make sure I didn't miss an important point. I need to make sure I understand why the labels *North, East, South* and *West* are so important on this map. The first paragraph on page 94 tells me they are directions that tell us which way to go.

2 Text Feature: Map

Teacher Think Aloud
The map on page 95 shows which way is north, east, south, and west. These are compass directions, and they're important because they never change. If I were at the Chester Zoo right now, I'd be able to find anything shown on this map as long as I knew which way was north, east, south, and west.

Literature Anthology

 Make Connections Have children think about how the specific features on a map can help them find their way.

Word Work

Quick Review
Build Fluency: Sound-Spellings
Display the **Word-Building Cards:** *ch, tch, wh, ph, th, sh, ng, nd, nk, nt, st, sk, mp, u, e, ea, sp, sn, sl, cr, fr, tr, o, pl, fl, cl.* Have children say the sounds. Repeat, and vary the pace.

MINILESSON 5 Mins

Phonemic Awareness

Phoneme Addition

OBJECTIVES

CCSS Know the spelling-sound correspondences for common consonant digraphs (two letters that represent one sound). **RF.1.3a**

CCSS Recognize and read grade-appropriate irregularly spelled words. **RF.1.3g**

CCSS Use conventional spelling for words with common spelling patterns and for frequently occurring irregular words. **L.1.2d**

Add phonemes to words

❶ **Model** Show children how to add a phoneme to a word to create a new word. *Listen carefully. I am going to say a word:* bun. *Now I am going to repeat the word and add the sound /ch/ to the end of the word to make a new word: /bun/ /ch/,* bunch. *The new word is* bunch.

❷ **Guided Practice/Practice** Have children practice adding a phoneme to a word. Guide practice with the first two. *I am going to say more sounds and words. Add the /ch/ sound to the end of the word to get a new word. Tell me the word.*

pin, /ch/ (pinch)	wren, /ch/ (wrench)
ran, /ch/ (ranch)	pun, /ch/ (punch)
in, /ch/ (inch)	bran, /ch/ (branch)

MINILESSON 5 Mins

Phonics

Build Words with *ch, -tch, wh, ph*

Review *The sound /ch/ is represented by the letters* ch. *It can also be represented by the letters* tch *at the end of a word. The sound /hw/ is represented by the letters* wh. *The sound /f/ can be represented by the letters* ph. *We'll use* **Word-Building Cards** *to build words with* ch, -tch, wh, *and* ph.

Place the letters *c, a, t, c, h. Let's blend the sounds together and read the word: /kaaach/. Now let's change the* c *to* h. *Blend the sounds and read the word: /haaach/,* hatch.

Continue with *latch, match, patch, pitch, ditch, hitch, itch, inch, pinch, punch, hunch, lunch, munch, crunch.*

Go Digital

Phonemic Awareness

Phonics

Structural Analysis

Spelling Word Sort

Visual Glossary

Structural Analysis

Inflectional Ending -*es*

Review Write the words *branch, branches, batch, batches, dress, dresses* and read them with children. Review that the -*es* ending means there is more than one. Remind children that when -*es* is added to a word, a syllable is added and the ending sound is /əz/.

Practice Write the following words: *box, bunch, brush, patch, mess.* Have children work in pairs to add -*es* to make the words plural and read the words aloud. Then have them write a sentence with each of the plural words.

Spelling

Word Sort with *ch, -tch, wh, ph*

Review Provide pairs of children with copies of the **Spelling Word Cards**. While one partner reads the words one at a time, the other partner should orally segment the word and then write the word. After reading all the words, partners should switch roles.

Practice Have children correct their own papers. Then have them sort the words by consonant digraph spelling pattern: *ch, -tch, wh, ph,* or none of these digraphs.

High-Frequency Words

around, by, many, place, walk

Review Display **Visual Vocabulary Cards** for high-frequency words *around, by, many, place, walk.* Have children Read/Spell/ Write each word.

→ Point to a word and call on a child to use it in a sentence.

→ Review last week's words using the same procedure.

Monitor and *Differentiate*

✔ **Quick Check**

Can children read and decode words with consonant digraphs *ch, -tch, wh, ph*?

Can children recognize and read high-frequency words?

⬇

Small Group Instruction

If No →	**Approaching**	Reteach pp. T368–T371
	ELL	Develop pp. T382–T389
If Yes →	**On Level**	Review pp. T376–T377
	Beyond Level	Extend pp. T380–T381

→ Language Arts

MINILESSON 5 Mins

Independent Writing

Go Digital

Writing

═ Make a capital letter.

Λ Add.

ⵑ Take out.

Proofreader's Marks

I see a fish.

Grammar

OBJECTIVES

CCSS With guidance and support from adults, focus on a topic, respond to questions and suggestions from peers, and add details to strengthen writing as needed. **W.1.5**

- Use irregular plural nouns
- Capitalize first word in a sentence
- Use periods at end of statements

ACADEMIC LANGUAGE

- *revise, delete, proofread*
- Cognate: *revisar*

Sentences That Explain

Revise

Explain to children that revising makes their ideas easier to understand.

Apply Writing Trait: Ideas Explain that as writers revise, they make sure all of their sentences are about one idea. Display the following sentences that explain information about the post office on a map:

1. The post office is by City Hall.

2. It sells stamps.

3. I like to get cards.

4. It is a place you can mail a package.

Read the sentences aloud. Guide children to identify the sentence that does not tell about the idea. Model deleting sentence 3.

 Peer Review Have children work in pairs to do a peer review. They should take notes about what they like most, questions they have for the author, and ideas they think the author could include. Have partners discuss these topics. Provide time for them to make revisions to their sentences.

Proofread/Edit

Apply Grammar Review proofreader's marks with children. Have them reread their drafts and fix mistakes. Remind them to make sure that:

→ all irregular plural nouns are spelled correctly.

→ the first word in each sentence is capitalized and statements end with periods.

→ all words are spelled correctly.

→ all sentences are complete.

 Peer Edit Next, have partners exchange their drafts and take turns reading for the mistakes above. Encourage partners to discuss and fix errors together as they read.

Final Draft

After children have edited their own papers and finished their peer edits, have them write their final draft. Encourage them to create or find a photo or other visual that relates to their writing. As children work, conference with them to provide guidance.

Grammar

Irregular Plural Nouns

1 Review Remind children that a plural noun names more than one, and some nouns change spelling when they are plural.

2 Practice Say the following sentences and have children tell you the correct noun to complete each sentence.

Two (man, men) sit at the desk. (men)

Three (women, woman) run around the block. (women)

I have two hands and two (foot, feet). (feet)

Six (child, children) play on the swings. (children)

 Talk About It Have partners work together to orally generate sentences with the words *people* and *mice*.

Mechanics: Capital Letters and Periods

1 Review Remind children that all statements begin with a capital letter and end with a period.

2 Practice Display the sentences below. Read each aloud. Have children fix the sentences as a class.

a Chick sat on an Egg? (A chick sat on an egg.)

my dog hid in the bush (My dog hid in the bush.)

Daily Wrap Up

→ Have children discuss the Essential Question using the oral vocabulary words. Ask: *How have you used a map this week?*

→ Prompt children to discuss the skills they practiced and learned today. Guide them to share examples of each skill.

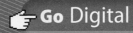

→ **Wrap Up the Week**
Integrate Ideas

RESEARCH AND INQUIRY

Follow the Map

OBJECTIVES

 Participate in shared research and writing projects (e.g., explore a number of "how-to" books on a given topic and use them to write a sequence of instructions). **W.1.7**

• Build background knowledge
• Research information using technology

ACADEMIC LANGUAGE
landmark, label

Make a Map

Review the steps in the research process. Tell children that today they will do a research project with a partner to learn more about maps.

STEP 1 Choose a Topic

Name areas or landmarks of your town to prompt brainstorming. Have children choose an area for which they would like to create a map.

STEP 2 Find Resources

Discuss how to use the selections, reference materials, and online sources to find out more about what to put on their maps. Have children use the Research Process Checklist online.

STEP 3 Keep Track of Ideas

Have children record their ideas in an Accordion Foldable®. Model recording details.

Dinah Zike's
FOLDABLES

Collaborative Conversations

Listen Carefully Review with children that as they engage in partner, small-group, and whole-group discussions, they should remember to:

→ always look at the speaker.

→ respect others by not interrupting them.

→ repeat others' ideas to check understanding.

STEP 4 **Create the Project: Map**

Explain the characteristics of a map.

→ **Locations** A map shows the location of places. In this project, the map will show the location of important streets, buildings, and other landmarks in your town, such as parks or rivers.

→ **Images** A map can have images that illustrate the information. For this project, your map will show images of important landmarks in your town, such as your school, big stores, and parks.

→ **Labels** A map can have labels. Your map will have labels that give the names of the streets and that identify the landmarks.

Have children create a map of their town or a section of town.

→ Guide them to label the streets and important features.

→ Have children display their maps. Give them the opportunity to comment on each others' maps.

ENGLISH LANGUAGE LEARNERS

SCAFFOLD

Beginning	Intermediate	Advanced/High
Use Sentence Frames Use sentence frames to help children discuss their maps. For example: *You can find _____ on this map.*	**Discuss** Guide children to focus on the most important details about their town. Ask: *What are some important places in your town? What are the most important streets?*	**Describe** Prompt children to elaborate on their maps. Ask them to explain why they chose to feature the landmarks and streets they did.

Materials

Reading/Writing Workshop
VOLUME 2

Literature Anthology
VOLUME 2

Literature Big Book
Me on the Map

Visual Vocabulary Cards
around
by
many
place
walk

Teaching Poster

Interactive Read-Aloud Cards

Word-Building Cards

Spelling Word Cards

→ Integrate Ideas

TEXT CONNECTIONS

Connect to Essential Question

OBJECTIVES

 Identify basic similarities and differences between two texts on the same topic (e.g., in illustrations, descriptions, or procedures). **RI.1.9**

• Develop answers to the Essential Question

• Make text connections to the world

ACADEMIC LANGUAGE

• *explore, identify, various*

• Cognates: *explorar, identificar, varios/as*

Text to Text

Remind children that all week they have been reading selections about how to find their way around. Tell them that now they can make connections across texts by thinking about how the selections were similar. Model comparing text using *Me on the Map* and *Which Way on the Map?*

Think Aloud Both selections are about maps. In *Me on the Map*, a girl explores maps of her room, her house, her street, her town, her state, her country, and Earth. In *Which Way on the Map?* readers explore a map of one town and identify different locations in that town.

 Complete the Organizer Have children use the graphic organizer on Teaching Poster 40 to organize the information from this week's selections.

→ Discuss and write about different types of information found on the maps in this week's selections.

→ Discuss various ways people use maps.

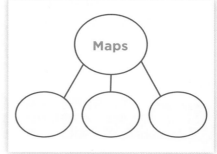
Teaching Poster

Text to Self

Have children talk about a time they or someone they were with used a map. *Where were you? What kind of map did you use? How did the map help you find your way around?*

Text to World

Provide a globe or world map. Point out your location. Then give children the opportunity to point to a place on the globe or map. *What location did you choose? Why? How might you get there?*

WRITE ABOUT READING *Analytical Writing*

OBJECTIVES

 Draw evidence from literary or informational texts to support analysis, reflection, and research. **W.4.9**

 Identify the reasons an author gives to support points in a text. **RI.1.8**

Analyze Main Topic and Key Details

Explain to children that as a group you will write about one of the selections that they have read this week.

Using the evidence in the text, think about how the author used key details to write about the topic.

Review the Main Topic and Details chart you completed for *Which Way On the Map?* Guide children to analyze the text evidence by asking "what" and "how" questions about the selection.

→ What details does the author give us about the main topic?

→ How did the author show what maps have on them?

→ What did you learn about maps from the selection?

Write an Analysis

Display the following sentence frames:

> *The author used the details _____ and _____ to explain the main topic.*
>
> *The author used _____ to show what maps have on them.*
>
> *The selection helped us learn that maps _____.*

Work with children to complete the sentence frames using details from *Which Way on the Map?*

Select another selection you have read this week. Work with children to complete similar sentence frames to write about the main topic and key details from the selection.

RESEARCH AND INQUIRY *SOCIAL STUDIES*

OBJECTIVES

 Participate in shared research and writing projects. **W.1.7**

Wrap Up the Project

 Guide children to share their maps. Have them use the Presentation Checklist online. *What important locations are on your map? How did you show them? Could someone use your map to find their way around?*

Word Work

Quick Review
Build Fluency: Sound-Spellings
Display the **Word-Building Cards:** *ch, tch, wh, ph, th, sh, ng, nd, nk, nt, st, sk, mp, u, e, ea, sp, sn, sl, cr, fr, tr, o, pl, fl, cl.* Have children say the sounds. Repeat, and vary the pace.

MINILESSON 5 Mins Phonemic Awareness

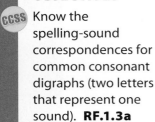

OBJECTIVES

CCSS Know the spelling-sound correspondences for common consonant digraphs (two letters that represent one sound). **RF.1.3a**

CCSS Decode regularly spelled one-syllable words. **RF.1.3b**

CCSS Read words with inflectional endings. **RF.1.3f**

Phoneme Blending

Review Guide children to blend phonemes to form words. *Listen as I say a group of sounds. Then blend those sounds to form a word.*

/ch/ /a/ /t/	/hw/ /e/ /n/	/p/ /u/ /n/ /ch/
/k/ /a/ /ch/	/g/ /r/ /a/ /f/	/hw/ /i/ /p/

Phoneme Segmentation

Review Guide children to segment phonemes in words. *I am going to say a word. Tell me the sounds you hear in the word.*

chill	graph	patch	pinch	fetch
which	itch	chest	when	inch

MINILESSON 5 Mins Phonics/Structural Analysis

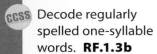

Blend and Build with *ch, -tch, wh, ph*

Review Have children read and say the words *chop, rich, itch, when,* and *graph.* Then have children follow the word-building routine with **Word-Building Cards** to build *whiz, whip, chip, hip, sip, snip, snitch, snatch, hatch, hat, chat, chin, pin, pinch, punch, lunch, crunch.*

Word Automaticity Help children practice word automaticity. Display decodable words and point to each word as children chorally read it. Test how many words children can read in one minute. Model blending words children miss.

Inflectional Ending *-es*

Review Have children explain when the *-es* ending is used. Then have children practice adding *-es* to form plural nouns, for words such as *lunch, patch, crutch, box, dish,* and *kiss.*

Go Digital

Phonemic Awareness

Phonics

Structural Analysis

Visual Glossary

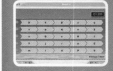

Fluency: Word Automaticity

Spelling

Word Sort with *ch, -tch, wh, ph*

Review Have children use the **Spelling Word Cards** to sort the weekly words by consonant digraphs. Remind children that four of the words do not have consonant digraphs *ch, -tch, wh,* or *ph.*

Assess Assess children on their abilities to spell words with consonant digraphs *ch, -tch, wh,* and *ph.* Say each word and provide a sentence so that children can hear the words used in a correct context. Then allow them time to write down the words. To challenge children, you may wish to provide an additional word in each word family in order to assess whether they understand the concept.

High-Frequency Words

around, by, many, place, walk

Review Display **Visual Vocabulary Cards** *around, by, many, place, walk.* Have children Read/Spell/Write each word. Have children write a sentence with each word.

Monitor and *Differentiate*

✓ Quick Check

Can children read and decode words with consonant digraphs *ch, -tch, wh, ph*?

Can children recognize and read high-frequency words?

⬇

Small Group Instruction

If No →	**Approaching**	Reteach pp. T368–T371
	ELL	Develop pp. T382–T389
If Yes →	**On Level**	Review pp. T376–T377
	Beyond Level	Extend pp. T380–T381

→ Language Arts

Independent Writing

OBJECTIVES

CCSS With guidance and support from adults, use a variety of digital tools to produce and publish writing, including in collaboration with peers. **W.1.6**

- Use irregular plural nouns
- Capitalize first word in a sentence
- Use periods at end of statements

ACADEMIC LANGUAGE

- *presentation, blog, organize*
- Cognates: *presentación, organizar*

Sentences That Explain

Prepare

Review guidelines for making presentations with children.

→ Provide time for children to finish preparing their presentations. Remind them to practice using their visuals if they have created any.

Present

Have children take turns giving presentations of their sentences. Remind them to speak clearly. When listening to other presenters, they should be polite and respectful, asking questions when appropriate and listening carefully when it is not appropriate to speak.

→ If possible, record the presentations so that children can self-evaluate.

Evaluate

Have children discuss their own presentations and evaluate their performance using the presentation rubric.

Use the teacher's rubric to evaluate children's writing. Have children add their writing to their Writer's Portfolio. Then have them discuss how they have changed and grown as writers this year.

Publish

After children finish presenting their sentences, discuss how they will publish their writing on a class blog. Guide them to use digital tools to create the blog. Suggest to children that you also post the map that illustrates the places they wrote about. Vote on how to organize the sentences, such as grouping students' writing by place.

Go Digital

Writing

Checklists

I see a fish.

Grammar

Grammar

Irregular Plural Nouns

1 Review Have children describe what plural nouns are and how they are used. Have them tell the difference between regular plural nouns and irregular plural nouns. Write and say the following sentence and have children tell you the plural nouns:

The children have fun playing chess with the men. (children, men)

Mice have four small feet. (mice, feet)

2 Practice Ask: *How do I know if a word is a plural noun?*

Write sentences that are missing irregular plural nouns. Read each sentence.

Two _____ use a map.

I see three _____ playing at school.

Have children work in pairs to complete each sentence with an irregular plural noun. Have pairs write the plural nouns on the board or dictate them to you to complete and share the sentences.

Mechanics: Capital Letters and Periods

1 Review Remind children that all statements begin with a capital letter and end with a period.

2 Practice Write the following sentences. Read each aloud. Have children fix the sentences.

the broth is Too Hot? (The broth is too hot.)

bread and fish are a Good lunch (Bread and fish are a good lunch.)

Wrap Up the Week

→ Review the Essential Question and encourage children to discuss using the oral vocabulary words.

→ Review with children that rereading parts of a selection and identifying the main topic and key details can help them better understand what they read.

→ Review words with consonant digraphs *ch*, *-tch*, *wh*, and *ph*.

→ Use the Visual Vocabulary Cards to review the Words to Know.

→ Remind children that nonfiction text explains facts about a topic.

Approaching Level

Leveled Reader:
How Maps Help

Lexile 130

 OBJECTIVES

 Identify the main topic and retell key details of a text. **RI.1.2**

Ⓒ With prompting and support, read informational texts appropriately complex for grade 1. **RI.1.10**

Reread for comprehension

Go
Digital

How Maps Help

Graphic Organizer

Retell

Before Reading

Preview and Predict

Have children turn to the title page. Read the title and the author's name and have children repeat. Preview the selection's photographs. Prompt children to predict what the selection might be about.

Review Genre: Informational Text/Nonfiction

Have children recall that informational text gives facts and details about real places, people, things, or events.

ESSENTIAL QUESTION

Remind children of the Essential Question: *How can you find your way around?* Set a purpose for reading: *Let's read to find out how maps help us find our way around.*

Remind children that as they read a selection, they can ask questions about what they do not understand or what they want to know more about.

During Reading

Guided Comprehension

As children whisper read *How Maps Help*, monitor and provide guidance, correcting blending and modeling the key strategies and skills.

Strategy: Reread

Remind children that sometimes they may misread a word or miss an important point. When they do, they can reread. Model using the strategy on page 4. Say: *The question at the end of the page asks how we can find "them." Who does them refer to? I'll reread the whole page.* Reread the page. *Now I see. Them refers to the animals in the park.*

Skill: Main Topic and Key Details

Remind children that the main topic is what the selection is about. The key details give information about the main topic. While reading, ask: *What is this selection mostly about? What do the details have in common?* Display the Main Topic and Key Details chart for children to copy.

Model recording children's answers in the boxes. Have children record the answers in their own charts.

Think Aloud As I read page 5, I see that the map shows where the animals live. This is a key detail. I'll write this on my chart. Then I'll look for more details. I can use them to help me identify the main topic.

Guide children to use the text and photographs to complete the chart.

After Reading

Respond to Reading

Have children complete the Respond to Reading on page 12.

Retell

Have children take turns retelling the selection using the **Retelling Cards** as a guide. Help children make a personal connection: *When have you used a map? What was it for?*

Model Fluency

Read the sentences, one at a time. Have children chorally repeat. Point out to children the phrasing you use when reading patterns or repeated phrases, such as the questions at the end of pages 4, 6, 8, and 10.

Apply Have children practice repeated readings with partners. Provide feedback as needed.

PAIRED READ ...

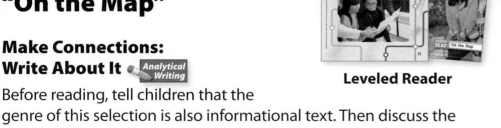

Leveled Reader

"On the Map"

Make Connections: Write About It *Analytical Writing*

Before reading, tell children that the genre of this selection is also informational text. Then discuss the Compare Texts direction. After reading, ask children to make connections between the information they learned from "On the Map" and *How Maps Help*. Ask: *What did both selections tell you about how maps help?*

FOCUS ON SOCIAL STUDIES

Children can extend their knowledge of maps by completing the social studies activity on page 16.

Literature Circles

Lead children in conducting a literature circle using the Thinkmark questions to guide the discussion. You may wish to discuss what children have learned about maps from both selections in the Leveled Reader.

Level Up

Level-up lessons available online.

IF children can read *How Maps Help* Approaching Level with fluency and correctly answer the Respond to Reading questions,

THEN tell children that they will read a more detailed selection.

- Use pages 5–7 of *How Maps Help* On Level to model using Teaching Poster 29 to list key details.

- Have children read the selection, checking their comprehension by using the graphic organizer.

Approaching Level

Phonemic Awareness

PHONEME SEGMENTATION

 TIER 2

OBJECTIVES

Segment spoken single-syllable words into their complete sequence of individual sounds (phonemes). **RF.1.2d**

 I Do Tell children they will be segmenting and counting sounds in words. *Listen as I say a word:* chop. *I will say each sound in* chop *and place one marker in each box of the* **Response Board** *for each sound. Listen:* /ch/ /o/ /p/. *Place three markers. Now I will count the markers. There are three sounds in* chop: /ch/ /o/ /p/.

 We Do *Let's do some together. I will say a word. Put a marker in each box for each sound. Listen:* /riiich/. *How many sounds do you hear? The sounds in* rich *are* /r/ /i/ /ch/. Repeat for these words:

pitch   graph   which   check   much

 You Do *It's your turn. I'll say some words. Put a marker in each box for each sound. Tell me the sounds.*

whip   branch   chat   match   hatch

PHONEME BLENDING

TIER 2

OBJECTIVES

Orally produce single-syllable words by blending sounds (phonemes), including consonant blends. **RF.1.2b**

 I Do Tell children they will be blending sounds to say words. *Listen as I say three sounds:* /ch/ /i/ /k/. *I'm going to blend the sounds together:* /ch/ /iii/ /k/, /chiiik/, chick.

 **We Do** *Let's do some together. Repeat these sounds:* /k/ /a/ /ch/. *Now let's blend the sounds:* /kaaach/, catch. Repeat the routine:

/g/ /r/ /a/ /f/   /hw/ /i/ /p/   /l/ /u/ /n/ /ch/   /ch/ /e/ /s/ /t/

 You Do *It's your turn. I'll say some sounds. Blend the sounds.*

/m/ /a/ /ch/   /hw/ /e/ /n/   /ch/ /i/ /m/ /p/   /i/ /n/ /ch/

PHONEME SEGMENTATION

OBJECTIVES

 Segment spoken single-syllable words into their complete sequence of individual sounds (phonemes). **RF.1.2d**

 I Do Explain to children that they will be segmenting, or separating, the sounds in words. *Listen as I say a word:* whiz. *I hear three sounds in* whiz: /hw/ /i/ /z/.

 We Do *Let's do some together. Listen :* inch. *What sounds do you hear? The sounds are:* /i/ /n/ /ch/. Repeat for:

crutch   chat   graph   ranch   such   whale

 You Do *Now it's your turn. I'll say a word. Tell me the sounds.*

chin   bench   white   which   chimp   hatch

PHONEME ADDITION

OBJECTIVES

 Isolate and pronounce initial, medial vowel, and final sounds (phonemes) in spoken single-syllable words. **RF.1.2c**

 I Do Tell children they will be adding phonemes. *Listen:* inch. *I will add /p/ to the beginning of* inch. *Listen* /p/, pinch. Inch *with /p/ at the beginning is* pinch.

 We Do *Let's do some together. Listen:* itch. *Let's add /r/ to the beginning of* itch. *Say it with me:* /rrr/ /iiich/, rich. Repeat for:

is, /hw/ (whiz)   itch, /d/ (ditch)   ranch, /b/ (branch)

You Do *It's your turn. Add the sound I say to make a new word.*

itch, /hw/ (which)   own, /f/ (phone)   arm, /ch/ (charm)

 ENGLISH LANGUAGE LEARNERS

For the **ELLS** who need **phonemic awareness**, **phonics** and **fluency** practice, use scaffolding methods as necessary to ensure children understand the meaning of the words. Refer to the Language Transfer Handbook for phonics elements that may not transfer in children's native languages.

→ Approaching Level

Phonics

CONNECT *ch, -tch* TO */ch/*, *wh* TO */hw/*, *ph* TO */f/*

 OBJECTIVES

Know and apply grade-level phonics and word analysis skills in decoding words. **RF.1.3**

I Do Display **Word-Building Card** *ch*. *These letters are lowercase* c *and* h. *Together they stand for /ch/. I am going to trace the letters* ch *while I say /ch/.* Trace *ch* while saying */ch/* five times. Repeat with *-tch, wh, ph*.

We Do *Now do it with me.* Have children take turns saying */ch/* while tracing *ch*. Repeat with *-tch, wh, ph*.

You Do Have children connect *ch* to */ch/* by saying */ch/* as they trace *ch* on paper. Then ask them to write *ch* while saying */ch/* five to ten times. Repeat with *-tch, wh, ph*.

Repeat, connecting the digraphs with their sounds throughout the week.

BLEND WORDS WITH *ch, -tch, wh, ph*

  OBJECTIVES

Decode regularly spelled one-syllable words. **RF.1.3b**

I Do Display Word-Building Cards *i, n, ch*. *This is the letter* i. *It stands for /i/. This is the letter* n. *It stands for /n/. These are the letters* c *and* h. *Together they stand for /ch/. I'll blend the sounds: /iiinnnch/,* inch.

We Do Guide children to blend the sounds and read: *chip, which, graph, catch*.

You Do Have children use Word-Building cards to blend and read: *itch, champ, whip, bunch, chop, pitch*.

Repeat, blend additional words with *ch, -tch, wh,* or *ph*.

You may wish to review Phonics with **ELL** using this section.

BUILD WORDS WITH *ch, -tch, wh, ph*

OBJECTIVES

 Decode regularly spelled one-syllable words. **RF.1.3b**

 Display Word-Building Cards *i, tch*. These are the letters i, t, c, h. I *stands for /i/.* T, c, *and* h *together stand for /ch/. I will blend /i/ /ch/ together: /iiich/,* itch. *The word is* itch.

 Now let's do some together. Place *p* in front of *itch. Let's blend and read this word: /p/ /i/ /ch/, /piiich/,* pitch. Change the *i* in *pitch* to *a. Let's blend and read this word: /paaach/,* patch.

 Have children build the words: *latch, patch, pitch, witch, which, whip, chip.*

BLEND WORDS WITH *ch, -tch, wh, ph*

OBJECTIVES

 Decode regularly spelled one-syllable words. **RF.1.3b**

 Display Word-Building Cards *wh, e, n.* These are the letters w *and* h. *Together they stand for /hw/. This is the letter* e. *It stands for /e/. This is the letter* n. *It stands for /n/. Listen as I blend: /hweeennn/,* when.

 Guide children to blend and read: *inch, pitch, chat,* and *whip.*

 Display the words to the right. Have children blend the words.

itch	whiff	chop	rich	chill	graph
whiz	much	catch	bunch	chest	branch
ship	chip	clip	thin	chin	chimp
thank	dish	crunch	which	thing	chunk

Chimp and Chick are the champs.

Chuck and Mitch sit on a bench and chat.

When did Chad make this graph?

BUILD FLUENCY WITH PHONICS

Sound-Spellings Fluency

Display the following Word-Building Cards: *ch, tch, wh, ph, th, sh, ng, nd, nk, nt, st, sk, mp, u, e, ea, sp, sn, sl, cr, fr, tr, o, pl, fl, cl.* Have children chorally say the sounds. Repeat and vary the pace.

Fluency in Connected Text

Have children review *Which Way on the Map?* in their Reading/Writing Workshop. Identify words with *ch, -tch, wh,* and *ph.* Blend words as needed.

Have children reread the selection on their own or with a partner.

→ Approaching Level

Structural Analysis

REVIEW INFLECTIONAL ENDING -es

OBJECTIVES

 Know and apply grade-level phonics and word analysis skills in decoding words. **RF.1.3**

Use words with inflectional ending -es

 I Do Review with children that we add -es to words that end in *ch, tch, sh, x, z*, or *ss* to make them mean "more than one." Write *dishes*. Read the word aloud. *The* -es *ending tells me that there is more than one dish. I'm going to use* dish *and* dishes *in sentences. I have one dish. She has three dishes.*

 We Do Write *foxes*. *Let's say this word:* foxes. *If we look at* foxes, *is there a word we know? I know that* -es *tells us that there is more than one fox. Let's use* fox *and* foxes *in sentences.*

 You Do Have children work with partners. Display words with -es endings. Ask children to create sentences that use both forms of the word correctly.

Repeat Have children write sentences for words with es.

RETEACH INFLECTIONAL ENDING -es

OBJECTIVES

 Know and apply grade-level phonics and word analysis skills in decoding words. **RF.1.3**

Use words with inflectional ending -es

 I Do Write *bench* and *benches*. Read the words aloud. Circle the letters *es* in *benches*. *The word* benches *means "more than one bench." We add* -es *to words that end in* ch, tch, sh, x, z, *or* ss *to make them mean "more than one."*

 We Do Write and read aloud *buzz*. *Let's add* -es. *Say* buzzes *with me:* buzzes. *Now let's use* buzz *and* buzzes *in sentences.*

Repeat this routine with the following examples:

box   lunch   dress

 You Do Have children add -es to nouns that end in *ch sh, x, s,* or *ss. Add* -es *to each word. Then say each word and use it in a sentence.* Guide children as needed.

patch   brush   bunch

Repeat Add -es to nouns that end in *ch tch, sh, x, z,* or *ss.*

High-Frequency Words

REVIEW

CCSS

OBJECTIVES

Recognize and read grade-appropriate irregularly spelled words. **RF.1.3g**

Review *around, by, many, place, walk*

 I Do Use **High-Frequency Word Cards** to **Read/Spell/Write** each high-frequency word. Use each word orally in a sentence.

 We Do Guide children to Read/Spell/Write each word on their **Response Boards**. Work together to generate oral sentences for the words.

 You Do Have partners work together to Read/Spell/Write the words *around, by, many, place,* and *walk.* Then have them use the words in sentences.

RETEACH

 CCSS

OBJECTIVES

Recognize and read grade-appropriate irregularly spelled words. **RF.1.3g**

 I Do Review the high-frequency words using the Read/Spell/Write routine. Write a sentence on the board for each word.

 We Do Guide children to use the Read/Spell/Write routine. Ask them to complete sentence starters: **(1)** *We run around the _____.* **(2)** *I am standing over by the _____.* **(3)** *She has many _____.* **(4)** *Is this a good place to _____?* **(5)** *Do you walk _____?*

 You Do Ask children to close their eyes, picture the word, and write it as they see it. Have children self-correct.

CUMULATIVE REVIEW

 CCSS

OBJECTIVES

Recognize and read grade-appropriate irregularly spelled words. **RF.1.3g**

Review previously taught high-frequency words

 I Do Display the High-Frequency Word Cards from the previous weeks. Use the Read/Spell/Write routine to review each word.

 We Do Guide children as they Read/Spell/Write the words on their Response Boards. Complete sentences for each word, such as: *Please eat _____.*

 You Do Show each card and have children chorally repeat. Mix and repeat.

Fluency Display the High-Frequency Word Cards. Point to the words in random order. Have children chorally read. Repeat at a faster pace.

Approaching Level

Comprehension

READ FOR FLUENCY

TIER 2

OBJECTIVES

 Read grade-level text orally with accuracy, appropriate rate, and expression. **RF.1.4b**

I Do Read pages 1 and 2 of the Practice Book selection. Model using appropriate phrasing when reading repeated patterns or phrases.

We Do Read the rest of the Practice Book selection and have children echo read each sentence after you. Point out how you read the repeated patterns and phrases.

You Do Have children work with a partner and take turns rereading the book aloud. Remind them to read the repeated patterns and phrases smoothly.

IDENTIFY KEY DETAILS

TIER 2

OBJECTIVES

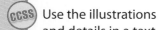 Ask and answer questions about key details in a text. **RI.1.1**

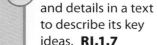 Use the illustrations and details in a text to describe its key ideas. **RI.1.7**

I Do Remind children that they have been reading informational text. Point out that as they read, they should look for key details, or important information. *Key details give me important information about the story. I look for key details in the pictures and words.*

We Do Read the first page of the Practice Book selection aloud. Model identifying details. *I read that many chicks hatch. Where do the chicks hatch?*

You Do Guide children to read the rest of the Practice Book selection. Prompt them to find and discuss details in the text and the pictures.

REVIEW MAIN TOPIC AND KEY DETAILS

OBJECTIVES

 Identify the main topic and retell key details of a text. **RI.1.2**

 I Do

Remind children that key details give important information about the main topic of an informational text. *When I read, I look for key details in the pictures and words. Then I use the key details to figure out the main topic. The main topic is what the selection is about.*

 We Do

Read the first two pages of the Practice Book selection together. Pause to discuss key details in the pictures and words. *What details do you see? What details do you read? We learn that chicks hatch on a farm. We also learn what kids do during recess.* Help children record the information on a Main Topic and Key Details chart.

 You Do

Have partners read the rest of the selection. Stop after each page to ask: *What key details do you learn on this page?* Help children add the details to the chart. Then help them use the details to figure out the main topic.

SELF-SELECTED READING

OBJECTIVES

 Identify the main topic and retell key details of a text. **RI.1.2**

 With prompting and support, read informational text appropriately complex for grade 1. **RI.1.10**

Apply the strategy and skill to read a text

Read Independently

Have children pick an informational text for sustained silent reading. Remind them to:

→ look for key details to help them understand what they read.

→ use details to identify the main topic, or what most of the selection is about.

→ reread to help them understand and remember details.

Read Purposefully

Have children record the key details on a Main Topic and Key Details chart. After reading, guide children to participate in a group discussion about the selection they read. Guide children to:

→ share their charts.

→ explain why the selection was informational text.

→ discuss how rereading helped them use key details to identify the main idea.

→ On Level

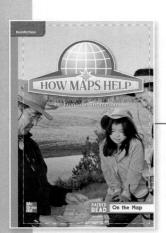

Lexile 230

OBJECTIVES

 Identify the main topic and retell key details of a text. **RI.1.2**

With prompting and support, read informational texts appropriately complex for grade 1. **RI.1.10**

Reread for comprehension

Leveled Reader: *How Maps Help*

Before Reading

Preview and Predict

Have children turn to the title page. Read the title and the author's name and have children repeat. Preview the selection's photographs. Prompt children to predict what the selection might be about.

Review Genre: Informational Text/Nonfiction

Have children recall that informational nonfiction text gives facts and details about real places, people, things, and events.

ESSENTIAL QUESTION

Remind children of the Essential Question: *How can you find your way around?* Set a purpose for reading: *Let's read to find out what we can learn from the maps in this selection.*

Remind children that as they read a selection, they can ask questions about what they do not understand or what they want to know more about.

During Reading

Guided Comprehension

As children whisper read *How Maps Help* monitor and provide guidance, correcting blending and modeling the key strategies and skills. Prompt children to use context to self-correct word recognition and understanding.

Strategy: Reread

Remind children that sometimes they may misread a word or miss an important point. They can reread the passage or an earlier part to make sure they understand. Model using the strategy on page 2. Say: *I read this page too quickly and want to be sure I understand why people use maps.* Reread the page. *How do maps help us?*

Skill: Main Topic and Key Details

Remind children that the main topic is the subject. The key details give information about the main topic. After reading, ask: *What are some key details we learned about maps?* Display a Main Topic and Key Details chart for children to copy.

Go Digital

How Maps Help

Main Topic		
Detail	Detail	Detail

Graphic Organizer

Retell

Model recording answers for children. Have children copy the answers into their own charts.

Think Aloud As I read, I will look for the important, or key, details. I see on page 5 the map shows where animals live. Page 7 shows trails on a map. I can use these details to help me figure out the main topic.

As children read, prompt them to complete the chart.

After Reading

Respond to Reading

Have children complete the Respond to Reading on page 12.

Retell

Have children take turns retelling the selection using the **Retelling Cards** as a guide. Help children make a connection by asking: *Have you or your family ever used a map? What did the map show? How did it help?*

Model Fluency

Read the sentences one at a time. Have children chorally repeat. Point out to children the phrasing you use when reading patterns or repeated phrases.

Apply Have children practice reading with partners. Tell them to use context to confirm and self-correct word recognition and understanding.

PAIRED READ ...

Leveled Reader

"On the Map"

Make Connections: Write About It

Before reading, say: *This selection's genre is also informational text.* Discuss the Compare Texts direction. Ask children to make connections between "On the Map" and *How Maps Help. What information is on both maps? How are they different?*

FOCUS ON SOCIAL STUDIES

Children can extend their knowledge of maps by completing the social studies activity on page 16.

Literature Circles

Lead children in conducting a literature circle using the Thinkmark questions to guide the discussion. You may wish to discuss what children have learned about maps from both selections in the Leveled Reader.

Level Up

Level-up lessons available online.

IF children can read *How Maps Help* On Level with fluency and correctly answer the Respond to Reading questions,

THEN tell children that they will read a more detailed selection.

- Use pages 5 and 7 of *How Maps Help* Beyond Level to model using Teaching Poster 29 to list key details.

- Have children read the selection, checking their comprehension by using the graphic organizer.

On Level

Phonics

BUILD WORDS WITH CONSONANT DIGRAPHS *ch, -tch, wh, ph*

OBJECTIVES

Decode regularly spelled one-syllable words. **RF.1.3b**

Build and decode words with consonant digraphs *ch, -tch, wh, ph*

I Do

Display **Word-Building Cards** *ch, i, n.* These are the letters c, h, i, n. *The letters* ch *together stand for /ch/,* i *stands for /i/,* n *stands /n/. I will blend the sounds together: /chiiinnn/,* chin. *The word is* chin.

We Do

Now let's do one together. Change *n* to *p. Let's blend and read the new word: /ch/ /i/ /p/, /chiiip/,* chip. *The new word is* chip.

You Do

Have children build and blend these words: *whip, which, rich, ranch, branch, brunch, crunch, crutch.*

Repeat with additional words with consonant digraphs *ch, -tch, wh,* or *ph.*

High-Frequency Words

REVIEW WORDS

OBJECTIVES

Recognize and read grade-appropriate irregularly spelled words. **RF.1.3g**

Review high-frequency words *around, by, many, place, walk*

I Do

Use the **Read/Spell/Write** routine to review *around, by, many, place,* and *walk.* Use each word orally in a sentence.

We Do

Guide children to Read/Spell/Write each word using their **Response Boards.** Work together to create oral sentences for the words.

You Do

Have partners work together to do the Read/Spell/Write routine on their own using the words *around, by, many, place,* and *walk.* Have them write sentences about this week's stories. Make sure that they include at least one high-frequency word in each sentence.

Comprehension

REVIEW MAIN TOPIC AND KEY DETAILS

OBJECTIVES

Identify the main topic and retell key details of a text. **RI.1.2**

 I Do Remind children that key details give important information about the main topic of an informational text. *When we read an informational text, we look for key details in the words and pictures. Key details help us identify the main topic, or what the selection is mostly about.*

 We Do Read the first page of the Practice Book selection aloud. Discuss key details in the words and pictures. *Where are the chicks? What do they do?*

 You Do Guide children to read the rest of the Practice Book selection. Remind them to look for key details as they read. Then have partners use the details to identify the main topic.

SELF-SELECTED READING

OBJECTIVES

With prompting and support, read informational texts appropriately complex for grade 1. **RI.1.10**

Apply the strategy and skill to read a text

Read Independently

Have children pick an informational text for sustained silent reading. Remind them to:

→ look for key details to help them understand what they read.

→ use details to identify the main topic.

→ reread to help them understand and remember details.

Read Purposefully

Have children record details on a Main Topic and Key Details chart. After reading, guide partners to:

→ share and compare their charts.

→ discuss how rereading helped them use key details to identify the main idea.

→ discuss how nonfiction text is different from fiction selections.

→ Beyond Level

Lexile 420

OBJECTIVES

 Identify the main topic and retell key details of a text. **RI.1.2**

 With prompting and support, read informational texts appropriately complex for grade 1. **RI.1.10**

Reread for comprehension

Leveled Reader:
How Maps Help

Go Digital

How Maps Help

Main Topic

Detail	Detail	Detail

Graphic Organizer

Before Reading

Preview and Predict

Read the title and the author's name. Have children preview the title page and the photographs. Ask: *What do you think this book will be about?*

Review Genre: Informational Text/Nonfiction

Have children recall that informational text gives facts and details about real places, people, things, and events. Prompt children to name key characteristics of informational text. Tell them to look for these characteristics as they read the Leveled Reader.

ESSENTIAL QUESTION

Remind children of the Essential Question: *How can you find your way around?* Set a purpose for reading: *Let's find out how maps help us find our way around.*

During Reading

Guided Comprehension

Have children whisper read *How Maps Help*. Have them place self-stick notes next to difficult words. Remind children that when they come to an unfamiliar word, they can look for familiar spellings. They will need to break longer words into smaller chunks and sound out each part.

Monitor children's reading. Stop periodically and ask open-ended questions to facilitate rich discussion, such as: *What does the author want us to know about maps?* Build on children's responses to develop deeper understanding of the text.

Strategy: Reread

Remind children that sometimes they may misread a word or miss an important point. Say: *If you get confused or do not understand some information or what is happening, reread the part that you do not understand. You may need to read text earlier in the selection as well.*

Skill: Main Topic and Key Details

Remind children that the main topic is the subject. The key details give information about the main topic. After reading, ask: *How did the key details help you figure out the main topic?* Display a Main Topic and Key Details chart for children to copy.

Model how to record the information. Have children fill in their chart.

Think Aloud On page 4, I read that maps can help us find animals in the park. This is a key detail. I can look for more key details to determine the main topic. I'll write the details and main topic in my chart.

After Reading

Respond to Reading

Have children complete the Respond to Reading on page 12.

Retell

Have children take turns retelling the selection. Help them make a personal connection by writing about a time when they used a map. *When have you used a map? How did it help you?*

PAIRED READ ...

Leveled Reader

"On the Map"

Make Connections: Write About It ● *Analytical Writing*

Before reading "On the Map," have children preview the title page and prompt them to identify the genre. Discuss the Compare Texts direction.

After reading, have children work with a partner to discuss the information they learned in "On the Map" and *How Maps Help*. Ask children to make connections by comparing and contrasting the selections.

FOCUS ON SOCIAL STUDIES

Children can extend their knowledge of maps by completing the social studies activity on page 16.

Literature Circles

Lead children in conducting a literature circle using the Thinkmark questions to guide the discussion. You may wish to discuss what children have learned about maps from both selections in the Leveled Reader.

Gifted and Talented

SYNTHESIZE Challenge children to write about how they might find a place if there were no maps. Encourage them to include personal experiences about getting lost and tell how a "no maps" world would affect how people travel.

EXTEND Have children use facts they learned from the week or do additional research to find out more about maps.

Beyond Level

Vocabulary

ORAL VOCABULARY: SYNONYMS

OBJECTIVES

 Use sentence-level context as a clue to the meaning of a word or phrase. **L.1.4a**

Determine the meaning of domain-specific words

 I Do Review the meaning of the oral vocabulary word *locate*. Write the sentence: *I can locate the school on the map.* Read the sentence aloud, and have children repeat. Discuss what it means to *locate*.

Remind children that a synonym is a word that means almost the same thing as another word. *To locate something means to find it. Synonyms for* locate *are* find, discover, detect, *or* spot.

 We Do Have children take turns using the words *find*, *discover*, *detect*, and *spot* in sentences. Help them understand the differences between the words.

 You Do Have children draw pictures or maps that illustrate the sentences they created using the synonyms above.

Gifted and Talented **Extend** Have partners use the words *find*, *discover*, *detect*, and *spot* in a short skit. Suggest that the skit focuses on two characters trying to locate something. Challenge them to use the synonyms for *locate*.

Comprehension

REVIEW MAIN TOPIC AND KEY DETAILS

OBJECTIVES

Identify the main topic and retell key details of a text. **RI.1.2**

 I Do Remind children that they should look for key details to help them figure out the main topic of informational texts. Prompt them to explain that the main topic is what the selection is mostly about. *How can key details help you figure out the main topic?*

 We Do Guide children in reading the first page of the Practice Book selection aloud. Prompt them to discuss key details. *What important details did you read and see? Why are they important?*

 You Do Have children read the rest of the Practice Book selection independently. Remind them to look for key details and use the details to identify the main topic.

SELF-SELECTED READING

OBJECTIVES

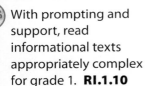
With prompting and support, read informational texts appropriately complex for grade 1. **RI.1.10**

Apply the strategy and skill to read a text

Read Independently

Have children pick an informational text for sustained silent reading. Remind them to look for key details that will help them figure out the main idea.

Read Purposefully

Have children record important details on a Main Topic and Key Details chart. After reading, guide children to:

→ share and compare their charts with partners.

→ record information about the selection and what they learned from it in a reading response journal.

 Independent Study Have children create a book poster for an important scene in the selection they read. Challenge them to write a few sentences about their selection and why they chose to illustrate the scene.

English Language Learners

Reading/Writing Workshop

 OBJECTIVES

 Identify the main topic and retell key details of a text. **RI.1.2**

Ccss With prompting and support, read informational texts appropriately complex for grade 1. **RI.1.10**

Shared Read
Which Way on the Map?

Go Digital

Which Way on the Map?

Main Topic		
Detail	Detail	Detail

Graphic Organizer

Before Reading

Build Background

Read the Essential Question: *How can you find your way around?*

→ Explain the meaning of the Essential Question. If possible, display a map and say: *I can use a map when I want to find a certain place or location. Some maps use small pictures to show buildings. I can use a map to find the street names and figure out where to go.*

→ **Model an answer:** *If I want to find the library, I can use a map. First, I look for the picture or name of the building. Then I look for the street names. I can follow the streets and figure out where to turn.*

→ Ask children a question that ties the Essential Question to their own background knowledge. *What maps have you seen? What did they look like?* Ask partners to share their answers.

During Reading

Interactive Question-Response

→ Ask questions that help children understand the meaning of the text after each paragraph.

→ Reinforce the meanings of key vocabulary by providing meanings embedded in the questions.

→ Ask children questions that require them to use key vocabulary.

→ Reinforce the comprehension strategies and skills of the week by modeling.

Which Way on the Map?

Pages 94–95

Point to the title. *Listen as I read the title of this nonfiction selection.* Point to each word as you read it. *This title asks a question. Let's read it together:* "Which Way on the Map?"

Point to the picture of the map. *This picture shows a map. Why do people use maps?* (to learn how to get somewhere) *A map usually shows streets and roads. Some show places, such as buildings, too. What places are on this map?* (school, playground, post office)

Pages 96–97

Listen as I reread the first sentence: "Mitch and Steph live in a big town." *Point to the map on page 97. This is a map of their town. It shows buildings in their town.*

Explain and Model High-Frequency Words
Point to the word *walk* and have children say it with you. *Let's say the letters in this word: w, a, l, k. Show me how you walk.*

 What places do you see on the map?

Pages 98–99

Listen as I read the first two sentences: "This place has red bricks. Many children go here." *What do you think this place is?* (school) *Let's find the picture of the school on the map.*

Explain and Model the Skill *The words tell me that Mitch and Steph go to this school. This is a key detail that could help me figure out the main topic.*

Explain and Model the Phonics Write: *Mitch, Steph.* Say each name and have children repeat. Then circle the letters *-tch* and *-ph. In the name* Mitch, *the letters* tch *stand for the /ch/ sound. In the name* Steph, *the letters* ph *stand for the /f/ sound.*

 Map the way you get to school each day. What buildings do you pass?

Pages 100–101

Let's look at the photo on page 100. What is this place? (playground) *Point to the first sentence. Let's read this sentence together:* "This place is by a lake." *What do you see at a lake?* (water, rocks, trees, fish)

Listen as I read what people do at this place: "People chat on benches. Mitch and Steph will run and play catch." *What does the word* chat *mean?* (talk) *What do you use to play catch?* (ball) *Let's pretend to play catch.* Role-play throwing and catching a ball with children.

 How do you get to the playground from school? How do you get there from home?

Pages 102–103

Let's look at the photo. This place is the post office. Say it with me: post office. *What do people do there?* (buy stamps, mail letters and packages) *Find the post office on the map.*

Explain and Model the Strategy *If something in the selection doesn't make sense, you can reread and figure it out. You can also look at the illustrations to help. If you don't understand what people do at a post office, reread the text and think about what it means. The text tells us that Mitch and Steph got stamps and dropped off a letter in the box.*

 How can a map help people? (People can use a map to find a place and figure out how to get there.)

After Reading

Make Connections

→ Review the Essential Question.

→ English Language Learners

Lexile 60

 OBJECTIVES

Identify the main topic and retell key details of a text. **RI.1.2**

 With prompting and support, read informational texts appropriately complex for grade 1. **RI.1.10**

Reread for comprehension

ACADEMIC LANGUAGE

reread

Leveled Reader:
How Maps Help

Before Reading

Preview

Read the title. Ask: *What is the title? Say it again*. Repeat with the author's name. Preview the photographs. Have children describe the photos. Use simple language to tell about each page. Follow with questions, such as: *What do we use maps for?*

ESSENTIAL QUESTION

Remind children of the Essential Question: *How can you find your way around?* Say: *Let's read to find out how maps help us find our way around.* Encourage children to ask for help when they do not understand a word or phrase.

During Reading

Interactive Question-Response

Pages 2–3 *Let's read these pages together. Why do we need a map?* (We are at a park.) *Find the word that tells the size of the park.* (big) *Look at the photo. Which park are we visiting?* (Yellowstone National Park)

Pages 4–5 *Look at the pictures on page 4. What animals are in the park?* (deer, beaver, eagle) *Now look at the map on page 5. With a partner, point to the places where you can locate each animal.*

Pages 6–7 *Look at the picture on page 6. What is the family doing?* (hiking; walking) *How did they know where to find hiking trails?* (They used a map.) *Trace the three hiking trails on the map on page 7.*

Pages 8–9 *A family is having a picnic. How did they know where to find a picnic place?* (They used a map. It has a picnic table symbol next to the places with eating areas.) *Look at the map on page 9. How many picnic places are located in the park?* (twelve)

Pages 10–11 *The family is ready to go home. How will they find their way out of the park?* (They are looking at a map.) *How do maps help us when we visit a big place like the park?*

Go Digital

How Maps Help

Graphic Organizer

Retell

After Reading

Respond to Reading

Revisit the Essential Question. Ask children to work with partners to answer the questions on page 12. Pair children with peers of varying language abilities.

Retell

Model retelling using the **Retelling Card** prompts. Say: *Look at the photographs. Use details to help you retell the selection.* Help children make personal connections by asking: *When have you or someone you know used a map?*

Phrasing Fluency: Patterns and Repeated Phrases

Read the pages in the book, one at a time. Help children echo read the pages expressively and with appropriate phrasing. Remind them to use appropriate phrasing when reading patterns or repeated phrases.

Apply Have children practice reading with partners. Pair children with peers of varying language abilities. Provide feedback as needed.

PAIRED READ ...

"On the Map"

Make Connections: Write About It

Leveled Reader

Before reading, tell children to note that this text is nonfiction. Then discuss the Compare Texts direction.

After reading, ask children to make connections between the information they learned from "On the Map" and *How Maps Help.* Prompt children by providing a sentence frame: *Maps help us _____.*

FOCUS ON SOCIAL STUDIES

Children can extend their knowledge of maps by completing the social studies activity on page 16.

Literature Circles

Lead children in conducting a literature circle using the Thinkmark questions to guide the discussion. You may wish to discuss what children have learned about maps from both selections in the Leveled Reader.

Level Up

Level-up lessons available online.

IF children can read *How Maps Help* **ELL Level** with fluency and correctly answer the Respond to Reading questions,

THEN tell children that they will read a more detailed version of this selection.

• Use pages 5 and 7 of *How Maps Help* **On Level** to model using Teaching Poster 29 to list key details.

• Have children read the selection, checking their comprehension by using the teaching poster.

English Language Learners
Vocabulary

PRETEACH ORAL VOCABULARY

OBJECTIVES

 Produce complete sentences when appropriate to task and situation. **SL.1.6**

LANGUAGE OBJECTIVE

Use oral vocabulary words

 I Do Display images from the **Visual Vocabulary Cards** one at a time to preteach the oral vocabulary words *locate* and *route*.

 We Do Display each image again and explain how it illustrates or demonstrates the word. Model using sentences to describe each image.

You Do Display the words again. Have partners talk about how the picture demonstrates the word.

Beginning	Intermediate	Advanced/High
Have children draw pictures for the words. Say sentences about children's pictures for them to repeat.	Help children act out each word. Then say a sentence frame about the actions for children to complete.	Have partners draw or cut pictures from magazines to illustrate each word. Have them use their pictures to make a collage.

PRETEACH ELL VOCABULARY

OBJECTIVES

 Produce complete sentences when appropriate to task and situation. **SL.1.6**

LANGUAGE OBJECTIVE

Use ELL vocabulary words

 I Do Display images from the Visual Vocabulary Cards one at a time and follow the routine to preteach the ELL Vocabulary words *direction* and *location*. Say each word and have children repeat it. Define the word in English.

We Do Display each image again and explain how it illustrates or demonstrates the word. Model using sentences to describe the image.

 You Do Display the word again and have children say the word and then spell it. Provide opportunities for children to use the words in speaking and writing. Provide sentence starters.

Beginning	Intermediate	Advanced/High
Say a sentence about an image. Help children say sentences about their pictures.	Ask questions about the images. Have children answer them. Provide sentence frames if needed.	Have children draw pictures for the words. Help them say sentences for their pictures.

High-Frequency Words

REVIEW WORDS

OBJECTIVES

Recognize and read grade-appropriate irregularly spelled words. **RF.1.3g**

LANGUAGE OBJECTIVE

Use high-frequency words *around, by, many, place, walk*

Display the **High-Frequency Word Cards** for *around*, *by*, *many*, *place*, and *walk*. Read each word. Use the **Read/Spell/Write** routine to teach each word. Have children write the words on their **Response Boards**.

Write sentence frames on separate lines. Track the print as you guide children to read and complete the sentences: **(1)** *When I look around, I see _____.* **(2)** *What do you see by _____?* **(3)** *I have many _____.* **(4)** *This place is _____.* **(5)** *My pals and I walk _____.*

Display the High-Frequency Word Cards from the previous weeks. Display one card at a time as children chorally read the word. Mix and repeat. Note words that children need to review.

Beginning	Intermediate	Advanced/High
Have children choose and read a word. Say a sentence for the word, and have children repeat.	Have one partner say a word and the other use it in a sentence. Then have partners switch roles.	Have partners take turns saying a sentence for a word and finding the card for the word used in the sentence.

RETEACH WORDS

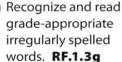

OBJECTIVES

Recognize and read grade-appropriate irregularly spelled words. **RF.1.3g**

LANGUAGE OBJECTIVE

Use high-frequency words

Display each Visual Vocabulary Card and say the word aloud. Define the word in English and, if appropriate, in Spanish. Identify any cognates.

Point to the image again and explain how it illustrates or demonstrates the word. Have children repeat the word. Engage children in structured partner-talk about the image as prompted on the back of the card. Ask children to chorally say the word three times.

Display each visual card in random order, hiding the word. Have children identify and define the word in their own words.

Beginning	Intermediate	Advanced/High
Say a word. Have children find its picture. Use the word in a sentence and have children repeat.	Have children complete sentence frames for the words. Ask them to illustrate their sentences.	Ask a question using each vocabulary word. Help children use the word in an answer: *Can you turn around in a circle? Yes, I can turn around.*

English Language Learners
Writing/Spelling

WRITING TRAIT: IDEAS

OBJECTIVES

 CCSS With guidance and support from adults, focus on a topic, respond to questions and suggestions from peers, and add details to strengthen writing as needed. **W.1.5**

LANGUAGE OBJECTIVE

Use details in sentences

I Do Explain that writers use details to give important information. Write and read these sentences: *This place is big. Pigs and chicks live here.* Help children identify important details. Ask what the place is. (farm)

We Do Read aloud page 98 of *Which Way on the Map?* Ask children which details give information. (red bricks; children go here) Explain that thinking about the hints, or details, helps us figure out that the place is a school. Repeat with pages 100 and 102.

You Do Have partners come up with an idea about a place they know well. Then have them write three detailed sentences about the place.

Beginning	Intermediate	Advanced/High
Say sentences about a place. Have children repeat each sentence and point out the details.	Provide sentence frames about a place. Have children use details to complete the sentences.	Have children draw pictures to support their sentences.

WORDS WITH CONSONANT DIGRAPHS *ch, -tch, wh, ph*

OBJECTIVES

 CCSS Use conventional spelling for words with common spelling patterns and for frequently occurring irregular words. **L.1.2d**

LANGUAGE OBJECTIVE

Spell words with consonant digraphs *ch, -tch, wh, ph*

I Do Read aloud the spelling words on page T326. Segment the first word into sounds and attach a spelling to each sound. Point out the /hw/ sound spelled *wh*. Read aloud, segment, and spell the remaining words. Have children repeat.

We Do Say a sentence for the first spelling word on page T326. Then, say the word with a consonant digraph slowly and ask children to repeat. Have them write the word. Repeat the process for the remaining sentences.

You Do Display the words. Have children work with partners to check their spelling lists. Have children correct misspelled words on their list.

Beginning	Intermediate	Advanced/High
Help children say the words and copy them with the correct spelling.	After children correct their words, have partners take turns spelling each word.	Challenge children to think of other words that have *ch, -tch, wh,* or *ph*.

Grammar

IRREGULAR PLURAL NOUNS

OBJECTIVES

 Demonstrate command of the conventions of standard English grammar and usage when writing or speaking. **L.1.1**

LANGUAGE OBJECTIVE

Use irregular plural nouns

Language Transfers Handbook

Cantonese, Haitian Creole, Hmong, Korean, Vietnamese, and Khmer do not use a plural marker. Children may use the singular form of the noun. Say phrases like *one child, two children* as you hold up one or two fingers. Have children repeat.

 I Do Remind children that a noun names a person, place, or thing. *We add -s or -es to most nouns to make them mean "more than one," but some words change spellings to make them mean "more than one."* Write *child* and *children* on the board. Read the words aloud. Child *means "one."* Have one child stand. *One child is standing.* Children *means "more than one."* Have three children stand. *Three children are standing.*

We Do Write the sentence pairs below on the board. Read each sentence pair aloud. Have children echo-read. Then ask them to circle the plural of the underlined word.

One <u>man</u> jumps. Two men run.

I stand on one <u>foot</u>. You stand on two feet.

This <u>leaf</u> fell down. Many leaves are on the tree.

 You Do Write and read aloud the following sentences:

One <u>mouse</u> went up. Two mice went down.

One <u>person</u> left. Most people are still here.

I lost one <u>tooth</u>. You lost two teeth.

Have partners copy the sentences. Then ask them to circle the plural of each underlined noun. Circulate, listen, and note each child's language use and proficiency.

Beginning	Intermediate	Advanced/High
Write *man, foot, leaf, tooth, child, men, feet, leaves, teeth,* and *children.* As you read each word, have children point to or draw a picture for it. Help them label their pictures.	Write *man, foot, leaf, tooth, child, men, feet, leaves, teeth,* and *children* on word cards. Read the singular nouns, and have children match them to their plurals.	Have partners write *man, foot, leaf, tooth, child,* on word cards. Have children take turns choosing a word, naming its plural, and using the plural in a sentence.

PROGRESS MONITORING

Weekly Assessment

✔**COMPREHENSION:**	✔**PHONEMIC AWARENESS:**	✔**PHONICS/STRUCTURAL ANALYSIS/HIGH-FREQUENCY WORDS:**
Main Topic and Key Details **RI.1.2**	Phoneme Segmentation and Counting **RF.1.2d**	Consonant Digraphs *ch, -tch, wh, ph* **RF.1.3a**
	Phoneme Addition **RF.1.2c**	*-es* (plural nouns) **L.1.1c**
	Phoneme Blending **RF.1.2b**	*around, by, many, place, walk* **RF.1.3g**

Conduct group fluency assessments.

Assess fluency for one group of children per week using the **Letter Naming, Phoneme Segmentation,** and **Sight Word Fluency** assessments in *Reading Wonders Fluency Assessment.*

Go Digital! http://connected.mcgraw-hill.com

Using Assessment Results

TESTED SKILLS	If ...	Then ...
COMPREHENSION	Children answer 0–3 multiple-choice items correctly . . .	. . . assign Lessons 85–87 on Main Idea and Details from the *Tier 2 Comprehension Intervention online PDFs.*
PHONEMIC AWARENESS	Children answer 0–1 multiple-choice items correctly . . .	. . . assign Lessons 67–71 on Phoneme Segmenting, Lessons 98–99 on Phoneme Addition (Add an Initial Sound), and Lessons 62–66 on Phoneme Blending from the *Tier 2 Phonemic Awareness Intervention online PDFs.*
PHONICS/ STRUCTURAL ANALYSIS/HFW	Children answer 0–5 multiple-choice items correctly . . .	. . . assign Lesson 53 on Short Vowels: Digraphs (*wh, ch, tch, ph*) and Lesson 54 on Plurals (*-s, -es*) from the *Tier 2 Phonics/Word Study Intervention online PDFs.*

Response to Intervention

Use children's assessment results to assist you in identifying children who will benefit from focused intervention.

Use the appropriate sections of the *Placement and Diagnostic Assessment* to designate children requiring:

TIER 2 **Intervention Online PDFs**

TIER 3 **WonderWorks Intervention Program**

REVIEW AND EXTEND

Reader's Theater

I Speak, I Say, I Talk

Genre Play

Fluency Accuracy, Rate, and Expression

I SPEAK, I SAY, I TALK
by Arnold L. Shapiro

Solo 1: Cats purr.
Solo 2: Lions roar.
Solo 3: Owls hoot.
Solo 4: Bears snore.
Solo 5: Crickets creak.
Solo 6: Mice squeak.
Solo 7: Sheep baa.
All: But I SPEAK!
Solo 1: Monkeys chatter.
Solo 2: Cows moo.
Solo 3: Ducks quack.
Solo 4: Doves coo.

Reading Digitally

TIME FOR KIDS "Help Your Community!"

Comprehension Close Reading

Study Skills Take Notes

Research Navigate Links to Information

Go Digital!

Level Up Accelerating Progress

From
APPROACHING
To **ON LEVEL**

From
ON LEVEL
To **BEYOND LEVEL**

From
ENGLISH LANGUAGE LEARNERS
To **ON LEVEL**

From
BEYOND LEVEL
To **SELF-SELECTED TRADE BOOK**

Advanced Level **Trade Book**

ASSESS

Presentations

Research and Inquiry
Project Presentations

Project Rubric

Writing
Writing Presentations

Writing Rubric

Unit Assessments

UNIT 2 TEST

FLUENCY

Evaluate Student Progress

Use the McGraw-Hill Reading Wonders e-Assessment reports to evaluate children's progress and help you make decisions about small group instruction and assignments.

→ Student and Class Assessment Report

→ Student and Class Standards Proficiency Report

→ Student Profile Summary Report

Jim Craigmyle/Corbis

SUGGESTED LESSON PLAN

		DAY 1	DAY 2
READING			
Whole Group	Reader's Theater "I Speak, I Say, I Talk" "Help Your Community!"	**Reader's Theater,** T394–T395 "I Speak, I Say, I Talk" Assign Roles Model Fluency: Phrasing, Rate and Prosody **Research and Inquiry,** T398–T400 Reliable Sources Group Project	**Reader's Theater,** T394–T395 "I Speak, I Say, I Talk" Model Fluency: Phrasing, Rate and Prosody *Research and Inquiry Projects*

DIFFERENTIATED INSTRUCTION Level Up to Accelerate

Small Group	**Approaching Level**	**Level Up to On Level** *Meerkat Family,* T404	**Level Up to On Level** *Meerkat Family,* T404
	On Level	**Level Up to Beyond Level** *Meerkat Family,* T405	**Level Up to Beyond Level** *Meerkat Family,* T405
	Beyond Level	**Level Up to Self-Selected Trade Book,** T407	**Level Up to Self-Selected Trade Book,** T407
	English Language Learners	**Level Up to On Level** *Meerkat Family,* T406	**Level Up to On Level** *Meerkat Family,* T406

Writing Process LANGUAGE ARTS

Whole Group	**Writing**	**Unit Writing** Prepare to Present Your Writing, T402	**Unit Writing** Discuss Peer Feedback, T402

DAY 3	DAY 4	DAY 5
Reading Digitally, T396	**Reading Digitally,** T397	**Research and Inquiry,** T400
TIME FOR KIDS. "Help Your Community!" *Analytical Writing*	TIME FOR KIDS. "Help Your Community!"	Presentation
Close Reading	Write About Reading	✓ **Unit Assessment,** T408–T409
	Reader's Theater, T394	
	Performance	
Research and Inquiry Projects	**Research and Inquiry Projects**	

DIFFERENTIATED INSTRUCTION

Level Up to On Level	**Level Up to On Level**	**Level Up to On Level**
Meerkat Family, T404	"I Live in a House!" T404	Literature Circle, T404
Level Up to Beyond Level	**Level Up to Beyond Level**	**Level Up to Beyond Level**
Meerkat Family, T405	"I Live in a House!" T405	Literature Circle, T405
Level Up to Self-Selected	**Level Up to Self-Selected**	**Level Up to Self-Selected**
Trade Book, T407	**Trade Book,** T407	**Trade Book,** T407
Level Up to On Level	**Level Up to On Level**	**Level Up to On Level**
Meerkat Family, T406	"I Live in a House!" T406	Literature Circle, T406

Unit Writing	**Unit Writing**	**Unit Writing**
Rehearse Your Presentation, T402	Present Your Writing, T402–T403	Portfolio Choice, T403
	Evaluate Your Presentation, T402–T403	

Reader's Theater

Go Digital!

Teacher's Resource PDF Online

OBJECTIVES

CCSS Read grade-level text with purpose and understanding. **RF.1.4a**

CCSS Read grade-level text orally with accuracy, appropriate rate, and expression. **RF.1.4b**

CCSS Use context to confirm or self-correct word recognition and understanding, rereading as necessary. **RF.1.4c**

I Speak, I Say, I Talk

Introduce the Play

Explain that *I Speak, I Say, I Talk* is a play that tells about the sounds different animals make and the ways children can communicate with their voices. Distribute scripts and the Elements of Drama handout from the **Teacher's Resource PDF Online**.

→ Review the features of a play.

→ Discuss the meaning of "solo" (a part read by one person) and explain that the characters in this play are not "characters" in the usual sense. Point out that the setting of the play is not specified; the setting could be any place.

Shared Reading

Model reading the play as children follow along in their scripts.

Focus on Vocabulary Stop and discuss any vocabulary words that children may not know. You may wish to teach:

→ creak
→ coyotes
→ chatter
→ squawk
→ doves

Model Fluency As you come to each part, state the name of each character and read the part, emphasizing the appropriate phrasing and expression.

Discuss Each Role

→ After reading the play, ask children to identify the difference between each character's part and the part everyone reads.

→ Ask children to note the rhyming words in the play.

Assign Roles

To accommodate all the children in the class, divide the class into groups to set up two or more casts. The casts can work on their scripts simultaneously. Or you might change the character names to reflect more than seven solos.

Practice the Play

Have children use highlighters to mark their parts in the script. Each day, allow children time to practice their parts. Pair fluent readers with less fluent readers. Pairs can echo-read or chorally read their parts. As needed, work with less fluent readers to mark pauses in their script, using one slash for a short pause and two slashes for longer pauses.

Throughout the week have children work on the Reader's Theater **Workstation Activity Card 25**.

Once children have practiced reading their parts several times, allow them time to practice performing the script.

Perform the Play

→ Have groups take turns "performing" their script for the rest of the class.

→ Remind children to focus on their scripts as the play is being performed and to read along, even when it is not their turn to speak.

→ Remind children to talk slowly and say each word loudly so their voices can be heard.

→ Talk with children about ways they could make their performances more enjoyable for the audience.

ACTIVITIES

PLAYING WITH SOUNDS

I Speak, I Say, I Talk tells about sounds that animals make. Help children brainstorm a list of other sounds. Then have them write their own plays about sounds.

1. Suggest that children think of things that make noise at school, home, or outside.

2. Using *I Speak, I Say, I Talk* as a model, have partners or small groups write their own plays. For example:

Solo 1: Bells ring.
Solo 2: Clocks tick.
Solo 3: Horns honk.
All: But I SING!

3. Have partners or groups take turns performing their plays for classmates.

ADD ACTIONS

Help children to create the animal sounds in *I Speak, I Say, I Talk* and act out the parts of some of the animals. For example, when:

→ Solo 2 says, "Lions roar," they can open their mouths wide and roar.

→ Solo 3 says, "Owls hoot," they can move their arms up and down like wings, and hoot.

→ Solo 6 says, "Mice squeak," they can twitch their noses and squeak.

Allow time for children to practice. Then read aloud the play again, having children act out their lines.

ELL ENGLISH LANGUAGE LEARNERS

→ Review the definitions of difficult words including *bears, monkeys, neigh, bats, bees,* and *talk.*

→ Pair an ELL child with a fluent reader who is reading the same part. Have each reader take turns reading the lines.

→ During practice sessions, shadow behind an ELL child. Read each line and then have the child echo-read the line.

Reading Digitally

Go Digital!

OBJECTIVES

Know and use various text features (e.g., headings, tables of contents, glossaries, electronic menus, icons) to locate key facts or information in a text. **RI.1.5**

Write opinion pieces in which they introduce the topic or name the book they are writing about, state an opinion, supply a reason for the opinion, and provide some sense of closure. **W.1.1**

ACADEMIC LANGUAGE

hyperlink, search engine, interactive, bookmarking

Help Your Community!

Before Reading

Preview Scroll through the online article "Help Your Community!" at **http://connected.mcgraw-hill.com** and point out the text features such as **lists** and **headings**. Explain how to use the **interactive features** in this article. Tell children that you will read the article together first and then use the features.

Close Reading Online

Take Notes Scroll back to the top and read the article aloud. As you read, ask questions about helping out and showing community spirit. Model taking notes using a Details chart. After each section, have partners discuss each particular way of showing community spirit. Encourage them to use text evidence as they discuss what they learned. Help children use context clues to understand domain-specific terms, such as *community, spirit, senior center,* and *citizens.*

Access Interactive Elements Have children access the interactive elements by clicking on or rolling over each feature. Discuss what information these elements add to the text.

Reread Tell children they will reread parts of the article to help them answer a specific question: *How can you show community spirit?*

Navigate Links to Information Point out that online texts may include hyperlinks. Hyperlinks help you go from the Web page you are on to another Web page that tells more about the topic.

Model how to use a hyperlink to jump to another Web page. Discuss information on the new Web page. Before navigating back, demonstrate bookmarking the page so children can return to it at another time.

WRITE ABOUT READING — *Analytical Writing*

Retell Review children's charts. Model using the information to retell "Help Your Community!"

Ask partners to draw pictures of three ways to show community spirit. Help them write a sentence that tells why each activity is important. Invite children to share their pictures to help them retell the article.

Make Connections Have children compare what they learned about community spirit with what they learned about communities in other texts they read in this unit.

TAKE A STAND

Be a Good Citizen

Discuss what it means to be a good citizen. Then have children discuss how community spirit is one way to be a good citizen.

Ask children if they think it is important to be a good citizen. Have partners share opinions. Ask them to use information from the article or linked Web pages to support their opinion.

→ How might a community change if everyone in it decided to be a good citizen?

→ What would happen if no one wanted to be a good citizen?

RESEARCH ONLINE

Key Words Explain that when children do research online, they need to use key words, or words that help them find information on a topic. Point out that they should type in the most important words related to the topic and should not use words like *a, an,* and *the.*

Ask children what key words they might use to find out more about community spirit or how to be a good citizen. List their ideas. Type in some of their suggestions on a child-friendly search engine. Demonstrate how different sites pop up when you use different key words.

INDEPENDENT STUDY

Investigate

Choose a Topic Brainstorm other ways that children help out in their communities. For example, they might ask: *What other things can kids do to show community spirit?*

Conduct Internet Research Have children conduct an Internet search. Type in the URL for a child-friendly search engine. Enter key words and click Search. Then, click on a link on the results page to go to a site.

Present Help children use their research to make a poster about community spirit or use presentation software to share it with others.

RESEARCH AND INQUIRY

The Big Idea: *What makes a community?*

Assign the Projects Have children work in five groups, with each group assigned one of the five projects that follow, or let groups self-select their project. Before children begin researching, present these minilessons.

Research Skill: Collecting Information

OBJECTIVES

 Participate in shared research and writing projects (e.g., explore a number of "how-to" books on a given topic and use them to write a sequence of instructions). **W.1.7**

 With guidance and support from adults, recall information from experiences or gather information from provided sources to answer a question. **W.1.8**

Collecting Information

→ After children select a research topic, explain that they will need to collect information about that topic. Guide them to make a list of possible resources. Model how to make a list by naming classroom resources, such as books, magazines, or encyclopedias.

→ Discuss library resources and different types of reference materials available, including appropriate online search engines. Point out that resources such as maps may be helpful for some projects.

→ After children generate a list of classroom and library resources, explain that they can begin their research with one or two resources that they think will be most helpful. If these resources do not provide enough information, they can move on to other resources they have identified. Starting with one or two resources can help keep the children from becoming overwhelmed with too much information.

Evaluating Sources

→ As children work on their research project, guide them to evaluate their resources. Explain that sometimes a resource is not very helpful, and they may need to look for other resource options.

→ Guide them to analyze their resources by asking questions, such as: *What kind of information can I find in this book/source? Does the information help me with my project? Does it include facts? Will photos help me?*

Go Digital

 **COLLABORATE**
Manage and assign Projects online. Children can also work with their group online.

Choose a Project!

1 A Question List

ESSENTIAL QUESTION
What jobs need to be done in a community?

Goal
Research teams will choose a job in the community and make a list of questions they have about that job. Teams figure out a way to find the answers to their questions.

2 A Diorama

ESSENTIAL QUESTION
What buildings do you know? What are they made of?

Goal
Research teams will make a diorama of a building in the community. They will include labels to describe the building materials.

3 A Collage

ESSENTIAL QUESTION
Where do animals live together?

Goal
Research teams will think of ways to add to the animal habitat collage created in Week 3. They will research other animals that live in that habitat.

STEM

4 A Plan

ESSENTIAL QUESTION
How do people help out in the community?

Goal
Research teams will choose one classroom improvement idea from their Week 4 list. Then they will interview people to write and illustrate a plan for making the improvement.

5 A Map

ESSENTIAL QUESTION
How can you find your way around?

Goal
Research teams will select more town details from previous research that are important to them, such as sidewalks or park benches, and add them to the maps they created in Week 5.

RESEARCH AND INQUIRY

Distribute the Research Roadmap online PDF. Have children use the roadmap to complete the project.

Conducting the Research

STEP 1 **Set Research Goals**

Discuss the Big Idea question and the research project. Each group should:

→ develop a research plan that helps focus their research.

→ discuss what they want to find out about their topic.

STEP 2 **Identify Sources**

Have the group brainstorm where they can find the information they need. Sources might include:

→ reliable online sources ending in *.edu, .org,* or *.gov.*

→ examples of maps.

→ classroom and library books and magazines that provide text and photos.

Remind children that they should make a list of possible resources before they begin the project.

STEP 3 **Find and Record Information**

Have children review the strategies for collecting information presented on page T398. Then have them conduct their research. Remind children to evaluate their sources to find the ones that are most useful for their project.

STEP 4 **Organize and Summarize**

After team members have completed their research, they can review the information they collected. Help children decide what information is necessary to complete the project. Help team members:

→ summarize their findings and decide on their final message.

→ connect the key ideas of their projects to the unit theme, "Our Community."

STEP 5 **Complete and Present**

Guide children to complete the project.

→ Ensure children work together to create each part of the project.

→ Encourage them to use various media in their presentations.

→ Have teams take turns presenting their work.

Audience Participation

→ Remind children to be active listeners by remaining quiet and making sure they understand the presentation.

→ Have children discuss how the presentation relates to the Unit Theme.

Review and Evaluate

Distribute the online PDF of the Student Checklist. Use the following Teacher Checklist and Project Rubric to evaluate children's research and presentations.

Student Checklist

- ☑ Did you choose a research topic?
- ☑ Did you use several sources to find information about your topic?

Presenting

- ☑ Did you practice your presentation?
- ☑ Did you speak clearly and loudly enough for others to hear?
- ☑ Did you give important facts and details about your topic?
- ☑ Did you answer the Essential Question?
- ☑ Did you use pictures, audio recordings, or other materials to make your presentation exciting for your audience?

Teacher Checklist

Assess the Research Process

- ☑ Selected a focus.
- ☑ Used sources to gather information.
- ☑ Used time effectively and collaborated well.

Assess the Presentation

- ☑ Presented information clearly and concisely.
- ☑ Maintained a consistent focus by staying on-topic.
- ☑ Used appropriate gestures.
- ☑ Maintained eye contact.
- ☑ Used appropriate visuals and technology.
- ☑ Spoke clearly and at an appropriate rate.

Assess the Listener

- ☑ Listened quietly and politely.
- ☑ Listened actively and asked questions to clarify understanding.

Project Rubric

4 Excellent	3 Good	2 Fair	1 Unsatisfactory
→ Presents the information clearly	→ Presents the information adequately	→ Attempts to present information	→ May show little grasp of the task
→ Includes many details	→ Provides adequate details	→ May offer few or vague details	→ May present irrelevant information
→ May include many relevant observations	→ Includes relevant observations	→ May include few or irrelevant personal observations	→ May reflect extreme difficulty with research or presentation

Celebrate Share Your Writing

Presentations

Giving Presentations

Now is the time for children to share one of their pieces of writing that they have worked on throughout the unit.

You may wish to invite parents or children from other classes to attend the presentations.

Preparing for Presentations

Tell children that they will present their writing. They will need to practice and prepare to do that. Guide children to use digital tools to prepare their work for presentation.

Allow children time to rehearse their presentation. Make sure they reread their writing several times. Encourage them to be aware of question marks and exclamation marks as they read.

Children should consider any visuals or props that they may want to use to accompany their writing. Discuss some options.

→ Do they have photos to accompany their writing, such as their piece about community workers?

→ Do they have illustrations to accompany their presentation, such as of the characters or setting of their fantasy stories?

→ Do they have visuals or props to accompany their sentences that explain?

Provide time for children to practice their presentations with a partner. Share the following Speaking Checklist to help them focus on important parts of the presentation. Discuss each point on the checklist.

Speaking Checklist

Review the Speaking Checklist with children as they practice.

- ☑ Have your notes and visuals ready.
- ☑ Take a few deep breaths.
- ☑ Speak clearly and slowly.
- ☑ Speak loudly so everyone can hear.
- ☑ Make sure everyone can see your visuals.

Jim Craigmyle/Corbis

Listening to Presentations

Remind children that they not only will take on the role of a presenter, but they will also be part of the audience for their classmates' presentations. As a listener, children have an important role. Review with them the following Listening Checklist.

Listening Checklist

During the presentation

- ☑ Look at the speaker and listen carefully.
- ☑ Think about something during the presentation that interests you.
- ☑ Write one question about the presentation.
- ☑ Remain quiet and still during the presentation.

After the presentation

- ☑ Only speak when it is your turn.
- ☑ Comment on something that interested you during the presentation.
- ☑ If someone else makes the same comment first, tell why you agree.

Portfolio Choice

Ask children to select one finished piece of writing, as well as a revision to include in their writing portfolio. As children consider their choices, have them use the checklist below.

Published Writing

Does your writing:

→ focus on one main idea?

→ include a beginning, middle, and end?

→ include details to support the main idea?

→ use commas in a series correctly?

→ have few or no spelling errors?

Sample Revisions

Did you choose a revised entry that:

→ uses singular and plural nouns correctly?

→ shows a clearer focus on a main idea?

→ includes added details to support the main idea?

→ contains a stronger beginning, middle, and end?

  **Go Digital**

PORTFOLIO
Children can submit their writing to be considered for inclusion in their digital portfolio. Children's portfolios can be shared with parents.

Level Up Accelerating Progress

Leveled Reader

Level Up Lessons **also available online**

Approaching Level to On Level

Meerkat Family

Before Reading

Preview Discuss what children remember about the information they learned about meerkats. Tell them they will be reading a more detailed version of *Meerkat Family*.

High-Frequency Words Use the **High-Frequency Word Cards** to review the high-frequency words. Use the routine on the cards.

ACT During Reading

OBJECTIVES

 Identify the main topic and retell key details of a text. **RI.1.2**

 With prompting and support, read informational text appropriately complex for grade 1. **RI.1.10**

▷ **Specific Vocabulary** Review the following science words that are new for this title. Model how to use the photographs and sentences to determine their meaning. *eyes   tails   hunt   watch*

▷ **Connection of Ideas** Children may need help connecting ideas from one page to the next. Point out that on each page children learn something new about meerkats. Have children tell what new information about meerkats they learned after reading each successive page.

▷ **Sentence Structure** Help children understand the use of rhetorical questions. See pages 2, 4, 6, and 10. For example, chorally read page 2. Have children repeat the question. Ask: *Do you need to answer this question to understand the page?* (no) *Why do you think the author added this question to the page?* (Sample answer: To get the reader more interested in meerkats.) For other examples of rhetorical questions, have children find where the author provides the answer.

After Reading

Ask children to complete the Respond to Reading on page 12 using the new information from the On Level text. After children finish the Paired Read, have them hold Literature Circles.

Leveled Reader

OBJECTIVES

 Identify the main topic and retell key details of a text. **RI.1.2**

 With prompting and support, read informational text appropriately complex for grade 1. **RI.1.10**

On Level
to Beyond Level

Meerkat Family

Level Up Lessons also available online

Before Reading

Preview Discuss what children remember about meerkats. Tell them they will be reading a more detailed version of *Meerkat Family*.

High-Frequency Words Use the **High-Frequency Word Cards** to review the high-frequency words. Use the routine on the cards.

A C T During Reading

▶ **Specific Vocabulary** Review the following science words that are new for this title. Model how to use the meaning of the sentence and the photographs to determine their meaning.

groups   mice   claws   tunnels   pups   sound

▶ **Connection of Ideas** Children may need help connecting ideas. After reading each page, model retelling information to connect ideas from that page to the previous one. For example, after reading page 4 say: *On page 3 we learned what meerkats look like. They have spotted fur and black noses. On this page we learned that they also have long tails.*

▶ **Sentence Structure** This sentence structure is more complex than in the On Level text. To help children understand the information, follow this routine when reading complex or compound sentences such as the second sentence on page 4:

Read it aloud: *They have long tails that help them stand.*

Break it down: *They have long tails. Their tails help them stand.*

Have children then read the sentence aloud.

After Reading

Ask children to complete the Respond to Reading on page 12 using the new information from the Beyond Level text. After children finish the Paired Read, have them hold Literature Circles.

Level Up Accelerating Progress

Leveled Reader

OBJECTIVES

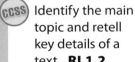 Identify the main topic and retell key details of a text. **RI.1.2**

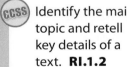 With prompting and support, read informational text appropriately complex for grade 1. **RI.1.10**

English Language Learners to On Level

Meerkat Family

 **Level Up Lessons** also available online

Before Reading

Preview Remind children informational text tells facts about real people, things, and events. Talk about what facts they remember about meerkats, then tell them they will be reading a more detailed version of *Meerkat Family*.

High-Frequency Words Use the **High-Frequency Word Cards** to review the high-frequency words. Use the routine on the cards.

A C T During Reading

▶ **Specific Vocabulary** Help children name elements in each photograph, now that there are no labels. Then review the following science words that are new for this title. Model how to use the illustrations to determine their meaning. Review any cognates. *eyes   tail   hunt   watch*

▶ **Connection of Ideas** Help children connect ideas from one page to the next. Point out on each page children learn something new about meerkats. Guide children to use the photos to help them tell what new information they learned after reading each page.

▶ **Sentence Structure** Help children understand why the author asks questions. See pages 2, 4, 6, and 10. For example, chorally read page 2. Have children repeat the question. Ask: *Who does the author want to answer question?* (the reader) *What do you think the answer is?* (yes) *How did this question help you?* (Sample answers: It made me look closer at the meerkat. It got me more interested.) For other examples of rhetorical questions, have children find where the author provides the answer.

After Reading

Ask children to complete the Respond to Reading on page 12 using the new information from the On Level text. After children finish the Paired Read, have them hold Literature Circles.

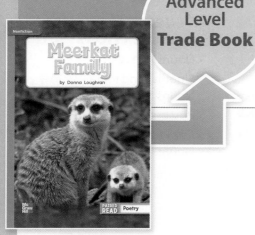

Advanced Level Trade Book

Leveled Reader

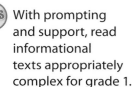

OBJECTIVES

CCSS With prompting and support, read informational texts appropriately complex for grade 1. **RI.1.10**

Beyond Level
to Self-Selected Trade Book

Independent Reading

Level Up Lessons **also available online**

Before Reading

Together with children identify the particular focus of their reading based on the text they choose. Children who have chosen the same title can work together to closely read the selection.

Close Reading

Taking Notes Assign a graphic organizer for children to use to take notes as they read. Reinforce a specific comprehension focus from the unit by choosing one of the graphic organizers that best fits the book.

Examples:	
Fiction	**Informational Text**
Character, Setting, Events	Main Topic and Key Details
Character, Setting, Events chart	Main Topic and Details chart

Make and Confirm Predictions Remind children that as they read they can think about what will happen next or what information will be provided next. Have them write down predictions as they read each section. Then have them record whether each prediction was correct as they read on. Encourage them to revise their predictions as needed.

After Reading

Write About Text

Have children use their notes, graphic organizers, and the information they shared in their discussions to write a response to the reading.

Examples:	
Fiction	**Informational Text**
Which character did you like best? Why?	What is the main topic of this book? What details helped you identify the main topic?

SUMMATIVE ASSESSMENT

Unit Assessment

CCSS **TESTED SKILLS**

✓ COMPREHENSION:	✓ PHONEMIC AWARENESS:	✓ PHONICS/STRUCTURAL AWARENESS/HIGH-FREQUENCY WORDS:	✓ ENGLISH LANGUAGE CONVENTIONS:
• Character, Setting, Events **RL.1.1, RL.1.3** • Use Illustrations **RL.1.7** • Main Topic and Key Details **RI.1.2**	• Phoneme Isolation **RF.1.2c** • Phoneme Blending **RF.1.2b** • Phoneme Substitution **RF.K.2e**	• Short Vowel: *u* **RF.1.3b** • Ending Consonant Blends: *-nd, -nk, -nt, -st, -sk, -mp, -sp* **RF.1.3** • Consonant Digraphs *th, sh, -ng, ch, -tch, wh, ph* **RF.1.3a** • Inflectional Endings: *-ed* and *-ing* **RF.1.3f** • Contractions with *'s* **RL.1.1** • High-Frequency Words **RF.1.3g**	• Nouns **L.1.2c** • Singular and Plural Nouns **L.1.1b** • Possessive Nouns **L.1.1b** • Common and Proper Nouns **L.1.1b**

Assessment Includes

→ Pencil-and-paper administration

→ Online administration

Additional Assessment Options

Assess fluency using the **Letter Naming Fluency (LNF)**, **Phoneme Segmentation Fluency (PSF)**, and **Sight Word Fluency (SWF)** assessments in *Fluency Assessment.*

Running Records

Use the instructional reading level determined by the Running Record calculations for regrouping decisions. Children at Level 4 or below should be provided reteaching on specific Comprehension skills.

Using Assessment Results

TESTED SKILLS	If ...	Then ...
COMPREHENSION	Children answer 0–7 items correctly ...	... reteach tested skills using the *Tier 2 Comprehension Intervention online PDFs.*
PHONEMIC AWARENESS	Children answer 0–3 items correctly ...	... reteach tested skills using the *Tier 2 Phonemic Awareness online PDFs.*
PHONICS/ STRUCTURAL ANALYSIS/HFW	Children answer 0–8 items correctly ...	... reteach tested skills using the *Tier 2 Phonics/Word Study online PDFs.*
ENGLISH LANGUAGE CONVENTIONS	Children answer 0–4 items correctly ...	... reteach necessary skills using the **online Grammar Reproducibles.**
WRITING	Children score less than the benchmark score on the constructed responses ...	... reteach necessary skills using the Write About Reading lessons in the *Tier 2 Comprehension Intervention online PDFs.*
FLUENCY	Children name 0–33 letters correctly in LNF OR have 0–22 phonemes correct in PSF OR have an accuracy rate less than 50% in SWF ...	... reteach tested skills using the *Tier 2 Phonemic Awareness Intervention online PDFs* and/or the *Tier 2 Phonics/Word Study Intervention online PDFs.*

Response to Intervention

Use the appropriate sections of the *Placement and Diagnostic Assessment* as well as children's assessment result to designate children requiring:

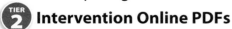 **Intervention Online PDFs**

 **WonderWorks Intervention Program**

Reevaluate Student Grouping

View the *McGraw-Hill Reading Wonders e-Assessment* Class Achievement Reports available for this Unit Assessment. Note children who are below the overall proficiency level for the assessment, and use the reports to assign small group intervention for children with similar needs.

Reading Complex Text

Your Own Texts

Program Information

Scope and Sequence

Index

 Correlations

Reading Complex Text

Your Own Texts **T412**

Program Information

Scope and Sequence. **BM1**

Index **BM10**

 Correlations **CCSS1**

For Additional Resources

Theme Bibliography

Literature and Informational Text Charts

Word Lists

Core Reading

 www.connected.mcgraw-hill.com

READING Complex Text

Close Reading Routine

Read the Text *What does the author tell us?*

Select the Text

Depending on the needs of individual children, choose a book to:

→ read aloud with children.

→ have children read alone.

Model Note-Taking

Invite children to generate questions about aspects of the text that might be confusing for them. Model simple note-taking on the board or on chart paper. Encourage children to note:

→ difficult vocabulary words or phrases.

→ details that are not clear.

→ information that they do not understand.

Together, complete a graphic organizer with important information from the text.

Reread the Text *What does the text mean?*

Ask Text-Dependent Questions/Generate Questions

Reread the text with children and discuss shorter passages from the text. As a group:

→ generate questions about the text.

→ answer questions using text evidence.

Write About the Text *Think about what the author wrote.*

Have children draw a picture and write a short response to the text. Based on their ability, children may respond to the text by labeling their picture, writing a short caption, or writing a sentence that uses evidence from the text to support their ideas.

Use Your Own Text

Classroom Library lessons available online.

Read-Aloud Books

The True Story of the 3 Little Pigs!

Genre Fiction

Lexile 570

Cactus Hotel

Genre Nonfiction

Lexile 700

Read-Alone Books

The Cow That Went OINK

Genre Fiction

Lexile 270

or

Choose from your own Trade Books

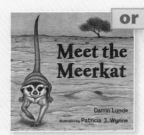

Meet the Meerkat

Genre Nonfiction

Lexile 340

Teacher's Choice

Use this model with a text of your choice. Go online for title specific classroom library book lessons.

Select a Read-Aloud book or a Read-Alone book.
Select a text that provides an opportunity to model application of the comprehension skills and strategies taught during the unit.

Present an Essential Question. You may want to use the Unit Big Idea: *What makes a community?*

Using the Classroom Library

Selecting a Book For each unit, the classroom library includes two Read-Aloud titles for you to read with the class and two Read-Alone titles for independent reading. There is a mix of fiction and informational nonfiction.

Reading Together Use the Read-Aloud titles to model close reading. Model taking notes, and prompt children to ask and answer text-dependent questions and to participate in writing about the text. You may choose to read the selection in multiple readings.

Independent Reading If children are ready to engage in close reading independently, select a Read-Alone title. Assign the Read-Alone title and guide children to take notes, ask and answer text-dependent questions, and write about the text.

"Cover" from the book *Cactus Hotel* by Brenda Z. Guiberson. Illustrated by Megan Lloyd. Copyright text © 1991 by Brenda Z. Guiberson. Illustrations © 1991 by Megan Lloyd. Reprinted by permission of Henry Holt and Company, LLC.; Meet the Meerkat. Text copyright © 2007 by Darrin Lunde. Illustrations copyright © 2007 by Patricia J. Wynne. Used with permission by Charlesbridge Publishing, Inc. All rights reserved.

READING Complex Text

Use Your Own Text

Read the Text   *What does the author tell us?*

Read Together

Read the text aloud. You may also invite more advanced readers to select a book to read alone and respond to independently.

Take Notes

As you read, model asking and answering text-dependent questions and taking simple notes on difficult parts of the text. Model taking notes on:

→ details or parts of the text that are unclear.

→ unfamiliar words.

→ important information.

→ connections between information or events.

→ the genre of the text.

Model how to use a graphic organizer, chosen from within the unit, to take notes on important details from the text. Together with children, use the information from the graphic organizer to retell the selection.

Teacher Think Aloud As I read, I ask myself questions about the text, such as, "What is the topic of this selection?" "What are the important details?" and "How do the details support the main topic?" I can find the answers to my questions using the text or illustrations. I can also take notes about things I don't understand and about important information in the text. Asking questions and taking notes helps me to understand a text better by making me think more carefully about what I'm reading.

 Help children access the complex text features of the text. Scaffold instruction on the following features as necessary:

→ Prior Knowledge   → Purpose

→ Genre   → Specific Vocabulary

→ Organization   → Sentence Structure

→ Connection of Ideas

Reread the Text *How does the author tell us?*

Ask Text-Dependent Questions/Generate Questions

Reread shorter passages of the text with children, focusing on how the author provides information or develops the characters, setting, and plot. Based on the selection you are reading, focus on key elements such as the following:

Literature Selections	**Informational Text**
Character, Setting, and Plot	Key Details
Word Choice	Main Topic
Genre	Text Structure
Character's Point of View	Text Features
Theme	Genre

Invite children to share questions they have about the text. As each child shares a question, return to the text together and model how to find text evidence to answer the question. Model how to:

→ point out the exact place within the text you found the evidence.

→ reread and paraphrase the section of the text that supports the answer.

→ discuss how well the evidence answers the question.

→ identify when an answer to a question cannot be found in the text.

Write About the Text *Think about what the author wrote.*

Essential Question

Have children respond to the Essential Question as it relates to the text by drawing a picture and labeling it, writing a caption, or writing a complete sentence. Children can work with a partner and use their notes and graphic organizer to locate evidence from the text that can be used to answer the question.

SCOPE & SEQUENCE

	K	1	2	3	4	5	6
READING PROCESS							
Concepts About Print/Print Awareness							
Recognize own name							
Understand directionality (top to bottom; tracking print from left to right; return sweep, page by page)	✔						
Locate printed word on page	✔						
Develop print awareness (concept of letter, word, sentence)	✔						
Identify separate sounds in a spoken sentence	✔						
Understand that written words are represented in written language by a specific sequence of letters	✔						
Distinguish between letters, words, and sentences	✔						
Identify and distinguish paragraphs							
Match print to speech (one-to-one correspondence)	✔						
Name uppercase and lowercase letters	✔						
Understand book handling (holding a book right-side-up, turning its pages)	✔						
Identify parts of a book (front cover, back cover, title page, table of contents); recognize that parts of a book contain information	✔						
Phonological Awareness							
Recognize and understand alliteration							
Segment sentences into correct number of words							
Identify, blend, segment syllables in words		✔					
Recognize and generate rhyming words	✔	✔					
Identify, blend, segment onset and rime	✔	✔					
Phonemic Awareness							
Count phonemes	✔	✔					
Isolate initial, medial, and final sounds	✔	✔					
Blend spoken phonemes to form words	✔	✔					
Segment spoken words into phonemes	✔	✔					
Distinguish between long- and short-vowel sounds	✔	✔					
Manipulate phonemes (addition, deletion, substitution)	✔	✔					
Phonics and Decoding/Word Recognition							
Understand the alphabetic principle	✔	✔					
Sound/letter correspondence	✔	✔	✔	✔			
Blend sounds into words, including VC, CVC, CVCe, CVVC words	✔	✔	✔	✔			
Blend common word families	✔	✔	✔	✔			

KEY ✔ = Assessed Skill
Tinted panels show skills, strategies, and other teaching opportunities.

	K	1	2	3	4	5	6
Initial consonant blends		✔	✔	✔			
Final consonant blends		✔	✔	✔			
Initial and medial short vowels	✔	✔	✔	✔	✔	✔	✔
Decode one-syllable words in isolation and in context	✔	✔	✔	✔			
Decode multisyllabic words in isolation and in context using common syllabication patterns		✔	✔	✔	✔	✔	✔
Distinguish between similarly spelled words	✔	✔	✔	✔	✔	✔	✔
Monitor accuracy of decoding							
Identify and read common high-frequency words, irregularly spelled words	✔	✔	✔	✔			
Identify and read compound words, contractions		✔	✔	✔	✔	✔	✔
Use knowledge of spelling patterns to identify syllables		✔	✔	✔	✔	✔	✔
Regular and irregular plurals	✔	✔	✔	✔	✔	✔	✔
Long vowels (silent *e*, vowel teams)	✔	✔	✔	✔	✔	✔	✔
Vowel digraphs (variant vowels)		✔	✔	✔	✔	✔	✔
r-Controlled vowels		✔	✔	✔	✔	✔	
Hard/soft consonants		✔	✔	✔	✔	✔	✔
Initial consonant digraphs		✔	✔	✔	✔	✔	
Medial and final consonant digraphs		✔	✔	✔	✔	✔	
Vowel diphthongs		✔	✔	✔	✔	✔	✔
Identify and distinguish letter-sounds (initial, medial, final)	✔	✔	✔				
Silent letters		✔	✔	✔	✔	✔	✔
Schwa words				✔	✔	✔	✔
Inflectional endings		✔	✔	✔	✔	✔	✔
Triple-consonant clusters		✔	✔	✔	✔	✔	
Unfamiliar and complex word families				✔	✔	✔	✔
Structural Analysis/Word Analysis							
Common spelling patterns (word families)		✔	✔	✔	✔	✔	✔
Common syllable patterns		✔	✔	✔	✔	✔	✔
Inflectional endings		✔	✔	✔	✔	✔	✔
Contractions		✔	✔	✔	✔	✔	✔
Compound words		✔	✔	✔	✔	✔	✔
Prefixes and suffixes		✔	✔	✔	✔	✔	✔
Root or base words			✔	✔	✔	✔	✔
Comparatives and superlatives			✔	✔	✔	✔	✔
Greek and Latin roots			✔	✔	✔	✔	✔
Fluency							
Apply letter/sound knowledge to decode phonetically regular words accurately	✔	✔	✔	✔	✔	✔	✔
Recognize high-frequency and familiar words	✔	✔	✔	✔	✔	✔	✔
Read regularly on independent and instructional levels							
Read orally with fluency from familiar texts (choral, echo, partner, Reader's Theater)							
Use appropriate rate, expression, intonation, and phrasing		✔	✔	✔	✔	✔	✔
Read with automaticity (accurately and effortlessly)		✔	✔	✔	✔	✔	✔
Use punctuation cues in reading		✔	✔	✔	✔	✔	✔

BM1

	K	1	2	3	4	5	6
Adjust reading rate to purpose, text difficulty, form, and style							
Repeated readings							
Timed readings		✔	✔	✔	✔	✔	✔
Read with purpose and understanding		✔	✔	✔	✔	✔	✔
Read orally with accuracy		✔	✔	✔	✔	✔	✔
Use context to confirm or self-correct word recognition		✔	✔	✔	✔	✔	✔

READING LITERATURE

Comprehension Strategies and Skills

	K	1	2	3	4	5	6
Read literature from a broad range of genres, cultures, and periods		✔	✔	✔	✔	✔	✔
Access complex text	✔	✔	✔	✔	✔	✔	✔
Build background							
Preview and predict							
Establish and adjust purpose for reading							
Evaluate citing evidence from the text							
Ask and answer questions	✔	✔	✔	✔	✔	✔	✔
Inferences and conclusions, citing evidence from the text	✔	✔	✔	✔	✔	✔	✔
Monitor/adjust comprehension including reread, reading rate, paraphrase							
Recount/Retell	✔	✔					
Summarize			✔	✔	✔	✔	✔
Story structure (beginning, middle, end)	✔	✔	✔	✔	✔	✔	✔
Visualize							
Make connections between and across texts		✔	✔	✔	✔	✔	✔
Point of view		✔	✔	✔	✔	✔	✔
Author's purpose							
Cause and effect	✔	✔	✔	✔	✔	✔	✔
Compare and contrast (including character, setting, plot, topics)	✔	✔	✔	✔	✔	✔	✔
Classify and categorize		✔	✔				
Literature vs informational text	✔	✔	✔				
Illustrations, using	✔	✔	✔	✔			
Theme, central message, moral, lesson		✔	✔	✔	✔	✔	✔
Predictions, making/confirming	✔	✔	✔				
Problem and solution (problem/resolution)		✔	✔	✔	✔	✔	✔
Sequence of events	✔	✔	✔	✔	✔	✔	✔

Literary Elements

	K	1	2	3	4	5	6
Character	✔	✔	✔	✔	✔	✔	✔
Plot development/Events	✔	✔	✔	✔	✔	✔	✔
Setting	✔	✔	✔	✔	✔	✔	✔
Stanza				✔	✔	✔	✔
Alliteration						✔	✔
Assonance						✔	✔
Dialogue							
Foreshadowing						✔	✔

KEY ✔ = Assessed Skill
Tinted panels show skills, strategies, and other teaching opportunities.

	K	1	2	3	4	5	6
Flashback						✔	✔
Descriptive and figurative language		✔	✔	✔	✔	✔	✔
Imagery					✔	✔	✔
Meter					✔	✔	✔
Onomatopoeia							
Repetition		✔	✔	✔	✔	✔	✔
Rhyme/rhyme schemes		✔	✔	✔	✔	✔	✔
Rhythm		✔	✔				
Sensory language							
Symbolism							
Write About Reading/Literary Response Discussions							
Reflect and respond to text citing text evidence		✔	✔	✔	✔	✔	✔
Connect and compare text characters, events, ideas to self, to other texts, to world							
Connect literary texts to other curriculum areas							
Identify cultural and historical elements of text							
Evaluate author's techniques, craft							
Analytical writing							
Interpret text ideas through writing, discussion, media, research							
Book report or review							
Locate, use, explain information from text features		✔	✔	✔	✔	✔	✔
Organize information to show understanding of main idea through charts, mapping							
Cite text evidence	✔	✔	✔	✔	✔	✔	✔
Author's purpose/ Illustrator's purpose							

READING INFORMATIONAL TEXT

Comprehension Strategies and Skills

	K	1	2	3	4	5	6
Read informational text from a broad range of topics and cultures	✔	✔	✔	✔	✔	✔	✔
Access complex text		✔	✔	✔	✔	✔	✔
Build background							
Preview and predict	✔	✔	✔				
Establish and adjust purpose for reading							
Evaluate citing evidence from the text							
Ask and answer questions	✔	✔	✔	✔	✔	✔	✔
Inferences and conclusions, citing evidence from the text	✔	✔	✔	✔	✔	✔	✔
Monitor and adjust comprehension including reread, adjust reading rate, paraphrase							
Recount/Retell	✔	✔					
Summarize			✔	✔	✔	✔	✔
Text structure	✔	✔	✔	✔	✔	✔	✔
Identify text features		✔	✔	✔	✔	✔	✔
Make connections between and across texts	✔	✔	✔	✔	✔	✔	✔
Author's point of view					✔	✔	✔	✔
Author's purpose		✔	✔				
Cause and effect	✔	✔	✔	✔	✔	✔	✔

	K	1	2	3	4	5	6
Compare and contrast	✔	✔	✔	✔	✔	✔	✔
Classify and categorize		✔	✔				
Illustrations and photographs, using	✔	✔	✔	✔			
Instructions/directions (written and oral)		✔	✔	✔	✔	✔	✔
Main idea and key details	✔	✔	✔	✔	✔	✔	✔
Persuasion, reasons and evidence to support points/persuasive techniques						✔	✔
Predictions, making/confirming	✔	✔					
Problem and solution		✔	✔	✔	✔	✔	✔
Sequence, chronological order of events, time order, steps in a process	✔	✔	✔	✔	✔	✔	✔

Writing About Reading/Expository Critique Discussions

	K	1	2	3	4	5	6
Reflect and respond to text citing text evidence		✔	✔	✔	✔	✔	✔
Connect and compare text characters, events, ideas to self, to other texts, to world							
Connect texts to other curriculum areas							
Identify cultural and historical elements of text							
Evaluate author's techniques, craft							
Analytical writing							
Read to understand and perform tasks and activities							
Interpret text ideas through writing, discussion, media, research							
Locate, use, explain information from text features		✔	✔	✔	✔	✔	✔
Organize information to show understanding of main idea through charts, mapping							
Cite text evidence		✔	✔	✔	✔	✔	✔
Author's purpose/Illustrator's purpose							

Text Features

	K	1	2	3	4	5	6
Recognize and identify text and organizational features of nonfiction texts		✔	✔	✔	✔	✔	✔
Captions and labels, headings, subheadings, endnotes, key words, bold print	✔	✔	✔	✔	✔	✔	✔
Graphics, including photographs, illustrations, maps, charts, diagrams, graphs, time lines	✔	✔	✔	✔	✔	✔	✔

Self-Selected Reading/Independent Reading

	K	1	2	3	4	5	6
Use personal criteria to choose own reading including favorite authors, genres, recommendations from others; set up a reading log							
Read a range of literature and informational text for tasks as well as for enjoyment; participate in literature circles							
Produce evidence of reading by retelling, summarizing, or paraphrasing							

Media Literacy

	K	1	2	3	4	5	6
Summarize the message or content from media message, citing text evidence							
Use graphics, illustrations to analyze and interpret information	✔	✔	✔	✔	✔	✔	✔
Identify structural features of popular media and use the features to obtain information, including digital sources				✔	✔	✔	✔
Identify reasons and evidence in visuals and media message							
Analyze media source: recognize effects of media in one's mood and emotion							
Make informed judgments about print and digital media							
Critique persuasive techniques							

KEY ✔ = Assessed Skill
Tinted panels show skills, strategies, and other teaching opportunities.

WRITING

	K	1	2	3	4	5	6
Writing Process							
Plan/prewrite							
Draft							
Revise							
Edit/proofread							
Publish and present including using technology							
Teacher and peer feedback							
Writing Traits							
Conventions		✔	✔	✔	✔	✔	✔
Ideas		✔	✔	✔	✔	✔	✔
Organization		✔	✔	✔	✔	✔	✔
Sentence fluency		✔	✔	✔	✔	✔	✔
Voice		✔	✔	✔	✔	✔	✔
Word choice		✔	✔	✔	✔	✔	✔
Writer's Craft							
Good topic, focus on and develop topic, topic sentence			✔	✔	✔	✔	✔
Paragraph(s); sentence structure			✔	✔	✔	✔	✔
Main idea and supporting key details			✔	✔	✔	✔	✔
Unimportant details							
Relevant supporting evidence			✔	✔	✔	✔	✔
Strong opening, strong conclusion			✔	✔	✔	✔	✔
Beginning, middle, end; sequence		✔	✔	✔	✔	✔	✔
Precise words, strong words, vary words			✔	✔	✔	✔	✔
Figurative and sensory language, descriptive details							
Informal/formal language							
Mood/style/tone							
Dialogue				✔	✔	✔	✔
Transition words, transitions to multiple paragraphs				✔	✔	✔	✔
Select focus and organization			✔	✔	✔	✔	✔
Points and counterpoints/Opposing claims and counterarguments							
Use reference materials (online and print dictionary, thesaurus, encyclopedia)							
Writing Applications							
Writing about text	✔	✔	✔	✔	✔	✔	✔
Personal and fictional narrative (also biographical and autobiographical)	✔	✔	✔	✔	✔	✔	✔
Variety of expressive forms including poetry	✔	✔	✔	✔	✔	✔	✔
Informative/explanatory texts	✔	✔	✔	✔	✔	✔	✔
Description	✔	✔	✔	✔			
Procedural texts		✔	✔	✔	✔	✔	✔
Opinion pieces or arguments	✔	✔	✔	✔	✔	✔	✔
Communications including technical documents		✔	✔	✔	✔	✔	✔
Research report	✔	✔	✔	✔	✔	✔	✔
Responses to literature/reflection				✔	✔	✔	✔

	K	1	2	3	4	5	6
Analytical writing							
Letters		✔	✔	✔	✔	✔	✔
Write daily and over short and extended time frames; set up writer's notebooks							
Penmanship/Handwriting							
Write legibly in manuscript using correct formation, directionality, and spacing							
Write legibly in cursive using correct formation, directionality, and spacing							

SPEAKING AND LISTENING

Speaking

	K	1	2	3	4	5	6
Use repetition, rhyme, and rhythm in oral texts							
Participate in classroom activities and discussions							
Collaborative conversation with peers and adults in small and large groups using formal English when appropriate							
Differentiate between formal and informal English							
Follow agreed upon rules for discussion							
Build on others' talk in conversation, adding new ideas							
Come to discussion prepared							
Describe familiar people, places, and things and add drawings as desired							
Paraphrase portions of text read alone or information presented							
Apply comprehension strategies and skills in speaking activities							
Use literal and nonliteral meanings							
Ask and answer questions about text read aloud and about media							
Stay on topic when speaking							
Use language appropriate to situation, purpose, and audience							
Use nonverbal communications such as eye contact, gestures, and props							
Use verbal communication in effective ways and improve expression in conventional language							
Retell a story, presentation, or spoken message by summarizing							
Oral presentations: focus, organizational structure, audience, purpose							
Give and follow directions							
Consider audience when speaking or preparing a presentation							
Recite poems, rhymes, songs							
Use complete, coherent sentences							
Organize presentations							
Deliver presentations (narrative, summaries, research, persuasive); add visuals							
Speak audibly (accuracy, expression, volume, pitch, rate, phrasing, modulation, enunciation)							
Create audio recordings of poems, stories, presentations							

Listening

	K	1	2	3	4	5	6
Identify musical elements in language							
Determine the purpose for listening							
Understand, follow, restate, and give oral directions							
Develop oral language and concepts							
Listen openly, responsively, attentively, and critically							

KEY	✔ = Assessed Skill Tinted panels show skills, strategies, and other teaching opportunities.

	K	1	2	3	4	5	6
Listen to identify the points a speaker makes							
Listen responsively to oral presentations (determine main idea and key details)							
Ask and answer relevant questions (for clarification to follow up on ideas)							
Identify reasons and evidence presented by speaker							
Recall and interpret speakers' verbal/nonverbal messages, purposes, perspectives							

LANGUAGE

Vocabulary Acquisition and Use

	K	1	2	3	4	5	6
Develop oral vocabulary and choose words for effect							
Use academic language		✔	✔	✔	✔	✔	✔
Identify persons, places, things, actions		✔	✔	✔			
Classify, sort, and categorize words	✔	✔	✔	✔	✔	✔	✔
Determine or clarify the meaning of unknown words; use word walls		✔	✔	✔	✔	✔	✔
Synonyms, antonyms, and opposites		✔	✔	✔	✔	✔	✔
Use context clues such as word, sentence, paragraph, definition, example, restatement, description, comparison, cause and effect		✔	✔	✔	✔	✔	✔
Use word identification strategies		✔	✔	✔	✔	✔	✔
Unfamiliar words		✔	✔	✔	✔	✔	✔
Multiple-meaning words		✔	✔	✔	✔	✔	✔
Use print and online dictionary to locate meanings, pronunciation, derivatives, parts of speech		✔	✔	✔	✔	✔	✔
Compound words		✔	✔	✔	✔	✔	✔
Words ending in -er and -est		✔	✔	✔	✔	✔	
Root words (base words)		✔	✔	✔	✔		✔
Prefixes and suffixes		✔	✔	✔	✔	✔	✔
Greek and Latin affixes and roots			✔	✔	✔	✔	✔
Denotation and connotation					✔	✔	✔
Word families		✔	✔	✔	✔	✔	✔
Inflectional endings		✔	✔	✔	✔	✔	✔
Use a print and online thesaurus			✔	✔	✔	✔	✔
Use print and online reference sources for word meaning (dictionary, glossaries)		✔	✔	✔	✔	✔	✔
Homographs				✔	✔	✔	✔
Homophones			✔	✔	✔	✔	✔
Contractions		✔	✔	✔			
Figurative language such as metaphors, similes, personification				✔	✔	✔	✔
Idioms, adages, proverbs, literal and nonliteral language			✔	✔	✔	✔	✔
Analogies							
Listen to, read, discuss familiar and unfamiliar challenging text							
Identify real-life connections between words and their use							
Use acquired words and phrases to convey precise ideas							
Use vocabulary to express spatial and temporal relationships							
Identify shades of meaning in related words	✔	✔	✔	✔	✔	✔	✔
Word origins				✔	✔	✔	✔
Morphology				✔	✔	✔	✔

	K	1	2	3	4	5	6
Knowledge of Language							
Choose words, phrases, and sentences for effect							
Choose punctuation effectively							
Formal and informal language for style and tone including dialects							
Conventions of Standard English/Grammar, Mechanics, and Usage							
Sentence concepts: statements, questions, exclamations, commands		✔	✔	✔	✔	✔	✔
Complete and incomplete sentences; sentence fragments; word order		✔	✔	✔	✔	✔	✔
Compound sentences, complex sentences				✔	✔	✔	✔
Combining sentences		✔	✔	✔	✔	✔	✔
Nouns including common, proper, singular, plural, irregular plurals, possessives, abstract, concrete, collective		✔	✔	✔	✔	✔	✔
Verbs including action, helping, linking, irregular		✔	✔	✔	✔	✔	✔
Verb tenses including past, present, future, perfect, and progressive		✔	✔	✔	✔	✔	✔
Pronouns including possessive, subject and object, pronoun-verb agreement, indefinite, intensive, reciprocal; correct unclear pronouns		✔	✔	✔	✔	✔	✔
Adjectives including articles, demonstrative, proper, adjectives that compare		✔	✔	✔	✔	✔	✔
Adverbs including telling how, when, where, comparative, superlative, irregular		✔	✔	✔	✔	✔	✔
Subject, predicate; subject-verb agreement		✔	✔	✔	✔	✔	✔
Contractions		✔	✔	✔	✔	✔	✔
Conjunctions				✔	✔	✔	✔
Commas			✔	✔	✔	✔	✔
Colons, semicolons, dashes, hyphens						✔	✔
Question words							
Quotation marks			✔	✔	✔	✔	✔
Prepositions and prepositional phrases, appositives		✔	✔	✔	✔	✔	✔
Independent and dependent clauses						✔	✔
Italics/underlining for emphasis and titles							
Negatives, correcting double negatives					✔	✔	✔
Abbreviations			✔	✔	✔	✔	✔
Use correct capitalization in sentences, proper nouns, titles, abbreviations		✔	✔	✔	✔	✔	✔
Use correct punctuation		✔	✔	✔	✔	✔	✔
Antecedents				✔	✔	✔	✔
Homophones and words often confused			✔	✔	✔	✔	✔
Apostrophes				✔	✔	✔	✔
Spelling							
Write irregular, high-frequency words	✔	✔	✔				
ABC order	✔	✔					
Write letters	✔	✔					
Words with short vowels	✔	✔	✔	✔	✔	✔	✔
Words with long vowels	✔	✔	✔	✔	✔	✔	✔
Words with digraphs, blends, consonant clusters, double consonants		✔	✔	✔	✔	✔	✔
Words with vowel digraphs and ambiguous vowels		✔	✔	✔	✔	✔	✔
Words with diphthongs		✔	✔	✔	✔	✔	✔

KEY ✔ = Assessed Skill
Tinted panels show skills, strategies, and other teaching opportunities.

	K	1	2	3	4	5	6
Words with *r*-controlled vowels		✔	✔	✔	✔	✔	✔
Use conventional spelling		✔	✔	✔	✔	✔	✔
Schwa words				✔	✔	✔	✔
Words with silent letters			✔	✔	✔	✔	✔
Words with hard and soft letters				✔	✔	✔	✔
Inflectional endings including plural, past tense, drop final *e* and double consonant when adding *-ed* and *-ing*, changing *y* to *i*		✔	✔	✔	✔	✔	✔
Compound words		✔	✔	✔	✔	✔	✔
Homonyms/homophones			✔	✔	✔	✔	✔
Prefixes and suffixes		✔	✔	✔	✔	✔	✔
Root and base words (also spell derivatives)				✔	✔	✔	✔
Syllables: patterns, rules, accented, stressed, closed, open				✔	✔	✔	✔
Words with Greek and Latin roots						✔	✔
Words from mythology						✔	✔
Words with spelling patterns, word families		✔	✔	✔	✔	✔	✔

RESEARCH AND INQUIRY

Study Skills

	K	1	2	3	4	5	6
Directions: read, write, give, follow (includes technical directions)			✔	✔	✔	✔	✔
Evaluate directions for sequence and completeness				✔	✔	✔	✔
Use library/media center							
Use parts of a book to locate information							
Interpret information from graphic aids		✔	✔	✔	✔	✔	✔
Use graphic organizers to organize information and comprehend text		✔	✔	✔	✔	✔	✔
Use functional, everyday documents				✔	✔	✔	✔
Apply study strategies: skimming and scanning, note-taking, outlining							

Research Process

	K	1	2	3	4	5	6
Generate and revise topics and questions for research					✔	✔	✔	✔
Narrow focus of research, set research goals					✔	✔	✔	✔
Find and locate information using print and digital resources		✔	✔	✔	✔	✔	✔
Record information systematically (note-taking, outlining, using technology)					✔	✔	✔	✔
Develop a systematic research plan					✔	✔	✔	✔
Evaluate reliability, credibility, usefulness of sources and information						✔	✔
Use primary sources to obtain information					✔	✔	✔
Organize, synthesize, evaluate, and draw conclusions from information							
Cite and list sources of information (record basic bibliographic data)					✔	✔	✔
Demonstrate basic keyboarding skills							
Participate in and present shared research							

Technology

	K	1	2	3	4	5	6
Use computer, Internet, and other technology resources to access information							
Use text and organizational features of electronic resources such as search engines, keywords, e-mail, hyperlinks, URLs, Web pages, databases, graphics							
Use digital tools to present and publish in a variety of media formats							

INDEX

A

Abbreviations, 5: T179, T189, T196, T204, T214

Academic Language, Units 1–6: T8, T10, T16, T18, T20, T26, T28, T30, T36, T38, T42, T44, T46, T50, T86, T88, T94, T96, T98, T104, T106, T08, T114, T116, T120, T128, T164, T166, T172, T174, T176, T182, T184, T186, T192, T194, T198, T202, T206, T242, T244, T250, T252, T254, T260, T262, T264, T270, T272, T276, T278, T280, T284, T320, T322, T328, T330, T332, T338, T340, T342, T348, T350, T354, T356, T358, T362. *See also* Vocabulary Acquisition: domain-specific; Vocabulary Acquisition: general vocabulary.

Access Complex Text

connection of ideas, **1:** T31, T187, T265, **3:** T187, **4:** T113B, T113F, **5:** T35B, T35D, T113B, T113C, T113H, T113J, T113N, **6:** 35B, T35J, T269B, T269G

genre, **2:** T265, **3:** T343, **4:** T347B, **5:** T191B, T191F, T347B, **6:** T269B, T269C

organization, **1:** T31, T109, T265, **2:** T31, T187, T343, **3:** T31, T187, **4:** T191B, T191K, T269B, T269G, T269J, T269O, T347B, T347D, **5:** T35B, T35E, T191B, T191C, T269B, T269F, T269I, **6:** T35B, T35C, T113B, T113F, T347B, T347D

prior knowledge, **1:** T109, **2:** T265, **3:** T109, T265, **4:** T35B, T35D, **5:** T347D, **6:** T191B, T191F, T191L

purpose, **1:** T343, **2:** T187, T343, **3:** T31, T343, **4:** T113B, T113C, **6:** T113B, T113E, T347B

sentence structure, **1:** T187, **2:** T31, **4:** T191B, T191C, **5:** T113B, T113E, T113G, T113I, T113O, T269B, T269C

specific vocabulary, **1:** T343, **2:** T109, **3:** T109, T265, **5:** T347B, **6:** T35H

Accuracy. *See* Fluency.

Adjectives. *See* Grammar.

Alliteration. *See* Literary Devices and Elements: alliteration.

Alphabet, 1: S6, S12

Alphabetic Order, 1: T257, T267, T275, T283, T292, **4:** T23, T33, T40, T48, T58

Analytical Writing, 2: T53, T63, T67, T73, T131, T141, T145, T151, T287, T297, T301, T307, **3:** T53, T63, T67, T73, T209, T219, T223, T229, **4:** T53, T63, T73, **5:** T53, T63, T73, **6:** T53, T63, T73, T287, T297, T301, T307. *See also* Write About Reading.

Answering Questions. *See* Comprehension Strategies: ask and answer questions.

Antonyms. *See* Vocabulary Skills and Strategies.

Approaching Level Options

comprehension, **1:** T60–T61, T138–T139, T216–T217, T294–T295, T372–T373, **2:** T60–T61, T138–T139, T216–T217, T294–T295, T372–T373, **3:** T60–T61, T138–T139, T216–T217, T294–T295, T372–T373, **4:** T60–T61, T138–T139, T216–T217, T294–T295, T372–T373, **5:** T60–T61, T138–T139, T216–T217, T294–T295, T372–T373, **6:** T60–T61, T138–T139, T216–T217, T294–T295, T372–T373

fluency, **1:** T60, T138, T216, T294, T372, **2:** T60, T138, T216, T294, T372, **3:** T60, T138, T216, T294, T372, **4:** T60, T138, T216, T294, T372, **5:** T60, T138, T216, T294, T372, **6:** T60, T138, T216, T294, T372

high-frequency words, **1:** T59, T137, T215, T293, T371, **2:** T59, T137, T215, T293, T371, **3:** T59, T137, T215, T293, T371

Leveled Reader lessons, **Units 1–6:** T52–T53, T130–T131, T208–T209, T286–T287, T364–T365

Level Up, **Units 1–6:** T53, T131, T209, T287, T365, T404

phonemic/phonological awareness, **Units 1–6:** T54–T55, T132–T133, T210–T211, T288–T289, T366–T367

phonics, **Units 1–6:** T56–T57, T134–T135, T212–T213, T290–T291, T368–T369

self-selected reading, **Units 1–6:** T61, T139, T217, T295, T373

structural analysis, **Units 1–6:** T58, T136, T214, T292, T370

words to know, **4:** T59, T137, T215, T293, T371, **5:** T59, T137, T215, T293, T371, **6:** T59, T137, T215, T293, T371

Ask and Answer Questions. *See* Comprehension Strategies.

Assessment

checklists

listening, **1:** T401, T403, **2:** T401, T403, **3:** T401, **4:** T401, T403, **5:** T401, T403, **6:** T401, T403

portfolio choice, **1:** T403, **2:** T403, **3:** T403, **4:** T403, **5:** T403, **6:** T403

presentation, **1:** T401, **2:** T401, **3:** T401, **4:** T401, **5:** T401, **6:** T401

project rubric, **1:** T401, **2:** T401, **3:** T401, **4:** T401, **5:** T401, **6:** T401

research process, **1:** T401, **2:** T401, **3:** T401, **4:** T401, **5:** T401, **6:** T401

speaking, **1:** T402, **2:** T402, **3:** T402, **4:** T402, **5:** T402, **6:** T402

end-of-week, **Units 1–6:** T77A–T77B, T155A–T155B, T233A–T233B, T311A–T311B, T389A–T389B

fluency, **1:** T408, **2:** T408, **3:** T408, **4:** T408, **5:** T408, **6:** T408

portfolio, **1:** T50, T128, T206, T284, T362, T403, **2:** T50, T128, T206, T284, T362, T403, **3:** T50, T128, T206, T284, T362, T403, **4:** T50, T128, T206, T284, T362, T403, **5:** T50, T128, T206, T284, T362, T403, **6:** T50, T128, T206, T284, T362, T403

Start Smart, **1:** S94–S95

Summative Assessment, **1:** T408–T409, **2:** T408–T409, **3:** T408–T409, **4:** T408–T409, **5:** T408–T409, **6:** T408–T409

Key 2 = Unit 2

unit assessment, **1:** T408–T409, **2:** T408–T409, **3:** T408–T409, **4:** T408–T409, **5:** T408–T409, **6:** T408–T409

Author's Craft

character in illustrations, **5:** T113Q

details, **1:** T191H

dialogue, **2:** T113F, T269E, T269I, **4:** T269M

genre, **4:** T191O, T269Q

narrator, **3:** T113I

organization, **3:** T269H, **5:** T191D, T191G

punctuation, **1:** T35E

repetition, **2:** T35D, T191G, **3:** T191D, **4:** T191E, T191L, **5:** T35H, T113F, T113H, T113O, T269D, **6:** T35E, T191K

rhyme/humor, **3:** T35I

sentence structure **1:** T113D, T191E, **2:** T191D, **4:** T113J

text structure, **1:** T269H, **6:** T35M

word choice, **3:** T35E, T35F, **4:** T35D, T191D, T191G, **5:** T35F, T113D, **6:** T191H, T269E, T269K

Author/Illustrator's Purpose, 1: T35G, T113H, T191H, T269H, **2:** T35H, T113I, T191G, T269I, **3:** T35I, T113I, T191I, T269H, **4:** T35J, T113J, T191O, T269Q, **5:** T35H, T113Q, T191J, T269O, **6:** T35M, T113K, T191P, T269P

Authors/Illustrators, Main Selection

Adler, David, **5:** T191J

Ancona, George, **6:** T113K

Arnold, Tedd, **4:** T269Q

Bernasconi, Pablo, **2:** T113I

Bogacki, Tomek, **1:** T113H

Cohen, Miriam, **2:** T269I

Crews, Nina, **1:** T269H

Cronin, Doreen, **6:** T35M

Cummings, Pat, **1:** T35G

Egielski, Richard, **3:** T191I

Finton, Nancy, **2:** T191G

Garland, Michael, **1:** T191H

Henkes, Kevin, **5:** 113Q

Jenkins, Steve, **4:** T191O

Keats, Ezra Jack, **5:** 269O

Lewin, Betsy, **6:** T35M

Lin, Grace, **6:** 269P

Lobel, Arnold, **5:** 35H

Mann, Rachel, **4:** 113J

McDermott, Gerald, **4:** 35J

Morales, Magaly, **3:** 113I

Nguyen, Vincent, **2:** T35H

Novek, Minda, **3:** 269H

Rumford, James, **6:** 191P

Sayre, April Pulley, **4:** 191O

Yee, Herbert Wong, **3:** T35I

Beyond Level Options

comprehension, **Units 1–6:** T69, T147, T225, T303, T381

Gifted and Talented, **Units 1–6:** T67, T145, T223, T301, T379, T407

Leveled Reader Lessons, **Units 1–6:** T66–T67, T144–T145, T222–T223, T300–T301, T378–T379

self-selected reading, **Units 1–6:** T69, T147, T225, T303, T381

vocabulary, **Units 1–6:** T68, T146, T224, T302, T380

Big Book, Reading and Sharing, 1: T10–T11, T31, T88–T89, T109, T166–T167, T187, T244–T245, T265, T322–T323, T343, **2:** T10–T11, T31, T88–T89, T109, T166–T167, T187, T244–T245, T265, T322–T323, T343, **3:** T10–T11, T31, T88–T89, T109, T166–T167, T187, T244–T245, T265, T322–T323, T343, **4:** T10–T11, T31, T88–T89, T109, T166–T167, T187, T244–T245, T265, T322–T323, T343, **5:** T10–T11, T31, T88–T89, T109, T166–T167, T187, T244–T245, T265, T322–T323, T343, **6:** T10–T11, T31, T88–T89, T109, T166–T167, T187, T244–T245, T265, T322–T323, T343

Big Idea/Big Question, 1: xii–xiii, T390, **2:** xii–xiii, T390, **3:** xii–xiii, T390, **4:** xii–xiii, T390, **5:** xii–xiii, T390, **6:** xii–xiii, T390

Biography. *See* Genre: informational text/nonfiction.

Blending. *See* Phonemic Awareness: phoneme blending.

Book, Parts of. *See* Print Awareness.

Build Background, 1: S8, S20, S38, S50, S68, T8, T86, T164, T242, T320, **2:** T8, T86, T164, T242, T320, **3:** T8, T86, T164, T242, T320, **4:** T8, T86, T164, T242, T320, **5:** T8, T86, T164, T242, T320, **6:** T8, T86, T164, T242, T320

Capitalization. *See* Grammar.

Cause and Effect. *See* Comprehension Skills.

CCSS Correlations, Units 1–6: CCSS1–CCSS24

Central Message. *See* Comprehension Skills, theme.

Characters. *See* Comprehension Skills.

Classroom Library, 1: T413–T415, **2:** T413–T415, **3:** T413–T415, **4:** T413–T415, **5:** T413–T415, **6:** T413–T415

Close Reading, 1: T26–T27, T31, T35A–T35H, T39–T39B, T104–T105, T109, T113A–T113J, T117–T117B, T182–T183, T187, T191A–T191J, T195A–T195B, T260–T261, T265, T269A–T269H, T273, T338–T339, T343, T347A–T347E, T351, T412, **2:** T26–T27, T31, T35A–T35G, T39A–T39B, T104–T105, T109, T113A–T113H, T117A–T117B, T182–T183, T187, T191A–T191F, T195, T260–T261, T265, T269A–T269H, T273A–T273B,

B

C

T338–T339, T343, T347A–T347E, T351, T412, **3:** T26–T27, T31, T35A–T35H, T39A–T39B, T104–T105, T109, T113A–T113H, T117A–T117B, T182–T183, T187, T191A–T191H, T195–T195B, T260–T261, T265, T269A–T269G, T273A–T273B, T338–T339, T343, T347A–T347E, T351, T412, **4:** T26–T27, T35A–T35J, T39–T39B, T104–T105, T113A–T113J, T117A–T117B, T182–T183, T191A–T191H, T195A–T195B, T260–T261, T269A–T269Q, T273A–T273B, T338–T339, T347A–T347E, T351, T412, **5:** T26–T27, T35A–T35G, T39–T39B, T104–T105, T113A–T113P, T117–T117B, T182–T183, T191A–T191I, T195A–T195B, T260–T261, T269A–T269N, T273A–T273B, T338–T339, T347A–T347E, T351, T412, **6:** T26–T27, T35A–T35L, T39–T39B, T104–T105, T113A–T113J, T117, T182–T183, T191A–T191O, T195A–T195B, T260–T261, T269A–T269O, T273A–T273B, T338–T339, T347A–T347E, T351, T412

Collaborative Conversations, 1: T9, T44, T87, T122, T165, T200, T243, T278, T321, T356, **2:** T9, T44, T87, T122, T165, T200, T243, T278, T321, T356, **3:** T9, T44, T87, T122, T165, T200, T243, T278, T321, T356, **4:** T9, T44, T87, T122, T165, T200, T243, T278, T321, T356, **5:** T9, T44, T87, T122, T165, T200, T243, T278, T321, T356, **6:** T9, T44, T87, T122, T165, T200, T243, T278, T321, T356

add new ideas, **1:** T321, T356, **2:** T9, T44, **3:** T87, T122, **6:** T243, T278

ask and answer questions, **1:** T278, **2:** T243, T278, **4:** T9, T44, **5:** T9, T243, T278, **6:** T9, T44

be open to all ideas, **1:** T165, T200, T243, **3:** T9, T44, T321, T356, **4:** T87, T122, T321, T356, **5:** T165, T200, **6:** T321, T356

listen carefully, **1:** T9, T44, **2:** T165, T200, T321, T356, **3:** T243, T278, **4:** T243, T278, **5:** T87, T122, T321, T356, **6:** T87, T122

take turns talking, **1:** T87, T122, **2:** T87, T122, **3:** T165, T200, **4:** T165, T200, **5:** T44, **6:** T165, T200

Compare and Contrast. *See* Comprehension Skills.

Comparing Texts, 1: S32, S62, S92, T39, T46, T53, T63, T67, T73,

T117, T124, T131, T141, T145, T151, T195A, T202, T209, T219, T223, T229, T280, T287, T297, T301, T351, T358, T365, T375, T379, T385, **2:** T39A, T46, T53, T63, T67, T73, T117A, T124, T131, T141, T145, T151, T195, T202, T209, T219, T223, T229, T273A, T280, T287, T297, T301, T351, T358, T365, T375, T379, T385, **3:** T39A, T46, T53, T63, T67, T73, T117A, T124, T131, T141, T145, T151, T191A, T202, T209, T219, T223, T229, T273A, T280, T287, T297, T301, T351, T358, T365, T375, T379, T385, **4:** T39, T46, T53, T63, T67, T73, T117A, T124, T131, T141, T145, T151, T195, T202, T209, T219, T223, T229, T273A, T280, T287, T297, T301, T351, T358, T365, T375, T379, T385, **5:** T39, T46, T53, T63, T67, T73, T117, T124, T131, T141, T145, T151, T195A, T202, T209, T219, T223, T229, T273A, T280, T287, T297, T301, T351, T358, T365, T375, T379, T385, **6:** T39, T46, T53, T63, T67, T73, T117, T124, T131, T141, T145, T151, T195A, T202, T209, T219, T223, T229, T273A, T280, T287, T297, T301, T351, T358, T365, T375, T379, T385

Complexity of Text. *See* Access Complex Text.

Compound Words. *See* Phonics/Word Analysis: structural analysis.

Comprehension Skills

author's purpose, **6:** T105, T113B, T113C, T113G, T113I, T113J, T113L, T125, T339, T347B, T347C, T347E, T359

cause and effect, **3:** T183, T191B, T191D, T191E, T191G, T191H, T191J, T203, **4:** T31, T35G, T265, T269F, T269J, **5:** T113B, T113G, T113I, T113K, T113L, T113P, T113R, T347B, T347C, T347E, T347F, **6:** T113F, T183, T191B, T191D, T191F, T191I, T191M, T191N, T191O, T191Q, T191R, T343, T347C

character, setting, events, **2:** T27, T35B, T35C, T35D, T35E, T35F, T35G, T35I, T47, T105, T113B, T113D, T113E, T113F, T113H, T113J, T125, T261, T269B, T269C, T269D, T269E, T269F, T269H, T269J, T281, **3:** T35D, T113D, **4:** T269I

connections within text

compare and contrast, **3:** T261, T269B, T269C, T269E, T269F, T269G, T269I, T269J, T281, **4:** T109, T113D, T113H, T191F

problem and solution, **5:** T183, T191B, T191E, T191G, T191H, T191I, T191K, T191L, T203, **6:** T109, T113E

sequence, **3:** T339, T347B, T347C, T347E, T347F, T359, **4:** T187, T191J, T339, T347C, T347D, T347E, T347F, T359, **5:** T187, T191C, T191H

details, **1:** S14, S26, S44, S56, S74, S86

key details, **1:** T27, T35B, T35C, T35D, T35E, T35F, T35H, T47, T105, T113B, T113D, T113E, T113F, T113G, T113I, T113J, T125, T183, T191B, T191C, T191D, T191E, T191G, T191I, T191J, T203, T261, T269B, T269D, T269E, T269F, T269G, T269I, T269J, T281, T339, T347B, T347C, T347D, T347E, T347F, T359, **2:** T113F, T191C, T269C, T269G, T347D, **4:** T113L, T191I, **5:** T269D, **6:** T113E, T191E

main idea and key details, **4:** T105, T113D, T113E, T113G, T113I, T113K, T113L, T125, T183, T191D, T191I, T191M, T191N, T191P, T203, T343, **5:** T343

main topic and key details, **2:** T183, T191B, T191D, T191E, T191F, T191H, T203, T339, T347B, T347C, T347D, T347E, T347F, T359, **3:** T269D, T347C, T347D

plot, **3:** T27, T35B, T35C, T35G, T35H, T35J, T47, T191C, **4:** T27, T31, T35B, T35E, T35G, T35I, T47, T265, **5:** T31, T35F, T109, **6:** T183, T191B, T191D, T191F, T191I, T191M, T191N, T191O, T191Q, T191R

cause and effect, **4:** T31, T265, **5:** T113B, T113G, T113I, T113K, T113L, T113P, T113R, **6:** T35G, T183, T191B, T191D, T191F, T191I, T191M, T191N, T191O, T191Q, T191R

problem and solution, **5:** T261, T269B, T269C, T269F, T269G,

T269L, T269N, T269P, T281, **6:** T265, T269D, T269H, T269N

sequence, **3:** T105, T125, T191C, **4:** T27, T35B, T35E, T35G, T35I, **5:** T31, T35F, T109, T113M

point of view, **4:** T261, T269E, T269F, T269H, T269K, T269O, T269P, T269R, T281, **5:** T27, T35B, T35C, T35D, T35E, T35G, T35I, T35J, T47, T265, T269E, T269H, T269L, **6:** T31, T35G

reasons to support ideas, **1:** T35H, T47, T113I–T113J, T191I–T191J, T202, T269I–T269J, **2:** T35I–T35J, T47, T113J, T124, T191H, T202, T269J, T280, **3:** T35J, T47, T113J, T191J, T202, T269I–T269J, T347F, T358, **4:** T35K–T35L, T47, T113K–T113L, T124, T191P, T202, T269R, T280, T347F, T358, **5:** T35I–T35J, T47, T113R, T124, T191K–T191L, T202, T269P, T280, T347F, T358, **6:** T35N, T47, T113L, T124, T191Q–T191R, T202, T269Q–T269R, T280, T347F, T358

story structure, **3:** T27, T105, T183, **4:** T27, T269B, T269G, T269O, **5:** T35B, T35E, T105, T261, T269B, T269F, T269I, **6:** T35B, T35C, T183

text structure, **3:** T339, **4:** T191B, T191K, T339, T347B, T347D, T339, **5:** T105, T191B, T191C, **6:** T113B, T113F, T347B, T347D

theme, **6:** T27, T35B, T35D, T35F, T35I, T35K, T35L, T35N, T47, T187, T191L, T261, T269B, T269C, T269F, T269H, T269L, T269M, T269O, T269Q, T269R, T281

use illustrations/photographs, **1:** T27, T338, **2:** T105, T187, T265, T343, **3:** T21, **4:** T269G

Comprehension Strategies

ask and answer questions, **1:** S14, S26, T191D, T245, T251, T255, T265, T269B, T269C, T269E, T273, T323, T329, T333, T343, T347B, T347D, T351, **2:** T35F, T113D, **4:** T11, T21, T35C, T35H, T39, T89, T95, T99, T113B, T113C, T113E, T113F, T113H, T117B, T167, T173, T177, T191B, T191C, T191E, T195, T269C, T269N, **5:** T113M, T167, T173, T177, T191D, T191F, T245, T251, T255, T269B, T269E, T273A,

T323, T329, T333, T347B, T351, **6:** T35C, T113H, T191C

make and confirm predictions, **2:** T11, T17, T21, T31, T35B, T35C, T35E, T35F, T39B, T89, T95, T99, T109, T113B, T113C, T113E, T117A, **3:** T11, T17, T21, T31, T35B, T35D, T35F, T35G, T39A, T89, T95, T99, T109, T113B, T113D, T113E, T113F, T113G, T117A, T167, T173, T177, T187, T191B, T191E, T191F, T191H, T195, **4:** T35E, T35F, T191K, T191L, T269L, **5:** T11, T17, T21, T35B, T35D, T39, T89, T95, T99, T113C, T113E, T113J, T113K, T113L, T117, T191C, T269F, T269I, T269J, T269K, **6:** T35I, T35J, T191H, T269E, T269F

reread, **1:** S56, T269C, **2:** T167, T173, T177, T187, T191B, T191D, T191E, T195, T245, T251, T255, T265, T269B, T269D, T269F, T273A, T323, T329, T333, T343, T347B, T347C, T351, **3:** T35C, T113C, T191C, T245, T251, T255, T265, T269B, T269C, T269E, T273B, T323, T329, T333, T343, T347B, T347D, T351, **4:** T191H, **5:** T35C, T113O, T117A, **6:** T11, T17, T21, T31, T35B, T35F, T39A, T89, T95, T99, T109, T113B, T113D, T117, T269I, T323, T329, T333, T343, T347B, T347D, T351

visualize, **1:** S74, S86, T11, T17, T21, T31, T35B, T35C, T35D, T39A, T89, T109, T113B, T113C, T113E, T117, T117A, T167, T173, T177, T187, T191B, T191F, **3:** T269D, **4:** T191M, T245, T251, T255, T269B, T269D, T269E, T269L, T273A, T323, T329, T333, T347B, **5:** T113D, T191E, T269J, T269M, **6:** T167, T173, T177, T191B, T191G, T191J, T195A, T245, T251, T255, T269B, T269G, T269K, T269N, T273A

Computer Activities, Units 1–6: T2–T3, T44, T80–T81, T158–T159, T236–T237, T278, T314–T315, T396–T397, T398–T401

Computer Literacy, 1: T396–T397, **2:** T396–T397, **3:** T396–T397, **4:** T396–T397, **5:** T396–T397, **6:** T396–T397

Concepts of Print

book handling, **1:** S22, T10, T88, T166

directionality, **1:** S4, S10, S34, S76, S82, S88, **2:** T10

distinguish letters, words, sentences, **1:** S10, S16, S28, S46, S58, S76

parts of a book, **1:** S28, S52, T10, T88

reading across pages, **1:** T322

reading across page turns, **2:** T10, T166, T244, **3:** T244

return sweeps, **1:** S34, S76, T166, **2:** T10

sentence capitalization, **1:** S22, S34, S52, S58, S70, **2:** T88, T166, **3:** T10

sentence length, **1:** S88

sentence punctuation, **1:** S22, S28, S40, S52, S58, **2:** T10, T88, T166, **3:** T10, T88, T166

text treatment, **1:** S58, S70, T322, **2:** T244, **3:** T166, T322

tracking print, **1:** S10, S46, S76, S82, T10, T166

word length, **1:** S46

Connect to Content

science, **1:** T191J, T269J, **2:** T191H, T269J, **3:** T113C, T113J, T269J, **4:** T35F, T113L, T191P, T269K, T269R, T347F, **5:** T35J, T113F, T113R, T191I, T269M, T347F

social studies, **1:** T269J, T347F, **2:** T35J, T269, T347F, **3:** T269J, T347F, **4:** T347F, **6:** T269Q, T347F

See also Research and Inquiry; Science; Social Studies; Workstation Activities.

Conventions. *See* Grammar.

Corrective Feedback, 1: T13, T33, T91, T111, T169, T189, T247, T267, T325, T345, **2:** T13, T33, T91, T111, T169, T189, T247, T267, T325, T345, **3:** T13, T33, T91, T111, T169, T189, T247, T267, T325, T345, **4:** T13, T33, T91, T111, T169, T189, T247, T267, T325, T345, **5:** T13, T33, T91, T111, T169, T189, T247, T267, T325, T345, **6:** T13, T33, T91, T111, T169, T189, T247, T267, T325, T345

Critical Thinking, 1: T35H, T46–T47, T113I, T124–T125, T191I, T202–T203, T269I, T280–T281, T347F, T358–T359, **2:** T35J, T46–T47, T113J,

T124–T125, T191H, T202–T203, T269J, T280–T281, T347F, T358–T359, **3:** T35J, T46–T47, T113J, T124–T125, T191J, T202–T203, T269I, T280–T281, T347F, T358–T359, **4:** T35K, T46–T47, T113K, T124–T125, T191P, T202–T203, T269R, T280–T281, T347F, T358–T359, **5:** T35I, T46–T47, T113R, T124–T125, T191K, T202–T203, T269R, T280–T281, T347F, T358–T359, **6:** T35N, T46–T47, T113L, T124–T125, T191Q, T202–T203, T269Q, T280–T281, T347F, T358–T359

See also **Essential Questions; Make Connections.**

Cross-Curricular Connections. *See* Research and Inquiry; Science; Social Studies; Workstation Activities: science, social studies.

D

Daily Warm-Up, 1: S4, S10, S16, S22, S28, S34, S40, S46, S52, S58, S64, S70, S76, S82, S88

Decodable Text, 1: T60, T138, T216, T294, T372, **2:** T60, T138, T216, T294, T372, **3:** T60, T138, T216, T294, T372, **4:** T60, T138, T216, T294, T372, **5:** T60, T138, T216, T294, T372, **6:** T60, T138, T216, T294, T372

Decoding. *See* Phonics/Word Analysis.

Diagrams, *See* Text Features.

Dialogue, 6: T31, T49, T60

Dictation, 1: T14, T92, T170, T248, T326, **2:** T14, T92, T170, T248, T326, **3:** T14, T92, T170, T248, T326, **4:** T14, T92, T170, T248, T326, **5:** T14, T92, T170, T248, T326, **6:** T14, T92, T170, T248, T326

Dictionary, Using. *See* Vocabulary Skills and Strategies.

Differentiated Instruction, 1: T4–T7, T80–T83, T158–T161, T236–T239, T314–T317, **2:** T4–T7, T80–T83, T158–T161, T236–T239, T314–T317, **3:** T4–T7, T80–T83, T158–T161, T236–T239, T314–T317, **4:** T4–T7, T80–T83, T158–T161, T236–T239, T314–T317, **5:** T4–T7, T80–T83, T158–T161, T236–T239, T314–T317, **6:** T4–T7, T80–T83, T158–T161, T236–T239, T314–T317

See also **Approaching Level Options; Beyond Level Options; English Language Learners; On Level Options.**

Digital Learning, Units 1–6: xiii, T2–T3, T8, T10, T12, T14, T16, T18, T20, T22, T24, T26, T28, T30, T32, T34, T36, T38, T40, T42, T48, T50, T80–T81, T86, T88, T90, T92, T94, T96, T98, T100, T102, T104, T106, T108, T110, T112, T114, T116, T118, T120, T126, T128, T158–T159, T164, T166, T168, T170, T172, T174, T176, T178, T180, T182, T184, T186, T188, T190, T192, T194, T196, T198, T204, T206, T236–T237, T242, T244, T246, T250, T252, T254, T256, T258, T260, T262, T264, T266, T268, T270, T272, T274, T276, T282, T284, T314–T315, T320, T322, T324, T326, T328, T330, T332, T334, T336, T338, T340, T342, T344, T346, T348, T350, T352, T354, T360, T362, T396–T397

See also **Computer Literacy.**

Domain-Specific Vocabulary. *See* Vocabulary Acquisition, domain-specific.

E

English Language Learners

beginning, intermediate, advanced, **1:** S9, S21, S33, S39, S51, S63, S69, S93, T9, T11, T19, T37, T45, T87, T89, T97, T115, T123, T165, T167, T175, T193, T201, T243, T245, T253, T271, T279, T321, T323, T331, T349, T357, **2:** T9, T11, T19, T37, T39, T45, T87, T89, T97, T115, T117, T123, T165, T167, T175, T193, T201, T243, T245, T253, T271, T273, T279, T321, T323, T331, T349, T357, **3:** T9, T11, T19, T37, T45, T87, T89, T97, T115, T117, T123, T165, T167, T175, T193, T201, T243, T245, T253, T271, T273, T279, T321, T323, T331, T349, T357, **4:** T9, T11, T19, T37, T45, T87, T89, T97, T115, T117, T123, T165, T167, T175, T193, T201, T243, T245, T253, T271, T273, T279, T321, T323, T331, T349, T357, **5:** T9, T11, T19, T37, T45, T87, T89, T97, T115, T117, T123, T165, T167,

T175, T193, T201, T243, T245, T253, T271, T273, T279, T321, T323, T331, T349, T357, **6:** T9, T11, T19, T37, T45, T87, T89, T97, T115, T117, T123, T165, T167, T175, T193, T201, T243, T245, T253, T271, T273, T279, T321, T323, T331, T349, T357

build background, **1:** T9, T87, T165, T243, T321, **2:** T9, T87, T165, T243, T321, **3:** T9, T87, T165, T243, T321, **4:** T9, T87, T165, T243, T321, **5:** T9, T87, T165, T243, T321, **6:** T9, T87, T165, T243, T321

comprehension, **1:** T11, T31, T35H, T109, T113J, T167, T187, T191J, T245, T265, T269J, T323, T333, T347F, **2:** T11, T31, T35J, T89, T109, T113J, T167, T187, T191H, T245, T265, T269J, T323, T333, T347F, **3:** T11, T31, T35J, T60–T61, T89, T109, T113J, T167, T187, T191J, T245, T265, T269J, T323, T333, T347F, **4:** T11, T31, T35L, T89, T109, T113L, T167, T187, T191P, T245, T265, T269R, T323, T333, T347F, **5:** T11, T31, T35J, T89, T109, T113R, T167, T187, T191L, T245, T265, T269P, T323, T347F, **6:** T11, T31, T35N, T89, T109, T113L, T167, T187, T191R, T245, T265, T269R, T323, T347F

grammar, **1:** T19, T29, T77, T97, T107, T155, T175, T185, T233, T253, T263, T311, T331, T341, T389, **2:** T19, T29, T77, T97, T107, T155, T175, T185, T233, T253, T263, T311, T331, T341, T389, **3:** T19, T29, T77, T97, T107, T155, T175, T185, T233, T253, T263, T311, T331, T341, T389, **4:** T19, T29, T77, T97, T107, T155, T175, T185, T233, T253, T263, T311, T331, T341, T389, **5:** T19, T29, T77, T97, T107, T155, T175, T185, T233, T253, T263, T311, T331, T341, T389, **6:** T19, T29, T77, T97, T107, T155, T175, T185, T233, T253, T263, T311, T331, T341, T389

high-frequency words, **1:** T75, T153, T231, T309, T387, **2:** T75, T153, T231, T309, T387, **3:** T75, T153, T231, T309, T387

Leveled Reader Lessons, **1:** T72–T73, T150–T151, T228–T229, T306–T307, T384–T385, **2:** T72–T73, T150–T151, T228–T229, T306–T307, T384–T385, **3:** T72–T73, T150–T151, T228–T229,

T306–T307, T384–T385,
4: T72–T73, T150–T151, T228–
T229, T306–T307, T384–T385,
5: T72–T73, T150–T151, T228–
T229, T306–T307, T384–T385,
6: T72–T73, T150–T151, T228–
T229, T306–T307, T384–T385

Level Up, **1:** T73, T151, T229, T307,
T385, T406, **2:** T73, T151, T229,
T307, T385, T406, **3:** T73, T151,
T229, T307, T385, T406, **4:** T73,
T151, T229, T307, T385, T406,
5: T73, T151, T229, T307, T385,
T406, **6:** T73, T151, T229, T307,
T385, T406

phonemic awareness, **1:** T13, T169,
T247, T325, **2:** T169, T247, T325,
3: T13, T91, T169, T247, T325,
4: T13, T91, T169, T247, T325,
5: T13, T91, T169, T247, T325,
6: T13, T91, T169, T247, T325

Readers Theater, **1:** T394–T395,
2: T395, **3:** T395, **4:** T395, **5:** T395,
6: T395

Research and Inquiry, **1:** T45, T123,
T201, T279, T357, **2:** T45, T123,
T201, T279, T357, **3:** T45, T123,
T201, T279, T357, **4:** T45, T123,
T201, T279, T357, **5:** T45, T123,
T201, T279, T357, **6:** T45, T123,
T201, T279, T357

shared read lessons, **1:** T70–T71,
T148–T149, T226–T227, T304–
T305, T382–T383, **2:** T70–T71,
T148–T149, T226–T227, T304–
T305, T382–T383, **3:** T70–T71,
T148–T149, T226–T227, T304–
T305, T382–T383, **4:** T70–T71,
T148–T149, T226–T227, T304–
T305, T382–T383, **5:** T70–T71,
T148–T149, T226–T227, T304–
T305, T382–T383, **6:** T70–T71,
T148–T149, T226–T227, T304–
T305, T382–T383

spelling, **1:** T24, T76, T92, T102,
T154, T170, T180, T190, T232,
T248, T258, T310, T326, T336,
T388, **2:** T14, T24, T76, T92, T103,
T154, T170, T180, T190, T232,
T248, T258, T310, T326, T336,
T388, **3:** T14, T24, T76, T92, T103,
T154, T170, T180, T190, T232,
T248, T258, T310, T326, T336,
T388, **4:** T14, T24, T76, T92, T103,
T154, T170, T180, T190, T232,
T248, T258, T310, T326, T336,
T388, **5:** T24, T76, T92, T103,
T154, T170, T180, T190, T232,

T248, T258, T310, T326, T336,
T388, **6:** T14, T24, T76, T92, T103,
T154, T170, T180, T190, T232,
T248, T258, T310, T326, T336,
T388

variations in language, **1:** S6, T13,
T169, T247, T325, **2:** T169, T247,
T325, **3:** T13, T91, T169, T247,
T325, **4:** T13, T91, T169, T247,
T325, **5:** T13, T91, T169, T247,
T325, **6:** T13, T91, T169, T247,
T325

vocabulary, **1:** S66, T23, T74, T101,
T152, T179, T230, T257, T308,
T335, T386, **2:** T23, T74, T101,
T152, T179, T230, T257, T308,
T335, T386, **3:** T23, T74, T101,
T152, T179, T230, T257, T308,
T335, T386, **4:** T23, T74, T101,
T152, T179, T230, T257, T308,
T335, T386, **5:** T23, T74, T101,
T152, T179, T230, T257, T308,
T335, T386, **6:** T23, T74, T101,
T152, T179, T230, T257, T308,
T335, T386

writing, **1:** T37, T76, T115, T154,
T193, T232, T271, T310, T349,
T388, **2:** T37, T76, T115, T154,
T193, T232, T271, T310, T349,
T388, **3:** T37, T76, T115, T154,
T193, T232, T271, T310, T349,
T388, **4:** T37, T76, T115, T154,
T193, T232, T271, T310, T349,
T388, **5:** T37, T76, T115, T154,
T193, T232, T271, T310, T349,
T388, **6:** T37, T76, T115, T154,
T193, T232, T271, T310, T349,
T388

Essential Questions, **Units 1–6:** T8,
T16, T20, T30, T35A, T38, T52, T62,
T66, T72, T86, T94, T98, T108, T113A,
T116, T130, T140, T144, T150, T164,
T172, T176, T186, T191A, T194,
T208, T218, T222, T228, T242, T250,
T254, T264, T269A, T272, T286,
T296, T300, T306, T320, T328, T332,
T342, T347A, T350, T364, T374,
T378, T384, T415

Expository Text. *See* **Genre:**
informational text/nonfiction.

Extended Complex Text, **1:** T412–
T415, **2:** T412–T415, **3:** T412–T415,
4: T412–T415, **5:** T412–T415,
6: T412–T415

F

Fiction. *See* Genre: literature/fiction.

Fluency

building, **1:** S13, S24, S31, S36, S42,
S48, S54, S61, S67, S72, T12, T22,
T32, T40, T48, T90, T100, T110, T118,
T126, T168, T178, T188, T196, T204,
T246, T256, T266, T274, T282, T324,
T334, T344, T352, T360, **2:** T12, T22,
T32, T40, T48, T90, T100, T110, T118,
T126, T168, T178, T188, T196, T204,
T246, T256, T266, T274, T282, T324,
T334, T344, T352, T360, **3:** T12, T22,
T32, T40, T48, T90, T100, T110, T118,
T126, T168, T178, T188, T196, T204,
T246, T256, T266, T274, T282, T324,
T334, T344, T352, T360, **4:** T12, T22,
T32, T40, T48, T90, T100, T110, T118,
T126, T168, T178, T188, T196, T204,
T246, T256, T266, T274, T282, T324,
T334, T344, T352, T360, **5:** T12, T22,
T32, T40, T48, T90, T100, T110, T118,
T126, T168, T178, T188, T196, T204,
T246, T256, T266, T274, T282, T324,
T334, T344, T352, T360, **6:** T12, T22,
T32, T40, T48, T90, T100, T110, T118,
T126, T168, T178, T188, T196, T204,
T246, T256, T266, T274, T282, T324,
T334, T344, T352, T360

choral reading, **1:** T33, T59, T265,
T343, T371, **2:** T31, T59, T371,
3: T31, T59, T109, T265, T371,
4: T31, T59, T109, T137, T265,
5: T31, T59, T109, T187, **6:** T31,
T60, T137, T187, T215, T265, T293

connected text, **Units 1–6:** T57,
T135, T213, T291, T369

echo reading, **1:** T109, **2:** T294,
4: T49, T127, T205, T283, **5:** T49,
T127, T138, T205, T283, **6:** T205

expression (prosody), **4:** T187, T205,
T216, **5:** T265, T283, T294, **6:** T31,
T49, T60

intonation, **1:** T109, T138, **2:** T31,
T60, T265, T294, **3:** T31, T60,
T343, T372, **4:** T31, T49, T60,
T343, T361, T372, **5:** T109, T127,
T138, T343, T361, T372, **6:** T109,
T127, T138, T187, T205, T216

modeling, **1:** T31, T60, T109, T138,
T187, T216, T265, T294, T343,
T372, **2:** T31, T60, T109, T138,
T187, T216, T265, T294, T343,
T372, **3:** T31, T60, T109, T138,

T187, T216, T265, T294, T343, T372, **4:** T31, T48, T60, T109, T138, T187, T216, T265, T294, T343, T372, **5:** T31, T60, T109, T138, T187, T216, T265, T294, T343, T372, **6:** T31, T60, T109, T138, T187, T216, T265, T294, T343, T361, T372

partner reading, **1:** T17, T95, T173, T251, T329, **2:** T17, T95, T173, T251, T329, **3:** T17, T95, T173, T251, T329, **4:** T17, T95, T173, T251, T329, **5:** T17, T95, T173, T251, T329, **6:** T17, T95, T173, T251, T329

phrasing, **1:** T31, T60, T187, T216, T265, T294, T343, **2:** T187, T216, T343, T371, **3:** T265, T294, **4:** T109, T127, T138, T265, T283, T294, **5:** T31, T49, T60, T187, T205, T216, **6:** T265, T283, T294, T343, T361, T372

read dialogue, **6:** T31, T49, T60

read exclamations, **2:** T31, T60, **5:** T109, T127, T138

read patterns, **1:** T187, T216, T265, T294, **2:** T187, T216, **4:** T187, T205, T216, **5:** T265, T283, T294

read questions, **2:** T31, T60, **3:** T31, T60, **4:** T31, T49, T60, T343, T361, T372, **6:** T109, T127, T138

read with purpose and understanding, **Units 1–6:** T26, T35A–T35F, T39–T39B, T52–T53, T61, T62–T63, T65, T66–T67, T69, T72–T73, T104, T113A–T113J, T117, T130–T131, T139, T140–T141, T143, T144–T145, T147, T150–T151, T182, T191A–T191J, T195–T195B, T208–T209, T217, T218–T219, T221, T222–T223, T225, T228–T229, T260, T269A–T269J, T273, T286–T287, T295, T296–T297, T299, T300–T301, T303, T306–T307, T338, T347A–T347F, T351, T364–T365, T373, T374–T375, T377, T378–T379, T381, T384–T385

repeated phrases, **1:** T187, T216, T265, T294, **2:** T187, T216, T343, T371

reread, **6:** T109, T127, T283, T343, T361

sentence punctuation, **1:** T31, T60, T187, T216, T343, T371, **3:** T265, T294, **4:** T109, T127, T138, T265,

T283, T294, **5:** T31, T49, T60, T187, T205, T216, T343, T361, T372, **6:** T187, T205, T216, T265, T283, T294

sound-spelling, **1:** S13, S24, S31, S36, S42, S48, S54, S61, S67, S72, T12, T22, T32, T40, T48, T90, T100, T110, T118, T126, T168, T178, T188, T196, T204, T246, T256, T266, T274, T282, T324, T334, T344, T352, T360, **2:** T12, T22, T32, T40, T48, T90, T100, T110, T118, T126, T168, T178, T188, T196, T204, T246, T256, T266, T274, T282, T324, T334, T344, T352, T360, **3:** T12, T22, T32, T40, T48, T90, T100, T110, T118, T126, T168, T178, T188, T196, T204, T246, T256, T266, T274, T282, T324, T334, T344, T352, T360, **4:** T12, T22, T32, T40, T48, T90, T100, T110, T118, T126, T168, T178, T188, T196, T204, T246, T256, T266, T274, T282, T324, T334, T344, T352, T360, **5:** T12, T22, T32, T40, T48, T90, T100, T110, T118, T126, T168, T178, T188, T196, T204, T246, T256, T266, T274, T282, T324, T334, T344, T352, T360, **6:** T12, T22, T32, T40, T48, T90, T100, T110, T118, T126, T168, T178, T188, T196, T204, T246, T256, T266, T274, T282, T324, T334, T344, T352, T360

use context to confirm and self-correct, **1:** T31, T35F, T60, T61, T65, T69, T109, T113C, T113G, T138, T139, T143, T147, T191G, T216, T217, T221, T225, T265, T269B, T269C, T269E, T269G, T294, T295, T299, T303, T343, T347B, T347D, T347E, T372, T373, T377, T381, **2:** T31, T35E, T35F, T35G, T60, T61, T65, T69, T109, T113C, T113E, T113H, T138, T139, T143, T147, T191B, T191D, T191E, T191F, T216, T217, T221, T225, T265, T269B, T269D, T269F, T269G, T269H, T283, T294, T295, T299, T303, T343, T347B, T347C, T347E, T361, T372, T373, T377, T381, **3:** T31, T35C, T35D, T35H, T49, T60, T61, T65, T69, T109, T113D, T113E, T113F, T113H, T127, T138, T139, T143, T147, T187, T191C, T191F, T191H, T205, T216, T217, T221, T225, T265, T269B, T269C, T269E, T269G, T283, T294, T295, T299, T303,

T343, T347B, T347D, T347E, T361, T372, T373, T377, T381, **4:** T31, T35C, T35F, T35I, T49, T60, T61, T65, T69, T109, T113I, T127, T138, T139, T143, T147, T187, T191H, T191L, T191N, T205, T216, T217, T221, T225, T265, T269L, T269P, T283, T294, T295, T299, T303, T343, T347E, T361, T372, T373, T377, T381, **5:** T31, T35C, T35D, T35G, T49, T60, T61, T65, T69, T109, T113K, T113L, T113O, T113P, T127, T138, T139, T143, T147, T187, T191I, T205, T216, T217, T221, T225, T265, T269I, T269J, T269N, T283, T294, T295, T299, T303, T343, T347E, T361, T372, T373, T377, T381, **6:** T31, T35B, T35F, T35J, T35L, T49, T60, T61, T65, T69, T109, T113B, T113D, T113J, T127, T138, T139, T143, T147, T187, T191H, T191O, T205, T216, T217, T221, T225, T265, T269F, T269I, T269O, T283, T294, T295, T299, T303, T343, T347B, T347D, T347E, T361, T372, T373, T377, T381

word automaticity, **Units 1–6:** T35, T48, T113, T126, T191, T204, T269, T282, T325, T347, T360

word stresses, **1:** T109, T138, **2:** T265, T294, **3:** T343, T372

Folktale. *See* Genre: literature.

G

General Vocabulary. *See* Vocabulary Acquisition, general vocabulary.

Genre

comparing. *See* Comparing Texts.

focus on, **6:** T287, T297, T301, T307

informational text/nonfiction, S26, S56, S86, **1:** T260, T269A, T338, T347A, **2:** T338, T347A, **3:** T117A, T260, T269A, T338, T347A, **4:** T104, T113A, T182, T338, T347A, **5:** T182, T191A, T338, **6:** T104, T113A, T338, T347A

biography, **5:** T191A–T191L

nonfiction article, **1:** T39, T117A, T195A, T351, **2:** T39A, T117A, T191A, T273A, T351, **3:** T39A, T273A, T351, **4:** T39A, T117A,

T191A, T273A, T351, **5:** T39A, T117, T273A, T347A, T351, **6:** T39, T195A, T273A, T351

procedural/how-to article, **5:** T273A, **6:** T273A

science, **1:** T195B, T347B, **2:** T191A, **3:** T117A, **4:** T39A, T113A, T117A, T191A, T273A, **5:** T39A, T117–T117B, T273A, T347A, **6:** T195A

social studies, **1:** T39B, T117B, T269J, **2:** T39A, T117A, T347A, T351, **3:** T269A, T273A, T347A, **4:** T347A, T351, **5:** T191A, T351, **6:** T39, T113A, T273A, T347A, T351

literature/fiction, S14, S44, S74

fantasy, **1:** T104, T113A, T182, T191A, **2:** T104, T113A, T260, T269A, **3:** T26, T35A, **4:** T260, T269A, **5:** T26, T35A, T104, T113A, **6:** T26, T35A

folktale, **3:** T182, T191A, **4:** T26, T35A

play/drama, **3:** T104, T113A

realistic fiction, **1:** T26, T35A, **2:** T26, T35A, **5:** T260, T269A, **6:** T182, T191A, T260, T269A

poetry, **1:** xii, S8, S20, S38, S50, S68, S80, T273, **2:** xii, T195, **3:** xii, T195–T195B, **4:** xii, T195, **5:** xii, T195A–T195B, **6:** xii, T117

Gifted and Talented, 1: T68, T69, T146, T147, T224, T225, T302, T303, T380, T381, **2:** T68, T69, T146, T147, T224, T225, T302, T303, T380, T381, **3:** T68, T69, T146, T147, T224, T225, T302, T303, T380, T381, **4:** T68, T69, T146, T147, T224, T225, T302, T303, T380, T381, **5:** T68, T69, T146, T147, T224, T225, T302, T303, T380, T381, **6:** T68, T69, T146, T147, T224, T225, T302, T303, T380, T381

Grammar

adjectives, **5:** T97, T107, T115, T121, T129, T155

articles, **5:** T253, T263, T271, T277, T285, T311

that compare, **5:** T175, T185, T193, T199, T207, T233

adverbs

that tell how, **6:** T331, T341, T349, T355, T363, T389

that tell when, **4:** T331, T341, T349, T355, T363, T389

apostrophes

contractions, **2:** T97, T107, T115, T121, T129, **3:** T331, T341, T349, T355, T363, T389, **4:** T19, T29, T37, T43, T51

possessive nouns, **2:** T175, T185, T193, T199, T207, T233

capitalization

days, months, and holidays, **5:** T175, T185, T193, T199, T207, **6:** T97, T107, T115, T121, T129

pronoun *I*, **6:** T19, T29, T37, T43, T51, T77

proper nouns, **2:** T253, T263, T271, T277, T285, **4:** T175, T185, T193, T199, T207, **5:** T19, T29, T37, T43, T51, T175, T185, T193, T199, T207, **6:** T97, T107, T115, T121, T129

sentence beginnings, **1:** T19, T29, T37, T43, T51, T77, T175, T185, T193, T199, T207, T233, T331, T341, T349, T355, T363, T389, **2:** T331, T341, T349, T355, T363, **4:** T97, T107, T115, T121, T129, **5:** T97, T107, T115, T121, T129

titles, books and plays, **3:** T97, T107, T115, T121, T129

titles, names, **5:** T331, T341, T349, T355, T363, T389, **6:** T331, T341, T349, T355, T363

combining sentences, **5:** T19, T29, T37, T43, T51, T77

commas

in a series, **2:** T19, T29, T37, T43, T51, **3:** T19, T29, T37, T42, T51, T77, T175, T185, T193, T199, T207, **4:** T331, T341, T349, T355, T363, T389

in dates, **3:** T253, T263, T271, T277, T285, **6:** T253, T263, T271, T277, T285

in letter greetings and closings, **6:** T253, T263, T271, T277, T285

conjunctions, **5:** T19, T29, T37, T43, T51, T77

contractions, **2:** T97, T107, T115, T121, T129, **3:** T331, T341, T349, T355, T363, T389, **4:** T19, T29, T37, T42, T51

with *not,* **3:** T331, T341, T349, T355, T363, T389, **4:** T19, T29, T37, T42, T51

days, months, and holidays, **5:** T175, T185, T193, T199, T207, **6:** T97, T107, T115, T121, T129

determiners, **5:** T253, T263, T271, T277, T285, T311, **6:** T97, T107, T115, T121, T129, T155, T175, T185, T193, T199, T207, T233

end marks

exclamation points, **1:** T253, T263, T271, T277, T285, T311, T331, T341, T349, T355, T363, T389, **4:** T97, T107, T115, T121, T129, **5:** T97, T107, T115, T121, T129

period, **1:** T97, T107, T115, T121, T129, T155, T175, T185, T193, T199, T207, T233, T331, T341, T349, T355, T363, T389, **2:** T331, T341, T349, T355, T363, **4:** T97, T107, T115, T121, T129, **5:** T97, T107, T115, T121, T129

question mark, **1:** T253, T263, T271, T277, T285, T311, T331, T341, T349, T355, T363, T389, **4:** T97, T107, T115, T121, T129, **5:** T97, T107, T115, T121, T129

exclamations, **1:** T253, T263, T271, T277, T285, T311, T331, T341, T349, T355, T363, T389, **4:** T97, T107, T115, T121, T129, **5:** T97, T107, T115, T121, T129

nouns, **2:** T19, T29, T37, T43, T51, T77, T97, T107, T115, T121, T129, T155

common, **2:** T253, T263, T271, T277, T285, T311

plural, **2:** T97, T107, T115, T121, T129, T155, T331, T341, T349, T355, T363, T389

possessive, **2:** T175, T185, T193, T199, T207, T233

proper, **2:** T253, T263, T271, T277, T285, T311

possessives

nouns, **2:** T175, T185, T193, T199, T207, T233

pronouns, **6:** T97, T107, T115, T121, T129, T155

prepositional phrases, **5:** T331, T341, T349, T355, T363, T389 prepositions, **5:** T331, T341, T349, T355, T363, T389

pronouns, **6:** T19, T29, T37, T43, T51, T77, T97, T107, T115, T121, T129, T155, T175, T185, T193, T199, T207, T233, T253, T263, T271, T277, T285, T311

  indefinite, **6:** T175, T185, T193, T199, T207, T233

  personal, **1:** S28, S40, S64, **6:** T19, T29, T37, T43, T51, T77, T253, T263, T271, T277, T285, T311

  possessive, **6:** T97, T107, T115, T121, T129, T155

questions, **1:** T253, T263, T271, T277, T285, T311, T331, T341, T349, T355, T363, T389, **4:** T97, T107, T115, T121, T129, **5:** T97, T107, T115, T121, T129

sentences, **1:** T19, T29, T37, T43, T51, T77, T175, T185, T193, T199, T207, T233, T331, T341, T349, T355, T363, T389

  capitalization, **1:** T19, T29, T37, T43, T51, T77, T175, T185, T193, T199, T207, T233, T331, T341, T349, T355, T363, T389

  compound, **5:** T19, T29, T37, T43, T51, T77

  declarative, **1:** T175, T185, T193, T199, T207, T233, T331, T341, T349, T355, T363, T389, **2:** T331, T341, T349, T355, T363, **4:** T97, T107, T115, T121, T129, **5:** T97, T107, T115, T121, T129

  exclamatory, **1:** T253, T263, T271, T277, T285, T311, T331, T341, T349, T355, T363, T389, **5:** T97, T107, T115, T121, T129

  punctuation. *See* Grammar: end marks.

speaking activities, **1:** T19, T29, T37, T43, T97, T107, T115, T121, T175, T185, T193, T199, T253, T263, T271, T277, T331, T341, T349, T355, **2:** T19, T29, T37, T43, T97, T107, T115, T121, T175, T185, T193, T199, T253, T263, T271, T277, T331, T341, T349, T355, **3:** T19, T29, T37, T43, T97, T107, T115, T121, T175, T185, T193, T199, T253, T263, T271, T277, T331, T341, T349, T355, **4:** T19, T29, T37, T43, T97, T107, T115, T121, T175, T185, T193, T199,

T253, T263, T271, T277, T331, T341, T349, T355, **5:** T19, T29, T37, T43, T97, T107, T115, T121, T175, T185, T193, T199, T253, T263, T271, T277, T331, T341, T349, T355, **6:** T19, T29, T37, T43, T97, T107, T115, T121, T175, T185, T193, T199, T253, T263, T271, T277, T331, T341, T349, T355

statements, **1:** T175, T185, T193, T199, T207, T233, T331, T341, T349, T355, T363, T389, **2:** T331, T341, T349, T355, T363, **4:** T97, T107, T115, T121, T129, **5:** T97, T107, T115, T121, T129

titles

  books, plays, **3:** T97, T107, T115, T121, T129, **4:** T253, T263, T271, T277, T285, **5:** T253, T263, T271, T277, T285

  names, **5:** T331, T341, T349, T355, T363, **6:** T331, T341, T349, T355, T363

  underlining, **3:** T97, T107, T115, T121, T129, **4:** T253, T263, T271, T277, T285, **5:** T253, T263, T271, T277, T285

upper- and lowercase letters, **1:** T13, T91, T169, T247, T325, **2:** T13, T91, T169, T247, T325, **3:** T13, T91, T169, T247, T325, **4:** T13, T91, T169, T247, T325, **5:** T13, T91, T169, T247, T325, **6:** T13, T91, T169, T247, T325

verbs, **3:** T19, T29, T37, T43, T51, T77

  future-tense verbs, **3:** T175, T185, T193, T199, T207, T233

  go and *do*, **4:** T175, T185, T193, T199, T207, T233

  has and *have*, **4:** T97, T107, T115, T121, T129, T155

  is and *are*, **3:** T253, T263, T271, T277, T285, T311

  past-tense verbs, **3:** T175, T185, T193, T199, T207, T233

  plural verbs, **3:** T97, T107, T115, T121, T129, T155

  present-tense verbs, **3:** T97, T107, T115, T121, T129, T155

  see and *saw*, **4:** T253, T263, T271, T277, T285, T311

was and *were*, **4:** T19, T29, T37, T43, T51, T77

word order, **1:** T97, T107, T115, T121, T129, T155, T331, T341, T349, T355, T363, T389

Graphic Organizers

charts

  author's purpose chart, **6:** T105, T113C, T113G, T113I, T113J, T339, T347B, T347C, T347E

  cause and effect chart, **3:** T183, T191B, T191D, T191E, T191G, T191H, T191J, **5:** T105, T113B, T113H, T113L, T113P, T339, T347C, T347E, **6:** T183, T191D, T191F, T191I, T191N, T191O

  character/setting/events chart, **2:** T27, T35B, T35D, T35E, T35G, T35I, T105, T113B, T113D, T113E, T113F, T113H, T261, T269B, T269C, T269D, T269F, T269H, T269J

  details chart, **1:** T27, T35B, T35C, T35D, T35E, T35F, T35H, T105, T113B, T113D, T113F, T113G, T191B, T191C, T191D, T191E, T191G, T269B, T269D, T269E, T269F, T269G, T339, T347B, T347D, T347E

  main idea and details chart, **4:** T105, T113D, T113E, T113G, T113I, T113K, T183, T191D, T191I, T191M, T191N, T191P

  main topic and details chart, **2:** T183, T191B, T191D, T191E, T191F, T339, T347B, T347C, T347E

  one-column chart, **5:** T106, T321

  point of view chart, **4:** T261, T269E, T269F, T269H, T269K, T269O, T269P, T269R, **5:** T27, T35C, T35E, T35G

  problem and solution chart, **5:** T183, T191B, T191E, T191G, T191H, T191I, T261, T269C, T269G, T269L, T269N, T269P

  sequence chart, **1:** T330, **2:** T96, T106, **3:** T105, T113B, T113C, T113E, T113H, T339, T347B, T347C, T347E, **4:** T27, T35E, T35G, T35I, T35K, T330, T339, T340, T347C, T347D, T347E, T347F, **5:** T18, T28, T330, T340, **6:** T18, T28 theme chart, **6:** T27, T35B, T35D, T35F, T35I, T35K, T35L, T261, T269C, T269F, T269H, T269L, T269M, T269O, T269Q

two-column chart, **1:** T9, T46, T87, T124, T252, **3:** T165, **4:** T87, T124, **5:** T124, T202, T243, T280

list, **1:** S9, S15, S27, S33, S39, S45, S51, S69, S75, S81

Venn diagram, **2:** T87, T124, **3:** T243, T261, T269C, T269E, T269F, T269G, T269I, T280, **4:** T9, T46

word web, **1:** S87, S93, T18, T28, T96, T106, T174, T243, T321, T358, **2:** T9, T18, T28, T46, T165, T174, T184, T202, T243, T252, T262, T280, T321, T330, T340, T358, **3:** T9, T18, T28, T46, T87, T96, T106, T124, T174, T184, T252, T262, T321, T330, T340, T358, **4:** T18, T28, T96, T106, T165, T174, T184, T202, T243, T252, T262, T280, T321, T358, **5:** T9, T46, T87, T96, T174, T184, T252, T262, **6:** T9, T46, T87, T96, T106, T165, T174, T184, T202, T243, T252, T262, T280, T321, T330, T340, T358

H

Handwriting. *See* Penmanship.

High-Frequency Words, 1: S7, S13, S19, S25, S31, S37, S43, S49, S55, S61, S67, S73, S79, S85, S91, T15, T25, T35, T41, T49, T59, T64, T75, T93, T103, T113, T119, T127, T137, T142, T153, T171, T181, T191, T197, T205, T215, T220, T231, T249, T259, T269, T275, T283, T293, T298, T309, T327, T337, T347, T353, T361, T371, T376, T387, **2:** T15, T25, T35, T41, T49, T59, T64, T75, T93, T103, T113, T119, T127, T137, T142, T153, T171, T181, T191, T197, T205, T215, T220, T231, T249, T259, T269, T275, T283, T293, T298, T309, T327, T337, T347, T353, T361, T371, T376, T387, **3:** T15, T25, T35, T41, T49, T59, T64, T75, T93, T103, T113, T119, T127, T137, T142, T153, T171, T181, T191, T197, T205, T215, T220, T231, T249, T259, T269, T275, T283, T293, T298, T309, T327, T337, T347, T353, T361, T371, T376, T387, **4:** T14–T15, T25, T34–T35, T41, T49, T59, T64,

T75, T92–T93, T102–T103, T112–T113, T119, T127, T137, T142, T153, T170–T171, T180–T181, T190–T191, T197, T205, T215, T220, T231, T248–T249, T258–T259, T268–T269, T275, T283, T293, T298, T309, T327, T336–T337, T346–T347, T353, T361, T371, T376, T387, **5:** T14–T15, T25, T34–T35, T41, T49, T59, T64, T75, T92–T93, T102–T103, T112–T113, T119, T127, T137, T142, T153, T170–T171, T180–T181, T190–T191, T197, T205, T215, T220, T231, T248–T249, T258–T259, T268–T269, T275, T283, T293, T298, T309, T326–T327, T336–T337, T346–T347, T353, T361, T371, T376, T387, **6:** T14–T15, T24–T25, T34–T35, T41, T49, T59, T64, T75, T92–T93, T102–T103, T112–T113, T119, T127, T137, T142, T153, T170–T171, T180–T181, T190–T191, T197, T205, T215, T220, T231, T248–T249, T258–T259, T268–T269, T275, T283, T293, T298, T309, T326–T327, T337, T346–T347, T353, T361, T371, T376, T387

word bank, **1:** T35, T113, T191, T269, T347, **2:** T35, T113, T191, T269, T347, **3:** T35, T113, T191, T269, T347, **4:** T35, T113, T191, T269, T347, **5:** T35, T113, T191, T269, T347, **6:** T35, T113, T191, T269, T347

I

Illustrations/Photographs, Use, 1: T27, T261, T338, **2:** T105, T187, T265, T343, **3:** T21, **4:** T269G

Illustrator's Craft

characters' actions, **2:** T113I

characters in illustrations, **5:** T113Q

collage, **5:** T191J

color, **5:** T269O, **6:** T191P

details, **1:** T113H, **3:** T191I, **6:** T269P

facial expressions, **1:** T35G, **4:** 269G

illustrations, **4:** 35J

points of view, **2:** T35H

Independent Reading, 1: T61, T65, T69, T139, T143, T147, T217, T221, T225, T295, T299, T303, T373, T377, T381, T413, **2:** T61, T65, T69, T139, T143, T147, T217, T221, T225, T295,

T299, T303, T373, T377, T381, T413, **3:** T61, T65, T69, T139, T143, T147, T217, T221, T225, T295, T299, T303, T373, T377, T381, T413, **4:** T61, T65, T69, T139, T143, T147, T217, T221, T225, T295, T299, T303, T373, T377, T381, T413, **5:** T61, T65, T69, T139, T143, T147, T217, T221, T225, T295, T299, T303, T373, T377, T381, T413, **6:** T61, T65, T69, T139, T143, T147, T217, T221, T225, T295, T299, T303, T373, T377, T381, T413

Inflected Form. *See* Phonics/Word Analysis: structural analysis.

Informational Text. *See* Genre.

Interactive Read-Aloud, 1: T10–T11, T21, T88–T89, T99, T166–T167, T177, T244–T245, T322–T323, T333, **2:** T10–T11, T21, T88–T89, T99, T166–T167, T177, T244–T245, T322–T323, T333, **3:** T10–T11, T21, T88–T89, T99, T166–T167, T177, T244–T245, T322–T323, T333, **4:** T10–T11, T21, T88–T89, T99, T166–T167, T177, T244–T245, T322–T323, T333, **5:** T10–T11, T21, T88–T89, T99, T166–T167, T177, T244–T245, T322–T323, T333, **6:** T10–T11, T21, T88–T89, T99, T166–T167, T177, T244–T245, T322–T323, T333

Intervention Program, 1: T4–T7, T77A–T77B, T80–T83, T155A–T155B, T158–T161, T233A–T233B, T236–T239, T311A–T311B, T314–T317, T389A–T389B, T408–T409, **2:** T4–T7, T77A–T77B, T80–T83, T155A–T155B, T158–T161, T233A–T233B, T236–T239, T311A–T311B, T314–T317, T389A–T389B, T408–T409, **3:** T4–T7, T77A–T77B, T80–T83, T155A–T155B, T158–T161, T233A–T233B, T236–T239, T311A–T311B, T314–T317, T389A–T389B, T408–T409, **4:** T4–T7, T77A–T77B, T80–T83, T155A–T155B, T158–T161, T233A–T233B, T236–T239, T311A–T311B, T314–T317, T389A–T389B, T408–T409, **5:** T4–T7, T77A–T77B, T80–T83, T155A–T155B, T158–T161, T233A–T233B, T236–T239, T311A–T311B, T314–T317, T389A–T389B, T408–T409, **6:** T4–T7, T77A–T77B, T80–T83, T155A–T155B, T158–T161, T233A–T233B, T236–T239, T311A–T311B, T314–T317, T389A–T389B, T408–T409

Tier 2 Intervention, **1:** T54, T56, T60, T132, T134, T138, T210,

T212, T216, T288, T290, T294, T366, T368, T372, T409, **2:** T54, T56, T60, T132, T134, T138, T210, T212, T216, T288, T290, T294, T366, T368, T372, T409, **3:** T54, T56, T60, T132, T134, T138, T210, T212, T216, T288, T290, T294, T366, T368, T372, T409, **4:** T54, T56, T60, T132, T134, T138, T210, T212, T216, T288, T290, T294, T366, T368, T372, T409, **5:** T54, T56, T60, T132, T134, T138, T210, T212, T216, T288, T290, T294, T366, T368, T372, T409, **6:** T54, T56, T60, T132, T134, T138, T210, T212, T216, T288, T290, T294, T366, T368, T372, T409

Tier 3 Intervention, **1:** T409, **2:** T409, **3:** T409, **4:** T409, **5:** T409, **6:** T409

J

Journal Writing. *See* Writer's Notebook.

K

Key Details. *See* Comprehension Skills.

L

Language. *See* Grammar; Spelling; Vocabulary Acquisition.

Lesson Plans, Suggested Weekly,
1: S2–S3, T4–T5, T82–T83, T160–T161, T238–T239, T316–T317, **2:** T4–T5, T80–T81, T158–T159, T236–T237, T314–T315, **3:** T4–T5, T80–T81, T158–T159, T236–T237, T314–T315, **4:** T4–T5, T80–T81, T158–T159, T236–T237, T314–T315, **5:** T4–T5, T80–T81, T158–T159, T236–T237, T314–T315, **6:** T4–T5, T80–T81, T158–T159, T236–T237, T314–T315

Leveled Reader lessons. *See under* Approaching Level Options; Beyond

Level Options; English Language Learners; On Level Options.

Level of Complexity. *See* Access Complex Text.

Level Up, 1: T404–T407, **2:** T404–T407, **3:** T404–T407, **4:** T404–T407, **5:** T404–T407, **6:** T404–T407

Library, 1: T412–T415, **2:** T412–T415, **3:** T412–T415, **4:** T412–T415, **5:** T412–T415, **6:** T412–T415

Listening. *See also* Collaborative Conversations.

checklists, **1:** T401, T403, **2:** T401, T403, **3:** T401, T403, **4:** T401, T403, **5:** T401, T403, **6:** T401, T403

following directions, **1:** S13, S73

for a purpose, **1:** T11, T21, T89, T99, T177, T187, T245, T255, T323, T333, **2:** T11, T21, T89, T99, T177, T187, T245, T255, T323, T333, **3:** T11, T21, T89, T99, T177, T187, T245, T255, T323, T333, **4:** T11, T21, T89, T99, T177, T187, T245, T255, T323, T333, **5:** T11, T21, T89, T99, T177, T187, T245, T255, T323, T333, **6:** T11, T21, T89, T99, T177, T187, T245, T255, T323, T333

speaking and listening skills

ask and answer questions, **1:** T278, **2:** T243, T278, **4:** T9, T44, **5:** T9, T243, T278, **6:** T9, T44

build on others' conversations, **1:** T321, T356, **2:** T9, T44, **3:** T87, T122, **6:** T243, T278

follow agreed upon rules, **1:** T9, T44, T87, T122, **2:** T87, T122, T165, T200, T321, T356, **3:** T165, T200, T243, T278, **4:** T165, T200, T243, T278, **5:** T44, T87, T122, T321, T356, **6:** T87, T122, T165, T200

presentations, **1:** T47, T50, T125, T128, T203, T206, T281, T284, T356, T359, T402–T403, **2:** T47, T50, T125, T128, T203, T206, T281, T284, T356, T359, T402–T403, **3:** T47, T50, T125, T128, T203, T206, T281, T284, T356, T359, T402–T403, **4:** T47, T50, T125, T128, T203, T206, T281, T284, T356, T359, T402–T403, **5:** T47, T50, T125, T128, T203,
T206, T281, T284, T356, T359, T402–T403, **6:** T47, T50, T125, T128, T203, T206, T281, T284, T356, T359, T402–T403

Listening Comprehension, 1: S8, S14, S20, S26, S32, S38, S44, S50, S56, S62, S68, S74, S80, T10–T11, T21, T60, T88–T89, T99, T166–T167, T177, T244–T245, T322–T323, T333, **2:** T10–T11, T21, T60, T88–T89, T99, T166–T167, T177, T244–T245, T322–T323, T333, **3:** T10–T11, T21, T60, T88–T89, T99, T166–T167, T177, T244–T245, T322–T323, T333, **4:** T10–T11, T21, T60, T88–T89, T99, T166–T167, T177, T244–T245, T322–T323, T333, **5:** T10–T11, T21, T60, T88–T89, T99, T166–T167, T177, T244–T245, T322–T323, T333, **6:** T10–T11, T21, T60, T88–T89, T99, T166–T167, T177, T244–T245, T322–T323, T333

Literacy Workstations. *See* Workstation Activities.

Literary Devices and Elements

alliteration, **2:** xii, **5:** T195, T195A, T195B

onomatopoeia, **4:** xii

repetition, **2:** T194, T195, **5:** xii

rhyme, **1:** xii, T272, T273, **3:** T194, T195A, T195B

rhythm, **3:** xii

sensory words, **4:** T194, T195, **6:** T116, T117

structure, **6:** xii

Literary Response. *See also* Respond to Reading: literature.

personal response, **1:** S32, S62, S92, T21, T35H, T39B, T99, T113J, T117B, T187, T191J, T195B, T255, T269J, T273, T343, T347F, T351, **2:** T21, T35J, T39B, T99, T113J, T117B, T187, T191H, T195, T255, T269J, T273B, T343, T347F, T351, **3:** T21, T35J, T39B, T99, T113J, T117B, T187, T191J, T195B, T255, T269J, T273B, T343, T347F, T351, **4:** T21, T35L, T39B, T99, T113L, T117B, T187, T191P, T195, T255, T269R, T273B, T343, T347F, T351, **5:** T21, T35J, T39B, T99, T113R, T117B, T187, T191L, T195B, T255, T269P, T273B, T343, T347F, T351, **6:** T21, T35N, T39B, T99, T113L,

T117, T187, T191R, T195B, T255, T269R, T273B, T343, T347F, T351

Literature Circles, Units 1–6: T53, T63, T66, T73, T131, T141, T145, T151, T109, T219, T223, T229, T287, T297, T301, T307, T365, T375, T379, T385

Literature Selections, Main

A Lost Button (Lobel), **5:** T35A–T35G

Animal Teams (Mann), **4:** T113A–T113I

At a Pond (Finton), **2:** T191A–T191F

Big Yuca Plant, The (Morales), **3:** T113A–T113H

Building Bridges, **5:** T347A–T347D

Click, Clack, Moo: Cows That Type (Cronin), **6:** T35A–T35C

Flip (Garland), **1:** T191A–T191G

Friends (Crews), **1:** T269A–T269G

From Cows to You, **3:** T347A–T347D

Fun with Maps, **2:** T347A–T347D

Gingerbread Man, The (Egielski), **3:** T191A–T191H

Go, Pip! (Bogacki), **1:** T113A–T113G

Happy Birthday, U.S.A.!, **6:** T347A–T347D

Hi! Fly Guy (Arnold), **4:** T269A–T269P

How Bat Got Its Wings (McDermott), **4:** T35A–T35I

Kitten's First Full Moon (Henkes), **5:** T113A–T113P

Koko and Penny, **4:** T347A–T347D

Lissy's Friends (Lin), **6:** T269A–T269O

Long Ago and Now (Novek), **3:** T269A–T269G

Meet Rosina (Ancona), **6:** T113A–T113J

Move It!, **1:** T347A–T347D

Nat and Sam (Cummings), **1:** T35A–T35F

Nell's Books (Cohen), **2:** T269A–T269H

On My Way to School (Yee), **3:** T35A–T35H

Pigs, the Wolf, and the Mud, The (Tarlow), **2:** T113A–T113H

Rain School (Rumford), **6:** T191A–T191O

Red Hat, The (Torres), **2:** T35A–T35G

Thomas Edison, Inventor (Adler), **5:** T191A–T191I

Vulture View (Sayre), **4:** T191A–T191N

Whistle for Willie (Keats), **5:** T269A–T269N

Literature Selections, Paired

"Abuelita's Lap" (Mora), **6:** T117

"Bats! Bats! Bats!" **4:** T39–T39B

"Busy As a Bee," **4:** T117A–T117B

"Firefighters at Work," **2:** T39A–T39B

"Food Chart, A," **3:** T351

"From Horse to Plane," **3:** T273A–T273B

"Higglety, Pigglety, Pop!"; "Hey! Diddle, Diddle"; "Star Light," **3:** T195A–T195B

"Homes Around the World," **2:** T117A–T117B

"How Plants Grow," **3:** T117A–T117B

"I Live Here," **1:** T117–T117B

"It's About Time," **3:** T39A–T39B

"Kids Can Help!" **2:** T273A–T273B

"Making Paper Shapes," **6:** T273A–T273B

"March On!" **6:** T39–T39B

"Meet the Insects," **4:** T273A–T273B

"Moon, The," **5:** T117–T117B

"North, East, South, or West?" **2:** T351

"Rainy Weather," **6:** T195A–T195B

"Rules at School," **1:** T39–T39B

"Saving Mountain Gorillas," **4:** T351

"Shake! Strike! Strum!" **5:** T273A–T273B

"Small Joy," **5:** T351

"Sort It Out," **5:** T39–T39B

"There Are Days and There Are Days," **1:** T273

"Using Diagrams," **1:** T351

"Way Down Deep," **2:** T195

"What Pets Need," **1:** T195A–T195B

"When It's Snowing" (Fisher), **4:** T195

"Windshield Wipers" and "Scissors" (Dotlich), **5:** T195A–T195B

"Young Nation Grows, A," **6:** T351

Lowercase Letters, 1: T13, T91, T169, T247, T325, **2:** T13, T91, T169, T247, T325, **3:** T13, T91, T169, T247, T325, **4:** T13, T91, T169, T247, T325, **5:** T13, T91, T169, T247, T325, **6:** T13, T91, T169, T247, T325

M

Main Idea, *See* Comprehension Skills.

Make Connections, 1: S32, S62, S92, T21, T35H, T39B, T53, T63, T67, T73, T99, T113J, T117B, T131, T141, T145, T151, T191J, T195B, T209, T219, T223, T229, T255, T269J, T273, T287, T297, T301, T307, T351, T365, T375, T379, T385, **2:** T21, T35J, T39B, T53, T63, T67, T73, T99, T113J, T117B, T131, T141, T145, T151, T191H, T195B, T209, T219, T223, T229, T255, T269J, T273B, T287, T297, T301, T307, T351, T365, T375, T379, T385, **3:** T21, T35J, T39B, T53, T63, T67, T73, T99, T113J, T117B, T131, T141, T145, T151, T191J, T195B, T209, T219, T223, T229, T255, T269J, T273B, T287, T297, T301, T307, T351, T365, T375, T379, T385, **4:** T21, T35L, T39B, T53, T63, T67, T73, T99, T113L, T117B, T131, T141, T145, T151, T191P, T195, T209, T219, T223, T229, T255, T269R, T273B, T287, T297, T301, T307, T351, T365, T375, T379, T385, **5:** T21, T35J, T39B, T53, T63, T67, T73, T99, T113R, T117B, T131, T141, T145, T151, T191L, T195B, T209, T219, T223, T229, T255, T269P, T273B, T287, T297, T301, T307, T351, T365, T375, T379, T385, **6:** T21, T35N, T39B, T53, T63, T67, T73, T99, T113L, T117, T131, T141, T145, T151, T191R, T195B, T209, T219, T223, T229, T255, T269R, T273B, T287, T297, T301, T307, T351, T365, T375, T379, T385

Maps. *See* Text Features.

Media Literacy. *See* Reading Digitally.

Meet the Author/Illustrator, 1: T35G, T113H, T191H, T269H, **2:** T35H,

T113I, T191G, T269I, **3:** T35I, T113I, T191I, T269H, **4:** T35J, T113J, T191O, T269Q, **5:** T35H, T113Q, T191J, T269O, **6:** T35M, T113K, T191P, T269P

Meet the Photographer, 6: T113K

N

Narrative Text. *See* Writing Text Types/Purposes.

Nonfiction. *See* Genre.

Note-Taking, 1: T44, T122, T200, T278, T356, T400, T412, **2:** T44, T122, T200, T278, T356, T398, T412, **3:** T44, T122, T200, T278, T356, T398, T412, **4:** T44, T122, T200, T278, T356, T412, **5:** T44, T122, T200, T278, T356, T398, T412, **6:** T44, T122, T200, T278, T356, T398, T412

Nouns. *See* Grammar.

O

On Level Options

comprehension, **Units 1–6:** T65, T143, T221, T299, T377

Leveled Reader Lessons, **Units 1–6:** T62–T63, T140–T141, T218–T219, T296–T297, T374–T375

Level Up, **Units 1–6:** T63, T141, T219, T297, T375, T405

phonics, **Units 1–6:** T64, T142, T220, T298, T376

self-selected reading, **Units 1–6:** T65, T143, T221, T299, T377

vocabulary, **Units 1–6:** T64, T142, T220, T298, T376

words to know, **4:** T64, T142, T220, T298, T376, **5:** T64, T142, T220, T298, T376, **6:** T64, T142, T220, T298, T376

Online Articles, 1: T396–T397, **2:** T396–T397, **3:** T396–T397, **4:** T396–T397, **5:** T396–T397, **6:** T396–T397

Oral Blending, 1: S17, S35, S53, S65, S71, T13, T23, T32, T48, T55, T91, T101, T110, T126, T132, T169, T178,

T179, T188, T204, T210, T247, T257, T266, T282, T325, T335, T344, T360, T367, **2:** T12, T23, T32, T48, T54, T55, T91, T101, T110, T126, T133, T178, T179, T204, T210, T247, T257, T266, T282, T289, T325, T335, T344, T360, T366, **3:** T12, T23, T32, T48, T91, T101, T110, T126, T132, T169, T179, T188, T204, T211, T247, T257, T266, T282, T289, T334, T360, T366, **4:** T32, T48, T55, T126, T132, T178, T204, T210, T344, T366, **5:** T32, T48, T55, T110, T126, T132, T188, T204, T266, T282, T288, T324, T352, T360, T366, T367, **6:** T110, T132, T266, T282, T288, T334, T366

Oral Language/Vocabulary, 1: T8, T20, T30, T68, T74, T86, T98, T108, T116, T146, T152, T164, T176, T186, T194, T224, T230, T242, T254, T264, T272, T302, T308, T320, T332, T342, T350, T380, **2:** T8, T20, T30, T38, T68, T74, T86, T98, T108, T116, T146, T152, T164, T176, T186, T194, T224, T230, T242, T254, T264, T272, T302, T308, T320, T332, T342, T350, T380, **3:** T8, T20, T30, T38, T68, T74, T86, T98, T108, T116, T146, T152, T164, T176, T186, T194, T224, T230, T242, T254, T264, T272, T302, T308, T320, T332, T342, T350, T380, **4:** T8, T10, T20, T30, T38, T68, T74, T86, T88, T98, T108, T116, T146, T152, T164, T166, T176, T186, T194, T224, T230, T242, T244, T254, T264, T272, T302, T308, T320, T322, T332, T342, T350, T380, **5:** T8, T10, T20, T30, T38, T68, T74, T86, T88, T98, T108, T116, T146, T152, T164, T166, T176, T186, T194, T224, T230, T242, T244, T254, T264, T272, T302, T308, T320, T322, T332, T342, T350, T380, **6:** T8, T10, T20, T30, T38, T68, T74, T86, T88, T98, T108, T116, T146, T152, T164, T166, T176, T186, T194, T224, T230, T242, T244, T254, T264, T272, T302, T308, T320, T322, T332, T342, T350, T380

Oral Presentation

Research and Inquiry, **1:** T47, T125, T203, T281, T359, **2:** T47, T125, T203, T281, T359, **3:** T47, T125, T203, T281, T359, **4:** T47, T125, T203, T281, T359, **5:** T47, T125, T203, T281, T359, **6:** T47, T125, T203, T281, T359

writing, **1:** T50, T128, T206, T284, T358, T402–T403, **2:** T50, T128, T206, T284, T358, T402–T403,

3: T50, T128, T206, T284, T358, T402–T403, **4:** T50, T128, T206, T284, T358, T402–T403, **5:** T50, T128, T206, T284, T358, T402–T403, **6:** T50, T128, T206, T284, T358, T402–T403

P

Paired/Partners, 1: T17, T42, T44–T45, T95, T120, T122–T123, T173, T198, T200–T201, T251, T276, T278–T279, T329, T354, T356–T357, **2:** T17, T42, T44–T45, T95, T120, T122–T123, T173, T198, T200–T201, T251, T276, T278–T279, T329, T354, T356–T357, **3:** T17, T42, T44–T45, T95, T120, T122–T123, T173, T198, T200–T201, T251, T276, T278–T279, T329, T354, T356–T357, **4:** T17, T42, T44–T45, T95, T120, T122–T123, T173, T198, T200–T201, T251, T276, T278–T279, T329, T354, T356–T357, **5:** T17, T42, T44–T45, T95, T120, T122–T123, T173, T198, T200–T201, T251, T276, T278–T279, T329, T354, T356–T357, **6:** T17, T42, T44–T45, T95, T120, T122–T123, T173, T198, T200–T201, T251, T276, T278–T279, T329, T354, T356–T357

Peer Conferences, 1: T42, T120, T198, T276, T354, **2:** T42, T120, T198, T276, T354, **3:** T42, T120, T198, T276, T354, **4:** T42, T120, T198, T276, T354, **5:** T42, T120, T198, T276, T354, **6:** T42, T120, T198, T276, T354

Penmanship, 1: S13, S25, S43, S55, S73, S85, T13, T91, T169, T247, T325, **2:** T13, T91, T169, T247, T325, **3:** T13, T91, T169, T247, T325, **4:** T13, T91, T169, T247, T325, **5:** T13, T91, T169, T247, T325, **6:** T13, T91, T169, T247, T325

correct writing position, **1:** T325, **5:** T325

spacing, words and sentences, **3:** T325

staying on the lines, **6:** T325

uppercase and lowercase letters, **1:** T13, T91, T169, T247, T325, **2:** T13, T91, T169, T247, T325, **3:** T13, T91, T169, T247, T325, **4:** T13, T91, T169, T247, T325, **5:** T13, T91, T169, T247, T325, **6:** T13, T91, T169, T247, T325

Personal Narrative. *See* Writing Text Types/Purposes.

Phonemic Awareness

contrast sounds, **1:** T168, T196, T210, **4:** T188, T211, **5:** T12, T54

phoneme addition, **2:** T334, T352, **3:** T22, T54, **4:** T360, T367, **5:** T196, T211, **6:** T352, T366

phoneme blending, **1:** S17, S35, S53, S65, S71, T32, T48, T55, T110, T126, T132, T178, T204, T210, T282, T360, T367, **2:** T12, T32, T48, T54, T55, T110, T126, T133, T178, T204, T210, T266, T282, T289, T344, T360, T366, **3:** T48, T126, T132, T188, T204, T211, T282, T289, T334, T360, T366, **4:** T32, T48, T55, T126, T132, T178, T204, T210, T344, T366, **5:** T32, T48, T55, T110, T126, T132, T188, T204, T266, T282, T288, T324, T352, T360, T366, T367, **6:** T110, T132, T266, T282, T288, T334, T366

phoneme categorization, **1:** T100, T246, T288, T324, T352, T366, **2:** T168, T196, T210, T256, T274, T288, T289, **4:** T22, T54, T168, T196, T210, T246, T288, T324, T352, T366, **5:** T22, T40, T54, T168, T210, T344, T366, **6:** T90, T118, T132, T168, T196, T210, T211

phoneme deletion, **1:** T367, **3:** T100, T118, T133, T344, T367, **4:** T334, T360, T367, **5:** T118, T133, **6:** T344, T367

phoneme identity, **1:** S5, **2:** T100, T118, T132, **3:** T12, T40, T54, **4:** T90, T118, T132, T256, T274, T288, **6:** T12, T54

phoneme isolation, **1:** S11, S41, T22, T40, T54, **2:** T22, T40, T54, T55, T246, T288, **3:** T256, T274, T288, **5:** T256, T274, T288, T289

phoneme reversal, **6:** T100, T133, T324, T367

phoneme segmentation, **1:** S77, S83, T48, T55, T126, T133, T204, T211, T256, T282, T289, T334, T360, T366, **2:** T48, T126, T133, T204, T211, T324, T360, T366, T367, **3:** T48, T54, T110, T126, T132, T178, T196, T204, T211, T246, T266, T282, T288, T289, T324, T352, T360, T366, T367, **4:** T48, T55, T100, T126, T133, T204, T211, T266, T282, T289, **5:** T48, T55, T204, T210, T334, T360, T367, **6:** T22, T48, T55, T126, T178, T204, T210, T256, T274, T288

phoneme substitution, **1:** T188, T211, **2:** T188, T211, **3:** T32, T56, **4:** T211, T282, T289, **5:** T100, T126, T133, T178, T211, T246, T282, T289 **6:** T48, T126, T133, T188, T204, T211, T282, T289

Phonics/Word Analysis

analyze errors, **1:** T24, T102, T180, T258, T336, **2:** T24, T102, T180, T258, T336, **3:** T24, T102, T180, T258, T336, **4:** T24, T102, T180, T258, T336, **5:** T24, T102, T180, T258, T336, **6:** T24, T102, T180, T258, T336

articulation, **1:** T24, T102, T180, T258, T336, **2:** T24, T102, T180, T258, T336, **3:** T24, T102, T180, T258, T336, **4:** T24, T102, T180, T258, T336, **5:** T24, T102, T180, T258, T336, **6:** T24, T102, T180, T258, T336

closed syllables, **2:** T259, T269, T272, T282, T292

contractions, **2:** T101, T111, T119, T127, T136, **3:** T23, T33, T41, T49, T58

corrective feedback, **1:** T13, T33, T91, T111, T169, T189, T247, T267, T325, T345, **2:** T13, T33, T91, T111, T169, T189, T247, T267, T325, T345, **3:** T13, T33, T91, T111, T169, T189, T247, T267, T325, T345, **4:** T13, T33, T91, T111, T169, T189, T247, T267, T325, T345, **5:** T13, T33, T91, T111, T169, T189, T247, T267, T325, T345, **6:** T13, T33, T91, T111, T169, T189, T247, T267, T325, T345

decoding, **1:** T13, T91, T169, T247, T335, **2:** T13, T91, T169, T247, T335, **3:** T13, T91, T169, T247, T335, **4:** T13, T91, T169, T247, T335, **5:** T13, T91, T169, T247, T335, **6:** T13, T91, T169, T247, T335

multisyllabic words. *See* Phonics/Word Analysis: structural analysis: inflectional endings; Phonics/Word Analysis: syllabication patterns.

letter-sound correspondence, consonant blends

end blends, **2:** T168–T169, T178–T179, T188–T189, T196, T204, T212–T213, T220

l-blends, **1:** T168–T169, T178–T179, T188–T189, T196, T204, T212–T213, T220

r-blends, **1:** T324–T325, T334–T335, T344–T345, T352, T360, T368–T369, T376

s-blends, **1:** S66, T324–T325, T334–T335, T344–T345, T352, T360, T368–T369, T376

three-letter blends, **6:** T246–T247, T256–T257, T266–T267, T274, T282, T290–T291, T298

letter-sound correspondences, consonant digraphs

/ch/*ch*, /tch/*tch*, **2:** T324–T325, T334–T335, T344–T345, T352, T360, T368–T369, T376

/f/*ph*, **2:** T246–T247, T256–T257, T266–T267, T274, T282, T290–T291, T298

/k/*ck*, **1:** S66–S67

/ng/*ng*, **2:** T246–T247, T256–T257, T266–T267, T274, T282, T290–T291, T298

/wh/*wh*, **2:** T246–T247, T256–T257, T266–T267, T274, T282, T290–T291, T298

letter-sound correspondences, consonants

/b/*b*, **1:** S60–S61

/d/*d*, **1:** S48–S49

/f/*f*, **1:** S36–S37

final double consonants, **1:** S30, S60

/g/*g* (hard *g*), **1:** S78–S79

/h/*h*, **1:** S48–S49

/j/*g* (soft *g*), **3:** T168–T169, T178–T179, T188–T189, T196, T204, T212–T213, T220

/j/*j*, **1:** S90–S91

/k/*c* (hard *c*), **1:** S36–S37

/k/*k*, *ck*, **1:** S66–S67

/ks/*x*, **1:** S84–S85

/kw/*qu*, **1:** S84–S85

/l/*l*, **1:** S60–S61

/m/*m*, **1:** S6

/n/*n*, **1:** S24–S25

/p/*p*, **1:** S18–S19

/r/*r*, **1:** S24–S25

/s/*c* (soft *c*), **3:** T168–T169, T178–T179, T188–T189, T196, T204, T212–T213, T220

/s/*s*, **1:** S6–S7

silent letters (*kn*, *gn*), **6:** T168–T169, T178–T179, T188–T189, T196, T204, T212–T213, T220

silent letters (*wr*), **6:** T168–T169, T178–T179, T188–T189, T196, T204, T212–T213, T220

/t/*t*, **1:** S18–S19

/v/*v*, **1:** S84–S85

/w/*w*, **1:** S78–S79

/y/*y*, **1:** S90–S91

/z/*s*, **1:** S48

/z/*z*, **1:** S90–S91

letter-sound correspondences, long vowels

final *e* (*o_e*, *u_e*, *e_e*), **3:** T246–T247, T256–T257, T266–T267, T274, T282, T290–T291, T298

long *a* (*a*, *ai*, *ay*), **4:** T12–T13, T22–T23, T32–T33, T40, T48, T56–T57, T62

long *a* (*a_e*), **3:** T12–T13, T22–T23, T32–T33, T40, T48, T56–T57, T62

long *e* (*e*, *ee*, *ea*, *ie*), **4:** T90–T91, T100–T101, T110–T111, T118, T126, T134–T135, T142

long *e* (*y*, *ey*), **4:** T324–T325, T334–T335, T344–T345, T352, T360, T368–T369, T376

long *i* (*i*, *y*, *igh*, *ie*), **4:** T246–T247, T256–T257, T266–T267, T274, T282, T290–T291, T298

long *i* (*i_e*), **3:** T90–T91, T100–T101, T110–T111, T118, T126, T134–T135, T142

long *o* (*o*, *oa*, *ow*, *oe*), **4:** T168–T169, T178–T179, T188–T189, T196, T204, T212–T213, T220

y as long *e*, **4:** T324–T325, T334–T335, T344–T345, T352, T360, T368–T369, T376

y as long *i*, **4:** T246–T247, T256–T257, T266–T267, T274, T282, T290–T291, T298

letter-sound correspondences, *r*-controlled vowels

/âr/*air*, *are*, *ear*, **6:** T324–T325, T334–T335, T344–T345, T352, T360, T368–T369, T376

/är/*ar*, **5:** T12–T13, T22–T23, T32–T33, T40, T48, T56–T57, T62

/ôr/*or*, *ore*, *oar*, **5:** T168–T169, T178–T179, T188–T189, T196, T204, T212–T213, T220

/ûr/*er*, *ir*, *ur*, *or*, **5:** T90–T91, T100–T101, T110–T111, T118, T126, T134–T135, T142

letter-sound correspondences, short vowels (single letters)

short *a*, **1:** S12–S13, T12–T13, T22–T23, T32–T33, T40, T48, T56–T57, T62

short *e*, **1:** S54, **2:** T12–T13, T22–T23, T32–T33, T40, T48, T56–T57, T64

short *i*, **1:** S30–S31, T90–T91, T100–T101, T110–T111, T118, T126, T134–T135, T142

short *o*, **1:** S42–S43, T246–T247, T256–T257, T266–T267, T274, T282, T290–T291, T298

short *u*, **1:** S72–S73, **2:** T90–T91, T100–T101, T110–T111, T118, T126, T134–T135, T142

letter-sound correspondences, vowel digraphs

/ā/*ay*, *ai*, *a*, **4:** T12–T13, T22–T23, T32–T33, T40, T48, T56–T57, T62

/e/*ea* (as in *bread*), **2:** T12–T13, T22–T23, T32–T33, T40, T48, T56–T57, T62

/ē/*ea* (as in *eat*), **4:** T90–T91, T100–T101, T110–T111, T118, T126, T134–T135, T142

/ē/*ee*, **4:** T90–T91, T100–T101, T110–T111, T118, T126, T134–T135, T142

/ē/*ie* (as in *chief*), **4:** T90–T91, T100–T101, T110–T111, T118, T126, T134–T135, T142

/ī/*ie* (as in *pie*), **4:** T246–T247, T256–T257, T266–T267, T274, T282, T290–T291, T298

/ī/*igh*, **4:** T246–T247, T256–T257, T266–T267, T274, T282, T290–T291, T298

/ô/*a*, *au*, *aw*, *augh*, *al*, **6:** T90–T91, T100–T101, T110–T111, T118, T126, T134–T135, T142

/ō/*o*, *oa*, *oe*, *ow*, **4:** T168–T169, T178–T179, T188–T189, T196, T204, T212–T213, T220

/ü/*oo*, *ou*, *u_e*, *ue*, *ew*, *ow* (as in *soon*), **6:** T12–T13, T22–T23, T32–T33, T40, T48, T56–T57, T64

/ù/*oo* (as in *foot*), **3:** T324–T325, T334–T335, T344–T345, T352, T360, T368–T369, T376

letter-sound correspondences, vowel diphthongs

oy, oi, **5:** T324–T325, T334–T335, T344–T345, T352, T360, T368–T369, T376

ou, ow, **5:** T246–T247, T256–T257, T266–T267, T274, T282, T290–T291, T298

silent letters (*wr*, *kn*, *gn*), **6:** T168–T169, T178–T179, T188–T189, T196, T204, T212–T213, T220

structural analysis

abbreviations, **5:** T179, T189, T196, T204, T214

alphabetical order, **1:** T257, T267, T275, T283, T292, **4:** T23, T33, T40, T48, T58

comparative inflectional endings *-er*, *-est*, **5:** T282, T292

compound words, **4:** T335, T345, T352, T360, T370, **6:** T179, T189, T191D, T196, T204, T214, T269I

contractions

with *not*, **3:** T23, T33, T41, T49, T58

with *'s*, **2:** T101, T111, T119, T127, T136

double final consonants, words with, **1:** T101, T111, T119, T127, T136

inflectional ending -*ed*, **2:** T23, T33, T41, T49, T58, **3:** T179, T189, T196, T204, T214, **4:** T257, T267, T274, T282

inflectional ending -*er*, **5:** T101, T111, T118, T126, T136

inflectional ending -*es*, **1:** T23, T33, T41, T49, T58, **4:** T257, T267, T274, T282

inflectional endings -*ing* and -*ed*, **2:** T179, T189, T197, T205, T214, **3:** T179, T189, T196, T204, T214, **4:** T259, T269, T272, T282, T292, **5:** T113C, **6:** T282

plural nouns, **1:** T179, T189, T196, T204, T214, **3:** T101, T111, T118, T126, T136

irregular, **5:** T23, T33, T40, T48, T58

possessives, **1:** T335, T345, T353, T360, T370

prefixes, **4:** T101, T111, T118, T126, T136, T302

suffixes, **3:** T380, **5:** T146, T269K, **6:** T23, T33, T40, T48, T58

syllabication patterns

closed syllables, **2:** T259, T269, T272, T282, T292

final stable syllables, **5:** T352, T360, T370

open syllables, **4:** T179, T189, T196, T204, T214

r-controlled vowel syllables, **6:** T335, T345, T352, T360, T370

vowel-consonant-silent *e* syllables, **3:** T259, T269, T272, T282, T292

vowel team syllables, **6:** T101, T111, T118, T126, T136

Phonological Awareness

alliteration, **1:** T90, T118, T132, T133, **3:** T90, T133

blend phonemes, **1:** S17, S35, S53, S65, S71, T32, T48, T55, T110, T126, T132, T178, T204, T210, T282, T360, T367, **2:** T12, T32, T48, T54, T55, T110, T126, T133, T178, T204, T210, T266, T282, T289, T344, T360, T366, **3:** T48, T126, T132, T188, T204, T211, T282, T289, T334, T360, T366, **4:** T32, T48, T55, T126, T132, T178, T204, T210, T344, T366, **5:** T32, T48, T55, T110, T126, T132, T188, T204, T266, T282, T288, T324, T352, T360, T366, T367, **6:** T110, T132, T266, T282, T288, T334, T366

generate rhyme, **1:** T274, T288, **2:** T90, T132, **3:** T168, T210, **4:** T12, T40, T54, T110, T133, **5:** T90, T132, **6:** T32, T54

identify rhyming words, **1:** S29, S59, S89, T12, T54, T274, T288, **2:** T90, T132, **3:** T168, T210, **4:** T12, T40, T54, T110, T133, **5:** T90, T132, **6:** T32, T54

isolate initial, medial, and final sounds, **1:** S11, S41, T22, T40, T54, **2:** T22, T40, T54, T55, T246, T288, **3:** T256, T274, T288, **5:** T256, T274, T288, T289

segment words into phonemes, **1:** S77, S83, T48, T55, T126, T133, T204, T211, T256, T282, T289, T334, T360, T366, **2:** T48, T126, T133, T204, T211, T324, T360, T366, T367, **3:** T48, T54, T110, T126, T132, T178, T196, T204, T211, T246, T266, T282, T288, T289, T324, T352, T360, T366, T367, **4:** T48, T55, T100, T126, T133, T204, T211, T266, T282, T289, **5:** T48, T55, T204, T210, T334, T360, T367, **6:** T22, T48, T55, T126, T178, T204, T210, T256, T274, T288

syllable addition, **6:** T246, T289, T360

syllable deletion, **6:** T40, T360

syllable segmentation, **1:** S23, S47

Photographers' Craft, 6: T113K

Photographs. *See* Comprehension Skills, use illustrations/ photographs.

Predictions, Making/Confirming. *See* Comprehension Strategies, make and confirm predictions.

Predictions and Purposes, Return to, 1: T35F, T113G, T191G, T269G, T347E, **2:** T35G, T113H, T191F, T269H, T347E, **3:** T35H, T113H, T191H, T269G, T347E, **4:** T35I, T113I, T191N, T269P, T347E, **5:** T35G, T113P, T191I, T269N, T347E, **6:** T35L, T113J, T191O, T269O, T347E

Prefixes. *See* Phonics/Word Analysis: structural analysis.

Print Awareness

identify letters and words, **1:** S10, S16, S22, S82, T10

parts of a book, **1:** S28, S40, S52, T10

print-to-speech match, **1:** S46, T10

sound-to-letter correspondence, **1:** S82, S88

spacing between words and sentences, **1:** S22, S40

Publishing Celebrations, 1: T402–T403, **2:** T402–T403, **3:** T402–T403, **4:** T402–T403, **5:** T402–T403, **6:** T402–T403

Purpose for Reading, 1: T10, T35A, T35F, T88, T113A, T113G, T177, T191A, T191G, T244, T269A, T269G, T323, T347A, T347E, **2:** T10, T35A, T35G, T89, T113A, T113H, T177, T191A, T191F, T245, T269A, T269H, T323, T347A, T347E, **3:** T10, T35A, T35H, T89, T113A, T113H, T177, T191A, T191H, T245, T269A, T269G, T323, T347A, T347E, **4:** T11, T35A, T35I, T89, T113A, T113I, T177, T191A, T191N, T245, T269A, T269P, T323, T347A, T347E, **5:** T11, T35A, T35G, T89, T113A, T113P, T191A, T191I, T245, T269A, T269N, T323, T347A, T347E, **6:** T11, T35A, T35L, T89, T113A, T113J, T191A, T191O, T245, T269A, T269O, T323, T347A, T347E

R

Range of Reading. *See* Access Complex Text.

Read Aloud. *See* Interactive Read Aloud.

Reader's Theater, 1: T394–T395, **2:** T394–T395, **3:** T394–T395, **4:** T394–T395, **5:** T394–T395, **6:** T394–T395

Read Independently, Units 1–6: T61, T65, T69, T139, T143, T147, T217, T221, T225, T295, T299, T303, T373, T377, T381

Reading Across Texts, 1: T39B, T117B, T195B, T273, T351, **2:** T39B, T117B, T195, T273B, T351, **3:** T39B, T117B, T195, T273B, T351, **4:** T39B, T117B, T195, T273B, T351, **5:** T39B, T117B, T195A, T273B, T351, **6:** T39B, T117, T195A, T273A, T351

Reading Digitally, 1: T396–T397, **2:** T396–T397, **3:** T396–T397, **4:** T396–T397, **5:** T396–T397, **6:** T396–T397

Read Together. *See* Shared Reading.

Realistic Fiction. *See* Genre.

Rereading, 1: S32, S34, S56, S62, S92, T31, T109, T187, T265, T269C, T343, T415, **2:** T31, T109, T167, T173, T177, T187, T191B, T191D, T191E, T195, T245, T251, T255, T265, T269B, T269D, T269F, T273A, T323, T329, T333, T343, T347B, T347C, T351, T415, **3:** T31, T35C, T109, T113C, T187, T191C, T245, T251, T255, T265, T269B, T269C, T269E, T273B, T323, T329, T333, T343, T347B, T347D, T351, T415, **4:** T21, T99, T177, T191H, T255, T333, T415, **5:** T21, T35C, T99, T113O, T117A, T177, T255, T333, T415, **6:** T11, T17, T21, T31, T35B, T35F, T39A, T89, T95, T99, T109, T113B, T113D, T117, T255, T269I, T323, T329, T333, T343, T347B, T347D, T351, T415

Research and Inquiry, 1: T44–T45, T47, T122–T123, T125, T200–T201, T203, T278–T279, T281, T356–T357, T359, T398–T401, **2:** T44–T45, T47, T122–T123, T125, T200–T201, T203, T278–T279, T281, T356–T357, T359, T398–T401, **3:** T44–T45, T47, T122–T123, T125, T200–T201, T203, T278–T279, T281, T356–T357, T359, T398–T401, **4:** T44–T45, T47, T122–T123, T125, T200–T201, T203, T278–T279, T281, T356–T357, T359, T398–T401, **5:** T44–T45, T47, T122–T123, T125, T200–T201, T203, T278–T279, T281, T356–T357, T359, T398–T401, **6:** T44–T45, T47, T122–T123, T125, T200–T201, T203, T278–T279, T281, T356–T357, T359, T398–T401

Research and Study Skills, 1: T398, **2:** T398, **3:** T398, **4:** T398, **5:** T398, **6:** T398. *See also* Research and Inquiry.

asking questions, **4:** T398

collecting information, **2:** T398

finding resources, **3:** T398

select a topic, **1:** T398

taking notes, **5:** T398

using a variety of resources, **1:** T398

using key words, **6:** T398

Respond to Reading

informational text, **1:** S26, S56, S86, T269I–T269J, T347F, **2:** T191H, T347F, **3:** T269I–T269J, T347F, **4:** T11, T113K–T113L, T191P, T323, T347F, **5:** T167, T191K–T191L, T347F, **6:** T113L, T245, T323, T347F

literature, **1:** S14, S44, S86, T35H, T113I–T113J, T191I–T191J, T269I–T269J, **2:** T35I–T35J, T113J, T269J, **3:** T35J, T113J, T191J, **4:** T35K–T35L, T89, T167, T245, T269R, **5:** T11, T89, T35I–T35J, T113R, T245, T269P, T323, **6:** T11, T35N, T89, T167, T191Q–T191R, T269Q–T269R

Response to Intervention. *See* Intervention Program.

Retelling, 1: T31, T35H, T109, T113F, T113I, T187, T191F, T191I, T265, T269D, T269I, T343, T347C, T347F, **2:** T31, T35I, T109, T113G, T113J, T187, T191H, T265, T269J, T343, T347F, **3:** T31, T35J, T109, T113J, T187, T191J, TT265, T269I, T343, T347F, **4:** T11, T35K, T89, T113K, T167, T191P, T245, T269R, T323, T347F, **5:** T11, T35I, T89, T113R, T167, T191K, T245, T269P, T323, T347F, **6:** T11, T35E, T35N, T89, T113L, T167, T191Q, T245, T269Q, T323, T347F

Rhyme/Rhyming Words, 1: xii, T272, T273, **3:** T194, T195A, T195B. *See also* Phonemic Awareness: generate rhyme, identify rhyming words.

Rhythm, 3: xii

Routines

following directions, **1:** S13, S73

high-frequency words, **1:** S7, S37, S67

interactive writing, **1:** S81

oral vocabulary, **1:** T8, T20, T86, T98, T164, T176, T242, T254, T320, **2:** T8, T20, T86, T98, T164, T176, T242, T254, T320, **3:** T8, T20, T86, T98, T164, T176, T242, T254, T320, T332, **4:** T8, T15, T86, T93, T164, T166, T171, T242, T249, T320, T327, **5:** T8, T15, T86, T93, T164, T166, T171, T242, T249, T320, T327, **6:** T8, T15, T86, T93, T164, T171, T242, T249, T320, T327

retellings, **1:** S32, S62, S92

S

Science, 1: T191J, T209, T219, T223, T229, T365, T375, T379, T385, **2:** T191H, **3:** T113C, T113J, T131, T141, T145, T151, **4:** T35F, T113L, T131, T141, T145, T151, T209, T219, T223, T229, T269K, T269R, T287, T297, T301, T307, **5:** T35J, T113F, T113R, T131, T141, T145, T151, T191I, T209, T219, T223, T229, T269M, T287, T297, T301, T307, T347F, **6:** T209, T219, T223, T229

informational text, **1:** T195A–T195B, T347A–T347F, T351, **2:** T191A–T191H, **3:** T117A–T117B, T351, **4:** T39A–T39B, T113A–T113L, T117A–T117B, T191A–T191B, T273A–T273B, **5:** T39A–T39B, T117–T117B, T273A–T273B, T347A–T347F, T351, **6:** T195A–T195B

Scope and Sequences, Units 1–6: T416–T423

Self-Selected Reading, Units 1–6: T61, T65, T69, T139, T143, T147, T217, T221, T225, T295, T299, T303, T373, T377, T381

Sensory Words. *See* Literary Devices and Elements.

Shared Reading, Units 1–6: T16–T17, T70–T71, T94–T95, T148–T149, T172–T173, T226–T227, T250–T251, T304–T305, T328–T329, T382–T383

Small Group Options, Units 1–6: T4–T5, T82–T83, T160–T161, T238–T239, T316–T317

See also Approaching Level Options; Beyond Level Options; English

Language Learners; On Level Options.

Social Studies, 1: T53, T63, T67, T73, T269J, T287, T297, T301, T307, **2:** T35J, T131, T141, T145, T151, T269J, T365, T375, T379, T385, **3:** T53, T63, T67, T73, T269J, T287, T297, T301, T307, T347F, **4:** T347F, T365, T375, T379, T385, **6:** T269R, T347F, T365, T375, T379, T385

informational text, **1:** T39–T39B, T117–T117B, T269A–T269J, **2:** T39A–T39B, T117A–T117B, T273A–T273B, T347A–T347F, T351, **3:** T39A–T39B, T269A–T269J, T273A–T273B, T347A–T347F, **4:** T347A–T347F, T351, **5:** T191A–T191L, T351, **6:** T39–T39B, T113A–T113L, T273A–T273B, T347A–T347F, T351

Speaking. *See also* Collaborative Conversations; Research and Inquiry; Writing Process: publish and present.

appropriate facts/relevant details, **1:** T47, T50, T125, T128, T203, T206, T281, T284, T359, T362, T398–T401, T402–T403, **2:** T47, T50, T125, T128, T203, T206, T281, T284, T359, T362, T398–T401, T402–T403, **3:** T47, T50, T125, T128, T203, T206, T281, T284, T359, T362, T398–T401, T402–T403, **4:** T47, T50, T125, T128, T203, T206, T281, T284, T359, T362, T398–T401, T402–T403, **5:** T47, T50, T125, T128, T203, T206, T281, T284, T359, T362, T398–T401, T402–T403, **6:** T47, T50, T125, T128, T203, T206, T281, T284, T359, T362, T398–T401, T402–T403

checklists, **1:** T401, T403, **2:** T401, T403, **3:** T401, T403, **4:** T401, T403, **5:** T401, T403, **6:** T401, T403

complete sentences, **1:** T47, T50, T125, T128, T203, T206, T281, T284, T359, T362, T398–T401, T402–T403, **2:** T47, T50, T125, T128, T203, T206, T281, T284, T359, T362, T398–T401, T402–T403, **3:** T47, T50, T125, T128, T203, T206, T281, T284, T359, T362, T398–T401, T402–T403, **4:** T47, T50, T125, T128, T203, T206, T281, T284, T359, T362, T398–T401, T402–T403, **5:** T47, T50, T125, T128, T203, T206,

T281, T284, T359, T362, T398–T401, T402–T403, **6:** T47, T50, T125, T128, T203, T206, T281, T284, T359, T362, T398–T401, T402–T403

create recordings, **Units 1–6:** T50, T128, T206, T284, T362

descriptive words, using, **5:** T96, T106, T114–T115, T120–T121, T128, T174, T184, T192–T193, T198–T199, T206

Reader's Theater, **1:** T394–T395, **2:** T394–T395, **3:** T394–T395, **4:** T394–T395, **5:** T394–T395, **6:** T394–T395

reciting poems and rhymes, **1:** S8, S20, S38, S50, S68, S80

retelling. *See* Retelling.

Spelling

analyze errors, **1:** T24, T102, T180, T258, T336, **2:** T24, T102, T180, T258, T336, **3:** T24, T102, T180, T258, T336, **4:** T24, T102, T180, T258, T336, **5:** T24, T102, T180, T258, T336, **6:** T24, T102, T180, T258, T336

assess, **1:** T49, T127, T205, T283, T361, **2:** T49, T127, T205, T283, T361, **3:** T49, T127, T205, T283, T361, **4:** T49, T127, T205, T283, T361, **5:** T49, T127, T205, T283, T361, **6:** T49, T127, T205, T283, T361

dictation, **1:** T14, T92, T170, T248, T326, **2:** T14, T92, T170, T248, T326, **3:** T14, T92, T170, T248, T326, **4:** T14, T92, T170, T248, T326, **5:** T14, T92, T170, T248, T326, **6:** T14, T92, T170, T248, T326

pretest, **1:** T14, T92, T170, T248, T326, **2:** T14, T92, T170, T248, T326, **3:** T14, T92, T170, T248, T326, **4:** T14, T92, T170, T248, T326, **5:** T14, T92, T170, T248, T326, **6:** T14, T92, T170, T248, T326

review, **1:** T41, T49, T119, T127, T197, T205, T275, T283, T353, T361, **2:** T41, T49, T119, T127, T197, T205, T275, T283, T353, T361, **3:** T41, T49, T119, T127, T197, T205, T275, T283, T353, T361, **4:** T41, T49, T119, T127, T197, T205, T275, T283, T353,

T361, **5:** T41, T49, T119, T127, T197, T205, T275, T283, T353, T361, **6:** T41, T49, T119, T127, T197, T205, T275, T283, T353, T361

spelling words, **1:** T14, T92, T170, T248, T326, **2:** T14, T92, T170, T248, T326, **3:** T14, T92, T170, T248, T326, **4:** T14, T92, T170, T248, T326, **5:** T14, T92, T170, T248, T326, **6:** T14, T92, T170, T248, T326

Spelling Patterns

words with *air, are, ear,* **6:** T326, T336, T346, T353, T361, T388

words with *ch, -tch, wh, ph,* **2:** T326, T336, T346, T353, T361, T388

words with diphthongs

oi, oy, **5:** T326, T336, T346, T353, T361, T388

ou, ow, **5:** T248, T258, T268, T275, T283, T310

word sort, **Units 1–6:** T24, T34, T41, T49, T102, T119, T127, T180, T190, T197, T205, T258, T268, T275, T283, T326, T336, T346, T353

words with /ā/*a, ai, ay,* **4:** T14, T24, T34, T41, T49, T76

words with /ē/*e, ee, ea,* **4:** T92, T102, T112, T119, T127, T154

words with end blends, **2:** T170, T180, T190, T197, T205, T232

words with /ī/*i, y, igh, ie,* **4:** T248, T258, T268, T275, T283, T310

words with *l*-blends, **1:** T170, T180, T190, T197, T205, T232

words with long *a: a_e,* **3:** T14, T24, T34, T41, T49, T76

words with long *e: y, ey,* **4:** T326, T336, T346, T353, T361, T388

words with long *i: i_e,* **3:** T92, T102, T112, T119, T127, T154

words with /ō/*o, oa, ow, oe,* **4:** T170, T180, T190, T197, T205, T232

words with *o_e, u_e,* **3:** T248, T258, T268, T275, T283, T310

words with *-ook, -ood,* **3:** T326, T336, T346, T353, T361, T388

words with *r-* and *s*-blends, **1:** T326, T336, T346, T353, T361, T388 words with *r*-controlled vowels,

/är/*ar,* 5: T14, T24, T34, T41, T49, T76

/ôr/*or, ore, oar,* 5: T170, T180, T190, T197, T205, T232

/ûr/*er, ir, ur, or,* 5: T92, T102, T112, T119, T127, T154

words with short *a*, 1: T14, T24, T34, T41, T49, T76

words with short *e*, 2: T14, T24, T34, T41, T49, T76

words with short *i*, 1: T92, T102, T112, T119, T127, T154

words with short *o*, 1: T248, T258, T268, T275, T283, T310

words with short *u*, 2: T92, T102, T112, T119, T127, T154

words with soft *c, g, dge*, 3: T170, T180, T190, T197, T205, T232

words with *th, sh, -ng*, 2: T248, T258, T268, T275, T283, T310

words with three-letter blends, 6: T248, T258, T268, T275, T283, T310

words with variant vowel /ô/, 6: T92, T102, T112, T119, T127, T154

words with variant vowel /ü/, 6: T14, T24, T34, T41, T49, T76

words with *wr, kn, gn*, 6: T170, T180, T190, T197, T205, T232

Start Smart, 1: S1–S95

Structural Analysis. *See* Phonics/Word Analysis.

Study Skills. *See* Research and Study Skills.

Syntax. *See* Vocabulary Skills and Strategies: context clues.

T

Talk About It, 1: xii, T9, T19, T29, T37, T43, T87, T97, T107, T115, T121, T165, T175, T185, T193, T199, T243, T253, T263, T271, T277, T321, T331, T341, T349, T355, 2: xii, T9, T19, T29, T37, T43, T87, T97, T107, T115, T121, T165, T175, T185, T193, T199, T243, T253, T263, T271, T277, T321, T331, T341, T349, T355, 3: xii, T9, T19, T29, T37, T43, T87, T97, T107, T115, T121, T165, T175, T185, T193, T199, T243, T253, T263, T271, T277, T321, T331, T341, T349, T355, 4: xii, T9, T19, T29, T37, T43, T87, T97, T107, T115, T121, T165, T175, T185, T193, T199, T243, T253, T263, T271, T277, T321, T331, T341, T349, T355, 5: xii, T9, T19, T29, T37, T43, T87, T97, T107, T115, T121, T165, T175, T185, T193, T199, T243, T253, T263, T271, T277, T321, T331, T341, T349, T355, 6: xii, T9, T19, T29, T37, T43, T87, T97, T107, T115, T121, T165, T175, T185, T193, T199, T243, T253, T263, T271, T277, T321, T331, T341, T349, T355

Technology. *See* Computer Literacy.

Text Connections

make connections across texts, 1: T39B, T117B, T195B, T273, T351, 2: T39B, T117B, T195, T273B, T351, 3: T39B, T117B, T195, T273B, T351, 4: T39B, T117B, T195, T273B, T351, 5: T39B, T117B, T195A, T273B, T351, 6: T39B, T117, T195A, T273A, T351

Text Complexity. *See* Access Complex Text.

Text Evidence, 1: T35H, T113I–T113J, T191I–T191J, T269I–T269J, T347F, 2: T35I–T35J, T113J, T191H, T269J, T347F, 3: T35J, T113J, T191J, T269I–T269J, T347F, 4: T35K–T35L, T113K–T113L, T191P, T269R, T347F, 5: T35I–T35J, T113R, T191K–T191L, T269P, T347F, 6: T35N, T113L, T191Q–T191R, T269Q–T269R, T347F

text to self, 1: S32, S62, S92, T46, T124, T202, T280, T358, 2: T46, T124, T202, T280, T358, 3: T46, T124, T202, T280, T358, 4: T46, T124, T202, T280, T358, 5: T46, T124, T202, T280, T358, 6: T46, T124, T202, T280, T358

text to text, 1: S32, S62, S92, T46, T124, T202, T280, T358, 2: T46, T124, T202, T280, T358, 3: T46, T124, T202, T280, T358, 4: T46, T124, T202, T280, T358, 5: T46, T124, T202, T280, T358, 6: T46, T124, T202, T280, T358

text to world, 1: S32, S62, S92, T46, T124, T202, T280, T358, 2: T46, T124, T202, T280, T358, 3: T46, T124, T202, T280, T358, 4: T46, T124, T202, T280, T358, 5: T46, T124, T202, T280, T358, 6: T46, T124, T202, T280, T358

Text Features

bold print, 1: T116, T117, T117A, T117B, 3: T38, T39B

book parts, 1: S28, S40, S52, T10

captions, 2: T117, T117B, 3: T273, T273A, T273B, 4: T117, T117A, T117B, T350, T351, 5: T116, T117, T117A, T117B, T350, T351, 6: T38, T39, T39A, T39B

chart, 3: T350, T351, 4: T38, T39, T39A, T39B

diagrams, 1: T350, T351, 3: T117, T117B

directions, 5: T273, T273B, 6: T273, T273B

headings, 4: T273, T273B, 6: T195, T195A, T195B

illustrations, 5: T39, T39A, T39B

labels, 1: T166, T195, T195A, T195B, T347C, 2: T39, T39A, T39B, T322

list, 2: T273, T273B

map, 2: T350, T351, 6: T350, T351

photographs, 1: T38, T39, T39A, T39B

Theme Projects. *See* Research and Inquiry.

Time for Kids, 4: T347A–T347F, T396–T397, 5: T347A–T347F, T396–T397, 6: T347A–T347F, T396–T397

U

Uppercase Letters, 1: T13, T91, T169, T247, T325, 2: T13, T91, T169, T247, T325, 3: T13, T91, T169, T247, T325, 4: T13, T91, T169, T247, T325, 5: T13, T91, T169, T247, T325, 6: T13, T91, T169, T247, T325

V

Vocabulary Acquisition. *See also* Vocabulary Skills and Strategies.

domain-specific, **1:** T39A, T117, T195A, T343, **2:** T39A, T109, T117A, T273A, **3:** T39A, T109, T117A, T265, **4:** T39, T117A, T273A, **5:** T39, T117, T195A, T273A, T347B, **6:** T35D, T35H, T39, T117, T195A, T273A

expanding, **1:** T41, T119, T197, T275, T253, **2:** T41, T119, T197, T275, T253, **3:** T41, T119, T197, T275, T253, **4:** T41, T119, T197, T275, T253, **5:** T41, T119, T197, T275, T253, **6:** T41, T119, T197, T275, T253

general vocabulary, **1:** S7, S13, S19, S25, S31, S37, S43, S49, S55, S61, S67, S73, S79, S85, S91, T15, T25, T35, T41, T49, T93, T103, T113, T119, T127, T171, T181, T191, T197, T205, T249, T259, T269, T275, T283, T327, T337, T343, T347, T353, T361, **2:** T15, T25, T35, T41, T49, T93, T103, T109, T113, T119, T127, T171, T181, T191, T197, T205, T249, T259, T269, T275, T283, T327, T337, T347, T353, T361, **3:** T15, T25, T35, T41, T49, T93, T103, T109, T113, T119, T127, T171, T181, T191, T197, T205, T249, T259, T265, T269, T275, T283, T327, T337, T347, T353, T361, **4:** T14–T15, T25, T34–T35, T41, T49, T92–T93, T102–T103, T112–T113, T119, T127, T170–T171, T180–T181, T190–T191, T197, T205, T248–T249, T258–T259, T268–T269, T275, T283, T327, T337, T347, T353, T361, **5:** T14–T15, T25, T34–T35, T41, T49, T92–T93, T102–T103, T112–T113, T119, T127, T170–T171, T180–T181, T190–T191, T197, T205, T248–T249, T258–T259, T268–T269, T275, T283, T326–T327, T336–T337, T346–T347, T347B, T353, T361, **6:** T14–T15, T24–T25, T34–T35, T35D, T35H, T41, T49, T92–T93, T102–T103, T112–T113, T119, T127, T170–T171, T180–T181, T190–T191, T197, T205, T248–T249, T258–T259, T268–T269, T275, T283, T326–T327, T337, T346–T347, T353, T361

introduce, **4:** T15, T93, T171, T249, T327, **5:** T15, T93, T171, T249, T327, **6:** T15, T93, T171, T249, T327

multiple-meaning words, **1:** T224, T380, **2:** T68, **4:** T68, **5:** T302, **6:** T224, T380

oral vocabulary, **1:** T8, T20, T30, T68, T74, T86, T98, T108, T146, T152, T164, T176, T186, T224, T230, T242, T254, T264, T302, T308, T320, T332, T342, T380, T386, **2:** T8, T20, T30, T68, T74, T86, T98, T108, T146, T152, T164, T176, T186, T224, T230, T242, T254, T264, T302, T308, T320, T332, T342, T380, T386, **3:** T8, T20, T30, T68, T74, T86, T98, T108, T146, T152, T164, T176, T186, T224, T230, T242, T254, T264, T302, T308, T320, T332, T342, T380, T386, **4:** T8, T20, T30, T68, T74, T86, T98, T108, T146, T152, T164, T166, T176, T186, T224, T230, T242, T254, T264, T302, T308, T320, T332, T342, T380, T386, **5:** T8, T20, T30, T68, T74, T86, T98, T108, T146, T152, T164, T176, T186, T224, T230, T242, T254, T264, T302, T308, T320, T332, T342, T380, T386, **6:** T8, T20, T30, T68, T74, T86, T98, T108, T146, T152, T164, T176, T186, T224, T230, T242, T254, T264, T302, T308, T320, T332, T342, T380, T386

reinforce, **4:** T25, T103, T181, T259, T337, **5:** T25, T103, T181, T259, T337, **6:** T25, T103, T181, T259, T337

review, **4:** T49, T59, T64, T75, T127, T137, T142, T153, T205, T215, T220, T231, T283, T293, T298, T309, T361, T371, T376, T387, **5:** T49, T59, T64, T75, T127, T137, T142, T153, T205, T215, T220, T231, T283, T293, T298, T309, T361, T371, T376, T387, **6:** T49, T59, T64, T75, T127, T137, T142, T153, T205, T215, T220, T231, T283, T293, T298, T309, T361, T371, T376, T387

selection/story words, **1:** T35A, T113A, T191A, T269A, T347A, **2:** T35A, T113A, T191A, T269A, T347A, **3:** T35A, T113A, T191A, T269A, T347A, **4:** T35A, T113A, T191A, T269A, T347A, **5:** T35A, T113A, T191A, T269A, T347A, **6:** T35A, T113A, T191A, T269A, T347A

vocabulary words, **4:** T15, T93, T171, T249, T327, **5:** T15, T93, T171, T249, T327, **6:** T15, T93, T171, T249, T327

words in context, **4:** T25, T103, T181, T259, T337, **5:** T25, T103, T181, T259, T337, **6:** T25, T103, T181, T259, T337

words that describe, **1:** T96, T106, T114–T115, T120–T121, T128, T174, T184, T192–T193, T198–T199, T206

Vocabulary Skills and Strategies. *See also* Phonics/Word Analysis.

antonyms, **1:** T146, T302, **2:** 302, **3:** T68, **5:** T68, **6:** T68, T113

clarify meaning of unfamiliar words, **4:** T113, T269, **5:** T35

compound words, **6:** T269

context clues, **1:** T113C, T269G, **3:** T269F, **4:** T113, T113F, T191J, T269, T269H, **5:** T35

dictionary, using, **4:** T35C, T269C, **6:** T35H

inflectional endings, **5:** T347

metaphors, **6:** T347

multiple-meaning words, **1:** T224, T380, **2:** T68, **3:** T113F, T224, **4:** T68, **5:** T302, **6:** T224, T380

prefixes, **4:** T302, **5:** T191

root words, **4:** T347

shades of meaning/intensity, **5:** T113

similes, **6:** T191

suffixes, **3:** T380, **5:** T146, T269

synonyms, **1:** T68, **2:** T146, T380, **3:** T224, **4:** T191F, T224, **5:** T380, **6:** T35

word categories, **4:** T191, T191H

Vowels. *See* Phonics/Word Analysis.

W

Ways to Confirm Meaning. *See* Comprehension Strategies, ask and answer questions, make and confirm predictions, reread; Vocabulary Skills and Strategies, context clues.

Weekly Contract, Units 1–6: T2, T80, T158, T236, T314

Words to Know. *See* High-Frequency Words.

Workstation Activities

    phonics/word study, **Units 1–6:** T3, T81, T159, T237, T315

    reading, **Units 1–6:** T3, T81, T159, T237, T315

    science/social studies, **Units 1–6:** T3, T81, T159, T237, T315

    writing, **Units 1–6:** T3, T81, T159, T237, T315

Write About Reading, 1: T47, T125, T203, T281, T359, T415, **2:** T47, T125, T203, T281, T359, T415, **3:** T47, T125, T203, T281, T359, T415, **4:** T21, T47, T99, T125, T177, T203, T255, T281, T333, T359, T415, **5:** T21, T47, T99, T125, T177, T203, T255, T281, T333, T359, T415, **6:** T21, T47, T99, T125, T177, T203, T255, T281, T333, T359, T415

Write to Sources. *See* Write About Reading.

Writer's Checklist, 1: T403, **2:** T403, **3:** T403, **4:** T403, **5:** T403, **6:** T403

Writer's Notebook, 1: T21, T99, T177, T255, T333, **2:** T21, T99, T177, T255, T333, **3:** T21, T99, T177, T255, T333, **4:** T21, T99, T177, T255, T333, **5:** T21, T99, T177, T255, T333, **6:** T21, T99, T177, T255, T333

Writing

    analytical writing, **1:** T47, T125, T203, T281, T359, **2:** T47, T125, T203, T281, T359, **3:** T47, T125, T203, T281, T359, **4:** T47, T125, T203, T281, T359, **5:** T47, T125, T203, T281, T359, **6:** T47, T125, T203, T281, T359

    analyze writing models, **1:** T36–T37, T114–T115, T192–T193, T270–T271, T348–T349, **2:** T36–T37, T114–T115, T192–T193, T270–T271, T348–T349, **3:** T36–T37, T114–T115, T192–T193, T270–T271, T348–T349, **4:** T36–T37, T114–T115, T192–T193, T270–T271, T348–T349, **5:** T36–T37,

T114–T115, T192–T193, T270–T271, T348–T349, **6:** T36–T37, T114–T115, T192–T193, T270–T271, T348–T349

    independent, **1:** S33, S63, S93, **Units 1–6:** T36–T37, T42–T43, T50, T114–T115, T120–T121, T192–T193, T198–T199, T206, T270–T271, T276–T277, T284, T348–T349, T354–T355, T362

    interactive, **1:** S21, S27, S51, S57, S81, S87, T28, T106, T184, T262, T340, **2:** T28, T106, T184, T262, T340, **3:** T28, T106, T184, T262, T340, **4:** T28, T106, T184, T262, T340, **5:** T28, T106, T184, T262, T340, **6:** T28, T106, T184, T262, T340

    shared, **1:** S9, S15, S39, S45, S69, S75, T18, T96, T174, T252, T330, **2:** T18, T96, T174, T252, T330, **3:** T18, T96, T174, T252, T330, **4:** T18, T96, T174, T252, T330, **5:** T18, T96, T174, T252, T330, **6:** T18, T96, T174, T252, T330

    varying sentence length and structure. *See* Writing Traits, sentence fluency, varying sentence length; Writing Traits, sentence fluency, varying sentence types.

Writer's Portfolio, 1: T50, T128, T206, T284, T362, T403, **2:** T50, T128, T206, T284, T362, T403, **3:** T50, T128, T206, T284, T362, T403, **4:** T50, T128, T206, T284, T362, T403, **5:** T50, T128, T206, T284, T362, T403, **6:** T50, T128, T206, T284, T362, T403

Writing Process

    brainstorm, **1:** S9, S15, S21, S27, S33, S39, S45, S51, S57, S63, S69, S75, S87, S93, T18, T36, T96, T114, T174, T192, T252, T270–T271, T330, T348, **2:** T18, T36, T96, T114, T174, T192, T252, T270–T271, T330, T348, **3:** T18, T36, T96, T114, T174, T192, T252, T270–T271, T330, T348, **4:** T18, T36, T96, T114, T174, T192, T252, T270, T330, T348, **5:** T18, T36, T96, T114, T174, T192, T252, T270, T330, T348, **6:** T18, T36, T96, T114, T174, T192, T252, T270, T330, T348

    draft, **1:** T37, T115, T193, T271, T349, **2:** T37, T115, T193, T271, T349, **3:** T37, T115, T193, T271, T349, **4:** T37, T115, T193, T271, T349,

    5: T37, T115, T193, T271, T349, **6:** T37, T115, T193, T271, T349

    evaluate, **1:** T50, T128, T206, T284, T362, T402–T403, **2:** T50, T128, T206, T284, T362, T402–T403, **3:** T50, T128, T206, T284, T362, T402–T403, **4:** T50, T128, T206, T284, T362, T402–T403, **5:** T50, T128, T206, T284, T362, T402–T403, **6:** T50, T128, T206, T284, T362, T402–T403

    focus and plan, **Units 1–6:** T18, T96, T174, T252, T330

    plan/prewrite, **Units 1–6:** T36, T114, T192, T270, T348

    proofread/edit, **Units 1–6:** T42, T120, T198–T199, T276, T354

    publish and present, **1:** T50, T128, T206, T284, T362, T402–T403, **2:** T50, T128, T206, T284, T362, T402–T403, **3:** T50, T128, T206, T284, T362, T402–T403, **4:** T50, T128, T206, T284, T362, T402–T403, **5:** T50, T128, T206, T284, T362, T402–T403, **6:** T50, T128, T206, T284, T362, T402–T403

    revise, **Units 1–6:** T42, T120, T198, T276, T354

    write, Start Smart, **1:** S9, S15, S21, S27, S33, S39, S45, S51, S57, S63, S69, S75, S71, S87, S93

Writing Text Types/Purposes

    informative/explanatory, **1:** T96, T106, T114–T115, T120–T121, T128, T174, T184, T192–T193, T198–T199, T206, **2:** T174, T184, T192–T193, T198–T199, T206, T330, T340, T348–T349, T354–T355, T362, **4:** T96, T106, T114–T115, T120–T121, T128, T174, T184, T192–T193, T198–T199, T206, T330, T340, T348–T349, T354–T355, T362, **5:** T18, T28, T36–T37, T42–T43, T50, T96, T106, T114–T115, T120–T121, T128, T330, T340, T348–T349, T354–T355, T362, **6:** T330, T340, T348–T349, T354–T355, T362

    describing sentences, **1:** T96, T106, T114–T115, T120–T121, T128, T174, T184, T192–T193, T198–T199, T206

    explaining sentences, **2:** T174, T184, T192–T193, T198–T199, T206, T330, T340, T348–T349,

T354–T355, T362, **4:** T330, T340, T348–T349, T354–T355, T362, **5:** T18, T28, T36–T37, T42–T43, T50, T330, T340, T348–T349, T354–T355, T362

letters, **6:** T174, T184, T192–T193, T198–T199, T206, T252, T262, T270–T271, T276–T277, T284

narratives, **1:** T18, T28, T36–T37, T42–T43, T50, T252, T262, T270–T271, T276–T277, T284, T330, T340, T348–T349, T354–T355, T362, **5:** T174, T184, T192–T193, T198–T199, T206

describing sentences, **1:** T96, T106, T114–T115, T120–T121, T128, T174, T184, T192–T193, T198–T199, T206

folktale, **4:** T18, T28, T36–T37, T42–T43, T50

poems, **3:** T18, T28, T36–T37, T42–T43, T50, T174, T184, T192–T193, T198–T199, T206

story, **2:** T18, T28, T36–T37, T42–T43, T50, T96, T106, T114–T115, T120–T121, T128, T252, T262, T270–T271, T276–T277, T284, **6:** T18, T28, T36–T37, T42–T43, T50

thank-you note, **6:** T96, T106, T114–T115, T120–T121, T128

using descriptive words, **4:** T18, T28, T36–T37, T42–T43, T50

opinion, **3:** T96, T106, T114–T115, T120–T121, T128, T252, T262, T270–T271, T276–T277, T284, T330, T340, T348–T349, T354–T355, T362, **4:** T252, T262, T270–T271, T276–T277, T284, **5:** T252, T262, T270–T271, T276–T277, T284

Writing Traits

ideas

describing details, **1:** T96, T106, T114–T115, T120–T121, T128, T174, T184, T192–T193, T198–T199, T206

focus on single event, **1:** T18, T28, T36–T37, T42–T43, T50

focus on single idea, **2:** T18, T28, T36–T37, T42–T43, T50

main idea, **2:** T174, T184, T192–T193, T198–T199, T206

main idea and details, **6:** T330, T340, T348–T349, T354–T355, T362

reason for opinion, **3:** T252, T262, T270–T271, T276–T277, T284, T330, T340, T348–T349, T354–T355, T362

supporting details, **2:** T330, T340, T348–T349, T354–T355, T362

organization

beginning, middle, end, **2:** T96, T106, T114–T115, T120–T121, T128, T252, T262, T270–T271, T276–T277, T284

compare and contrast, **1:** T252, T262, T270–T271, T276–T277, T284

concluding sentence, **4:** T174, T184, T192–T193, T198–T199, T206, T252, T262, T270–T271, T276–T277, T284

introduce the topic, **4:** T96, T106, T114–T115, T120–T121, T128

order of events, **1:** T330, T340, T348–T349, T354–T355, T362

steps in an order, **5:** T330, T340, T348–T349, T354–T355, T362

sentence fluency

use complete sentences, **5:** T18, T28, T36–T37, T42–T43, T50, T252, T262, T270–T271, T276–T277, T284

varying sentence length, **6:** T18, T28, T36–T37, T42–T43, T50

varying sentence types, **6:** T252, T262, T270–T271, T276–T277, T284

voice

use your own voice, **6:** T96, T106, T114–T115, T120–T121, T128, T174, T184, T192–T193, T198–T199, T206

word choice

describing adjectives, **5:** T96, T106, T114–T115, T120–T121, T128

figurative language, **4:** T18, T28, T36–T37, T42–T43, T50

sensory details, **3:** T18, T28, T36–T37, T42–T43, T50

strong verbs, **3:** T174, T184, T192–T193, T198–T199

time-order words, **5:** T174, T184, T192–T193, T198–T199, T206

use specific words, **3:** T96, T106, T114–T115, T120–T121, T128

words that tell order, **4:** T330, T340, T348–T349, T354–T355, T362

Common Core State Standards Correlations

English Language Arts

College and Career Readiness Anchor Standards for READING

The K–5 standards on the following pages define what students should understand and be able to do by the end of each grade. They correspond to the College and Career Readiness anchor standards below by number. The CCR and grade-specific standards are necessary complements—the former providing broad standards, the latter providing additional specificity—that together define the skills and understandings that all students must demonstrate.

Key Ideas and Details

1. Read closely to determine what the text says explicitly and to make logical inferences from it; cite specific textual evidence when writing or speaking to support conclusions drawn from the text.

2. Determine central ideas or themes of a text and analyze their development; summarize the key supporting details and ideas.

3. Analyze how and why individuals, events, and ideas develop and interact over the course of a text.

Craft and Structure

4. Interpret words and phrases as they are used in a text, including determining technical, connotative, and figurative meanings, and analyze how specific word choices shape meaning or tone.

5. Analyze the structure of texts, including how specific sentences, paragraphs, and larger portions of the text (e.g., a section, chapter, scene, or stanza) relate to each other and the whole.

6. Assess how point of view or purpose shapes the content and style of a text.

Integration of Knowledge and Ideas

7. Integrate and evaluate content presented in diverse media and formats, including visually and quantitatively as well as in words.

8. Delineate and evaluate the argument and specific claims in a text, including the validity of the reasoning as well as the relevance and sufficiency of the evidence.

9. Analyze how two or more texts address similar themes or topics in order to build knowledge or to compare the approaches the authors take.

Range of Reading and Level of Text Complexity

10. Read and comprehend complex literary and informational texts independently and proficiently.

Common Core State Standards
English Language Arts

Grade 1

Each standard is coded in the following manner:

Strand	Grade Level	Standard
RL	1	1

Reading Standards for Literature

Key Ideas and Details		*McGraw-Hill Reading Wonders*
RL.1.1	Ask and answer questions about key details in a text.	**READING/WRITING WORKSHOP:** Unit 1: 24, 25, 44, 45, 64, 65 Unit 2: 44, 45, 84, 85 Unit 3: 24, 25, 64, 65 Unit 4: 88, 89 Unit 5: 130, 131, 190, 191 Unit 6: 232, 233, 272, 273 **LITERATURE ANTHOLOGY:** Unit 1: 19, 41, 63 Unit 2: 21, 43, 81 Unit 3: 23, 45, 67, 73 Unit 4: 29, 89, 125 Unit 5: 155, 195, 225, 255 Unit 6: 295, 325, 357, 393 **LEVELED READERS:** Unit 1, Week 1: *We Like to Share* (O), *Class Party* (B) Unit 1, Week 2: *A Trip to the City* (O), *Harvest Time* (B) Unit 1, Week 3: *Mouse's Moon Party* (A), *Pet Show* (O) Unit 2, Week 1: *Pick Up Day* (A), *Ben Brings the Mail* (O), *At Work with Mom* (B) Unit 2, Week 2: *What a Nest!* (A), *Staying Afloat* (O) Unit 2, Week 4: *The Sick Tree* (A), *Squirrels Help* (O), *Wow, Kitty!* (B) Unit 3, Week 1: *Busy's Watch* (A), *Kate Saves the Date!* (O) Unit 3, Week 2: *Corn Fun* (A), *Yum, Strawberries!* (O) Unit 3, Week 3: *The Magic Paintbrush* (O) Unit 4, Week 1: *Fly to the Rescue!* (O) Unit 4, Week 4: *The Hat* (O) Unit 5, Week 1: *Nuts for Winter* (A), *Dog Bones* (O), *Spark's Toys* (B) Unit 5, Week 2: *Hide and Seek* (O) Unit 5, Week 4: *Thump, Jangle, Crash* (A), *Down on the Farm* (O) Unit 6, Week 1: *Two Hungry Elephants* (A), *What a Feast!* (O) Unit 6, Week 3: *Snow Day* (A), *Heat Wave* (O), *Rainy Day Fun* (B) Unit 6, Week 4: *The Quilt* (A), *Latkes for Sam* (O) **YOUR TURN PRACTICE BOOK:** 7, 17, 42, 44, 50, 117, 127, 147, 150, 162, 193, 205, 210, 217, 229, 241, 246, 253, 258, 277, 282, 301, 306, 313, 318 **READING WORKSTATION ACTIVITY CARDS:** 1, 3, 8, 14, 16, 23, 26, 28 **WRITING WORKSTATION ACTIVITY CARDS:** 9 **INTERACTIVE READ-ALOUD CARDS:** Unit 1, Week 5: 2, 4 Unit 2, Week 2: 3, 4 Unit 3, Week 2: 4 Unit 3, Week 3: 4 Unit 3, Week 5: 4 Unit 4, Week 1: 3, 4 Unit 4, Week 5: 4 Unit 5, Week 1: 4 Unit 5, Week 2: 4 Unit 5, Week 4: 2, 4 Unit 5, Week 5: 3, 4 Unit 6, Week 1: 4 Unit 6, Week 2: 2, 4 Unit 6, Week 3: 3, 4 **TEACHER'S EDITION:** Unit 1: T183, T191B, T191C, T191I, 191J, T221, T222, T223, T407, T412, T413 Unit 2: T412, T413, T415 Unit 3: T191J, T412, T413, T415 Unit 4: T11, T21, T35C, T35H, T167, T177, T191B, T191C, T191D, T191E, T191F, T191G, T191H, T191I, T191J, T191K, T191L, T191M, T191N, T191O, T191P, T269N, T407, T412, T413, T415 Unit 5: T245, T255, T261, T269D, T269E, T300, T322, T333, T407, T412, T413, T415 Unit 6: T35C, T191C, T407, T412, T413, T415 www.connected.mcgraw-hill.com: **RESOURCES: Units 1–6: Student Practice:** Genre Study, Approaching Reproducibles, Beyond Reproducibles, ELL Reproducibles, **Graphic Organizers:** Graphic Organizers, **Cards:** Retelling Cards

Reading Standards for Literature

Key Ideas and Details		McGraw-Hill Reading Wonders
RL.1.2	Retell stories, including key details, and demonstrate understanding of their central message or lesson.	**READING/WRITING WORKSHOP:** Unit 1: 24, 25, 44, 45, 64, 65 **Unit 4:** 28, 29 **Unit 5:** 150, 151 **Unit 6:** 232, 233, 272, 273, 292, 293 **LITERATURE ANTHOLOGY:** Unit 1: 19, 40, 63 **Unit 2:** 21, 42, 81 **Unit 3:** 23, 45, 67 **Unit 4:** 29, 125 **Unit 5:** 155, 195, 255 **Unit 6:** 295, 357, 393 **LEVELED READERS:** Unit 1, Week 3: *Pet Show* (O) **Unit 2, Week 1:** *Pick Up Day* (A), *Ben Brings the Mail* (O), *At Work with Mom* (B) **Unit 3, Week 3:** *The Magic Paintbrush* (O) **Unit 4, Week 1:** *Fly to the Rescue!* (O), *The Hat* (O) **Unit 5, Week 2:** *Little Blue's Dream* (A), *Hide and Seek* (O) **Unit 5, Week 4:** *Down on the Farm* (O), *Going on a Bird Walk* (B) **Unit 6, Week 4:** *The Quilt* (A), *Latkes for Sam* (O), *Patty Jumps!* (B) **YOUR TURN PRACTICE BOOK:** 138, 274, 277, 282, 310, 313 **READING WORKSTATION ACTIVITY CARDS:** 2, 6, 14, 16, 23 **WRITING WORKSTATION ACTIVITY CARDS:** 9 **INTERACTIVE READ-ALOUD CARDS:** Unit 1, Week 2: 4 **Unit 1, Week 5:** 4 **Unit 2, Week 2:** 3, 4 **Unit 3, Week 2:** 4 **Unit 3, Week 3:** 4 **Unit 3, Week 5:** 4 **Unit 4, Week 1:** 3, 4 **Unit 4, Week 5:** 4 **Unit 5, Week 1:** 4 **Unit 5, Week 2:** 4 **Unit 5, Week 4:** 4 **Unit 5, Week 5:** 3, 4 **Unit 6, Week 1:** 4 **Unit 6, Week 2:** 4 **Unit 6, Week 3:** 4 **TEACHER'S EDITION:** Unit 1: S32, T31, T109, T113I, T113J, T187, T191F, T414, T415 **Unit 2:** T35I, T35J, T345 **Unit 3:** T31, T113J, T187, T191I, T191J, T269J **Unit 4:** T11, T35K, T35L, T269R **Unit 5:** T11, T35I, T89, T113R, T245, T269P, T297, T414, T415 **Unit 6:** T11, T27, T35B, T35D, T35E, T35N, T89, T191Q, T191R, T269B, T269C, T300, T301 www.connected.mcgraw-hill.com: **RESOURCES: Units 1–6: Cards:** Retelling Cards **Media:** Fluency Passages **Graphic Organizers:** Graphic Organizers, Think Aloud Clouds **Student Practice:** Approaching Reproducibles, Beyond Reproducibles, ELL Reproducibles
RL.1.3	Describe characters, settings, and major events in a story, using key details.	**READING/WRITING WORKSHOP:** Unit 2: 24, 25, 44, 45, 84, 85 **Unit 3:** 24, 25, 44, 45, 64, 65 **Unit 4:** 28, 29 **Unit 5:** 150, 151, 190, 191 **Unit 6:** 272, 273 **LITERATURE ANTHOLOGY:** Unit 1: 19, 41, 63 **Unit 2:** 21, 43, 81 **Unit 3:** 23, 45, 67 **Unit 4:** 29, 125 **Unit 5:** 155, 195, 255 **LEVELED READERS:** Unit 1, Week 1: *We Like to Share* (O) **Unit 1, Week 3:** *Pet Show* (O) **Unit 2, Week 1:** *Ben Brings the Mail* (O) **Unit 2, Week 2:** *Staying Afloat* (O) **Unit 2, Week 4:** *The Sick Tree* (A), *Squirrels Help* (O) **Unit 3, Week 1:** *Busy's Watch* (A), *Kate Saves the Date!* (O) **Unit 5, Week 1:** *Dog Bones* (O) **Unit 6, Week 1:** *What a Feast!* (O) **YOUR TURN PRACTICE BOOK:** 42, 44, 50, 104, 107, 114, 117, 124, 127, 144, 147, 150, 154, 157, 190, 193, 198, 202, 205, 210, 214, 217, 222, 226, 229, 234, 238, 241, 246, 250, 258, 277, 298, 301, 306, 313, 318 **READING WORKSTATION ACTIVITY CARDS:** 1, 2, 3, 4, 6, 7, 8, 12, 13, 16, 23, 28 **WRITING WORKSTATION ACTIVITY CARDS:** 9, 23 **INTERACTIVE READ-ALOUD CARDS:** Unit 2, Week 2: 4 **Unit 3, Week 3:** 2 **Unit 3, Week 5:** 2, 4 **Unit 4, Week 1:** 4 **Unit 4, Week 5:** 4 **Unit 5, Week 1:** 4 **Unit 5, Week 2:** 3, 4 **Unit 5, Week 4:** 2, 4 **Unit 5, Week 5:** 3, 4 **Unit 6, Week 1:** 4 **Unit 6, Week 2:** 4 **Unit 6, Week 3:** 3, 4 **TEACHER'S EDITION:** Unit 1: T27, T35D, T35E, T35F, T35H, T105, T113D, T183 **Unit 2:** T27, T35B, T35E, T35F, T35G, T35I, T35J, T47, T69, T70, T71, T72, T73, T113E, T113F, T138, T139, T140, T141, T271B, T271C, 271D, T296, T297 **Unit 3:** T27, T35C, T35G, T35H, T35J, T52, T53, T69, T70, T71, T72, T73, T113B, T113C, T113G, T113H, T113J, T147, T148, T149, T150 **Unit 4:** T27, T31, T35E, T35G, T35I, T35L, T52, T53, T60, T61, T62, T63, T65, T66, T67 **Unit 5:** T27, T31, T35C, T35D, T35F, T60, T65, T104, T105, T138, T139, T269C, T269F, T269G, T269H, T305, T206, T307, T407, T415 **Unit 6:** T35D, T35F, T35I, T35K, T182, T183, T216 www.connected.mcgraw-hill.com: **RESOURCES: Units 1–6: Graphic Organizers:** Graphic Organizers **Cards:** Retelling Cards **Student Practice:** Approaching Reproducibles, Beyond Reproducibles, ELL Reproducibles
Craft and Structure		*McGraw-Hill Reading Wonders*
RL.1.4	Identify words and phrases in stories or poems that suggest feelings or appeal to the senses.	**READING/WRITING WORKSHOP:** Unit 1: 7 **Unit 2:** 7 **Unit 3:** 7 **Unit 4:** 11 **Unit 5:** 113 **Unit 6:** 215 **LITERATURE ANTHOLOGY:** Unit 1: 84, 85 **Unit 2:** 62, 63 **Unit 3:** 68, 69, 70, 71, 72, 73 **Unit 4:** 90, 91 **Unit 5:** 222, 223, 224, 225 **Unit 6:** 324, 325 **READING WORKSTATION ACTIVITY CARDS:** 21 **WRITING WORKSTATION ACTIVITY CARDS:** 13, 15 **INTERACTIVE READ-ALOUD CARDS:** Unit 3, Week 3: 1 **TEACHER'S EDITION:** Unit 1: T272, T273 **Unit 2:** T194, T195 **Unit 3:** T18, T35E, T35F, T35I, T76, T194, T195A, T195B **Unit 4:** T194, T195 **Unit 5:** T35H, T195, T195A, T195B **Unit 6:** T116, T117, T269K www.connected.mcgraw-hill.com: **RESOURCES: Media:** Images

Reading Standards for Literature

RL.1.5	Explain major differences between books that tell stories and books that give information, drawing on a wide reading of a range of text types.	**LITERATURE ANTHOLOGY:** Unit 1: 47, 67, 83, 93 **Unit 2:** 21, 25, 43, 47, 61, 81, 93 **Unit 3:** 23, 27, 45, 66, 89, 101 **Unit 4:** 29, 55, 89, 125, 137 **Unit 5:** 155, 195, 221, 255, 267 **Unit 6:** 295, 323, 357, 393, 405 **LEVELED READERS:** Unit 1, Week 1: *We Like to Share* (0), *Class Party* (B) **Unit 1, Week 2:** *What Can We See?* (A), *A Trip to the City* (0), *Where I Live*, pp. 13–16 (0), *Harvest Time* (B) **Unit 1, Week 3:** *Mouse's Moon Party* (A), *Pet Show* (0), *Polly the Circus Star* (B) **Unit 1, Week 4:** *Friends Are Fun* (A, 0, B) **Unit 1, Week 5:** *We Can Move!* (A, 0, B) **Unit 2 Week 1:** *Pick Up Day* (A), *Ben Brings the Mail* (0), *At Work with Mom* (B) **Unit 2, Week 2:** *What a Nest!* (A), *Stone Castles*, pp. 13–16 (A), *Staying Afloat* (0), *City Armadillo, Country Armadillo* (B) **Unit 2, Week 3:** *Meerkat Family* (A, 0, B) **Unit 2, Week 4:** *The Sick Tree* (A), *Squirrels Help* (0), *Sharing Skills*, pp. 13–16 (B) **Unit 2, Week 5:** *How Maps Help* (A, 0, B) **Unit 3, Week 1:** *Busy's Watch* (A), *Kate Saves the Date!* (0), *Uncle George Is Coming!* (B) **Unit 3, Week 3:** *How Coquí Got Her Voice* (A), *The Magic Paintbrush* (0), *The Storytelling Stone* (B) **Unit 4, Week 1:** *The King of the Animals* (A), *Lions and Elephants*, pp. 13–16 (A), *Fly to the Rescue!* (0), *Animal Traits*, pp. 13–16 (0), *Hummingbird's Wings* (B) **Unit 4, Week 2:** *Penguins All Around* (A, 0, B) **Unit 4, Week 4:** *Come One, Come All* (B) **Unit 5, Week 1:** *Nuts for Winter* (A), *Dog Bones* (0), *Spark's Toys* (B) **Unit 5, Week 5:** *What Is a Yurt?* (A, 0, B) **Unit 6, Week 1:** *Two Hungry Elephants* (A), *What a Feast!* (0), *Beware of the Lion!* (B) **Unit 6, Week 4:** *The Quilt* (A), *Latkes for Sam* (0) **TEACHER'S EDITION:** Unit 1: S14, S32, S56, S62, S92, T113F, T269F **Unit 2:** T26, T113G, T191H, T260, T269E, T338 **Unit 3:** T35E, T269D **Unit 4:** T26, T35H, T113H, T191I, T269D, T347D **Unit 5:** T35C, T35J, T113K, T182, T191L, T269P, T338, T347F **Unit 6:** T26, T35J, T113L, T191R, T269J, T347F **www.connected.mcgraw-hill.com: RESOURCES: Units 1–6: Teacher Resources:** Theme Bibliography, Literature/Informational Text Chart, Book Talk, Reader Response **Graphic Organizers:** Graphic Organizers
RL.1.6	Identify who is telling the story at various points in a text.	**READING/WRITING WORKSHOP:** Unit 2: 24, 25, 44, 45, 84, 85 **Unit 3:** 24, 25 **Unit 4:** 88, 89 **Unit 5:** 130, 131 190, 191 **Unit 6:** 272, 273 **LITERATURE ANTHOLOGY:** Unit 4: 125 **Unit 5:** 155 **TEACHER'S EDITION:** Unit 3: T26, T113B, T113I **Unit 4:** T261, T269E, T269F, T269H, T269K, T269O, T269R **Unit 5:** T26, T27, T35B, T35C, T35D, T35E, T35G, T35I, T35J, T395 **www.connected.mcgraw-hill.com: RESOURCES: Graphic Organizers:** Graphic Organizers

Integration of Knowledge and Ideas		*McGraw-Hill Reading Wonders*
RL.1.7	Use illustrations and details in a story to describe its characters, setting, or events.	**READING/WRITING WORKSHOP:** Unit 4: 88, 89 **Unit 5:** 130, 131 **LITERATURE ANTHOLOGY:** Unit 1: 63 **Unit 2:** 21, 42, 81 **Unit 3:** 23 **LEVELED READERS:** Unit 1, Week 1: *A Fun Day* (A) **Unit 2, Week 1:** *Pick Up Day* (A), *Ben Brings the Mail* (0), **Unit 6, Week 3:** *Heat Wave* (0) **YOUR TURN PRACTICE BOOK:** 44, 144, 147, 150, 154, 190, 193, 198, 202, 205, 210, 214, 246, 250, 258, 277, 298 **READING WORKSTATION ACTIVITY CARDS:** 2, 4, 28 **INTERACTIVE READ-ALOUD CARDS:** Unit 6, Week 1: 4 **Unit 6, Week 2:** 2, 4 **TEACHER'S EDITION:** Unit 1: T35E, T35F, T35G, T104, T105, T113H, T113I, T216 **Unit 2:** T27, T35I, T35J, T261, T269D, T269G, T269J, T308 **Unit 3:** T113D, T141, T167, T191D, T208, T298 **Unit 4:** T11, T35B, T35J, T71, T269G **Unit 5:** T35C, T269D, T269P, T305, T306, T307, T323 **Unit 6:** T183, T191E, T191I, T191P, T227, T269G, T269P, T306, T307 **www.connected.mcgraw-hill.com: RESOURCES: Graphic Organizers:** Graphic Organizers; **Media:** Images; **Cards:** Retelling Cards; Student Practice Approaching Reproducibles 44, 144, 147, 150, 154, 190, 193, 198, 202, 205, 210, 214, 246, 250, 258, 277, 298; Beyond Reproducibles 44, 144, 147, 150, 154, 190, 193, 198, 202, 205, 210, 214, 246, 250, 258, 277, 29, ELL Reproducibles 44, 144, 147, 150, 154, 190, 193, 198, 202, 205, 210, 214, 246, 250, 258, 277, 298
RL.1.8	(Not applicable to Literature)	
RL.1.9	Compare and contrast the adventures and experiences of characters in stories.	**READING/WRITING WORKSHOP:** Unit 2: 24, 25, 44, 45, 84, 85 **Unit 3:** 64, 65 **Unit 4:** 88, 89 **Unit 5:** 130, 131, 150, 151 **Unit 6:** 272, 273 **LEVELED READERS:** Unit 3, Week 3: *How Coquí Got Her Voice* (A), *The Magic Paintbrush* (0) **READING WORKSTATION ACTIVITY CARDS:** 23 **INTERACTIVE READ-ALOUD CARDS:** Unit 6, Week 1: 3 **TEACHER'S EDITION:** Unit 1: T124, T202 **Unit 2:** T124 **Unit 3:** T124, T191I, T202 **Unit 4:** T46 **Unit 5:** T46, T124, T280 **Unit 6:** T46, T202 **www.connected.mcgraw-hill.com: RESOURCES: Units 1–6: Graphic Organizers:** Graphic Organizers

Reading Standards for Literature

Range of Reading and Level of Text Complexity		McGraw-Hill Reading Wonders
RL.1.10	With prompting and support, read prose and poetry of appropriate complexity for grade 1.	**READING/WRITING WORKSHOP: Unit 1:** 7, 14–23, 34–43, 54–63 **Unit 2:** 7, 14–23, 34–43, 74–83 **Unit 3:** 7, 14–23, 34–43, 54–63 **Unit 4:** 11, 18–27, 78–87 **Unit 5:** 113, 120–129, 140–149, 180–189 **Unit 6:** 215, 222–231, 262–271, 282–291 **LITERATURE ANTHOLOGY: Unit 3, Week 2:** *The Big Yuca Plant,* 28 **Unit 3, Week 3:** *The Gingerbread Man,* 50 **Unit 3, Week 4:** *Mother Goose Rhymes,* 68 **Unit 4, Week 1:** *How Bat Got Its Wings,* 10 **Unit 4, Week 4:** *When It's Snowing,* 90 **Unit 5, Week 1:** *A Lost Button,* 140 **Unit 5, Week 2:** *Kitten's First Full Moon,* 162 **Unit 5, Week 3:** *Windshield Wipers,* 222 **Unit 6, Week 2:** *Abuelita's Lap,* 324 **Unit 6, Week 3:** *Rain School,* 236 **LEVELED READERS: Unit 1, Week 4:** *I Like to Play,* pp. 13–16 (A, O, B) **Unit 2, Week 3:** *I Live in a House!* (A, O, B) **Unit 4, Week 3:** *Ducklings,* pp. 13–16 (A, O), pp. 12–16 (B) **Unit 5, Week 3:** *Fly Away, Butterfly,* pp. 13–16 (A, O) **Unit 6, Week 2:** *Fire!* pp. 13–16 (A, O); pp. 12–16 (B) **YOUR TURN PRACTICE BOOK:** 5, 6, 15, 16, 25, 26, 35, 36, 42, 45, 46, 50, 55, 56, 65, 66, 75, 76, 85, 86, 105, 106, 115, 116, 125, 126, 145, 146, 155, 156, 191, 192, 203, 204, 215, 216, 227, 228, 239, 240, 251, 252, 275, 276, 299, 300, 311, 312 **READING WORKSTATION ACTIVITY CARDS:** 1, 2, 3, 4, 6, 7, 8, 12, 14, 16, 20, 23, 25, 26, 28 **TEACHER'S EDITION: Unit 1:** T16, T17, T52, T53, T140, T141, T412, T413, T414 **Unit 2:** T16, T17, T35A, T61, T62, T63, T297, T298, T299, T305, T306, T307 **Unit 3:** T65, T66, T67, T94, T95, T113A, T130, T131, T172, T173, T191B, T191C, T195, T195, T195A, T195B, T225 **Unit 4:** T16, T17, T191B, T219, T299, T303, T304, T305, T306, T307 **Unit 5:** T16, T17, T35D, T69, T70, T71, T72, T73, T143, T144, T145, T260, T261, T295, T296, T306, T307 **Unit 6:** T35B, T35H, T61, T62, T63, T151, T217, T303, T407 **LITERATURE BIG BOOKS: Unit 1, Week 1:** *This School Year Will be the Best* **Unit 1, Week 2:** *Alicia's Happy Day* **Unit 1, Week 3:** *Cool Dog, School Dog* **Unit 2, Week 1:** *Millie Waits for the Mail* **Unit 2, Week 2:** *The 3 Little Dassies* **Unit 2, Week 3:** *Babies in the Bayou* **Unit 3, Week 1:** *A Second is a Hiccup* **Unit 3, Week 2:** *Mystery Vine* **Unit 3, Week 3:** *Interrupting Chicken* **Unit 3, Week 4:** *The Last Train* www.connected.mcgraw-hill.com: **RESOURCES: Units 1–6: Teacher Resources:** Theme Bibliography, Literature/Informational Texts Chart **Student Practice:** Approaching Reproducibles, Beyond Reproducibles, ELL Reproducibles

Reading Standards for Informational Text

Key Ideas and Details		*McGraw-Hill Reading Wonders*
RI.1.1	Ask and answer questions about key details in a text.	**READING/WRITING WORKSHOP:** Unit 1: 84–85, 104–105 Unit 2: 64–65, 104–105 Unit 3: 84–85, 104–105 Unit 4: 48–49, 68–69 **LITERATURE ANTHOLOGY:** Unit 1: 83, 93, 94, 95 Unit 2: 61, 88, 89, 91, 93 Unit 3: 26, 49, 75, 89, 101, 103 Unit 4: 35, 55, 89, 137 Unit 5: 221, 267 Unit 6: 301, 323, 405 **LEVELED READERS:** Unit 1, Week 4: *Friends Are Fun* (A, O, B) Unit 2, Week 3: *Meerkat Family* (A, O, B) Unit 2, Week 5: *How Maps Help* (A, O, B) Unit 3, Week 4: *Schools Then and Now* (A, O, B) Unit 3, Week 5: *Apples from Farm to Table* (A, O, B) Unit 4, Week 2: *Penguins All Around* (A, O, B) Unit 4, Week 3: *Go, Gator!* (A, O, B) Unit 5, Week 3: *The Wright Brothers* (A, O, B) Unit 5, Week 5: *What Is a Yurt?* (A, O, B) Unit 6, Week 2: *Helping Me, Helping You!* (A, O, B) Unit 6, Week 5: *It's Labor Day!* (A, O, B) **YOUR TURN PRACTICE BOOK:** 94, 97, 100, 137, 161, 169, 181, 221, 257, 265, 270, 286, 289, 294, 305, 317, 322, 325, 330 **READING WORKSTATION ACTIVITY CARDS:** 5, 9, 11, 13, 15, 27 **WRITING WORKSTATION ACTIVITY CARDS:** 27, 29, 30 **INTERACTIVE READ-ALOUD CARDS:** Unit 1, Week 3: 4 Unit 2, Week 1: 3, 4 Unit 2, Week 3: 1, 4 Unit 2, Week 4: 3, 4 Unit 2, Week 5: 1, 3, 4 Unit 3, Week 1: 4 Unit 3, Week 4: 4 Unit 4, Week 2: 2, 4 Unit 4, Week 3: 1, 4 Unit 4, Week 4: 3, 4 Unit 5, Week 3: 4 Unit 5, Week 4: 4 Unit 6, Week 5: 3, 4 **TEACHER'S EDITION:** Unit 1: T244, T245, T269C, T322, T323, T332, T333, T338, T339, T358, T374, T375, T404, T412, T413 Unit 2: T218, T374, T394, T395, T407, T412, T413, T415 Unit 3: T255, T261, T265, T260, T261, T269C, T269I, T269J, T294, T358, T372, T389, T394, T395, T407, T412, T413, T415 Unit 4: T89, T99, T105, T113C, T113E, T117B, T130, T140, T144, T148, T149, T167, T183, T191C, T191F, T191H, T208, T216, T218, T222, T227, T228 Unit 5: T167, T191D, T208, T218, T222, T280, T338, T339, T364, T374, T379, T382, T383 Unit 6: T113F, T113G, T113H, T113I, T113J, T113L, T124, T372, T394, T395, T407, T412 www.connected.mcgraw-hill.com: **RESOURCES:** Units 1–6: Graphic Organizers: Graphic Organizers, Think Aloud Clouds **Tier 2 Intervention:** Comprehension **Student Practice:** Approaching Reproducibles, Beyond Reproducibles, ELL Reproducibles
RI.1.2	Identify the main topic and retell key details of a text.	**READING/WRITING WORKSHOP:** Unit 2: 64, 65, 104, 105 Unit 4: 48, 49, 68, 69 **LITERATURE ANTHOLOGY:** Unit 1: 83, 93 Unit 2: 61, 93 Unit 3: 89 Unit 4: 55, 89 Unit 5: 221 Unit 6: 323 **LEVELED READERS:** Unit 2, Week 3: *Meerkat Family* (A, O, B) Unit 2, Week 5: *How Maps Help* (A, O, B) Unit 4, Week 2: *Penguins All Around* (A, O, B) Unit 4, Week 3: *Go, Gator!* (A, O, B) **YOUR TURN PRACTICE BOOK:** 94, 97, 100, 166, 169, 174, 178, 181, 186, 197, 305, 317, 330 **READING WORKSTATION ACTIVITY CARDS:** 5, 10, 11, 27 **WRITING WORKSTATION ACTIVITY CARDS:** 24, 27 **INTERACTIVE READ-ALOUD CARDS:** Unit 1, Week 3: 4 Unit 2, Week 1: 4 Unit 2, Week 3: 2, 4 Unit 2, Week 4: 3, 4 Unit 2, Week 5: 1, 3, 4 Unit 3, Week 1: 4 Unit 3, Week 4: 4 Unit 4, Week 2: 4 Unit 4, Week 3: 1, 4 Unit 4, Week 4: 4 Unit 5, Week 3: 4 Unit 6, Week 4: 4 Unit 6, Week 5: 4 **TEACHER'S EDITION:** Unit 1: T261, T265, T269D, T269E, T269F, T269G, T269H, T269I, 269J, T342 Unit 2: T182, T183, T191B, T191D, T191E, T191F, T191H, T218, T219, T220, T221, T227, T228, T229, T230, T231, T383, T384, T385, T396, T387, T397, T405 Unit 3: T269I, T269J, T307, T338, T339, T347C, T347D, T347E, T347F, T375 Unit 4: T89, T105, T113G, T113K, T124, T125, T151, T245, T347B, T347C, T347E, T347F, T379 Unit 5: T167, T191H, T191K, T191L, T223, T385, T414, T415 Unit 6: T109, T131, T245, T347F, T359 www.connected.mcgraw-hill.com: **RESOURCES:** Units 1–6: Graphic Organizers: Graphic Organizers, Think Aloud Clouds **Tier 2 Intervention:** Comprehension **Student Practice:** Approaching Reproducibles, Beyond Reproducibles, ELL Reproducibles **Cards:** Retelling Cards

Reading Standards for Informational Text

Key Ideas and Details		McGraw-Hill Reading Wonders
RI.1.3	Describe the connection between two individuals, events, ideas, or pieces of information in a text.	**READING/WRITING WORKSHOP:** Unit 3: 84, 85, 104, 105 **Unit 4:** 38–47, 108, 109 **Unit 5:** 170, 171, 210, 211 **LITERATURE ANTHOLOGY:** Unit 1: 94, 95 **Unit 2:** 61, 93 **Unit 3:** 49, 89, 101 **Unit 4:** 35, 37–53, 55, 89, 137 Unit 5: 221, 267 **Unit 6:** 323 **LEVELED READERS:** Unit 2, Week 5: *How Maps Help* (A, O, B) **Unit 3, Week 5:** *Apples from Farm to Table* (A, O, B) **Unit 4, Week 4:** *Wings,* pp. 13–16 (A) **Unit 4, Week 5:** *Teach a Dog!* (A, O, B) **Unit 5, Week 5:** *What Is a Yurt?* (A, O, B) **Unit 6, Week 5:** *It's Labor Day!* (A, O, B) **YOUR TURN PRACTICE BOOK:** 100, 134, 137, 257, 262, 265, 270, 317 **READING WORKSTATION ACTIVITY CARDS:** 9, 13, 15, 17 **INTERACTIVE READ-ALOUD CARDS:** Unit 6, Week 4: 4 Unit 6, Week 5: 3 **TEACHER'S EDITION:** Unit 1: T281, T347B, T347E, T347F, T404, T405, T406 **Unit 2:** T183, T202, T404, T405, T406 **Unit 3:** T261, T269B, T269E, T269I, T269J, T281, T286, T287, T295, T296, T297, T299, T300, T301, T303, T304, T305, T306, T307, T365, T373, T375, T377, T379, T381, T385, T404, T405 **Unit 4:** T105, T109, T113D, T113F, T113H, T404, T405, T406 **Unit 5:** T183, T187, T191B, T191E, T191H, T191I, T208, T209, T216, T217, T218, T219, T223, T225, T226, T227, T228, T229, T339, T347C, T347E, T347F, T339, T364, T365, T373, T375, T377, T379, T384, T385 **Unit 6:** T113D, T113E, T125, T404, T405, T406 www.connected.mcgraw-hill.com: **RESOURCES: Units 1–6: Student Practice:** Approaching Reproducibles, Beyond Reproducibles, ELL Reproducibles **Graphic Organizers:** Graphic Organizers **Interactive Games & Activities:** Comprehension

Craft and Structure		McGraw-Hill Reading Wonders
RI.1.4	Ask and answer questions to help determine or clarify the meaning of words and phrases in a text.	**TEACHER'S EDITION:** Unit 2: T176, T273A, T396 **Unit 3:** T269F **Unit 4:** T113, T113F, T191G, T347 **Unit 5:** T347 **Unit 6:** T113F www.connected.mcgraw-hill.com: **RESOURCES: Units 1–6: Media:** Visual Glossary **Tier 2 Intervention:** Vocabulary **Interactive Games & Activities:** Vocabulary
RI.1.5	Know and use various text features (e.g., headings, tables of contents, glossaries, electronic menus, icons) to locate key facts or information in a text.	**READING/WRITING WORKSHOP:** Unit 2: 61, 94–103 **Unit 3:** 74–83, 96, 98, 103 **Unit 4:** 43, 45, 47, 98–107 Unit 5: 162, 164, 166, 200–209 **Unit 6:** 302–311 **LITERATURE ANTHOLOGY:** Unit 1: 94, 95 **Unit 2:** 59 **LEVELED READERS:** Unit 2, Week 5: *How Maps Help* (B) **Unit 3, Week 4:** *Schools Then and Now* (B) **Unit 4, Week 2:** *Penguins All Around* (B) **Unit 6, Week 5:** *It's Labor Day!* (O,B) **YOUR TURN PRACTCE BOOK:** 19, 29, 49, 59, 69, 99, 109, 119, 139, 149, 161, 173, 197, 209, 221, 233, 269, 281, 305, 329 **READING WORKSTATION ACTIVITY CARDS:** 18, 19, 20 **TEACHER'S EDITION:** Unit 1: T38, T39A, T39B, T338, T347C, T347F, T350, T351, T396, T415 **Unit 2:** T117, T117B, T274, T275, T275B, T338, T347A, T350, T351, T385, T396, T415 **Unit 3:** T260, T273, T273A, T322, T338, T350, T351, T396, T415 **Unit 4:** T38, T39A, T39B, T104, T273, T273B, T280, T338, T396, T415 **Unit 5:** T38, T39, T116, T117A, T396, T415 **Unit 6:** T195, T195A, T195B, T338, T350, T396, T415 www.connected.mcgraw-hill.com: **RESOURCES: Media:** Images; Time for Kids Online Articles; **Collaborate:** Projects; **Student Practice:** Approaching Reproducibles 19, 29, 49, 59, 69, 99, 109, 119, 139, 149, 161, 173, 197, 209, 221, 233, 269, 281, 305, 329, Beyond Reproducibles 19, 29, 49, 59, 69, 99, 109, 119, 139, 149, 161, 173, 197, 209, 221, 233, 269, 281, 305, 329; ELL Reproducibles 19, 29, 49, 59, 69, 99, 109, 119, 139, 149, 161, 173, 197, 209, 221, 233, 269, 281, 305, 329
RI.1.6	Distinguish between information provided by pictures or other illustrations and information provided by the words in a text.	**READING/WRITING WORKSHOP:** Unit 1: 84, 85, 104, 105 **Unit 2:** 104, 105 **Unit 5:** 210, 211 **YOUR TURN PRACTICE BOOK:** 173, 181, 209, 233, 269, 281 **READING WORKSTATION ACTIVITY CARDS:** 20 **INTERACTIVE READ-ALOUD CARDS:** Unit 1, Week 1: 4 Unit 1, Week 3: 4 Unit 1, Week 4: 4 Unit 2, Week 1: 4 Unit 2, Week 3: 4 Unit 2, Week 4: 4 Unit 2, Week 5: 3, 4 Unit 3, Week 1: 4 Unit 3, Week 4: 4 Unit 4, Week 2: 4 Unit 4, Week 3: 3, 4 Unit 4, Week 4: 2, 4 Unit 5, Week 3: 4 Unit 6, Week 4: 3, 4 Unit 6, Week 5: 4 **TEACHER'S EDITION:** Unit 1: T39B, T269C, T269E, T269F, T347B, T347C **Unit 2:** T35C, T39A, T191C, T347D, T350, T351 **Unit 3:** T269D **Unit 4:** T182 **Unit 5:** T182, T273, T338, T350, T351 **Unit 6:** T113E, T113F, T113H, T338 www.connected.mcgraw-hill.com: **RESOURCES: Media:** Images; Graphic Organizers; **Student Practice:** Approaching Reproducibles 173, 181, 209, 233, 269, 281, Beyond Reproducibles 173, 181, 209, 233, 269, 281, ELL Reproducibles 173, 181, 209, 233, 269, 281 **Interactive Games & Activities:** Comprehension

Reading Standards for Informational Text

Integration of Knowledge and Ideas		*McGraw-Hill Reading Wonders*
RI.1.7	Use the illustrations and details in a text to describe its key ideas.	**READING/WRITING WORKSHOP:** Unit 1: 104, 105 Unit 2: 104, 105 **LITERATURE ANTHOLOGY:** Unit 1: 83, 93, 95 Unit 2: 59, 61 Unit 3: 49, 89, 103 **LEVELED READERS:** Unit 1, Week 1: *A Fun Day* (A), *Our Classroom Rules,* pp. 13–16 (B) Unit 3, Week 1: *Make a Clock,* pp. 13–16 (A) Unit 3, Week 4: *Schools Then and Now* (A, O, B) Unit 4, Week 3: *Go, Gator!* (A, O, B) Unit 4, Week 4: *Wings,* pp. 13–16 (A) Unit 5, Week 1: *Sort by Color,* pp. 13–16 (A) **YOUR TURN PRACTICE BOOK:** 99, 100, 137, 166, 169, 174, 181, 186, 221, 233, 269, 270, 281, 294, 305, 317, 330 **READING WORKSTATION ACTIVITY CARDS:** 20 **INTERACTIVE READ-ALOUD CARDS:** Unit 1, Week 1: 1, 2, 4 Unit 1, Week 3: 4 Unit 1, Week 4: 4 Unit 2, Week 1: 4 Unit 2, Week 3: 4 Unit 2, Week 4: 2, 4 Unit 2, Week 5: 3, 4 Unit 3, Week 1: 4 Unit 3, Week 4: 4 Unit 4, Week 2: 4 Unit 4, Week 3: 3, 4 Unit 4, Week 4: 2, 4 Unit 5, Week 3: 4 Unit 6, Week 4: 3, 4 Unit 6, Week 5: 4 **TEACHER'S EDITION:** Unit 1: T38, T261, T269D, T269E, T269F, T269G, T304, T305, T306, T307, T347D, T347E, T347F, T372, T373, T374, T375 Unit 2: T39, T117, T191B, T191C, T191D, T191G, 191H, T274, T275, T349B, T349C, T349D, T349E, T349F, T385, T386, T387 Unit 3: T39, T269D, T269I, T269J, T273, T273B, T287, T307, T350, T365, T372, T383, T384, T385 Unit 4: T38, T149, T150, T167, T191G, T191I, T1910, T229, T245, T339, T365, T374, T375, T384, T385 Unit 5: T38, T39, T39A, T39B, T191B, T191D, T228, T347F, T372 Unit 6: T31, T38, T39A, T113E, T113F, T113G, 113H, T113I, T113K, T113L, T148, T149, T150, T151, T273, T273A, T338, T339, T347B, T347C, T347D, T365, T383 www.connected.mcgraw-hill.com: **RESOURCES: Media:** Images; **Student Practice:** Approaching Reproducibles 99, 100, 137, 166, 169, 174, 181, 186, 221, 233, 269, 270, 281, 294, 305, 317, 330, Beyond Reproducibles 99, 100, 137, 166, 169, 174, 181, 186, 221, 233, 269, 270, 281, 294, 305, 317, 330, ELL Reproducibles 99, 100, 137, 166, 169, 174, 181, 186, 221, 233, 269, 270, 281, 294, 305, 317, 330
RI.1.8	Identify the reasons an author gives to support points in a text.	**READING/WRITING WORKSHOP:** Unit 6: 252, 253, 312, 313 **LITERATURE ANTHOLOGY:** Unit 6: 323, 405 **LEVELED READERS:** Unit 6, Week 2: *Helping Me, Helping You!* (A, O, B) Unit 6, Week 5: *It's Labor Day!* (A, O, B) **WRITING WORKSTATION ACTIVITY CARDS:** 26 **TEACHER'S EDITION:** Unit 1: T260, T261, T269D, T269F, T281, T359 Unit 2: T183, T191F, T203, T359 Unit 3: T261, T282, T347D, T330, T359 Unit 4: T105, T113C, T113E, T125, T359 Unit 5: T183, T203, T339, T359 Unit 6: T104, T105, T113C, T113G, T113I, T125, T339, T347C, T359 www.connected.mcgraw-hill.com: **RESOURCES: Units 1–6: Cards:** Retelling Cards, **Graphic Organizers:** Graphic Organizers
RI.1.9	Identify basic similarities in and differences between two texts on the same topic (e.g., in illustrations, descriptions, or procedures).	**LITERATURE ANTHOLOGY:** Unit 1: 84, 94 Unit 2: 22, 44, 61, 62, 82, 94 Unit 3: 24, 46, 90, 102 Unit 4: 30, 56, 59, 90, 126, 138, 139 Unit 5: 156, 201, 222, 256, 268 Unit 6: 296, 301, 324, 394, 406 **LEVELED READERS:** Unit 1, Week 5: *What's Under Your Skin?* pp. 13–16 (A, O, B) Unit 2, Week 5: *On the Map,* pp. 13–16 (A, O); pp. 12–16 (B) Unit 3, Week 4: *School Days,* pp. 13–16 (A, O, B) Unit 4, Week 1: *Lions and Elephants,* pp. 13–16 (A, O); pp. 12–16 (B) Unit 4, Week 2: *Penguins All Around* (A, O, B), *Animals Work Together,* pp. 13–16 (A, O), pp. 12–16 (B) Unit 4, Week 5: *Teach a Dog!* (A, O, B), *Working with Dolphins,* pp. 13–16 (A, O), pp. 12–16 (B) **READING WORKSTATION ACTIVITY CARDS:** 22 **TEACHER'S EDITION:** Unit 1: S32, S62, S92, T39B, T46, T124, T280, T351, T358, T379, T385 Unit 2: T46, T39B, T117B, T191H, T195, T202, T275B, T353, T360, T361, T367, T381, T387 Unit 3: T117B, T273B, T280, T286, T287, T297, T307, T358, T359, T379 Unit 4: T39B, T117B, T124, T131, T141, T145, T151, T202, T209, T219, T273B, T280, T287, T297, T301, T307, T351, T358, T365, T375, T379, T385 Unit 5: T39B, T117B, T202, T209, T219, T223, T273B, T280, T281, T297, T301, T351, T358, T365, T375, T385 Unit 6: T195B, T273B, T280, T287, T297, T301, T307, T351, T358, T365, T375, T379, T385 www.connected.mcgraw-hill.com: **RESOURCES: Units 1–6: Graphic Organizers:** Graphic Organizers **Cards:** Retelling Cards

Reading Standards for Informational Text

Range of Reading and Level of Text Complexity	McGraw-Hill Reading Wonders
RI.1.10 With prompting and support, read informational texts appropriately complex for grade 1.	**READING/WRITING WORKSHOP:** Unit 1: 94–103 **Unit 2:** 54–63, 94–103 **Unit 3:** 74–83, 94–103 **Unit 4:** 38–47, 58–67, 98–107 **Unit 5:** 160–169, 200–209 **Unit 6:** 242–251, 302–311 **LITERATURE ANTHOLOGY:** These Units reflect the range of text complexity found throughout the book. **Unit 1, Week 4:** *Friends,* 68 **Unit 2, Week 5:** *Fun with Maps,* 86 **Unit 3, Week 4:** *Long Ago and Now,* 74 **Unit 4, Week 2:** *Animal Teams,* 36 **Unit 4, Week 5:** *Koko and Penny,* 130 **Unit 5, Week 3:** *Thomas Edison, Inventor,* 202 **Unit 6, Week 5:** *Happy Birthday, U.S.A.!,* 398 **LEVELED READERS: Unit 1, Week 1:** *We Share,* pp. 13–16 (O) **Unit 2, Week 2:** *What a Nest!,* pp. 13–16 (A), *Staying Afloat,* pp. 13–16 (O), *City, Armadillo, Country Armadillo,* pp. 13–16 (B) **Unit 3, Week 4:** *Schools Then and Now* (A, O, B) **Unit 4, Week 3:** *Go, Gator!* (A, O, B) **Unit 5, Week 1:** *Dog Bones,* pp. 13–16 (O) **Unit 6, Week 4:** *Latkes for Sam,* pp. 13–16 (O) **TEACHER'S EDITION: Unit 1:** T39A, T117, T195A, T250, T251, T269A, T328, T329, T347A, T373, T374, T375, T404, T405, T406, T407 **Unit 2:** T39A, T117A, T172A, T173, T191A, T328, T329, T340, T341, T383, T384, T385, T386, T387, T412, T413, T414 **Unit 3:** T39A, T117A, T250, T251, T269A, T286, T287, T304, T305, T306, T307, T328, T329, T347A, T377, T378, T379 **Unit 4:** T39, T94, T95, T113A, T140, T141, T226, T227, T328, T329, T382, T383 **Unit 5:** T117, T172, T173, T191A, T208, T209, T221, T222, T223, T338, T339, T381, T382, T383, T384, T385 **Unit 6:** T94, T95, T113A, T195A, T273A, T328, T329, T347A **LITERATURE BIG BOOKS: Unit 1, Week 4:** *Friends All Around* **Unit 1, Week 5:** *Move!* **Unit 2, Week 4:** *The Story of Martin Luther King, Jr.* **Unit 2, Week 5:** *Me on the Map* **Unit 3, Week 5:** *Where Does Food Come From?* www.connected.mcgraw-hill.com: **RESOURCES: Unit 1: Teacher Resources:** Theme Bibliography, Literature/Informational Text Chart **Student Practice:** Approaching Reproducibles, Beyond Reproducibles, ELL Reproducibles

Reading Standards: Foundational Skills

Print Concepts		*McGraw-Hill Reading Wonders*
RF.1.1	Demonstrate understanding of the organization and basic features of print.	
RF.1.1a	Recognize the distinguishing features of a sentence (e.g., first word, capitalization, ending punctuation).	**TEACHER'S EDITION:** Unit 1: S34, S64, T28, T29, T185, T207, T349 **Unit 2:** T88, T166, T331, T341, T349, T363 **Unit 3:** T19, T29, T51 **Unit 4:** T107, T115, T121 **Unit 5:** T97, T107, T115, T129 www.connected.mcgraw-hill.com: **RESOURCES:** Units 1–5: Student Practice: Grammar Practice **Interactive Games & Activities:** Writing & Grammar

Phonological Awareness		*McGraw-Hill Reading Wonders*
RF.1.2	Demonstrate understanding of spoken words, syllables, and sounds (phonemes).	
RF.1.2a	Distinguish long from short vowel sounds in spoken single-syllable words.	**TEACHER'S EDITION:** Unit 1: T168, T196 **Unit 4:** T22, T168, T196, T246 www.connected.mcgraw-hill.com: **RESOURCES: Unit 3: Interactive Games & Activities:** Phonemic Awareness **Cards:** Word-Building Cards **Tier 2 Intervention:** Phonemic Awareness **Unit 4: Interactive Games & Activities:** Phonemic Awareness **Cards:** Word-Building Cards **Tier 2 Intervention:** Phonemic Awareness
RF.1.2b	Orally produce single-syllable words by blending sounds (phonemes) including consonant blends.	**YOUR TURN PRACTICE BOOK:** SS1, SS2, SS6, SS7, SS11, SS13, SS14, SS18, SS19, SS23, SS25, SS26, SS30, SS31, SS35, 1, 41, 121, 171 **PHONICS WORKSTATION ACTIVITY CARDS:** 5, 15, 16, 20, 23, 28, 29 **TEACHER'S EDITION:** Unit 1: S53, S65, S71, T32, T55, T91, T110, T132, T168, T178, T210, T282, T289 **Unit 2:** T12, T48, T110, T126, T178 **Unit 3:** T126, T188, T282, T334, T360 **Unit 4:** T32, T48, T178, T204, T282, T344 **Unit 5:** T32, T110, T126, T188, T266, T282, T288, T324, T325, T352, T366, T367 **Unit 6:** T110, T266, T282, T334 www.connected.mcgraw-hill.com: **RESOURCES: Units 1–6: Interactive Games & Activities:** Phonemic Awareness **Student Practice:** Phonics/Spelling Practice, Approaching Reproducibles, Beyond Reproducibles, ELL Reproducibles **Cards:** Word-Building Cards
RF.1.2c	Isolate and pronounce initial, medial vowel, and final sounds (phonemes) in spoken single-syllable words.	**YOUR TURN PRACTICE BOOK:** SS1, SS2, SS6, SS7, SS11, SS13, SS14, SS18, SS19, SS23, SS25, SS26, SS30, SS31, SS35, 31, 39, 129, 245 **TEACHER'S EDITION:** Unit 1: S5, S11, S41, T22, T40, T100, T188, T324 **Unit 2:** T22, T40, T54, T55, T100, T118, T132, T168, T188, T198, T212, T213, T246, T258, T276, T290, T291, T369 **Unit 3:** T12, T40, T256, T274 **Unit 4:** T22, T23, T54, T90, T110, T118, T132, T133, T168, T188, T196, T210, T211, T246, T288, T289, T324, T352, T366, T367 **Unit 5:** T12, T22, T40, T168, T256, T274, T288, T289, T334, T366 **Unit 6:** T12, T90, T118, T132, T133, T168, T196, T210, T211, T289, T366, T367 www.connected.mcgraw-hill.com: **RESOURCES: Units 1–6: Interactive Games & Activities:** Phonemic Awareness **Student Practice:** Phonics/Spelling Practice, Approaching Reproducibles, Beyond Reproducibles, ELL Reproducibles **Cards:** Word-Building Cards
RF.1.2d	Segment spoken single-syllable words into their complete sequence of individual sounds (phonemes).	**TEACHER'S EDITION:** Unit 1: S77, S83, T48, T204, T256, T266, T282, T334, T360 **Unit 2:** T48, T126, T204, T282, T324, T360 **Unit 3:** T48, T110, T126, T178, T196, T246, T288, T360, T367 **Unit 4:** T48, T100, T126, T266, T282 **Unit 5:** T48, T204, T334, T360 **Unit 6:** T22, T48, T126, T178, T204, T210, T256, T274, T288, T367 www.connected.mcgraw-hill.com: **RESOURCES: Units 1–6: Interactive Games & Activities:** Phonemic Awareness **Student Practice:** Phonics/Spelling Practice **Tier 2 Intervention:** Phonemic Awareness **Cards:** Word-Building Cards

Phonics and Word Recognition		*McGraw-Hill Reading Wonders*
RF.1.3	Know and apply grade-level phonics and word analysis skills in decoding words.	
RF.1.3a	Know the spelling-sound correspondences for common consonant digraphs (two letters that represent one sound).	**READING/WRITING WORKSHOP:** Unit 2: 72, 73, 92, 93 **PHONICS WORKSTATION ACTIVITY CARDS:** 9, 10 **TEACHER'S EDITION:** Unit 2: T246, T247, T250, T251, T256, T257, T266, T267, T324, T325, T328, T329 **Unit 6:** T168, T169, T172, T173, T179, T188, T189 **YOUR TURN PRACTICE BOOK:** SS25, 13, 18, 23, 25, 26, 28, 29, 31, 33, 49, 91, 93, 103 www.connected.mcgraw-hill.com: **RESOURCES: Unit 2: Tier 2 Intervention:** Phonics **Cards:** Sound-Spelling Cards **Teacher Resources:** Sound-Spelling Songs **Interactive Games & Activities:** Phonics **Student Practice:** Phonics/Spelling Practice, Approaching Reproducibles, Beyond Reproducibles, ELL Reproducibles **Unit 6: Tier 2 Intervention:** Phonics **Cards:** Sound-Spelling Cards **Teacher Resources:** Sound-Spelling Songs **Interactive Games & Activities:** Phonics **Student Practice:** Phonics/Spelling Practice, Approaching Reproducibles, Beyond Reproducibles, ELL Reproducibles

Reading Standards: Foundational Skills

Phonics and Word Recognition		McGraw-Hill Reading Wonders
RF.1.3b	Decode regularly spelled one-syllable words.	**READING/WRITING WORKSHOP:** Unit 1: 12, 13, 32, 33, 52, 53, 72, 73, 92, 93 **Unit 2:** 12, 13, 32, 33, 52, 53, 72, 73, 92, 93 **Unit 3:** 12, 13, 32, 33, 52, 72, 73, 92, 93 **Unit 4:** 16, 17, 56, 57, 76, 77, 96, 97 **Unit 5:** 118, 119, 138, 139, 158, 159, 178, 179, 198, 199 **Unit 6:** 220, 221, 240, 241, 260, 261, 280, 281, 300, 301 **YOUR TURN PRACTICE BOOK:** SS3, SS4, SS9, SS10, SS15, SS16, SS21, SS22, SS27, SS28, SS33, SS34, 1, 3, 5, 6, 8, 11, 13, 15, 16, 18, 19, 21, 23, 25, 26, 28, 29, 31, 33, 35, 36, 39, 41, 43, 45, 46, 49, 51, 53, 55, 56, 59, 61, 62, 63, 65, 66, 69, 71, 73, 75, 76, 79, 81, 82, 83, 85, 86, 91, 92, 93, 95, 96, 101, 102, 103, 105, 106, 111, 112, 113, 115, 116, 119, 121, 122, 123, 125, 126, 129, 133, 135, 136, 138, 141, 142, 143, 145, 146, 151, 152, 155, 156, 159, 163, 164, 167, 168, 171, 175, 176, 179, 180, 183, 187, 188, 191, 192, 195, 199, 200, 203, 204, 207, 211, 212, 215, 216, 219, 223, 224, 227, 228, 231, 235, 236, 239, 240, 243, 245, 247, 248, 251, 252, 253, 255, 257, 259, 260, 263, 264, 267, 271, 272, 275, 276, 279, 283, 284, 287, 288, 291, 295, 296, 299, 300, 303, 307, 308, 311, 312, 315, 319, 320, 323, 324, 327 **PHONICS WORKSTATION ACTIVITY CARDS:** 3, 6, 7, 8, 9, 10, 11, 12, 13, 14, 15, 16, 17, 18, 19, 20, 21, 22, 23, 24, 25, 26, 27, 28, 29, 30 **TEACHER'S EDITION:** Unit 1: S30, S31, S48, S49, T32, T33, T110, T111, T196, T266, T267, T368, T369 **Unit 2:** T32, T33, T118, T119, T188, T189, T215, T252, T253, T336, T337 **Unit 3:** T16, T17, T168, T169, T266, T267, T324, T325 **Unit 4:** T17, T22, T23, T32, T33, T64, T95, T101, T134, T135, T173, T188, T189, T212, T213, T250, T251, T290, T291, T324, T325, T328, T329, T346 **Unit 5:** T12, T13, T126, T127, T212, T213, T324, T325, T344, T345, T368, T369 **Unit 6:** T16, T17, T22, T23, T32, T33, T40, T48, T56, T57, T64, T90, T91, T94, T95, T100, T101, T134, T135, T142, T168, T169, T172, T173, T188, T189, T196, T197, T204, T205, T212, T213, T246, T247, T250, T251, T256, T257, T266, T267, T274, T275, T290, T291, T298, T324, T325, T328, T329, T334, T335, T344, T345, T352, T353, T368, T369, T376 www.connected.mcgraw-hill.com: **RESOURCES:** Units 1–6: Tier 2 Intervention: Phonics **Cards:** Word-Building Cards, Spelling Word Cards **Interactive Games & Activities:** Phonics **Student Practice:** Approaching Reproducibles, Beyond Reproducibles, ELL Reproducibles
RF.1.3c	Know final -e and common vowel team conventions for representing long vowel sounds.	**READING/WRITING WORKSHOP:** Unit 3: 12–13, 32–33, 72–73 **Unit 4:** 16, 17, 36, 37, 56, 57, 76, 77, 96, 97 **Unit 6:** 220, 221 **YOUR TURN PRACTICE BOOK:** 101, 103, 111, 113, 131, 133, 138, 151, 159, 163, 171, 175, 183, 187, 195, 199, 207, 271, 279, 292 **PHONICS WORKSTATION ACTIVITY CARDS:** 3, 11, 12, 13, 14, 16, 17, 18, 19, 20 **TEACHER'S EDITION:** Unit 3: T12, T13, T17, T22, T23, T32, T40, T48, T56, T57, T64, T90, T91, T100, T101, T110, T111, T118, T126, T134, T135, T142, T210, T246, T247, T256, T257, T290, T291 **Unit 4:** T12, T13, T22, T23, T24, T32, T33, T40, T48, T56, T57, T64, T76, T90, T91, T101, T110, T111, T118, T119, T126, T127, T134, T142, T168, T169, T213, T220, T246, T247, T256, T257, T266, T267, T282, T290, T291, T334, T335, T352, T353, T360, T361, T368, T369, T376, T388 www.connected.mcgraw-hill.com: **RESOURCES:** Unit 3: Tier 2 Intervention: Phonics **Cards:** Word-Building Cards, Spelling Word Cards **Interactive Games & Activities:** Phonics **Student Practice:** Approaching Reproducibles, Beyond Reproducibles, ELL Reproducibles **Unit 4: Tier 2 Intervention:** Phonics **Cards:** Word-Building Cards, Spelling Word Cards **Interactive Games & Activities:** Phonics **Student Practice:** Approaching Reproducibles, Beyond Reproducibles, ELL Reproducibles
RF.1.3d	Use knowledge that every syllable must have a vowel sound to determine the number of syllables in a printed word.	**YOUR TURN PRACTICE BOOK:** 138, 328 **TEACHER'S EDITION:** Unit 2: T179, T257 **Unit 3:** T257 **Unit 4:** T179, T214 **Unit 5:** T335, T370 **Unit 6:** T101, T335, T370 www.connected.mcgraw-hill.com: **RESOURCES:** Cards: Word-Building Cards **Interactive Games & Activities:** Phonics
RF.1.3e	Decode two-syllable words following basic patterns by breaking the words into syllables.	**READING/WRITING WORKSHOP:** Unit 2: 73, 93 **Unit 4:** 56, 57, 76, 77, 94, 95, 96, 97 **Unit 5:** 116, 117, 118, 119, 139, 156, 157, 158, 159, 176, 177, 178, 179, 196, 197, 198, 199 **Unit 6:** 220, 221, 240, 241, 260, 261, 280, 281, 298–301 **YOUR TURN PRACTICE BOOK:** 138, 184, 208, 268, 304, 314, 328 **PHONICS WORKSTATION ACTIVITY CARDS:** 8, 28 **TEACHER'S EDITION:** Unit 2: T257, T267, T275, T283 **Unit 3:** T257, T267, T275, T283 **Unit 4:** T179, T189, T196, T204 **Unit 5:** T335, T345, T352, T360 **Unit 6:** T101, T111, T118, T126, T179, T335, T345, T360 www.connected.mcgraw-hill.com: **RESOURCES:** Cards: Word-Building Cards, Student Practice Approaching Reproducibles 138, 184, 208, 268, 304, 314, 328, Beyond Reproducibles 138, 184, 208, 268, 304, 314, 328, ELL Reproducibles 138, 184, 208, 268, 304, 314, 328

Reading Standards: Foundational Skills

RF.1.3f	Read words with inflectional endings.	**READING/WRITING WORKSHOP:** Unit 1: 52, 53, 72, 73, 92, 93 Unit 2: 32, 33, 73 Unit 3: 32, 33, 72, 92, 93 Unit 4: 16, 17, 36, 37, 56, 57, 76, 77 Unit 5: 118, 139, 178, 179, 198 Unit 6: 240, 260, 261, 280, 281 **YOUR TURN PRACTICE BOOK:** 8, 28, 58, 78, 98, 118, 128, 148, 196, 225, 232, 249, 256, 266, 316 **PHONICS WORKSTATION ACTIVITY CARDS:** 8, 13, 15 **TEACHER'S EDITION:** Unit 1: T23, T33, T179, T189, T197, T205 Unit 2: T23, T33, T41, T49, T179, T189, T199, T206, T216, T337, T347, T354, T362 Unit 3: T101, T111, T119, T127, T179, T189, T205, T214, T335, T345, T352, T360, T370 Unit 4: T257, T267, T274, T282, T353 Unit 5: T101, T111, T118, T126, T136, T257, T267, T274, T282, T392 Unit 6: T40, T257, T267, T274, T282 www.connected.mcgraw-hill.com: **RESOURCES: Units 1–6: Cards:** Word-Building Cards **Student Practice:** Phonics/Spelling Practice, Approaching Reproducibles, Beyond Reproducibles, ELL Reproducibles
RF.1.3g	Recognize and read grade-appropriate irregularly spelled words.	**READING/WRITING WORKSHOP:** Unit 1: 10, 11, 30, 31, 50, 51, 70, 71, 90, 91 Unit 2: 10, 11, 30, 31, 50, 51, 70, 71, 90, 91 Unit 3: 10, 11, 30, 31, 50, 51, 70, 71, 90, 91 Unit 4: 14, 74, 94 Unit 5: 116, 156, 176, 177, 196 Unit 6: 218, 238, 258, 298, 299 **YOUR TURN PRACTICE BOOK:** 188, 200, 220, 296 **PHONICS WORKSTATION ACTIVITY CARDS:** 28 **TEACHER'S EDITION:** Unit 1: T15, T16, T17, T92, T93, T94, T95, T171, T172, T173, T327, T328, T329 Unit 2: T15, T16, T17, T93, T94, T95, T103, T171, T172, T173, T249, T250, T251, T327, T328, T329, T337 Unit 3: T15, T16, T17, T25, T93, T94, T95, T249, T250, T251 Unit 4: T14, T15, T16, T17, T49, T112, T113, T180, T181, T258, T259, T326, T327 Unit 5: T14, T25, T26, T17, T92, T93, T94, T95, T170, T171, T172, T173, T248, T249, T250, T251, T346, T347 Unit 6: T24, T25, T102, T248, T249, T250, T252, T326, T327, T328, T329 www.connected.mcgraw-hill.com: **RESOURCES: Units 1–6: Cards:** High-Frequency Word Cards, Spelling Word Cards, Word-Building Cards **Student Practice:** Approaching Reproducibles, Beyond Reproducibles, ELL Reproducibles

Fluency		***McGraw-Hill Reading Wonders***
RF.1.4	Read with sufficient accuracy and fluency to support comprehension.	
RF.1.4a	Read grade-level text with purpose and understanding.	**YOUR TURN PRACTICE BOOK:** SS3, SS4, SS9, SS10, SS15, SS16, SS21, SS22, SS27, SS28, SS33, SS34, 5, 6, 11, 12, 13, 15, 16, 18, 21, 22, 23, 25, 26, 28, 31, 32, 33, 35, 36, 42, 43, 45, 46, 47, 55, 56, 65, 66, 75, 76, 82, 85, 86, 95, 96, 99, 101, 103, 105, 106, 109, 111, 113, 115, 116, 121, 123, 125, 126, 131, 132, 133, 135, 136, 138, 139, 141, 143, 145, 146, 149, 151, 155, 156, 157, 159, 161, 163, 167, 168, 169, 171, 173, 175, 179, 180, 181, 183, 185, 187, 191, 192, 193, 195, 197, 199, 203, 204, 205, 207, 209, 211, 215, 216, 219, 221, 223, 227, 228, 231, 233, 235, 239, 240, 241, 243, 247, 251, 252, 255, 257, 259, 263, 264, 265, 267, 269, 271, 275, 276, 277, 279, 281, 283, 287, 288, 289, 291, 293, 295, 299, 300, 301, 303, 305, 307, 311, 312, 313, 315, 317, 319, 323, 324, 325, 327, 329 **READING WORKSTATION ACTIVITY CARDS:** 1, 2, 3, 4, 5, 6, 7, 8, 9, 10, 11, 12, 13, 14, 15, 16, 17, 19, 21, 22, 23, 24, 25, 26, 27, 28 **TEACHER'S EDITION:** Unit 1: T16, T17, T104, T105, T250, T251, T328, T329 Unit 2: T94, T95, T182, T183 Unit 3: T94, T95, T280, T281, T394, T395 Unit 4: T104, T105, T172, T173, T394, T395 Unit 5: T16, T17, T260, T261, T328, T329, T343, T394, T395 Unit 6: T94, T95, T182, T183, T328, T329, T343, T344, T395 www.connected.mcgraw-hill.com: **RESOURCES: Units 1–6: Student Practice:** Reader's Theater, Approaching Reproducibles, Beyond Reproducibles, ELL Reproducibles
RF.1.4b	Read grade-level text orally with accuracy, appropriate rate, and expression.	**YOUR TURN PRACTICE BOOK:** 157, 169, 181, 193, 205, 241, 265, 277, 289, 301, 313, 325 **READING WORKSTATION ACTIVITY CARDS:** 24, 25 **TEACHER'S EDITION:** Unit 1: T31, T113, T127, T191, T265, T394, T395 Unit 2: T31, T63, T109, T141, T151, T187, T221, T267, T299, T394, T395 Unit 3: T31, T63, T141, T187, T219, T265, T294, T343, T375, T394, T395 Unit 4: T31, T49, T109, T187, T205, T219, T265, T297, T343, T361, T375, T394, T395 Unit 5: T31, T49, T63, T109, T127, T141, T187, T205, T265, T283, T297, T343, T361, T375, T394, T395 Unit 6: T31, T49, T63, T109, T127, T141, T187, T205, T219, T283, T297, T343, T361, T375, T394, T395 www.connected.mcgraw-hill.com: **RESOURCES: Units 1–6: Media:** Fluency Passages **Student Practice:** Reader's Theater, Approaching Reproducibles, Beyond Reproducibles, ELL Reproducibles **Tier 2 Intervention:** Comprehension **Interactive Games & Activities:** Fluency
RF.1.4c	Use context to confirm or self-correct word recognition and understanding, rereading as necessary.	**YOUR TURN PRACTICE BOOK:** 53, 73, 83, 103, 112, 123, 132, 133, 142, 152, 164, 175, 176, 183, 187, 188, 200, 201, 207, 212, 219, 223, 231, 236, 237, 243, 259, 260, 272, 284, 295, 296, 303, 308, 319, 320 **TEACHER'S EDITION:** Unit 1: T39, T394, T395 Unit 2: T394, T395 Unit 3: T394, T395 Unit 4: T394, T395 Unit 5: T394, T395 Unit 6: T394, T395 www.connected.mcgraw-hill.com: **RESOURCES: Units 1–6: Student Practice:** Reader's Theater, Approaching Reproducibles, Beyond Reproducibles, ELL Reproducibles **Media:** Fluency Passages **Interactive Games & Activities:** Fluency

College and Career Readiness Anchor Standards for WRITING

The K–5 standards on the following pages define what students should understand and be able to do by the end of each grade. They correspond to the College and Career Readiness anchor standards below by number. The CCR and grade-specific standards are necessary complements—the former providing broad standards, the latter providing additional specificity—that together define the skills and understandings that all students must demonstrate.

Text Types and Purposes

1. Write arguments to support claims in an analysis of substantive topics or texts, using valid reasoning and relevant and sufficient evidence.

2. Write informative/explanatory texts to examine and convey complex ideas and information clearly and accurately through the effective selection, organization, and analysis of content.

3. Write narratives to develop real or imagined experiences or events using effective technique, well-chosen details, and well-structured event sequences.

Production and Distribution of Writing

4. Produce clear and coherent writing in which the development, organization, and style are appropriate to task, purpose, and audience.

5. Develop and strengthen writing as needed by planning, revising, editing, rewritings, or trying a new approach.

6. Use technology, including the Internet, to produce and publish writing and to interact and collaborate with others.

Research to Build and Present Knowledge

7. Conduct short as well as more sustained research projects based on focused questions, demonstrating understanding of the subject under investigation.

8. Gather relevant information from multiple print and digital sources, assess the credibility and accuracy of each source, and integrate the information while avoiding plagiarism.

9. Draw evidence from literary or informational texts to support analysis, reflection, and research.

Range of Writing

10. Write routinely over extended time frames (time for research, reflection, and revision) and shorter time frames (a single sitting or a day or two) for a range of tasks, purposes, and audiences.

CCSS Common Core State Standards
English Language Arts
Grade 1

Writing Standards

Text Types and Purposes	*McGraw-Hill Reading Wonders*
W.1.1 Write opinion pieces in which they introduce the topic or name the book they are writing about, state an opinion, supply a reason for the opinion, and provide some sense of closure.	**READING/WRITING WORKSHOP:** Unit 3: 46, 86, 106 Unit 4: 90 Unit 5: 192 **READING WORKSTATION ACTIVITY CARDS:** 14 **WRITING WORKSTATION ACTIVITY CARDS:** 4, 11, 26, 30 **TEACHER'S EDITION:** Unit 3: T106, T114, T115, T128, T262, T270, T271, T276, T277, T284, T340, T348, T349, T354, T355, T362 Unit 4: T262, T270, T271, T276, T277, T284 Unit 5: T262, T270, T271, T276, T277, T284 www.connected.mcgraw-hill.com: **RESOURCES:** Units 1–6: Teacher Resources: Writer's Checklists/Proofreading Marks
W.1.2 Write informative/explanatory texts in which they name a topic, supply some facts about the topic, and provide some sense of closure.	**READING/WRITING WORKSHOP:** Unit 2: 66, 106 Unit 4: 50, 70, 110 Unit 5: 132, 212 Unit 6: 314 **LITERATURE ANTHOLOGY:** Unit 2: 60, 80 Unit 3: 44, 88 Unit 4: 54 **LEVELED READERS:** Unit 4, Week 3: *Go, Gator!* p. 16 (B) Unit 5, Week 3: *The Wright Brothers*, p. 16 (B) Unit 6, Week 5: *It's Labor Day!* p. 16 (O, B) **READING WORKSTATION ACTIVITY CARDS:** 10 **SCIENCE & SOCIAL STUDIES WORKSTATION ACTIVITY CARDS:** 9, 19, 27 **READING WORKSTATION ACTIVITY CARDS:** 5, 6, 9, 10, 27, 28, 29 **TEACHER'S EDITION:** Unit 4: T106, T114, T115, T120, T121, T128, T184, T192, T193, T198, T199, T206, T340, T348, T349, T354, T355, T362 Unit 5: T340, T348, T349, T354, T355, T362 Unit 6: T340, T348, T349, T354, T355, T362 www.connected.mcgraw-hill.com: **RESOURCES:** Units 1–6: Teacher Resources: Writer's Checklists/Proofreading Marks
W.1.3 Write narratives in which they recount two or more appropriately sequenced events, include some details regarding what happened, use temporal words to signal event order, and provide some sense of closure.	**READING/WRITING WORKSHOP:** Unit 1: 26, 46, 106 Unit 2: 26, 46, 86 Unit 4: 30 Unit 5: 172 Unit 6: 234 **LITERATURE ANTHOLOGY:** Unit 3: 22, 66 Unit 4: 124 Unit 5: 154, 254 Unit 6: 322 **LEVELED READERS:** Unit 2, Week 1: *Ben Brings the Mail*, p. 16 (O,B) Unit 3, Week 3: *The Storytelling Stone*, p. 16 (B) Unit 4, Week 1: *Fly to the Rescue!* p. 16 (O), *Hummingbird's Wings*, p. 16 (B) Unit 5, Week 1: *Spark's Toys* (B) Unit 6, Week 1: *Beware of the Lion!* p. 16 (B) Unit 6, Week 4: *Patty Jumps!* (B) **READING WORKSTATION ACTIVITY CARDS:** 10, 16 **WRITING WORKSTATION ACTIVITY CARDS:** 21, 23 **TEACHER'S EDITION:** Unit 2: T262, T270, T271, T276, T277, T284 Unit 4: T28, T36, T37, T42, T43, T50 Unit 5: T184, T192, T193, T198, T199, T206 Unit 6: T28, T36, T37, T42, T43, T50 www.connected.mcgraw-hill.com: **RESOURCES:** Units 1–6: Teacher Resources: Writer's Checklists/Proofreading Marks

Writing Standards

Production and Distribution of Writing		McGraw-Hill Reading Wonders
W.1.4	(Begins in grade 3)	
W.1.5	With guidance and support from adults, focus on a topic, respond to questions and suggestions from peers, and add details to strengthen writing as needed.	**WRITING WORKSTATION ACTIVITY CARDS:** 1, 2, 3, 4, 5, 6, 7, 8, 9, 10, 11, 12, 13, 14, 15, 16, 17, 18, 19, 20, 21, 22, 23, 24, 25, 26, 27, 28, 29, 30 **TEACHER'S EDITION: Unit 1:** T42, T43, T120, T121, T174, T198, T199, T252, T276, T277, T330, T354, T355 **Unit 2:** T42, T43, T120, T121, T174, T198, T199, T252, T276, T277, T330, T354, T355 **Unit 3:** T42, T43, T120, T121, T174, T198, T199, T252, T276, T277, T330, T354, T355 **Unit 4:** T42, T43, T120, T121, T174, T198, T199, T252, T276, T277, T330, T354, T355 **Unit 5:** T42, T43, T120, T121, T174, T198, T199, T252, T276, T277, T330, T354, T355 **Unit 6:** T42, T43, T120, T121, T174, T198, T199, T252, T276, T277, T330, T354, T355 www.connected.mcgraw-hill.com: **RESOURCES: Units 1–6: Graphic Organizers:** Graphic Organizers **Teacher Resources:** Writer's Checklists/Proofreading Marks
W.1.6	With guidance and support from adults, use a variety of digital tools to produce and publish writing, including in collaboration with peers.	**TEACHER'S EDITION: Unit 1:** T36, T50, T114, T122, T128, T192, T206, T270, T284, T348, T362, T397, T398, T399, T400, T401, T402 **Unit 2:** T36, T50, T114, T128, T192, T206, T270, T284, T348, T362, T397, T398, T399, T400, T401, T402 **Unit 3:** T36, T50, T114, T128, T192, T206, T270, T284, T348, T362, T397, T398, T399, T400, T401, T402 **Unit 4:** T36, T50, T114, T128, T192, T206, T270, T284, T348, T362, T397, T398, T399, T400, T401, T402 **Unit 5:** T36, T50, T114, T128, T192, T206, T270, T284, T348, T362, T397, T398, T399, T400, T401, T402 **Unit 6:** T36, T50, T114, T128, T192, T206, T270, T284, T348, T362, T397, T398, T399, T400, T401, T402 www.connected.mcgraw-hill.com: **RESOURCES: Units 1–6: Time for Kids Online Articles, Research & Inquiry:** Weekly Lessons **Teacher Resources:** Writer's Checklists/Proofreading Marks; **Digital Resources and Tools:** Writer's Workspace; Graphic Organizers; My Binder (My Work, My Portfolio); Collaborate (Projects)

Research to Build and Present Knowledge		McGraw-Hill Reading Wonders
W.1.7	Participate in shared research and writing projects (e.g., explore a number of "how-to" books on a given topic and use them to write a sequence of instructions).	**TEACHER'S EDITION: Unit 1:** T44, T45, T47, T122, T123, T203, T278, T279, T281, T356, T357, T359, T379, T397, T398, T399, T400, T401 **Unit 2:** T44, T45, T47, T122, T123, T125, T203, T204, T205, T281, T358, T359, T361, T397, T398, T399, T400, T401 **Unit 3:** T44, T45, T47, T122, T123, T125, T200, T201, T203, T278, T279, T281, T356, T357, T359, T397, T398, T399, T400, T401 **Unit 4:** T44, T45, T47, T122, T123, T125, T200, T201, T203, T278, T279, T281, T356, T357, T359, T397, T398, T399, T400, T401 **Unit 5:** T44, T45, T47, T122, T123, T125, T200, T201, T278, T279, T281, T356, T357, T359, T397, T398, T399, T400, T401 **Unit 6:** T47, T122, T123, T125, T200, T201, T203, T278, T279, T281, T356, T357, T359, T397, T398, T399, T400, T401 www.connected.mcgraw-hill.com: **RESOURCES: Units 1–6: Research & Inquiry:** Weekly Lessons **Teacher Resources:** Writer's Checklists/Proofreading Marks **Graphic Organizers:** Foldables
W.1.8	With guidance and support from adults, recall information from experiences or gather information from provided sources to answer a question.	**LEVELED READERS: Unit 1, Week 3:** *A Mouse in the House*, pp. 13–16 (A), *Love That Llama!* pp. 13–16 (O), *Birds That Talk*, pp. 13–16 (B) **Unit 1, Week 4:** *I Like to Play*, pp. 13–16 (A, O, B) **Unit 2, Week 3:** *I Live in a House!* (A, O, B) **Unit 4, Week 2:** *Animals Work Together!* pp. 13–16 (A, O); pp. 12–16 (B) **Unit 4, Week 3:** *Ducklings* (A) **Unit 4, Week 4:** *Let's Look at Insects!* pp. 13–16 (O), *Compare Insects*, pp. 13–16 (B) **Unit 5, Week 2:** *Hello, Little Dipper!* pp. 13–16 (A), *Our Sun Is a Star!* pp. 13–16 (O), *Sunrise and Sunset*, pp. 13–16 (B) **Unit 5, Week 3:** *Fly Away, Butterfly*, pp. 13–16 (A, O); pp. 12–16 (B) **Unit 6, Week 5:** *Four Voyages*, pp. 13–16 (A, O); pp. 12–16 (B) **SCIENCE & SOCIAL STUDIES WORKSTATION ACTIVITY CARDS:** 4, 5, 6, 7, 8, 9, 10, 11, 12, 13, 14, 15, 16, 17, 18, 19, 20, 22, 23, 24, 25, 26, 27, 28, 29, 30 **WRITING WORKSTATION ACTIVITY CARDS:** 1, 2, 3, 4, 5, 6, 7, 8, 9, 10, 11, 12, 13, 14, 15, 16, 17, 18, 19, 20, 21, 22, 23, 24, 25, 26, 27, 29, 30 **INTERACTIVE READ-ALOUD CARDS: Unit 1, Week 3:** 1 **Unit 3, Week 1:** 1, 3 **Unit 5, Week 1:** 3 **Unit 5, Week 2:** 1 **Unit 5, Week 4:** 1 **Unit 6, Week 2:** 1 **Unit 6, Week 5:** 2 **TEACHER'S EDITION: Unit 1:** T200, T398, T399, T400 **Unit 2:** T398, T399, T400 **Unit 3:** T200, T201, T398, T399, T400, T401 **Unit 4:** T122, T398, T399, T400 **Unit 5:** T44, T122, T200, T201, T278, T398, T399, T400 **Unit 6:** T44, T125, T278, T398, T399, T400 www.connected.mcgraw-hill.com: **RESOURCES: Units 1–6: Research & Inquiry:** Weekly Lessons, Note-taking Tools **Graphic Organizers:** Graphic Organizers
W.1.9	(Begins in grade 4)	

Range of Writing		McGraw-Hill Reading Wonders
W.1.10	(Begins in grade 3)	

College and Career Readiness Anchor Standards for SPEAKING AND LISTENING

The K–5 standards on the following pages define what students should understand and be able to do by the end of each grade. They correspond to the College and Career Readiness anchor standards below by number. The CCR and grade-specific standards are necessary complements—the former providing broad standards, the latter providing additional specificity—that together define the skills and understandings that all students must demonstrate.

Comprehension and Collaboration

1. Prepare for and participate effectively in a range of conversations and collaborations with diverse partners, building on others' ideas and expressing their own clearly and persuasively.

2. Integrate and evaluate information presented in diverse media and formats, including visually, quantitatively, and orally.

3. Evaluate a speaker's point of view, reasoning, and use of evidence and rhetoric.

Presentation of Knowledge and Ideas

4. Present information, findings, and supporting evidence such that listeners can follow the line of reasoning and the organization, development, and style are appropriate to task, purpose, and audience.

5. Make strategic use of digital media and visual displays of data to express information and enhance understanding of presentations.

6. Adapt speech to a variety of contexts and communicative tasks, demonstrating command of formal English when indicated or appropriate.

CCSS Common Core State Standards
English Language Arts
Grade 1

Speaking and Listening Standards

Comprehension and Collaboration		McGraw-Hill Reading Wonders
SL.1.1	Participate in collaborative conversations with diverse partners about *grade 1 topics and texts* with peers and adults in small and larger groups.	
SL.1.1a	Follow agreed-upon rules for discussions (e.g., listening to others with care, speaking one at a time about the topics and texts under discussion).	**PHONICS WORKSTATION ACTIVITY CARDS:** 3, 10, 11, 12, 17, 18, 19, 20, 22, 23, 24, 30 **READING WORKSTATION ACTIVITY CARDS:** 1, 2, 3, 4, 5, 6, 7, 8, 9, 10, 11, 12, 13, 14, 15, 16, 17, 19, 20, 21, 22, 23, 24, 25, 26, 27, 28 **TEACHER'S EDITION:** Unit 1: T9, T87, T165 Unit 2: T87, T122, T165, T200, T321, T356, T403 Unit 3: T9, T165, T200, T243, T278, T321, T356, T403 Unit 4: T87, T122, T165, T200, T243, T278, T356, T403 Unit 5: T44, T87, T122, T165, T200, T321, T403 Unit 6: T87, T122, T165, T200, T321, T356, T403 www.connected.mcgraw-hill.com: **RESOURCES:** Units 1–6: **Media:** Images, Videos **Teacher Resources:** Speaking and Listening Checklists
SL.1.1b	Build on others' talk in conversations by responding to the comments of others through multiple exchanges.	**READING WORKSTATION ACTIVITY CARDS:** 2, 5, 10, 13, 16 **TEACHER'S EDITION:** Unit 1: T321, T356, T403 Unit 2: T9, T44, T403 Unit 3: T87, T122, T403 Unit 4: T403 Unit 5: T403 Unit 6: T278, T403 www.connected.mcgraw-hill.com: **RESOURCES:** Units 1–6: **Media:** Images, Videos **Teacher Resources:** Speaking and Listening Checklists
SL.1.1c	Ask questions to clear up any confusion about the topics and texts under discussion.	**TEACHER'S EDITION:** Unit 1: T165, T245, T269C, T403 Unit 2: T403 Unit 3: T321, T356, T403 Unit 4: T9, T44, T122, T403 Unit 5: T9, T243, T278, T403 Unit 6: T9, T44, T321, T403 www.connected.mcgraw-hill.com: **RESOURCES:** Units 1–6: **Graphic Organizers:** Graphic Organizers, Think Aloud Clouds **Teacher Resources:** Speaking and Listening Checklists
SL.1.2	Ask and answer questions about key details in a text read aloud or information presented orally or through other media.	**READING WORKSTATION ACTIVITY CARDS:** 2, 6, 11, 13, 14 **INTERACTIVE READ-ALOUD CARDS:** Unit 1, Week 1: 1, 2, 4 Unit 1, Week 2: 1, 3, 4 Unit 1, Week 3: 4 Unit 1, Week 4: 4 Unit 2, Week 3: 4 Unit 2, Week 4: 2 Unit 3, Week 1: 4 Unit 3, Week 2: 4 Unit 3, Week 3: 2, 4 Unit 3, Week 4: 1, 3, 4 Unit 3, Week 5: 4 Unit 4, Week 1: 3 Unit 4, Week 2: 2, 4 Unit 4, Week 3: 1, 3, 4 Unit 4, Week 4: 2 Unit 5, Week 1: 4 Unit 5, Week 2: 4 Unit 5, Week 3: 4 Unit 5, Week 4: 4 Unit 5, Week 5: 4 Unit 6, Week 1: 4 Unit 6, Week 2: 4 Unit 6, Week 3: 4 Unit 6, Week 4: 4 **TEACHER'S EDITION:** Unit 1: S8, S14, S26, S38, S44, S50, S56, S68, S74, S80, S86, T50, T245, T255, T403 Unit 2: T20, T99, T177, T255, T403 Unit 3: T11, T21, T31, T89, T99, T109, T167, T177, T245, T255, T333, T403 Unit 4: T11, T21, T89, T99, T167, T177, T255, T333, T403 Unit 5: T21, T99, T245, T255, T333, T403 Unit 6: T21, T99, T333, T403 www.connected.mcgraw-hill.com: **RESOURCES:** Units 1–6: **Graphic Organizers:** Think Aloud Clouds **Teacher Resources:** Speaking and Listening Checklists
SL.1.3	Ask and answer questions about what a speaker says in order to gather additional information or clarify something that is not understood.	**TEACHER'S EDITION:** Unit 1: T128, T165, T243, T403 Unit 2: T50, T243, T403 Unit 3: T9, T321, T362, T403 Unit 4: T9, T87, T206, T321, T403 Unit 5: T9, T165, T243, T284, T403 Unit 6: T9, T50, T321, T403 www.connected.mcgraw-hill.com: **RESOURCES:** Units 1–6: **Research & Inquiry:** Note-taking tools **Graphic Organizers:** Graphic Organizers **Teacher Resources:** Speaking and Listening Checklists

Speaking and Listening Standards

Presentation of Knowledge and Ideas		McGraw-Hill Reading Wonders
SL.1.4	Describe people, places, things, and events with relevant details, expressing ideas and feelings clearly.	**LITERATURE ANTHOLOGY: Unit 1:** 47, 63, 85, 86, 94, 95 **Unit 2:** 25, 43, 47 **Unit 5:** 195, 259 **Unit 6:** 392 **LEVELED READERS: Unit 1, Week 2:** *My Home,* pp. 13–16 (A), *Where I Live,* pp. 13–16 (O), *Where We Live,* pp. 13–16 (B) **Unit 2, Week 3:** *I Live in a House!* pp. 13–16 (A, O, B) **Unit 2, Week 4:** *The Sick Tree* (A), *Squirrels Help* (O) **Unit 3, Week 4:** *School Days,* pp. 13–16 (A, O); pp. 12–16 (B) **Unit 4, Week 1:** *Animal Traits,* pp. 13–16 (O) **Unit 4, Week 5:** *Working with Dolphins,* pp. 13–16 (A, O); pp. 12–16 (B) **Unit 5, Week 1:** *Nuts for Winter* (A), *Spark's Toys* (B) **Unit 5, Week 2:** *Hello, Little Dipper!* pp. 13–16 (A), *Our Sun Is a Star!* pp. 13–16 (O), *Sunrise and Sunset,* pp. 13–16 (B) **Unit 6, Week 4:** *The Quilt* (A), *Latkes for Sam* (O) **Unit 6, Week 5:** *Four Voyages,* pp. 13–16 (A, O); pp. 12–16 (B) **PHONICS WORKSTATION ACTIVITY CARDS:** 4, 10, 11, 19, 26 **READING WORKSTATION ACTIVITY CARDS:** 1, 2, 3, 4, 7, 8, 9, 10, 13, 15 **SCIENCE & SOCIAL STUDIES WORKSTATION ACTIVITY CARDS:** 2, 3, 4, 5, 6, 7, 8, 9, 10, 12, 13, 14, 15, 16, 17, 18, 19, 20, 21, 22, 23, 24, 25, 26, 27, 28, 29, 30 **WRITING WORKSTATION ACTIVITY CARDS:** 1, 2, 3, 4, 5, 6, 7, 8, 9, 10, 11, 12, 13, 14, 15, 16, 17, 19, 20, 21, 22, 23, 24, 25, 26, 27, 28, 29 **INTERACTIVE READ-ALOUD CARDS: Unit 1, Week 1:** 2 **Unit 1, Week 2:** 3 **Unit 1, Week 3:** 3 **Unit 3, Week 1:** 2, 3 **Unit 3, Week 2:** 1 **Unit 3, Week 4:** 1 **Unit 6, Week 4:** 3 **TEACHER'S EDITION: Unit 1:** S26, S50, S74, T9, T46, T87, T98, T124, T280, T321 **Unit 2:** T9, T87, T203, T245, T321 **Unit 3:** T9, T87, T89, T113J, T165, T243, T321 **Unit 4:** T9, T87, T165, T243, T269R **Unit 5:** T9, T87, T113R, T165, T243, T273, T321 **Unit 6:** T87, T177, T243 **www.connected.mcgraw-hill.com: RESOURCES: Unit 1: Graphic Organizers:** Graphic Organizers
SL.1.5	Add drawings or other visual displays to descriptions when appropriate to clarify ideas, thoughts, and feelings.	**LITERATURE ANTHOLOGY: Unit 1:** 18, 40, 62, 82 **Unit 2:** 20, 42, 80 **Unit 3:** 22, 44, 66, 88 **Unit 4:** 28, 88, 124 **Unit 5:** 194 **Unit 6:** 356, 392 **LEVELED READERS: Unit 1, Week 2:** *Where I Live,* pp. 13–16 (O) **Unit 1, Week 3:** *Love That Llama!* pp. 13–16 (O) **Unit 1, Week 4:** *I Like to Play,* pp. 13–16 (A, O, B), *What's Under Your Skin?* pp. 13–16 (A, O, B) **Unit 2, Week 3:** *I Live in a House!* pp. 13–16 (A, O, B) **Unit 2, Week 4:** *Squirrels Help* (O) **Unit 2, Week 5:** *On the Map,* pp. 13–16 (A, O); pp. 12–16 (B) **Unit 3, Week 4:** *School Days,* pp. 13–16 (A, O); pp. 12–16 (B) **Unit 4, Week 1:** *Animal Traits,* pp. 13–16 (O) **Unit 4, Week 3:** *Ducklings,* pp. 13–16 (A, O); pp. 12–16 (B) **Unit 4, Week 5:** *Working with Dolphins,* pp. 13–16 (A, O); pp. 12–16 (B) **Unit 5, Week 3:** *Fly Away, Butterfly,* pp. 13–16 (A, O); pp. 12–16 (B) **Unit 6, Week 1:** *What a Feast* (O) **Unit 6, Week 2:** *Fire!* pp. 13–16 (A, O); pp. 12–16 (B) **Unit 6, Week 4:** *Latkes for Sam* (O) **YOUR TURN PRACTICE BOOK:** 165, 189, 225, 249, 261, 285 **PHONICS WORKSTATION ACTIVITY CARDS:** 1, 3, 4, 6, 8, 9, 10, 16, 17, 18, 20, 21, 22, 25, 26, 29 **READING WORKSTATION ACTIVITY CARDS:** 1, 2, 3, 4, 5, 6, 7, 8, 9, 10, 11, 12, 13, 15, 17, 19, 20, 23, 26, 27, 28 **SCIENCE & SOCIAL STUDIES WORKSTATION ACTIVITY CARDS:** 2, 3, 4, 5, 6, 7, 8, 9, 10, 12, 13, 14, 15, 16, 17, 18, 19, 20, 21, 22, 23, 24, 25, 26, 27, 28, 29, 30 **WRITING WORKSTATION ACTIVITY CARDS:** 1, 2, 3, 4, 5, 6, 7, 9, 10, 13, 14, 17, 20, 21, 22, 23, 24, 25, 26, 27, 28, 29 **TEACHER'S EDITION: Unit 1:** T43, T45, T47, T50, T121, T123, T191J, T279, T355, T362 **Unit 2:** T43, T50, T121 **Unit 3:** T121, T199, T206, T277, T279, T362 **Unit 4:** T43, T121, T123, T128, T199, T206, T284, T357 **Unit 5:** T43, T121, T123, T199, T206, T277, T284, T362 **Unit 6:** T43, T50, T121, T123, T128, T206, T277, T284, T362 **www.connected.mcgraw-hill.com: RESOURCES: Units 1–6: Research & Inquiry:** Weekly Lessons **Student Practice:** Approaching Reproducibles, Beyond Reproducibles, ELL Reproducibles
SL.1.6	Produce complete sentences when appropriate to task and situation.	**LEVELED READERS: Unit 3, Week 1:** *Busy's Watch* (A), *Kate Saves the Date!* (O), *Uncle George Is Coming!* (B) **Unit 3, Week 4:** *School Days,* pp. 13–16 (A, O); pp. 12–16 (B) **Unit 5, Week 2:** *Sunrise and Sunset,* pp. 13–16 (B) **Unit 5, Week 3:** *Fly Away, Butterfly* pp. 13–16 (A, O); pp. 12–16 (B) **Unit 6, Week 1:** *Two Hungry Elephants* (A) **Unit 6, Week 2:** *Fire!* pp. 13–16 (A, O); pp. 12–16 (B) **YOUR TURN PRACTICE BOOK:** 2, 12, 17, 22, 32, 51, 52, 58, 61, 62, 71, 72, 81, 91, 92, 93, 101, 111, 151, 165, 189, 211, 221, 225, 249, 261, 285, 314 **PHONICS WORKSTATION ACTIVITY CARDS:** 1, 2, 4, 5, 6, 7, 8, 9, 10, 11, 12, 14, 15, 18, 19, 20, 21, 22, 23, 24, 25, 26, 27, 29 **READING WORKSTATION ACTIVITY CARDS:** 10 **SCIENCE & SOCIAL STUDIES WORKSTATION ACTIVITY CARDS:** 2, 4, 5, 6, 7, 8, 9, 12, 14, 15, 17, 18, 19, 20, 23, 24, 25, 26, 27, 28, 30 **WRITING WORKSTATION ACTIVITY CARDS:** 1, 2, 3, 4, 5, 6, 7, 8, 9, 10, 11, 12, 13, 14, 15, 16, 17, 18, 19, 20, 21, 22, 23, 24, 25, 26, 27, 28, 29, 30 **INTERACTIVE READ-ALOUD CARDS: Unit 1, Week 4:** 3 **Unit 1, Week 5:** 1 **Unit 2, Week 1:** 1 **Unit 2, Week 3:** 3 **Unit 3, Week 4:** 2 **Unit 4, Week 1:** 2 **Unit 4, Week 4:** 1 **Unit 5, Week 5:** 2 **Unit 6, Week 3:** 1 **TEACHER'S EDITION: Unit 1:** S5, S14, T19, T37, T43, T175, T185, T193, T341, T355 **Unit 2:** T9, T19, T29, T175, T193 **Unit 3:** T37, T43, T87, T165, T253, T271 **Unit 4:** T9, T107, T191, T253, T263, T321 **Unit 5:** T19, T29, T185, T199, T277 **Unit 6:** T9, T19, T29, T165, T243, T253, T263 **www.connected.mcgraw-hill.com: RESOURCES: Units 1–6: Student Practice:** Approaching Reproducibles, Beyond Reproducibles, ELL Reproducibles

College and Career Readiness Anchor Standards for LANGUAGE

The K–5 standards on the following pages define what students should understand and be able to do by the end of each grade. They correspond to the College and Career Readiness anchor standards below by number. The CCR and grade-specific standards are necessary complements—the former providing broad standards, the latter providing additional specificity—that together define the skills and understandings that all students must demonstrate.

Conventions of Standard English

1. Demonstrate command of the conventions of standard English grammar and usage when writing or speaking.

2. Demonstrate command of the conventions of standard English capitalization, punctuation, and spelling when writing.

Knowledge of Language

3. Apply knowledge of language to understand how language functions in different contexts, to make effective choices for meaning or style, and to comprehend more fully when reading or listening.

Vocabulary Acquisition and Use

4. Determine or clarify the meaning of unknown and multiple-meaning words and phrases by using context clues, analyzing meaningful word parts, and consulting general and specialized reference materials, as appropriate.

5. Demonstrate understanding of word relationships and nuances in word meanings.

6. Acquire and use accurately a range of general academic and domain–specific words and phrases sufficient for reading, writing, speaking, and listening at the college and career readiness level; demonstrate independence in gathering vocabulary knowledge when encountering an unknown term important to comprehension or expression.

CCSS Common Core State Standards
English Language Arts
Grade 1

Language Standards

Conventions of Standard English		*McGraw-Hill Reading Wonders*
L.1.1	Demonstrate command of the conventions of standard English grammar and usage when writing or speaking.	
L.1.1a	Print all upper- and lowercase letters.	**YOUR TURN PRACTICE BOOK:** SS5, SS8, SS12, SS17, SS20, SS24, SS29, SS32, SS36 **TEACHER'S EDITION: Unit 1:** T13, T91, T169, T247 **Unit 2:** T13, T91, T169, T247, T325 **Unit 3:** T13, T91, T169, T247 **Unit 4:** T13, T91, T169, T247, T325 **Unit 5:** T13, T91, T169, T247 **Unit 6:** T13, T91, T169, T247 www.connected.mcgraw-hill.com: **RESOURCES: Unit 1: Student Practice:** Grammar Practice, Approaching Reproducibles, Beyond Reproducibles, ELL Reproducibles **Interactive Games & Activities:** Writing & Grammar
L.1.1b	Use common, proper, and possessive nouns.	**READING/WRITING WORKSHOP: Unit 2:** 27, 47, 67, 87, 107 **YOUR TURN PRACTICE BOOK:** 2, 32, 49, 59, 92, 102, 112, 132, 152, 165, 176, 200, 213, 237, 248, 260, 261, 272, 273, 284, 296, 297, 321 **PHONICS WORKSTATION ACTIVITY CARDS:** 5 **TEACHER'S EDITION: Unit 2:** T28, T29, T184, T185, T199, T262, T272, T276, T277 **Unit 4:** T199 **Unit 5:** T42, T121 www.connected.mcgraw-hill.com: **RESOURCES: Unit 2: Student Practice:** Grammar Practice, Approaching Reproducibles, Beyond Reproducibles, ELL Reproducibles **Interactive Games & Activities:** Writing & Grammar **Unit 4: Student Practice:** Grammar Practice, Approaching Reproducibles, Beyond Reproducibles, ELL Reproducibles **Interactive Games & Activities:** Writing & Grammar **Unit 5: Student Practice:** Grammar Practice, Approaching Reproducibles, Beyond Reproducibles, ELL Reproducibles **Interactive Games & Activities:** Writing & Grammar
L.1.1c	Use singular and plural nouns with matching verbs in basic sentences (e.g., *He hops; We hop*).	**READING/WRITING WORKSHOP: Unit 3:** 47, 87 **Unit 4:** 31, 51 **YOUR TURN PRACTICE BOOK:** 2, 8, 220 **PHONICS WORKSTATION ACTIVITY CARDS:** 5 **TEACHER'S EDITION: Unit 2:** T106, T017 **Unit 3:** T97, T106, T107, T253, T263, T271, T277, T285 **Unit 4:** T19, T29, T37, T42, T43, T51 www.connected.mcgraw-hill.com: **RESOURCES: Units 3: Student Practice:** Grammar Practice, Approaching Reproducibles, Beyond Reproducibles, ELL Reproducibles **Interactive Games & Activities:** Writing & Grammar **Unit 4:** Approaching Reproducibles, Beyond Reproducibles, ELL Reproducibles, Grammar Practice, Interactive Games & Activities (Writing & Grammar)
L.1.1d	Use personal, possessive, and indefinite pronouns (e.g., *I, me, my; they, them, their; anyone, everything*).	**READING/WRITING WORKSHOP: Unit 6:** 235, 254, 255, 275, 295 **YOUR TURN PRACTICE BOOK:** SS3, SS4, SS9, SS10, SS15, SS16, SS21, SS22, SS27, SS28, SS33, SS34, 32, 152, 296, 308, 309 **WRITING WORKSTATION ACTIVITY CARDS:** 21 **TEACHER'S EDITION: Unit 6:** T19, T29, T37, T42, T43, T51, T97, T107, T115, T121, T129, T175, T185, T193, T198, T199, T207, T253, T263, T271, T276, T277, T285 www.connected.mcgraw-hill.com: **RESOURCES: Unit 6: Student Practice:** Grammar Practice, Approaching Reproducibles, Beyond Reproducibles, ELL Reproducibles **Interactive Games & Activities:** Writing & Grammar

Language Standards

Conventions of Standard English		McGraw-Hill Reading Wonders
L.1.1e	Use verbs to convey a sense of past, present, and future (e.g., *Yesterday I walked home; Today I walk home; Tomorrow I will walk home*).	**READING/WRITING WORKSHOP:** Unit 3: 27, 47, 67 **Unit 4:** 71, 91 **YOUR TURN PRACTICE BOOK:** 58, 78, 225 **PHONICS WORKSTATION ACTIVITY CARDS:** 5 **TEACHER'S EDITION:** Unit 3: T97, T107, T115, T120, T121, T129, T175, T185, T193, T198, T199, T207, T253, T263, T271, T276, T277, T285 **Unit 4:** T19, T29, T42, T43, T51, T175, T185, T193, T198, T199, T207, T253, T263, T271, T276, T277, T285 www.connected.mcgraw-hill.com: **RESOURCES:** Unit 3: Student Practice: Grammar Practice, Approaching Reproducibles, Beyond Reproducibles, ELL Reproducibles **Interactive Games & Activities:** Writing & Grammar **Unit 4: Student Practice:** Grammar Practice, Approaching Reproducibles, Beyond Reproducibles, ELL Reproducibles **Interactive Games & Activities:** Writing & Grammar
L.1.1f	Use frequently occurring adjectives.	**READING/WRITING WORKSHOP:** Unit 5: 152–153, 173 **YOUR TURN PRACTICE BOOK:** SS15, SS16, SS33, SS34, 22, 42, 52, 62, 92, 102, 112, 122, 132, 142, 152, 153, 164, 165, 176, 185, 189, 200, 201, 212, 213, 236, 237, 248, 256, 272, 293, 309, 320 **WRITING WORKSTATION ACTIVITY CARDS:** 17, 22, 25 **TEACHER'S EDITION:** Unit 5: T97, T106, T107, T115, T120, T121, T129, T175, T185, T193, T199, T207 www.connected.mcgraw-hill.com: **RESOURCES:** Unit 5: Student Practice: Grammar Practice, Approaching Reproducibles, Beyond Reproducibles, ELL Reproducibles **Interactive Games & Activities:** Writing & Grammar
L.1.1g	Use frequently occurring conjunctions (e.g., *and, but, or, so, because*).	**READING/WRITING WORKSHOP:** Unit 5: 133 **YOUR TURN PRACTICE BOOK:** SS15, SS16, SS21, SS22, 164 **TEACHER'S EDITION:** Unit 5: T19, T28, T29, T37, T42, T43, T51 www.connected.mcgraw-hill.com: **RESOURCES:** Unit 5: Student Practice: Grammar Practice, Approaching Reproducibles, Beyond Reproducibles, ELL Reproducibles **Interactive Games & Activities:** Writing & Grammar
L.1.1h	Use determiners (e.g., articles, demonstratives).	**READING/WRITING WORKSHOP:** Unit 5: 193 **YOUR TURN PRACTICE BOOK:** SS3, SS4, SS9, SS10, SS15, SS16, SS21, SS22, SS27, SS28, SS33, SS34 **TEACHER'S EDITION:** Unit 5: T253, T262, T263, T271, T276, T277, T285 www.connected.mcgraw-hill.com: **RESOURCES:** Unit 5: Student Practice: Grammar Practice, Approaching Reproducibles, Beyond Reproducibles, ELL Reproducibles **Interactive Games & Activities:** Writing & Grammar
L.1.1i	Use frequently occurring prepositions (e.g., *during, beyond, toward*).	**READING/WRITING WORKSHOP:** Unit 5: 213 **YOUR TURN PRACTICE BOOK:** SS9, SS10, SS33, SS34, 72, 92, 122, 142, 152, 164, 176, 200, 260, 308 **TEACHER'S EDITION:** Unit 5: T331, T340, T341, T349, T354, T355, T363 www.connected.mcgraw-hill.com: **RESOURCES:** Unit 5: Student Practice: Grammar Practice, Approaching Reproducibles, Beyond Reproducibles, ELL Reproducibles **Interactive Games & Activities:** Writing & Grammar
L.1.1j	Produce and expand complete simple and compound declarative, interrogative, imperative, and exclamatory sentences in response to prompts.	**READING/WRITING WORKSHOP:** Unit 1: 107 **Unit 5:** 132–133 **Unit 6:** 294–295 **YOUR TURN PRACTICE BOOK:** 2, 12, 17, 22, 51, 52, 58, 61, 62, 71, 72, 81, 91, 92, 93, 101, 111, 148, 151, 165, 189, 211, 221, 225, 249, 261, 285, 314 **PHONICS WORKSTATION ACTIVITY CARDS:** 1, 2, 4, 9, 10, 11, 12, 15, 17, 18, 19, 22, 23, 29, 30 **SCIENCE & SOCIAL STUDIES WORKSTATION ACTIVITY CARDS:** 2, 4, 5, 6, 7, 8, 9, 12, 14, 15, 17, 18, 19, 20, 23, 24, 25, 26, 27, 28, 30 **WRITING WORKSTATION ACTIVITY CARDS:** 1, 2, 3, 4, 5, 6, 7, 8, 9, 10, 11, 12, 13, 14, 15, 16, 17, 18, 19, 20, 21, 22, 23, 24, 25, 26, 27, 28, 29, 30 **TEACHER'S EDITION:** Unit 1: T19, T28, T37, T43, T51, T175, T185, T193, T198, T199, T253, T263, T271, T277, T285, T363 **Unit 5:** T19, T29, T37, T43, T51 www.connected.mcgraw-hill.com: **RESOURCES:** Unit 1: Student Practice: Grammar Practice, Approaching Reproducibles, Beyond Reproducibles, ELL Reproducibles **Interactive Games & Activities:** Writing & Grammar **Graphic Organizers:** Graphic Organizers **Teacher's Resources:** Writer's Checklists/Proofreading Marks
L.1.2	Demonstrate command of the conventions of standard English capitalization, punctuation, and spelling when writing.	
L.1.2a	Capitalize dates and names of people.	**READING/WRITING WORKSHOP:** Unit 2: 86–87 **TEACHER'S EDITION:** Unit 2: T263, T277, T285 **Unit 4:** T97, T175, T185, T193, T207 **Unit 5:** T175, T185, T193, T199, T207 **Unit 6:** T97, T107, T120, T115, T129 www.connected.mcgraw-hill.com: **RESOURCES:** Units 1–6: Student Practice: Grammar Practice, **Interactive Games & Activities:** Writing & Grammar **Teacher Resources:** Writer's Checklists/Proofreading Marks

Language Standards

L.1.2b	Use end punctuation for sentences.	**READING/WRITING WORKSHOP:** Unit 1: 47, 87, 107 **TEACHER'S EDITION:** Unit 1: T97, T107, T115, T121, T129, T175, T185, T207, T253, T263, T271, T277, T285, T331, T341, T349, T355, T366 **Unit 2:** T331, T341, T349, T355, T363 **Unit 4:** T97, T107, T115, T120, T121, T129 **Unit 5:** T97, T107, T115, T121, T129 **www.connected.mcgraw-hill.com: RESOURCES:** Units 1–5: Student Practice: Grammar Practice, **Interactive Games & Activities:** Writing & Grammar **Teacher Resources:** Writer's Checklists/Proofreading Marks
L.1.2c	Use commas in dates and to separate single words in a series.	**READING/WRITING WORKSHOP:** Unit 3: 27 **TEACHER'S EDITION:** Unit 2: T19, T28, T29, T37, T43, T51 **Unit 3:** T19, T28, T29, T37, T42, T43, T51, T175, T185, T198, T199, T207, T253, T263, T271, T276, T277, T285 **Unit 4:** T331, T341, T349, T354, T355, T363 **Unit 6:** T175, T185, T193, T198, T199, T207, T253, T263, T271, T276, T277, T285 **www.connected.mcgraw-hill.com: RESOURCES:** Units 1–6: Student Practice: Grammar Practice, **Interactive Games & Activities:** Writing & Grammar **Teacher Resources:** Writer's Checklists/Proofreading Marks
L.1.2d	Use conventional spelling for words with common spelling patterns and for frequently occurring irregular words.	**YOUR TURN PRACTICE BOOK:** 196, 220, 232, 256 **PHONICS WORKSTATION ACTIVITY CARDS:** 1, 2, 3, 4, 5, 6, 7, 8, 9, 10, 11, 12, 13, 14, 15, 16, 17, 18, 19, 20, 21, 22, 23, 24, 25, 26, 27, 28, 29, 30 **TEACHER'S EDITION:** Unit 1: T14, T92, T170, T196, T274 **Unit 2:** T25, T92, T93, T112, T113, T190, T191 **Unit 3:** T34, T35, T103, T180, T181, T258, T259, T326, T327 **Unit 4:** T92, T93, T170, T171, T268, T269, T336, T337, T346, T347 **Unit 5:** T14, T49, T119, T180, T353 **Unit 6:** T41, T127, T248, T283, T326, T327, T361 **www.connected.mcgraw-hill.com: RESOURCES:** Units 1–6: Student Practice: Phonics/Spelling Practice, Approaching Reproducibles, Beyond Reproducibles, ELL Reproducibles **Interactive Games & Activities:** Phonics **Cards:** Spelling Word Cards, Sound-Spelling Cards **Teacher Resources:** Sound-Spelling Songs
L.1.2e	Spell untaught words phonetically, drawing on phonemic awareness and spelling conventions.	**PHONICS WORKSTATION ACTIVITY CARDS:** 1, 2, 3, 4, 5, 6, 7, 8, 9, 10, 11, 12, 13, 14, 15, 16, 17, 18, 19, 20, 21, 22, 23, 24, 25, 26, 27, 28, 29, 30 **TEACHER'S EDITION:** Unit 1: T14, T92, T170, T248, T326 **Unit 2:** T14, T92, T170, T248, T326 **Unit 3:** T15, T92, T170, T248, T326 **Unit 4:** T15, T170, T248, T326 **Unit 5:** T14, T92, T170, T248, T326 **Unit 6:** T14, T92, T170, T248, T326 **www.connected.mcgraw-hill.com: RESOURCES:** Units 1–6: Student Practice: Phonics/Spelling Practice, Approaching Reproducibles, Beyond Reproducibles, ELL Reproducibles **Interactive Games & Activities:** Phonemic Awareness **Cards:** Spelling Word Cards, Sound-Spelling Cards **Teacher Resources:** Sound-Spelling Songs

Knowledge of Language	*McGraw-Hill Reading Wonders*
L.1.3	(Begins in grade 2)

Vocabulary Acquisition and Use	*McGraw-Hill Reading Wonders*
L.1.4	Determine or clarify the meaning of unknown and multiple-meaning words and phrases based on *grade 1 reading and content,* choosing flexibly from an array of strategies.

L.1.4a	Use sentence-level context as a clue to the meaning of a word or phrase.	**READING/WRITING WORKSHOP:** Unit 4: 15, 35, 55, 75, 95 **Unit 5:** 117, 137, 157, 177, 197 **Unit 6:** 218, 239, 259, 279, 299 **YOUR TURN PRACTICE BOOK:** 170, 194 **INTERACTIVE READ-ALOUD CARDS:** Unit 1, Week 1: 3 **Unit 4, Week 2:** 3 **Unit 5, Week 3:** 3 **Unit 6, Week 3:** 2 **TEACHER'S EDITION:** Unit 1: T195A **Unit 2:** T39A, T113C, T224, T269G, T273A **Unit 3:** T39A, T113F, T269F, T273A **Unit 4:** T113, T113F, T117A, T191J, T269, T269H **Unit 5:** T35, T39, T117, T224, T273A **Unit 6:** T39, T113G, T146, T195A, T273A, T302 **www.connected.mcgraw-hill.com: RESOURCES:** Units 1–6: Student Practice: Approaching Reproducibles, Beyond Reproducibles, ELL Reproducibles **Interactive Games & Activities:** Vocabulary **Cards:** Visual Vocabulary Cards
L.1.4b	Use frequently occurring affixes as a clue to the meaning of a word.	**YOUR TURN PRACTICE BOOK:** 172, 206, 218, 242, 254, 280 **PHONICS WORKSTATION ACTIVITY CARDS:** 17 **TEACHER'S EDITION:** Unit 4: T101, T111, T118, T126, T136 **Unit 5:** T146, T191, T269, T269K **Unit 6:** T23, T33, T58, T191J **www.connected.mcgraw-hill.com: RESOURCES:** Units 3–6: Student Practice: Approaching Reproducibles, Beyond Reproducibles, ELL Reproducibles **Interactive Games & Activities:** Vocabulary **Cards:** Visual Vocabulary Cards

Language Standards

Vocabulary Acquisition and Use		McGraw-Hill Reading Wonders
L.1.4c	Identify frequently occurring root words (e.g., *look*) and their inflectional forms (e.g., *looks, looked, looking*).	**YOUR TURN PRACTICE BOOK:** 118, 128, 148, 196, 266, 316 **TEACHER'S EDITION:** Unit 4: T146, T347, T347D Unit 5: T113C, T269K, T347 Unit 6: T41, T119, T191J, T197 www.connected.mcgraw-hill.com: **RESOURCES: Units 3–6: Student Practice:** Approaching Reproducibles, Beyond Reproducibles, ELL Reproducibles **Interactive Games & Activities:** Vocabulary **Cards:** Visual Vocabulary Cards
L.1.5	With guidance and support from adults, demonstrate understanding of figurative language, word relationships and nuances in word meaning.	
L.1.5a	Sort words into categories (e.g., colors, clothing) to gain a sense of the concepts the categories represent.	**TEACHER'S EDITION:** Unit 4: T191G, T191H Unit 6: T35K, T191M www.connected.mcgraw-hill.com: **RESOURCES: Units 1–6: Cards:** High-Frequency Word Cards, Visual Vocabulary Cards **Teacher Resources:** Word Games and Activities, Word Lists **Interactive Games & Activities:** Vocabulary
L.1.5b	Define words by category and by one or more key attributes (e.g., a duck is a bird that swims; a *tiger* is a large cat with stripes).	**TEACHER'S EDITION:** Unit 4: T191G, T191H Unit 6: T35K, T191M www.connected.mcgraw-hill.com: **RESOURCES: Units 1–6: Cards:** High-Frequency Word Cards, Visual Vocabulary Cards **Teacher Resources:** Word Games and Activities, Word Lists **Interactive Games & Activities:** Vocabulary
L.1.5c	Identify real-life connections between words and their use (e.g., note places at home that are *cozy*).	**TEACHER'S EDITION:** Unit 1: T20, T30, T194 Unit 2: T38, T39A, T116 Unit 3: T30, T38, T116 Unit 4: T186, T332 Unit 5: T186, T194, T264, T272 Unit 6: T30, T264 www.connected.mcgraw-hill.com: **RESOURCES: Units 1–6: Cards:** High-Frequency Word Cards, Visual Vocabulary Cards **Teacher Resources:** Word Games and Activities, Word Lists **Interactive Games & Activities:** Vocabulary
L.1.5d	Distinguish shades of meaning among verbs differing in manner (e.g., *look, peek, glance, stare, glare, scowl*) and adjectives differing in intensity (e.g., *large, gigantic*) by defining or choosing them or by acting out the meanings.	**YOUR TURN PRACTICE BOOK:** 177, 189, 230 **TEACHER'S EDITION:** Unit 4: T191D, T191G, T302 Unit 5: T113 Unit 6: T191K www.connected.mcgraw-hill.com: **RESOURCES: Units 1–6: Cards:** High-Frequency Word Cards, Visual Vocabulary Cards **Teacher Resources:** Word Games and Activities, Word Lists **Interactive Games & Activities:** Vocabulary
L.1.6	Use words and phrases acquired through conversations, reading and being read to, and responding to texts, including using frequently occurring conjunctions to signal simple relationships (e.g., *because*).	**WRITING WORKSTATION ACTIVITY CARDS:** 26 **INTERACTIVE READ ALOUD CARDS:** Unit 1: Weeks 1–4 Unit 2: Weeks 1–4 Unit 3: Weeks 1–4 Unit 4: Weeks 1–4 Unit 5: Weeks 1–4 Unit 6: Weeks 1–4 **TEACHER'S EDITION:** Unit 1: T30, T38, T66, T108, T116, T194, T254, T255, T264, T332, T342 Unit 2: T20, T30, T38, T98, T108, T116, T176, T186, T194, T264, T272, T332 Unit 3: T20, T30, T38, T108, T116, T176, T186, T194, T254, T264, T272, T332, T342, T397 Unit 4: T20, T30, T98, T108, T116, T176, T186, T194, T254, T264, T272, T332 Unit 5: T20, T30, T38, T98, T108, T116, T176, T186, T194, T254, T264, T272, T332, T342 Unit 6: T20, T30, T38, T98, T108, T116, T176, T186, T194, T254, T264, T272, T332, T342 www.connected.mcgraw-hill.com: **RESOURCES: Units 1–6: Student Practice:** Grammar Practice **Interactive Games & Activities:** (Writing & Grammar) **Cards:** Retelling Cards, Visual Vocabulary Cards